ST AUGUSTINE OF HIPPO

LIFE AND CONTROVERSIES

ST AUGUSTINE
OF HIPPO

Life and Controversies

GERALD BONNER

77310

SCM PRESS LTD
BLOOMSBURY STREET LONDON

FIRST PUBLISHED 1963
© SCM PRESS LTD 1963
PRINTED IN GREAT BRITAIN BY
WESTERN PRINTING SERVICES LTD
BRISTOL

TO MY MOTHER

CONTENTS

ABBREVIATIONS
commonly employed in the references

CIL	*Corpus Inscriptionum Latinarum*
CSEL	*Corpus Scriptorum Ecclesiasticorum Latinorum*, Vienna
CSHB	*Corpus Scriptorum Historiae Byzantinae*, Bonn
dCD	*De Civitate Dei* (see Bibliography)
ET	English translation
FT	French translation
Hefele-Leclercq	Hefele-Leclercq, *Histoire des Conciles d'après les documents originaux*, tom. II¹, Paris, 1908
JEH	*Journal of Ecclesiastical History*, London
JRS	*Journal of Roman Studies*, London
JTS	*Journal of Theological Studies*, Oxford
Mansi	J. D. Mansi, *Sacrorum Conciliorum Collection nova et amplissima*, Florence, 1759
MGH	*Monumenta Germaniae Historica*, Berlin
MPG	Migne, *Patrologia Graeca*, Paris
MPL	Migne, *Patrologia Latina*, Paris
Pauly-Wissowa, *Real-Encyclopädie*	*Real-Encyclopädie der klassischen Altertumswissenschaft*, Stuttgart, 1894 (in progress)
Rev. béned.	*Revue bénédictine*, Maredsous
ZNW	*Zeitschrift für die neutestamentliche Wissenschaft*, Münster i. W.

PREFACE

IN VIEW of the vast quantity of literature which St Augustine has inspired, there is almost a moral obligation laid upon any writer adding to the sum to justify his action and to explain why, in his opinion, his book is a necessary contribution to the already formidable total. In the case of an English author, justification is the easier in that there is a relative scarcity of recent English works on Augustine—a scarcity which, while it throws into relief the merits of those actually existing, compares unfavourably with the position on the Continent and, indeed, with English writing itself a few decades ago.

This apparent neglect is the more strange when we remember that Augustine has often been invoked as a patron by almost all the communions of Western Christendom. Catholic and Protestant have vied with one another in claiming his teaching for their own. There was, indeed, a recession during the nineteenth century, when Roman Catholics looked to St Thomas Aquinas as the guide to Christian doctrine, while Protestants tended to recoil from the more extreme statements of Augustine on Predestination and the fate of the unbaptized. The twentieth century, however, has seen a resurgence of Augustinian studies, and it was a matter for some comment at the Third International Conference on Patristic Studies at Oxford in 1959 how Augustinian themes predominated among the many communications offered.

What is the reason for this abiding influence? Why should Augustine continue to preoccupy the minds of so many Christian students? One answer is obvious enough: his importance in the history of Christian thought. Whether we approve or disapprove, no one will dispute the power which Augustine exercised in the theology and culture of Europe from his own lifetime until the rise of scholasticism and for a long while afterwards so that, in the later Middle Ages and in the disputes of the Reformation, his name and doctrine were continually invoked. But this historical importance is not, in the present writer's opinion, the proper justification for the study of Augustine, which is to be found, rather, in his personality, in the depth of his experience of God, and in his extraordinary flair for communicating that experience to others. This is what sets Augustine apart from the other Fathers of the Church. In terms of intellectual ability he has little advantage over the Greek Fathers, except possibly in the range of his interests. Where he can claim the advantage is in his ability (at least where Western Christians are concerned) to touch the heart. Frederick Van der Meer expresses the matter admirably when he says: '[Augustine] is the father of Western piety and, despite his intellectualism, the teacher of all who are unable to live by argument alone.' And who, in the Christian life, would wish to do so?

The present work deals with Augustine's life and with three of the great controversies which preoccupied him at various periods throughout his whole Christian career: the Manichaean; the Donatist; and the Pelagian. In the first, he was concerned to refute a tendency, which constantly reappears in human thought, to regard the visible and material world as something evil and sordid—a denial, in fact, of the significance of the Incarnation. In the second, he deals with unity in the Mystical Body of Christ, His Church; while, in the third, he is concerned to defend the need for Grace, which is the indwelling of the Holy Spirit, the Sanctifier, against those who trusted in their own righteousness. All these issues are of vital importance for Christian doctrine and Christian living at all times and in all places, and Augustine's answers are as relevant today as they were when he wrote. We do not have to accept him in every particular in order to benefit from reading him. We may at times disagree. But to read him is to be reminded of what Christian faith and Christian life involve, for Augustine, to quote Van der Meer again, was 'an unconditional Christian'.

The object of the present work is twofold: to provide the general reader with an up-to-date account of the aspects of Augustine's life which have been described and, at the same time, to supply the student of theology or history with a textbook giving adequate references to original texts and modern studies. Accordingly, while no previous knowledge on the part of the reader is assumed and all quotations in the text are translated, the documentation is more considerable than is usual with books of this type. There is, inevitably, a danger that the book will fall between two stools, by being too technical for the general reader and not sufficiently learned for the student; but because of Augustine's importance and the relative scarcity of works in English, it seemed permissible to offer the work to the public with all its imperfections on its head. The author hopes, at a later date, to extend the study to cover other aspects of Augustine's works: his trinitarian theology, his ethics, and his philosophy.

The present book has been written during various periods of not over-abundant leisure during the past six years, and the circumstances of composition have contributed not a little to its approach and form. During these years, I have been helped and encouraged by many friends to whom I shall always be grateful. To select any for specific mention is a somewhat invidious task; but in view of the debt I owe, like so many others, to the University of Oxford, I will presume to mention three Oxford men as being, in some sense, representative of the rest: Sir Maurice Bowra, Warden of Wadham College; the Rev. Dr Thomas M. Parker, Fellow and Chaplain of University College; and the Rev. Fr T. Corbishley, S.J., sometime Master of Campion Hall. To these, to the SCM Press and, in particular, to Miss Jean Cunningham, and to all my other friends, I offer my sincere thanks. It is hardly necessary to add the time-honoured formula that, while what is good in the book I owe to others, its faults and imperfections are my own. Every student of Augustine must be conscious of the Master's words: *Nemo habet de suo, nisi mendacium et peccatum.*

I

Introduction

Cur mundus militat sub vana gloria,
Cuius prosperitas est transitoria?
Tam cito labitur eius potentia
Quam vasa figuli, quae sunt fragilia.

ANON., once ascribed to Jacapone da Todi

Et mundus transit et concupiscentia eius. Qui autem facit voluntatem Dei,
manet in aeternum.

I IOAN. 2.17

THE STUDY of the life and writings of Augustine of Hippo is most profitable when it is based upon some general knowledge of the age in which he lived. It is, of course, true that the distinctive quality of a great thinker is that his thought transcends the time and place of origin and speaks directly to other men in later ages and in places far removed; but since no genius, however elevated, is wholly emancipated from his age and circumstances, it follows that our understanding is immeasurably enhanced if we know something of his social and intellectual environment. This is particularly true of St Augustine. Living as he did in some of the most critical decades of European history—it is often said that he was a man living on the frontiers of two worlds, the ancient world which was passing away and the medieval world which was coming into being—Augustine of Hippo was continually compelled to concern himself with contemporary issues. It is some measure of his greatness that many of his answers not only influenced the centuries immediately succeeding his own, but remain a living force to this day. For this reason, an outline sketch of the age will be attempted before we turn to the man.

The lifetime of Augustine (354–430) spans a decisive period in the history of the Roman state. At the time of his birth, the fabric of the Empire, although battered, seemed secure and capable of resisting whatever pressures might be applied, whether internal or from without. When he died, the majestic structure was already falling into ruins, so far as the Latin-speaking provinces of the west were concerned. The German tribes, who had for centuries been a dangerous menace on the northern frontiers of the Empire, had crossed the barrier of the Rhine, poured through Gaul and Spain and, in the persons of the Vandals and the Alans, had invaded Africa, a province which they were to capture and occupy for a century, before the reconquest by the Byzantine army of the Emperor Justinian in 533. Fifty years after Augustine's death in 430, the last legal emperor of the west, Julius Nepos, died in exile at Salona, in Dalmatia.[1] Constitutionally, the whole Empire, from Gaul to the Persian frontier, now came under the direct rule of the Emperor Zeno, reigning at Constantinople[2]—a legal fiction recognized by the barbarian chieftain Odovacar, who had made himself ruler of Italy in 476 after deposing the young emperor Romulus Augustulus, a puppet who had been invested with the imperial insignia when the rightful emperor Nepos fled from Ravenna in 475.[3] In political fact, the effective rulers of western Europe were the barbarian kings who had established themselves as the successors of the Roman administration. Zeno's recognition of Odovacar as the imperial governor of Italy merely set the seal of legality on a process which was developing when Augustine breathed his last in his episcopal city of Hippo on 28 August 430, with the army of the Vandal king Gaiseric encamped around the walls.

The character of the social organization into which Augustine was born and which the German invasions so radically transformed was determined by the circumstances which brought it into being. The imperial system, created by Augustus to replace the incompetent and morally bankrupt administration of the Republic and consolidated by his successors, gave the Mediterranean world a period of peace and stability which endured for two centuries and which almost justifies the celebrated encomium of Gibbon: 'If a man were called to fix the period in the history of the world during which the condition of the human race was most happy and prosperous, he would, without hesitation, name that which elapsed from the death of Domitian to the succession of Commodus.'[4] In the third century of the Christian era, however, there came change and deterioration. Within the boundaries of the Empire, the failure to establish any effective system of hereditary succession offered continual temptation to ambitious military commanders to make a bid for imperial power, with the result that for more than fifty years of the third century, the history of the Roman state is one of revolt and civil war. To this unrest were added the horror of disease —the soldiers of Marcus Aurelius had brought back the Plague from the

---

[1] The deposition of Romulus Augustulus in 476 is the traditional date for the end of the Roman Empire in the west; but Romulus was a usurper, not recognized at Constantinople.
[2] See A. A. Vasiliev, *History of the Byzantine Empire*, 2nd ed., Madison, 1958, i, 107.
[3] See J. B. Bury, *History of the Later Roman Empire*, London, 1923, i, 405.
[4] Gibbon, *Decline and Fall*, ed. Bury, i, 78. Gibbon says nothing of the horror of slavery, which disfigures the whole social life of the ancient world.

east, and its spectre was to haunt Europe for fifteen centuries—and the misery of financial instability, when successive emperors met financial deficits by the pernicious expedient of debasing the coinage—a policy which reached its climax when Gallienus (260–8) flooded the market with a worthless billon (silver-washed) currency, which was hardly distinguishable from copper. At the same time, internal confusion was accompanied by renewed pressure on the frontiers of the Empire. In the north, the German peoples, after two centuries of relative quiescence, were again on the move. Marcus Aurelius spent much of his reign campaigning against them. In 251 the Emperor Decius fell in battle against the Goths; and although they were checked by Gallienus, it was not until their rout by Claudius Gothicus in 269 that Rome enjoyed a temporary respite.

In the east the situation was equally perilous. The rise of the able and aggressive Sassanian dynasty in Persia confronted Rome with an enemy such as she had not known since the days of the Parthian Empire. In 260 the Emperor Valerian, while campaigning against the Persians, was taken prisoner by Shâpuhr I and ended his days in captivity—a disgrace unparalleled in Roman history. The Persian advance was subsequently checked, but the mischief was done. At the death of the Emperor Gallienus in 268, the situation was such that it seemed that the Roman Empire was already in a state of dissolution.

But the end had not yet come. The campaigns of Claudius Gothicus (died of the Plague in January 271 after a reign of only twenty-one months) and Aurelian (271–5) restored the military situation in the north and east. Thereafter, the labours of Diocletian (284–305) and Constantine the Great (312–37) effected a stabilization and a recovery. It is difficult in a few words to do justice to the work of these last two men. In a very real sense they can be called the saviours of the Roman Empire and yet, in another sense, their reconstitution (which involved a good deal of consolidation of work begun by their predecessors) may be criticized and regretted. Briefly, it had two results. First, a recognition of the fact that the administration of the Empire was beyond the scope of any one man, however able; a consideration which led, after various experiments under Diocletian, to the establishment of a dyarchy, with two emperors, one in the west, at Rome, Milan or Ravenna, and one in the east at Constantinople. This practical division of authority involved no suggestion that the Empire had been divided. On the contrary, it was an article of political faith that the Roman state was one and indivisible, and had been so, ever since the foundation of Rome. The two emperors of east and west exercised a single *imperium*. Decrees issued in one capital were ratified in the other and held good throughout the Empire. Nevertheless, the administrative division of the Empire marks a stage in the dissolution of the organism created by Augustus and enlarged and maintained by the emperors who followed him, for it amounted to an admission that troubled conditions no longer made it possible for the Empire to be run from a single capital. Furthermore, the nature of the division tended to widen the gulf between the richer, Greek-speaking provinces of the east and the poorer, Latin-speaking provinces of the west. Co-operation remained possible, and for centuries the Byzantine rulers remembered their western inheritance but, in the long run, it was in a Hellenic culture that the political tradition of imperial Rome was preserved, after the Latin homeland had fallen to the barbarian invader.

The second result of the reforms of Diocletian and Constantine was an extension of autocratic government to all departments of life. Essentially, this was a military measure, necessary in a beleaguered world, such as the Roman Empire had become. Its final development and archetype was to be the Byzantine autocracy, ruled by an emperor who was both the successor of the Caesars and God's vicegerent upon earth, and standing as the bulwark of Europe against the armies of Islam. There was, however, a price to be paid for this reorganization, for life in a beleaguered fortress is rarely a source of joy to the besieged, and the background of the world of the later Roman Empire, like the background of the Byzantine world, is one of sadness.

The reorganization of Diocletian and Constantine involved, besides a division of the Empire into east and west, a complete separation of military and civil administration. In the past it had proved too easy for an ambitious provincial governor with an army at his back to set himself up as a rival emperor. From now on, the civil authority was not to have command of troops, while military commanders were drawn increasingly from barbarian volunteers who, by reason of their origins, could never aspire to the imperial dignity which, as they themselves acknowledged, was the prerogative of the Roman alone. To pay these commanders and the troops they led and to meet the huge expense of imperial administration it was essential that taxes should be regularly forthcoming. A pure coinage was re-established and with it a new system of taxation, of which the main feature was that a tax in kind was substituted for a tax in money. Throughout the Empire, a unit of assessment of land, the *iugum*, was introduced, to be equal to the poll-tax on the individual, the *caput*. The actual area of the *iugum* varied according to the nature of the land, whether it was agricultural or used for vines or olives. A similar principle was employed in assessing the labour value of the *caput*. A man's labour was reckoned at one *caput*, a woman's at half this value, and animals were rated proportionately lower.

From this system, it was possible for the government to calculate, with the minimum of trouble, the income it could expect to receive from the taxation. In theory, the burden was supposed to be equitably imposed; in practice, it proved an abominable oppression, since it made no provision for the ravages of pestilence or the effects of a bad harvest. To the system of taxation was added another incubus, that of compulsory state service. Everywhere hereditary services were imposed on the various classes of society, and there came into being a caste system, in which each man followed his father's profession and met his obligations. While promotion to the higher ranks of society was not impossible, it was a jealously guarded privilege. Particularly wretched was the condition of the middle classes, the so-called *decuriones*, who furnished the councils of the provincial cities, since they were not only liable to pay taxes themselves, but were responsible for the collection of the poll-tax from their fellow citizens and any deficiency had to be made good from their own pockets. The miseries of the office were such that the decurionate soon became a very select body—select, because no one wanted to join it, while its members made strenuous efforts to get out. Membership of the provincial city senate, once an honour, now became a punishment, and not a few of the monks who fled to the Egyptian deserts were attracted, not so much by the ascetic life as by a desire to escape from their unenviable social position. The government, of course, had no hesitation in restoring such deserters to their duties, and it had been well said that 'in the later fourth century "hunt the decurion" became, as it were, the sport of the imperial bureaucracy'.[1]

Supreme as was the misery of the decurion, the peasant led a wretched enough life, the victim alike of the landlord, the tax-collector, and the recruiting-sergeant. The Christian apologist, Lactantius, admittedly a biased witness where Diocletian is concerned, paints a grisly picture of the governmental machine in action, wringing money from the people in order to maintain the massive fabric of the Roman order. It was not that the government desired to afflict its subjects; rather, the fault lay in the clumsy and brutal method that it employed, with a sublime confidence in the righteousness of its exactions which was to remain a feature of the imperial government for centuries to come. Very illuminating in this respect are the views of an East Roman merchant whom the Byzantine historian, Priscus,

[1] H. M. D. Parker, *A History of the Roman World from AD 138 to 337*, 2nd ed., London, 1958, 289.

found living in the camp of Attila the Hun in 449, nineteen years after the death of Augustine. This Roman renegade, after being captured by the Huns, had purchased his freedom with booty gained in their service, and now lived among them in far greater comfort than he had enjoyed in his home town of Viminacium, where peace was even more wretched than war on account of the pitiless collection of taxes and the helplessness of poor men before the law courts.[1] Similarly, in the next century, the Emperor Justinian frequently exhorts his tax-officials to have 'pure hands'; but his finance minister, John of Cappadocia, keeps a torture chamber in the dungeons of his official residence for the benefit of recalcitrant taxpayers.[2] These considerations provide a fitting commentary both on the justice of the complaints of the merchant living among the Huns and on the laboured and unconvincing reply by which Priscus sought to justify the condition of affairs in the Roman Empire.

In an age of material hardship, it was not a matter for wonder that men turned increasingly to religion to shed some ray of consolation on a world which offered so little. Gone were the days of scepticism, of the atheism of a Julius Caesar or the mockery of a Lucian of Samosata. 'The fourth century is above all an age dominated by the unseen.'[3] Just as the self-confidence of the Greek city state of the fifth century BC gave way to the doubts and fears of the Hellenistic age, so the old state religion of Rome failed utterly to satisfy the emotional needs of the Romans of the Empire. From the east came the mystery religions; the worship of Isis; Mithraism; and Christianity itself. For three centuries, the religion of the Crucified Jew had been gaining ground, particularly in the eastern provinces, in the face of fierce, but spasmodic and short-lived, persecutions, which produced many apostasies but also the heroic martyrdoms which inspired others to endure. The triumph of Christianity, from a worldly point of view, came in the early fourth century, when the Emperor Constantine adopted it as his own religion, thereby becoming, if not the first,[4] certainly the greatest of the imperial converts to the faith of Christ. The sincerity of

---

[1] Priscus, *Exc. de Legat.*, in L. Dindorf, *Historici Graeci Minores*, vol. i, Leipzig, 1870, 305–7. There is a translation of this passage in Bury, *Later Roman Empire*, i, 283–4. On the episode, see E. A. Thompson, *A History of Attila and the Huns*, Oxford, 1948, 184–7.
[2] John Lydus, *De Magistratibus*, iii, 57. *CSHB*, Pars xxi, 250.
[3] H. St L. B. Moss, *The Birth of the Middle Ages*, London, 1947, 13.
[4] Eusebius, *H.E.*, VI, 34, records a tradition that the Emperor Philip (244–9) was a Christian, and is followed by Orosius, *Historia*, vii, 20. 'This evidence is unhistorical and must be rejected' (Parker, *Roman World*, 157). On the other hand, the tradition is accepted by H. Grégoire, *Les persécutions dans l'empire romain* (Academie Royale de Belgique: Classe des lettres et des sciences morales et politiques, Tom. xlvi, Fasc. I), Brussels, 1951, 11: 'L'empereur qui célébra, en 248 après J.-C., naturellement, le millième anniversaire de la fondation de Rome, était chrétien. Le fait, souvent méconnu, est pour moi établi.'

the emperor's conversion has been much discussed, and very different estimates formed of his motives and character; but today few scholars would question the view that Constantine's profession of Christianity was a matter of genuine conviction, and not of political calculation.[1] It is significant that, from the point of view of worldly ambition, Constantine could hope to gain little from adopting the Christian religion. The Church was still a minority, with most of its members concentrated in the eastern provinces of the Empire. Constantine, who came from the west, would therefore have been better advised to cling to the monotheistic sun worship of his predecessors, which was essentially the religion of the army. But the final blow to theories of self-interest is given by the foundation, in 330, of Constantinople, 'New Rome', which was to equal old Rome in all but one particular—New Rome was a Christian city, whose pagan temples were for ornament and not for use, and where the emperor built many Christian churches, while the city on the Tiber long remained obstinately attached to her pagan traditions. This conservative love of the old religion was particularly marked in the ancient senatorial families, and Augustine himself observed that, in the mid-fourth century, almost all the Roman nobility was inspired with enthusiasm for pagan rites and mysteries.[2] From this atmosphere Constantine, who aspired (so he said) to be the Bishop of those without the Church, sought to escape by a new foundation. The idea of an imperial city in the east was not new; Diocletian had had his capital at Nicomedia; and the device of a divided administration is similarly Diocletianic. But the specifically Christian city on the Bosporus is a new conception, and marks a turning-point in Roman history. This does not mean that Christianity immediately became the official religion of

[1] For a convenient summary of views, see Norman Baynes, *Constantine the Great and the Christian Church* (Proceedings of the British Academy, xv), London, 1929. More recently, A. H. M. Jones, *Constantine and the Conversion of Europe*, London, 1948, 79–102; 'Notes on the Genuineness of the Constantinian Documents in Eusebius's Life of Constantine', in *JEH* v (1954), 196–200; Kurt Aland, 'Eine Wende in der Konstantin-Forschung?' in *Forschungen und Fortschritte*, Bd. 28, Heft 7 (July 1954).

[2] *Conf.*, VIII, ii, 3. Speaking of the conversion of the rhetorician and Platonist Victorinus, which is to be placed between 353 and 357, Augustine says: '[Victorinus] . . . usque ad illam aetatem venerator idolorum sacrorumque sacrilegorum particeps, quibus tunc tota fere Romana nobilitas inflata spirabat populo Osirim et *omnigenum deum monstra et Anubem latratorem*, quae aliquando

contra Neptunum et Venerem contraque Minervam

tela tenuerunt et a se victis iam Roma supplicabat.' During the second half of the fourth century, it seems that a number of noble Roman families became Christians. See Pierre de Labriolle, *La réaction païenne: Etude sur la polémique antichrétienne du Ier au VIe siècle*, Paris, 1948, 340–3; P. R. L. Brown, 'Aspects of the christianization of the Roman Aristocracy' in *JRS* li (1961), 1–11. There may well have been a pagan element in the hostility shown to St Jerome, after the death in 384 of the noble young widow Blesilla, said to have been brought about by excessive austerities, practised under Jerome's direction.

the Roman Empire. Rather, it secured an official, and a privileged, position, together with an inevitable appeal for the time-server and the fair-
weather proselyte. The short-lived pagan reaction under the Emperor
Julian (361–3) served only to demonstrate how little positive power remained in paganism as a rival to Christianity. Julian struggled with a
single-minded devotion to restore the ancient cults, but he found no
response among the pagans themselves. His friend and admirer, the loyal
soldier and honest historian Ammianus Marcellinus, thought Julian superstitious, rather than a correct observer of the rites,[1] while to others he was
an embarrassing fanatic. With his death, his attempted restoration of
paganism came to an end and the eventual triumph of the Church was
assured. Under the emperors Gratian (367–83) and Theodosius the Great
(378–95) a new phase is reached in the history of the Church—the introduction of definite anti-pagan legislation although, like so much of the
legislation of the later Empire, it does not seem to have been universally
enforced. Paganism was a long time dying. Even in Christian Constantinople in the sixth century, we are told that John of Cappadocia, Justinian's
hated taxation minister, 'gave no thought at all to God; and if ever he did
visit a church as if to pray and keep vigil, he did not behave in the least like
a Christian, but putting on a rough cloak proper for a priest of the old
faith which people are now accustomed to call Hellenic, he would repeat all
through the night certain unholy words which he had previously rehearsed,
that the emperor might be brought still more under his influence and he
himself be immune from harm by anyone.'[2] Just how numerous men like
John of Cappadocia were in the sixth century we cannot be sure, and in
any case our informant, Procopius, is an unreliable witness, with a personal axe to grind. There can, however, be no doubt that, while the end of
the fourth century and the beginning of the fifth saw the final victory of
Christianity,[3] there nevertheless remained many admirers of the old cults,
from aristocrats like the poet Rutilius Namatianus or the historian Count
Zosimus or Volusianus, with whom Augustine corresponded on the
subject of the Incarnation and the Virgin Birth,[4] to provincials like the

[1] Ammianus Marcellinus, *Historia*, XXV, 4, 17: '. . . superstitiosus magis quam sacro-
rum legitimus observator.' To the somewhat frivolous Christian city of Antioch, Julian
was simply ridiculous.
[2] Procopius, *De Bello Persico*, i, 25. *CSHB*, Pars ii, vol. i, p. 131. I give the translation
by P. N. Ure, *Justinian and his Age*, London, 1951, 204.
[3] See P. de Labriolle, op. cit., p. 467: 'On constate chez les défenseurs du christianisme, dans la dernière partie du IVe siècle et du début du Ve, une alacrité joyeuse,
expansive, un ton de certitude et de victoire, où se décèle la sécurité d'une situation
religieusement et politiquement trop forte pour que l'intellectualisme païen puisse doré-
navant l'ébranler.'
[4] Aug., *Epp.* 135, 137. See Brown, art. cit., pp. 7–8.

grammarian Maximus of Madauros, to whose epistolary overtures the saint sent a somewhat brusque reply.[1]

From the consideration of the Church as a whole, extending from Britain to Syria and even beyond the boundaries of the Empire where the Roman armies had never extended her sway, it is necessary to examine more closely that part which was established in Africa, in which Augustine was to exercise his ministry. The diocese[2] of Africa consisted in the fourth century, as a result of the Diocletianic reorganization of the Empire, of the provinces of Tripolitania, Byzacena, Africa Proconsularis or Zeugitana, Numidia, Mauretania Sitifensis and Mauretania Caesariensis—an area roughly equivalent to the present-day Tripolitanian littoral, Tunisia and Algeria. It fell within the western or Latin-speaking part of the Empire, and could boast of having given to Latin literature the dramatist Terence and the philosopher Lucius Apuleius, the author of the celebrated *Golden Ass*. Its population was not, however, Roman in origin, but was the product of the fusion of many races and peoples. The oldest inhabitants, the Berber peoples, destined to play an important part in North African history and to endure in the face of repeated foreign invasions, so that their language is still spoken in central Algeria to this day, formed the nucleus of the population. On the high plains of Numidia, lying between the mountain masses of the Kabylie to the north-west and the Aures mountains to the south, the effect of Latin culture had been relatively small (though the security afforded by Roman arms had led to considerable material prosperity founded upon the cultivation of the olive), but nearer the coast, in the urbanized country of forest and fertile valleys known as the Tell, Latin was widely spoken and generally familiar. It seems likely indeed that Augustine himself came of Berber stock, though his culture and outlook were thoroughly Roman. But besides the Berber influence there was that which had been exercised by Carthage from the earliest days of Phoenician settlement in the ninth century before Christ to her destruction by Rome in 146 BC—and after, for Punic continued to be spoken down

---

[1] Aug., *Ep.* 17.

[2] 'Diocese' is here used in the civil and not the ecclesiastical sense. Diocletian had divided the Empire into four Prefectures: of the East; of Illyricum; of Italy; and of the Gauls. These were in turn divided into dioceses, administered by a *vicarius* or civil governor. The dioceses again were divided into provinces, under governors called variously *consulares, correctores* or *praesides*. There was thus a chain of command from the *praeses* (or his equivalent) to the *vicarius*, and from him to the Pretorian Prefect, in charge of the Prefecture. The diocese of Africa came within the prefecture of Italy but, by a special privilege, the governor of Africa Proconsularis continued to bear the old republican title of Proconsul and was responsible directly to the emperor, without the intermediary of either *vicarius* or Pretorian Prefect. See Bury, *Later Roman Empire*, i, 25–28; B. H. Warmington, *The North African Provinces from Diocletian to the Vandal Conquest*; and Ch. A. Julien, *Histoire de l'Afrique du Nord*, 2e éd., Paris, 1956, i, 199–200.

to Augustine's own day, while the Emperor Septimius Severus, who marched from his command on the Danube to seize power at Rome in 193 and died at York in 211 while on campaign against the tribes of Caledonia, was a native of the Phoenician settlement of Leptis Magna in Tripolitania, and a member of an old Phoenician family.

To the admixture of Berber and Punic blood which made up much of the population of Roman Africa must be added that of Roman colonists. Carthage herself had been refounded by Augustus in 29 BC, after the abortive attempt by Gaius Gracchus a century earlier, and by the fourth century had become the great metropolis of Africa, in size second only to Rome in the western part of the Empire. The heterogeneous population of Africa showed traces of its mixed origins. Besides the more obvious characteristics of Mediterranean peoples: a taste for wine and women, and an easygoing generosity (like that of the thief who explained to Augustine that although he got his fortune by stealing he gave money to the poor), there went a sternness and a gloomy superstition which could easily break out into outbursts of religious fanaticism—traits which are readily explicable if it is remembered that the old Berber deity, called Saturn by the Romans, was a jealous and implacable being, who had to be propitiated with human or substitute sacrifices, while the Carthaginian worship of Baal Hammon notoriously included the offering of children—a practice which scandalized the Greeks and the Romans.

The origins of African Christianity are shrouded in mystery. At the end of the second century the Church of Carthage suddenly appears as an organized body. The source of that church is unknown, but those who have studied the matter most carefully consider that it was probably Rome, and there is no good reason to question this view. The first document of African Christianity which we possess (which is, incidentally, the earliest original Christian Latin document known)[1] is the record of the trial and condemnation of a little group of Christians of Scillium (of unknown location) at Carthage, before the proconsul, Vigellius Saturninus, on 16 July 180. Then, at the turn of the second century, appears the first great Christian Latin writer, Quintus Septimus Florens Tertullianus. We have no knowledge of the dates of his birth or death, but he was probably born about 160 and lived, according to St Jerome, to a very great age. He was a Carthaginian, but visited Rome. Tertullian was a man of vast erudition, particularly with regard to law and philosophy, and a ready writer,

---

[1] The Latin translation of the first epistle of St Clement of Rome is to be assigned to the first half of the second century and is therefore older. See Christine Mohrmann, 'Les origines de la latinité chrétienne à Rome', *Vigiliae Christianae*, iii (1949), 78.

employing a tortured but tremendously impressive style and always writing at white heat. A pamphleteer of genius, he lashed pagans and heretics alike with the bitterest invective; but his own temperament was too stormy and his confidence in his own judgement too great for him to remain in the Catholic Church. In his later years he joined the Montanists, a sect of enthusiasts from Asia Minor, given to prophesying and visions. But even the Montanists failed to satisfy the exacting standards required by Tertullian and, at the end of his life, he broke away from them to form his own private sect of Tertullianists, which survived as a tiny community in the city of Carthage until Augustine's own lifetime, when the survivors were quietly received back into the Catholic Church, their own peculiar tenet that the soul was material being regarded as not sufficiently serious to justify their exclusion.[1] Tertullian's defection to the Montanists naturally rendered the whole corpus of his writings suspect to good Catholics. 'By his subsequent error,' declared St Hilary of Poitiers, 'he took away authority from his orthodox writings',[2] and this might well have been the verdict of the whole Church, had it not been for the attitude of St Cyprian (executed in 258), the great martyr bishop of the Church of Carthage. A whole-hearted admirer of Tertullian's genius, Cyprian was an assiduous student of his works, and the phrase by which he would ask for a book: 'Give me the master!'[3] was a sufficient reassurance for any tender soul uneasy about Tertullian's orthodoxy, for St Cyprian was the great enemy of all schism and separation. Posterity has confirmed St Cyprian's opinion of one of the outstanding writers of the early Church.

Thus, at the beginning of the third century, the African Church already possessed a writer of genius. But it was not only in literature that her strength lay. The spirit of martyrdom which, as we have seen, ushers in her stormy history was strong, and the lists of her martyrs was steadily growing. In the year 203[4] there suffered in the amphitheatre of Carthage a young matron of good family, Vibia Perpetua, with a band of humble companions, including a slave girl, Felicitas. The account of their martyrdom, with an introduction perhaps written by Tertullian himself, has given us the most beautiful of the Acts of the Martyrs.[5] And behind this heroic spirit of witness for Christ and willing self-sacrifice, the administration of

---

[1] Aug., *De Haeres.*, 86.

[2] Hilarius Pictaviensis, *Commentarius in Matthaeum*, v, 1: 'consequens error hominis detraxit scriptis probabilibus auctoritatem.' *MPL* ix, 943.

[3] Hieronymus, *De Viris Illustribus*, 54. *MPL* xxiii, 661, 663.

[4] For a discussion of the date, see Monceaux, *Histoire littéraire de l'Afrique chrétienne*, Paris, 1901, i, 71–72.

[5] Editions are J. Armitage Robinson, *Texts and Studies*, Cambridge, 1891, and E. Knopf, *Ausgewählte Märtyrerakten*, Tübingen, 1929.

the Church was steadily consolidated. Seventy bishops met in council under the presidency of Agrippinus of Carthage, some time after AD 200,[1] and about this time also Christian communities would appear to have been established, not only in the cities of Proconsular Africa, in the coastal area, around the modern Tunis and Bizerte, but as far east as Leptis Magna, near the modern Homs in Tripolitania, and westwards as far as Setif, in modern Algeria.[2] Enthusiasm and organization alike meant that the time was ripe for a great ecclesiastical leader who, by his inspiration, would weld the African Christian communities into a formidable body in the eyes of the Roman world. Such a leader was found in the person of St Cyprian of Carthage, born probably about 210, brought up as a pagan, converted through the influence of a venerable priest called Caecilianus, and baptized, probably at Easter 246. He was consecrated bishop not long after his baptism at the demand of the people and against his own will. During the years of his episcopate, by sheer force of character and apparently without any design on his own part, St Cyprian became the acknowledged spokesman of the African bishops and, after his execution in 258, the most popular saint of Africa.[3]

It is not possible within the limits of the present narrative to deal with St Cyprian's life at any length, but two episodes must be mentioned, because of their influence upon subsequent African Church history. The first concerns St Cyprian's attitude to the treatment of the *lapsi*—those Christians who had fallen away in time of persecution, and offered sacrifice to the gods of the heathen, denying their Lord. Behind the little heroic band of martyrs who remained faithful to the death in the time of tribulation and the no less heroic confessors, who bore witness to their Christianity but who languished in prison, whether by accident or the deliberate design of the pagan government, deprived of the opportunity to shed their blood for Christ, there was another group, probably very numerous, which did not endure but which, when threatened with death or torture, apostasized and offered incense to the genius of the emperor. When the persecution had, for the moment, subsided, many of these were seized with remorse and begged for absolution and for permission to receive the sacraments once more. As to the propriety of granting that request, there was a difference of opinion; for there was in Africa, and indeed throughout the

---

[1] Cyprian, *Epp.* 71, 4; 73, 3. *CSEL* iii, 2, 774, 780.
[2] Frend, *The Donatist Church*, 88.
[3] Although marked by sectarian prejudice, E. W. Benson, *Cyprian: His life, his times and his work*, London, 1897, is still the best biography in English, while there is an excellent short life in French by Paul Monceaux, *Saint Cyprien*, Paris, 1914. The chapter 'Saint Cyprien et son temps', in the same author's *Histoire littéraire*, ii, 1902, is fundamental. There is a good chapter in Frend, op. cit., pp. 125–40.

whole of the Christian Church, a rigorist element which held that there could be no hope of pardon in this world for the man who had renounced his baptism and crucified Christ afresh by offering sacrifice to pagan gods. Only a lifetime of penitence and exclusion from the sacraments could await such a sinner, at the end of which he might hope, after death, to obtain the pardon which the Church on earth dared not bestow. In considering the grim nature of this sentence, it is necessary to remember the extreme view taken in the early Church with regard to any mortal sin committed after baptism, a view which explains the common practice of clinical baptism, that is, of deferring baptism until the approach of death, and thereby reducing the possibility of grave sin after its reception.

At the opposite extreme to the rigorists stood another group, holding a more optimistic view of the position of the lapsed. According to these, the lapsed could be absolved from their guilt by the intercessions of the Confessors, who had been willing to shed their blood for Christ but had not, in fact, been put to death. Already in the Church, the martyr and the confessor were held in particular veneration—it was felt that they had, by their sufferings, acquired a power of intercession with God. So far as this view concerns the martyrs, the question is a theological one and need not be considered in this context; but as regards the confessors, who were still on earth and among the faithful in the flesh, the problem was very acute, since certain of them assumed that they could themselves absolve penitents in virtue of their own merits as confessors, without reference to the bishop.

St Cyprian's handling of the matter revealed an admirable temper, in which firmness was combined with gentleness. A council of African bishops which met at Carthage in the spring of 251 under his presidency declared that the *libellatici*—those who had not actually sacrificed but who had, by devious means, secured certificates of sacrifice from the authorities to avoid molestation—should be reconciled after penance, while the *thurificati*—those who had offered sacrifice—should do penance and only be admitted to communion if in danger of death.[1] A year later, at Easter, these too were readmitted.[2]

The treatment of the lapsed was, however, only a part of the problem which confronted the African bishops at the end of the Decian persecution. Divergent views over the treatment of these same lapsed caused the uncompromising elements of the rigorist party to go into schism from the remainder of the fellow Christians, loudly proclaiming that they alone held

[1] Cyprian, *Ep.* 55, 17. *CSEL* iii (2), 635–6.
[2] Id., *Epp.* 56, 2; 57, 1. *CSEL* iii (2), 648–9, 650–1.

the faith undefiled. At Carthage the situation was soon brought under control and the dissidents excommunicated. At Rome, however, the situation was more serious. There, the rigorist party was led by a certain Novatian, an austere man and an able theologian, who contrived to get himself consecrated bishop in opposition to pope Cornelius, the rightful occupant of the see. In the early stages of the Novatianist schism, the position at Rome was not clear to the African Church, and the council which excommunicated the Carthaginian schismatics felt unable to declare for either Roman party without due inquiry. Accordingly, a deputation was sent to Rome and, on its recommendations, the African bishops extended their official recognition to Cornelius and excommunicated Novatian.

It was in connection with these disputes that St Cyprian wrote one of his most famous works, the treatise *De Catholicae Ecclesiae Unitate* (*On the Unity of the Christian Church*). In it he emphasized the view, which was to have portentous consequences in the history of African Christianity, that since the Church is one, there can be no spiritual life among those who separate themselves from her. 'There is one head, one origin, one mother prolific with offspring; of her are we born, by her milk we are nourished, by her spirit we are quickened.'[1] A man cannot have God for a father who does not have the Church for a mother. If there had been any escape from the waters of the Flood outside the ark of Noah, there might have been some escape for those outside the Church.[2] St Cyprian presses to its logical conclusion the Dominical saying: *He that is not with Me is against Me; and he that gathereth not with Me scattereth.*

The second incident in St Cyprian's career which particularly concerns us occurred towards the end of his life. This is the controversy with St Stephen, bishop of Rome, as to whether heretics who returned to the communion of the Church, having been already baptized in their heretical sect, should be rebaptized, as was the custom in Africa and in the Greek-speaking churches of Asia Minor. The principle underlying this practice is the principle which animates the *De Unitate*: that outside the Church there can be no valid ministry since there is no valid spirituality. Nor can there be valid martyrdom. A schismatic may be put to death for the name of Christ, but he cannot be regarded as a martyr because he has violated the first principle of martyrdom, since he does not possess fraternal charity. Such a man may be killed, but he cannot be crowned.[3] This, however, was

---

[1] *De Unitate*, 5: 'Unum tamen caput est et origo una et una mater fecunditatis successibus copiosa; illius fetu nascimur, illius lacte nutrimur, spiritu eius animamur.' *CSEL* iii (1), 214.
[2] Ibid., 6.
[3] Ibid., 14: 'occidi talis potest, coronari non potest.' *CSEL* iii (1), 223.

an argument which had been directed against men who were schismatic in conduct but orthodox in belief. Far worse was the case of those who, to the sin of schism, added that of holding and teaching false doctrine. From the Cyprianic point of view, it was impossible that such men could validly administer the sacraments.

These opinions brought St Cyprian into collision with St Stephen in the spring of 256. In the early part of the preceding year, Cyprian had been asked by a certain Magnus whether converts from the Novatian schism should be rebaptized.[1] The bishop of Carthage did not hesitate. In a long letter he recommended rebaptism, appealing to Scripture and to the tradition of the African Church. An African council which met in the same year,[2] and which was attended by thirty-one bishops, endorsed Cyprian's recommendation. In the spring of 256 another council, this time consisting of seventy-one members, reaffirmed the previous decision, and communicated the reaffirmation by a letter to Stephen of Rome.[3] The Roman church did not follow the African practice of rebaptizing, and it is difficult to believe that Cyprian was not aware of this. The African council's decision cannot have failed to be very unwelcome at Rome, where the Novatian schism, which had been crushed relatively easily in Africa, still remained a formidable problem. No doubt Stephen of Rome was glad to receive into communion any Novatianist who cared to come over without introducing an added obstacle by insisting on rebaptism, or by emphasizing that, elsewhere, they would certainly have been rebaptized. At all events, he replied to the African bishops' communication with a forceful letter, requiring Cyprian to observe the Roman custom, and claiming the right to impose it upon other churches, both African and Oriental. To this command was added the threat of excommunication for those who refused to obey.[4]

St Cyprian was not unduly alarmed by this outburst. He had always in the past treated the occupant of the Roman see with respect, but with the respect due to a *primus inter pares*, since Cyprian held that all bishops were equal and independent, except in matters of faith.[5] He obtained the support of the churches of Asia Minor, who were at one with those of Africa on the subject of rebaptism. Then, on 1 September 256, yet another council, convoked by him and numbering eighty-seven bishops from all over

[1] Cyprian, *Ep.* 69, 1. *CSEL* iii (2), 749–50.
[2] *Ep.* 70. *CSEL* iii (2), 766–70.
[3] *Ep.* 72, 1. *CSEL* iii (2), 775–6.
[4] *Epp.* 74, 1; 75, 25. *CSEL* iii (2), 799; 826–7.
[5] *De Unitate*, 4, 5; *Epp.* 69, 17; 73, 26. Cf. Paul Monceaux, *Histoire littéraire*, ii, 228: 'Il estimait que toutes les Eglises étaient égales et tous les évêques indépendents, sauf sur les questions de foi.'

North Africa, assembled at Carthage and gave him unanimous support.[1]

By one of the ironies of history, we have no detailed knowledge of the outcome of the dispute, and cannot tell whether Stephen carried out his threat to excommunicate Cyprian. All that can be said is that the quarrel between the church of Rome and the churches of Africa and Asia Minor did not have immediately serious results. Stephen died in 257, apparently as a martyr, and Cyprian seems to have been on good terms with his successor, pope Xystus. On a superficial examination, the incident might be considered closed.

In the history of African Christianity, unfortunately, it was to have the gravest consequences. After his martyrdom in 258, Cyprian's thought and teaching became the dominating influence upon African doctrine both for good and ill. Certain aspects acquired a lasting and not very happy fame in a movement which is to be counted as one of the most remarkable in the history of the Christian Church. That movement was Donatism.

The Donatist schism was a product of the persecution which began with Diocletian's first edict against Christianity on 23 February 303. Wiser and more merciful than his predecessors, the emperor did not wish to proceed to extremes against the Church but hoped, rather, by bringing pressure to bear upon the clergy to render the laity leaderless, and so bring about general apostasy. Hence, a new technique was applied to the method of persecution—a demand for the surrender of the Scriptures to the authorities. Many clergy obeyed the order, or handed over what they said were the sacred writings, but were in fact heretical books, denounced by the Church, and fit fuel for the imperial bonfire. As a consequence, the great issue which arose after the persecution was ended was not that of *libellatici* and *thurificati*, as in Cyprian's day, but of *traditores*—'handers over'—those who had committed the sin of *traditio*, by surrendering God's Word to His enemies. Such persons were universally condemned, and the ingenuity of those who had avoided the surrender of the Scriptures by handing over some spurious work was not calculated to excite the admiration of their fellows. Among such contrivers was Mensurius, the bishop of Carthage who, in a letter to Secundus, bishop of Tigisis and primate of

---

[1] *Sententiae episcoporum numero LXXXVII de haereticis baptizandis. CSEL* iii [1], 435ff. The dispute between Cyprian and Stephen has itself been the subject of much controversy, particularly between Roman and Anglican apologists, since the latter have, for obvious reasons, frequently appealed to the example of St Cyprian in defence of their own position. Stephen has been the object of a good deal of criticism, even from those who consider him to have been in the right; but his conduct may well deserve more sympathy than it usually receives. See N. Zernov in the *Church Quarterly Review*, cxvii (Jan. 1934), 304ff. Zernov's views are accepted by T. G. Jalland, *The Church and the Papacy*, London, 1944, 168–74.

Numidia, described how he ordered certain heretical works to be deposited in the Basilica Novorum at Carthage, which were surrendered to the officer of the proconsul as the Scriptures.[1] Mensurius died in 311. Next year his archdeacon, Caecilian, was elected as his successor. Although popular with the citizens of Carthage, Caecilian was disliked by the rigorist group in the Carthaginian church. During the persecution, he had supported Mensurius in discouraging attempts to seek martyrdom by deliberately provoking the authorities. It was alleged that in 304 he had allowed a party of Christians from Abitina (probably the modern Chaoud near Medjez el Bab in the Mejerda valley) to starve to death, in their Carthaginian prison, and had even stationed armed guards at the doors to prevent the faithful from bringing them food. How true these accusations may have been we do not know. On the face of it, they seem extravagant. However, the victims of any persecution include men of doubtful character and motive, as well as genuinely innocent persons. In the third century the sceptical Lucian of Samosata had written a satire on the life and death of the charlatan Proteus, alias Peregrinus, who at one point in his disreputable career affected Christianity, and had accordingly been arrested in a time of persecution:

> During the time that he was in prison, the Christians, looking upon it as a general misfortune, tried every means to get him released. Then, when this was found impossible, their attention to him in all other ways was zealous and unremitting. From early dawn you might see widows and orphans waiting at the prison doors; and the men of rank among them even bribed the jailers to allow them to pass the night with him inside the walls. Then they brought in to him there sumptuous meals, and read their sacred books together; and this good Peregrinus (for he was then called so) was termed by them a second Socrates. There came certain Christians, too, from some of the cities of Asia, deputed by their community to bring him aid, and to counsel and encourage him. For they are wonderfully ready whenever their public interest is concerned —in short, they grudge nothing; and so much money came in to Peregrinus at that time, by reason of his imprisonment, that he made a considerable income by it. For these poor wretches persuade themselves that they shall be made immortal, and live for everlasting; so that they despise death, and some of them offer themselves to it voluntarily.[2]

Such was the case with one rogue in the third century; and in spite of the malice and contempt which inspire Lucian's writing, his story serves

[1] Aug., *Breviculus Collationis*, III, xiii, 25.
[2] Lucian, *Peregrinus*, 12, 13. Tr. by W. Lucas Collins, *Lucian*, Edinburgh/London, 1873, 170-1.

as a reminder that not everyone who went to prison as a declared Christian was necessarily anxious only to bear witness to Christ. It is conceivable that the persons against whom Caecilian was supposed to have taken drastic action were men of the stamp of Peregrinus.

Whatever the reason, a powerful body of Caecilian's enemies, encouraged by a rich woman called Lucilla, a Spaniard living at Carthage, who had never forgotten or forgiven the archdeacon for having rebuked her at one time for kissing the alleged bone of a martyr before receiving communion, set themselves up in opposition to Caecilian. An objection to the validity of his consecration was found in the fact that one of his consecrating bishops, Felix of Apthungi, was said to have been a *traditor*. This accusation was taken up by the bishops of the province of Numidia whose primate, Secundus of Tigisis, was highly offended at not having been invited to exercise his traditional right to consecrate the bishop-elect of Carthage. Accordingly, the Numidians declared that Caecilian had not been validly consecrated, and proceeded to elect and consecrate a servant of Lucilla, Majorinus, in Caecilian's place. So the dispute became a schism. After the death of Majorinus, which occurred shortly after his consecration, probably as early as the summer of 313, a successor was found in the person of Donatus of Casae Nigrae, the man who, more than any other, built up the schismatic church, so that he ultimately bestowed his name upon it, and men spoke of Donatism and the Donatist Church.

The theological position of the Donatists was the logical development of one aspect of St Cyprian's doctrine of the unity of the Church, and the invalidity of sacraments administered outside her. The position of the *traditor* is that of the schismatic or the heretic. He has, by his own action, cut himself off from the body of the Church, and cannot therefore bring forth fruit. The view was pithily expressed by one of Secundus of Tigisis' Numidian colleagues at the very beginning of the schism.

In His Gospel the Lord says: *I am the true vine and My Father is the husbandman. Every branch in Me that beareth not fruit He cutteth off and casteth it away ; and every branch that beareth fruit, He cleanseth it.* Thus, unfruitful branches are to be cut off and cast aside. So *thurificati, traditores* and those who, being in schism, are ordained by *traditores*, cannot remain within the Church of God unless they are reconciled through penance, with wailing acknowledgement [of their fault]. Hence no one ought to communicate with Caecilian, who has been ordained by *traditores* in schism.[1]

[1] *Inter opera* Aug., *C. Fulgentium*, 26 (citing Iohan. 15, 2). *MPL* xliii, 774. Tr. by Frend, op. cit., p. 20.

Sentiments such as these found a ready echo in the hearts of many African Christians, particularly among the country-dwellers of the High Plains to the south and west of the coast-line of Tunisia and modern Algeria. Here popular enthusiasm could rejoice in being the Church of the Saints, free from the taint of association with *traditores* and the sons of *traditores*, and holding fast to the traditions of the great Cyprian, the most popular of African saints. Nor was this enthusiasm shaken by the demolition of the factual assumptions on which it reposed; for apart from the fact that a considerable number of enthusiastic Donatists had apparently themselves been guilty of *traditio*—including their leader Donatus, or so the Catholics declared—investigation into the conduct of Felix of Apthungi, the ostensible cause of the whole dispute, vindicated him completely. As early as 313 Majorinus and his party appealed to the Emperor Constantine, asking for judges to be appointed from Gaul to settle the dispute. Constantine referred the appeal to the bishop of Rome, pope Miltiades, instructing him to investigate the matter with the assistance of the bishops of Cologne, Autun, and Arles. Miltiades does not seem to have greatly cared for the tone of the imperial letter, which might be thought to treat him rather as if he were a senior civil servant, and accordingly added fifteen other bishops to the court, thereby transforming 'an imperial commission of inquiry' into a Church council.[1]

The council gave judgement in favour of Caecilian. The Donatists declined to accept the verdict. Constantine allowed an appeal, and another and larger council met at Arles in 314. Here, thirty-three bishops confirmed the Roman decision. At the same time an independent commission under the proconsul of Africa, Aelianus, declared Felix of Apthungi innocent of the charge of having surrendered or burned the Scriptures. The Donatists refused to accept the decisions either of the council or of the commission. In 321 the exasperated Constantine turned to coercion to make them conform, but the effort lasted for only three months. Donatism was too strong and, in the next few years, it was to go from strength to strength. Within a generation it had become the religion of a very large part—according to St Jerome, almost the whole[2] —of Africa.

The subsequent history of Donatism and Augustine's struggle against it will be discussed at length in a later chapter. For the moment it is only

---

[1] A. H. M. Jones, *Constantine and the Conversion of Europe*, 109.
[2] Hieron., *De Viris Illustr.*, 93: 'Donatus, a quo Donatiani per Africam sub Constantinio Constantinoque pullulaverunt, asserens, a nostris Scripturas in persecutione Ethnicis traditas, totam pene Africam et maxime Numidiam, sua persuasione decepit.' *MPL* xxiii, 695.

necessary to consider its effect upon African Christianity at the middle of the fourth century. Because of the Donatist schism, the once united Church of Africa was torn asunder, with altar set up against altar and mutual hatred replacing fraternal charity. The significance of this division could not be lost on any thoughtful African Christian in the fourth century, and it was to dominate Augustine's mind during the whole of his Christian ministry. It is Donatism which differentiates the religious history of Africa from that of other provinces of the Roman Empire. Some parallel can be found in the east in the case of the Nestorians and the Monophysites, but here vitally important Christological issues were involved, compared with which the issues in dispute between the Donatists and the African Catholics were of only secondary importance. In his later years Augustine described the Donatists as heretics in order that the imperial laws against heresy might be invoked against them; but in his dealings with the Donatists themselves, he always emphasized that there was no doctrinal difference between them. Essentially, the issue was one of schism, not heresy.

If we reflect upon the characteristics of the world, the province and the church in which Augustine of Hippo lived and worked, we find strange contrasts, and an environment which is both like our own and also very unlike. On the one hand, there is much in the administration—the bureaucracy and the chain of command—which resembles our own age and society, at least in states of a collectivist and totalitarian structure. Furthermore, there is a sense of unity imparted by the Roman Empire, which is lacking in the Middle Ages, except as a nostalgic memory. Travel, if not particularly speedy, was relatively safe and easy at the time of Augustine's birth, when the Mediterranean was still a Roman lake; and during the saint's lifetime, St Jerome could leave Italy and settle at Bethlehem, and yet keep up a correspondence with his friends in western Europe, although it must be admitted that this correspondence, which relied upon the good nature of travellers (for there was no postal service for private individuals), was a slow business, and might lead to misunderstanding and ill-feeling when letters went astray, as happened once in the case of Augustine. Nevertheless, even with this limitation, we can observe in the later Empire a lack of parochialism, an awareness of the world beyond the individual's particular locality, which recalls at times the ethos of the twentieth century. In the course of this study, it will appear that events and developments in Italy, and even in Palestine, considerably affected the situation in Africa when Augustine was bishop.

Yet, having said this, it is also true that, if the later Empire was in some respects very like our own world, it was in others profoundly different. Indeed, if we except Christianity—and this is an exception which, for many people, including the writer, will invalidate the comparison—there is a case for holding that the Roman Empire approached less nearly to our own civilization than to that of classical China. In both these civilizations we find certain impressive similarities: a great political unit ruled autocratically by a single monarch, the Vicegerent of God[1]; an administration recruited from an educated class whose minds had been formed largely by the study of literature; and a certain sense of unity, a conviction that one's own civilization is the only valid one, from which all peoples should, if they were capable of so doing, learn, and that those who were not partakers in it were barbarians. This attitude on the Chinese side was expressed in 1793 in the famous reply of the Emperor Ch'ien-lung to the request of the British government through the mission of Lord Macartney that diplomatic and commercial relations should be established between their respective kingdoms:

> As to your entreaty to send one of your nationals to be accredited to my Celestial Court and to be in control of your country's trade with China, this request is contrary to all usage of my dynasty and cannot possibly be entertained. . . . Our ceremonies and code of laws differ so completely from your own that, even if your envoy were able to acquire the rudiments of our civilisation, you could not possibly transplant our manners and customs to your alien soil. . . . Swaying the wide world, I have but one aim in view, namely, to maintain a perfect governance and to fulfil the duties of the State. . . . I set no value on objects strange or ingenious, and have no use for your country's manufactures.[2]

The calm assumption which lay behind the Chinese emperor's message —an assumption which was to be rudely shattered less than half a century later when, by the Treaty of Nanking of 1842, China was forced to cede Hong Kong to Britain and to open five ports south of the Yangtze to foreign residents and trade—is paralleled in Italy at the beginning of the fifth century of the Christian Era by the Christian poet Prudentius who, anxious to emphasize the difference between Christianity and paganism, declares without hesitation:

> There is the same gulf fixed between the Roman world and that of the barbarians as between bipeds and quadrupeds, or between a dumb brute and a creature endowed with speech. There is also the same

[1] It is true that the later Roman Empire was in practice administered by two or more emperors reigning simultaneously, but there was no division of the *imperium*. The *potestas imperialis* remained one.

[2] F. Whyte, *China and Foreign Powers*, London, 1927, Appendix I, p. 39.

B

distance between those who duly follow the precepts of God, and ridiculous cults and those who follow their errors.[1]

There could be no more fitting comment upon the unquestioning assumption of superiority with which the Roman of the later Empire viewed the world outside than this almost unthinking comparison made, not by a pagan littérateur, but by the first great Christian Latin poet.

But—again like China—beneath this assumption of superiority, an assumption based primarily upon literary considerations ('If we lose our eloquence,' said the rhetorician Libanius, 'what will be left to distinguish us from the barbarians?'),[2] there was a spiritual void, a dark world peopled with demons and hostile powers, always waiting to seize their victim. The unseen dominated men's lives. They were haunted by fear of magic and the Evil Eye, to whose malefic influence the numerous prophylactic phallic symbols found in the excavations of Roman towns in Africa bear eloquent witness.[3] Astrology, which has so often been the curse of human intellectual progress, by imposing the dead hand of fate upon men's freedom, exercised a terrible fascination, despite the denunciation of men of science[4] and divines. Augustine, as a bishop, had frequently to denounce astrology, and emphasize that the notion of an ineluctable fate is destructive of any sort of morality.[5] There is no reason to think that African congregations of the fourth and fifth centuries were greatly inferior in intelligence to ourselves. While they lacked the theological sophistication which made their fellow Christians in the Greek-speaking part of the Empire discuss trinitarian doctrine avidly, and brought crowds to hear the sermons of a brilliant thinker like St Gregory Nazianzen at Constantinople, it is likely that Augustine's flock at Hippo were as well informed about Christian doctrine as the inhabitants of a modern parish. Where they differed was in the background to their belief. It is not merely that they were, by present-day standards, ignorant of many facts about the nature of the physical world familiar to any schoolboy today; nor was it simply that, for most of them, life was physically hard and uncertain, while even those who were relatively well off and had money and property did not enjoy many

[1] Prudentius, Contra Symmachum, II, 816–19. CSEL lxi, 276.

>Sed tantum distant Romana et barbara, quantum
>quadrupes abiuncta est bipedi vel muta loquenti,
>quantum etiam, qui rite dei praecepta sequuntur,
>cultibus a stolidis et eorum erroribus absunt.

[2] Libanius, Ep. 372.
[3] See Frend, The Donatist Church, 102–3; id., 'The Gnostic-Manichaean Tradition in North Africa', in JEH iv (1953), 18–19.
[4] Like Vindicianus, proconsul of Africa and former physician, who advised Augustine, as a young man, to give up his interest in astrology. See Conf., IV, iii, 4–6.
[5] See Van der Meer, Saint Augustin: Pasteur d'ames, i, 115–26.

minor luxuries which the ordinary citizen of a progressive European state in the twentieth century takes for granted (the luxury of a private bathroom would be quite a good example). The great intellectual difference was that the members of Augustine's congregation lived their lives under a continual threat of attack by unseen forces, numerous, powerful, and inspired by hostility to mankind. And behind these demon armies was the inexorable deity Fate (*Fatum*, *'Ανάγκη*), whose unalterable decree could be read in the stars by those who had the skill, and the unforeseeable element Chance (*Fortuna*, *Τύχη*), whose intervention could suddenly fling a man into the power of Fate. It was into this demon-haunted and Fate-dominated world that the Gospel brought its message of hope. Fate and Chance were not the final arbiters of human destiny. Divine Providence, which was not an abstract, impersonal thing, but the decree of God, who was *Φιλάνθρωπος*, the Lover of Mankind, offered freedom from the powers which had dominated the pre-Christian world. The Word made Flesh released man from the power of the demon armies which lay in wait to destroy him. The significance of the words of the Seventy recorded by St Luke (10.17): *Lord, even the demons are subject to us in Thy name*, makes little impact at the present time, when most people have no belief in demons at all and even orthodox Christians give little thought to the power of Satan and his angels, but the wonder and delight which they expressed were very well understood in the fourth century.

St Augustine is a product of his age and it should not, therefore, be a matter for surprise that his thought and teaching bear traces of its influence. On many issues, and those the most important, he outsoars the limitations of his contemporaries in a manner befitting one of the greatest of the great teachers of Christianity. Elsewhere, however, Augustine's knowledge and opinions are those of a man of the later Roman Empire—an educated man and a Christian, but a man subject to the influences of his time and place. It is this fact which explains the slight shock which we sometimes experience, when reading him, by coming upon some piece of naïveté or brutality, which appears to be utterly at variance with his more inspired teaching. Nothing is gained by seeking to discount the less attractive aspects of Augustine's life and thought but, at the same time, allowance must be made for the circumstances and conventions of another period of human history. It is with a willingness to recognize these circumstances and conventions that we may profitably embark upon our study of Augustine's career.

2

Augustine's Life: I

Herr! ich steh in deinem Frieden,
Ob ich lebe, ob ich sterbe;
Starb mein Heiland doch hienieden,
Dass ich sein Verdienst erwerbe.

Will der Schmetterling zum Lichte,
Muss die Larve er zerbrechen;
So hast du dies Haus vernichtet,
Meine Freiheit auszusprechen.

CLEMENS BRENTANO

AURELIUS AUGUSTINE, bishop of Hippo, saint and Doctor of the Church, was born at Thagaste, the modern Souk-Ahras in Tunisia, on 13 November 354.[1] Of his family origins we are ignorant; but there is no reason to suppose that he was of any but Berber stock,[2] while the name Aurelius[3] suggests that his family were among the many who were enfranchised by the famous edict of Caracalla of 212, whereby almost all the freemen of the Empire became Roman citizens.[4] The point, however, is an academic one. In appearance, Augustine would probably not have differed from other dwellers on the western Mediterranean littoral, while he spoke Latin as naturally as any inhabitant of Italy of his own day or as a French *colon* living in Algeria in the twentieth century spoke French.[5] In determining a man's race, culture is a more significant factor than blood;[6] and nowhere do we find Augustine thinking of himself as anything other than a Latin-speaking Roman. The population of Thagaste was no doubt mostly of Berber stock; but Latin would have been the language of the

[1] *De Beata Vita*, i, 6: 'Idibus Novembris mihi natalis dies erat.'
[2] See H. I. Marrou, *Saint Augustin et l'augustinisme*, 11: 'Le calcul des probabilités permet d'inférer qu'il était sans doute de pure race berbère.'
[3] Aurelius is presumably his *nomen* and Augustinus his *cognomen*. We have no information about any *praenomen*.
[4] Septimius Severus, the father of Caracalla, had adopted Marcus Aurelius as his fictitious father and with him the whole Antonine house as his ancestry. See H. M. D. Parker, *A History of the World from AD 138 to 337*, 2nd ed., 66.
[5] It is, perhaps, hardly necessary to remark that there was nothing even remotely negroid about Augustine. Evidence, if any were needed, would be found in *Enar. in Ps.* 73, 16: 'Æthiopes enim nigri sunt'—an explanation given by Augustine to his congregation, without any suggestion that either he or they are of a similar hue.
[6] Or, as Marrou delightfully puts it: 'ce qui compte, c'est la civilisation et non les chromosomes.' Op. cit., p. 11.

administration and of the educated classes in their private affairs,[1] and it is doubtful whether Augustine ever acquired more than a smattering of the old Punic language spoken by the families of Phoenician extraction, still less a knowledge of Berber.[2]

Augustine's father, Patricius, was a *decurio* of Thagaste,[3] a person of some local consequence but of limited financial resources.[4] Indeed, when a bishop, Augustine was to protest against those who offered him costly robes as presents befitting his episcopal position: 'It is not becoming for Augustine who is poor, and who is the son of poor parents. Would you have men say that in the Church I found means to obtain richer clothing than I could in my father's house or in the pursuit of secular employment? That would be a shame to me.'[5] The relative poverty of Augustine's family is hardly surprising. The wretched condition of the curial class to which the *decuriones* belonged was notorious in the fourth century, when the exactions of the imperial taxation from its members together with the social demands made upon them as members of the civic aristocracy made their lives a burden, causing many of them to flee into the solitudes of the deserts, there to join the ranks of the monks, from which they were angrily recalled by imperial edicts. Augustine's social status, then, was a relatively humble one—Professor Marrou describes him as belonging to the petty bourgeoisie on the way to proletarianization[6]—and could not compare with, for example, St Ambrose, the son of one of the highest civil officials of the Roman Empire, or St John Chrysostom, whose father was a general. He did not even have the advantage of St Jerome, as a young man, of frequenting the best circles of Roman society.[7] The milieu into which

---

[1] John J. O'Meara, *The Young Augustine*, London, 1954, 24–25. Cf. *De Magistro*, xiii, 44.

[2] W. H. C. Frend, *The Donatist Church*, 57–58, thinks that the language of the people of Hippo itself, as of other Roman towns of Carthaginian origin, was Punic, and that Berber was the language of the peoples of the Numidian plains. He compares the distribution of Libyan (Berber) and Punic in Roman times with the modern distribution of Berber and Arabic speaking areas, 'though Arabic is spoken far more extensively than ever Punic was'. Frend's arguments were first put forward by him in an article 'A Note on the Berber Background in the Life of Augustine', in *JTS* xviii (1942), 188–91. They were taken up and amplified by Christian Courtois, 'Saint Augustin et le problème de la survivance de Punique', in *Revue Africaine*, xxxiv (1950), 259–82, who denies any survival of Punic after the third century AD. Frend does not go so far as this; and see *contra* Marcel Simon in *Revue d'Histoire et de Philosophie religieuse*, xxvi (1946), cited by J. Lecerf, 'St Augustin et les survivances puniques', in *Augustinus Magister*, i, 32 q.v.

[3] Possidius, *Vita Augustini*, 1: 'de numero curialium'.

[4] *Conf.*, II, iii, 5: 'municeps Thagastensis admodum tenuis'.

[5] Aug., *Serm.* 356, 13.

[6] *Saint Augustin et l'augustinisme*, 12: '. . . à une petite bourgeoisie en voie de prolétarisation.'

[7] See Gustave Bardy, *L'Église et les derniers Romains*, 8e éd., Paris, 1948, 58–59; though Bardy tends to underestimate the possibilities open to Augustine as Public Orator of Milan (see *Conf.*, VI, vi, 9; xi, 19–20; Marrou, op. cit., p. 20).

Augustine was born was that of small-town society, with the additional
disadvantage of progressive impoverishment and legislation which desired
to make membership of a class hereditary. However, there were ways of
escape for persons of outstanding ability, as both Augustine and his friend
Alypius were to discover, even before they embarked upon a clerical career.[1]

At the time of his son's birth, Patricius was still a pagan, being baptized
only a little before his death, which occurred when Augustine was about
seventeen.[2] Although a violent,[3] and not very refined personality, he seems
to have had a genuine concern for his son's welfare and an appreciation of
his intellectual qualities, evidenced by his determination to secure for him
the best possible education;[4] while the consideration which he showed
towards his wife, recorded by Augustine as an example of his mother's
charm and virtue,[5] may well reflect no little credit upon Patricius himself.
The picture left by Augustine of his father is not a very detailed one, and
it is clear that they had little in common;[6] but the general impression of
the town-counsellor of Thagaste is not so unfavourable as certain writers
have chosen to assume.

Of Augustine's mother, Monica,[7] we know more, thanks to the enthusiasm with which her son speaks of her. 'To her merit', he wrote after his
conversion, 'I think I owe everything that is best in me.'[8] Her name may
indicate that she was of Berber stock.[9] Unlike her husband, she was an
enthusiastic Christian and it was, no doubt, due to her influence that
Augustine, at his birth, was 'signed with Christ's cross, and seasoned with
His salt',[10] to dedicate him to the service of God and to exorcize the devil,

[1] For Alypius' secular profession, see *Conf.*, VI, x, 16.
[2] *Conf.*, II, iii, 6: 'Sed ubi sexto illo et decimo anno interposito otio ex necessitate
domestica feriatus ab omni schola cum parentibus esse coepi . . . ille [Patricius] adhuc
catechumenus, et hoc recens, erat.'
[3] Ibid., IX, ix, 19: 'Erat vero ille praeterea sicut benivolentia praecipuus, ita ira fer-
vidus.'
[4] Ibid., II, iii, 5: 'Et anno quidem illo intermissa erant studia mea, dum mihi reducto
a Madauris, in qua vicina urbe iam coeperam litteraturae atque oratoriae percipiendae
gratia peregrinari, longinquioris apud Carthaginem peregrinationis sumptus praepara-
bantur animositate magis quam opibus patris, municipis Thagastensis admodum tenuis.'
[5] Ibid., IX, ix, 19.
[6] Though it is an exaggeration to say, as does Rebecca West, *St Augustine*, London,
ed. of 1938, 25: 'He speaks of him always in a tone of hatred and moral reprobation,
which was probably quite unjustified.'
[7] 'Monnica' is the form given in the MSS., which Frend describes (*The Donatist
Church*, 230) as 'a Berber name, perhaps derived from the Libyan deity Mon worshipped
in the neighbouring town of Thibilis'. It seems, however, pedantic to depart from the
form which has been adopted as an English name.
[8] *De Beata Vita*, i, 6: '. . . in primis nostra mater, cuius meriti credo esse omne quod
vivo.'   [9] See *n*[7] supra.
[10] *Conf.*, I, xi, 17: 'Audieram enim ego adhuc puer de vita aeterna promissa nobis per
humilitatem domini dei nostri descendentis ad superbiam nostram et signabar iam signo
crucis eius et condiebar eius sale iam inde ab utero matris meae, quae multum speravit in te.'

thus making him a catechumen;[1] though in accordance with the practice
of the times, baptism was deferred, until he should have passed the stormy
years of his youth, when sins of the flesh were commonly deemed unavoidable, at least in the case of a man. Nevertheless, there is no evidence
to show that, in his childhood, Augustine received any thorough or satisfy-
ing instruction in the Christian faith. 'I had heard while yet a boy', he says,
'of the eternal life, promised to us through the humility of our Lord God,
descending to our pride',[2] and when, as a child, he fell sick, he begged that
he might be baptized—a wish that would have been granted, but for his
immediate recovery. He seems, however, to have had little real understanding of Christian belief, apart from a regard for Christ which never
deserted him. The reason for this is probably not far to seek. Monica,
though a saint, was not an educated woman; and although Augustine, in
later years, regarded her intellect with admiration,[3] she was certainly unqualified to deal with the problems which were in his youth to perplex her
brilliant son. Her influence on Augustine was to be that of a much-loved
and strong-willed mother, of whose personal devotion there could be no
doubt;[4] but it was to be an influence of exhortation and example, and not
of the intellect. It was, without question, an abiding influence, and it is
not by chance, when speaking of his reverence for the name of Christ, that
Augustine declares: 'This name of my Saviour, Thy Son, O Lord, my
tender heart had piously drunk in, deeply treasured even with my mother's
milk.'[5] Nor should we underestimate the determination with which
Monica set herself to follow her son's career, even when he seemed to be
hopelessly alienated from the Catholic Church. On the famous occasion

[1] See B. Busch, 'De initiatione Christiana sec. Sanctum Augustinum', in *Ephemerides
liturgicae*, Anno 52, no. 2, 159–78; 'De modo quo S. Augustinus descripserit initiationem
Christianam,' ibid., Anno 52, no. 4, 385–483, esp. 419–24; *De initiatione Christiana sec. S.
Augustinum*, Rome, 1939, 48–65.
[2] *Conf.*, I, xi, 17, cited supra, p. 38, *n*[10].
[3] *De Beata Vita*, ii, 10: 'Cui ego arridens atque gestiens: Ipsam, inquam, prorsus,
mater, arcem philosophiae tenuisti. nam tibi procul dubio verba defuerunt, ut non sicut
Tullius te modo panderes, cuius de hac sententia verba ista sunt. . . . In quibus verbis
illa sic exclamabat, ut obliti penitus sexus eius magnum aliquem virum considere nobiscum crederemus me interim, quantum poteram, intellegente, ex quo illa et quam divino
fonte manarent.' *De Ordine*, I, xi, 31: 'Atque interea mater ingressa est quaesivitque a
nobis, quid promovissemus; nam et ei quaestio nota erat. cuius et ingressum et roga-
tionem cum scribi nostra more iussissem: Quid agitis? inquit; numquidnam in illis quos
legitis libris etiam feminas umquam audivi in hoc genus disputationes inductas? Cui
ego: . . . Nec deerit, mihi crede, tale hominum genus, cui plus placeat hoc ipsum, quia
mecum philosopharis, quam si quid hic aliud aut iucunditatis aut gravitatis invenerit.
nam et feminae sunt apud veteres philosophatae et philosophia tua mihi plurimum
placet.'
[4] See the comments of O'Meara, *The Young Augustine*, 33–38.
[5] *Conf.*, III, iv, 8. Tr. by Albert C. Outler, *Augustine: Confessions and Enchiridion*
(The Library of Christian Classics, Vol. VII), London, 1955, 65.

when Augustine quitted Carthage for Rome, she followed him to the harbour, desiring either to keep him in Africa or to go with him to Italy, with the result that her son lied to his mother—and such a mother! he interjects, parenthetically—and escaped to sea.[1] Père Henry comments: 'This was not harshness, as some have thought, but the sign of a conscience pierced by her powerful and maternal tenderness.'[2] Without rejecting this judgement, it is possible to see in the deception another element: a harassed son anxious to escape from a much-loved, but dominating, mother. Historical parallels are apt to be misleading; but there is surely something almost nineteenth-century in the relationship between Monica and Augustine: the strong-willed and pious mother, who continues to exercise a powerful influence over a son who has fallen into unbelief, but who still reveres his mother's religious views, even when he no longer shares them, and who is ultimately brought back to the faith in which she has never wavered. It is noteworthy that Monica seems never to have entertained any serious doubt as to her son's destiny to return to the true Church.[3]

At the time of her son's birth, Monica was twenty-three.[4] Besides Augustine, she had at least two other children,[5] a son, Navigius, and a daughter, whose name we do not know, though there is a tradition that she was called Perpetua.[6] This daughter was married, widowed, and later

---

[1] *Conf.*, V, viii, 15.   [2] Paul Henry, *La vision d'Ostie*, Paris, 1938, 50.

[3] See Henry, op. cit., pp. 48–52; O'Meara, op. cit., pp. 33–34. It is difficult to understand how so great a scholar as T. A. Lacey came to the opinion that Monica, in Augustine's youth, was a 'pious but rather frivolous girl' (*Nature, Miracle, and Sin*, London, 1916, 8). My own impression is, that if there were any trait which was conspicuously absent from St Monica's character, it was frivolity, since even the notorious episode of her youthful wine-drinking (*Conf.*, IX, viii, 18) is not particularly frivolous. On the contrary, St Monica seems to have been a very serious person indeed, and even her humour (see *De Beata Vita*, ii, 16) has a grim note. Otto Seeck's comment (*Geschichte des Untergangs der antiken Welt*, vi, Stuttgart, 1920, 9–10), although it springs from his rooted distaste for Christianity, is not without some justice: 'Augustin hatte das Unglück, eine gar zu liebevoll Mutter zu besitzen. Die brave Monnica gehörte zu den glücklichen Naturen, die den Zweifel nie gekannt haben und ihn daher bei andern als sündliche Abnormität betrachten.' The fairest verdict upon her seems to me to be that of R. L. Ottley, *Studies in the* Confessions *of St. Augustine*, London, 1919, 5: 'Monnica was by no means faultlessly virtuous and wise; she had a touch of African fanaticism; she cherished some worldly ambitions, and in her upbringing of Augustine made some grave mistakes which the providence of God overruled for good. But at least she taught him to pray and to hold in reverence the sacred name of Christ. Moreover, he probably inherited from her a certaint enacity of purpose which in the long run triumphed over hindrances. Certainly her influence kept alive in him a capacity for faith which was destined in due time to lift him into the fellowship *of the saints in light.*'

[4] She died at Rome in the autumn of 387, when she was in her fifty-sixth year, and her son nearly thirty-three. *Conf.*, IX, xi, 28.

[5] *Conf.*, IX, ix, 22: 'Nutrierat *filios* totiens eos parturiens, quotiens abs te deviare cernebat.' This may imply more sons than Augustine and Navigius; but it clearly need not.

[6] This name is assigned to her, for example, in a British Museum MS. of 1407—Harley MS. 3081, f. 101: 'De sancta Monica matre sancti Augustini. Monica mater sancti

became the superior of a religious community for women.[1] When she died in about 423, dissensions broke out among her nuns, and seem to have been the occasion of Augustine sending them a letter of exhortation embodying a rule of life, which was to become the basis of the medieval Rule of St Augustine.[2] It is possible that Monica bore another daughter, the mother of Augustine's nephew, Patricius,[3] who was, in Augustine's old age, a subdeacon and a member of his uncle's monastic community at Hippo.[4] Little is known of the children of Patricius and Monica, other than Augustine himself. Eclipsed by their brilliant brother, they are hardly more than figures who appear from time to time in the course of his life, and have interest only in so far as they affect him. Our ignorance of their lives and characters is to be regretted; though it is something to be able to say that, so far as we know, they all lived Christian lives and died in the faith.

Our knowledge of Augustine's life comes from four main sources. First, from the *Confessions*—his own account of his career from his birth to his baptism, and the subsequent death of his mother at Rome, in the autumn of 387. Secondly, the *Life* by his friend and fellow bishop, Possidius of Calama (Guelma), which is primarily concerned with his career from his ordination until his death at Hippo in 430, when the Vandals were besieging the town. Thirdly, we have the evidence afforded by Augustine's writings, in particular by his letters, his sermons, and the work called the *Retractationes*, composed towards the end of his life in 426, in which he

Augustini: cuius historia trahitur ex sententia sancti Augustini ex nono Confessionum, et ex duabus epistolis quas Augustinus scripsit sue sorori Perpetue virgini. "Hortor te," inquit Augustinus, "dilecta sponsa Cristi ut Deo studeas in omnibus placere; sicut et caram matrem novisti perfecisse . . ." ' This spurious letter is printed by L. V. E. Bougaud, *Histoire de sainte Monique*, Paris, 1861, 466–9. On Monica's family, see Bougaud, op. cit., pp. 31–34.

[1] Possidius, *Vita*, 26: 'Feminarum intra domum eius [Augustini] nulla umquam conversata est, nulla mansit, ne quidem germana soror, quae vidua Deo serviens multo tempore usque in diem obitus sui praeposita ancillarum Dei vixit, sed nec fratris sui filiae, quae pariter Deo serviebant, quas personas sanctorum episcoporum concilia in exceptis posuerunt.'

[2] *Ep.* 211, 4: 'Perseverate in bono proposito et non desiderabitis mutare praepositam, qua in monasterio illo per tam multos annos perseverante et numero et aetate crevistis, quae vos mater non utero sed animo suscepit. omnes enim, quae illuc venistis, ibi eam aut sanctae praepositae sorori meae servientem, placentem aut etiam ipsam praepositam, quae vos suscepit, invenistis.' See Appendix B, pp. 396–7.

[3] Such is the view of Bardy, *Saint Augustin*, 7é éd., 26.

[4] Aug., *Serm.*, 356, 3: 'Nuntio ergo vobis unde gaudeatis. Omnes fratres et clericos meos, qui mecum habitant, presbyteros, diaconos, subdiaconos, et Patricium nepotem meum, tales inveni, quales desideravi. . . . Nepos autem meus ex quo conversus est, et mecum esse coepit, impediebatur et ipse aliquid de agellulis suis agere invita usufructuaria matre sua, quae hoc anno defuncta est. Inter ipsum et sorores eius sunt quaedam in Christi adiutorio cito finienda: ut et ipse faciat quod servum Dei decet, quod ipsa professio, et ista exigit lectio.'

passed in review all his works published up to that time, explained the circumstances which led to their composition, and indicated points on which he had changed his opinion or modified it in the light of subsequent reflection or fresh evidence. Finally, we have evidence afforded by the writings of others, both friends and enemies.

Of these four classes of source materials, it is plain that the *Confessions* are of particular importance, inasmuch as they represent Augustine's own account of his early career and of the circumstances which brought him into the Catholic Church.[1] The question then arises: to what extent are we able to draw on the *Confessions* as an historical source? Even if they are to be regarded as autobiography—and they are autobiographical only in a somewhat wide use of the word[2]—the fact that they were written in 397 at the earliest means that a decade had already elapsed between Augustine's conversion and baptism, so that, at the time when he began to write about his religious evolution, he was bishop of Hippo and the most distinguished theologian in Africa. In the very nature of things, he would tend to regard his past life in the light of his present spiritual condition, and we must be prepared to make allowance for this in using the *Confessions* as a biographical source. But does this mean that we are justified in taking the *Confessions* at their face value in gathering facts for recording Augustine's life?

For hundreds of years—one may say indeed from Augustine's own lifetime until the last decades of the nineteenth century—almost all readers had done precisely that. From then onwards, a number of scholars, among whom the names of Gaston Boissier, Adolf von Harnack, Friedrich Loofs, L. Gourdon, H. Becker, W. Thimme and, above all, Prosper Alfaric, are outstanding,[3] have argued against the value of the *Confessions* as an historical source. The crucial point of their attack turned upon the apparent

[1] Among modern studies of the *Confessions*, two are of outstanding importance: Pierre Courcelle, *Recherches sur les* Confessions *de saint Augustin*, Paris, 1950; and Michele Pellegrino, *Le 'Confessioni' di sant' Agostino*, Rome, 1956. Unfortunately, neither of these two excellent books is available in English translation. John J. O'Meara, *The Young Augustine*, 1954, takes into account Courcelle's work, acknowledging its importance, while rejecting some of its theses—rightly, in the present writer's opinion. Among older works, R. L. Ottley, *Studies in the* Confessions *of St Augustine*, 1919, may profitably be consulted. Among more general writings on Augustine's career may be mentioned Professor H. I. Marrou, *Saint Augustin et l'augustinisme*, Paris [1956], ET, London [1957]—a brilliant little book. Still useful and stimulating is W. Montgomery, *St Augustine: Aspects of his life and thought*, 1914. The same cannot be said of Rebecca West, *St Augustine*, 1933, which should be used with care or avoided altogether.

[2] 'Le *Confessiones* dunque non sono, essenzialmente, un' autobiografia: nell' autobiografia il protagonista è sempre lo scrittore, mentre in esse non è Agostino, ma il Signore.' A. G. Amatucci, *Storia della letteratura latina cristiana*, 2a ed., Turin, 1955, 236.

[3] A good summary of the course of the attack on the reliability of the *Confessions* is given by J. J. O'Meara, 'Augustine and Neo-Platonism', in *Recherches augustiniennes*, i, Paris, 1958, 91–111.

contrast between the account given in the *Confessions* of the circumstances of Augustine's conversion and baptism, and the mood of three dialogues held at Cassiciacum immediately after the conversion, and recorded in three treatises: the *Contra Academicos*, the *De Beata Vita*, and the *De Ordine*, all written in 386 and displaying, in the opinion of the critics, a mood of detachment and philosophical preoccupation very different from that painted by Augustine in the *Confessions*. This view found its clearest expression in Alfaric's declaration that, morally and intellectually, it was to Neo-Platonism, and not to Christianity, that Augustine was converted in 386.[1]

Besides the alleged conflict between the evidence of the *Confessions* and that of the contemporary dialogues in which, it was held, the evidence of the dialogues must be accepted, another consideration was urged: the form of the *Confessions* themselves. They are the work of a rhetorician, in an age when rhetoric was governed by stringent rules of convention, and when fact was readily subordinated to the interests of style.[2] It is this consideration which leads so judicious a scholar as M. Pierre Courcelle to regard the whole circumstantial account given by Augustine of his religious experience and conversion under the fig-tree at Milan as a literary convention, and the fig-tree itself as a symbol taken from the Gospel of St John.[3] So Augustine becomes at best a mere literary artist and, at worst, something less attractive: a man deliberately prepared to write untruths about the deepest and most decisive moments of his life to satisfy the literary tastes of his audience.

It must be emphasized, however, that at no time did the critics of the factual accuracy of the *Confessions* enjoy an unchallenged domination of the intellectual scene. Numerous scholars came forward to defend the traditional view,[4] and after the appearance of Charles Boyer's epoch-making

---

[1] P. Alfaric, *L'évolution intellectuelle de saint Augustin*, Paris, 1918, i, 399: 'Moralement comme intellectuellement, c'est au Néoplatonisme qu'il s'est converti, plutôt qu'à l'Evangile.'

[2] 'Die ganzen „Bekentnisse" sind durch und durch rhetorisch; sie wimmeln von Antithesen, Gleichklängen und allen andern Kunststücken der Schule. Auch in seine Beichte will Augustin glänzen, obgleich er vorgibt, die Mittel dieses Glanzes zu verachten.' Seeck, *Gesch. des Untergangs d. antiken Welt*, vi, 4. There is, however, no good ground for his assertion: 'Offenbare Lügen in seine Beichte aufzunehmen, hütet sich Augustin; doch dem lieben Hergott alles zu sagen, war überflüssig, weil er es ja doch schon von selbst wusste; die Menschen aber, die das Buch lesen sollten, brauchten nicht alles zu wissen. Schon in seiner Form ist das ganze Werk eine grosse Unwahrkraftigheit.' Such a statement springs rather from personal antipathy than from any serious evaluation of the evidence.

[3] Courcelle, *Recherches*, 193–202. See the comments on this by O'Meara, *The Young Augustine*, 182–90; and Pellegrino, *Le 'Confessioni' di sant' agostino*, 116–18.

[4] F. Wörter, *Die Geistesentwicklung des hl. Aurelius Augustinus*, Paderborn, 1892; J. Martin, 'St. Augustin à Cassiciacum', in *Annales de philosophie chrétienne*, Dec. 1898, 307; E. Portalié, *DTC*, art. 'Augustin', col. 2273; Louis de Mandadon, 'Les premières

study, *Christianisme et néo-platonisme dans la formation de saint Augustin*,[1] it became very difficult for anyone to deny the sincerity of Augustine's conversion to Christianity in 386. Indeed, it is probably true to say that, at the present time, the majority of Augustinian scholars would accept the historical veracity of the *Confessions*, and that the period of doubt will be hereafter seen only as an episode in the history of the study of Augustine.[2]

It is beyond the scope of this study to embark on a general examination of the nature of the *Confessions* and the reasons why their evidence may be accepted, in all major matters, with confidence. It is, however, both possible and desirable to adduce certain general considerations which support their claim to be a valid source of evidence.

In the first place, one may question the inherent probability of anyone holding the theological opinions of Augustine when he came to write the *Confessions* deliberately incorporating material which he knew to be untrue. He might have done so, but it is most unlikely. If we reject this possibility, as do most of those who reject the *Confessions* as an historical source, we have still to ask whether a man of Augustine's ability, to whom his religion was his life, would be incapable of recalling the precise circumstances of his conversion and of the events leading up to it. In any case, the *Confessions* were written only about a decade after the conversion of the author; and if we accept the evidence of modern autobiographies, written by men who have reached an advanced age, for the events and experiences of their youth, we have no good grounds for rejecting that of a man still in his early forties, and in his intellectual prime. We need not labour the point; Augustine had both the motive and the capacity for giving accurate information about his early career when he came to write the *Confessions*.

Again, it may be observed that certain facts which have been urged to invalidate the testimony of the *Confessions*, may, upon consideration, serve rather to confirm it. One such example is the claim that Augustine makes a too sharp division of his life before his conversion, which he paints in the blackest hues and contrasts with the joy and peace which he found after he had received the grace of God. There is no question that Augustine judged himself extremely harshly, and was influenced in this, no doubt, by his

impressions catholiques de saint Augustin', in *Études*, 20 May and 5 June 1909; W. Montgomery, *St Augustine: Aspects of his life and thought*, 1914; A. Hatzfeld, *St Augustin*, 5e éd., Paris, 1898; T. Bret, *La conversion de saint Augustin*, Geneva, 1900. See O'Meara, 'Augustine and Neo-Platonism', 94.
[1] Paris, 1920; new edition, Rome, 1953.
[2] An excellent discussion of the historical value of the *Confessions* will be found in Pellegrino, op. cit., pp. 161–74.

doctrine of Original Sin; but it is important to make a distinction between the sins which he records, and the judgements which he passes upon them. The fact that he appears to place too much emphasis upon certain youthful sins, such as the dawning of concupiscence and its indulgence, or the famous episode of robbing the pear-tree—and it should be remembered that these are sins, and that the critic may well be at fault for under-estimating, rather than Augustine for exaggerating them—in no way dis-proves the historical reality of the events he describes. Again, the calm and balance which appears in the account of the dialogues of Cassiciacum, and which is supposed to be wholly foreign to the highly emotional mood recorded in the *Confessions* at the time of the conversion, far from in-validating the account given in the latter tends rather to support it, as being psychologically very probable.[1] No one can remain keyed up to a condition of emotional excitement indefinitely; a period of calm, even of spiritual flatness, succeeds, particularly when a vital decision has been made and there is now no turning back. Even when the decision is a disagreeable one, as when, for example, a general informs his troops that he intends to attack in the morning and that heavy casualties are to be expected, there is a sense of relief when the orders have been given—at least one is no longer stretched upon the rack of anticipation. How much greater is the relief when one battle has been won, and the way ahead clear! Inevitably, a sense of anticlimax sets in, and the victor requires some time to adjust himself to new circumstances, felicitous though they may be. If he is wise, he will make good use of that time, as Augustine did at Cassiciacum, by con-solidating the ground gained. But a man will be altogether exceptional if he remains in the condition of excitement which prevailed during the battle and the moment of victory. The spirit and mind require rest and refresh-ment no less than the body.

Furthermore, it may be noted that modern research tends to regard the problem of Augustine's conversion in a rather different light from that in which it was seen by the critics at the beginning of the century. It is not necessary to speak in terms of *either* Christianity *or* Neo-Platonism,[2] any more than it would be necessary today, in discussing the conversion of a modern intellectual, to talk about either Christianity or Existentialism. Augustine thought that he could have a synthesis of the philosophy and

[1] See the comment of Pellegrino, op. cit., pp. 170-1: 'Ma giustamente è stato osser-vato che i due documenti rispecchiano due momenti successivi ed hanno una natural-issima spiegazione psicologica: alla tensione estenuante della lotta, conchiusa con la vittoria definitava, doveva succedere un periodo di distensione in cui l'uomo, nella riflessione calma e serena, potesse rendersi conto di quanto era avvenuto in lui e pre-pararsi ad affrontare le ulteriori tappe del suo cammino.'
[2] See O'Meara, 'Augustine and Neo-Platonism', 94-95.

the religion, as did many other Christians of his age,[1] always with the proviso that, in the last resort, when the two systems conflicted, Neo-Platonism would have to give way to Christianity. Viewed in this light, the philosophical nature of the discussions at Cassiciacum which followed the crisis of conversion loses much of its significance as an argument against the sincerity of Augustine's newly acquired orthodoxy. But the matter does not rest there; for the dialogues of Cassiciacum are not without expressions of Catholic Christianity,[2] while the fact that Augustine's mother participated at her son's request in the conversations is in itself a guarantee that they were Christian in outlook.[3]

There remains the question of the style, which bears the marks of the rhetorician. Are we justified in declining to accept evidence supplied by a work full of figures of speech and the literary devices of a decadent age? The charge is not a new one; in Augustine's own lifetime it was levelled against him by the Donatist grammarian, Cresconius, who reproached Augustine for being a rhetorician and sought to utilize the verse of Proverbs: *By great eloquence thou shalt not escape sin.* Augustine retorted that his opponent had misrepresented the text; what Scripture condemns is not eloquence but superfluity of words.[4] Superfluity is a vice and is condemned, but eloquence, the ability to speak well, enables us to express our thoughts in the best possible way, and may certainly be used provided we think rightly.[5] Now by eloquence, Augustine understood the same as did other men of his day, and he was perfectly prepared to employ it, when it seemed likely to edify his hearers or readers.[6] The austere Donatists were an exception; most men of Augustine's age enjoyed fine language, as they conceived it, and would not easily have understood the modern feeling that eloquence implies insincerity, and that strong convictions should be expressed in an artless fashion. Augustine shared the views of his contemporaries; and he was sufficiently a product of the rhetorical schools to

---

[1] See Étienne Gilson, *La philosophie au Moyen Age*, 3e éd., Paris, 1947, 115-38; Courcelle, 'Plotin et saint Ambrose', in *Revue de philologie*, lxxvi (1950), 29-56; *Recherches*, 92-138.

[2] Pellegrino, op. cit., pp. 167-74 gives numerous examples.

[3] See Henry, *La vision d'Ostie*, 56-58.

[4] Prov. 10.19; following the Septuagint: Ἐκ πολυλογίας οὐκ ἐκφεύξῃ ἁμαρτίαν. Vulgate: In multiloquio non deerit peccatum. R.V. In the multitude of words there wanteth not transgression.

[5] *Contra Cresconium*, I, i, 2-ii, 3: '. . . putes: *ex multa eloquentia non effugies peccatum*, cum dictum non sit "ex multa eloquentia", sed "ex multiloquio". multiloquium autem est superflua locutio, vitium scilicet loquendi amore contractum. . . . eloquentia vero facultas dicendi est congruenter explicans quae sentimus, qua tunc utendum est cum recta sentimus. . . . cum me videres a nonnullis putari eloquentem, ut a me lectoris auditorisve studium deterreres, accusandam existimasti eloquentiam.'

[6] See Marrou, *Saint Augustin et la fin de la culture antique*, 4e éd., Paris, 1958, 505-40.

admire certain techniques of his day, which are not calculated to appeal to later generations. Fortunately, his religious ardour and the genius for language with which he had been endowed saved him from the worst excesses, and enabled him, in the *Confessions*, to produce a work which is not only a religious but also a literary classic.[1] Unfortunately, by the standards of the twentieth century, his concessions to the taste of his age sometimes detract from the book and inspire a feeling of disquiet and distrust.[2] It is, however, a little unjust to reproach an author for failing to write for readers whose mother tongue would be different from his own and who would not be born for centuries after his death. We must judge the style of the *Confessions* by the age; and it is unreasonable to condemn the good faith of the author because he writes in a fashion which does not appeal to us. 'I do not like her name', said Jaques, and received the very proper reply: 'There was no thought of pleasing you when she was christened.' Augustine loved the truth; he was determined to avoid obscurity; but when he was converted at the age of thirty-two he had behind him twenty years of the practice of rhetoric and thirteen years of teaching it.[3] It is no reproach to him that he failed to free his style completely from the discipline which he had so long and ardently cultivated. One may agree with Mr Moss that 'a feverish sincerity glows through the *Confessions*'.[4]

We are therefore justified in accepting the *Confessions* as supplying valid evidence for the career of Augustine. At the same time, we must understand that they are not, and were never intended to be, an autobiography in the modern sense of the term. Neither are they simply an acknowledgement of sin, nor a declaration of actions and opinions in the manner of Rousseau's *Confessions* or (in the field of fiction) by Alfred de Musset's *Confession d'un enfant du siècle*. Augustine's *Confessions* are not like any of these, and anyone who reads them in the hope of being regaled with scabrous detail is likely to be disappointed.

What are the *Confessions*? They comprise thirteen books, of which only nine can properly be called autobiographical, although even in these Augustine is more concerned to praise the greatness and the mercy of God than to dwell upon his own career. The tenth book is a survey of the writer's spiritual and psychological condition at the time of composition. In this, it does not directly follow upon the ninth, which brings to an end the story of Augustine's life from his infancy until his conversion, baptism, and the

---

[1] 'Tutto è naturale e spontaneo in questo scritto, anche la lingua garbatamente vuole avvicinarsi a quella parlata senza perdere di dignità.' Amatucci, op. cit., pp. 236–7.
[2] See Pellegrino, op. cit., pp. 178–9.
[3] Marrou, op. cit., pp. 553–4.
[4] H. St L. B. Moss, *The Birth of the Middle Ages*, 32.

48 ST AUGUSTINE OF HIPPO

death of his mother. Between that date and the writing of the *Confessions* more than a decade elapsed. Augustine was ordained, was consecrated bishop of Hippo, and became a notable figure in the African Church. But nothing is said of this in the tenth book; Augustine apparently decided that, whatever might be his own joy and gratitude to God for those ten years, his fellow Christians would derive no spiritual benefit from reading about them, and therefore passes directly to the discussion of his spiritual condition at the time of writing. Even more curiously, in the last three books he abandons himself entirely, and devotes all his powers to the praise and adoration of God in contemplating the mysteries of the creation in a commentary on the first chapter of Genesis. It is customary for readers of the *Confessions* to devote their attention to the first nine books, to pay some regard to the tenth, and to neglect the last three. This practice has given an added emphasis to the tendency to treat the whole work as if it were essentially autobiographical. It is, however, foreign to the intention of Augustine. He wrote the thirteen books as a unit, and by ignoring the last three, the balance of the whole is upset, and much of the object lost.[1]

To understand the nature of the *Confessions*, we must first understand the sense of the word *confiteri* in Augustine's terminology. It has, indeed, the meaning of the English verb *to confess*, but is not limited to the sense of confession of sin—a meaning which it was already acquiring in Christian language in Augustine's day, and against which he protests in his sermons. 'There are some of the faithful', he says, 'who are so little informed that, when they hear Scripture speaking of confession, they immediately beat their breasts as if there could be no confession other than of sins, and as if they had been warned to confess them.'[2] Augustine, of course, fully recognizes this sense of confession of sin; but it is not his primary meaning, which is that of confession of praise to God. 'Dost Thou laugh at me for asking such things?' he asks. 'Or dost Thou command me to praise and confess unto Thee only what I know? I confess to Thee, O Lord of heaven and earth, giving praise to Thee for that first being and my infancy of which I have no memory.'[3] The very opening words of the *Confessions* are a confession of praise:

[1] Courcelle, op. cit., pp. 20–29; Pellegrino, op. cit., pp. 11, 142–51.
[2] *Serm.* 29, ii, 2: 'Confessio aut laudantis est, aut poenitentis. Sunt enim parum eruditi, qui cum audierint confessionem in Scripturis, tanquam nisi peccatorum esse non possit, continuo tundunt pectora; velut iam moneantur confiteri peccata. Sed ut noverit Charitas vestra, non ad sola peccata pertinere confessionem, audiamus illum, de quo dubitare non possumus quod nullum omnino habebat peccatum, exclamantem et dicentem: *Confiteor tibi, Pater, Domine caeli et terrae.*' Cf. *Serm.* 67, i, 1; *Enarr. in Ps.* 7, 19; 44, 33; 105, 2.
[3] *Conf.*, I, vi, 9–10.

*Great art Thou, O Lord, and greatly to be praised; great is Thy power,
and infinite is Thy wisdom.*[1] And man desires to praise Thee, for he is a
part of Thy creation; he bears his mortality about with him, and carries
the evidence of his sin and the proof that *Thou dost resist the proud.*[2] Still
he desires to praise Thee, this man who is only a small part of Thy
creation. Thou hast prompted him, that he should delight to praise
Thee, for Thou hast made us for Thyself and restless is our heart until
it comes to rest in Thee.[3]

This is the first, and primary, sense of confession in Augustine's use of
the word: confession of praise and thanks to God for His mighty works and
for His goodness and mercy to His creation. This is the note on which the
Confessions open, and it is repeated at the beginning of Book XI, when the
saint turns from his own life to the contemplation of God revealed in His
creation.[4] This is what gives unity to the apparently unrelated elements of
the book: the narration of Augustine's past life; his examination of his
spiritual and psychological condition at the time of writing; and the commentary on Genesis; all these are written to the greater glory of God.

Nevertheless, the conception of confession as confession of sins is
present in Augustine's mind as he prepares to recount the sins of his youth,
and the flaws and weaknesses which are yet unhealed:

The house of my soul is too narrow for Thee to come in to me; let it be
enlarged by Thee. It is in ruins; do Thou restore it. There is much
about it which must offend Thy eyes; I confess and know it. But who
will cleanse it? Or to whom shall I cry but to Thee? *Cleanse Thou me
from my secret faults, O Lord, and keep back Thy servant from strange
sins.*[5] *I believe, and therefore do I speak.*[6] But Thou, O Lord, Thou
knowest. *Have I not confessed my transgressions unto Thee, O my God;
and hast not Thou put away the iniquity of my heart?*[7] *I do not contend in
judgement with Thee,*[8] who art Truth itself; and I would not deceive
myself, *lest my iniquity lie even to itself.*[9] I do not, therefore, contend in
judgement with Thee, for *if Thou, Lord, shouldst mark iniquities, O Lord,
who shall stand?*[10]

A third significance can be found in Augustine's use of the word confession: confession of faith.[11] It is to be found particularly in the last three

[1] Ps. 144.3 [145.3]; 146.5 [147.5].   [2] Jac. 4.6.
[3] *Conf.*, I, i, 1. Tr. by Outler, p. 31.
[4] Ibid., XI, i, 1: 'Cur ergo tibi tot rerum narrationes digero? Non utique ut per me
noveris ea, sed affectum meum excito in te et eorum, qui haec legunt, ut dicamus omnes:
magnus dominus et laudabilis valde. Iam dixi et dicam: amore amoris tui facio istuc.'
[5] Ps. 18.13, 14 [19.12, 13].   [6] Ps. 115.10 [116.10].
[7] Ps. 31.5 [32.5].   [8] Job 9.3.
[9] Ps. 26.12 in the Vulgate version.
[10] Ps. 129.3 [130.3]. *Conf.*, I, v, 6. Tr. by Outler, p. 34.
[11] Courcelle, op. cit., pp. 19–20; Pellegrino, op. cit., p. 11.

books of the *Confessions*,[1] where it serves to place the theological commentary into perspective with the rest of the work; but the two fundamental significations are confession of praise, and confession of sins. God, indeed, does not require to be told the sins of His creatures, which He knows already: 'and what is there in me that could be hidden from Thee, O Lord, to whose eyes the abysses of man's conscience are naked, even if I were unwilling to confess it to Thee?',[2] but Augustine's fellow Christians wish to hear his confession,[3] and the saint gratifies this desire, in the hope that it will encourage some of his readers in their own spiritual life;[4] will procure prayers both for Augustine's dead parents,[5] and for Augustine himself;[6] and for another and deeper reason, which includes these others —the sense of the coinherence of all members of the Body of Christ,[7] and of the love which desires to communicate with others and share with them its thoughts and memories:

This, then, is the fruit of my confessions (not of what I was, but of what I am), that I may not confess before Thee alone, in a secret exultation with trembling and a secret sorrow with hope, but also in the ears of the believing sons of men—who are the companions of my joy, and sharers of my mortality, my fellow citizens and fellow pilgrims—those who have gone before and those who are to follow after, as well as the comrades of

[1] E.g. *Conf.*, XIII, xii, 13: 'Procede in confessione, fides mea; dic domino deo tuo: sancte, sancte, sancte, domine deus meus, *in nomine tuo baptizati sumus*, pater et fili et spiritu sancte, in nomine tuo baptizamus, pater et fili et spiritus sancte, quia et apud nos in Christo suo *fecit deus caelum et terram*, spiritales et carnales ecclesiae suae, et terra nostra antequam acciperet formam doctrinae, *invisibilis erat et inconposita*, et ignorantiae tenebris tegebamur, quoniam *pro iniquitate erudisti hominem*, et *iudicia tua sicut multa abyssus.*'
[2] *Conf.*, X, ii, 2: 'Et tibi quidem, domine, cuius oculis nuda est abyssus humanae conscientiae, quid occultum esset in me, etiamsi nollem confiteri tibi?'
[3] Ibid., X, iii, 3.
[4] Ibid., X, iii, 4: 'Verum tamen tu, medice meus intime, quo fructu ista faciam, eliqua mihi. Nam confessiones praeteritorum malorum meorum, quae remisisti et texisti, ut beares me in te, mutans animam meam fide et sacramento tuo, cum leguntur et audiuntur, excitant cor, ne dormiat in desperatione et dicat: "Non possum," sed evigilet in amore misericordiae tuae et dulcidine gratiae tuae, qua potens est omnis infirmus, qui sibi per ipsam fit conscius infirmitatis suae. Et delectat bonos audire praeterita mala eorum, qui iam carent eis, nec ideo delectat, quia mala sunt, sed quia fuerunt et non sunt.'
[5] Ibid., IX, xiii, 37: 'Et inspira, domine meus, deus meus, inspira servis tuis, fratribus meis, filiis tuis, dominis meis, quibus et corde et voce et litteris servio, ut quotquot haec legerint, meminerint ad altare tuum Monnicae, famulae tuae, cum Patricio, quondam eius coniuge, per quorum carnem introduxisti me in hanc vitam, quemadmodum nescio.'
[6] Ibid., X, iv, 5: 'Sed quo fructu id volunt? An congratulari mihi cupiunt, cum audierint, quantum ad te accedam munere tuo, et orare pro me, cum audierint, quantum retarder pondere meo? Indicabo me talibus. Non enim parvus est fructus, domine deus meus, ut *a multis tibi gratiae agantur* de nobis et a multis rogeris pro nobis. Amet in me fraternus animus quod amandum doces, et doleat in me quod dolendum doces.'
[7] For this social instinct in Augustine, see J. M. Le Blond, *Les conversions de saint Augustin*, Paris, 1950, 27–30.

my present way. These are Thy servants, my brothers, whom Thou desirest to be Thy sons. They are my masters, whom Thou hast commanded me to serve if I desire to live with and in Thee. But this Thy Word would mean little to me if it commanded in words alone, without Thy prevenient action. I do this, then, both in act and word. I do this under Thy wings, in a danger too great to risk if it were not that under Thy wings my soul is subject to Thee, and my weakness known to Thee. I am insufficient, but my Father liveth for ever, and my Defender is sufficient for me. For He is the Selfsame who did beget me and who watcheth over me; Thou art the Selfsame who art all my good. Thou art the Omnipotent, who art with me, even before I am with Thee. To those, therefore, whom Thou commandest me to serve, I will declare, not what I was, but what I now am, and what I will continue to be. But I do not judge myself. Thus, therefore, let me be heard.[1]

This declaration makes clear how widely the purpose of the *Confessions* differs from that of the modern autobiography; and Courcelle is right in saying that Augustine's principal purpose is not historical, but theological.[2] It is for this reason that he omits narrative details which he regards as irrelevant to his object: praise of God; and confession of sin to God in the presence of his fellows, to help them in their Christian lives, to obtain their prayers, and to further that sense of unity in the bond of charity which is the essence of his doctrine of the Church. At the same time, the fact that the work is not an autobiography does not mean that the events recounted in it are not historical or that it may not confidently be used for biographical purposes.[3] The *Confessions*, indeed, not only may be used by the historian, but must be used; and they represent our most important source for the early life of their author.

The first book of the *Confessions* presents a vivid picture of Augustine's childhood. He looks back upon his infancy and, although he cannot remember it, reconstructs it from the behaviour of other infants whom he had observed. He wonders from this about the alleged innocency of childhood, recognizing in a manner which anticipates in a remarkable way the conclusions of certain schools of modern psychology, that the infant's mind is the seat of violent desires and emotions, and very far removed from the popular idea of childish innocence.

---

[1] *Conf.*, X, iv, 6. Tr. by Outler, p. 204. See Pellegrino, op. cit., p. 14.

[2] Courcelle, op. cit., p. 27: 'Même pour les neuf premiers livres, il est evident, après ce que j'ai dit de l'emploi du mot *confession*, que le dessein principal d'Augustin n'est pas historique, mais théologique.'

[3] 'Non sono dunque le *Conf.* un'autobiografia nel senso commune della parola, da cui possiamo attenderci il racconto ordinato e completo delle vicende dell'autore. . . . Ma se autobiografio è rappresentazione commosa e potente del dramma che s'agita nell'intimo dell'uomo e degli avvenimenti che dànno significato e valore a tutta la sua vita (per Agostino, la conversione), nessun'opera ne merita più di questa il nome.' Pellegrino, op. cit., pp. 15, 16.

The infant's innocence lies in the weakness of his body and not in the
infant mind [he declares]. I have myself observed a baby to be jealous,
though it could not speak; it was livid as it watched another infant at the
breast. Who is ignorant of this? Mothers and nurses tell us that they
cure these things by I know not what remedies. But is this innocence,
when the fountain of milk is flowing fresh and abundant, that another
who needs it should not be allowed to share it, even though he requires
such nourishment to sustain his life? Yet we look leniently on such
things, not because they are not faults, or even small faults, but because
they will vanish as the years pass. For, although we allow such things in
an infant, the same things could not be tolerated patiently in an adult.[1]

From infancy, Augustine turns to childhood, recalling his school-days,
and the miseries he then suffered. The educational system of the later
Roman Empire was marked by two characteristics, which were to have a
long-continuing influence upon western culture: a preoccupation with
literature;[2] and the regular employment of the rod as a spur to diligence.
The brutality of the schoolmaster was an accepted convention; and we
find Ausonius, a kind-hearted man, painting a grisly picture of the school-
room, with its instruments of torture—the ferule, the rod, and the tawse.[3]
In the face of this menace, the best that Ausonius can offer by way of
encouragement in the poem addressed to his little grandson, is to exhort
the child to show courage: 'fear betrays a degenerate spirit'; and to urge
him to comfort himself with the reflection that his own father and mother
went through the same ordeals, and have survived to bring peace to his
grandfather's age—the sort of unconvincing consolation which age is only
too prone to offer to youth. Augustine, for his part, thanks to his indolence
and taste for play was very often the victim of the scholastic disciplinary
system of the day. Like many another child in similar circumstances, he
prayed most earnestly that he might escape punishment, to find that not
only was his prayer unanswered, but that his parents merely regarded his
beatings as a joke.[4] The recollection of these childhood punishments still
remained with him as a bishop; and he recalls bitterly the shallowness of

---

[1] *Conf.*, I, vii, 11. Tr. by Outler, p. 37.
[2] For the aims and method of Roman education in the fourth century AD, see Aubrey
Gwynn, *Roman Education from Cicero to Quintilian*, Oxford, 1926; T. J. Haarhoff,
Schools of Gaul, 2nd ed., Johannesburg, 1958; and particularly H. I. Marrou, *Saint
Augustin et la fin de la culture antique*, 4e éd., 1958 and *Histoire de l'éducation dans l'antiquité*, 3e éd., Paris, 1955 (ET, London, 1956).
[3] See Haarhoff, op. cit., p. 95. For the Roman schoolmaster's armoury, see the *Dictionnaire d'archéologie chrétienne et de liturgie*, art. 'Châtiments'.
[4] *Conf.*, I, ix, 14: 'Nam puer coepi rogare te, *auxilium et refugium meum*, et in tuam
invocationem rumpebam nodos linguae meae et rogabam te parvus non parvo affectu, ne
in schola vapularem. Et cum me non exaudiebas, *quod non erat ad insipientiam mihi*, ride-
bantur a maioribus hominibus usque ab ipsis parentibus, qui mihi accidere mali nihil
volebant, plagae meae, magnum tunc et grave malum meum.'

his masters, who were not ashamed to boast of their lusts provided they could do so in a good literary style.[1] He records the difficulty he had with Greek and asks why he found the language so difficult.[2] (The difficulty was to beset him all his life. Unlike St Ambrose and St Jerome, he never really mastered the language; and although, as a bishop, he found time amid his many preoccupations to rub up his rusty Greek, and acquire a practical working knowledge for his studies, he never became a finished scholar.[3]) In his own Latin language, however, he excelled. He loved the poets, especially Virgil, breaking his heart for Dido, self-slain for love of Aeneas, and delighting in 'the most sweet spectacle of vanity, the wooden horse, heavy with armed men, and burning Troy, and the shade of Creusa'.[4] His studies prospered; his father determined to send him to the schools of Carthage, the great university of North Africa and second only to Rome as a centre of learning in the western part of the Empire. With this object in mind Augustine, in the sixteenth year of his age, returned to Thagaste from the neighbouring town of Madauros, where he had been at school, to spend a year at home, during which time his father hoped to save a little money in order to face the expenses of the university.[5] It was during this year at home that Augustine, according to his own account, fell into serious sin.[6] There is no reason to underestimate his misconduct; the age and society were lustful, and chastity as a masculine virtue has never been over-esteemed on the shores of the Mediterranean. On the other hand—and it is a practice by no means confined to the Mediterranean —we have Augustine's own declaration that he was in the habit of exaggerating his misdeeds when talking with his friends, and of making himself appear a greater rake than he actually was.[7] Unfortunately, he received no encouragement from his father in the matter of chastity, but was rather encouraged in his lusts by the older man's hope of grand-children.[8] His mother, indeed, warned him against fornication and adultery; but her aspiring son paid no heed to such womanish counsels.[9] The satisfaction of lust was not, however, the only pleasure that sin could provide; to it he added theft. Near his home stood a not very desirable

---

[1] Conf., I, xviii, 28.   [2] Ibid., I, xiv, 23.
[3] See Appendix A: 'Augustine's knowledge of Greek', pp. 394–5.
[4] Conf., I, xiii, 22.   [5] Ibid., II, iii, 5.   [6] Ibid., 6.
[7] Conf., II, iii, 7: 'Sed nesciebam et praeceps ibam tanta caecitate, ut inter coaetaneos meos puderet me minoris dedecoris, quoniam audiebam eos iactantes flagitia sua et tanto gloriantes magis, quanto magis turpes essent, et libebat facere non solum libidine facti verum etiam laudis. Quid dignum est vituperatione nisi vitium? Ego ne vituperarer, vitiosior fiebam, et ubi non suberat, quo admisso aequarer perditis, fingebam me fecisse quod non feceram, ne viderer abiectior, quo eram innocentior, et ne vilior haberer, quo eram castior.'   [8] Ibid., 6.
[9] Ibid., 7: 'Qui mihi monitus muliebres videbantur, quibus obtemperare erubescerem.'

pear-tree which Augustine, with some disreputable companions, raided one night, afterwards throwing the stolen fruit to the pigs.[1] Certain critics have found the episode of the pear-tree ridiculously trivial and wondered why the saint should chronicle, with loudly declared regret, what seems essentially a schoolboy prank.[2] To ask such a question suggests that the questioner has missed the point of the story. It is not that Augustine regarded robbing the pear-tree as the worst sin of his life but that he was appalled, on reflection, by the apparent lack of motive for the deed. Sins, he says, are commonly committed because the sinner has some particular good in mind which he wishes to enjoy as the result of his sin; for example, a man kills another because he covets his wife or his goods, or burns to avenge an injury;[3] but the object of the theft of the pears was nothing of this sort. Augustine was not hungry and, had he been so, he had better fruit of his own at home.[4] The motive then was not material; it was malice pure and simple—a pleasure in doing evil.[5] In this schoolboy escapade, we find proof of the spiritual nature of sin, and hence its importance in the mind of Augustine.[6] The motive of the apparently motiveless action is a perverse desire to emulate the divine omnipotence,[7] which springs from what Augustine was afterwards to regard in *The City of God* as the architect of the Earthly City—love of self to the contempt of God.[8] In this sense the theft of the pears, even more than unchastity, is the great sin of Augustine's adolescence, and for this reason it forms a fitting climax to the sins of his childhood.

> I came to Carthage, where a cauldron of unholy loves was seething and bubbling all around me. I was not in love as yet, but I was in love with love; and, from a hidden hunger, I hated myself for not feeling more intensely a sense of hunger. I was looking for something to love, for I was in love with loving, and I hated security and a smooth way, free

[1] *Conf.*, II, iv, 9.
[2] E.g. Frederic W. Farrar (the author of the Victorian classic, *Eric : or, Little by Little*) in *The Lives of the Fathers*, ii, London, 1907, 414: 'A good many schoolboys have robbed orchards, but surely no other schoolboy expresses his remorse in language so heart-breaking as that used by this young African!'
[3] *Conf.*, II, v, 11.
[4] Ibid., II, vi, 12: 'Erat mihi enim meliorum copia, illa autem decerpsi, tantum ut furarer.'
[5] Ibid., II, vi, 14: 'Quid ergo in illo furto dilexi et in quo dominum meum vel vitiose atque perverse imitatus sum? An libuit facere contra legem saltem fallacia, quia poten-tatu non poteram, ut mancam libertatem captivus imitarer faciendo inpune quod non liceret tenebrosa omnipotentiae similitudine? Ecce est ille servus fugiens dominum suum et consecutus umbram. O putretudo, o monstrum vitae et mortis profunditas! Potuitne libere quod non licebat, non ob aliud, nisi quia non licebat?'
[6] See J. M. Le Blond, *Les conversions de saint Augustin*, 68–71.
[7] *Conf.*, II, vi, 14, cited above, *n*[5].
[8] *dCD*, XIV, xxviii: 'Fecerunt itaque civitates duas amores duo, terrenam scilicet amor sui usque ad contemtum Dei, caelestem vero amor Dei usque ad contemtum sui.'

from snares. Within me I had a dearth of that inner food which was
Thyself, my God—although that dearth caused me no hunger. And I
remained without any appetite for incorruptible food—not because I
was already filled with it, but because the emptier I became the more
I loathed it.[1]

In these words, Augustine introduces his third book, which begins with
his student life at Carthage. The passage is a famous one, and was employed by T. S. Eliot as the conclusion of the third part of *The Waste Land*:

> To Carthage then I came
>
> Burning burning burning burning
> O Lord Thou pluckest me out
> O Lord Thou pluckest
>
> burning

—and there are few better descriptions of the eager desires and hungers of
youth, which are satisfied, as Christians believe and as Augustine was to
discover, by the knowledge and love of the living God, but which he then
sought to find in human loves and affections. 'I rushed into love by which I
desired to be ensnared.'[2] A phrase of his: 'To love and to be loved was
sweet to me, and all the more when I gained the enjoyment of the body of
the person I loved. Thus I polluted the spring of friendship with the filth
of concupiscence and I dimmed its lustre with the slime of lust',[3] has given
rise to the suggestion that at this time he indulged in homosexual affairs.[4]
For this opinion, there is not a particle of evidence. Interpreted in the most
damaging way, Augustine's language hardly points to more than juvenile
experiments, often alleged to be a common feature of life at English
boarding-schools; but there is nothing whatever in his voluminous writing
which justifies such an interpretation and everything that we know of his

---

[1] *Conf.*, III, i, 1. Tr. by Outler, p. 61.
[2] *Conf.*, III, i, 1: 'Rui etiam in amorem, quo cupiebam capi.'
[3] Ibid.: 'Amare et amari dulce mihi erat magis, si et amantis corpore fruerer. Venam
igitur amicitiae coinquinabam sordibus concupiscentiae candoremque eius obnubilabam
de tartaro libidinis.'
[4] 'The language he uses in the *Confessions*,' says Dr Farrar, '—especially in II, ii, 2 and
III, i, 1—has been interpreted as casting the very darkest shadow on his memory; but
when we read of the terms in which he expresses remorse for his schoolboy robbing of
the pear-tree, we interpret his phrases with less severity' (*Lives of the Fathers*, ii, 415 *n*[1]).
Miss West, *more suo*, does not hesitate: 'Certainly he confesses to homosexual relationships in a sentence which, with characteristic insight, puts its finger on the real offence of
homosexuality, by pointing out that it brings confusion of passion into the domain where
one ought to be able to practise calmly the art of friendship' (op. cit., p. 40). Professor
Marrou has, as always, the *mot juste*: 'De quelques expressions discrètes on a parfois
conclu qu'il avait été pédéraste (les homosexuels ne manquent jamais d'invoquer Augustin dans la litanie des héros de leur secte): c'est une erreur' (*Saint Augustin et l'augustinisme*, 24).

sexuality suggests a normal, heterosexual nature.[1] His remarks, indeed, are more likely to be inspired by recollections of the mistress with whom he became united about this time,[2] and who bore him the son, Adeodatus, whom he was to love tenderly, whose intellect he was to admire, and whose early death he was bitterly to lament, while submitting himself to the dispositions of God.[3] Since Augustine specifically declares that he was faithful to his mistress during their association[4]—an association which lasted for about fifteen years—the length of time which he devoted to dissipation in Carthage can hardly have amounted to more than a few months at the outside, and he was probably only a very modest rake.[5] There were, however, other delights at Carthage besides those of the flesh in their cruder forms. There were the theatres, which Augustine was to assail bitterly as a Christian apologist, but which now ravished him and which, besides the classical drama of Terence and Plautus whose influence Augustine the bishop was to consider so demoralizing,[6] afforded spectacles of pagan worship of the most uninhibited kind.[7] Sweeter still was the pleasure of success in the schools, where Augustine already excelled in rhetoric, the key to a successful legal career with hopes of advancement to the highest posts in the imperial administration.[8] And then, in the midst of these delights, came the event which he was later to regard as the first action of God in

[1] See B. Legewie, 'Die körperliche Konstitution und die Krankheiten Augustins', in *Miscellanea Agostiniana*, ii: *Studi Agostiniani*, Rome, 1931, 8–9: 'Wer das Sexualleben Augustins einigermassen kennt, der müss mit grösstem Befremden von der hie und da auftauchenden Behaupten Kenntnis nehmen, Augustin sei homosexuell gewesen. . . . Hier mag es genügen festzustellen: Augustin hatte eine normale sexuelle Konstitution.'

[2] At Cassiciacum in 386, Adeodatus was nearly fifteen (*Conf.*, IX, vi, 14). This gives the year of his birth as 372 and means that Augustine's association with his mistress began not later than 371, i.e. within a year of his going to Carthage.

[3] *Conf.*, IX, vi, 14: 'Est liber nostra, qui inscribitur *de Magistro*. Ipse [sc. Adeodatus] ibi mecum loquitur. Tu scis illius esse sensa omnia, quae inseruntur ibi ex persona conlocutoris mei, cum esset in annis sedecim. Multa enim alia mirabiliora expertus sum. Horrori mihi erat illud ingenium: et quis praeter te talium miraculorum opifex? Cito de terra abstulisti vitam eius, et securior eum recordor non timens quicquam pueritiae nec adulescentiae nec omnino homini illi.'

[4] Ibid., IV, ii, 2: 'In illis annis unam habebam non eo quod legitimum vocatur coniugio cognitam, sed quam indagaverat vagus amor inops prudentiae, sed unam tamen, ei quoque servans tori fidem.'

[5] See O'Meara, *The Young Augustine*, 55; Pellegrino, op. cit., pp. 46–47.

[6] See his comments on Terence, *Eunuchus*, III, v, 584–5, 590–1, *Conf.*, I, xvi, 26.

[7] *Conf.*, III, ii, 2–4. On the pagan nature of the Carthaginian stage, see Courcelle, op. cit., pp. 52–56; O'Meara, op. cit., pp. 52–55; Pellegrino, op. cit., pp. 47–48. Christians were not supposed to attend the theatres; see Augustine's reference in *De Civitate Dei*, I, xxxv, to faithless Christians 'qui etiam cum ipsis inimicis adversus Deum, cuius sacramentum gerunt, murmurare non dubitant, modo cum illis theatra, modo ecclesias nobiscum replentes'.

[8] *Conf.*, III, iii, 6: 'Habebant et illa studia, quae honesta vocabantur, ductum suum intuentem fora litigiosa, ut excellerem in eis, hoc laudabilior, quo fraudulentior. Tanta est caecitas hominum de caecitate etiam gloriantium. Et maior iam eram in schola rhetoris et gaudebam superbe et tumebam tyfo.'

placing his feet in the way to the heavenly Jerusalem. At the age of nine-teen, in the normal course of his studies, he read the treatise of Cicero called the *Hortensius*, and the reading changed his whole outlook. The *Hortensius* itself has perished, and survives today only in isolated frag-ments, but it is possible, from what Augustine tells us, to form an estimate of its nature. The work was an exhortation to philosophy, of the genre called by the Greeks λόγος προτρεπτικός, written by Cicero in 45 BC, when the Republican fortunes had finally foundered and the triumph of Julius Caesar, after successive victories at Pharsalus, Thapsus and Munda, had forced him into private life. Making the best of a bad bargain—for no one less willingly retired from political life[1]—the ageing orator set himself to compose a eulogy of philosophy, 'the discovery and the knowledge of nature, which alone makes the life of the gods praiseworthy'.[2] The reading of the *Hortensius* had an immediate effect on Augustine.

In the ordinary course of study [he wrote], I came upon a book of a cer-tain Cicero, whose language almost all admire, though not his heart.[3] This particular book of his contains an exhortation to philosophy and was called *Hortensius*. Now it was this book which quite definitely changed my whole attitude and turned my prayers toward Thee, O Lord, and gave me new hope and new desires. Suddenly every vain hope became worthless to me, and with an incredible warmth of heart I yearned for an immortality of wisdom and began now to arise that I might return to Thee. But it was not to sharpen my tongue further that I made use of that book, read when I was nineteen, when my father had been dead for two years, and my mother was providing the money for my study of rhetoric; what won me in it was not its style but its sub-stance.[4]

The reading of the *Hortensius* inspired Augustine by its praise of the love of wisdom; but one thing was lacking in the treatise: the name of Christ was not there; 'for this name, by Thy mercy, O Lord, this name of my Saviour, Thy Son, my tender heart had piously drunk in, deeply

[1] 'Philosophy was the haven from which he took refuge from the storms of life, but he was ready to put out to sea again when the storms had abated,' M. L. Clarke, *The Roman Mind*, London, 1956, 58.
[2] *Hortensius*, Fr. 42. Tr. by Clarke, op. cit., p. 58.
[3] '. . . in librum cuiusdam Ciceronis, cuius linguam fere omnes mirantur, pectus non ita.' This form of reference to a writer as famous as Cicero is regarded by Courcelle (op. cit., p. 57) as an expression of disdain, 'une concession faite par l'évêque d'Hippone, à la mode selon laquelle les chrétiens de l'époque affectent de mépriser la culture profane.' Pellegrino, op. cit., pp. 49–50 n[12], points out that Augustine refers both to Joshua (*Conf.*, XI, xxiii, 30: 'quia et cuiusdam voto cum sol stetisset) and to St Paul (XII, xv, 20: 'ait enim quidam servus tuus'), in this fashion, and denies any derogatory significance. The whole matter is exhaustively discussed by Maurice Testard, *Saint Augustin et Cicéron*, Paris, 1958, i, 11–19, who decides that no derogation is intended.
[4] *Conf.*, III, iv, 7. Tr. by Outler, pp. 64–65, somewhat modified.

treasured even with my mother's milk. And whatsoever was lacking that name, no matter how erudite, polished, and truthful, did not quite take complete hold of me.'[1]

So the reading of Cicero caused him to study the Scriptures; but the study was a disappointment, for he found, as St Jerome had done before him, that to a mind trained in the rhetorical tradition of the schools of the later Roman Empire, the language of the early Latin version of the Bible seemed a poor thing when compared with the style of Cicero.[2] In this frame of mind, he fell in with the sect which was to claim him for its own for more than nine years, against which he was to wage merciless warfare as a Catholic Christian convert and as a bishop, and which was to supply ecclesiastical controversialists in his later years with a convenient term of abuse to level against him. He became a Manichee.[3]

The religious system of the Manichees will be referred to hereafter in some detail and only a brief outline need be given at this stage. It was a faith founded upon the teaching of the Persian, Mani, who called himself 'the Apostle of Jesus Christ' and who, after a long and successful apostolate in the Persian Empire, was martyred under King Bahrâm I in 277. The question of whether Manichaeism is to be regarded as a Christian heresy or as an independent religion has been much discussed, but one thing is perfectly clear: that the Manichees thought of themselves as Christians, the only true Christians, indeed. Augustine himself bears witness to them by saying: 'Thus I fell among men, delirious in their pride, carnal and voluble, whose mouths were the snares of the devil—a trap made out of the mixture of the syllables of Thy name and the names of our Lord Jesus Christ and of the Paraclete.'[4] On the other hand, Manichaean theology was dualist, envisaging the world as the product of a struggle between two co-equal and co-eternal powers of Light and Darkness—a struggle which would not be ended until the end of time, when both would be finally separated and the world destroyed in a great conflagration. In the meantime, the aim of the faithful was to assist in the separation of Light from the mixture of Light and Darkness which constitutes the world in which we live. The way was by a rigorous asceticism, involving celibacy, poverty, and vegetarianism. Since a church organized on these lines would obviously have but a short continuance, the full Manichaean life was lived only by an élite minority, the so-called Elect, while the majority of the

---

[1] *Conf.*, III, iv, 8.

[2] Ibid., III, v, 9. On the attitude of the literary mind of the later Empire to the Latin Bible, see Marrou, *Saint Augustin et la fin de la culture antique*, 473–503. Cf. Testard, op. cit., i, 41–42.

[3] Ibid., III, vi, 10.

[4] *Conf.*, III, vi, 10. Tr. by Outler, p. 66.

faithful, known as Auditors or Hearers, were permitted to eat meat and drink wine, to marry and beget offspring, and to own property. Among their religious duties, the most important was the support of the mendicant Elect who were not permitted to fend for themselves.

The Manichaean attitude to Christ was an ambiguous one. Mani had called himself an Apostle of Jesus Christ and had taught that Jesus was the greatest of all religious teachers; while the abundant Manichaean literature which has come to light during the first half of the twentieth century reveals a love and devotion to Christ expressed in language which might often have come from orthodox Christian writing:

> Put in me a holy heart, my God: let an upright Spirit be new within me.
> The holy heart is Christ: if He rises in us, we also shall rise in Him.
> Christ has risen, the dead shall rise with Him. If we believe in Him,
> we shall pass beyond death and come to life.[1]

On the other hand, the Manichees rejected the reality of the Incarnation, regarding Jesus as a divine being who only seemed to be mortal. So the Manichaean bishop, Faustus, in controversy with St Augustine, was to declare: 'Christ was not a prophet, nor was he a prophet like Moses; for Moses was a man, and Christ was God; Moses was a sinner, Christ was holy; Moses was born of human coition, and Christ of a Virgin, according to you or, as I hold, not born at all.'[2] But the Manichaeans also held a pantheistic conception of Christ, seeing Him in the fruit hanging on the tree, 'Suffering Jesus, who is the life and salvation of man, suspended from every tree.'[3] Such a view is clearly inadmissible by orthodox Christian standards, and indicates that Manichaeism differed from Catholic Christianity in a way that other heresies did not.[4]

Moreover, this differentiation was emphasized by the Manichaean attitude to the Old Testament. To them Yahweh, the God of Abraham, of Isaac, and of Jacob, was an evil deity, and had nothing in common with the

[1] C. R. C. Allberry, *A Manichaean Psalm Book*, Part II, Stuttgart, 1938, 159, lines 21–23. It will be noted that the first verse is an echo of Ps. 50.12 [51.10]. Père Pierre Jean de Menasce, O.P., 'Augustin Manichéen,' in *Freundesgabe für Ernst Robert Curtius*, Bern, 1958, 89 n^1, draws attention to the Manichaean use of certain texts of the Old Testament, in spite of their theoretical rejection of this part of the canon. It would seem, however, that their choice was limited to the Psalms.
[2] *C. Faust.*, XVI, iv.
[3] Ibid., XX, ii: '. . . patibilem Iesum, qui est vita ac salus hominum, omni suspensus ex ligno'.
[4] O'Meara, op. cit., p. 58, apparently does not regard the Manichees as Christians: 'Between this time [of reading the *Hortensius*] and the time when he met St. Ambrose he was definitely not a Christian—*unless one regards the Manichees as Christians*' (italics mine). It is, of course, always difficult to decide at what point heterodoxy becomes independent; but the Manichees seem to me to have kept within the pale.

Father of Greatness revealed by Jesus. Hence they declined to accept the Old Testament,[1] or, indeed, any text of Scripture unfavourable to their theology, declaring all such to be forged interpolations. This anticipation of a certain type of Higher Criticism appealed to Augustine. He had found certain assertions of the Old Testament hard to accept, such as the statement that God created man in His own image, which Augustine could interpret only in anthropomorphic fashion, and he was scandalized by the polygamy of many of the patriarchs.[2] To his problems, the Manichees had an easy answer: the passages were spurious. Furthermore, they had a reply to a problem which haunted and perplexed him: the origin of evil. If God is good, how does evil arise? The Manichaean reply was deceptively simple: God is good, but evil exists independently of Him.[3]

In view of the savage nature of Augustine's denunciation of the intellectual side of Manichaeism after he had become a Catholic, and the (to us) obvious follies and contradictions of the sect, it may be asked how it was that he was attracted to Manichaeism in the first place, and thereafter remained in it for more than nine years. The reasons can be fairly easily established.

First, there was the Manichaean assertion that, while the Catholics relied on authority to establish their doctrine, they themselves appealed only to the reason. In the work *On the Usefulness of Belief* written by Augustine in 391 or 392, just after he had become a Catholic priest, he explained this very clearly:

> You know, Honoratus, that I fell among these people for no other reason than that they declared that they would put aside all overawing authority, and by pure and simple reason would bring to God those who were willing to listen to them, and so deliver them from all error. What else compelled me for nearly nine years to spurn the religion implanted in me as a boy by my parents, to follow these men and listen diligently to them, than that they said we were overawed by superstition and were bidden to believe rather than to reason, while they pressed no one to believe until the truth had been discussed and elucidated? Who would not be enticed by these promises, especially if he were an adolescent with a mind eager for truth, but made proud and garrulous by the disputes of learned men in school?[4]

[1] Although they were willing to incorporate portions of the OT in their own writings. See above, p. 59 n^1.
[2] *Conf.*, III, vii, 12.
[3] Ibid.: 'Quibus rerum ignarus perturbabar et recedens a veritate ire in eam mihi videbar, quia non noveram malum non esse nisi privationem boni usque ad quod omnino non est. Quod unde viderem, cuius videre usque ad corpus erat oculis et animo usque ad phantasma?'
[4] *De Utilitate Credendi*, i, 2. Tr. by John H. S. Burleigh, *Augustine: Earlier Writings* (The Library of Christian Classics, Vol. VI), London, 1953, 292.

To such a mind, the alleged rationalism of the Manichees made an obvious appeal, especially when it solved (or appeared to solve) the perplexing problem of evil and to reject the Old Testament which had seemed distasteful to him, both from its form and its content. But to these intellectual appeals must be added two others, of a more emotional nature: Manichaean austerity[1] and Manichaean religious enthusiasm. The austere lives of the Manichaean Elect must have impressed Augustine, especially in view of the difficulty which he himself found in living chastely. In this, they must have seemed much more impressive than the Catholics; for at this time, Augustine had heard nothing of the lives of the solitaries of the Egyptian Thebaid, and of their great exemplar and patron, St Anthony, who had died in 354—the year of Augustine's birth—aged one hundred and five years.[2] The enthusiasm with which Augustine learned of the deeds of these athletes of God, and the rôle which the image of continence played at the decisive moment of his conversion,[3] leave no doubt of the attraction which asceticism held for the young professor of rhetoric. He did not, indeed, attempt to emulate the lives of the Elect, but remained an Auditor throughout his Manichaean career; but it appears that he made unsuccessful efforts to obtain the gift of continence. It is perhaps significant that Adeodatus was Augustine's only son and was conceived before his father became a Manichee;[4] while Augustine prayed for chastity, but

[1] *De Moribus*, I, i, 2: 'Duae maxime sunt illecebrae Manichaeorum, quibus decipiuntur incauti, ut eos velint habere doctores; una, cum Scripturas reprehendunt, vel quas male intelligunt vel quas male intelligi volunt; altera, cum vitae castae et memorabilis continentiae imaginem praeferunt.'

[2] *Conf.*, VIII, vi, 14: 'Cui [sc. Ponticiano] ego cum indicassem illis me scripturis curam maximam inpendere, ortus est sermo ipso narrante de Antonio Aegyptio monacho, cuius nomen excellenter clarebat apud servos tuos, nos autem usque in illam horam latebat. Quod ille ubi conperit, inmoratus est in eo sermone insinuans tantum virum ignorantibus et admirans eandem nostram ignorantiam. Stupebamus autem audientes tam recenti memoria et prope nostris temporibus testatissima *mirabilia tua* in fide recta et catholica ecclesia. Omnes mirabamur, et nos, quia tam magna erant, et ille, quia inaudita nobis erant.' Augustine's reference to these divine wonders 'in fide recta et catholica ecclesia' may have the continence of the Manichaean Elect in mind. Augustine's ignorance of the life and times of St Anthony is the more curious, in that his reputation had already reached the west before St Athansius wrote his life (Athanasius, *Vita Antonii*, 93. *MPG* xxvi, 973 C). See Karl Heussi, *Der Ursprung des Mönchtums*, Tübingen, 1936, 100.

[3] Ibid., VIII, xi, 27: 'Aperiebatur enim ab ea parte, qua intenderam faciem et quo transire trepidabam, casta dignitas continentiae, serena et non dissolute hilaris, honeste blandiens, ut venirem neque dubitarem, et extendens ad me suscipiendum et amplectendum pias manus plenas gregibus bonorum exemplorum. Ibi tot pueri et puellae, ibi inventus multa et omnis aetas et graves viduae et virgines anus, et in omnibus ipsa continentia nequaquam sterilis, sed fecunda mater filiorum gaudiorum de marito te, domine.'

[4] Too much emphasis cannot, however, be placed upon this fact, since the Manichees apparently practised contraception. See below, p. 183 *n*[3].

with the secret and very human reservation that God would delay to
answer his prayer.[1]

Finally, we need not doubt that Augustine found much to attract him in
the spirituality of Manichaeism. The glowing sincerity of the Manichaean
psalms which have survived bears witness to a very real devotion to Christ,
even if conceived very differently from the Word made flesh of Catholic
Christianity. If the Manichees of Africa at all resembled their brethren of
Egypt, Augustine would have found in their liturgy the name of Christ
and the Persons of the Trinity given pre-eminence and a religious
emotion which may have been lacking among the Catholics whom he
knew. He tells us little about this aspect of Manichaeism in his writings;
but it seems likely that it existed.[2]

Augustine's conversion to Manichaeism outraged his mother. The
Manichees always inspired the greatest horror among orthodox Christians,
and for the first and only time in her life, Monica forbade her son the
house.[3] From this action she was dissuaded by a vision, in which she saw
herself standing upon a rule of wood, and beheld a handsome youth
coming towards her with a joyful and smiling countenance while she herself was wretched and mourning. The young man asked her the reason for
her grief, and she replied that she was mourning her son's perdition. The
youth then told her to be of good cheer, for where she was, her son should
also be.[4] Monica recounted the vision to Augustine, who attempted to
interpret it as foreshadowing his mother's conversion to Manichaeism, to
receive the immediate reply: 'No; for it was not told me that "where he is,
there you shall be" but "where you are, there he will be" '—a reply which
impressed Augustine more than the vision itself.[5] Monica was further
comforted by an interview with an aged bishop whom she had visited in
the hope that she might persuade him to remonstrate with her son and
refute his errors. This the old man declined to do, on the ground that
Augustine was, as yet, unteachable, being still puffed up with the novelty
of the heresy. 'Let him alone for a time,' the old man advised, 'and only
pray for him to God; and he himself will discover, by reading, what an
error it is, and what a great impiety.' The old bishop added that he had

[1] *Conf.*, VIII, vii, 17: 'At ego adulescens miser valde, miser in exordio ipsius adulescentiae, etiam petieram a te castitatem et dixeram: "Da mihi castitatem et continentiam, sed
noli modo." Timebam enim ne me cito exaudires et cito sanares a morbo concupiscentiae, quem malebam expleri quam exstingui.'
[2] See Menasce, art. cit., esp. pp. 87–93.
[3] *Conf.*, III, x, 19: 'Exaudisti [Domine] eam nec despexisti lacrimas eius, cum pro-
fluentes rigarent terram sub oculis eius in omni loco orationis eius: exaudisti eam. Nam
unde illud somnium, quo eam consolatus es, ut vivere mecum cederet et habere mecum
eandem mensam in domo? Quod nolle coeperat aversans et detestans blasphemias
erroris mei.'   [4] Ibid.   [5] Ibid., III, xi, 20.

himself once been a very active Manichee, but had left the sect of his own accord without anyone arguing with him. Such faith in the inevitability of gradualness had, however, little attraction for St Monica, and she redoubled her entreaties, with bitter tears; which caused the bishop to say, a shade testily: 'Go your way from me; as you live, it is impossible that the son of these tears should perish.'[1]

So for nine years Augustine continued a Manichee.[2] His studies prospered. 'During those years I taught the art of rhetoric. Conquered by the desire for gain, I offered for sale speaking skills with which to conquer others. And yet, O Lord, Thou knowest that I really preferred to have honest scholars (or what were esteemed as such) and, without tricks of speech, I taught these scholars the tricks of speech—not to be used against the life of the innocent, but sometimes to save the life of a guilty man.'[3] He was fascinated by the astrologers, and those who claimed to foretell the future—astrology played a prominent part in Manichaean doctrine— though on one occasion, when he was a candidate for a rhetorical competition, and was visited by a fortune-teller, who asked what Augustine would give him for secret rites to secure success, he gave the proud reply that, if the victor's crown were to be of imperishable gold, he would not suffer even a fly be slain for his victory[4]—a piece of self-denial dictated by the Manichaean ban upon the taking of animal life.[5] In the event, both his self-denial and his self-confidence were justified; for in 377, at a rhetorical contest at which the proconsul of Africa, Vindicianus, presided, Augustine was successful, and carried off the prize.[6] The proconsul, a former physician of great reputation, took an interest in the youthful professor of rhetoric, and attempted to dissuade him from his astrological interests,[7] as did also Augustine's friend Nebridius;[8] but neither could make any impression upon the convinced young Manichee, who had already contrived to make numerous converts to his faith from among his friends at Thagaste.[9]

The tide of success seemed to be flowing in Augustine's favour, when there occurred an event which was to shake him to the core. He had returned to Thagaste from Carthage and was teaching in his home town

[1] *Conf.*, III, xii, 21.
[2] Ten according to the calculation of Prof. Courcelle, op. cit., p. 78.
[3] *Conf.*, IV, ii, 2. Tr. Outler, p. 77. Testard, *Saint Augustin et Cicéron*, i, 45 sees this refusal to act against an innocent man as inspired by *De Officiis*, II, 51.
[4] Ibid., IV, ii, 3.   [5] O'Meara, op. cit., p. 95; Pellegrino, op. cit., p. 72.
[6] *Conf.*, IV, iii, 5. For the name of the proconsul, see VII, vi, 8.
[7] Ibid.   [8] Ibid., IV, iii, 6.
[9] See Courcelle, op. cit., pp. 69–70. Augustine had, indeed, included Nebridius among his converts; but was unable to persuade him to swallow astrology.

when one of his dearest friends, whom he had known since childhood and whom he had converted to Manichaeism, fell ill.[1] As he lay apparently at the point of death, baptism was administered—the clinical baptism for which Augustine had asked, during his childhood sickness,[2] but which he now despised, for the Manichees had no sacraments as the Catholics understood the term, though they gave the name of baptism to the ritual imposition of hands by which a convert joined the sect.[3] Augustine's friend, however, having received Catholic baptism, unexpectedly rallied and appeared to be making a successful recovery. Augustine visited him during his convalescence, and affected to treat the baptism as a matter for jesting. To his surprise, his friend[4] reproved him sternly, declaring that if Augustine wished their friendship to continue, he must abstain from such pleasantries. Augustine was astounded; but decided to refrain from argument until his friend should be well again, when he would be able to deal with him as he wished. God however decreed otherwise; for a few days later the young man suffered a relapse, and died before Augustine could reach him.[5] His death plunged Augustine into the depths of misery:

> My native place was a torture room to me and my father's house a strange unhappiness. And all the things I had done with him—now that he was gone—became a frightful torment. My eyes sought him everywhere, but they did not see him; and I hated all places because he was not in them, because they could not say to me: 'Look, he is coming', as they did when he was alive and absent.[6]

In these circumstances, life at Thagaste became intolerable and he was glad to escape to a teaching post at Carthage.[7] It is possible, however, to discern another motive in this remove, besides grief in his friend's death, to which Augustine makes allusion, not in the *Confessions* but in the *Contra Academicos*: the desire to further his academic career. Thagaste was only a small town, an *oppidum*, and a teacher of rhetoric there was not a person of any great consequence. Carthage was the leading university of Africa and a convenient stepping-stone to a chair of rhetoric in Italy. Augustine confided his desire to his friend and patron, Romanianus, who had already shown him much kindness from his student days onwards and whose goodness he had repaid by leading him into the Manichaean fold,[8] and who now, after some demur befitting a patriotic citizen of Thagaste

[1] *Conf.*, IV, iv, 7.   [2] Ibid., I, xi, 17.   [3] See below, p. 173.
[4] We do not know his name. 'Augustin a sans doute jugé que le nom de ce jeune homme de Thagaste, mort à la fleur de l'âge, était sans intérêt pour les lecteurs et la postérité' (Courcelle, op. cit., p. 41).
[5] *Conf.*, IV, iv, 8.   [6] Ibid., IV, iv, 9. Tr. Outler, p. 81.   [7] Ibid., IV, vii, 12.
[8] *C. Academicos*, I, i, 3: 'Ipsa [philosophia] me penitus ab illa superstitione, in quam te mecum praecipitem dederam, liberavit.'

anxious to retain in the town a young scholar of rising reputation, not only encouraged him, but bestowed upon him material help to enable him to establish himself at Carthage.[1]

Arrived at Carthage, Augustine did not disappoint either his own hopes or those of his friends. At the age of twenty-six or twenty-seven—he is not clear about the date[2]—he published a work (now lost) *De Pulchro et Apto* —'On the Fair and the Fit'—in two or three books—he is not clear about the number.[3] Augustine's vagueness about this work is hardly surprising. Many literary men of distinction are reluctant to recall too exactly their earliest publication; and it can easily be believed that, on purely literary grounds, the bishop of Hippo might be unsympathetic to the work of the young Manichaean rhetorician, who had no better taste, after writing his book, than to dedicate it to Hierius, an orator of Rome, whom he had never seen, but whose work he admired, and who (we may easily conjecture) might be a very useful friend for a rising young scholar, anxious to better himself.[4] 'To me it was a great matter that both my literary work and my zest for learning should be known by that man', declares Augustine, with a remarkably frank naïveté,[5] and there are few better ways of attracting a man's attention than by dedicating a book to him.

The subject of the *De Pulchro et Apto* was aesthetics, 'beauty' being regarded as a quality of an object inherent in itself, and 'fitness' as a quality in its relation to other objects.[6] When however Augustine attempted to turn his attention to the mind, he was hampered by his incapacity to think of any immaterial substance, or of evil except as a substance with a real life of its own.[7] More than this we do not know. It is usual to regard the *De Pulchro et Apto* as being written from a Manichaean standpoint,[8] and the materialism and the hypostatic conception of evil add support to such a view; but a careful study of what Augustine tells us about the book has caused M. Maurice Testard to see the philosophic background as Stoic rather than Manichaean, and the immediate influence Cicero, the great interpreter of Greek philosophic writing to the Latin world.[9] Perhaps the

---

[1] *C. Acad.*, II, ii, 3. Courcelle, op. cit., pp. 68–69; Pellegrino, op. cit., pp. 73–74.

[2] *Conf.*, IV, xv, 27: 'Et eram aetate annorum fortasse viginti sex aut septem, cum illa volumina scripsi.' [3] Ibid., IV, xiii, 20.

[4] Ibid., IV, xiv, 21: 'Quid est autem, quod me movit, domine deus meus, ut ad Hierium, Romanae urbis oratorem, scriberem illos libros? Quem non noveram facie, sed amaveram hominem ex doctrinae fama, quae illi clara erat, et quaedam verba eius audieram, et placuerant mihi.'

[5] Ibid., IV, xiv, 23: 'Et magnum quiddam mihi erat, si sermo meus et studia mea illi viro innotescerent.'

[6] Ibid., IV, xii, 20. Cf. Aug., *Ep.* 138, i, 5. [7] Ibid., IV, xv, 24.

[8] E.g. O'Meara, op. cit., p. 97: '*On the Beautiful and the Fitting*, as revealed in his account of it in the *Confessions*, was at once an ambitious rhetorical work and a public expression of his Manichaean faith.' [9] Testard, op. cit., vol. i, pp. 49–66.

C

safest course is to recognize frankly that we have no knowledge of the book other than what Augustine chooses to tell us; and what we do know points at least as much to the influence of Greek philosophy as to that of Manichaeism.[1]

Whatever the background to the *De Pulchro et Apto*, it would appear that, at the time when he was writing it, Augustine was still a convinced Manichee. During the next few years, however, his belief in that religion was to be badly shaken. Various factors were to contribute. One was the nature of Manichaeism itself, which although outwardly imposing was intellectually sterile: 'I observed that they were more clever and ready of wit in refuting others than firm and sure in proving their own doctrines.'[2] Another, and of particular importance, was the weakness of Manichaeism in the sphere of physical science. Augustine read widely—it was the fruit of that youthful study of the *Hortensius*. About a year after that influential reading, he came upon Aristotle's *Categories*, a work widely esteemed in Africa but little comprehended[3]—and understood it without any effort. We do not know what other books of Aristotle he read, if any.[4] No doubt Cicero supplied a good deal of his general information about physical science;[5] but whatever the source, he studied a number of works on astronomy,[6] and made the disquieting discovery that the facts recorded in these, and backed with a wealth of evidence, were utterly at variance with the cosmological doctrines of the Manichees. This discrepancy was a fatal flaw in Manichaeism, which claimed to be a direct revelation of the Holy Spirit on all matters, the more so since there had been no theological necessity for Mani to write upon such topics;[7] indeed, Augustine specifically declares that, as a Catholic Christian, he personally could patiently

---

[1] Cf. R. L. Ottley, *Studies in the* Confessions *of St Augustine*, 16: 'As a matter of fact nothing is now known of the juvenile essay which he regarded with such complacency: but the subject he chose is perhaps a slight indication that his mind was already turning in the direction of Platonism.'   [2] *De Util. Cred.*, i, 2. Tr. Burleigh, p. 292.

[3] *Conf.*, IV, xvi, 28: 'Et quid mihi proderat, quod annos natus ferme viginti, cum in manus meas venissent Aristotelica quaedam, quas appellant decem categorias—quarum nomine, cum eas rhetor Carthaginiensis, magister meus, buccis tyfo crepantibus conmemoraret et alii qui docti habebantur, tamquam in nescio quid magnum et divinum suspensus inhiabam—legi eas solus et intellexi? Quas cum contulissem cum eis, qui se dicebant vix eas magistris eruditissimis non loquentibus tantum, sed multa in pulvere depingentibus intellexisse, nihil inde aliud mihi dicere potuerunt, quam ego solus apud me ipsum legens cognoveram.'

[4] Marrou, *St Augustin et la fin de la culture antique*, 34: 'Le seul livre de lui [Aristote] qu'il ait certainement lu, ce sont les *Catégories*.'

[5] Testard, op. cit., i, pp. 67–68.

[6] *Conf.*, V, iii, 3: 'Et quoniam multa philosophorum legeram memoriaeque mandata retinebam, ex eis quaedam conparabam illis manichaeorum longis fabulis, et mihi probabiliora ista videbantur, quae dixerunt illi *qui tantum potuerunt valere, ut possent aestimare saeculum*, quamquam *eius dominum minime invenerint*.'

[7] Ibid., V. v, 8.

endure hearing a Christian brother speaking ignorantly on scientific matters,[1] though he thought it very disgraceful and pernicious if a pagan should hear a Christian talking nonsense on scientific matters and claiming the authority of the Scriptures for his views.[2] The intellectual dissatisfaction caused by study was increased by the dialectic of his friend, Nebridius, who was accustomed to baffle the Carthaginian Manichees by asking them what the powers of Darkness would have done if the good God, the Father of Greatness, had refused to fight with them; for if they replied that in that case the powers of Darkness would have wounded Him, they admitted that God could be hurt; but if on the other hand they declared that the powers of Evil could have done no harm to the Light, their whole elaborate account of the war between Light and Darkness which resulted in the creation of this imperfect world where Light and Darkness are mixed in a sordid and defiling fashion was utterly pointless: why should God engage in a needless and degrading struggle?[3] About this time, too, a Catholic apologist, Elpidius, came forward in Carthage against the Manichees, with a wealth of argument to which Augustine's co-religionists made only a very feeble reply in public. Privately, they explained to the Auditors that the text of the New Testament had been interpolated by persons of Judaizing tendencies, who desired to introduce the Jewish Law into the Christian faith. They did not, however, produce any uncorrupted copies of the text, and Augustine found their explanation wholly inadequate.[4] Finally, there was the uncomfortable consideration that the morals of some of the Manichaean Elect fell far below their ideal; while the fact that Manichaeism was a proscribed religion in the Roman Empire

[1] *Conf.*, V, v, 9: 'Cum enim audio christianum aliquem fratrem illum aut illum ista nescientem et aliud pro alio sentientem, patienter intueor opinantem hominem nec illi obesse video, cum de te, domine *creator omnium*, non credat indigna, si forte situs et habitus creaturae corporalis ignoret. Obest autem, si hoc ad ipsam doctrinae pietatis formam pertinere arbitretur et pertinacius affirmare audeat quod ignorat.'

[2] *De Gen. ad Litt.*, I, xix, 39: 'Turpe est autem nimis et perniciosum ac maxime cavendum, ut christianum de his rebus quasi secundum christianas litteras loquentem, ita delirare [quilibet infidelis] audiat, ut, quemadmodum dicitur, toto caelo errare conspiciens risum tenere vix possit. et non tam molestum est, quod errans homo diridetur, sed quod auctores nostri ab eis, qui foris sunt, talia sensisse creduntur, et cum magno eorum exitio, de quorum salute satagimus, tanquam indocti reprehenduntur atque respuuntur.' [3] *Conf.*, VII, ii, 3.

[4] Ibid., V, xi, 21: 'Iam enim Elpidii cuiusdam adversus eosdem manichaeos coram loquentis et disserentis sermones etiam apud Carthaginem movere me coeperant, cum talia de scripturis proferret, quibus resisti non facile posset. Et inbecilla mihi responsio videbatur istorum; quam quidem non facile palam promebant, sed nobis secretius, cum dicerent scripturas novi testamenti falsatas fuisse a nescio quibus, qui Iudaeorum legem inserere christianae fidei voluerunt, atque ipsi incorrupta exemplaria nulla proferrent.' *De Util. Cred.*, iii, 7: 'Quae vox mihi semper quidem, etiam cum eos audirem, invalidissima visa est: nec mihi soli, sed etiam tibi [sc. Honorato]—nam bene memini—et nobis omnibus, qui paulo maiorem diligintiam in iudicando habere conabamur, quam turba credentium.'

prevented its bishops from taking any action against the guilty, for fear that the criminals would denounce them to the secular authority by way of revenge.[1]

All these factors contributed to unsettling Augustine's mind with regard to his religion, but the most influential was undoubtedly the problem of the discrepancy between Manichaean dogma and the researches of the philosophers. To these problems, the Carthaginian Manichees had no answer, except to exhort Augustine to wait patiently until Faustus of Milevis, their great theologian, should visit Carthage. Faustus, they declared, would satisfy all Augustine's problems.[2]

When however Faustus did come to Carthage, about the year 383, he proved a complete disappointment. He was a man of high character, and a natural eloquence which he had improved by a certain amount of reading,[3] but he knew nothing of philosophy, and could merely repeat the usual Manichaean arguments in a rather more pleasing way. This, as Augustine comments, was rather like offering a thirsty man an empty cup of great value at the hands of a handsome cupbearer.[4] Augustine did not, indeed, leave the sect; but his enthusiasm was quenched. For Faustus personally he had only friendly feelings, and the professor of rhetoric was soon directing the reading of the Manichaean bishop.[5]

Although the encounter with Faustus produced no immediate and dramatic decision on Augustine's part, it must nevertheless be regarded as one of the decisive moments of his career.[6] Henceforth, he no longer desired to make any progress in the sect;[7] any thoughts which he had had of advancing to the grade of an Elect vanished; he decided to remain where he was, and await developments. Such a decision in any sect or, indeed, in any serious religion, is a very grave one; for no worth-while

---

[1] *De Moribus*, II, xix, 68. See Courcelle, op. cit., pp. 74–75.   [2] *Conf.*, V, vi, 10.

[3] Ibid., V, vi, 11: 'Et quia legerat aliquas Tullianas orationes et paucissimos Senecae libros et nonnulla poetarum et suae sectae si qua volumina latine atque conposite conscripta erant, et quia aderat cotidiana sermocinandi exercitatio, inde suppetebat eloquium, quod fiebat acceptius magisque seductorium moderamine ingenii et quodam lepore naturali.'

[4] Ibid., V, vi, 10: 'Sed quid ad meam sitim pretiosorum poculorum decentissimus ministrator?'

[5] Ibid., V, vii, 13: 'Refracto itaque studio, quod intenderam in Manichaei litteras, magisque desperans de ceteris eorum doctoribus, quando in multis, quae me movebant, ita ille nominatus apparuit, coepi cum eo pro studio eius agere vitam, quo ipse flagrabat in eas litteras, quas tunc iam rhetor Carthaginis adulescentes docebam, et legere cum eo sive quae ille audita desideraret sive quae ipse tali ingenio apta existimarem.'

[6] Courcelle, op. cit., p. 76, hardly notices the effect of the meeting with Faustus; O'Meara, op. cit., p. 102 and Pellegrino, op. cit., p. 80, do it more justice.

[7] *Conf.*, V, vii, 13: 'Ceterum conatus omnis meus, quo proficere in illa secta statueram, illo homine cognito prorsus intercidit, non ut ab eis omnino separarer, sed quasi melius quicquam non inveniens eo, quo iam quoquo modo inrueram, contentus interim esse decreveram, nisi aliquid forte, quod magis eligendum esset, eluceret.'

religious life is static and, if you do not advance, you are apt to find that you are retiring. There are occasions which can be clearly recognized as times of testing, when all a man can do is to hold fast, and pray for grace; but no one will regard such times with anything other than concern. It was into such a time of testing that Augustine now entered in his career as a Manichee, and its ultimate issue was to restore him to the Catholic Church.

It is probable that an immediate consequence of his disillusionment was his decision to remove himself to Rome. The motive for this decision, he says—and as he says so very seriously we cannot doubt that he actually believed this when he wrote the *Confessions*—was his disgust with the violence and indiscipline prevailing among the students of the university of Carthage,[1] those bands of *Eversores* or 'Destroyers' whose company he had himself avoided as an undergraduate.[2] At the same time, we must not underestimate the pull of ambition as a motive, perhaps not fully recognized, in Augustine's removal to the capital,[3] to which his loss of enthusiasm for the Manichaean ideal now gave free rein. His move from Thagaste to Carthage after his friend's death had been the first step upon the road; his action in dedicating the *De Pulchro et Apto* to Hierius of Rome, a man whom he had never seen, was a further move towards the goal—a goal which, as he was afterwards to reflect at Milan, might at the very least be a provincial governorship of the lowest grade.[4] At the time of quitting Carthage for Rome, it would seem that Augustine was still essentially a don on the make, freed from the restraints which the essentially anti-social outlook of Manichaeism had hitherto imposed.[5] His mother strongly opposed his departure, and Augustine was only able to set sail after deceiving her in a rather heartless fashion, by declaring that his intention was only to take leave of a friend. The trusting Monica retired into a little oratory dedicated to St Cyprian to pray, and in the night her faithless son

[1] *Conf.*, V, viii, 14.
[2] Ibid., III, iii, 6: 'Et maioriam eram in schola rhetoris et gaudebam superbe et tumebam tyfo, quamquam longe sedatior, domine, tu scis, et remotus omnino ab eversionibus, quas faciebant eversores—hoc enim nomen scaevum et diabolicum velut insigne urbanitatis est—inter quos vivebam pudore inpudenti, quia talis non eram.'
[3] See Ernesto Buonaiuti, *Il cristianesimo nell' Africa Romana*, Bari, 1928, 343.
[4] *Conf.*, VI, xi, 19: 'Suppetit amicorum maiorum copia: ut nihil aliud multum festinemus, vel praesidatus dari potest.' Labriolle, in his edition of the *Confessions*, i, 137 n[1], suggests that Augustine had in mind the presidency of a tribunal, rather than the governorship of a province, an interpretation which is accepted by Pellegrino, op. cit., p. 98: 'ora poteva sperare almeno una presidenza di tribunale.' Both Courcelle, op. cit., p. 83, and Marrou, *Augustin et l'augustinisme*, 20, however, think he had the provincial governorship in mind.
[5] 'All the same in 383 [Augustine] was still a Manichee. In that year he made up his mind to go at last to Rome, where, it had been arranged, he was received in Manichaean circles. There can be no doubt but that an important motive for doing so was to improve his position, which in effect he did.' O'Meara, *The Young Augustine*, 104.

set sail, leaving his mother to her orations and lamentations.[1] Arrived at Rome, he took lodgings at the house of a Manichaean Auditor,[2] and almost immediately succumbed to a violent attack of fever, which very nearly proved fatal.[3] When sick in his childhood, he had demanded the sacrament of baptism;[4] but now he made no such demand—which would, in any case, have been very badly received in a Manichaean household.[5] This failure to ask for baptism is proof of the fact that, however disappointed in Manichaeism Augustine might be, he was, as yet, far from seeing in Catholic Christianity the answer to his spiritual needs. He was still influenced by Manichaean conceptions, and considered the doctrine of the Incarnation unworthy of the deity, though he was, at the same time, dominated by the materialist conception of the universe, which made him unable to conceive of God except as a corporeal mass.[6] Moreover, precisely because of this materialistic outlook, he was forced to regard Evil as a substance. But, since he could not regard the good God as being the author of Evil, he was constrained to grant it an independent existence in the Manichaean fashion.[7] For this reason, he remained, outwardly, a Manichee. It was, indeed, his Manichaean friendships which caused him to remain in the sect, for which he felt little enthusiasm,[8] and it was through the influence and support of the Roman Manichees that he applied for and obtained the post of Public Orator at Milan,[9] in the autumn of 384.[10] His reason for

[1] *Conf.*, V, viii, 15.

[2] Ibid., V, x, 18: 'Et iungebar etiam tunc Romae falsis illis atque fallentibus sanctis: non enim tantum auditoribus eorum, quorum e numero erat etiam is, in cuius domo aegrotaveram et convalueram, sed eis etiam, quos electos vocant.'

[3] Ibid., V, ix, 16.   [4] Ibid., I, xi, 17.

[5] Ibid., V, ix, 16: 'Neque enim desiderabam in illo tanto periculo baptismum tuum et melior eram puer, quo illum de materna pietate flagitavi, sicut iam recordatus atque confessus sum.'

[6] Ibid., V, x, 19: '. . . multumque mihi turpe videbatur credere figuram te [Domine] habere humanae carnis et membrorum nostrorum liniamentis corporalibus terminari. Et quoniam cum de deo meo cogitare vellem, cogitare nisi moles corporum non noveram—neque enim videbatur mihi esse quicquam, quod tale non esset—ea maxima et prope sola causa erat inevitabilis erroris mei.'

[7] Ibid., V, x, 20: 'Hinc enim et mali substantiam quandam credebam esse talem et habere suam molem tetram et deformem, sive crassam, quam terram dicebant, sive tenuem atque subtilem, sicuti est aeris corpus: quam malignam mentem per illam terram repentem imaginantur. Et quia deum bonum nullam malam naturam, creasse qualiscumque me pietas credere cogebat, constituebam ex adverso sibi duas moles, utramque infinitam, sed malam angustius, bonam grandius, et ex hoc initio pestilentioso me cetera sacriligia sequebantur.'

[8] Ibid., V, x, 19: 'Nec dissimulavi eundem hospitem meum reprimere a nimia fiducia, quam sensi eum habere de rebus fabulosis, quibus manichaei libri pleni sunt. Amicitia tamen eorum familiarius utebar quam ceterorum hominum, qui in illa haeresi non fuissent. Nec eam defendebam pristina animositate, sed tamen familiaritas eorum—plures enim eos Roma occultabat—pigrius me faciebat quaerere praesertim desperantem in ecclesia tua, *domine caeli et terrae*.'

[9] Ibid., V, xiii, 23.

[10] For the date, see Courcelle, op. cit., pp. 78–83; O'Meara, op. cit., p. 115.

going, he says, was that he had received intelligence of the most distasteful kind about the behaviour of the undergraduate population of Rome. He had flung himself into his work as a teacher with enthusiasm, and had gathered a small following to whom and through whom he had begun to be known,[1] when he was informed that the Roman students, although they did not indulge in the violence of the Carthaginians, had another custom which many tutors might find yet more disagreeable: that of failing to pay their tuition fees. 'Yet now, my friends told me, many of the Roman students—breakers of faith, who, for love of money, set a small value on justice—would conspire together and suddenly transfer to another teacher, to evade paying their master's fees.'[2] Disconcerted by this news, Augustine was very willing to apply for the post of Public Orator at Milan and, thanks to the good offices of his Manichaean friends, he obtained it from Symmachus, the City Prefect of Rome, one of the most distinguished of the conservative Roman patricians who remained loyal to paganism and who now, by a strange irony, appointed to a chair of rhetoric a man destined to become one of the most bitter enemies of paganism which the Christian Church ever produced.

Augustine came to Milan on the eve of his thirtieth birthday, there to experience a conversion as dramatic as that which had followed his going to Carthage fourteen years earlier, but which was to have far more enduring consequences, both for himself and for the world. He had come to Carthage as a boy, in love with love, and anxious to experience all the pleasures that youth could provide; he came to Milan in a troubled spirit, having tasted the delights of youth, found them intoxicating, but unsatisfying, and craving for spiritual food. Fortunately for him, there was at Milan a teacher able to help him: St Ambrose, the most outstanding ecclesiastical figure of the day, the greatest figure among Italian clergy before pope Gregory the Great, a prelate who was not afraid to excommunicate an emperor for atrocities which had been committed in his name, as he did with the Emperor Theodosius after the massacre of Thessalonica, but who was also capable of the most exquisite diplomacy, as in the funeral oration on the murdered emperor Valentinian II.[3] Ambrose received Augustine with kindliness, when the young man paid

[1] *Conf.*, V, xii, 22: 'Sedulo ergo agere coeperam, propter quod veneram, ut docerem Romae artem rhetoricam, et prius domi congregare aliquos, quibus et per quos innotescere coeperam.'
[2] Ibid. Tr. Outler, pp. 109–10.
[3] See Augustine's tribute, *Conf.*, V, xiii, 23: 'Et veni Mediolanium ad Ambrosium episcopum, in optimis notum orbi terrae, pium cultorem tuum, cuius tunc eloquia strenue ministrabant adipem frumenti tui et laetitiam olei et sobriam vini ebrietatem populo tuo. Ad eum autem ducebar abs te nesciens, ut per eum ad te sciens ducerer.'

his official call, and quite won his heart,[1] since he may well have expected no very cordial reception as the nominee of Symmachus, the defender of paganism.[2] As a result of the interview, Augustine began to attend Ambrose's sermons, not, at first, out of any desire for instruction—for he did not expect to find the answer to his problems in the Catholic Church[3]— but with professional concern to satisfy himself that Ambrose's reputation as an orator was justified. Stylistic considerations, however, were soon forgotten in the interest of what the preacher was saying; for from Ambrose, Augustine learnt that the Scriptures could be defended against the attacks of the Manichees and that the passages which had disturbed him were to be understood, by the use of the allegorical method of interpretation, for *the letter killeth, but the Spirit giveth life*. These first sermons of Ambrose had their effect; they revealed that the Catholic religion had a reasoned defence and brought back for Augustine's consideration the claims of the religion of his childhood. He did not, however, yet see that he was justified in joining the Catholic Church merely because it had able apologists, nor in rejecting Manichaeism because its enemies were able to fight against it on equal terms. The Catholic Church no longer seemed conquered; but neither did it seem victorious.[4]

At the same time, Ambrose's sermons finally persuaded Augustine to start quite deliberately to search for some conclusive argument which would utterly discredit Manichaeism; and he realized that if he could once bring himself to conceive of a spiritual substance, the whole Manichaean theology would disintegrate. Unfortunately, this he found himself at that time wholly unable to do.

> Still, concerning the body of this world, nature as a whole—now that I was able to consider and compare such things more and more—I now decided that the majority of the philosophers held the more probable views. So, in what I thought was the method of the Academics—doubting everything and fluctuating between all the options—I came to the conclusion that the Manichaeans were to be abandoned. For I judged, even in that period of doubt, that I could not remain in a sect to which I preferred some of the philosophers. But I refused to commit the cure of my fainting soul to the philosophers, because they were without the

---

[1] Ibid.; 'Suscepit me paterne ille homo dei et peregrinationem meam satis episcopaliter dilexit. Et eum amare coepi, primo quidem non tamquam doctorem veri, quod in ecclesia prorsus desperabam, sed tamquam hominem benignum in me.'

[2] See O'Meara, op. cit., p. 117. Courcelle, op. cit., pp. 85–86 is unable to believe that Ambrose would have been so friendly on Augustine's first, and purely formal, social call; but there seems no reason for not accepting what Augustine actually says.

[3] *Conf.*, V, xiii, 23: '. . . non tamquam doctorem veri, *quod in ecclesia tua prorsus desperabam.*'

[4] Ibid., V, xiv, 24.

saving name of Christ. I resolved, therefore, to become a catechumen in the Catholic Church—which my parents had so much urged upon me—until something certain shone forth by which I might guide my course.[1]

This passage is of the greatest significance, as evidence of the effect which Ambrose's first sermons had upon Augustine. He had come to Milan still nominally a Manichee, having lost faith in physics as taught by Mani, and preferring the theories of the philosophers. However, he still clung to two Manichaean tenets: to their method of scriptural exegesis, despite the attacks of Elpidius; and to their materialism. Ambrose had destroyed his confidence in the first of these, and he had been feeling a distaste for the second. It was plain that he could no longer remain a Manichee, even in name.[2]

In the circumstances, he says, his decision was to adopt what he thought was the method of the Academics, 'doubting everything and fluctuating between all opinions'.[3] In view of the importance which the opinions of the New Academy assumed in Augustine's mind after his conversion, so that his first works after his baptism were three books, *Against the Academics*, it is worth considering what his decision at Milan really implied. In the first place, he did not suddenly become aware of Academic scepticism at Milan but was apparently already thinking about it while at Rome:

I was now half inclined to believe that those philosophers whom they call 'the Academics' were wiser than the rest in holding that we ought to doubt everything, and in maintaining that man does not have the power of comprehending any certain truth for, although I had not yet understood their meaning, I was fully persuaded that they thought just as they are commonly reputed to do.[4]

The history of the philosophic school called the Middle and the New Academy need not be dealt with in any detail here, since it seems reasonably certain that Augustine's knowledge of it was derived from Cicero, and not gained at first hand.[5] As the name implies, the Academics regarded themselves as the heirs of the Academy of Plato. Under Arcesilaus (315–241 BC) and Carneades (219–129 BC), a sceptical attitude was cultivated, largely in opposition to the materialism and dogmatism of the Stoics. The degree of scepticism varied in various Academic writers and they were not hostile to the practice of religion, as such. 'They did not contend that the arguments against the existence of gods were in the least stronger than the

[1] *Conf.*, V, xiv, 25. Outler, p. 112.
[2] See Testard, op. cit., i, 92.
[3] *Conf.*, V, xiv, 25: '. . . dubitans de omnibus atque inter omnia fluctuans.'
[4] Ibid., V, x, 19. Outler, p. 107.
[5] See O'Meara, op. cit., p. 111; Testard, op. cit., i, 93–97; Le Blond, op. cit., p. 100.

arguments in favour of popular beliefs. Their point was that the arguments for and against were precisely balanced. It was just as likely there were gods as that there were not.'[1] Carneades, however, laid particular emphasis on the negative arguments, precisely because he was attacking Stoicism, which strongly upheld the positive, and was accordingly regarded as the founder of the New Academy, as Arcesilaus of the Middle.[2] Cicero at times regarded himself as a follower of the New Academy,[3] and it was from him that Augustine gained his knowledge of, and approach to, the school.[4]

As has been remarked already, Augustine's decision to adopt the standpoint of the Academics was not made suddenly at Milan, but was apparently a revival of sentiments which were already being entertained at Rome. It is moreover significant that Augustine's scepticism was not complete; he was unwilling to abandon his faith in Christ and so became a Christian catechumen. How long he remained under the influence of the Academics, we do not know. Some words of his in the *De Beata Vita* suggest that it was for a long while,[5] but it can hardly have been more than three years at the most from his arrival at Rome in 383 to his conversion at Milan in August 386; while the decision deliberately to adopt Academic scepticism was only made at Milan at the end of 384 or the beginning of 385. Furthermore, it was a qualified decision. Augustine was not, by temperament, inclined to doubt but rather to believe, and he was determined to believe in Christ. Altogether, it is misleading to talk, in any but the widest sense, of a period of Academic scepticism in Augustine's life. It was, in fact, a very accommodating kind of scepticism.[6] Its real significance lies in the fact that it marks the final breach with Manichaeism.

The action of the drama now quickens. St Monica arrived in Milan, still pursuing her son for his spiritual welfare, and rapidly made a reputation for herself by her devotion and piety.[7] Although delighted by the

---

[1] Edwyn Bevan, *Later Greek Religion*, London, 1927, xxiii.
[2] See the comments of Augustine on Arcesilaus and Carneades in *C. Acad.*, III, xvii, 38-39.
[3] See Clarke, *The Roman Mind*, 55-56.
[4] *C. Acad.*, III, xx, 43: 'Hoc mihi de Academicis interim probabiliter, ut potui, persuasi. quod si falsum est, nihil ad me, cui satis est iam non arbitrari non posse ab homine inveniri veritatem. quisquis autem putat hoc sensisse Academicos, ipsum Ciceronem audiat. ait enim illis morem fuisse occultandi sententiam suam nec eam cuiquam, nisi qui secum ad senectutem usque vixisset, aperire consuesse. quae si autem ista, deus viderit; eam tamen arbitror Platonis fuisse.'
[5] *De Beata Vita*, i, 4: 'At ubi discussos eos [sc. Manichaeos] evasi maxime traiecto isto mari, *diu* gubernacula mea repugnantia omnibus ventis in mediis fluctibus Academici tenuerunt.'
[6] Cf. Testard, op. cit., i, 96; Benjamin B. Warfield, *Studies in Tertullian and Augustine*, New York, 1930, 136.
[7] *Conf.*, VI, i, 1; ii, 2.

news that Augustine was no longer a Manichee, she did not seem surprised, but only redoubled her prayers on his behalf.[1] Augustine was impressed by an incident which occurred soon after her arrival. In the African fashion, she had visited the tombs of the saints in the cathedral of Milan, taking with her offerings of food and wine—a practice known as the *refrigerium*[2] —only to be informed by the doorkeeper that Ambrose had prohibited the practice in his diocese. It smacked too much of the *Parentalia*[3] of the Roman pagan religion, and afforded a pretext for drunkenness.[4] Monica accepted this ruling without question; and her son was amazed that she so readily preferred the teachings of a foreign bishop to her own local practice;[5] though he could not help adding when he came to write the *Confessions* that his mother would, perhaps, have shown less alacrity in obeying a bishop whom she did not love as she did Ambrose.[6] At all events, she was sufficiently disconcerted by the veto and by the fact that the church of Milan did not fast on Saturdays, to persuade Augustine to seek an audience with Ambrose to ask for an explanation which was, when given, no more than local usage and the bishop's own authority![7] Thus Augustine, on his mother's behalf, maintained the friendly relations with Ambrose which had marked his arrival in Milan. Nevertheless, he did not contrive to have any intimate conversations with the bishop about his own spiritual troubles. Ambrose was too busy, and Augustine too shy, for an effective encounter.[8]

[1] Ibid., VI, i, 1.
[2] See *Dictionnaire d'archéologie chrétienne et de liturgie*, arts. 'Refrigerium' and 'Agape'; Van der Meer, *St Augustin: pasteur d'ames*, ii, 327–67.
[3] The feast in honour of dead parents, which lasted from February 13th to 21st. See Franz Altheim, *A History of Roman Religion*, ET by Harold Mattingly, London, 1938, 132. Ovid describes the ceremonies in the *Fasti*, II, 533–70.
[4] *Conf.*, VI, ii, 2.
[5] Ibid.
[6] Ibid.: 'Sed tamen videtur mihi, domine deus meus—et ita est *in conspectu tuo* de hac re cor meum—non facile fortasse de hac amputanda consuetudine matrem meam fuisse cessuram, si ab alio prohiberetur, quem non sicut Ambrosium diligebat.'
[7] Aug., *Epp.* 36, xiv, 32; 54, ii, 3. See Courcelle, op. cit., pp. 87–92; O'Meara, op. cit., p. 122. Ambrose's reasons are worth consideration: 'Respondit nihil se docere me posse, nisi quod ipse faceret, quia, si melius nosset, id potius observaret, cumque ego putassem nulla reddita ratione, auctoritate sola sua nos voluisse admonere, ne sabbato ieiunaremus, subsecutus est et ait mihi: "Cum Romam venio, ieiunio sabbato; cum hic sum, non ieiunio: sic etiam tu, ad quam forte ecclesiam veneris, eius morem serva, si cuiquam non vis esse scandalum' (Aug., *Ep.* 54, ii, 3). Cf. Ambrose's remarks in the *De Sacramentis* on the Milanese custom, not observed at Rome, whereby the bishop washed the feet of the newly baptized when they ascended from the font: 'In omnibus cupio sequi ecclesiam Romanam, sed tamen et nos hominis sensum habemus' (III, i, 5; *CSEL* lxxiii, 40).
[8] *Conf.*, VI, iii, 3: 'Nec ille sciebat aestus meos nec foveam periculi mei. Non enim quaerere ab eo poteram quod volebam, sicut volebam, secludentibus me ab eius aure atque ore catervis negotiosorum hominum, quorum infirmitatibus serviebat: cum quibus quando non erat, quod perexiguum temporis erat, aut corpus reficiebat necessariis sustentaculis aut lectione animum.'

Nevertheless, Augustine continued to attend Ambrose's sermons, and was delighted with what he heard. Whether these sermons can now be identified among Ambrose's surviving works is a matter for controversy, and need not be discussed here;[1] the essential fact that emerges is, that in his preaching Ambrose continued to confirm the impression which his earlier homilies had made upon his hearer. Augustine learned that he had accused the Catholic Church with a blind contentiousness. 'I had not yet discovered that it taught the truth, but I now knew that it did not teach what I had so vehemently accused it of.'[2] He was delighted that it did not hold that God was bounded by space like a human body[3] and that the Scriptures were to be understood in a spiritual and not a carnal sense,[4] but the influence of the Academics held him back; 'for my desire was to be as certain of invisible things as I was that seven and three are ten'.[5] Disillusioned with the Manichees, he was still reluctant to trust himself to Ambrose; but from that time, he began to prefer Catholic doctrine.[6] Gradually, too, he came to realize that there were a multitude of things in this life which had to be believed upon the evidence of others—including the identity of our parents—without which we should never act at all.[7] Furthermore, since it was clear that the unaided reason was in itself too weak to find out the truth; and since, on that account, it was necessary to have the authority of the Scriptures; Augustine began to think that God would not have given such eminent authority to Scripture throughout all lands if it had not been that through them His will might be believed in, and Himself sought.[8] He was, however, held back by certain difficulties of a non-intellectual, but very persuasive nature, notably by ambition.

I was still eagerly aspiring [he says] to honours, money, and matrimony; and Thou didst mock me. In pursuit of these ambitions I endured the most bitter hardships, in which Thou wast being the more gracious the

---

[1] Courcelle, op. cit., pp. 93–138 attempts to identify the sermons as those on the Hexameron, the *De Isaac* and *De bono Mortis*. He wishes to argue that Ambrose was teaching a form of Christian Neo-Platonism, and that it was from this that Augustine turned to study the Neo-Platonists for himself. Courcelle's views have been rejected by Christine Mohrmann in *Vigiliae Christianae*, v (October 1951), 249–54 and by W. Theiler in *Gnomon*, xxv (1953), 113–22. O'Meara, op. cit., pp. 118–20 agrees with this rejection. Testard, op. cit., i, 119–27 accepts Courcelle's suggestions, but urges the Ciceronian element in Ambrose's preaching.

[2] *Conf.*, VI, iv, 5: 'Etsi nondum conpertam vera docentem, non tamen ea docentem, quae graviter accusabam.'

[3] Ibid.   [4] Ibid., VI, iv, 6.   [5] Ibid. Outler, p. 118.

[6] Ibid., VI, v, 7: 'Ex hoc tempore quoque iam praeponens doctrinam catholicam modestius ibi minimeque fallaciter sentiebam iuberi, ut crederetur quod non demonstrabatur—sive esset quid, sed cui forte non esset, sive nec quid esset—quam illic temeraria pollicitione scientiae credulitatem inrideri et postea tam multa fabulosissima et absurdissima, quia demonstrari non poterant, credenda imperari.'

[7] Ibid.   [8] Ibid., VI, v, 8.

less Thou wouldst allow anything that was not Thee to grow sweet to me. Look into my heart, O Lord, Whose prompting it is that I should recall all this, and confess it to Thee. Now let my soul cleave to Thee, now that Thou hast freed her from that fast-sticking glue of death.[1]

The passage is of particular importance, since it shows very clearly how far Augustine's difficulties in the matter of accepting Catholic Christianity were from being exclusively intellectual. He was haunted by a fear—which his subsequent history was to justify—that to become a Catholic would be to sound the death-knell of his ambitions in the world at the very time when all the struggles of his career seemed likely to bear fruit. The old restlessness still burned within—'Thou hast made us for Thyself, and our heart is unquiet until it may repose in Thee'—but Augustine, like many another, feared to offer himself to the Divine Physician, in case he should be more thoroughly cured than he cared to be. His prayer was still that of his youth: 'Give me chastity and continence—but not yet.'[2] This aspect of Augustine's conversion can very easily be overlooked if we concentrate upon the more obvious interest of his philosophical development.[3] But the call of the World and of the Flesh was still very strong; and it is with this consideration in mind that we should read Augustine's account of an experience which occurred about this time, when he had to deliver a panegyric on the young emperor, Valentinian II, whose court was established at Milan.[4] To deliver a fitting encomium on a lad of fourteen, under the influence of a strong-willed and unscrupulous mother, was not an easy undertaking, especially when, as Augustine was well aware, the fulfilment of his ambitions depended very largely upon the success of his orations. He was, therefore, in no very cheerful frame of mind as he walked through the streets of Milan when, suddenly, he came upon a poor beggar, who had contrived to beg enough to enable him to reach a very happy stage of drunkenness. The sight brought home to Augustine the futility of all his efforts and the worry which he, and other worldlings, expended to obtain the same happiness which the beggar had purchased for a few begged pence. The beggar, certainly, had not gained true happiness, but Augustine was pursuing a happiness even further removed from true felicity. Both rhetor and beggar were intoxicated; but the beggar could sleep off

[1] *Conf.*, VI, vi, 9. Tr. Outler, p. 120..   [2] Ibid., VIII, vii, 17.
[3] Cf. Testard, op. cit., i, 131 n^2. See O'Meara, op. cit., pp. 126–8.
[4] Gustave Bardy, *Saint Augustin*, 7e éd., 78 and Courcelle, op. cit., pp. 80–82 both consider that the address was directly in praise of the emperor (as opposed to being occasioned by the consulship of the Frankish general Bauto in January 385), and Courcelle suggests that it was on the tenth anniversary of the reign on 22 November 385. This view is accepted by Pellegrino, op. cit., p. 95 n^{13}. O'Meara, op. cit., p. 127 does not commit himself.

his drunkenness in the night, while Augustine lay down with his and rose again with it in the morning.[1]

With worldly ambitions went a desire for a suitable marriage, not so much to gratify the demands of the flesh—Augustine had his mistress with him in Milan—as to supply the family connections necessary to forward his career. A match was arranged and, perhaps as an inevitable consequence, Augustine's mistress was dismissed. She returned to Africa, vowing to God that she would henceforth know no man. Her lover, less constant and impatient of the two-year delay imposed by the youth of his promised bride, promptly found himself another concubine.[2] Chastity seemed impossible for him, and a plan contrived with some of his friends, including Romanianus, his fellow-citizen and patron; Alypius, another citizen of Thagaste and a former pupil;[3] and Nebridius, his friend and admirer from Carthage,[4] for a philosophical community run on collegiate lines, came to nothing, because of the disagreement among those concerned as to whether wives could be tolerated.[5]

Augustine's behaviour in the dismissal of his mistress has been often and severely criticized and there is no doubt that, in this matter, he appears in a very unamiable light. The suggestion that, having become a Christian, he should have sought the woman out and married her, may be set aside as anachronistic. Such a course could hardly have suggested itself in the fourth century; and in any case, imperial legislation forbade marriages between persons of Augustine's social position and members of the lower ranks of society, to which his mistress presumably belonged.[6] What is far harder to explain and to forgive is the cold-blooded manner in which he discarded the companion of a dozen years, in order to ensure a socially advantageous marriage. This is a sort of disloyalty which is to be deplored at all times and in all places.

Nevertheless, even here we should be careful. Augustine discarded his mistress, it is true; but he did not do so lightly. 'My mistress was torn from my side as an impediment to my marriage, and my heart which clung to her was torn and wounded till it bled', he says,[7] and years after, as a bishop, he still dwelt on her memory, and did not presume to blame her.[8] For her part, the girl returned to Africa, 'vowing to God that she would henceforth know no other man'[9]—a vow which implies a considerable

---

[1] *Conf.*, VI, vi, 9-10.   [2] Ibid., VI, xv, 25.   [3] Ibid., VI, vii, 11.
[4] Ibid., VI, x, 17.   [5] Ibid., VI, xiv, 24.
[6] Marrou, *Augustin*, 24; Bardy, op. cit., pp. 83-84; O'Meara, op. cit., p. 129; Pellegrino, op. cit., p. 99.
[7] *Conf.*, VI, xv, 25.   [8] *De bono coniugali*, v, 5.
[9] *Conf.*, VI, xv, 25: 'Et illa in Africam redierat vovens tibi alium se virum nescituram, relicto apud me naturali ex illa filio meo.'

regard for the man who had cast her off. Her ultimate fate is unknown, and no good can come of romantic hypotheses about the later years of this unnamed woman. We can only hope that her generous loyalty was rewarded by the gift of a Christian end to her life, without pain or blame, and a right answer before the judgement seat of Christ.

Monica's part in the affair is not clear, though it is easy to explain the episode as a case of the pious, respectable, and strong-willed mother dominating her weaker son and exploiting his ambition in a not very Christian way. Possibly there is an element of truth in this picture; but Monica's position was not an easy one. Her son loudly proclaimed his inability to forgo the embraces of a woman.[1] In the circumstances, the only apparent way to make it possible for him to be baptized was to arrange for him to be married.[2] Her way may seem to be a brutal one; but it must be remembered that she believed her son's salvation to be at stake. It is easy to be unjust and cruel to another on behalf of those we love.

Augustine's spiritual condition in the period following the dismissal of his mistress was, perhaps, at its nadir. He was haunted by dreams of worldly success; he had just proved to himself that he was incapable of controlling the demands of his sexual appetite; he had been guilty of a great disloyalty to one who loved him. He seems, by his own admission, to have come very near to adopting an Epicurean position, in its crudest sense.

I discussed with my friends, Alypius and Nebridius, the nature of good and evil, maintaining that, in my judgement, Epicurus would have carried off the palm if I had not believed what Epicurus would not believe: that after death there remains a life for the soul, and places of recompense. And I demanded of them: 'Suppose we are immortal and live in the enjoyment of perpetual bodily pleasure, and that without any fear of losing it—why, then, should we not be happy or why should we search for anything else?'[3]

To these moral difficulties must be added the fact that his understanding was still darkened by the materialism which he had inherited from his Manichaean days, and to which he had, at that time, found no answer. He

[1] *Conf.*, VI, xi, 20: 'Putabam enim me miserum fore nimis, si feminae privarer amplexibus, et medicinam misericordiae tuae ad eandem infirmitatem sanandam non cogitabam, quia expertus non eram, et propriarum virium credebam esse continentiam, quarum mihi non eram conscius, cum tam stultus essem, ut nescirem, sicut scriptum est, neminem posse esse continentem, nisi tu dederis.'

[2] Ibid., VI, xiii, 23: 'Et instabatur inpigre, ut ducerem uxorem. Iam petebam, iam promittebatur maxime matre dante operam, quo me iam coniugatum baptismus salutaris ablueret, quo me in dies gaudebat aptari et vota sua ac promissa tua in mea fide conpleri animadvertebat.'

[3] Ibid., VI, xvi, 26. Tr. by Outler, pp. 132–3.

was, intellectually, still undecided. He preferred the Catholic Church to any other creed, but was perplexed by the fact of evil, for which he had no satisfactory explanation. It is significant that the conversation with Alypius and Nebridius which closes the sixth book of the *Confessions* deals with this most agonizing of problems: the origin of evil.

It was in this moment of doubt and despair that Augustine enjoyed an intellectual illumination even more important and influential than his reading of the *Hortensius* in his undergraduate days. He obtained, from a certain unknown, but very vainglorious person,[1] certain writings of the Neo-Platonist philosophers. This school, which claimed descent from Plato, but which had incorporated elements from other philosophic systems, including Aristotelianism, Stoicism and the Pythagoreans, is the dominating influence in philosophy, whether Christian or pagan, from the third to the sixth century. The two outstanding names among the Neo-Platonists are Plotinus (died 270) and his friend and biographer, Porphyry (232/3 to early fourth century), although it is clear that at least as much responsibility in the shaping of the system must be assigned to Philo of Alexandria (*c.* 25 BC to *c.* AD 40), the Jewish Platonist who devoted himself to the task of reconciling Jewish revelation with Greek philosophy. Neo-Platonism was both a philosophy and a way of life and had, superficially at least, not a little in common with Christian doctrine. The centre of all existence is the One (τὸ ἕν), the First or the Absolute, which Plotinus identified with the Good (τὸ ἀγαθόν) of Plato, and which is the God who is beyond all being. From the One's self-knowledge emanates Intelligence (νοῦς), called the Logos or the Word, containing the immaterial Ideas— the Platonic Forms—of all created things. From the Logos again emanates the World Soul. These three, the One, the Logos and the World Soul, form a triad. The external universe, as we experience it, owes its being to the imposition of the divine ideas on matter (ὕλη), which is the bare

---

[1] Ibid., VII, ix, 13: '. . . procurasti mihi per quendam hominem inmanissimo tyfo turgidum quosdam Platonicorum libros ex graeca lingua in latinam versos.' Courcelle, *Les lettres grecques en occident*, 2e éd., 125–8 and *Recherches*, 153–6, identifies this unnamed person with Mallius Theodorus, to whom Augustine dedicated the *De Beata Vita*, in which he says: 'Lectis autem Plotini [*al.* Platonis] paucissimis libris, cuius te esse studiosissimum accepi', etc. (i, 4). This view is rejected by Theiler, *Gnomon*, xxv (1953), 117 and O'Meara, op. cit., pp. 125–6, and it appears unlikely that Augustine would have used the phrase 'cuius te esse studiosissimum accepi' if Theodorus had actually presented the books to him. O'Meara, p. 152 suggests that the person 'puffed up with most unnatural pride' is Porphyry: 'We should not be put off by the words: "Thou procuredst for me by means of one . . ." as if they implied that the books were given to Augustine by someone who was not their author. Augustine is addressing God and stressing that in His Providence He was using a proud instrument for Augustine's good.' This, however, seems to strain the interpretation of the text. Pellegrino, op. cit., p. 103 *n* says roundly: '[O'Meara] scorge indicato qui Porfirio, il che appare impossibile.'

receptacle of forms, the 'subject of energy viewed by abstraction as existing apart from the energy which gives it meaning and existence. It is not
"material"; it is that intangible all-but-nothing which remains when we
abstract from an object of thought all that makes it a possible object of
thought.'[1] The human soul, lowest and last in the hierarchy of spiritual
beings, has yet a memory of its divine origin, and the life of man should be
a liberation from the fetters of this earthly life and a flight to the One—a
way of ascent and ecstasy for the few capable of it, and a way of discipline
and purgation for the many, who are incapable of the higher way.[2]

The Neo-Platonist works surprised Augustine by their unexpected
agreement with Christian doctrine:

> Therein I found, not indeed in the same words, but to the selfsame
> effect, enforced by many and various reasons that *in the beginning was the
> Word, and the Word was with God, and the Word was God. The same was
> in the beginning with God. All things were made by Him; and without Him
> was not anything made that was made.* That which was made by Him is
> *life, and the life was the light of men. And the light shined in darkness; and
> the darkness comprehended it not.* Furthermore, I read that the soul of
> man, though it *bears witness to the light,* yet itself *is not the light*; but the
> Word of God, being God, *is that true light that lights every man who
> comes into the world.* And further, that *He was in the world, and the world
> was made by Him, and the world knew Him not.* But that *He came unto
> His own, and His own received Him not. And as many as received Him, to
> them gave He power to become the sons of God, even to them that believed on
> His name*—this I did not find there.
>
> Similarly, I read there that God the Word was born *not of flesh nor of
> blood, nor of the will of man, nor the will of the flesh, but of God.* But, that
> *the Word was made flesh and dwelt among us*—I found this nowhere
> there.[3]

This reading dispelled the last shades of Augustine's Academic doubt:

> And I said: Is Truth, therefore, nothing, because it is not diffused
> through space—neither finite nor infinite? And Thou didst cry to me
> from afar: *I am that I am.* And I heard this, as things are heard in the
> heart, and there was no room for doubt. I should have more readily
> doubted that I am alive than that the Truth exists—the Truth which is
> *clearly seen, being understood by the things that are made.*[4]

---

[1] W. R. Inge, 'Plotinus': the annual lecture for a master mind, read at the British
Academy on 30 January 1929, reprinted in *Mysticism in Religion*, London, 2nd ed., 1959,
111.
[2] For accounts of Neo-Platonism, see O'Meara, op. cit., pp. 133-6; A. E. Taylor,
Platonism and its Influence, London [1925], 11-14; W. R. Inge, *The Philosophy of
Plotinus*, 3rd ed., 2 vols., London, 1929, *passim*; and James K. Feibleman, *Religious
Platonism*, London, 1959, esp. pp. 96-178.
[3] *Conf.*, VII, ix, 13-14. Tr. by Outler, pp. 144-5.
[4] Ibid., VII, x, 16 (Rom. 1.20). Outler, p. 147.

Furthermore, the problem of evil which had so long haunted Augustine's mind was answered by the Neo-Platonists. From them he learned that created things were real, in so far as they had their being from the Creator, but were unreal in so far as they did not share His immutability and were liable to be corrupted.[1] He also discovered that things remain good even when corrupted, for unless they were good, they could not be corrupted; but if they were deprived of all good, they would cease to be.[2]

Evil, then, the origin of which I had been speaking, has no substance at all; for if it were a substance, it would be good. For either it would be an incorruptible substance and so a supreme good, or a corruptible substance, which could not be corrupted unless it were good. I understood, therefore, and it was made clear to me that Thou madest all things good, nor is there any substance at all not made by Thee. And because all that Thou madest is not equal, each by itself is good, and the sum of all of them is very good, for our God made all things very good.[3]

There can be no doubt that the reading of the Neo-Platonists—'a very few books' or so Augustine declared not long afterwards[4]—had a profound effect upon his intellectual development. 'The reading of the Neo-Platonists . . .', says Professor O'Meara, 'left Augustine in a state of spiritual elevation.'[5] Did that spiritual elevation include any momentary experimental knowledge of God which would justify us talking of a mystical experience? Two passages in the *Confessions*[6] seem to give grounds for such a supposition.

And being admonished by these books [of the Platonists] to return into myself, I entered into my inward soul, guided by Thee. This I could do because Thou wast my helper. And I entered, and with the eye of my soul—such as it was—saw above the same eye of my soul and above my mind the Immutable Light. . . . When I first knew Thee, Thou didst lift me up, that I might see that there was something to be seen, though I was not yet fit to see it. And Thou didst beat back the weakness of my

---

[1] *Conf.*, VII, xi, 17: 'Et inspexi cetera infra te et vidi nec omnino esse nec omnino non esse: esse quidem, quoniam abs te sunt, non esse autem, quoniam id quod es non sunt. Id enim vere esse, quod incommutabiliter manet.'

[2] Ibid., VII, xii, 18: 'Et manifestatum est mihi, quoniam bona sunt, quae corrumpuntur, quae neque si summa bona essent, corrumpi possent, neque nisi bona essent, corrumpi possent, quia, si summa bona essent, incorruptibilia essent, si autem nulla bona essent, quid in eis corrumperetur, non esset. . . . Ergo si omni bono privabuntur, omnino nulla erunt: ergo quamdiu sunt, bona sunt.'

[3] Ibid. Tr. Outler, p. 148.

[4] *De Beata Vita*, i, 4: '. . . lectis autem Plotini [al. Platonis] paucissimis libris.'

[5] O'Meara, *The Young Augustine*, 141. For Augustine's own testimony, see *C. Acad.*, II, ii, 5.

[6] There is a third passage, discussed by Courcelle, *Recherches*, 157–63, in *Conf.*, VII, xx, 26.

sight, shining forth upon me Thy dazzling beams of light, and I trembled with love and fear. I realized that I was far away from Thee in the land of unlikeness, as if I heard Thy voice from on high: 'I am the food of strong men; grow and you shall feed on me; nor shall you change me, like the food of your flesh into yourself, but you shall be changed into My likeness.'[1]

. . . Thus by degrees I was led upward from bodies to the soul which perceives them by means of the bodily senses, and from there on to the soul's inward faculty, to which the bodily senses report outward things —and this belongs even to the capacities of the beasts—and thence on up to the reasoning power, to whose judgement is referred the experience received from the bodily sense. And when this power of reason within me also found that it was changeable, it raised itself up to its own intellectual principle, and withdrew its thoughts from experience, abstracting itself from the contradictory throng of fantasms in order to seek for that light in which it was bathed. Then, without any doubting, it cried out that the unchangeable was better than the changeable. From this it follows that the mind somehow knew the unchangeable, for, unless it had known it in some fashion, it could have had no sure ground for preferring it to the changeable. And thus with the flash of a trembling glance, it arrived at THAT WHICH IS. And I saw Thy invisibility understood by means of the things that are made. But I was not able to sustain my gaze. My weakness was dashed back, and I lapsed again into my accustomed ways, carrying along with me nothing but a loving memory of my vision, and an appetite for what I had, as it were, smelled the odour of, but was not yet able to eat.[2]

Taken at its face value, the language used by Augustine in these two passages suggests some sort of apprehension of the divine which might be regarded as a mystical experience. This was emphatically the view of Abbot Cuthbert Butler in a famous study on Western Mysticism when he remarked, with reference to these passages: 'There is a special interest in the circumstances that these experiences, evidently in full sense mystical, were pre-Christian, or at any rate pre-Catholic; and they are couched in great measure in the very language of Plotinus.'[3] It is, however, precisely their Plotinian element which raises doubts, in the minds of some readers, as to whether the word mystical may properly be applied to them. From the Christian point of view, a mystical experience is a revelation of God to favoured souls and is a grace, in that it does not follow upon human effort, although, in the case of most of the great mystics known to us, it usually follows upon prolonged and fervent prayer. The Plotinian ecstasy, on the other hand, is an intuitive and instantaneous vision of the One, which the

[1] Conf., VII, x, 16. Outler, pp. 146, 147.
[2] Ibid., VII, xvii, 23. Outler, pp. 151–2.
[3] Butler, Western Mysticism, 2nd ed., London, 1927, 43.

soul experiences by raising itself from the flux of visible and material things to the eternal forms of the intellectual world. Such an experience Plotinus seems to have had on more than one occasion during his life, and there is no reason to doubt either the sincerity of his belief or the reality of his vision. It differs, however, from Christian mysticism in that it is, essentially, an intellectual experience, and is procured by the effort of will of the contemplative. Was Augustine's experience at Milan, after reading the works of the Neo-Platonists, an experience of the Plotinian order? Such is the opinion of Professor Courcelle[1] and Gustave Bardy.[2] Père Henry, while recognizing the Plotinian influence on Augustine, holds that there was in the experience some element of a more supernatural character.[3] The precise nature of Augustine's experience will never, perhaps, be satisfactorily explained by the methods of historical investigation;[4] but it is significant that it is possible to interpret Augustine's description of his ascent in terms of epistemology,[5] while Professor O'Meara's comment is very germane: 'One will not readily believe that the ecstasy of contemplative union with the One was accorded [Augustine] at this early date.'[6] Perhaps the safest course is to regard Augustine's experiences at Milan on reading the Neo-Platonists as being, not so much a vision of God as a vision of the spiritual life, to which he had been a stranger for so many years and to which the Neo-Platonists helped him to return, and, if we feel that this does not go far enough, to recognize that it is possible for supernatural enlightenment to be given to the mind in an experiential, but not a strictly mystical, way, and to regard Augustine's experiences as coming within that category.[7]

The important fact is that, from the writings of the philosophers, Augustine turned to the epistles of St Paul, and read him with the greatest enthusiasm.[8] The weakness of the Neo-Platonist writings was the same omission which had jarred upon him when he read the *Hortensius*: the

[1] Courcelle, op. cit., p. 167. [2] Bardy, *Saint Augustin*, 7e éd., 91–92.
[3] *La vision d'Ostie*, 88–90. [4] Cf. Pellegrino, op. cit., pp. 106–7 n^{14}.
[5] So M. H. Carré, *Realists and Nominalists*, O.U.P., 1946 [on *Conf.*, VII, xvii, 23]: 'Bodies, sensation, inner sense, judgement, pure thought, intuition—such are the steps in Augustine's investigation of knowledge.'
[6] O'Meara, *The Young Augustine*, 139. Cf. David Knowles, *The English Mystical Tradition*, London, 1961, 26: 'We may add . . . that some of these experiences occurred either before or shortly after Augustine's conversion and baptism, when we should scarcely expect to meet with advanced mystical experiences.'
[7] See Knowles, op. cit., p. 27.
[8] *Conf.*, VII, xxi, 27: 'Itaque avidissime arripui venerabilem stilum spiritus tui et prae ceteris apostolum Paulum, et perierunt illae quaestiones, in quibus mihi aliquando visus est adversari sibi et non congruere testimoniis legis et prophetarum textus sermonis eius, et apparuit mihi una facies eloquiorum castorum, et *exultare cum tremore*'didici.' Cf. *C. Acad.*, II, ii, 5: '. . . itaque titubans properans haesitans arripio apostolum Paulum.'

name of Christ was not there. He was, however, hindered by the fact that his great regard for the name of Christ was not matched by any clear understanding of Christian doctrine about Him. For Augustine, Christ was merely a man of eminent wisdom, elevated far above the rest of humanity, as was proved by His virgin birth, who was sent to set mankind an example of despising earthly things for the sake of attaining immortality.[1] This emphasis upon the humanity of Christ, and the utter neglect of the doctrine of the Incarnation,[2] probably represent a reaction from the Manichaean denial of any human body to Christ.[3] (By a similar reaction, Augustine's friend Alypius, while recognizing the divinity of Christ, supposed the Catholic doctrine to be that the Word of God inhabited a human body, but had no human soul or mind.[4]) The reading of Scripture where the Neo-Platonist books left him unsatisfied revealed to Augustine Christian doctrine—the fact of sin, and the liberation of fallen humanity by the grace of Christ.[5] Now he was able to grasp both the strength and the weakness of the Neo-Platonist philosophers: they understood the need of the human soul to seek God, and to free itself from the restraints of lower things; but they had no power themselves to bring man to the beatific vision.

The books of the Platonists tell nothing of this. Their pages do not contain the expression of this kind of godliness—the tears of confession, Thy sacrifice, *a troubled spirit, a broken and a contrite heart*,[6] the salvation of Thy people, the *espoused City, the earnest of the Holy Spirit*,[7] the cup of our redemption. In them no man sings: *Shall not my soul be subject unto God, for from Him comes my salvation? He is my God and my salvation, my defender; I shall no more be moved.*[8] In them no one hears Him calling, *Come unto me all you who labour.*[9] They scorn to learn of Him *because He is meek and lowly of heart;*[10] for *Thou hast hidden these things from the wise and prudent and hast revealed them unto babes.*[11] For it is one thing to see the land of peace from a wooded mountain-top, and fail to find the way thither—to attempt impassable ways in vain, opposed and waylaid by fugitives and deserters under their captain, *the lion and the dragon*;[12] but it is quite another thing to keep to the highway that leads thither, guarded by the hosts of the heavenly Emperor, on which there are no deserters from the heavenly army to rob passers-by,

---

[1] *Conf.*, VII, xix, 25.

[2] Ibid.: 'Quid autem sacramenti haberet *verbum caro factum*, ne suspicari quidem poteram.'

[3] See Pellegrino, op. cit., p. 108.

[4] *Conf.*, VII, xix, 25. It is not clear whether Alypius evolved the Apollinarian heresy—which is what his views amount to—for himself, or learned it from others.

[5] Ibid., VII, xxi, 27.   [6] Ps. 50.19 [51.17].   [7] Apoc. 21.2; II Cor. 5.5.

[8] Ps. 61.2, 3 [62.1, 2].   [9] Matt. 11.28.   [10] Matt. 11.29.

[11] Matt. 11.25.

[12] Ps. 90.13 [91.13]. Cf. I Peter 5.8.

for they shun it as a torment. These thoughts sank wondrously into my heart, when I read that *least of Thy apostles*[1] and when I had considered all Thy works and trembled.[2]

This passage forms a convenient summary of Augustine's debt to the Neo-Platonists. Undoubtedly, it was great; but it is important not to misunderstand its nature. Neo-Platonism was at no time an alternative to Catholic Christianity but, rather, a philosophy which enabled Augustine more readily able to understand and accept Catholic Christianity. One must not overlook the surprise and delight with which Augustine came upon a body of philosophic doctrine which appeared to confirm Catholic teaching. One of the first and telling blows delivered at Manichaeism had been the discovery that their cosmological speculations were refuted by serious philosophers; now, philosophers appeared to be endorsing the Catholic faith. Curiously enough, Augustine read into Neo-Platonism elements which did not exist there, though they were a part of orthodox Christian doctrine. Thus, the Neo-Platonic triad: the One, the Logos, and the World Soul, is not the same as the Christian Trinity, but Augustine thought it was.[3] Again, from his reading of the Neo-Platonists, he was able to solve the problem which had for so long obsessed him, regarding the nature of evil. Evil, he learned, was not a substance, but a privation of good. So far, so good. Plotinus himself had declared that evil, if it is to exist at all, must be placed in the realm of non-being;[4] but he nevertheless goes on to assert that evil must exist independently,[5] and to identify it with Matter.[6] Here, Augustine never thinks to follow him, and it is clear that his doctrine of evil, though derived from one train of Neo-Platonist thought, is, essentially, of a very different order. The Neo-Platonists were an inspiration to him, but he did not accept all their teaching.[7] On the contrary, he adopted it only when it harmonized with Christian doctrine. If, as Professor Courcelle supposes, Ambrose was preaching a form of Christian Platonism from the bishop's throne in Milan,[8] this aspect of Augustine's attitude to Neo-Platonism is easily explained. If this is not the case—and powerful considerations can be urged against it[9]—then we must allow for a strong, positive influence of Catholic teaching even before the reading of the Neo-Platonists. There is no need to minimize their

---

[1] I Cor. 15.9.   [2] *Conf.*, VII, xxi, 27. Tr. by Outler, pp. 155-6.
[3] See M. F. Sciacca, *Saint Augustin et le Néoplatonisme*, Louvain–Paris, 1956, 4-6.
[4] Plotinus, *Enneads*, I, viii, 3.
[5] Ibid.   [6] Ibid., I, viii, 7.
[7] See Régis Jolivet, *Le problème du mal d'après saint Augustin*, 2e éd., Paris, 1936, 131-62; Sciacca, op. cit., pp. 13-15. See below, pp. 201-4.
[8] *Recherches*, 93-138.
[9] See O'Meara, 'Augustine and Neo-Platonism', *Recherches augustiniennes*, i, 99-101.

contribution to his conversion; but it is equally important not to exagger-
ate their function in his religious development.

The immediate result of Augustine's philosophical reading was to remove his intellectual doubt: 'I no longer desired to be more certain *of*
Thee, but more stable *in* Thee.'[1] But the moral difficulty remained. The
attractions of worldly success no longer fascinated him, but the more
beguiling seductions of the love of women still held his will in bondage.[2]
The challenge of Christianity, he felt, demanded a total response, an un-
reserved commitment; and although St Paul did not forbid marriage to
Christians, he nevertheless exhorted them to another and a better way.[3] In
his difficulty, Augustine went to visit an old priest, Simplicianus, the
spiritual father of Ambrose and destined to succeed him in the see of
Milan. Simplicianus had travelled, read much, and—it is significant—had
a taste for Neo-Platonism.[4] To him Augustine recounted the tangled history of his life, and when he mentioned that he had read certain Neo-
Platonist writings in the Latin translation of Marius Victorinus, a former
professor at Rome who had died a Christian, the old priest congratulated
him on his choice, saying that other philosophies were full of lies and
deceit, but that the Neo-Platonists were full of intimations of God and of
His Word.[5] Furthermore, he told Augustine of the circumstances of the
conversion of Victorinus, whom he had known personally; how the old
man, who had been a pagan until late in life, was led to accept Christianity
by his study of the Scriptures, and used to remark to Simplicianus: 'You
must know that I am already a Christian', to which Simplicianus would
reply: 'I shall not believe it or count you among the Christians until I see
you in the Church of Christ.' Victorinus used to try to meet this argument
with a joke: 'Do walls then make Christians?' for he was afraid of

[1] *Conf.*, VIII, i, 1: 'De vita tua aeterna certus eram, quamvis eam in *aenigmate* et quasi
per speculum videram; dubitatio tamen omnis de incorruptibili substantia, quod ab illa
esset omnis substantia, ablata mihi erat, nec certior de te, sed stabilior in te esse cupiebam.'
[2] Ibid., VIII, i, 1–2: 'De mea vero temporali vita nutabant omnia et mundandum erat
cor a fermento veteri; et placebat via ipse salvator et ire per eius angustias adhuc pige-
bat. . . . Videbam enim plenam ecclesiam, et alius sic ibat, alius autem sic. Mihi autem
displicebat, quod agebam in saeculo, et oneri mihi erat valde non iam inflammantibus
cupiditatibus, ut solebant, spe honoris et pecuniae ad tolerandam illam servitutem tam
gravem. Iam enim me illa non delectabant prae dulcedine tua et *decore domus tuae*, quam
dilexi, sed adhuc conligabar ex femina.'
[3] Ibid.: '. . . nec me prohibebat apostolus coniugari, quamvis exhortaretur ad melius
maxime volens omnes homines sic esse, ut ipse erat. Sed ego infirmior eligebam mol-
liorem locum et propter hoc unum voluebar in ceteris languidis et tabescens curis
marcidis, quod etin aliis rebus, quas nolebam pati, congruere cogebar vitae coniugali, cui
deditus obstringebar.'
[4] Courcelle, op. cit., pp. 171–2. The fact that, at this crisis of his life, Augustine turned
to Simplicianus and not to Ambrose is worth noting.
[5] *Conf.*, VIII, ii, 3.

offending his pagan friends by openly adopting Christianity. However, he gradually came to realize that failure to confess Christ on earth would lead to denial by Him in the presence of the angels, so one day, coming to Simplicianus, he said simply: 'Let us go to church; I want to become a Christian.' The Roman clergy, anxious to spare so distinguished a man the embarrassment of a public confession of faith, suggested that he might prefer to make it privately; but Victorinus refused to avail himself of this concession, and made his confession in public, and in the set form of words used by converts. And so, amidst general rejoicing, he was received into the Church.[1]

There can be no doubt that the story of Victorinus had a great effect upon Augustine. One of the weaknesses he had observed in the Neo-Platonists had been their pride.[2] From St Paul he had learned of Christian humility, whose head and pattern is Christ.[3] Now he was given an example of that humility in the story of Victorinus.[4] He yearned to imitate him—as Simplicianus had correctly judged, when he set out to recount the story.[5] When however Simplicianus went on to tell how, in the reign of Julian the Apostate, when the Christians were forbidden to teach literature and oratory, Victorinus preferred to resign his chair, rather than deny his master, Augustine thought him no less fortunate than happy, because he was thereby enabled to devote his whole time to the service of God, a thing which Augustine was longing to do, but was bound by the chain of his own will. 'The enemy held fast my will, and had made of it a chain, and had bound me tight with it. For out of the perverse will came lust, and the service of lust ended in habit, and habit, not resisted, became necessity.'[6] So Augustine made practical experience with the fact that *the flesh lusts against the spirit and the spirit against the flesh.*[7] 'On all sides, Thou didst show me that Thy words are true, and I, convicted by the truth, had nothing at all to reply but the drawling and drowsy words: "Presently; see, presently. Leave me alone a little while." But "presently, presently" had no present; and my "leave me alone a little while" went on for a long while.'[8]

It was then that the Providence of God offered to Augustine the final challenge. He and his friends, Alypius and Nebridius, were at that time

[1] *Conf.*, VIII, ii, 3–5.   [2] Ibid., VII, xx, 26.   [3] Ibid., VII, xxi, 27.
[4] As noted by Pellegrino, op. cit., pp. 112–13.
[5] *Conf.*, VIII, v, 10: 'Sed ubi mihi homo tuus Simplicianus de Victorino ista narravit, exarsi ad imitandum: ad hoc enim et ille narraverat.'
[6] Ibid. Tr. Outler, p. 164.   [7] Gal. 5.17.
[8] *Conf.*, VIII, v, 12: 'Et undique ostendenti vera te dicere, non erat omnino, quid responderem veritate convictus, nisi tantum verba lenta et somnolenta: "Modo", "ecce modo", "sine paululum". Sed "modo et modo" non habebat modum et "sine paululum" in longum ibat.' Outler, p. 165.

living together, devoting as much time as they could spare to reading and discussions on wisdom. On a certain day, when Nebridius was absent, Augustine and Alypius were visited by one Ponticianus, an African, and an official of the imperial court. In the course of conversation, Ponticianus noticed a book lying on a gaming-table in the room and took it up, supposing that it would be one of Augustine's rhetorical textbooks. To his surprise, it was a copy of the Epistles of St Paul. Ponticianus was a devout Christian and was delighted to find that Augustine was reading the Scriptures. In the conversation which followed, he told Augustine and Alypius of St Anthony of Egypt, the founder of monasticism, amazed that they had never heard of him before.[1] He next spoke more generally about the monastic life, revealing a fact of which they had hitherto been ignorant, that there was a monastery at Milan. He then told them of an experience of his own, when he was on duty with the emperor at Trier, and had gone for a walk one afternoon in the park outside the city walls, with three of his companions, members of the corps called the *agentes in rebus*, the secret police of the Roman Empire.[2] By chance, two of them came upon a cottage, where dwelt a little band of Christian hermits, and there they found a book—the *Life of St Anthony*, which one of them took up and began to read. Touched by what he found related there concerning the conversion and life of the great anchorite, he turned to his friend and announced his intention of abandoning the world and devoting himself to the service of God. The sudden conversion of the one so moved the other that he resolved to do likewise, and they became anchorites from that very hour. Shortly afterwards, Ponticianus and the fourth member of the party, who had been walking in another part of the gardens, came upon them, to remind them that it was time to return home. When they heard the decision which the two new solitaries had made, they felt themselves unable to leave the world; but congratulated their friends on their decision and requested their prayers, before they returned to their own duties at the palace. The two monks, however, setting their affections on heavenly things, remained in the cottage; while their affianced brides—for both were engaged to be married—when they heard what had come to pass, voluntarily took the veil.[3]

[1] *Conf.*, VIII, vi, 14.
[2] On this unpopular body, see O. Hirschfeld, 'Die *agentes in rebus*', in *Sitzungsberichte der berl. Akad.*, 1893, 421-4; J. B. Bury, *History of the later Roman Empire*, i, 30-31; and André Pigianiol, *L'empire chrétien, 325-395*, Paris, 1947, 316-17.
[3] *Conf.*, VIII, vi, 15. Courcelle, op. cit., pp. 183-7, suggests that one of the converts may have been St Jerome himself. This hypothesis has been attacked by G. Bardy, in *Sacris erudiri*, v (1953), 88 and W. Theiler in *Gnomon*, xxv (1953), 122. See Pellegrino, op. cit., p. 114 *n*[8].

The story touched Augustine's heart. In a flash, he recalled his past life, foul with sin. He remembered his youthful reading of the *Hortensius*, and of the sudden thirst for wisdom, whose very search ought to have been preferred above the treasures and kingdoms of this world. But he recalled how he had failed in that search, and had been wont to pray: 'Give me chastity and continence—but not yet!'[1] Ponticianus departed, but the storm continued to rage in Augustine's soul. With a great voice he cried to Alypius: 'What is the matter with us? What is this? What did you hear? The uninstructed start up and take heaven, and we—with all our learning but so little heart—see where we wallow in flesh and blood! Because others have gone before us, are we ashamed to follow, and not rather ashamed at our not following?'[2] With these words, he rushed from the house into the garden, closely followed by Alypius. Together they sat down with Augustine in a torment of indecision. He kept saying to himself: 'Let it be done now! let it be done now!' but his words did not seem to bring him to any decision.[3] It was as if his old lusts and ambitions, those trifles of trifles and vanities of vanities, were at his elbow, plucking at his sleeve and murmuring in his ear: 'Are you turning us away? Shall we never be with you again from this moment? Will this and that henceforth be forbidden to you for ever?' And by the phrase 'this and that' ('hoc et illud') they implied unmentionable vileness and shame.[4] But already their voice grew fainter; and there seemed to appear before Augustine's eyes the figure of Continence, with her attendant throng of men and women, young and old, virgin and widow, who seemed to say: 'Can you not do what these young men and maidens can? Or can any of them do it of themselves, and not rather in the Lord their God? The Lord their God gave me to them. Why do you stand in your own strength, and so stand not? Cast yourself on Him; fear not. He will not flinch and you will not fall. Cast yourself on Him without fear, for He will receive and heal you.'

And I blushed violently, for I still heard the muttering of those 'trifles' and hung suspended. Again she seemed to speak: 'Stop your ears against those unclean members of yours, that they may be mortified. They tell you of delights, but not according to the law of the Lord thy

[1] *Conf.*, VIII, vii, 16–17.
[2] Ibid., VIII, viii, 19. Outler, p. 170.
[3] Ibid., VIII, xi, 25: 'Dicebam enim apud me intus: "Ecce modo fiat, modo fiat", et cum verbo istum in placitum. Iam paene faciebam, et non faciebam, nec relabebar tamen in pristina, sed de proximo stabam et respirabam. Et item conabar et paulo minus ibi eram et paulo minus, iam iamque adtingebam et tenebam: et non ibi eram nec adtingebam nec tenebam, haesitans mori morti et vitae vivere, plusque in me valebat deterius inolitum, quam melius insolitum, punctumque ipsum temporis, quo aliud futurus eram, quanto propius admovebatur, tanto ampliorem incutiebat horrorem; sed non recutiebat retro nec avertebat, sed suspendebat.'
[4] Ibid., VIII, xi, 26.

God.' This struggle raging in my heart was nothing but the contest of self against self. And Alypius kept close beside me, and awaited in silence the outcome of my extraordinary agitation.[1]

In this mood, even the company of Alypius became intolerable, and Augustine left his side. He flung himself down under a fig-tree and wept bitterly, calling upon God. In an agony of spirit he cried out: 'How long, how long, tomorrow and tomorrow? Why not now? Why should there not be at this hour an end to my baseness?'[2] As if in answer, there came from a neighbouring house the voice of a child, whether boy or girl he could not tell, repeating the words: 'Take and read! take and read!' These words recalled to Augustine's mind the story he had heard from Ponticianus about the conversion of St Anthony, who had been turned to the solitary life by hearing the words of the Gospel read out in church: *If thou wouldest be perfect, go, sell that thou hast, and give to the poor, and thou shalt have treasure in heaven: and come follow Me.*[3] Accordingly, he hastened back to the bench where Alypius was sitting, and took up the copy of the Pauline Epistles which he had left lying there. His eyes lighted upon the text: *Not in rioting and drunkenness, not in chambering and wantonness, not in strife and envying, but put ye on the Lord Jesus Christ, and make not provision for the flesh to fulfil the lusts thereof.*[4] It was the answer to all his prayers. The fight was ended, and the battle won.[5]

Augustine closed the book, keeping a finger within to mark the place which he had found, and with a tranquil expression—'calm of mind, all passion spent'—began to tell Alypius what had happened. Alypius, for his part, revealed that a similar struggle had been raging in his own mind. He asked to see the text which Augustine had read and, reading on, found the words: *Him that is weak in the faith receive ye,*[6] which Augustine had not noticed, but which Alypius straightway applied to himself. They went to

---

[1] *Conf.*, VIII, xi, 27. Tr. by Outler, p. 175. This personification of the struggle between the vices and virtue in Augustine's mind is clearly a literary device (O'Meara, *The Young Augustine*, 178; Pellegrino, op. cit., p. 116), and in accordance with the classical tradition. The use of this literary device does not, however, detract from the historicity of the rest of the narrative.

[2] Ibid., VII, xii, 28.   [3] Matt. 19.21.   [4] Rom. 13. 13, 14.

[5] *Conf.*, VIII, xii, 29. Courcelle is unable to accept the famous 'Tolle, lege' episode as historical. To him (op. cit., pp. 197–202) it is merely a literary fiction, a repetition of the conversion at Trier, recorded by Ponticianus. O'Meara, op. cit., pp. 178–85 and Pellegrino, op. cit., pp. 116–20, esp. n[13], strongly criticize the position adopted by Courcelle, which does not seem to be defended by any really convincing argument, and his suggestion (p. 200) that the fig-tree beneath which Augustine cast himself down is imported from the episode of Nathanael (John 1.47–51) is arbitrary to the point of being absurd. One might equally well suggest that there was a significant, and possibly sinister, element in the narrative, since the Manichees believed that the fig-tree wept when its fruit was plucked! (*Conf.*, III, x, 18).

[6] Rom. 14.1.

tell St Monica, who was overwhelmed with joy, and blessed the God who had rewarded her beyond her expectations.

For Thou didst so convert me to Thee that I sought neither a wife nor any other of this world's hopes, but set my feet on that rule of faith which so many years before Thou hadst showed her in her dream about me.[1] And so Thou didst turn her grief into gladness more plentiful than she had ventured to desire, and dearer and purer than the desire she used to cherish of having grandchildren of my flesh.[2]

Augustine's conversion took place at the beginning of August 386.[3] He now felt moved to put into effect the plan which he had been entertaining for some time past, to remove himself from the schools of rhetoric, and to devote himself wholly to the service of God. Fortunately, there were only a few weeks before the end of term,[4] so he was able to finish his course of lectures and retire without much comment,[5] for he and his friends were agreed that there should be no ostentation,[6] which might give the impression that Augustine wished to attract attention and be considered a person of great consequence.[7] In the circumstances, he decided that it was best for him to make an undramatic resignation; and the fact that he had been ill that summer with pains in the lungs[8] and in the stomach[9] made such a decision practicable.[10]

When the vacation arrived, Augustine looked hopefully for some place where he could enjoy rest and refreshment, after the tension of the past months. He found it in the villa of Cassiciacum, situated at some distance from Milan,[11] the property of Verecundus, a Milanese citizen, a teacher of

---

[1] See *Conf.*, III, xi, 19–20.   [2] Ibid., VIII, xii, 30. Tr. by Outler, p. 177.
[3] See Pellegrino, op. cit., p. 119 n^{14}.
[4] Before the 'vintage vacation' from 22 August to 15 October.   [5] *Conf.*, IX, ii, 2.
[6] Ibid.: 'Consilium ergo nostrum erat coram te, coram hominibus autem nisi nostris non erat. Et convenerat inter nos, ne passim cuiquam effunderetur, quamquam tu nobis *a convalle plorationis ascendentibus* et cantantibus *canticum graduum* dederas *sagittas acutas et carbones vastatores adversus linguam subdolam* velut consulendo contradicentem et, sicut cibum assolet, amando consumentem.'   [7] Ibid., IX, ii, 3.
[8] Ibid., IX, ii, 4: 'Quin etiam quod ipsa aestate litterario labori nimio pulmo meus cedere coeperat et difficulter trahere suspiria doloribusque pectoris testari se saucium vocemque clariorem productioremve recusare, primo perturbaverat me, quia magisterii illius sarcinam paene iam necessitate deponere cogebat aut, si curari et convalescere potuissem, certe intermittere'; *C. Acad.*, I, i, 3: '. . . nisi me pectoris dolor ventosam professionem abicere et in philosophiae gremium confugere coegisset'; ibid., III, vii, 15; *De Beata Vita*, i, 4.
[9] *De Ordine*, I, ii, 5: 'Nam cum stomachi dolor scholam me deserere coegisset, qui iam, ut scis, etiam sine ulla tali necessitate in philosophiam confugere moliebar, statim me contuli ad villam familiarissimi nostri Verecundi.'
[10] O'Meara, op. cit., p. 191 points out that an additional factor in the decision to make an undramatic resignation may have been the desire to avoid hurting the feelings of pagan friends, including Augustine's patrons, with whom he desired to remain friendly.
[11] Variously identified with Cassago and Casciago. See Filippo Medea, 'La controversia sul "rus Cassiciacum", in *Miscellanea Agostiniana*, ii, 49–59; Pellegrino, op. cit., p. 122 n^2.

grammar and a generous and sincere friend. For Verecundus, the conversion of Augustine and Alypius was a painful blow, which he feared would put an end to their friendship; for although married to a Christian wife, he himself remained a pagan, held back by a disinclination to become a Christian unless he could embrace a life of celibacy.[1] His friends comforted him, with the assurance that their friendship was unaffected, and that his married condition was no obstacle to him becoming a Christian also.[2] (Ultimately, indeed, Verecundus was to be baptized on his death-bed and depart from life a servant of Christ.[3]) Nebridius, on the other hand, was delighted by their decision, which he was himself soon to imitate.[4] He was not, however, one of the little group which proceeded to Cassiciacum in the autumn of 386, and which included, besides Augustine and Alypius, Monica; Adeodatus, Augustine's illegitimate son; Navigius, his brother; Trygetius and Licentius, two of Augustine's pupils, for whom the stay at Milan was in the nature of a vacation reading-party; and two relatives of Augustine, Rusticus and Fastidianus.[5]

The weeks spent at Cassiciacum during the autumn of 386 have been the subject of much discussion among scholars, and it is important to try to come to some understanding of the nature of the holiday. The picture of Augustine and his friends passing their time in philosophic dialogues on the pattern of Plato against a pleasing rural background is not supported by the picture which Augustine paints in the three works written there.[6] It was the harvest season; and it is clear that Augustine and his friends did not merely not sit idle while the farm-labourers were actively engaged[7] but even, when necessary, got up early to lend a hand.[8] Men do not get up early to work in the fields simply to lend verisimilitude to an idyllic rural existence.[9] One does not easily imagine Horace doing so on his Sabine farm.

Again, Augustine's references to the reading of Virgil[10] do not indicate

---

[1] *Conf.*, IX, iii, 5.   [2] Ibid., IX, iii, 6.   [3] Ibid., IX, iii, 5.   [4] Ibid., IX, iii, 6.

[5] O'Meara, op. cit., p. 192, suggests that Nebridius' teaching duties as an assistant to Verecundus (*Conf.*, VIII, vi, 13) prevented him from joining the party at Cassiciacum; but it seems unlikely that, in the period of the university vacations, there would have been no school holidays.

[6] The *Contra Academicos*; the *De Beata Vita*; and the *De Ordine*.

[7] *C. Acad.*, I, v, 15: 'Nam disputare coeperamus sole iam in occasum declinante diesque paene totus cum in rebus rusticis ordinandis tum in recensione primi libri Vergilii peractus fuit.'

[8] Ibid., II, iv, 10: 'Maturius itaque solito lectos reliquimus paululumque cum rusticis egimus quod tempus urgebat.'

[9] This makes Frend's comment seem rather unfair: 'The ideal of Augustine and his friends was not the safeguarding of the city state or even the active farming of a villa, but *otium liberale*—the mere enjoyment of the fruits of a great rural domain.' 'Augustine's choice of Cassiciacum for his retirement in 387 [*sic*] is also indicative of this attitude' (*The Donatist Church*, Oxford, 1952, 235 and *n*[6]). The reference to *otium liberale* is to *De Ordine*, I, ii, 4.   [10] *C. Acad.*, I, v, 15; ibid., II, iv, 10; *De Ordine*, I, viii, 26.

a poetry-reading society, but something far more like a university tutorial. The two youths, Licentius and Trygetius, were with the party for the sake of their education[1] and Virgil was the standard author for the study of Latin poetry, as Cicero was for Latin prose. Since Augustine was giving up his post as an official teacher of rhetoric, it was desirable that he should find some other way of supporting himself and his dependants, and it is very likely that the tuition of these two was a source of income. As Montgomery remarks, most men have to go on with some daily work, whether passing through a spiritual crisis or not.[2]

Besides recognizing the essentially practical background to the stay at Cassiciacum, we must not overlook the evidence which exists to show that Augustine's mind was still much preoccupied with the spiritual crisis through which he had passed. He read the psalms, discovering, as many have done before and after him, the heights of spiritual aspiration and the deeps of spiritual insight which they contain.[3] He wrote to Nebridius, still remaining at Milan, about his experiences.[4] And he prayed, often with tears.[5] If his general mood was one of calm, following a spiritual crisis, it was a calm which could very easily turn to a condition of highly emotional excitement.[6] In the circumstances, the retreat to Cassiciacum, and the quiet life lived there, in the company of his mother, his son, and his friends, was perhaps the best preparation for baptism that he could have had. Its influence over his subsequent career as a Christian was profound, and it is probable that it was a determining factor in Augustine's decision, after he was baptized, to found and live in a Christian community.[7] He was by nature a gregarious person, for whom the eremitical life had little appeal, and at Cassiciacum he discovered the strength and joy which come from the Christian life lived in community.[8]

One episode during his life at the villa amazed and rather frightened

[1] *De Quant. Anim.* xxxi, 62: '. . . nostri illi adolescentes qui tunc mecum erant studiorum suorum gratia.' *De Beata Vita*, I, i, 6: '. . . Trygetius et Licentius, cives et discipuli mei.'

[2] W. Montgomery, *St. Augustine : Aspects of his life and thought*, 37. The whole of the chapter should be consulted regarding the stay at Cassiciacum.   [3] *Conf.*, IX, iv, 8.

[4] Ibid., IX, iv, 7. The correspondence with Nebridius in Augustine's letters are *Epp.* 3–14, of which 2 and 3 refer to the stay at Cassiciacum.

[5] *De Ordine*, I, viii, 22: 'Interea post paululum dies sese aperuit. surrexerunt illi et ego inlacrimans multa oravi'; ibid., I, x, 29: 'Satis mihi sint vulnera mea, quae ut sanentur, paene cotidianis fletibus deum rogans indigniorem tamen esse me, qui tam cito saner, quam volo, saepe memet ipse convinco.'

[6] Evidenced, for example, by the burst of tears which accompanied his rebuke to Trygetius and Licentius for their uncharitable behaviour, *De Ordine*, I, x, 30.

[7] See Paul Monceaux, 'Saint Augustin et saint Antoine: contribution à l'histoire du monachisme', in *Miscellanea Agostiniana*, ii, 61–89, esp. 69–70.

[8] There is a good chapter on the months at Cassiciacum in Farrar, *Lives of the Fathers*, ii, 452–71.

him. He was seized by a toothache, so sudden and agonizing that he was unable to talk. It came into his mind that, if he could ask his friends to pray for him, he might obtain some relief. Accordingly he wrote his request upon a wax tablet and showed it to them. They began to pray, and suddenly the pain was gone. Welcome as the relief was, the incident left Augustine terrified. There was terror in the divine Mercy no less than in the divine Judgement.[1]

Towards the end of the vintage vacation, Augustine informed the civic authorities of Milan that he was resigning his post of Public Orator, urging both his decision to serve God and the poor state of his health.[2] At the same time he wrote to Ambrose, informing the bishop of his past errors and present conversion, and asking advice as to suitable books to read. Ambrose recommended the prophecies of Isaiah, no doubt, says Augustine, because of all the books of the Old Testament, Isaiah foreshadows most clearly the Gospel and the calling of the Gentiles. But Augustine was, at that time, still too new in the faith to gain much profit from such an author; and after the first reading, laid it aside, intending to return to it when more familiar with the divine word.[3]

About the beginning of Lent, 387, Augustine and Alypius returned to Milan, to enrol themselves among the candidates for baptism in the following Easter. With them was Augustine's son, the young Adeodatus, a boy of remarkable intelligence and goodness, destined soon to be taken out of the world.[4] All three were baptized together becoming, in Augustine's word, contemporaries in the life of grace. 'And so,' he says, 'we were baptized and the anxiety about our past life left us.'[5]

Augustine, after his baptism, was in a mood of spiritual elevation and happiness:

> Nor did I ever have enough in those days of the wondrous sweetness of meditating on the depth of Thy counsels concerning the salvation of the human race. How freely did I weep in Thy hymns and canticles; how deeply was I moved by the voices of Thy sweet-speaking Church! The voices flowed into my ears; and the truth was poured forth into my heart where the tide of my devotion overflowed, and my tears ran down, and I was happy in all these things.[6]

The recollection of the beauty of the antiphonal chanting of the cathedral of Milan causes Augustine, at this point, to introduce into the *Confessions* an account of its introduction by St Ambrose (who found it in the Eastern

---

[1] *Conf.*, IX, iv, 12.
[2] Ibid., IX, v, 13: 'Renuntiavi peractis vindemialibus, ut scholasticis suis Mediolanenses venditorem verborum alium providerent, quod et tibi ego servire delegissem et illi professioni prae difficultate spirandi ac dolore pectoris non sufficerem.'
[3] Ibid.   [4] Ibid., IX, vi, 14.   [5] Ibid. Outler, p. 187.   [6] Ibid.

Church) into the church of Milan, and of the part which it played in sustaining the morale of the Catholics of Milan, during the persecution by the Empress Justina, a convinced Arian, then ruling the western part of the Empire on behalf of her son, who was still a minor.[1] This recollection in turn leads Augustine to the discovery of the alleged relics of the martyrs Gervasius and Protasius, whose miracles restrained the fury of the heretical empress,[2] and to recall how, at the time of the invention (17-19 June 386), he had been indifferent to these miracles, and how remembering this caused him to weep the more bitterly, a year later, when the beauty of the chant brought back to his mind the circumstances of its institution.[3]

Not long after his baptism, Augustine and Monica decided to return to Africa, and went accordingly to Ostia, on the Tiber, accompanied by Augustine's brother, Navigius; Adeodatus; the faithful Alypius; and by Evodius, a young compatriot from Thagaste, who had formerly served in the ranks of the *agentes in rebus*, but who had now resigned from his secular employment, and proposed to devote himself to the service of God.[4] At Ostia, on the Tiber, the party remained for a little while for rest and refreshment after the journey from Milan, before embarking for Africa. It was here that Augustine and Monica enjoyed together the experience which has become famous as the Vision of Ostia. The interpretation of this experience which has been, and remains, a battlefield for rival exegetes, is of the greatest importance, not merely in the career of Augustine, but for the history of Christian mysticism. Before it is discussed, however, it deserves quotation in full, both for the beauty of the language and for the fact that it marks the goal of Monica's life's work and is, in a certain sense, a memorial to her.

As the day approached on which she was to depart this life—a day which Thou knewest, but which we did not—it happened (though I believe it was by Thy secret ways arranged) that she and I stood alone, leaning in a certain window from which the garden of the house we occupied at Ostia could be seen. Here in this place, removed from the crowd, we were resting ourselves for the voyage after the fatigues of a long journey. We were conversing alone very pleasantly and *forgetting those things which are past, and reaching forward toward those things which are future.*[5] We were in the present—and in the presence of Truth (which Thou art)—discussing together what is the nature of the eternal life of the saints: which *eye has not seen, nor ear heard, neither has entered into the heart of man.*[6] We opened wide the mouth of our heart, thirsting for those supernal streams of Thy fountain, the *fountain of life, which is with Thee,*[7] that we might be sprinkled with its waters

[1] *Conf.*, IX, vii, 15. [2] See Courcelle, op. cit., pp. 139-53. [3] *Conf.*, IX, vii, 16.
[4] Ibid., IX, viii, 17. [5] Phil. 3.13. [6] I Cor. 2.9. [7] Ps. 35.10 [36.9].

according to our capacity and might in some measure weigh the truth of so profound a mystery.

And when our conversation had brought us to the point where the very highest of physical sense and the most intense illumination of physical light seemed, in comparison with the sweetness of that life to come, not worthy of comparison, nor even of mention, we lifted ourselves with a more ardent love toward *the Selfsame*,[1] and we gradually passed through all the levels of bodily objects, and even through the heaven itself, where the sun and moon and stars shine on the earth. Indeed, we soared higher yet by an inner musing, speaking and marvelling at Thy works.

And we came at last to our own minds and went beyond them, that we might climb as high as that region of unfailing plenty,[2] where Thou feedest Israel forever with the food of Truth,[3] where life is that Wisdom by whom all things are made, both which have been, and which are to be. Wisdom is not made, but is as she has been and forever shall be; for 'to have been' and 'to be hereafter' do not apply to her, but only 'to be', because she is eternal and 'to have been' and 'to be hereafter' are not eternal.[4]

And while we were thus speaking and straining after her, we just barely touched her by the whole effort of our hearts. Then with a sigh, leaving the *first fruits of the Spirit*[5] bound to that ecstasy, we returned to the sounds of our own tongue, where the spoken word had both beginning and end. But what is like to Thy Word, our Lord, who *remaineth in Himself* without becoming old, and *makes all things new*.[6]

What we said was something like this: If to any man the tumult of the flesh were silenced; and the phantoms of earth and waters and air were silenced; and the poles were silent as well; indeed, if the very soul grew silent to herself, and went beyond herself by not thinking of herself; if fancies and imaginary revelations were silenced; if every tongue and every sign and every transient thing—for actually if any man could hear them, all these would say, *We did not create ourselves, but were created by Him who abides for ever*[7]—and if, having uttered this, they too should be silent, having stirred our ears to hear Him who created them; and if then He alone spoke, not through them but by Himself, that we might hear His Word, not in fleshly tongue or angelic voice, nor sound of thunder, nor the obscurity of a parable,[8] but might hear Him—Him for whose sake we love these things—if we could hear Him without these, as we two now strained to do, we then with rapid thought might touch on

---

[1] *Conf.*, IX, x, 24: '. . . erigentes nos ardentiore affectu in *id ipsum*.' Cf. Ps. 4.9 (Vulgate): In pace in idipsum dormiam, et requiescam. Note the impression made upon Augustine by the reading of the Fourth Psalm at Cassiciacum, *Conf.*, IX, iv, 8–11, esp. 11: 'Et clamabam in consequenti versu clamore alto cordis mei: *o in pace! o in id ipsum! o quid dixit: obdormiam et somnum capiam?*' See Henry, *La Vision d'Ostie*, 40–42; A. Mandouze, 'L'extase d'Ostie', in *Augustinus Magister*, i, 70 *n*[4].

[2] Cf. Ezech. 34.14; but see Henry, op. cit., p. 23.   [3] Cf. Ps. 77.71 [78.71].
[4] Cf. Prov. 8.22–31.   [5] Rom. 8.23.
[6] Cf. Sap. 7.27.   [7] Ps. 99.3, 5 [100.3, 5]; Eccl. 18.1.
[8] *Conf.*, IX, x, 25: '. . . nec per aenigma similitudinis.' Cf. I Cor. 13.12: Videmus nunc per speculum in aenigmate.

D

that Eternal Wisdom which abides over all. And if this could be sustained, and other visions of a far different kind be taken away, and this one should so ravish and absorb and envelop its beholder in these inward joys that his life might be eternally like that one moment of knowledge which we now sighed after—would not *this* be the reality of the saying, *Enter into the joy of thy Lord*?[1] But when shall such a thing be? Shall it not be *when we shall all rise again*, and shall it not be that *all things will be changed*?[2]

Such a thought I was expressing, and if not in this manner and in these words,[3] still, O Lord, Thou knowest that on that day we were talking thus and that this world, with all its joys, seemed cheap to us even as we spoke. Then my mother said: 'Son, for myself I have no longer any pleasure in anything in this life. Now that my hopes in this world are satisfied, I do not know what more I want here or why I am here. There was indeed one thing for which I wished to tarry in this life, and that was that I might see you a Catholic Christian before I died. My God hath answered this more than abundantly, so that I see you now made His servant and spurning all earthly happiness. What more am I to do here?'[4]

Such was the Vision of Ostia. How is it to be understood?

For some readers, Augustine's words will seem to describe a mystical experience, as the words are understood in Christian theology. This was emphatically the view of Abbot Butler, who compared Augustine's teaching in this passage regarding the 'silencing of the faculties' as a preparation for contemplating God with that of so great a master of mystical theology as St John of the Cross in *The Ascent of Mount Carmel*.[5] Abbot Butler observed, however, in a footnote, that 'this passage is reminiscent of Plotinus', and later research, notably that of Père Henry[6] and Professor Courcelle,[7] has confirmed this observation. It is moreover significant that even so staunch a champion of Augustine's claim to be regarded as a mystic as Butler was moved to remark that 'western mystics commonly represent contemplation as attained to by and in absorption in prayer; but for Augustine it seems to have been primarily an intellectual process—informed, indeed, by intense religious warmth, but still primarily intellectual'.[8] Something of Butler's reserve seems to have been felt by Père

[1] Matt. 25.21.   [2] I Cor. 15.51.
[3] See Henry, op. cit., pp. 37–39; Mandouze, art. cit., p. 79 n^2.
[4] *Conf.*, IX, x, 23–26. Tr. Outler, pp. 192–4.
[5] Butler, *Western Mysticism*, 2nd ed., 44.
[6] Henry, *La Vision d'Ostie*, 15–26.   [7] Courcelle, *Recherches*, 222–6.
[8] Butler, op. cit., p. 46. Cf. John Burnaby, *Amor Dei. A Study of Saint Augustine's teaching on the Love of God as the motive of Christian Life*, London, 1938, 33: 'If Augustine is to be called a mystic, that and no other was the character of his mystical experience —a reflective ascent through the ordered values of the created world, inexplicably transformed into an instantaneous apprehension, not of any particular truth, but of *the* Truth, the Light that lighteneth every man.'

Cayré in his study, *La contemplation augustinienne*, where he speaks of the Vision of Ostia as a religious meditation.[1] For Professor O'Meara, the Vision was 'an intellectual and emotional experience quite above the ordinary . . .; but technical terms such as "mystical" and "ecstasy" should not lightly be employed of an intellectual and emotional experience devoid of any of the characteristic signs of mystical states, and described much later in language apparently, at least in part, borrowed from the Neo-Platonists'.[2] Nor are there wanting those who flatly deny that Augustine was a mystic at all.[3]

Owing to the diversity of opinions regarding the Vision of Ostia, it is clear that any judgement upon its nature must be, in part, subjective, and depend upon the degree to which it arouses a response in the reader. It is however likely that anyone who believes in the possibility of an experimental knowledge of God for certain favoured souls in this life, such as the mystics claim to enjoy, and who approaches Augustine's narrative without any preconceived opinion, will find it hard to doubt that the vision which was afforded to Monica and Augustine at Ostia comes within the class of mystical experiences as Christianity understands the term. The Neo-Platonist terminology employed by Augustine should not be misunderstood. In a minute analysis of the sources of the text of the Vision of Ostia, M. André Mandouze has shown that the very extent and multiplicity of Augustine's reference to Plotinus is an argument against the direct influence of Neo-Platonism on his thought. If one can find a reference to Plotinus in every few words of the account, and if such references consist largely in similarity of words and expressions, one must either regard the Vision of Ostia as a mosaic of citations, and so destroy its spiritual content, or recognize that it is misleading to talk of Plotinian sources in connection with it.[4] In any case, as Professor Courcelle has remarked, it is likely that the experience of Ostia was less Plotinian in reality than in the description in the *Confessions*[5]—an account written, it is worth recalling, when Augustine was a mature Christian and a bishop, with a far more critical attitude towards Neo-Platonism than he had shown as a neophyte. In any case, there are numerous, and significant, references to biblical texts in the Vision, as well as to Plotinus.[6]

---

[1] Cayré, op. cit., 2e éd., p. 214.

[2] O'Meara, *The Young Augustine*, 202–3.

[3] E. Hendriks, *Augustins Verhältnis zur Mystik. Eine patristische Untersuchung*, Würzberg, 1936, 176: 'Augustin war einer grosser Enthusiast; er war aber kein Mystiker.'

[4] Mandouze, 'L'extase d'Ostie', *Aug. Mag.*, i, 81.

[5] Courcelle, *Recherches*, 226.

[6] See Mandouze, art. cit., *Aug. Mag.*, i, 69–79 *notes*.

It may be argued that the Vision of Ostia (assuming that it is a mystical experience) is the only one of its kind of which we have any sure knowledge in Augustine's life, if we are agreed that the experiences of Milan fall outside the limits of Christian mysticism,[1] and that we should not expect such a favour to be granted so early in the Christian life. Such an argument overlooks the gratuitous nature of mystical experience; and it is to be remembered that, in the case of the celebrated Dame Julian of Norwich, whose claim to be counted among the mystics is a very strong one, her sixteen 'shewings' or revelations were imparted to her during an all-but-fatal illness in May 1373, when she was in her thirty-first year. Fifteen or more years afterwards she was shown the meaning of her revelations, but beyond this we cannot be sure that she had any further mystical experiences, in the strict sense of the term. It is not impossible that Augustine's case was similar, particularly in view of Professor O'Meara's suggestion that the mystical element in his nature was suppressed by the duties imposed upon him as a bishop.[2]

We may say then that while the nature of the Vision of Ostia is at present undecided, and likely to remain so, there is no decisive argument against the interpretation that it represented a mystical experience as the word is exemplified in the lives and teaching of the great Christian mystics, and not a little to commend such a view.[3]

The words uttered by Monica at the window of the house of Ostia seem to express a presentiment that she had finished her course, and accomplished the work which God had given her to do. Five days later she lay sick of a fever, and fell into a coma. Her sons hastened to her side; but she recovered consciousness and looked at them and asked: 'Where was I?' In their grief, neither Augustine nor Navigius was able to speak, and Monica then said: 'Here in this place shall you bury your mother.' Augustine kept silent, and restrained his tears; but Navigius, anxious to comfort her, expressed the hope that she would meet death in her own country and not abroad. Monica looked at him, unhappy at such earthly hopes; and then turning to Augustine she said: 'See how he speaks.' After a pause, she addressed both her sons: 'Lay this body where you will and let no care for it disturb you. This only I ask: that you will remember me at the altar of

---

[1] See *contra* Burnaby, op. cit., p. 32: 'There is no ground for the claim that the intervening "purgation" and reception into the Church gave to the so-called ecstasy of Ostia a "Christian" quality lacking to the earlier experience.'

[2] O'Meara, op. cit., p. 203.

[3] For a discussion of the present state of studies regarding Augustine's mysticism, see A. Mandouze, 'Où en est la question de la mystique augustinienne?', *Aug. Mag.*, iii, 103–63.

the Lord, wherever you are.'[1] With that she fell silent, and Augustine turned to his thoughts. He knew that his mother had always desired to be buried beside her husband and had been much concerned about providing for a suitable grave, and he felt a joy that God had released her from such a worldly concern. Later he was to learn that, during their stay at Ostia, she had been talking with some of his friends on the contempt a Christian should feel for this life, and the blessing of death. They had been amazed at such a spirit in a woman, and asked her if she did not dread the idea of being buried in strange earth, so far from her native city, to which she replied: 'Nothing is far for God, nor is there any fear that, in the Last Day, He will not know the spot from whence to raise me up.'[2]

And so on the ninth day of her sickness, in the fifty-sixth year of her life and the thirty-third of mine, that religious and devout soul was set loose from the body.[3]

'I closed her eyes,' says Augustine, 'and a great sadness flowed into my heart, ready to overflow in tears; but at the same time my eyes, at the strong command of my will, swallowed back their fountain to dryness; and the struggle was a great evil to me'.[4] The boy Adeodatus was unable to contain himself, but broke out into a wail of grief. He was, however, speedily checked by the others; such violent grief was incompatible alike with Roman fortitude and Christian hope.[5] Augustine, for his part, had the comforting memory that, in her last illness, his mother had praised his loving affection, and had recalled with joy that she had never heard him utter a harsh or reproachful word to her; but he felt himself stricken to the heart by her loss, and that his life, which had been one with hers, had been torn asunder.[6]

When Adeodatus had been quietened, Evodius took the psalter, and began to sing the Hundredth Psalm,[7] *I will sing of mercy and judgement*

---

[1] *Conf.*, IX, xi, 27. This episode inspired Matthew Arnold's sonnet:

'Oh could thy grave at home, at Carthage, be!'—
Care not for that and lay me where I fall,
Everywhere heard will be the judgement-call.
But at God's altar oh! remember me.

St Monica would hardly have been grateful to the English poet for misstating the place of her domicile; and she would probably have very much disliked the concluding lines:

Creeds pass, rites change, no altar standeth whole:
Yet we her memory, as she pray'd, will keep,
Keep by this: *Life in God, and union there!*

[2] *Conf.*, IX, xi, 28: ' "Nihil" inquit "longe est deo, neque timendum est, ne ille non agnoscat in fine saeculi, unde me resuscitet".'
[3] Ibid.   [4] Ibid., IX, xii, 29.
[5] Ibid.   [6] Ibid., IX, xii, 30.   [7] Ps. 101 in the A.V.

unto Thee, O Lord, while the whole household gave the responses.[1] The news of Monica's death spread abroad. Pious brethren and sisters came to prepare the body for burial, while Augustine, in another part of the house, tried to find something appropriate to say to his companions in what was a common loss. So well did he succeed in controlling his emotions that his hearers imagined him to be free from any deep sense of loss. But Augustine wrestled within himself, striving to control the surging grief which tormented him, and feeling a sense of anger that so ordinary and inevitable an event in human affairs as a death should have such power to move him, so that he found himself consumed with a twofold sadness.[2]

The corpse was taken out for burial and the eucharist offered at the graveside. Augustine remained dry-eyed. All the day he remained in the deepest unhappiness, praying that God would heal his sorrows. The thought came into his mind that his grief might be eased if he took a bath, believing that the Latin word for bath, *balneum*, came from the Greek, *balaneion*, which was, in turn, formed from *ballein*, to cast out, because it cast care out of the mind. Accordingly, he went to bathe, but found that he did not sweat away his grief by doing so.[3] Afterwards, he slept, and when he awoke, he found his grief had abated. Then, as he lay upon his bed, he called to mind the verses of St Ambrose's hymn:

> Deus, creator omnium,
> polique rector, vestiens
> diem decoro lumine,
> noctem soporis gratia,
>
> Artus solutos ut quies
> reddat laboris usui
> mentesque fessas allevet
> luctusque solvat anxios.

'O God, creator of all things and governor of the heavens, who clothest the day with the lovely light and night with the sweetness of sleep, that quiet may restore slackened limbs for their accustomed labour, and comfort

---

[1] The memory of this psalm, and its appropriateness to the circumstances, may well have lingered in Augustine's mind when he came to write his great work against Faustus the Manichee, thirteen years after the death of his mother, and three years after writing the *Confessions*. See *C. Faustum*, XXI, iii: 'Vos autem non valentes discernere, quid faciat deus beneficio, quid iudicio, quia et a corde et ab ore vestro longe est psalterium nostrum, ubi dicitur: *misericordiam et iudicium cantabo tibi, domine*, quicquid vos pro infirmitate humanae mortalitatis offenderit, alienatis omnino ab arbitrio et iudicio dei veri videlicet habentes paratum alterum deum malum, quem vobis non veritas ostendit, sed vanitas fingit.'

[2] *Conf.*, IX, xii, 31.

[3] It should be borne in mind that, to a Roman, a bath was essentially a sweat bath—what we should call a Turkish bath.

tired minds, and dissolve the anguish of grief.' The words were a charm to soften his heart, to release the tears which he had repressed and to call to his mind memories of his mother's goodness and charity.

> And now, O Lord [he declares], I confess it to Thee in letters! Read it who will, and comment how he will, and if he finds me to have sinned in weeping for my mother for part of an hour—that mother who was for a while dead to my eyes, who had for many years wept for me that I might live in Thy eyes—let him not laugh at me; but if he be a man of generous love, let him weep for my sins against Thee, the Father of all the brethren of Thy Christ.[1]

It has been observed that one of the sweetest things in Christianity is that it prevents entirely all hardening of the heart. Certainly, there are few more touching pages in literature than those in which the bishop of Hippo tells of his mother's last days and death. From a literary point of view, it is true, Augustine was fortunate in the events he had to describe. His mother finished her work and left him, so that we may say with truth that her death was also, in a sense, his own: the death of his youth, with its wasted years and vain searchings, and his rebirth into the Christian life. But even when this is conceded, there can be no mistaking the love which trans-figures the account of the Vision of Ostia, the last sickness, with its Christian resignation to death in an alien land and the simple request for remembrance at God's altar, and the death and burial, where Augustine stood with dry eyes and a weeping heart. But this is not quite all, for when Augustine came to write of these events, ten years after they occurred, he remembered also his father, and joined his name to that of Monica in his concluding sentences:

> Let her rest in peace with her husband, before and after whom she was married to no other man; whom she obeyed with patience, bringing fruit to Thee that she might also win him for Thee. And inspire, O my Lord my God, inspire Thy servants, my brothers; Thy sons, my mas-ters, whom with voice and heart and writings I serve, that as many of them as shall read these confessions may also at Thy altar remember Monica, Thy handmaid, together with Patricius, once her husband; by whose flesh Thou didst bring me into this life, in a manner I know not. May they with pious affection remember my parents in this transitory life, and remember my brothers under Thee our Father in our Catholic mother, and remember my fellow-citizens in the eternal Jerusalem, for which Thy people sigh in their pilgrimage from birth until their return. So be fulfilled what my mother desired of me—more richly in the prayers of so many gained for her through these confessions of mine than by my prayers alone.[2]

[1] Ibid., IX, xii, 33. Tr. by Outler, pp. 198–9, slightly modified.
[2] Conf., IX, xiii, 37. Outler, p. 200.

3

Augustine's Life: II

'Ο δέσμιος τοῦ Χριστοῦ 'Ιησοῦ ...
EPHESIANS 3.1

Thou mastering me
God! giver of breath and bread;
World's strand, sway of the sea;
Lord of living and dead;
Thou hast bound bones and veins in me, fastened me flesh,
And after it almost unmade, what with dread,
Thy doing: and dost thou touch me afresh?
Over again I feel thy finger and find thee.

GERARD MANLEY HOPKINS

WITH THE death of St Monica, the autobiographical element in the *Confessions* comes to an end and we must draw our material for the life of Augustine from other sources. From now on interest in Augustine the man is merged with, and to a certain degree surpassed by, interest in Augustine the thinker. It is, however, desirable to give a biographical framework, in order to lend coherence to the various aspects of Augustine's thought and teaching which will later be studied in isolation. Such a framework the present chapter attempts to supply.[1]

At the time of his mother's death, Augustine was at Ostia with his little party of friends, preparing to return to Africa. Monica's death seems to have altered his plans and delayed his return for a year.[2] The precise reason for this delay is not clear, but from certain words of Augustine,[3] it

---

[1] Studies of Augustine's life as a Christian are numerous and only a few can be mentioned. Among books of small size, W. J. Sparrow Simpson, *St Augustine's Episcopate*, London, 1944, and H. I. Marrou, *Saint Augustin et l'augustinisme* (E.T., London, 1957), are to be highly recommended. Gustave Bardy, *Saint Augustin*, 7e éd., is an excellent and full biography. Hugh Pope, *St Augustine of Hippo*, London, 1937, is a large and well-documented study, but omits all reference to certain highly important aspects of Augustine's career, e.g. the Pelagian controversy. Finally must be mentioned the large and extremely important book by F. Van der Meer, *Augustinus de Zielzorger*, Utrecht/Brussels, 1948 (ET, London, 1961), best studied in the revised French translation, *Saint Augustin: pasteur d'âmes*, 2 vols., Colmar–Paris, 1959.

[2] See Pope, op. cit., p. 102; Courcelle, *Recherches*, 227.

[3] *C. Litt. Pet.*, III, xxxv, 30: 'Inter multa etiam prorsus ad rem non pertinentia dicit Messiani proconsulis sententia me fuisse percussum, ut ex Africa fugerem, et propter hoc falsum, quod si non ipse confinxit, certe malivolis fingentibus malevole credidit, quam multa alia falsa consequenter non utcumque dicere, sed etiam scribere mira temeritate

seems to have been due to the unsettled conditions brought about by the rebellion of Maximus, the military governor of Britain, who had been raised to the purple by his soldiery in the spring of 385 and had established himself in Gaul after the assassination of the Emperor Gratian on 25 August of the same year.[1] In 387 Maximus' armies drove the young emperor Valentinian from Italy; his fleet controlled the sea, while Gildo, the Count of Africa, was on friendly terms with him.[2] In these circumstances, Augustine may well have deemed it prudent to remain in Italy until the political situation should become more settled, or at least a little clearer. Accordingly, he returned to Rome, where he and his friends took lodgings[3] and where, unable to bear the boasting of the Manichees about their alleged chastity, which they contrasted with the supposedly inferior morality of orthodox Christians, he wrote two books *On the Morals of the Catholic Church and of the Manichees*, in which he vehemently denounced the claims of his former co-religionists.[4] At Rome, too, he wrote the essay *De Quantitate Animae*[5] and began work on the treatise on free will, which was not, however, completed until his return to Africa,[6] after the defeat

---

non timuit, cum ego Mediolanum ante Bautonem consulem venerim eique consuli calendis Ianuariis laudem in tanto conventu conspectuque hominum pro mea tunc rhetorica professione recitaverim et ex illa peregrinatione *iam post Maximi tyranni mortem Africam repetiverim*, Manicheos autem Messianus proconsul audierit post consulatum Bautonis, sicut dies gestorum an eodem Petiliano insertus ostendit. quae si dubitantibus vel contra credentibus probare necesse esset, multos possem claros in saeculos viros testes locupletissimos adhibere totius illius temporis vitae meae.'

[1] On Maximus, see Gibbon, *Decline and Fall*, ed. Bury, iii, 161–7; Otto Seeck, *Gesch. des Untergangs d. antiken Welt*, v (1913), 182–216; Ernst Stein, *Gesch. des spätrömischen Reiches*, i, 316–20; and Pauly-Wissowa, *Real-Encyclopädie*, 14ter Bd. (1930), art. 'Maximus (Usurpator)', cols. 2546–55.

[2] Pacatus, *Panegyricus*, 38.2 (ed. Baehrens, *XII Panegyrici Latini*, 122), but see Pauly-Wissowa, 13ter Halbbd. (1910), art. 'Gildo', cols. 1360–3. Frend, *The Donatist Church*, 208 implies that Gildo changed sides.

[3] Aug., *Ep.* 162, 2 (ad Evodium): '. . . quamquam et illa si relegas, quae tibi iam diu nota sunt vel, nisi fallunt, fuerunt, quia ea fortasse oblitus es, quae te conferente mecum et sermocinante conscripsi, sive de animae quantitate, sive de libero arbitrio.' Cf. *Retract.*, i, 5–8 [5–9].

[4] *Retract.*, i, 6 [7]: 'Iam baptizatus autem cum Romae essem nec tacitus ferre possem Manicheorum iactantiam de falsa et fallaci continentia vel abstinentia, qua se ad inperitos decipiendos veris Christianis, quibus conparandi non sunt, insuper praeferunt, scripsi duos libros, unum de moribus ecclesiae catholicae et alteram de moribus Manicheorum.'

[5] Ibid., i, 7 [8]: 'In eadem urbe scripsi dialogum, in quo de anima multa quaeruntur ac disseruntur, id est unde sit, qualis sit, quanta sit, cur corpori fuerit data, cum ad corpus venerit qualis efficiatur, qualis cum abscesserit.'

[6] Ibid., i, 8 [9]: 'Cum adhuc Romae demoraremur, voluimus disputando quaerere, unde sit malum, et eo modo disputavimus, ut, si possemus, id quod de hac re divinae auctoritati subditi credebamus etiam ad intellegentiam nostram, quantum disserendo opitulante deo agere possemus, ratio considerata et pertractata perduceret. et quoniam constitit inter nos diligenter ratione discussa malum non exortum nisi ex libero voluntatis arbitrio, tres libri, quos eadem disputatio peperit, appellati sunt de libero arbitrio. quorum secundum et tertium in Africa iam Hippone Regio presbyter ordinatus, sicut tunc potui, terminavi.'

and execution of Maximus on 28 August 388.[1] Accordingly, it was at the end of the summer of 388 that Augustine finally reached Africa, which he had left five years before in search of quiet students and academic glory. He disembarked at Carthage, where he encountered his former pupil, Eulogius, now himself a teacher of rhetoric, who had a strange story to tell of an incident which had occurred during Augustine's stay in Italy. Eulogius, in preparing a portion of Cicero to read with his pupils on the following day, was baffled by a difficult passage. The same night, in a dream, he had a vision of Augustine, who explained the difficulty for him, while the subject of the dream was asleep at Milan, quite unaware of the extracurricular instruction which he appeared to be giving.[2] During their stay at Carthage, Augustine and Alypius lodged with a certain Innocent, a former civil servant and a devout Christian,[3] and were much impressed by his miraculous cure from agonizing haemorrhoids at the prayers of a group of clergy, including Saturninus, bishop of Uzalis, and Aurelius, deacon and future bishop of Carthage, who had come to visit him and offer their consolations.[4] The sojourn at Carthage did not last for more than a few days. Augustine was anxious to return home to Thagaste, and the memories which Carthage must have held of his student days, of his former mistress, and of his callous desertion of his mother were all more painful than pleasant. He therefore returned to Thagaste, and formed a religious community there, on the lines which he had envisaged in Italy before Monica's death.[5] He had been much impressed by reading in the Acts of the Apostles of how the Church of Jerusalem had had all things in common, and wished to follow the apostolic example.[6] Two other considerations

---

[1] Otto Seeck, *Regesten der Kaiser und Päpste für Jahre 311 bis 476 N. Chr.*, Stuttgart, 1919, 274 gives the date as 28th August; Courcelle, *Recherches*, 227 *n*[1] as 27th. The Benedictine editors in their *Life* of Augustine, III, i, 1 (reprinted *MPL* xxxii, 157–578) say: 'occisus est [Maximus] anno sequenti [sc. 388] quinto kalendas Augusti aut sexto kalendas septembris'. Sparrow Simpson, *St Augustine's Episcopate*, 4 accepts the July date (and unaccountably places Augustine's second visit to Rome *before* the death of Monica, which he is therefore obliged to transfer to 388). See Pauly-Wissowa, art. 'Maximus (Usurpator)', col. 2554 for various authorities. The majority give the month of August, and there seems no good reason to prefer, as does Courcelle, the date of 27th (given by Socrates, *EH* V, 14) to the 28th.

[2] *De Cura pro Mortuis Gerenda*, xi, 13.

[3] *dCD*, XXII, viii: 'Aput Carthaginem autem quis novit praeter admodum paucissimos salutem, quae facta est Innocentio, ex advocato vicariae praefecturae, ubi nos interfuimus et oculis adspeximus nostris? Venientes enim de transmarinis me et fratrem meum Alypium, nondum quidem clericos, sed iam Deo servientes, ut erat cum tota domo sua religiosissimus, ipse susceperat, et aput eum tunc habitabamus.'

[4] Ibid. See Bardy, *Saint Augustin*, 140–1.

[5] *Conf.*, IX, viii, 17: 'Simul eramus, simul habitaturi placito sancto. Quaerebamus, quisnam locus nos utilius haberet servientes tibi; pariter remeabamus in Africam . . .'

[6] Aug., *Serm.* 355, i, 2; Possidius, *Vita*, 5 (referring to Augustine's monastic foundation after he had become a priest).

somewhat modified his original plan: the example of the Christian communities he had seen at Rome, with their experienced directors, their ascetics, and the emphasis placed upon the religious living by the works of their hands, in contrast to the idleness of the Manichaean Elect;[1] and his own personal ideal of study and the association of scholarly and philosophic minds.[2] Accordingly, he sold the family property at Thagaste[3] and gathered around him his most faithful friends to form a monastic community,[4] including Evodius, the faithful Alypius, and his son Adeodatus. Nebridius, however, remained at Carthage with his mother, and besieged Augustine with letters, urging him to come to Carthage and proposing that some way should be found for them to live together,[5] to which Augustine replied that his commitments to the brethren at Thagaste made a visit to Carthage impossible, and reminded Nebridius of the feelings of his mother.[6] This affectionate correspondence was brought to an abrupt close by the death of Nebridius, and in the *Confessions* Augustine was to pay a moving tribute to the memory of his dead friend, which might well serve as an epitaph:

> Not long after our conversion and regeneration by Thy baptism, he also became a faithful member of the Catholic Church, serving Thee in perfect chastity among his own people in Africa, and bringing his whole household with him to Christianity. Then Thou didst release him from the flesh, and now he lives in Abraham's bosom. Whatever is signified by that term 'bosom', there lives my Nebridius, my sweet friend, Thy son by adoption, O Lord, and not a freedman any longer. There he lives; for what other place could there be for such a soul? There he lives in that abode of which he used to ask me so many questions—poor ignorant one that I was. Now he does not put his ear up to my mouth, but his spiritual mouth to Thy fountain, and drinks wisdom as he desires and as he is able—happy without end. But I do not believe that he is so inebriated by that draught as to forget me; since Thou, O Lord, who art the draught, art mindful of us.[7]

---

[1] *De Moribus*, I, xxxiii, 70. See Courcelle, *Recherches*, 232.

[2] On these three elements, see Paul Monceaux, 'Saint Augustin et saint Antoine: contribution à l'histoire du monachisme', in *Miscellanea Agostiniana*, ii, Rome, 1931, 70–72.

[3] Aug., *Ep.* 126, 7: '. . . nam si in me dilexerunt [Hipponienses], quod audierant paucis agellulis paternis contemptis ad dei liberam servitutem me fuisse conversum . . .'; ibid., 157, iv, 39: 'Ego, qui haec scribo, perfectionem, de qua dominus locutus est, quando ait diviti adulescenti: *Vade, vende omnia quae habes, et da pauperibus, et habebis thesaurum in caelo et veni, sequere me,* vehementer adamavi et non meis viribus sed gratia ipsius adiuvante sic feci. neque enim, quia dives non fui, ideo minus mihi inputabitur; nam neque ipsi apostoli, qui priores hoc fecerunt, divites fuerunt.'

[4] Possidius, *Vita*, 3: 'Ac placuit ei percepta gratia cum aliis civibus et amicis suis Deo pariter servientibus ad Africam et propriam domum agrosque remeare. Ad quos veniens, et in quibus constitutus ferme triennio et a se iam alienatis, cum his qui eidem adhaerebant Deo vivebat, ieiuniis, orationibus, bonis operibus in lege Domini meditans die ac nocte.' [5] Nebridius, *apud* Aug., *Ep.* 5.

[6] Aug., *Ep.* 10, 1. [7] *Conf.*, IX, iii, 6. Tr. Outler, p. 181.

The little community of Thagaste, though inspired by the ideals of monasticism, was not a monastery in the strict sense of the word, but was partly monastic and partly a society for study—one might almost say a religious college.[1] The dominating influence was unquestionably Augustine's. He was the eldest and the most distinguished and, once established in the quiet life of the society, he experienced a wonderful literary flowering, which amply confirmed the promise of the writings of Cassiciacum, Milan and Rome. He completed the first part of the treatise *De Musica*, which he had begun at Milan and which he had originally intended to write in twelve books, six on metre and six on harmony, but of which he only completed the section on metre, being unwilling to devote his energies to what was, essentially, secular composition.[2] At about the same time, he wrote the dialogue *The Master*, recording a discussion between himself and his son Adeodatus, on the relation between words and reality, which leads to the conclusion that there is only one teacher for mankind: *One is your teacher, even Christ*.[3] The form of the work is that of a Platonic dialogue similar to those composed at Cassiciacum, but it was certainly composed in Africa.[4] But where did it take place? Augustine was at pains, in the *Confessions*, to emphasize that Adeodatus' part in the conversation was a genuine one and not merely ascribed to him by the author: 'There is a book of mine, entitled *De Magistro*. It is a dialogue between Adeodatus and me, and Thou knowest that all things there put into the mouth of my interlocutor are his, though he was then only in his sixteenth year. Many other gifts even more wonderful I found in him. His talent was a source of awe to me.'[5] There is pathos in this declaration, for it was during the three years spent at Thagaste following their return to Africa that Adeodatus died,[6] and it is not unduly fanciful to see in the *De Magistro* a memorial to

[1] Monceaux, art. cit., p. 73; Bardy, op. cit., p. 145.

[2] *Retract.*, i, 5 [6]; i, 10 [11]. Cf. Aug., *Ep.* 101, 3.

[3] *De Magistro*, xiv, 46 [Matt. 23.10]; *Retract.*, i, 11 [12]. Trans. by John H. S. Burleigh, *Augustine: Earlier Writings* (The Library of Christian Classics, vol. vi), London, 1953, 64–101.

[4] *Retract.*, i, 11 [12]. Cf. i, 9 [10]: 'Iam vero in Africa constitutus scripsi duos libros de Genesi contra Manicheos . . . [10 (11)]: Deinde . . . sex libros de musica scripsi . . . [11 (12)]: Per idem tempus scripsi librum, cuius est titulus de magistro.'

[5] *Conf.*, IX, vi, 14. Tr. Outler, pp. 186–7.

[6] F. Van der Meer, *Saint Augustin: pasteur d'âmes*, i, 28 says that Adeodatus was eighteen at the time of his death, i.e. about 390; Marrou, *Saint Augustin et l'augustinisme*, 21 gives the date as 389, i.e. the date of the *De Magistro*. Bardy, op. cit., p. 149 remarks very rightly: 'Adéodat en effet a quitté ce monde, assez peu de temps après l'installation à Thagaste: le temps et les circonstances de sa mort nous sont inconnus', and suggests, very tentatively, that the dialogue may have taken place in Italy and the book have been composed after Adeodatus' death: 'C'eût été pour [Augustin] une douceur de revivre ainsi par la pensée avec ce fils trop vite retourné à Dieu qui lui avait demandé ce sacrifice afin de le posséder plus exclusivement à son service.' The suggestion is both attractive and reasonable.

the brilliant and much-loved son, who had been all too quickly taken from this world. Perhaps, then, the conversation took place in Italy, at Cassiciacum or Milan, but was not put into writing until after the death of Adeodatus, when it would have helped to relieve the pain of bereavement by reminding Augustine of the joy that he had known in his son's society.

Augustine's campaign against the Manichees, begun at Rome, was continued on his return to Africa. He wrote two books *On Genesis against the Manichees*, the first of many works of scriptural exegesis which were to come from his pen, in which he met the objections which the Manichees brought against the Scriptures by the use of allegorical interpretation, such as he learned from Ambrose of Milan—though he took care to add that if anyone could give the words of Genesis a literal interpretation consonant with Catholic faith, he must not merely be tolerated but applauded.[1] A more important treatise was that *Of True Religion*, dedicated to his friend and former patron, Romanianus. The *De Vera Religione* was completed about 390 and sent to Romanianus with a brief covering letter.[2] In this remarkable work, Christian Platonism in the best sense of the term, Augustine contended that Christ had fulfilled what Plato had commanded and achieved what Plato failed to do:

> After all the Christian blood shed, after all the burnings and crucifixions of the martyrs, fertilized by these things, churches have sprung up as far afield as among barbarian nations. That many thousands of youths and maidens disdain marriage and live in continence surprises no one; Plato, after having done so, feared the perverse opinion of his time to such a degree, that he is reported to have made sacrifice to nature, to blot out that past disdain as if it were a fault.[3] Views are accepted which it was once monstrous to maintain, even as it is monstrous now to dispute them. All over the inhabited world the Christian rites are entrusted to men who are willing to make professions and undertake the obligations required. Every day the precepts of Christianity are read in the churches and expounded by the priests. Those who try to fulfil them beat their breasts in contrition. Multitudes enter upon this way from every race, forsaking the riches and honours of this present world, desirous of dedicating their whole life to the one most high God. Islands once deserted and many lands formerly left in solitude are filled with monks.

[1] *Retract.*, i, 9 [10].
[2] Aug., *Ep.* 15; *Retract.*, i, 12 [13]. Augustine had already dedicated to Romanianus the *Contra Academicos*, the first of his writings as a Christian.
[3] *De Vera Rel.*, iii, 5: 'Si tot iuvenum et virginum milia contemnentium nuptias casteque viventium iam nemo miratur: quod cum fecisset Plato, usque adeo perversam temporum suorum timuit opinionem, ut perhibeatur sacrificasse naturae, ut tamquam peccatum illud aboleretur.' Professor Burleigh translates: 'That thousands of young men and maidens contemn marriage and live in chastity causes no one surprise. Plato might have suggested this, but he so dreaded the perverse opinion of his times that he is said to have given in to nature and declared continence to be no sin.'

In cities and towns, settlements[1] and villages, country places and private estates, there is openly preached and practised such a renunciation of earthly things and conversion to the one true God that daily throughout the entire world with almost one voice the human race makes response: *Lift up your hearts to the Lord*. Why, then, do we still admiringly yearn for the darkness of yesterday, and look for divine oracles in the entrails of dead cattle? Why, when it comes to disputation, are we so eager to mouth the name of Plato rather than to have the truth in our hearts. . . . If Plato and the rest of them, in whose names men glory, were to come to life again and find the churches full and the temples empty, and that the human race was being called away from desire for temporal and transient goods to spiritual and intelligible goods and to the hope of eternal life, and was actually giving its attention to these things, they would perhaps say (if they were the men they are said to have been): That is what we did not dare to preach to the people. We preferred to yield to popular custom rather than to bring the people over to our way of thinking and living.[2]

So, says Augustine, 'if these men could live their lives again today, they would see by whose authority measures are best taken for man's salvation and, with the change of a few words and sentiments, they would become Christians, as many Platonists of recent times have done'.[3] And they would become Christians, not as members of any heretical sect, but in the Catholic Church, strongly and widely spread throughout the world.[4] Augustine here proceeds to give an exposition of the Catholic faith,[5] indicating the lines upon which he was to build his later theology, and even speaking of two races of men—the impious, who bear the image of the earthly man from the beginning to the end of the world, and the righteous who, from Adam to John the Baptist, lead the life of the earthly man under a certain form of righteousness until the coming of Christ, by whose grace the Old Man is changed into the New, a change which will be finally completed at the Day of Judgement[6]—a division of humanity which would be finally elaborated in one of the most famous of his writings, *The City of God*.

Augustine's personality, reputation and literary activity combined to

---

[1] *Castella*, which Professor Burleigh renders 'castles'; but Augustine has in mind the settlements, generally fortified, of the non-Latin-speaking population. See Frend, *The Donatist Church*, 32, 49, 51, 52: 'In Mauretania Sitifensis the majority of the native *castella*, whose growth was so favoured by the third-century Emperors, were unchallenged Donatist bishoprics, and Donatist inscriptions have been found on these sites', 55, 73, 92 *n*[7]. The use of the word *castellum* to describe a fortified settlement is not unlike the development of the English *burgh* (borough) or the French *bourg*. An admirable description of a *castellum* will be found in André Berthier, *Tiddis: Antique Castellum Tidditanorum*, Algiers, 1951.
[2] *De Vera Rel.*, iii, 5–iv, 6. Tr. by Burleigh, pp. 228–9, slightly modified.
[3] Ibid., iv, 7. Burleigh, p. 229.
[4] Ibid., v, 9–vi, 10.   [5] Ibid., xi, 21–xxiii, 44.   [6] Ibid., xxvi, 48–xxvii, 50.

make him famous in North Africa, even in these early days of his Christian career. He was continually approached for advice on the widest
possible range of subjects. After he had become a bishop, he published a
collection of eighty-three questions which had been submitted to him for
an opinion from the earliest days of his return to Africa onwards, and his
answers.[1] In these circumstances, it was clear that he was exposed to the
danger which confronted every layman of talent in the fourth century:
that of forcible consecration to the episcopate. It was a matter of convention to affect extreme reluctance. The Apostle might commend the saying:
If a man desire the office of a bishop, he desireth a good work, but Christian
humility and a sense of the awful responsibility of the priesthood, which
finds expression in St John Chrysostom's treatise *De Sacerdotio*, forbade
any sincere Christian to submit to ordination except under protest. In
Augustine's case, there is no doubt that his desire to avoid ordination was
perfectly genuine. He had found his vocation in the religious life. He
wished to be a monk, not a minister. Three years at Thagaste had taught
him much about the cloister; he felt the need to organize his community in
a more regular fashion, in a new locality with an established rule.[2] But that
was all; and in order to avoid being consecrated against his will, he carefully avoided churches which he knew, at any time, to be without a
bishop.[3]

In the year 391, however, he had occasion to visit Hippo Regius, a
flourishing coastal city of considerable local importance though of no
great consequence outside Africa.[4] He went there in the hope of persuad-
ing a friend to embrace the religious life.[5] This friend was a member of the
agentes in rebus, the secret police, and had declared that if he could meet
Augustine personally and receive his counsels, he would probably be
moved to abandon the world and enter a monastery. The possibility of
enlisting a soul for God's service brought Augustine to Hippo as soon as
he heard of the declaration; but once arrived, he discovered that the would-
be monk's ardour had cooled, so that after a number of interviews, he was
still unwilling to renounce the world, though he kept promising to carry

---

[1] *De Diversis Quaestionibus LXXXIII (Retract.*, i, 25 [26]).
[2] This seems to be the point of Augustine's remark to his congregation at Hippo,
Serm. 355, i, 2: 'Ego, quem Deo propitio videtis episcopum vestrum, iuvenis veni ad
istam civitatem, ut multi vestrum noverunt. Quaerebam ubi constituerem monasterium,
et viverem cum fratribus meis.'
[3] Ibid.: 'Cavebam hoc, et agebam quantum poteram, ut in loco humili salvarer, ne in
alto periclitarer.'
[4] On Hippo, see Erwan Marec, *Hippone: antique Hippo Regius*, 2e éd., Algiers, 1954;
Van der Meer, op. cit., i, 47-67.
[5] Aug., *Serm.* 355, i, 2: 'Veni ad istam civitatem propter videndum amicum, quem
putabam me lucrari posse Deo, ut nobiscum esset in monasterio.'

out his intention.[1] During his enforced stay, Augustine had occasion to
attend divine service in the great church of Hippo. He went there without
any anxiety, for Hippo had a bishop, the venerable Valerius, and the
Nicene canons forbade any multiplication of bishops in a single see. What
Augustine did not know was that Valerius had for some time been
anxious to secure a presbyter to assist him in his duties. The bishop was
old. Moreover, he was a Greek, and found the task of preaching to a congregation predominantly Latin- or Punic-speaking a heavy burden.
Accordingly, in his sermon that day he spoke to the people about the
desirability of ordaining a presbyter for the city.[2] The congregation, well
aware of Augustine's reputation, began to demand that he should fill the
vacancy, and promptly dragged him before the bishop for ordination,
despite his tears and protests. His reluctance was misunderstood by some
of those present, who supposed that it proceeded from chagrin at not
being chosen to be a bishop, and they tried to console him by observing
that, although he was certainly worthy of a bishopric, the office of a presbyter came near to that of the episcopate in dignity.[3] At all events, they
had their way, and Augustine was ordained priest of Hippo, bringing with
him, as he was afterwards to remark, only the clothes he stood up in.[4]

Two immediate problems confronted the newly ordained priest. The
first was to secure an opportunity for study, in order to be able to discharge the duties of the office to which he had so unexpectedly been called
with some degree of success. He therefore wrote a formal letter to Valerius,
asking for some delay before he entered upon his responsibilities:

> First and foremost [he wrote], I beg your wise holiness to consider that
> there is nothing in this life, and especially in our own day, more easy and
> pleasant and acceptable to men than the office of a bishop or priest or
> deacon, if the duties be discharged in a mechanical or sycophantic way,
> but nothing more worthless and deplorable and meet for chastisement
> in the sight of God; and, on the other hand, that there is nothing in this
> life, and especially in our own day, more difficult, toilsome and hazar-

---

[1] Possidius, *Vita*, 3: 'Ac se ille de die in diem facturum pollicebatur, nec tamen in eius
tunc hoc implevit praesentia.'   [2] Ibid. 4.
[3] Ibid.: 'Nonnullis quidem lacrimas eius, ut nobis ipse rettulit, tunc superbe inter-
pretantibus et tamquam eum consolantibus et dicentibus quia et locus presbyterii, licet
ipse maiore dignus esset, propinquaret tamen episcopatui.' St Jerome, who as a presbyter
was very sensible of the dignity of the priesthood, and as a scholar was familiar with early
Church history, held somewhat the same opinion; see his *Ep.* 69, 3: 'In utraque epistula
[sc. I Tim. 3.1; Titus 1.5] sive episcopi sive presbyteri—quanquam apud veteres iidem
episcopi et presbyteri fuerint, quia illud nomen dignitatis est, hoc aetatis—iubentur
monogami in clerum adligi.' *CSEL* liv, 682. *Ep.* 146, 1, 2: 'Si auctoritas quaeritur, orbis
maior est Urbe . . . presbyter et episcopus, aliud aetatis, aliud dignitatis est nomen.'
CSEL lvi, 310, 311.
[4] Aug., *Serm.* 355, i, 2: 'Non attuli aliquid, non veni ad hanc Ecclesiam, nisi cum iis
indumentis quibus illo tempore vestiebar.'

dous, than the office of a bishop or priest or deacon, but nothing more blessed in the sight of God if our service be in accordance with our Captain's orders. But how that is to be done I learned neither in my boyhood nor in my youth, and just as I had begun to learn, I was compelled by reason of my sins to assume the sacred place at the helm, although I did not know how to hold an oar.

But I imagine that it was the Lord's intention to chastise me because I was bold enough to rebuke many sailors for their faults, as though I were a wiser and a better man, before experience had taught me the nature of their work. So, on being sent into their midst, I then began to realize how presumptuous were my rebukes, although even before that time I had concluded that this occupation was fraught with great hazards. That was the cause of those tears which some of the brethren noticed me shedding when I was newly ordained; they said all that they could to console me, but, although their intentions were good, their words had no bearing whatever on my trouble, as they did not know the reasons for my grief. But experience has revealed the hazards far, far more fully than even anticipation; it is not that I have observed some new breakers or storms unknown to me by previous observation or report or reading or meditation, but that I completely miscalculated my ability and strength to avoid them or endure them and reckoned it to be of some worth. But the Lord mocked me, and by actual experience sought to show me just what I am.[1]

Augustine went on to beg Valerius to grant him a little leisure to devote himself to the study of Holy Scripture, for which he had never previously had adequate time, and ended his letter with a moving appeal to Valerius 'in the name of the goodness and severity of Christ' to let him have his way.[2] Valerius was touched, and gave Augustine leave of absence as he desired. At the beginning of Lent 391 the new priest delivered his first addresses to the candidates for baptism, being himself, as he remarked, as much a beginner as they.[3]

The other problem facing Augustine at his ordination was how to come to terms with his sense of a monastic vocation. Fortunately bishop Valerius presented him with a garden close to the cathedral, in which he might build a monastery,[4] and here he established a new community. He was

---

[1] Aug., *Ep.* 21, 1–2. Tr. by J. H. Baxter, *St Augustine: Select Letters*, Loeb ed., 1930, 33, 35.   [2] Ibid., 6.
[3] Aug., *Serm.* 216, i, 1: 'Rudimenta ministerii nostri et vestri conceptus quo fidei concipitis utero generari coelesti gratia, adiuvanda sunt ore: ut et noster vos sermo salubriter alloquatur, et nos vester conceptus utiliter consoletur . . .'
[4] Aug., *Serm.* 355, i, 2: 'Et quia hoc disponebam, in monasterio esse cum fratribus, cognito instituto et voluntate mea, beatae memoriae senex Valerius dedit mihi hortum illum, in quo nunc est monasterium'; Possidius, *Vita*, 5: 'Factusque presbyter monasterium intra ecclesiam mox instituit et cum Dei servis vivere coepit secundum modum et regulam sub sanctis apostolis constitutam: maxime ut nemo quicquam proprium in illa societate haberet, sed eis essent omnia communia, et distribueretur unicuique sicut opus erat, quod iam ipse prior fecerat, dum de transmarinis ad sua remeasset.' For the archaeological evidence for Augustine's foundation, see Van der Meer, op. cit., i, 54.

joined by his friends from Thagaste, including Alypius, Evodius and Severus, while new recruits subsequently came forward: Possidius, the future bishop of Calama and Augustine's biographer; Profuturus, afterwards bishop of Cirta; Urban, the future bishop of Sicca; and Peregrinus, who was to preside over the church of Thenae.[1] It is possible that a written rule was provided, though we have no proof of this.[2] The little band of friends who for nearly three years had followed a common way of life at Thagaste was transformed into a regular religious community, and the period of Augustine's life which had begun at Cassiciacum was over.

Augustine entered upon his duties as priest of Hippo at the beginning of Lent 391. In Valerius he had an admirable bishop, whose high regard for his presbyter's brilliant qualities was wholly free from envy. He had long desired to have a priest who could preach to the people in fluent Latin, and now that he had secured Augustine, he encouraged him to do so. This provoked unfavourable comment in some quarters—it was not the custom in Africa for bishops to allow presbyters to preach before them[3]—but Valerius was a Greek, familiar with Oriental practice, where such restriction played no part. Furthermore, he was a generous man, who appreciated what a treasure the African Church had found and was determined that Augustine's qualities should be given every encouragement.[4] Other bishops began to follow Valerius' example,[5] among them Aurelius of Carthage, the same Aurelius whom Augustine had encountered on his return to Africa in 388. Aurelius, who was destined to play an important part in the struggle against the Donatists, was an admirer of Augustine, and the latter did not hesitate, in a letter written in 392, congratulating the new bishop of Carthage on his election, to add suggestions for the reform of abuses in the African Church, notably in the matter of the banquets held at the tombs of

---

[1] See Bardy, op. cit., p. 160. Brief biographical sketches are given by Pope, op. cit.' pp. 113–32.   [2] See Appendix B: 'Augustine as a monastic legislator'.

[3] St Jerome condemns this practice as due to envy or arrogance; see *Ep.* 52, 7: 'Pessimae consuetudinis est in quibusdam ecclesiis tacere presbyteros et praesentibus episcopis non loqui, quasi aut invideant aut non dignentur audire.' *CSEL* liv, 428.

[4] Possidius, *Vita*, 5: 'Sanctus vero Valerius ordinator eius, ut erat vir pius et Deum timens, exultabat et Deo gratias agebat, suas exauditas a Domino fuisse preces, quas se frequentissime fudisse narrabat, ut sibi divinitus homo concederetur talis, qui posset verbo Dei et doctrina salubri ecclesiam Domini aedificare, cui rei se homo natura Graecus minusque Latina lingua et litteris instructus minus utilem pervidebat. Et idem presbytero potestatem dedit se coram in ecclesia evangelium praedicandi ac frequentissime tractandi, contra usum quidem et consuetudinem Africanarum ecclesiarum: unde etiam eum nonnulli episcopi detrahebant. Sed ille vir venerabilis ac providus, in orientalibus ecclesiis id ex more fieri sciens et certus, et utilitati ecclesiae consulens, obtrectantium non curabat linguas, dummodo factitaretur a presbytero quod a se episcopo impleri minime posse cernebat.'

[5] Ibid.: 'Et postea currente et volante huiusmodi fama, bono praecedente exemplo, accepta ab episcopis potestate, presbyteri nonnulli coram episcopis populis tractare coeperunt [verbum Dei].'

the departed, which were apt to become the occasion for disorder and
drunkenness.[1] Some hint of the esteem in which Augustine was held by
his flock is found in this letter. He would like, he said, to come to Carthage
to talk the matter over with Aurelius, but was unable to do so; the people
would not wish him to be absent for so long.[2]

In the following year (393), the strength of Augustine's influence in
Africa received public recognition at the African council which assembled
at Hippo on 8 October, under the presidency of Aurelius. Here it was
resolved that bishops and clergy were to be forbidden to provide food in
churches, except in cases of necessity, and that they were, as far as possible,
to discourage the laity from so doing.[3] Augustine's words had borne fruit.
An even more impressive testimonial was however paid to his intellectual
stature by the council by an invitation to preach in the presence of the
assembled bishops, before whom he delivered a sermon *On Faith and
the Creed*, which he subsequently published at the request of some of the
audience.[4] In view of the fact that Augustine was a priest of less than three
years' standing and of the African tradition against priests preaching in the
presence of a bishop, no more generous tribute could have been paid to
his qualities by the African episcopate than this command to address an
important provincial council.[5]

Despite the demands made upon his time and energy now that he was a
presbyter, Augustine did not allow his pen to be idle. He completed the
work which he had begun at Rome, *On Free Will*. In this essay, he sought
to demonstrate that evil had no origin other than the freely exercised choice
of the will,[6] an argument aimed at the Manichaean doctrine that evil has a
real existence, independent of good. Another anti-Manichaean tract was
the book *On the Usefulness of Belief*, addressed to a friend, Honoratus,
whom Augustine had himself persuaded to become a Manichee,[7] and
whom he now wished to lead back from error to Catholic truth.[8] About the

---

[1] Aug., *Ep.* 22. See Van der Meer, op. cit., ii, 353–7.
[2] Ibid., ii, 9: 'absentiam enim meam tantum longe Hipponienses vehementer nimisque
formidant neque ullo modo mihi sic volunt credere ut et ego vobis.'
[3] 'Ut nulli episcopi vel clerici in ecclesia conviventur, nisi forte transeuntes hospi-
tiorum necessitate illic reficiantur. Populi autem ab huiusmodi conviviis, quantum fieri
potest, prohibeantur.' Mansi, iii, 923; Hefele-Leclercq, II, i, 88.
[4] *Retract.*, i, 16 [17]. Tr. Burleigh, op. cit., pp. 349–69.
[5] The Maximianist schism was at that time raging in the Donatist Church (see below,
pp. 247–9), and only four months earlier, on 24 June 393, the dissident Donatist bishops
had met at Cabarsussi and deposed Primianus, the Donatist bishop of Carthage. No
doubt the Catholic bishops assembled at Hippo were anxious to take advantage of internal dissensions in the ranks of their rivals, and several of the canons which they passed
appear to be aimed at the Donatists. See G. G. Willis, *Saint Augustine and the Donatist
Controversy*, London, 1950, 30–31.
[6] *Retract.*, i, 8 [9]. Tr. Burleigh, op. cit., pp. 113–217.
[7] *De Util. Cred.*, i, 2. Tr. Burleigh, op. cit., pp. 291–323.   [8] *Retract.*, i, 13 [14].

same time, he produced a book against the Manichaean belief that there were two souls in every human being, one good and the other evil, and that wrongdoing was not the responsibility of the individual, but the action of the evil soul.[1] Besides these works, Augustine published the minutes of a debate with Fortunatus the Manichee, held on two successive days in August 392 at the baths of Sossius, which resulted in the ruin of Fortunatus' reputation and his departure from the city to hide his humiliation;[2] began work on a literal commentary on Genesis, which he never completed;[3] and wrote an essay *Against Adimantus*, a Manichaean theologian who had written a book in which he opposed seemingly contradictory passages of the Old and New Testaments to demonstrate their incompatibility.[4]

At this period of his life, Augustine's efforts as a controversialist were directed against the Manichees rather than against the Donatists, but already he was preparing for the second great series of controversial writings. Soon after the Council of Hippo—probably at the beginning of 394—he wrote the *Psalm against the Party of Donatus*, an account of the origin and progress of the schism, written in a rough verse form and directed at the simplest and most humble believers, so that they might be provided with an answer to Donatist propaganda.[5] He also wrote a book *Against the Epistle of Donatus*, now lost.[6] If to these writings we add a commentary on the Epistle to the Galatians;[7] two books of homilies on the Sermon on the Mount[8] (which were, however, probably not completed until after his consecration);[9] two treatises on the Epistle to the Romans;[10] a work *On Lying*[11] and another *On Continence*,[12] together with a number of long letters (including one to St Jerome giving Augustine's views on scriptural translation, which was destined to have portentous, and wholly unexpected, consequences),[13] it will be seen that the literary flowering of the layman of Thagaste was more than maintained by the priest of Hippo.

By 395 Augustine's influence was already so great at Hippo that he was able to bring to an end the ceremony called the *laetitia*—'joy'—celebrated

---

[1] *Retract.*, i, 14 [15]: 'Post hunc librum scripsi adhuc presbyter contra Manicheos de duabus animabus, quarum dicunt unam partem dei esse, alteram de gente tenebrarum, quam non condiderit deus et quae sit deo coaeterna, et has ambas animas, unam bonam, alteram malam, in homine uno esse delirant.'
[2] Ibid., i, 15 [16]; *C. Fortun. Manich. Disput.*, Praef., 1–2; Possidius, *Vita*, 6.
[3] *Retract.*, i, 17 [18].   [4] Ibid., i, 21 [22].   [5] Ibid., i, 19 [20].
[6] Ibid., i, 20 [21].   [7] Ibid., i, 23 [24].   [8] Ibid., i, 18 [19].
[9] See Adolf Holl, *Augustins Bergpredigtexegese*, Vienna, 1960, 11 n[9].
[10] *Expositio quarundam propositionum ex Ep. ad Romanos* (*Retract.*, i, 22 [23]); *Epistolae ad Romanos inchoata expositio* (*Retract.*, i, 24 [25]).
[11] *Retract.*, i, 26 [27].   [12] Aug., *Ep.* 231, 7.
[13] Aug., *Ep.* 28 (included among Jerome's letters as *Ep.* 56).

on the feast of St Leontius on the fourth of May. This time-honoured celebration was the most open and flagrant manifestation of the banquets at the tombs, about which Augustine had written to Aurelius in 392 and which Ambrose had forbidden at Milan several years before. On the feast of St Leontius, Catholic and Donatist alike gave themselves up to wild excesses of gluttony and drunkenness. The Circumcellions, the physical force group of Donatism, were particularly notorious for their ritual drunkenness and frenzied dancing at the tombs of the martyrs,[1] but Catholics were only too ready to rival them, and Augustine was determined to bring the practice to an end. Valerius agreed with him, and he had the support of his friend Alypius, who had just been elected bishop of Thagaste.

A few days before the festival, Valerius reminded the people that the Council of Hippo of 393 had forbidden drinking and feasting in churches and forbade them to do so. The announcement was not well received; many persons resented the attempt to end a traditional and congenial celebration. With this unrest in mind, Augustine preached a sermon on Wednesday, 2 May, taking for his text the Dominical injunction: *Give not that which is holy to the dogs, neither cast your pearls before swine* (Matt. 7.6), and used these words to remind his hearers how shameful it was to commit in church outrages which they would not tolerate in their own homes. Contrary to Augustine's apprehensions, the sermon was well received, but the congregation was small in number.[2] The following day, which was the Ascension, the church was crowded, and Augustine made good use of the opportunity by taking for his theme the cleansing of the Temple and the expulsion of the money-changers. If, he asked, our Lord did not tolerate a legal traffic in animals necessary for the sacrifices then permitted, would He not expel with yet greater indignation and vehemence drunken revels which would be condemned in any place? Which more resembled a den of thieves: a place where necessary things are sold, or one where men drink to excess?[3] Augustine reminded his hearers that in the Jewish Temple, where the Body and Blood of Christ were not offered, there were no banquets and still less drunken orgies. Only once in their history had the Jews allowed themselves to become drunken with the excuse of a religious celebration, and that was when they had fallen into idolatry and were worshipping a golden calf of their own making.[4] He quoted St Paul: *Have ye not houses to eat and to drink in? or despise ye the church of God and shame*

---

[1] See Frend, *The Donatist Church*, 174–5 *n*[1].

[2] Aug., *Ep.* 29, 3: 'Sed haec quamvis grate accepta fuerint, tamen quia pauci convenerant, non erat satisfactum tanto negotio.'

[3] Ibid., 3.   [4] Ibid., 4.

them that have not ?[1] and himself read the passage from Galatians concerning the works of the flesh[2] to remind his hearers of the category of sins in which the Apostle places drunkenness.[3]

Augustine then handed back the book to the Reader[4] and led the congregation in prayer, before he embarked upon his final peroration. He held up before the eyes of his hearers the spectacle of Christ suffering for their sins, wounded and bloody. He begged them to have pity upon themselves, upon their priest, and upon their venerable pastor, Valerius, and warned them of the divine punishment which would fall upon those who failed to repent.[5] The people began to weep, and the preacher added his tears to theirs. When Augustine concluded his sermon, the victory seemed definitely won.

The affair was not, however, ended. Once removed from the spell of Augustine's oratory, spirits revived. The presbyter preached well, no doubt; but it was a heavy price for a good sermon to forgo a popular entertainment. So, on the following morning, St Leontius' Day, Augustine learned that there was a party of malcontents who were determined to hold their revelry in despite of the prohibition of their bishop and the eloquence of their priest. The news plunged him into deep dejection, for the attitude of some of the crowd was distinctly hostile.[6] He decided, if the worst came to the worst, to preach on the text from Ezekiel 33.9: *Nevertheless, if thou warn the wicked of his way to turn from it, and he turn not from his way ; he shall die in his iniquity, but thou hast delivered thy soul.* Then, if the people still refused to listen, he would shake the dust from his garments and leave them to their sin. Fortunately, things did not come to so desperate a pitch. A deputation of the discontented came to see him. He received them in a friendly fashion, and managed to convince them. He abandoned the projected sermon on the text from Ezekiel, and spoke instead on the origins of the *laetitia*, which he regarded as having sprung from concessions made in the early Church to pagan converts who found it difficult to abandon their traditional practices. Such concessions could not endure indefinitely, and

[1] I Cor. 11.22.
[2] Gal. 5.19–21.
[3] Aug., *Ep.* 29, 6.
[4] Readers were young boys with clear voices whose duty was to read the Scriptures in church. Julian the Apostate during his youth, when it was expedient to pass for a Christian, became a Reader in the church of Nicomedia (Socrates, *HE* III, 1). A Novel of Justinian (123, 54) forbade anyone to be ordained a Reader before the age of eighteen; but it is clear that Readers were frequently of a much younger age (the Council of Carthage of 397 decreed that Readers, when they came to years of puberty, must either marry or take vows of celibacy, while Victor Vitensis, *Historia Persecutionis*, III, 34, speaks of *lectores infantuli*).
[5] Aug., *Ep.* 29, 7.
[6] Ibid., 8.

in most churches overseas they had been abolished. In the case of the basilica of St Peter at Rome, where similar festivities took place and to which the defenders of the old order appealed, Augustine pointed out that the practice had many times been forbidden; but the church was a long way from the bishop's dwelling and the population of Rome very mixed, so that it was extremely difficult to enforce the ban. In any case, those who wished to honour St Peter would better do so by giving heed to his declaration that our past life should suffice us to have walked in drunkenness (I Peter 4.3) than by appealing to a practice which went on in his church in flagrant contradiction of his ideal.[1] In conclusion, Augustine begged the congregation to return later in the afternoon to celebrate the day with prayers and psalms as was fitting. The response to this appeal would indicate those whose guide was their reason and those whose guide was their belly. His answer was a crowded church. Valerius desired Augustine to preach again, which he was by no means anxious to do, but only to reach the end of an uncomfortable day. However, he obeyed; and the sound of revelry from the Donatist basilica near by[2] gave inspiration to his sermon and enabled him to contrast the dignified and spiritual worship of the Catholics with the dissipation of men whose god, as St Paul had said, was their belly (Phil. 3.19). To conclude, Augustine quoted the Apostle: *Meats for the belly and the belly for meats; but God shall destroy both it and them* (I Cor. 6.13), and urged his hearers to seek only the food which does not perish. The afternoon service continued until Vespers, which were duly sung, and Valerius and Augustine then left the church. A number of the congregation nevertheless remained, to sing psalms until the night came down. The day was over, to Augustine's great relief.[3]

The successful ending of the *laetitia* may well have decided Valerius to secure Augustine's consecration as coadjutor bishop of Hippo. The old man was approaching the end of his life. It was desirable that he should make provision for a suitable successor, and it was clear that delay was dangerous, if he wished to secure his nominee. Of the monastic community of Hippo, Alypius had already departed in 394 to become bishop of Thagaste, while Profuturus had followed him by being called to Cirta in the following year.[4] Augustine himself had been the object of an attempt at kidnapping, with a view to forcible consecration elsewhere, and it had been necessary to hide him, so that he should not fall into the hands of his

---

[1] Aug., *Ep.* 29, 10.
[2] For the possible location of the Donatist church at Hippo, see Van der Meer, op. cit., i, 54–55, who appeals to this incident to confirm the identification.
[3] Aug., *Ep.* 29, 11.
[4] Bardy, op. cit., p. 187.

admirers.[1] In the circumstances, Valerius wrote to Aurelius of Carthage, stating that he desired to see Augustine consecrated as his coadjutor, with the right of succession reserved to him. Aurelius fully approved of this proposal. Augustine, however, had scruples. He had never heard of co-adjutor bishops, and would not consent to be consecrated until several cases had been cited to him, both in Africa and overseas.[2] Neither he nor Valerius was aware at that time of the eighth canon of the Council of Nicaea, which declared that there may not be two bishops in one city,[3] and in after years Augustine was filled with remorse for what he deemed to be a lapse on his part, and managed to obtain an order that the canons of the councils should be read to bishops and presbyters before they were ordained.[4]

A more serious obstacle to Augustine's consecration than his own scruples was the attitude of Megalius, bishop of Calama, senior among the Numidian bishops by consecration and therefore accorded by their custom an honorary primacy. Megalius had formed an unfavourable opinion of Augustine and at first refused to have anything to do with his consecra-tion. A story had gone abroad that Augustine had given a love philtre to a married woman with the consent of her husband, and that under its in-fluence she had been led to commit adultery. This story Megalius re-counted in a letter to his episcopal colleagues with far-reaching results, for the Donatists were able to obtain copies, which they afterwards used in an attempt to discredit Augustine's reputation.[5] Megalius' accusation was in-vestigated by an episcopal commission, and it was established that the alleged love philtre was nothing more than a *eulogia*—a loaf of bread which

[1] Possidius, *Vita*, 8: 'Ille vero beatus senex Valerius caeteris ex hoc amplius exultans et Deo gratias agens de concesso sibi speciali beneficio, metuere coepit, ut est humanus animus, ne ab alia ecclesia sacerdote privata ad episcopatum quaereretur et sibi aufer-retur: nam ad id provenisset, nisi hoc idem episcopus cognito ad locum secretum eum transire curasset atque occultatum a quaerentibus minime inveniri fecisset.'

[2] Aug., *Epp.* 31, 4; 213, 4; Possidius, *Vita*, 8.

[3] Augustine was, in fact, unduly scrupulous, since the canon in question was concerned with the problem of Novatianist bishops who returned to Catholic unity, and how they were to be treated, by giving the Catholic bishop authority to employ them as presbyters in his city or as *chorepiskopoi*—rural bishops—in the country beyond the city. The prob-lem here was that the Novatianist bishops claimed to be the lawful bishops of the cities over which their Catholic rivals presided. (See the story told by Socrates, *HE*, vi, 22, about Sisinnius, the Novatianist bishop of Constantinople, and his encounter with St John Chrysostom. 'This city cannot have two bishops,' said Chrysostom. 'Neither does it,' replied Sisinnius.) The Fathers at Nicaea were not concerned with coadjutor bishops but with a problem similar to that which confronted the Catholics at the Conference of Carthage in 411, when it was proposed that the Catholic bishop of each see should take the Donatist as co-partner (*Gesta Coll. Carth.*, i, 16. MPL xi, 1267; Aug., *Ep.* 128, 3).

[4] Possidius, *Vita*, 8.

[5] *C. Litt. Pet.*, III, xvi, 19; *C. Cresconium*, III, lxxx, 92: '*Sed epistulam*, inquis, *principis vestri, qua nescio quid de te scripsit, cum te ordinari nollet, tenent non pauci nostrorum.*' Cf. *Gesta Coll. Carth.*, iii, 247. MPL xi, 1406.

had been blessed but not consecrated[1]—and that the whole affair was a misunderstanding transformed into a slander.[2] At this, Megalius humbly and unreservedly withdrew his accusation, asked for pardon, and presided at Augustine's consecration,[3] which took place probably about the middle of 395.[4] For some months he assisted Valerius, who died in 396; and then Augustine, at the age of forty-two, became bishop of Hippo, over which he was to rule for more than thirty years.

Augustine's succession to the see of Hippo affords a convenient point at which to devote some attention to him as a bishop of the Catholic Church. The eminent position which his genius has secured for him in the history of Christian thought tends to obscure the fact that his first concern lay always with the Christian community of Hippo over which he ruled. The writings which constitute his legacy to posterity and upon which his fame rests were in the nature of a spare-time occupation—occasional writings composed in the scanty leisure which episcopal routine afforded. For Augustine, a bishop's first and principal duty was the service of God and of his fellow Christians, 'Thy servants, my brothers; Thy sons, my masters', as he calls them,[5] and chief among these were the members of the church of Hippo, over whom he had been called to preside against his own inclination. It was the consciousness of his responsibilities to his people which caused Augustine, in a letter to St Paulinus of Nola, written soon after his consecration, to refer to the 'heavy burden of the episcopate' (*episcopatus sarcina*) which it had pleased Valerius to lay upon him.[6]

Of the nature of that burden it is necessary to say something. In a general fashion, it was the burden of duties and responsibilities which bishops continue to bear at the present time; but there were certain features which tend to differentiate a fourth-century bishop's office from that of his successors at the present day. The principal difference may be stated briefly as follows: in the age of the Fathers, the bishop habitually discharged duties which are today regarded as being those of the parish priest, while the presbyter was essentially one of the clergy gathered round the bishop and not an independent agent. Today, for most of his flock, a bishop is a rare and rather awful figure, who occasionally visits a parish

---

[1] The practice has survived in the rites of the Orthodox Church in the *antidoron*, which is distributed to non-communicants at the end of the Divine Liturgy.

[2] The serious nature of the accusation was accentuated by the fact that Augustine had been a Manichee, and the Manichees were believed to offer a peculiar Eucharist with an obscene Host.

[3] *C. Litt. Pet.*, III, xvi, 19; *C. Cresconium*, IV, lxiv, 79.

[4] Germain Morin in *Revue Bénédictine*, xl (1928), 366 proposes January 396, but see S. M. Zarb in *Angelicum*, 1933, 261–85. Casamassa, in *Enciclopedia italiana*, i, 915 places Augustine's consecration at the end of 396.   [5] *Conf.*, IX, xiii, 37; X, iv, 6.

[6] Aug., *Ep.* 31, 4. See Van der Meer, op. cit., i, 44–45.

church, but who normally remains aloof in a splendid isolation. The fourth-century bishop, on the other hand, while not inferior in dignity, was a much more familiar figure in the city over which he presided. One reason for this is that, in the early Church, the proportion of bishops was higher than it is today. Even quite small towns had their bishops, and in Africa in particular the episcopate was remarkably numerous.[1] At the famous Conference of Carthage of 411, where the Donatist schism was finally condemned, the first roll-call revealed that two hundred and sixty-six Catholic bishops faced two hundred and seventy-nine Donatists,[2] and feverish searching subsequently increased the number of the Catholics to two hundred and eighty-six. Seventy years later, under the domination of the Arian Vandals when Catholic Christianity was a persecuted sect in Africa, it was still possible to muster some four hundred bishops to assemble at Carthage at the command of King Hunneric in 484.[3] The large number of bishops naturally tended to make them discharge personally many duties which are today regarded as pertaining to a parish priest, and Augustine, as bishop of Hippo, would himself baptize and offer the Eucharist, duly assisted by his presbyters. Again, as a general rule, he would preach—we have already seen that the idea of a presbyter preaching in the presence of a bishop was unknown in Africa when Augustine was ordained and that Valerius was criticized for introducing it. But besides these sacerdotal functions there were others of an administrative nature. The bishop was, naturally, responsible for the finances of his church—a distraction which Augustine met by arranging for the more capable clergy to act as stewards in rotation, and to present him with the accounts at the end of the year.[4] Again, there were demands upon the bishop's time as a judge. He might find himself summoned to an episcopal commission held in his province to investigate a charge brought against a bishop or some other cleric, and to punish or absolve as it might deem fit.[5] In his own diocese, it was his regular duty to hear and decide the cases of his parishioners.[6] Episcopal jurisdiction steadily increased in the Christian Roman

---

[1] On the other hand, some dioceses were large, and included many villages in their territory, each served by its own parish priest. For these rural clergy, see Van der Meer, op. cit., i, 351–4. They were sometimes men of very independent character and, in relation to them and to their flocks, the fourth-century bishop more nearly resembled his modern successor than he did vis-à-vis the clergy and people of his cathedral town.

[2] *Gesta Coll. Carth.*, i, 213–14. *MPL* xi, 1350.

[3] See Ch. A. Julien, *Histoire de l'Afrique du nord*, 2e éd., Paris, 1956, i, 248. The *Notitia Provinciarum et Civitatum Africae* given by Victor Vitensis in his *Historia Persecutionis* (*CSEL* vii, 117–34) includes the names of many presbyters.

[4] Possidius, *Vita*, 24.   [5] Ibid., 21.

[6] See F. Martroye, 'Les plaidoiries devant la jurisdiction épiscopale au IVe siècle', in *Bulletin de la Société nationale des Antiquaires de France*, 1918, 136–7; Van der Meer, op. cit., i, 389–96.

Empire. Its origins can be discerned in the apostolic injunction that Christians should not go to law with Christians before a court of unbelievers
(I Cor. 6.1–6)—a text to which Augustine staunchly adhered[1] and in the
Roman legal device of *recepti arbitri*, by which litigants voluntarily made
contracts, one between themselves and another with an arbitrator, so that
cases might be settled out of court, according to principles independent of,
though not in conflict with, the formal law of Rome.[2] On the basis of these
two factors, the Christian court descending from apostolic times and the
legal device of *recepti arbitri*, the bishop's court secured an official place in
the Roman legal system. By an edict of 355, bishops were exempted from
accusation in public courts,[3] and their position in the official hierarchy was
duly enhanced. (The privilege was later extended to all clerics, with
notorious consequences in the later Middle Ages.) The status which the
episcopate thus acquired, combined with speed and lack of expense,
caused the episcopal courts to grow in popularity. In theory, episcopal
courts were supposed to confine themselves to religious matters, but
repeated imperial edicts commanding that criminal cases should be heard
in secular courts suggest that even here the judgement of a bishop was preferred to that of a professional lawyer.[4] Augustine, certainly, was a much-
sought-after arbitrator, and adjudicated carefully, in the spirit of the wit
who remarked that he would rather judge between strangers than between
his friends, since a just decision would gain one of the strangers, but
would lose one of the friends.[5] Whether or not Augustine lost friends we
do not know; but his services were so much in demand that he would, on
occasion, go without a meal for the whole day, in his anxiety to settle the
cases which had been brought before him.[6] At the end of his life in 426, he
was to appeal to his congregation to submit their problems, initially at
least, to the priest Heraclius, and so afford their bishop a little leisure for
scripture study.[7]

Besides his own responsibilities as a judge, the bishop was expected to
intervene, where necessary, with the secular authority to secure some
amelioration of the rigour of the law in the interest of Christian charity. A

[1] Possidius, *Vita*, 19.
[2] On *receptri arbitri* see W. K. Boyd, *The Ecclesiastical Edicts of the Theodosian Code*,
New York, 1905, 89–90.
[3] *Cod. Theod.*, XVI, 2, 12. See Boyd, op. cit., p. 93.
[4] *Cod. Theod.*, XVI, 2, 23; XVI, 11, 1; II, 35, 41; *Const. Sirm.*, 7. Boyd, op. cit.,
pp. 87–102.
[5] Possidius, *Vita*, 19.
[6] Ibid.
[7] Aug., *Ep.* 213, 6. For Augustine as a judge, see Mary E. Keenan, *The Life and Times
of St Augustine as revealed in his Letters* (Catholic University of America Patristic
Studies Vol. 45), Washington, D.C., 1935, 97–98.

less reputable convention was that he should use his influence with imperial officials in the interest of his dearest friends—a convention regrettably common at all times and in all places. This Augustine refused to do;[1] but he was willing to appeal in a deserving case, and usually contrived to obtain both his request and the good opinion of the official whom he petitioned. One of them, Macedonius, the *vicarius* of Africa, was so impressed by Augustine that he sent him an enthusiastic letter, which Possidius felt deserved quotation in his official biography:

> I am amazingly impressed by the wisdom I find, first in the books you have published, and now in this letter you have not thought it too much trouble to send to me, interceding for people in trouble. The books show a penetration, a learning and a piety to which nothing can be added; and the letter is written with such delicate restraint that, if I did not do what you tell me, I should have to put the blame on myself and not on the case. For you, my Lord—'venerable' indeed—and most esteemed father in God, do not, like most in your position, insist on extracting everything the petitioner wants, but confine yourself to what you think can rightly be asked of a judge with so many responsibilities, and recommend it with that accommodating tact that is the best way of settling difficulties amongst men of good will. For this reason I have given immediate effect to your recommendations, as, indeed, I had given you reason to expect.[2]

Macedonius' testimony is the more interesting because, when Augustine had first written, the Roman official had remarked: 'You say that it is the function of your episcopate to intercede on behalf of criminals, and that unless you obtain your request you will be offended, as if you had failed to receive your due. I very much doubt whether this claim can be justified from religion'[3]—only to receive a lengthy epistle,[4] almost a small treatise, on the duties of the Christian magistrate, which inspired the tribute recorded by Possidius.[5]

An even more remarkable testimony to the popular belief in the intercessory rôle of the bishop is afforded by an incident at the city of Calama, where Augustine's friend Possidius was bishop, in 408. Augustine, we know, would hear the cases of anyone who approached him, whether Christian or not, in his court;[6] but the appeal made to him on behalf of the

---

[1] Possidius, *Vita*, 20.
[2] Macedonius, *apud* Aug., *Ep.* 154, 1; Possidius, *Vita*, 20. Tr. by Frederick R. Hoare, *The Western Fathers*, London, 1954, 219.
[3] Aug., *Ep.* 152, 2.
[4] *Ep.* 153, written in AD 414.
[5] See Keenan, op. cit., pp. 98–101; Sparrow-Simpson, *The Letters of St Augustine*, London, 1919, 114–18.
[6] Possidius, *Vita*, 19: 'Interpellatus ergo a Christianis vel a cuiuscumque sectae hominibus causas audiebat diligenter ac pie.'

pagan population of Calama is both amazing in its audacity and remarkable in its conception of the character of a Christian bishop. On 1 June
408[1] the pagans of Calama staged a religious procession in defiance of the
law,[2] which developed into a noisy demonstration, accompanied by stone-
throwing, before the door of the Catholic church. A week later, after
Possidius had made a protest to the municipal authorities, another and
more serious riot broke out which, although temporarily checked by a
providential hail-storm, ended with an attempt to burn the church. At the
same time the deacons' lodgings, where church property was kept, were
sacked, and a monk found in the street was killed. Possidius was forced to
hide himself, and from his hiding-place could hear his would-be murderers
shouting: 'Where's the bishop? If we don't get him we'll have wasted our
time!' During the riot the decurions of the city, supposedly responsible
for keeping the peace, did nothing. When however the citizens came to
their senses, it was clear that the consequences of their behaviour were
likely to be extremely serious. Accordingly, when Augustine came to
Calama a little later to visit Possidius, a deputation waited upon him,
begging him to intercede on their behalf. One of them, a respectable pagan
called Nectarius who had taken no part in the riot, wrote to Augustine
urging him to see that there should be no punishment or judicial inquiry
—which would be accompanied by torture—in which the innocent should
suffer with the guilty. Nectarius admitted that the offence should be
punished with great severity by the law, 'but it is not for a bishop', he
argued, 'to seek anything but the welfare of men, or to deal with legal
affairs except for the betterment of the parties, and to obtain pardon from
Omnipotent God for the offences of others'.[3] Nectarius had a case to
argue, and it is not impossible that a faint suggestion of irony underlay
this statement of a bishop's duties; but it is significant that the pagan
client saw nothing incongruous in appealing to the Christian bishop in
such circumstances.

Charitable enterprises made further demands upon the bishop's time.
Public relief—except for the corn doles of the two capitals, Rome and
Constantinople, which were an exception—was unknown in the Roman

---

[1] Van der Meer, op. cit., i, p. 85, says after the execution of Stilicho; but Stilicho was
not beheaded until 22 August. See Seeck, *Regesten*, 314.

[2] Aug., *Ep.* 91, 8. The law in question was *Cod. Theod.*, XVI, 10, 19, dated 15 November 407, which was not promulgated at Carthage until June 408. See Van der Meer, op.
cit., i, p. 440 *n*[63].

[3] *Apud* Aug., *Ep.* 90: 'quod quidem si iuris publici rigore metiamur, debet plecti
severiore censura. sed episcopum fas non est nisi salutem hominibus impertire et pro
statu meliore causas adesse et apud omnipotentem deum veniam aliorum mereri
delictis.'

Empire, and it was here, outstandingly, that the philanthropy of the Christian Church affected contemporary life.[1] Augustine, says Possidius,

> never forgot his companions in poverty; and what he spent on them came from the same fund as supported him and those who lived with him, namely the income from the Church's property, and the offerings of the faithful.[2]

Like St Ambrose, he was prepared to melt down church plate for the redemption of captives, a proceeding which gave offence to some persons in the fourth century as it did to Lord Westbury in the nineteenth.[3] Augustine's views about church property were, indeed, very simple: it belonged to the poor, to the *plebs Christi*, and the bishop held it as a trustee.[4] The pagan Nectarius bore witness to the philanthropic activities of the Christian bishop; but Augustine was often handicapped by lack of funds[5] and wrote bitterly about the reluctance of his people to give to charitable causes.[6] Nevertheless, he refused to accept legacies, even though they would have been of value for the purposes of alms-giving, if by leaving them the testator disinherited the rightful heirs.[7]

Alms-giving was not, however, the only form in which the bishop's philanthropy found expression. Distress of any kind merited his attention, and we find Augustine writing a stiff letter to a landowner named Romulus, whose agent, Ponticanus, had collected the rents from the tenants of his master's estates and then absconded with the money, leaving the angry landlord attempting to wring a second payment from his miserable tenantry;[8] or engaged in correspondence with his fellow bishop, Benenatus of Tugutiana, about a young girl, not yet of marriageable years, whom a certain pagan, Rusticus, wished to marry to his son, and who herself announced that she wanted to be a nun—a proposal which Augustine was disposed to regard as the product of adolescent fancy, rather than any

---

[1] Keenan, op. cit., p. 147.   [2] Possidius, *Vita*, 23. Tr. Hoare, op. cit., p. 221.
[3] Possidius, *Vita*, 24. Westbury's comment, in a speech on 29 June 1869, was: 'What might be the opinion respecting St. Ambrose in the days when he lived I do not know; but I must say, with the modern ideas of property, that if St. Ambrose had been brought before me in equity I should not have hesitated to find him guilty of a breach of trust, and to make him refund the property.' (*Dict. Nat. Biog.*, iv, 430, art. 'Richard Bethell'.)
[4] Aug., *Ep*. 185, ix, 35: '. . . si autem privatim, quae nobis sufficiant, possidemus, non sunt illa nostra sed pauperum, quorum procurationem quodam modo gerimus, non proprietatem nobis usurpatione damnabili vindicamus.'
[5] Ibid., 126, 8: 'Restat ergo, ut iste pecuniae turpissimus appetitus ex obliquo in clericos et maxime in episcopum dirigatur. nos enim rebus ecclesiae dominari existimamur, nos opibus frui. postremo quicquid de istis nos accepimus, nos vel adhuc possidemus vel, ut placuit, erogavimus: nihil inde populo extra clericatum vel extra monasterium constituto nisi paucissimis indigentibus largiti sumus.'
[6] Ibid., 36, 7.   [7] Possidius, *Vita*, 24.
[8] Aug., *Ep*. 247. See Keenan, op. cit., p. 149; Van der Meer, op. cit., i, 398-9; Bardy, op. cit., p. 208.

genuine vocation.[1] The situation was complicated by the fact that Benenatus was favourable to the match, while the would-be bridegroom showed no disposition to become a Catholic. Augustine was determined to safeguard the interests, both spiritual and material, of the girl who was under the guardianship of the Church, and declined to allow any action to be taken, until she should have reached a suitable age to make her own decisions, and until her mother, who could not at that time be traced, should have been consulted.[2]

Hand in hand with this intervention in particular cases went the routine visitation of those who needed help or guidance. Here, Augustine adhered to apostolic precept, and visited only widows and the fatherless in their afflictions[3]—a rule probably designed to avoid any accusation of that cultivation of the rich and legacy-hunting which Jerome bitterly denounced in the clergy of his day. A similar consideration led Augustine to refuse invitations to feasts within his own diocese;[4] but if he were asked to visit the sick, to pray for them and lay his hand upon them, he came without delay.[5] He was, however, reluctant to visit female monasteries, except in cases of urgent necessity.[6]

If to these multifarious duties we add those of a specifically sacerdotal character: the administration of the sacraments and the preaching of the word, it will be apparent that any conscientious bishop of the fourth or fifth century was likely to be perpetually busy, and probably overworked. In the case of Augustine, however, we must add to his episcopal duties an astonishing literary output, which makes him not merely one of the most prolific of the Fathers, but also one of the most voluminous writers of all time. How he contrived to write so much is something of a miracle; Possidius says that he did it by living laborious days, and by working far into the night.[7] It is, of course, a truism that it is precisely the busy people who contrive to find time for extra work; but Augustine, although constitutionally sound, was delicate and liable to fall ill,[8] so that, in the circumstances, his achievement becomes the more amazing.

---

[1] *Ep.* 254: '. . . quia in his annis est, ut et, quod se dicit velle esse sanctimonialem, iocus sit potius garrientis quam sponsio profitentis.'
[2] For the incident, see Aug., *Epp.* 252–5. Keenan, op. cit., pp. 149–51; Bardy, op. cit., pp. 289–90.
[3] Jac. 1.27.   [4] Possidius, *Vita*, 27.   [5] Cf. Jac. 5.14, 15.
[6] Possidius, *Vita*, 27: 'In visitationibus vero modum tenebat ab apostolo definitum, ut non nisi pupillos et viduas in tribulationibus constitutas visitaret. Et si forte ab aegrotantibus ob hoc peteretur, ut pro eis in praesenti Dominum rogaret eisque manum imponeret, sine mora pergebat. Feminarum autem monasteria non nisi urgentibus necessitatibus visitabat.'
[7] Possidius, *Vita*, 24: 'Et id agebat in die laborans et in nocte lucubrans.'
[8] See B. Legewie, 'Die körperliche Konstitution und die Krankheiten Augustins', in *Miscellanea Agostiniana*, ii, 1–21; Van der Meer, op. cit., i, pp. 363–5.

Possidius gives a picture of Augustine's way of life which can be supplemented from his own writings. Augustine's elevation to the episcopate did not alter his desire to be a monk, but it was clear that a bishop's duties and responsibilities made life in the monastery by the great church at Hippo impossible. Other considerations apart, a bishop was expected to show hospitality, and the comings and goings of many guests were unsuited to a community where silence and meditation were essential.[1] Accordingly, Augustine left the monastery and resided in the bishop's house. He insisted, however, that his diocesan clergy who lived with him should lead a monastic life and become, in effect, canons regular. Every cleric who entered the bishop's household was required to renounce his possessions in favour of the church of Hippo, or another church, or his own family; to share with the bishop food and shelter; and to lead a life of chastity and poverty. At the beginning of 425, in his seventy-first year and about five years before his death, Augustine discovered that one of his priests, Januarius, had not, in fact, renounced all his property, but had retained it, nominally in trust for his daughter, and proposed to bequeath it to the church of Hippo, thereby disinheriting the girl. A violent explosion ensued. In two public sermons, Augustine denounced Januarius, declined to receive the legacy, and required all those who wished to continue to live with him to reaffirm their pledge of poverty. As for the others, he had in the past, he said, been accustomed to degrade any who refused to continue in the community life; now however he would relax his rule: those who were unable to support the renunciation of their goods might continue as clergy, but could find themselves some dwelling other than the clergy house of Hippo. Having extracted from all his clergy the promise of obedience, the old bishop continued:

> If any one has lived hypocritically and is found having property, I shall not permit him to make a testament, but I shall strike him from the list of my clergy. He can appeal against me to a thousand councils, he can sail where he likes to denounce me [Augustine is thinking of appeals to the imperial court and to the Roman curia], he can live where he likes; but so far as God gives me strength, he shall never be a cleric where I am bishop. You have heard, the clergy have heard. But I hope in our God and in His mercy, that as they have received my words with joy, they will observe them in pure faith.[2]

[1] Aug., *Serm.* 355, i, 2: 'Perveni ad episcopatum: vidi necesse habere episcopum exhibere humanitatem assiduam quibusque venientibus sive transeuntibus: quod si non fecisset episcopus, inhumanus diceretur. Si autem ista consuetudo in monasterio permissa esset, indecens esset. Et ideo volui habere in ista domo episcopii mecum monasterium clericorum.'

[2] Aug., *Serm.* 356, 14.

Augustine's own personal life was frugal in the extreme. His dress was modest and unostentatious, resembling that of his clergy, but, at the same time, he avoided any parade of poverty.[1] He commonly wore a *byrrhus* or coat, of a type worn also by laymen, and he protested against the action of well-meaning persons who sent him presents of costly clothing, which they deemed suitable for his episcopal station. 'Such a gift perhaps becomes the bishop, but it does not become Augustine, who is a poor man and born of poor parents.'[2] However he could, with exquisite tact and kindliness, make an exception to his rule of wearing the same dress as his clergy,[3] as was shown in the case of the pious Sapida, a consecrated virgin who sent him a tunic made with her own hands, originally destined for her brother Timothy, a deacon of Carthage, who had died before receiving his sister's present. Sapida presented the garment to Augustine, declaring that it would be a great comfort for her if he would accept it. The bishop had not the heart to refuse such a gift, but in the letter of thanks, in which he informed Sapida that he was already wearing the tunic,[4] he reminded her that she must seek for more solid consolations, remembering that her brother, for whom she had made an earthly garment, was now clothed with the incorruptible robe of immortality.[5]

Augustine's table was modest and frugal. For himself and his clergy, there were vegetables and pot-herbs, but meat was available for guests and for invalids, and wine was always served.[6] The reason for this abstemious diet is given in the tenth book of the *Confessions*, written soon after Augustine became a bishop, and of great value as evidence of his views and spiritual condition at that time. Possidius judged the passage of sufficient importance to quote in his biography, so it may well be quoted here also:

[1] Possidius, *Vita*, 22.
[2] Aug., *Serm.* 356, 13: 'Nolo talia offerat Sanctitas vestra, quibus ego solus quasi decentius utar; offerat mihi, verbi gratia, byrrhum pretiosum; forte decet episcopum, quamvis non deceat Augustinum, id est, hominem pauperem, de pauperibus natum. Modo dicturi sunt homines quia inveni pretiosas vestes, quas non potuissem habere vel in domo patris mei, vel in illa saeculari professione mea.'
[3] Possidius, *Vita*, 25: 'Cum ipso semper clerici una etiam domo ac mensa sumptibusque communibus alebantur et vestiebantur.'
[4] Aug., *Ep.* 263, 1: 'Missam abs te tunicam accepi et, quando haec ad te scripsi, ea me vestire iam coeperam.'
[5] Ibid., 4: 'Si enim, quia vestior, quoniam ille non potuit, ea veste, quam fratri texueras, te aliquid consolatur, quanto debes amplius et certius consolari, quia, cui fuerat praeparata, incorruptibili indumento nullo egens corruptione atque inmortalitate vestitur.'
[6] Possidius, *Vita*, 22: 'Mensa usus est frugali et parca, quae quidem inter olera et legumina etiam carnes aliquando propter hospites vel quosque infirmiores, semper autem vinum habebat.' Augustine's insistence upon wine, apart from natural good taste—he is the patron of theologians and brewers—would be an emphatic repudiation of charges that he was still a Manichee at heart, for the Manichees abhorred wine.

E

It is not that uncleanness of meat that I fear, but the uncleanness of an incontinent appetite. I know that permission was granted to Noah to eat every kind of flesh that was good for food; that Elias was fed with flesh; that John, blessed with a wonderful abstinence, was not polluted by the living creatures (that is, the locusts) on which he fed. And I also know that Esau was deceived by his hungering after lentils and that David blamed himself for desiring water, and that our King was tempted not by flesh but by bread. And, thus, the people in the wilderness truly deserved their reproof, not because they desired meat, but because in their desire for food they murmured against the Lord.[1]

Augustine's abstinence was directed, not by any ascetic disdain of the good things which God has created for the use of man, but by recognition of the danger of uncontrolled enjoyment of these good things, which leads to a neglect of God. 'I hear the voice of my God commanding: *Let not your heart be overcharged with surfeiting and drunkenness.*[2] Drunkenness is far from me. Thou wilt have mercy that it does not come near me. But "surfeiting" (*crapula*) sometimes creeps upon Thy servant. Thou wilt have mercy that it may be put far from me. *For no man can be continent unless Thou give it.*'[3] There is a certain consolation for lesser men in the spectacle of the great bishop, ten years after his conversion, admitting that, on occasion, he finds the pleasures of the table too strong for him.

The furnishings of Augustine's table were simple in the extreme. The only plate, if the term can be used, consisted of silver spoons; but the dishes were of clay, wood, or stone; not—as Possidius hastens to reassure us, jealous for the honour of his hero—because Augustine could not have had these things, but because he was determined to forgo them.[4] In accordance with the traditions of his order, he always showed hospitality, and took a delight in reading and discussion when at table. To guard against the possibility of malicious gossip, he caused a notice to be exhibited which read:

> Let him who takes pleasure in mauling the lives of the absent
> Know his own is not such as to fit him to sit at this table.[5]

---

[1] *Conf.*, X, xxxi, 46. Tr. by Outler, p. 229. Cited by Possidius, *Vita*, 22.

[2] Luc. 21.34.

[3] *Conf.*, X, xxxi, 45. Tr. Outler, p. 228.

[4] Possidius, *Vita*, 22: 'Cochlearibus tantum argenteis utens, ceterum vasa quibus mensae inferebantur cibi vel testea vel lignea vel marmorea fuerunt, non tamen necessitatis inopia, sed proposito voluntatis.'

[5] Ibid.: '. . . et contra pestilentiam humanae consuetudinis in ea [mensa] scriptum ita habebat:

> Quisquis amat dictis absentum rodere vitam
> Hac mensa indignam noverit esse suam.'

Tr. by Hoare, *The Western Fathers*, 221. For the origin of this distich, see Pellegrino, *Vita di s. Agostino*, 220 n[16].

Nor had he any intention of allowing this warning to be a dead letter. On one occasion, when he was entertaining an episcopal party, composed of close friends, the conversation began to infringe the prohibition. Augustine then declared in great wrath that either the notice would have to be expunged or he, the host, would have to retire to his cell and leave the feast.[1] He also attempted to check any tendency to swearing among his clergy by a form of sconcing. A certain statutory number of draughts of wine was permitted to each person dining at the episcopal board, and one of these was forfeited every time a man swore.[2]

Augustine's dealings with women were marked by the greatest possible discretion. His reluctance to visit female religious communities has already been noticed. Nor would he permit any woman to stay at his house, not even his own sister, a widow who presided over a community of nuns, or his brother's daughters, who had also taken religious vows.[3] The society of such relations was not forbidden by the canons of the councils,[4] but Augustine forbade it on the grounds that while no ill conclusions could be drawn from the company of blood relations, such persons would be accompanied by other women and would, in any case, have female visitors, whose presence might give offence and scandal to weaker brethren, and constitute a temptation to the residents of the house.[5] The bishop was careful, for his own part, never to receive a woman except in the presence of members of his clergy, even on matters of a confidential nature.[6] This may seem exaggerated precaution, but it must be remembered that Augustine was an African dealing with Africans in a part of the world where the reticences and conventions of modern society were unknown. In the circumstances, his behaviour was wise and the mark of a man in whom the natural impulses were strong and who was determined to control them in himself and to ensure that they gave no occasion for stumbling in others.[7] Indeed, Augustine's attitude to sexuality, in view of his doctrine of the part played by concupiscence in the transmission of Original Sin, was a remarkably sane one, and very far from the extreme views which have been held by certain other Christian teachers. Like the Apostle, he preferred

[1] Possidius, *Vita*, 22.
[2] Ibid., 25.
[3] Ibid., 26.
[4] Council of Nicaea, can. 3; Council of Carthage, 397 can. 17.
[5] Possidius, *Vita*, 26.
[6] Ibid.: 'Ob hoc ergo dicebat, numquam debere feminas cum servis Dei, etiam castissimis, una manere domo, ne, ut dictum est, aliquod scandalum vel offendiculum tali exemplo poneretur infirmis. Et si forte ab aliquibus feminis ut videretur vel salutaretur rogabatur, numquam sine clericis testibus ad eum intrabant, vel solus cum solis numquam est locutus nec si secretorum aliquid interesset.'
[7] See O'Meara, *The Young Augustine*, 198–9.

that all men should be even as he, and rated the life of dedicated virginity above that of marriage; but he regarded Christian marriage as a noble thing, and deprecated any attempt to disparage it.

A good example of Augustine's view will be found in his letter[1] to Ecdicia, a Christian woman with a Christian husband, and the mother of a son. One day, without consulting her husband, she decided to take a vow of continence and to live with him thereafter as a sister and not as a wife. Such a decision was not uncommon in the early Church, and Augustine specifically approves of it,[2] but it had to be by joint consent—*pari consensu* —so that neither spouse defrauded the other of the marriage debt. This requirement Ecdicia failed to observe; but her husband, a sincere Christian, agreed with her, and for some time the couple lived together in edifying continence. Ecdicia, however, was not satisfied. She assumed the black garb of a widow or a religious, in defiance of her husband's wishes, and proceeded to squander his goods in alms, without any regard for the well-being of her small son. Two foreign monks, of doubtful antecedents, enjoyed her hospitality and, in her husband's absence, she transferred most of his property to them. Exasperated by her behaviour, her husband abandoned her, broke his vow of continence, and committed adultery.

It was in these circumstances that Ecdicia wrote to Augustine, no doubt believing that he would approve of her conduct. If so, she was to be disillusioned. Augustine informed her that she was wrong in the first instance to live with her husband as a sister and not as a wife if he were reluctant to do so, and referred her to St Paul's first Epistle to the Corinthians[3] for information about the duties of the married, which she had apparently either not heard or not understood. She was further told that she was wrong to offend her husband in matters of dress. She had been wrong again to give away his possessions in alms to the two monks without his knowledge or consent. By so doing she had deprived him of an opportunity of sharing in charitable deeds to which, if she had acted differently, she might have persuaded him. With greater consideration, she would have postponed giving her alms to the poor lest she should anger her husband and cause him to recoil from his religion, to the detriment of his immortal soul. Which is better: to give bread to the hungry, or save a soul from the devil? She was further told that, as a married woman, she had no right to say:

[1] Aug., *Ep.* 262.
[2] *De Serm. Dom. in Monte*, I, xiv, 39: 'Beatiora sane coniugia iudicanda sunt, quae sive filiis procreatis, sive etiam ista terrena prole contempta, continentiam inter se pari consensu servare potuerint: quia neque contra illud preceptum fit, quo Dominus dimitti coniugem vetat; non enim dimittit, qui cum ea non carnaliter, sed spiritualiter vivit.'
[3] I Cor. 7.1–17. Aug., *Ep.* 262, 3–4.

I will do what I will with my own, and reminded about St Peter's teaching on the subjection of the wife to the husband.[1] Finally, she was informed that she should have considered her son's welfare. Augustine set a high value on the prerogatives of a mother,[2] but he did not consider that these included the right to give away in charity what would become the property of her son. Ecdicia was reminded of the words of the Apostle: *If any provideth not for his own, and specially his own household, he hath denied the faith, and is worse than an unbeliever*,[3] and Augustine ended his letter by exhorting her to ask her husband's forgiveness and to promise that, if he would adhere to his profession of continence, she would obey him in all matters. In the meantime, it was unnecessary to remind her that her son was under his father's control rather than hers.[4] The lack of sympathy which she received from the ascetic bishop must have been a great disappointment to the enthusiastic votary.

Throughout his long episcopate, in addition to his duties as bishop of Hippo, Augustine worked and wrote for the benefit of the whole Church of Christ. A large proportion of his writing was of a polemical nature, aimed at the enemies of Catholic Christianity. Very roughly speaking, Augustine's career as a Christian writer can be divided into three periods. In the first, he was mainly concerned with attacking and refuting the Manichees. During the second, he was preoccupied with the Donatist schismatics; while in the third, he was concerned with the Pelagians. At the same time, throughout the three periods, he was at work on treatises on biblical, dogmatic and moral theology, among which the great work *On the Trinity* enjoys an undisputed pre-eminence. But all this does not exhaust Augustine's range. His ability as a controversialist found further employment in writing against the Arians;[5] against the Priscillianists;[6] and against the pagans, of which last the best-known example is the famous *City of God*.[7] Hermeneutics was enriched by the four books *On Christian Doctrine*, a study of historical importance for the justification which it supplied for

---

[1] I Peter 3.5–6. *Ep.* 262, 7.

[2] See his view in *Ep.* 254, on the disposal of the young girl who was a ward of the Church: 'Fortassis enim, quae nunc non apparet, apparebit et mater, cuius voluntatem in tradenda filia omnibus, ut arbitror, natura praeponit.' Such a view runs counter to the Roman idea of the *patria potestas*. [3] I Tim. 5.8. *Ep.* 262, 8.

[4] *Ep.* 262, 11: 'filium autem vestrum, quoniam de legitimis eum et honestis nuptiis suscepisti, magis in patris quam in tua esse potestate quis nesciat? et ideo ei negari non potest, ubicumque illum esse cognoverit et iure poposcerit; ac per hoc, ut secundum tuam voluntatem nutriri in dei possit nutriri et erudiri sapientia, necessaria illi est etiam vestra concordia.'

[5] *Contra Sermonem Arianorum Liber* (AD 418); *Collatio cum Maximiano Arianorum Episcopo* and *Contra Maximinum* (428).

[6] *Contra Priscillianistas et Origenistas* (AD 415).

[7] See also Aug., *Ep.* 102 ad Deogratiam (*Sex Quaestiones contra paganos*).

the reading by Christians of pagan literature.[1] The booklet *On Catechising the Uninstructed*, addressed to the Carthaginian deacon Deogratias in 400, is a manual on the technique of imparting the Christian faith to would-be converts; the *Enchiridion*, written for a certain Laurentius in 421, is, as the name implies, a short handbook of Christian doctrine;[2] while the work *On Heresies to Quodvultdeus* is of interest as a translation from the Greek by Augustine, with additions supplied by the translator for the benefit of the clergy of Carthage.[3]

It is convenient to trace the history of Augustine's career as a bishop in terms of his polemical writings. This is not because they are necessarily his best (though some, like the *De Spiritu et Littera*, produced by the Pelagian controversy, are among his finest writings[4] while the *De Trinitate* itself is partly directed against the Arian heresy), but because they are of great importance for establishing certain characteristic features of Augustinian theology, and because they can be related to his practical activities, in a way which his more dispassionate writings cannot be. Augustine's literary campaigns against the Donatists and the Pelagians were accompanied by active participation in African councils and by correspondence with Rome and with the Eastern Churches. His books against the Manichees, the Donatists and the Arians were supplemented by public disputations, taken down by stenographers—a numerous and very efficient profession in the ancient world—and thereafter distributed by Augustine for propaganda purposes. By studying these various controversies in turn, the course of Augustine's life can be followed in a roughly chronological sequence. This is the method adopted by Possidius, Augustine's first biographer, and this is the method which will be followed in the present book.

The earlier part of Augustine's episcopate, up to about AD 405, is dominated by the struggle against the Manichaean heresy, in which he had spent so many years and from which he had recoiled so violently. As a

---

[1] Begun in 397, the work originally only extended to III, xxv, 35. It was completed only in 427, when the remainder of Book III and the whole of Book IV were added. See *Retract.*, ii, 30 [4]: 'Libros de doctrina Christiana cum inperfectos conperissem, perficere malui quam eis sic relictis ad alia retractanda transire. conplevi ergo tertium, qui scriptus fuerat usque ad eum locum, ubi commemoratum est ex evangelio testimonium de muliere, quae *fermentum abscondit in tribus mensuris farinae, donec totum fermentaretur*. addidi etiam novissimum librum et quatuor libris opus illud inplevi.'

[2] *Retract.*, ii, 89 [63]: 'Scripsi etiam librum de fide, spe, caritate, cum ad me, ad quem scriptus est, postulasset, ut aliquod opusculum haberet meum de suis manibus non recessurum: quod genus Graeci *Enchiridion* vocant.'

[3] See Pierre Courcelle, *Les lettres grecques en occident*, 2e éd., Paris, 1948, 192–3; Luguori G. Müller, *The De Haeresibus of St Augustine* (Catholic University of America Patristic Studies Vol. 90), Washington, D.C., 1956, 30–37.

[4] See the comment of William Bright, *Select anti-Pelagian Treatises of St Augustine*, Oxford, 1880, xxi: '. . . a book which, perhaps, next to the *Confessions* tells us most of the thoughts of that "rich, profound and affectionate mind", on the soul's relation to its God.'

newly baptized Christian, during the year passed at Rome after his mother's death, he had produced his work, *On the Morals of the Catholic Church and on the Morals of the Manichees*, in which he had attacked the high claims made by the Manichees for continence. His two works, *On Genesis against the Manichees* and *On Free Will*, begun in Italy but only completed after his return to Africa, continued the assault, as did the books *On True Religion* (389-90) and *On the Usefulness of Belief* (391-2), and the book *On the two Souls* (391-2). While still a priest, Augustine had a public debate against the Manichee, Fortunatus, and so discredited him that he departed from Hippo to hide his shame.[1] This method of public disputation appealed to Augustine; in 404, he held a similar debate, the Manichaean protagonist being, on this occasion, a certain Elect called Felix who, at the close of the debate, agreed to become a Catholic.[2] In the next year, Augustine wrote what is, perhaps, the most important of his anti-Manichaean works, *On the Nature of Good*, one of the most significant in a series which had begun in 396-7 with the publication of the book *Against the Epistle which the Manichees call 'of the Foundation'*, and which continued with the massive thirty-three books *Against Faustus the Manichee* (400)—the same Faustus who had failed so disastrously to settle Augustine's intellectual difficulties seventeen years before.

In his writings against the Manichees, Augustine had a threefold objective. First, to refute Manichaean dualism, by demonstrating that God was the sole author and creator of all that exists, and that all that exists must be, in so far as it is is of divine creation, good. To do so, he drew upon an idea which he had found in the Neo-Platonists, but which he developed in his own way, that Evil had no positive existence, but was merely a privation of Good. Absolute Evil, as the Manichees conceived in their Kingdom of Darkness, is a mere figment of the imagination, for if a thing were to become absolutely evil, it would become, literally, No-thing, and cease to exist. So long as a thing exists, it has some good in it. Evil men, inasmuch as they are men, are good; they are evil, inasmuch as they try to oppose the will of God. Even the devil, as a created being, is good.[3] From

---

[1] Possidius, *Vita*, 6. *Retract.*, i, 15 [16].

[2] *De Actis cum Felice Manichaeo*, II, xxii. Cf. *Retract.*, ii, 34 [8].

[3] Cf. the developed statement of this doctrine in the *Enchiridion, passim*, and esp. iv, 12, 13: 'Naturae igitur omnes, quoniam naturarum prorsus omnium Conditor summe bonus est, bonae sunt; sed quia non sicut earum Conditor summe atque incommutabiliter bonae sunt, ideo in eis et minui bonum et augeri potest. Sed bonum minui malum est; quamvis, quantumcumque minuatur, remaneat aliquid necesse est (si adhuc natura est) unde natura sit. . . . Ac per hoc nullum est quod dicitur malum, si nullum sit bonum. Sed bonum omni malo carens, integrum bonum est; cui vero inest malum, vitiatum vel vitiosum bonum est: nec malum unquam potest esse ullum, ubi bonum est nullum.'

this it follows that the Manichaean hatred of matter and of the body is wholly wrong. Both are God's creations, and therefore good. They become evil only when being desired or employed in a manner which God has forbidden.

Secondly, Augustine had to meet the attacks which the Manichees brought against the Bible, and especially against the books of the Old Testament and to show that the Manichaean habit of only accepting those parts of Scripture which suited them was mistaken and unsatisfactory. Finally, he had to deal with the Manichaean argument that the Catholic Church was hostile to reason, and commanded men to believe, while they themselves argued their case rationally, and constrained no one to belief. We shall see later how Augustine dealt with these objections.

It has been suggested that the year 405 marks a stage in Augustine's career, and that he subsequently showed less interest in Manichaean controversy and devoted himself to attacking the Donatists. Like all generalizations, this is somewhat misleading, for before 405 Augustine had written a number of anti-Donatist treatises, from the *Psalmus contra Partem Donati*, composed while he was still a priest in 394, to the three books *Against the Epistle of Parmenian* in 400 and three more *Against the Letters of Petilian*, written between 401 and 403; but the year 405 marked the intensification of the attempt to suppress Donatism by the Roman imperial authorities, by the promulgation of a series of decrees commanding the schismatics to return to Catholic unity, and under this impulse the Catholic clergy began a parallel intensification of their own campaign to win (or to constrain) conversions. The joint efforts of the Catholic Church and the Roman state culminated in the famous Conference of Carthage of 411, when Donatism was finally condemned and every resource of the secular arm deployed to bring it to an end. It is easy to think of the year 411 as the great triumph of Augustine over the Donatists, and the victorious conclusion of his long-continued efforts to restore them to the Catholic fold; but this judgement needs to be modified in the light of our available evidence, for it is clear that Donatism was by no means annihilated in 411, and as late as 418 Augustine was still debating with Donatist bishops (on that occasion, unsuccessfully) to bring them over to the Catholic side.

In writing against the Donatists, Augustine had to debate questions very different from those which had preoccupied him when the Manichees were concerned. The Donatists, for practical purposes, were orthodox Christians, schismatic but not heretical. It is true that, in the course of the struggle against them, the Catholic bishops invoked the imperial laws against heresy, but this is to be regarded rather as a reprisal measure

against the violence of their fanatical Circumcellions, than as a denunciation of the religious beliefs of the Donatist Church. So far as the creeds
were concerned, the Donatists accepted them as much as the Catholics.
Where they differed was in their conception of the nature of the Church.
Inheriting an African tradition of great antiquity, they held that deadly
sin on the part of the minister invalidated the sacraments administered by
him, and maintained that the sacraments of the African Catholics were
invalid because, in the past, Catholic clergy had been guilty of betraying
their trust, and of handing over the Holy Scriptures to the pagan and per-
secuting Roman government. By this action they had put themselves outside the One True Church of Christ, and their descendants were likewise
excluded, since the sacraments they had received were invalid.

Against this view, Augustine argued that the Donatist conception of the
Church was an erroneous one, and that they confused the Church Militant
upon earth with the Church Triumphant in heaven. As long as the world
endured, the Church will have unworthy members, who will be finally
excluded only at the Last Judgement. In the meantime, it was not for any
man to anticipate this final separation, and anyone who abandoned the
Church because he found its members unworthy, was himself guilty of a
greater sin than theirs—the sin of schism, which is an offence against Charity.

Furthermore, the Donatist attitude to the sacraments was wrong. Their
minds were preoccupied with the man who administered them; if he were
sinful, then the sacraments which he administered were no sacraments, for
his sin had destroyed his sacerdotal character. Augustine, however, argued
that the true administrator of the sacraments is Christ. The priest is only
an agent through whom Christ chooses to work, and the validity of the
sacraments cannot be destroyed by his character, any more than the rays
of the sun become impure through shining through a sewer. Certainly,
such sacraments cannot benefit anyone who receives them unless he is
within the Church—the Donatists eat and drink to their own condemnation; but the sacraments themselves are valid, can be received, if necessary,
by a Catholic to his advantage, and become effective for good once the
schismatic or sinful minister is reconciled to the Church. There is, therefore, no question of repeating them; and the Donatist practice of rebaptizing converts from Catholicism is not merely superfluous, but sinful.
Donatists who make their peace with the Catholic Church are received,
but not rebaptized or reordained.

The struggle with the Donatists was long and bitter. After the Conference of Carthage of 411, they were proscribed and ordered to return to
the unity of the Catholic Church, with all the resources of the Roman state

deployed to coerce them to return. However, despite many conversions, the hard core of Donatism remained untouched and unyielding. In 418, Augustine had a public disputation with Emeritus, the Donatist bishop of Caesarea (the modern Cherchel, in Algeria) which he had visited on behalf of the bishop of Rome. It would have been a great triumph for Augustine if he could have won Emeritus over, but all his eloquence failed, in the face of obstinate silence on the part of the Donatist. Augustine had to leave Caesarea with his hopes unfulfilled, and the only satisfaction which he could draw from his visit was that he managed to persuade the citizens to abandon the *caterva*—'crowd' or 'band'—a yearly battle, with the city divided into two factions, in which lives were regularly lost.[1] No doubt this was some consolation; but the failure of his main objective must have been bitter. Two years later, the two books *Against Gaudentius* constitute Augustine's last publication against Donatism.

Augustine's struggle with the Pelagians is the last of the three great controversies of his life, and death overtook him while he was still engaged upon it. Pelagianism differed from both Manichaeism and Donatism, in that these were religious groups clearly and deliberately outside Catholic communion—the former by its doctrine, the latter by its own volition. The Pelagians, on the other hand, were a group within the Church, whose opinions could be, and were, reconcilable with perfect credal orthodoxy, and who claimed, indeed, to represent genuine Christian tradition. They were also by far the most formidable opponents whom Augustine had to encounter. The Manichees he had easily cut to pieces. The Donatists, although they were made of tougher material and were generally impervious to logic, preferring to deal in personal abuse and innuendo, were not his equals in dialectic. With the Pelagians, however, the case was otherwise. They were astute and forceful controversialists, well able to score debating points and extremely skilful in appealing to what may be called Christian commonsense, in order to maintain their thesis.[2] Augustine, after his first brush with them, spoke of their intellect with respect[3] and, as

---

[1] *De Doctrina Christiana*, IV, xxiv, 53. See Farrer, *Lives of the Fathers*, ii, 485; Bardy, op. cit., p. 218; Van der Meer, op. cit., ii, p. 202.

[2] See, for example, the technique of Caelestius, illustrated in *De Perfectione Iustitiae Hominis*, I, ii, 1: ' "Ante omnia", inquit, "interrogandus est qui negat hominem sine peccato esse posse, quid sit quodcumque peccatum: quod vitari potest an quod vitari non potest. si quod vitari non potest, peccatum non est; si quod vitari potest, potest homo sine peccato esse, quod vitari potest. nulla enim ratio vel iustitia patitur saltem dici peccatum, quod vitari nullo modo potest." '

[3] E.g. *De Nat. et Grat.*, vi, 6: 'Acute quippe videntur haec dici, sed in sapientia verbi, qua evacuatur crux Christi, *non est ista sapientia desursum descendens*. nolo quod sequitur dicere, ne amicis nostris, quorum fortissima et celerrima ingenia non in perversum, sed in directum currere volumus, facere existimemur iniuriam.' Cf. Aug., *Ep.* 186, v, 13; xi, 37.

the struggle progressed, he was given fresh evidence both of their skill in debate, and of their strategy, in appealing from one council to another and in presenting their case in a manner to make it acceptable to devout Christians. Pelagianism, which took its name from the British monk Pelagius, but which was elaborated and promulgated by disciples rather than by Pelagius himself, was a movement which desired to call men to a more perfect observance of the Christian life by appealing to their conscience and their will. The Pelagians saw in the good actions of men an example of co-operation between God and man. Unhappily, they emphasized the human element in such a way as to suggest that man was able to be good and to do good with his own natural forces. As an inevitable consequence, they undervalued the Fall and denied that it injured Adam's descendants. Every man, in their opinion, starts his earthly career with the same powers and the same capacity for good which Adam enjoyed in Paradise before the Fall. Holding such views, they naturally had no doctrine of Original Sin, though they were prepared to accept the tradition of infant baptism, a concession which Augustine was to urge against them, in view of the fact that there is only one baptism for the remission of sins.

Against the Pelagian views Augustine wrote continually from the publication of his three books, *On the Deserts and Remission of Sins*, in 412[1] to his death eighteen years later, when he was engaged on a massive refutation of Julian of Eclanum, the most formidable of the Pelagian apologists.[2] In his anti-Pelagian writing, Augustine placed all his emphasis on the helplessness of man to do any good whatsoever without the Grace of God, and upon the disastrous consequences of Adam's sin for his posterity unless cleansed by baptism. In the heat of controversy his views, never very gentle, hardened into a stern and even terrifying doctrine, which seems at times to be strangely at variance with the emphasis which he places, in other writings, on Charity as the characteristic quality of the Divine nature. However this may be, the legacy which the Pelagian controversy left to western Europe has been one of a most influential and enduring character, and no Christian can fail to feel anything other than gratitude to Augustine for insisting that it is utterly impossible for man to do anything good, without the Grace of Christ. The Augustinian doctrine of Predestination is another matter. Few theologians would today maintain

---

[1] *Retract.*, ii, 59 [33]: 'Venit etiam necessitas, quae me cogeret adversus Pelagianam heresem scribere, contra quam, cum opus erat, non scriptis, sed sermonibus et conlocutionibus agebamus, ut quisque nostrum poterat aut debebat. missis ergo mihi a Carthagine quaestionibus eorum, quas rescribendo dissolverem, scripsi primum tres libros, quorum titerlus est: de peccatorum meritis et remissione.'

[2] See Aug., *Ep.* 224, 2, written between 427 and 428.

it in its full rigour; but it is at least worth remembering that the Pelagian alternative: that man is capable of holiness by his natural endowments and his own efforts, was a disastrous alternative and far more foreign to the spirit of the Gospel.

Other controversies occupied Augustine's attention. Paganism in Africa was a dying cult, but it still had adherents, some of whom were men of intellect and ability,[1] while the rank and file was capable of sudden outbreaks of savage violence, as the ugly incident at Calama in 408 demonstrated.[2] But the days of paganism were numbered. Imperial legislation (supported by Christian violence which could, on occasion, equal that of the pagans, as the murder of Hypatia at Alexandria in 415 tragically demonstrated)[3] decreed the closing of the pagan temples, and the old faith found few martyrs.[4] The weakness of paganism lay in the fact that, although it answered an emotional need and offered the worshipper much that was gracious and moving, it was not a faith for which men would easily die, since it held little hope for the future and inspired little loyalty.[5] From the Christian point of view the menace in paganism lay, not in its theology— it had none—nor in its attractiveness as a rival—Julian the Apostate's attempt to refurbish it and set it up as a serious alternative to Christianity had had little success in his life, and had collapsed ludicrously after his death—but in the fashion in which it influenced society, and conditioned, often unconsciously, the thoughts and actions of the ordinary Christian believer.[6] Not a few Christians believed in keeping a foot in both camps, frequented the theatres and the circus, wore amulets, consulted sooth-sayers, and had a healthy respect for the powers of the demons. For such persons any disaster, whether natural or human, was a trial to faith, and the sack of Rome by Alaric the Goth in 410 was a terrifying portent. The sacred city, the home of the Roman race, which had been preserved in-violate while she worshipped the old gods, had fallen to a barbarian after she had adopted Christianity. The pagans drew the obvious conclusions; the simpler and more superstitious Christians wondered and wavered. To deal with their doubts and fears, Augustine set to work upon a refutation which, begun in 413, was not finally completed until 426, by which time it had extended to twenty-two books. This majestic work was the famous

---

[1] See Van der Meer, op. cit., i, pp. 72–80.   [2] See above, pp. 124–5.
[3] Socrates, *EH* VII, 15 (ed. Bright, Oxford, 1878, 295–6). Socrates deplores the murder, declaring that it brought the greatest opprobrium on St Cyril and on the whole church of Alexandria, and adds that nothing can be more alien to the spirit of Christianity than episodes of this nature. On the episode, see Bury, *History of the later Roman Empire*, i, 217–20.   [4] See Van der Meer, op. cit., i, pp. 80–92.
[5] This was not true of the Mystery cults or of Mithraism.
[6] Van der Meer, op. cit., i, pp. 93–138.

City of God, perhaps the most influential of all Augustine's writings and certainly one of the most famous. Because of its size and the range of questions which it discusses it forms, with the *Confessions*, a valuable introduction to the study of Augustine's thought as a whole.

Towards the end of his life, Augustine found himself increasingly and unpleasantly aware of the problems raised by Arianism. This heresy, first openly maintained by Arius, a fourth-century presbyter of Alexandria, affirmed that God the Son, the Second Person of the Trinity, was a created being, created before time, worthy of divine honours and immeasurably exalted over other creatures but still, in the last resort, created and inferior to God the Father. This doctrine, which has an obvious appeal for simple minds, was condemned by the Council of Nicaea in 325; but it had many influential adherents, and for more than half a century the battle against it raged throughout the Christian east and, to a lesser extent, in the west. The names of St Athanasius, St Basil of Caesarea, St Gregory of Nyssa, St Gregory Nazianzen, St Hilary of Poitiers, and St Ambrose of Milan are eminent among the champions of Christian orthodoxy and the doctrine of Nicaea. The Council of Constantinople of 381 finally condemned Arianism, and the orthodox Roman emperors set about suppressing it in east and west. Unfortunately for the Catholics, there was one element in the social order where Arianism continued to flourish, and that was the army, now largely composed of German barbarian soldiery. The German tribes—Goths, Sueves, Vandals, Alans and the rest—had been converted to Christianity by the labours of Ulfilas, the apostle of the Goths, who had, unhappily, adopted Arianizing views, so that his converts learned Arianism from their missionary, and cherished a bitter hatred of Nicene orthodoxy and especially of the word *homoöusios*—'of the same substance'—which has long been the crucial test in defining Catholic belief. Thus wherever the Goths went, either as soldiers of the Roman Emperor or as invaders, hoping to secure lands and loot for themselves, they carried with them Arianism and, when they were able, made strenuous efforts to convert the local Catholic population to their way of thinking.

During the last years of Augustine's episcopate, the presence of Gothic troops in Africa and the fact that certain Roman officials showed Arianizing tendencies made it inevitable that the bishop of Hippo should be called in to defend Catholic doctrine and to refute error. One case of this nature was the disputation with Count Pascentius, a high-ranking official,[1] disliked for his rigour in exacting the payment of taxes and for his attacks on

---

[1] He was *comes domesticorum*, a commander in one of the corps of imperial household troops (see Bury, op. cit., i, pp. 37–38), belonging to the grade of *spectabilis*.

Nicene Christianity.[1] Augustine was challenged by him to a public debate and accepted; but the encounter proved, in the event, to be a farce. At the very beginning, when Augustine proposed that minutes of the proceedings should be taken by shorthand writers, the Count objected that to have such a record taken would compromise him in the eyes of the law. Accordingly the debate was of a purely informal character and the results unsatisfactory. The Count was no theologian, and the only thing clear in his mind was dislike of the term *homoöusios*. He announced that his ideal of Christian orthodoxy was Auxentius, the former Arian bishop of Milan and the rival and enemy of St Ambrose. Alypius of Thagaste, who was present, then put the question: was Auxentius a true Arian, or was he not rather a Eunomian—a follower of Eunomius of Cyzicus, the founder of Anomoianism, the extreme left wing of Arianism, which held that the Son was wholly unlike (*anomoios*) the Father? Pascentius had never heard of such theological refinements but cheerfully declared that he anathematized Arius and Eunomius equally, and called upon the Catholics, for their part, to anathematize *homoöusios*. When it was explained to him that *homoöusios* was not a person but a technical term in theology, he demanded that the Catholics should show him the word in the Bible, in which event he would forthwith enter into communion with them.[2] Augustine replied that the proper course was rather to decide what the term implied, and then consider whether it could be found, in that sense, in the Scriptures. He further asked if the term which Pascentius had himself employed, that *the Father is unbegotten*, could be found in Scripture, in which case he asked Pascentius to show him the passage. At this, one of the Count's Arian supporters asked: did Augustine then believe that the Father had been begotten? and receiving the obvious reply, proclaimed with the pride of a triumphant logician that if the Father were not begotten, He must be unbegotten. Augustine agreed, and pointed out that here was an example of a reason being given to justify the use of a term not found in Scripture. A similar case could be made out for the employment of the term *homoöusios*.[3]

[1] Possidius, *Vita*, 17: 'Praeterea cum quodam etiam Pascentio comite domus regiae Arriano qui per auctoritatem suae personae fisci vehementissimus exactor, fidem catholicam atrociter ac iugiter oppugnabat et quamplurimos sacerdotes Dei simpliciore fide viventes dicacitate et potestate exagitabat et perturbabat, interpositis honoratis et nobilibus viris, apud Carthaginem ab illo provocatus coram contulit.'
[2] Aug., *Ep*. 238, i, 4: '. . . tum continuo flagitasti, ut et nos anathematizaremus ὁμοούσιον, quasi quisquam homo esset, qui hoc vocaretur, sicut Arrius et Eunomius. deinde vehementer exigebas, ut hoc verbum tibi in scripturis ostenderemus, et statim nobis communicares.'
[3] Ibid., i, 5: 'cui ego: "Vides", inquam, "posse fieri, ut etiam de verbo, quod in scriptura dei non est, reddatur tamen ratio, unde recte dici ostendatur. sic ergo et

A debate of this sort was not likely to be of much value to anybody. After a recess for luncheon, the discussion was resumed, this time with shorthand writers in attendance.[1] The Count, however, talked so fast that the stenographers were not able to keep up with him, and when Augustine called upon him to observe the terms of their agreement, Pascentius accused him of trying to secure a written statement which could be used against him in a legal action under the imperial laws against heresy. In a moment of impatience, Augustine used language which he immediately regretted, and for which he subsequently apologized to Pascentius,[2] but the mischief was done. Pascentius became more and more confused in the statement of his beliefs and finally descended to mere abuse, declaring that it would have been better if they had never met, since Augustine's reputation far exceeded his performance.[3] On this note, the meeting broke up. Augustine subsequently sent a long letter to Pascentius, describing the debate from his own point of view and adding an exposition of Catholic doctrine.[4] The Count did not bother to read this and, when Augustine reinforced it with a second,[5] sent a short, contemptuous reply,[6] in which he likened Augustine to a man who, having drunken his fill of slime, could obtain no benefit from fresh water, and hinted that there would be no profit in any further correspondence. Pascentius could not, however, resist firing a parting shot: if there are three Persons, which of them is God? or is there one Person in three forms?[7] Augustine, in his reply, naturally vehemently repudiated any suggestion that Catholics believed in a three-formed Person and added, apropos of Pascentius' metaphor of the muddy water, that if he, Augustine, had changed his views after luncheon on the day of the debate, Pascentius' accusation would have referred, not to water but to wine.[8] This short reply brought the very unsatisfying correspondence to an end.

ὁμοούσιον, quod in auctoritate divinorum librorum cogebamur ostendere, etiamsi vocabulum ipsum non ibi inveniamus, fieri posse, ut illud inveniamus, cui hoc vocabulum recte adhibitum iudicetur." '

[1] Ibid., i, 6: '. . . et constituimus, post meridianum tempus ut adessent notarii ad excipienda verba nostra atque inter nos ista, quantum possemus, diligentius tractaremus.'

[2] Ibid., i, 7: 'ubi cum postulassem, commemorans antemeridianum placitum nostrum, ut ea, quae dixeras, dictare potius dignareris, tunc exclamasti calumniam parere nos tibi et ideo verba tua conscripta velle retinere. ibi quid responderim, recordari non libet atque utinam nec tu memineris.'

[3] Ibid., i, 8: 'tunc indignanter dixisti melius fuisse, ut famam mean semper audires, eo quod longe inferiorem me expertus esses, quam tibi illa iactasset.'

[4] Aug., *Ep.* 238.   [5] *Ep.* 239.   [6] Pascentius, *apud* Aug., *Ep.* 240.

[7] *Ep.* 240: 'rescribit mihi sanctitas tua patrem deum, filium deum, spiritum sanctum deum, sed unum deum. quis e tribus unus deus? an forte una est persona triformis, quae hoc nomine nuncupatur?'

[8] Aug., *Ep.* 241, 1: 'neque enim aqua caenosa ingurgitatum me iudicares sed perfidiae, quod multo peius est, ebrietate submersum, si non talis post prandium redissem, qualis ante prandium recessissem.'

Another Arian with whom Augustine had dealings was a certain Elpidius, who conceived the rather optimistic hope of converting him to Arianism. Accordingly, he sent him not only a work by an Arian bishop for his perusal, but also a recommendation that he should undertake a long journey to visit Bonosus and Jason, two Arian sages who, according to Elpidius, would be able to solve all Augustine's difficulties. To this, Augustine sent a friendly reply,[1] in which he referred, with some light irony, to the difficulties which such a journey would entail, and promised to write a refutation of the Arian bishop's book. Another of Augustine's correspondents, a physician called Maximus, had formerly been an Arian but had been converted after hearing one of the bishop's sermons. To him Augustine wrote jointly with Alypius, urging him to bring others to the faith which he now accepted, and providing him with an exposition of Catholic doctrine.[2]

Augustine's most formidable opponent among the Arians was a bishop named Maximinus, who accompanied the Gothic army under the command of Count Sigisvult, which the Empress Galla Placidia sent to Africa in 428, to take action against the rebel general, Count Boniface. Maximinus speedily complained that Augustine was interfering in his affairs—perhaps by propaganda among the Gothic soldiers of the garrison of Hippo[3]—and took grievous offence at the language of one of Augustine's sermons.[4] Accordingly, a debate was arranged, and both contestants demonstrated their familiarity with Holy Scripture in support of their principles. Maximinus was an able controversialist and was, moreover, extremely loquacious, so that Augustine had to endure the unfamiliar, and no doubt very distasteful, experience of not being able to interject a reply. Night found the Arian still speaking, with the result that he was afterwards able to claim a victory and assert that the famous Augustine had been unable to meet his arguments.[5] To refute these allegations, Augustine produced a long work in two books, the first designed to show that Maximinus had failed to meet his objections, the second to refute the Arian bishop's own doctrines. To this Maximinus vouchsafed no reply, though he had promised, before he left Hippo, to answer whatever Augustine might urge in writing.[6]

[1] Aug., *Ep.* 242, 1: 'Quis nostrum esset in fide vel cognitione trinitatis, alia quaestio est. gratum sane habeo, quod me quamvis incognitum facie tamen, quia errare credidisti, revocare ab errore conatus es.'

[2] Aug., *Ep.* 170.

[3] Such is the suggestion of Van der Meer, op. cit., i, p. 206.

[4] Aug., *Serm.* 140, 4; *C. Max. Ar.*, II, xxii, 1.

[5] Possidius, *Vita*, 17. See Van der Meer, op. cit., i, pp. 206–7; Bardy, *Saint Augustin*, 460–1.

[6] *Coll. cum Maximino*, 26: 'Maximinus [scripsit]: Cum explicueris hunc libellum, et ad me transmiseris, si non ad omnia responsum debeo, tunc ero culpabilis.'

It might well be thought that the demands made upon Augustine by his episcopal duties, his theological writings and controversial activities would have left him no time for other employment. But this was not the case. Augustine was a great preacher, one of the greatest in the early Church, and occupied a place in the Latin west which rivals that of St John Chrysostom in the Greek east. His sermons were delivered, not only at Hippo, where he preached as part of his episcopal duties, but in other African cities as well, and particularly in the metropolis of Carthage, to which he was frequently invited. Augustine's sermons are characterized both by profundity and by spontaneity, for the preacher did not read his sermons from a prepared script but, as a general rule, delivered extempore whatever the Lord put into his mouth—*quod Dominus donaverit*[1] is Augustine's own description of the method. These unprepared sermons were taken down by professional stenographers whose speed and accuracy, proverbial in the later Roman Empire, has received a striking testimonial in the case of Sermon 37 of Augustine's collected works, which has come down to us, not from a single archetype but from two absolutely independent transcripts made at the time when it was delivered by two different stenographers, which nevertheless give an identical text. The popularity of the preacher ensured that there would be a market for copies of his sermons, and the shorthand writers who took them down became Augustine's first editors, for there is no evidence that he himself ever thought of publishing his homilies, though it is possible that he may have revised some of the texts. Various collections of his sermons grew and multiplied. Certain of these, including the famous *Enarrationes in Psalmos* and the *Tractatus in Iohannem*, were copied and recopied in the Middle Ages. Inevitably, in the course of their transmission, many spurious sermons were added to those of Augustinian origin and passed for Augustine's own compositions. From the Renaissance onwards, generations of scholars have laboured to separate the chaff from the grain. The Benedictines of St Maur, in the epoch-making edition of Augustine's works which they published between 1679 and 1700, printed three hundred and sixty-three sermons which they regarded as genuine, and thirty-two more of doubtful authenticity.[2] In the next two hundred and fifty years, scholars discovered and printed more and more sermons attributed to Augustine so that Dom Germain Morin, in his edition of 1930,[3] calculated that there existed no less than six hundred and forty sermons discovered since the

[1] Aug., *Serm.*, 151, i, 1.
[2] The sermons were in Tome V, which appeared in 1683.
[3] G. Morin, *Sancti Augustini Sermones post Maurinos reperti* (*Miscellanea Agostiniana*, vol. I), Rome, 1930, p. viii.

Benedictine edition, of which he considered that only one hundred and thirty-eight were genuine. Since then, fresh material has come to light, thanks particularly to the labours of Dom Cyrile Lambot who, in 1961, published the first volume of a critical edition of the sermons designed, ultimately, to include all those known to scholarship.[1]

Besides his preaching, Augustine engaged in a voluminous correspondence. Some of his letters, indeed, are miniature treatises in themselves, and were so regarded in medieval times, as happened in the case of the letter to Paulina, written about 413, which was included by the Benedictines among Augustine's letters and numbered 147, but which is generally referred to in the manuscripts as the *Liber de Videndo Deo*. By contrast, other letters are extremely short, being simply the routine matter of a bishop's correspondence. An example of this type is provided by a letter written about the same date as that to Paulina, and immediately preceding it in the Benedictine edition (*Ep.* 146), addressed to Pelagius, at a time when the relations between the two men were still friendly. Pelagius had sent messages of greeting to Augustine,[2] to which the recipient responded using all the—to modern ears—slightly exaggerated language of the epistolary style of the ancient world, which he later felt constrained to justify, when Pelagius employed the letter to create the impression that Augustine was in sympathy with his views.[3]

The range of Augustine's correspondents was very wide, extending from high officials like Count Boniface, the military commander in Africa and Count Marcellinus, the imperial commissioner charged with the settlement of the Donatist controversy, to the studious girl, Florentina, who had wished for his advice on a point in her studies which perplexed her, but was too shy to write without the bishop's permission[4] or to the

---

[1] *Sancti Aurelii Augustini Sermones de Vetere Testamento id est Sermones* I–L (*Corpus Christianorum Series Latina* xli) recensuit Cyrillus Lambot, Tournholt, 1961. Dom Lambot's publications in preparation for the work appeared mainly in the *Revue bénédictine*. For bibliographies see Lambot, op. cit., pp. xxxi–xxxv and *Sancti Augustini Sermones Selecti Duodeviginti* (*Stromata*, Fasc. I), Utrecht–Brussels, 1950, 11–12. An important book on St Augustine considered as a preacher is Maurice Pontet, *L'exégèse de s. Augustin prédicateur*, Paris [1945]. See also Bardy, op. cit., pp. 212–63; Van der Meer, op. cit., ii, pp. 205–64; Pope, op. cit., pp. 139–94.

[2] See Georges de Plinval, *Pélage: ses écrits, sa vie, et sa réforme*, Lausanne, 1943, 214 n[1].

[3] *De Gest. Pel.*, xxvi, 51: 'Dixi eum quippe in salutationem dominum, quod epistolari more etiam non christianis quibusdam scribere solemus neque id mendaciter, quoniam omnibus ad salutem, quae in Christo est, consequendam debemus quodam modo liberam servitutem. dixi dilectissimum, quod et nunc dico et si iratus fuerit, adhuc dicam, quoniam nisi erga eum dilectionem tenuero, illo irascente ipse mihi magis nocebo. Dixi desideratissimum, quoniam valde cupiebam cum praesente aliquid colloqui; iam enim audieram contra gratiam, qua iustificamur, quando hinc aliqua commemoratio fieret, aperta eum contentione conari.'   [4] *Ep.* 266.

religious, Sapida, who had sent him a tunic she had made for her dead brother.[1] Nor was Augustine's letter-writing confined to Africa. He wrote regularly to St Paulinus, bishop of Nola and ex-consul, a charming character who, after selling his goods and embracing a life of poverty, saw no reason to renounce the pleasures of friendship. More famous still was the correspondence which Augustine exchanged with St Jerome, which extended over a period of twenty-one years and which admirably illustrates the misunderstandings which can arise when letters depend for their transportation upon the good will of private persons, some of whom may be tempted to display them, or even circulate copies en route, if the reputations of the writers are likely to arouse interest. Jerome, after a stormy career, came to live at Bethlehem. He was sensitive and easily offended, well aware of his own scholarship, which far exceeded that of any of his contemporaries, and conscious of the fact that it had never had the recognition which it deserved. To him Augustine wrote,[2] probably in 394 before his consecration,[3] offering gratuitous advice about Jerome's translation of the Old Testament (Augustine, for pastoral reasons, thought that the authoritative text should be the Greek of the Septuagint; Jerome, with a scholar's instinct, preferred to go direct to the Hebrew) and, with better reason, protesting against Jerome's explanation of the famous dispute between St Peter and St Paul, recorded in Galatians (2.12ff.) which, according to Jerome, was merely simulated in order to rebuke and refute the exclusiveness of Jewish converts to Christianity. Such an explanation, with its suggestion of deliberate dissimulation on the part of the Apostles, shocked Augustine to the core. How could the veracity of Holy Scripture be defended if Christians adopted theories like these?

Unfortunately, Augustine's language was tactless, his letters miscarried, and Jerome was quick to take offence. For years the unhappy dispute dragged on, provoking some bitter and wounding observations from Jerome, a past-master in the art of sarcasm. We do not know whether Jerome came, ultimately, to accept Augustine's view, though some hint may be afforded by a remark in Jerome's *Dialogue against the Pelagians*, written in 415, some ten years after his last exchange with Augustine on this particular matter. Commenting upon the text that a priest or bishop must be blameless, Jerome refers to St Paul's assertion that St Peter did not walk in accordance with the truth of the Gospel, so that Barnabas was carried away by his dissimulation, and asks why any man should wonder if

---

[1] *Ep.* 263.
[2] *Ep.* 28.
[3] He calls Jerome his 'fellow-presbyter'; but continues to use the term in later correspondence (*Epp.* 67 and 71), so the evidence is not conclusive.

he is not credited with the blamelessness which even the chief of the Apostles did not possess.[1] At all events, the menace of Pelagianism united Augustine and Jerome, and we find Augustine writing to St Jerome on the thorny problem of the origin of the human soul,[2] while the latter pays the bishop of Hippo generous compliments in his reply.[3]

Throughout his episcopate, Augustine's reputation steadily grew. The condemnation of Donatism at the Conference of Carthage in 411 was recognized as being due in no small measure to his personal efforts. His fame even penetrated to the eastern parts of the Empire. At the Synod of Diospolis Pelagius, with the haughty question: 'What is Augustine to me?' shocked the Greek bishops there assembled; how dared he speak so scornfully of the man who, by his zeal for the faith, had restored unity to Africa?[4] (This reputation did not endure among the east Romans. By the ninth century the Patriarch Photius, one of the most learned of Byzantine scholars, knew Augustine by name as the man who, with Aurelius, had crushed the Pelagian heresy; but he had no real knowledge of him or of his writings.[5] The Greeks were not in the habit of looking to Latin authors for lessons in theology, and it was not until the later Middle Ages that Augustine found Greek translators, beginning with Maximus Planudes in the thirteenth century.[6])

In the west, however, Augustine reigned supreme during the last twenty years of his life, not only in North Africa and Italy—an area naturally in touch with North Africa—but elsewhere, in Gaul and Spain. It was to him that Hilary wrote from Sicily on behalf of Timasius and James, who were being corrupted by Pelagianism, with a request that Augustine would refute Pelagius' teaching; it was to him that Paul Orosius journeyed from Spain, perturbed by the survival of Priscillianism in his native land; it was to his authority that Prosper of Aquitaine appealed in his struggle against

---

[1] Hieron., *Dialogus adv. Pelagianos*, I, 22. *MPL* xxiii, 515-16.

[2] Aug., *Ep.* 166, written in 415.

[3] Hieron., *apud* Aug., *Ep.* 172, written at the end of 415 or in 416. On the correspondence between Augustine and Jerome, see W. J. Sparrow-Simpson, *The Letters of St Augustine*, London, 1919, 216-54; Pope, op. cit., 212-27. On the correspondence in general, see Sparrow-Simpson and Pope, and Bardy, op. cit., pp. 265-99.

[4] Orosius, *Liber Apologeticus*, 4: 'Intromissum Pelagium unanimiter omnes interrogastis, an haec, quibus Augustinus episcopus respondisset, se docuisse cognosceret. ilico ille respondit: "et quis est mihi Augustinus?" cumque universi acclamarent, blasphemantemin episcopum, ex cuius ore Dominus universae Africae unitatis indulserit sanitatem, non solum a conventu illo verum ab omni ecclesia pellendum, episcopus Iohannes ilico eum, hominem videlicet laicum in consessu presbyterorum, reum haereseos manifestae in medio catholicorum sedere praecepit et deinde ait: "Augustinus ego sum." ' *CSEL* v, 607-8.

[5] Photius, *Bibliotheca*, Cod. LIII. *MPG* ciii, 93B; Cod. LIV; ibid., col. 96C.

[6] For Planudes, see the article 'Maximus Planudes' by Carl Wendel in Pauly-Wissowa, *Real-Encyclopädie*, Neue Bearbeitung, 4oer Halbb., 1950, 2202-53, esp. 2241.

the so-called Semi-Pelagians of Provence. Less than nine months after his death, Pope Celestine admirably expressed the view of western Christians in a solemn tribute to his memory. 'The life and merits of Augustine, that man of holy memory, always kept him in Our communion, nor was he ever assailed by so much as a suspicion of evil. We remember him as a man of such great wisdom that he was always reckoned by Our predecessors among the greatest teachers.'[1] This verdict would have been enthusiastically endorsed by Augustine's flock at Hippo, though their pastor himself might, on occasion, have wished that they had shown their appreciation of his merits by a greater deference to his authority. A particularly flagrant example of their indiscipline was the disgraceful incident in the spring of 411, when they attempted to secure the forcible ordination of the rich young Roman aristocrat Pinianus, in the hope of benefiting from his liberality. Despite Augustine's protests they insulted and menaced Alypius, who was Pinianus' host, and when Augustine categorically refused to ordain Pinianus against his will, they extracted from the Roman patrician a promise that he would remain at Hippo unconditionally, though it appears that Pinianus was subsequently released from his oath, for he later joined Jerome at Bethlehem and ended his life in Italy, the abbot of a community of thirty monks.[2]

It was not, however, destined that Augustine's life should close on a note of triumph in the worldly sense of the word, but in circumstances which, by all reasonable standards, would seem to mark the ruin of his life's work and the failure of all his hopes. Throughout his lifetime, the menace of the German peoples to the Roman world had been steadily increasing, a menace which would ultimately sweep away the structure of the western part of the Empire and leave in its place the independent partially Romanized barbarian kingdoms from which would develop the sovereign states of the Middle Ages. In 378 a band of Goths who had sought shelter within the boundaries of the Roman Empire against the attacks of the Huns and had been mercilessly exploited by Roman officials, rose in revolt, defeating and killing the Emperor Valens at the battle of Adrianople. The Roman defeat was retrieved by the genius of the Emperor Theodosius the Great but, after his death in 395, when the administration of the Empire was divided between his sons, Honorius and Arcadius, and the courts at Ravenna and Constantinople pursued independent and, at times,

---

[1] Coelestinus, *Ep.* 21, ii, 3: 'Augustinum sanctae recordationis virum pro vita sua atque meritis in nostra communione semper habuimus, nec umquam hunc sinistrae suspicionis saltem rumor aspersit: quem tantae scientiae olim fuisse meminimus, ut inter magistros optimos etiam ante a meis semper decessoribus haberetur.' *MPL* l, 530.
[2] The affair of Pinianus is described by Aug., *Epp.* 125, 126.

mutually hostile courses, the situation steadily deteriorated. St Jerome, writing in 396 to console his friend, Heliodorus, on the death of his nephew, Nepotian, drew a picture of the miseries of human existence from the events of his age:

> I will say no more of the calamities of individuals; I come now to the frail fortunes of human life, and my soul shudders to recount the downfall of our age. For twenty years and more the blood of Romans has every day been shed between Constantinople and the Julian Alps. Scythia, Thrace, Macedonia, Thessaly, Dardania, Dacia, Epirus, Dalmatia, and all the provinces of Pannonia, have been sacked, pillaged and plundered by Goths and Sarmatians, Quadians and Alans, Huns and Vandals and Marcomanni. How many matrons, how many of God's virgins, ladies of gentle birth and high position, have been made the sport of these beasts! Bishops have been taken prisoners, presbyters and other clergymen of different orders murdered. Churches have been overthrown, horses stabled at Christ's altar, the relics of martyrs dug up.
>
> > Sorrow and grief on every side we see
> > And death in many a shape.
>
> The Roman world is falling, and yet we hold our heads erect instead of bowing our necks. . . . Happy is Nepotian, for he does not see these sights nor hear these cries. We are the unhappy, who either suffer ourselves or see our brothers suffer.[1]

This, however, was only the beginning of a season of calamities. In 410 Alaric the Goth, nominally an ally of the Roman state and a general in the service of the emperor, sacked Rome. This action was a great moral shock; but it was less of a mortal blow to Roman authority than the crossing of the Rhine near Moguntiacum (the modern Mainz) by vast bands of Vandals, Suevians and Alans on the last day of December 406 and the subsequent invasion of Gaul. Two years later, in the autumn of 409, after ravaging Gaul, the invaders crossed into Spain. Here they succeeded in establishing themselves and the Vandals, under King Gunderic, settled in the southern Spanish province of Baetica. Gunderic died in 428 and was succeeded by

---

[1] Hieron. *Ep.* 60, 16, 17; *CSEL* liv, 570–1, 572. Tr. by F. A. Wright. It is interesting to compare this letter of Jerome's with the famous letter of consolation by Servius Sulpicius to Cicero on the death of his daughter Tullia in 45 BC (*Ad Fam.* IV, 5). Both Sulpicius and Jerome draw attention to the miseries of the present world, but there is a 'certain and sure hope' in the Christian Father, which is absent from the pagan writer: 'Nullus dolor est, quem non longinquitas temporis minuat ac molliat: hoc te exspectare tempus tibi turpe est ac non ei rei sapientia tua te occurrere. Quod si qui etiam inferis sensus est, qui illius in te amor fuit pietasque in omnis suos, hoc certe illa te facere non vult.' Cf. Jerome: 'Scimus quidem Nepotianum nostrum esse cum Christo et sanctorum mixtum choris, quod hic nobiscum eminus rimabatur in terris et aestimatione quaerebat, ibi videntem comminus dicere: *Sicut audivimus, ita et vidimus in civitate domini virtutum, in civitate dei nostri*, sed desiderium absentiae eius ferre non possumus, non illius, sed nostram vicem dolentes' (*Ep.* 60, 7. *CSEL* liv, 555).

his brother, Gaiseric, one of the ablest and most ruthless of all the German leaders.

The Roman military commander in North Africa was Count Boniface, an old friend of Augustine. As a young officer he had become acquainted with the bishop of Hippo and in 417 had approached him for information about the difference between Donatists and Arians. Augustine had written to him, congratulating him on the fact that, among the demands and distractions of his military duties, he showed interest in the affairs of God.[1] Some time later, after the death of his wife, Boniface announced that he felt moved to abandon his army career and enter a monastery. He was dissuaded from doing this by Augustine and Alypius. They were aware of his military talents and argued that he could observe a vow of continence in the world and live a holy life, but that it was his duty to remain in his command.[2] However, despite what Bury called his 'profession of orthodox zeal and hypocritical pretences', Boniface married again, and his second wife was an Arian.[3] She exercised great influence over him, and caused his daughter to receive Arian baptism.[4] His character deteriorated. He neglected his duties and failed to guard the province from the incursion of hostile tribes from beyond the frontiers. Augustine drew a melancholy contrast between the feats of the young Boniface at the head of his battalion and the inactivity of the commander-in-chief with the army of Africa at his back.[5] Rumours went abroad that the man who had formerly desired to become a monk now found the embraces of a wife insufficient and had turned to concubines.[6]

Boniface had hitherto enjoyed a successful career in the imperial service[7] and had been rewarded in 425 with the title of *Comes Domesticorum*, one of the commanders of the *Domestici*, a select body of household troops who were independent of the commander-in-chief, the *Magister Militum*. Success appears, however, to have been his undoing. He began to entertain hopes of yet greater advancement, and his inactivity in the face of local enemies may have been due, as Augustine hinted in a letter designed to bring Boniface to a better frame of mind,[8] to preparations to make himself absolute ruler in Africa. So at least it seemed to the imperial court at Ravenna, and in 427 Boniface was ordered home to give an account of himself. He refused to come and was declared a public enemy. An army

---

[1] Aug., *Ep.* 185, i, 1.   [2] Ibid., 189.
[3] Her name was Pelagia and she was very rich. There is no support for the suggestion that she was a relative of the Vandal, Gaiseric.   [4] Aug., *Ep.* 220, 4.   [5] Ibid., 7.
[6] Ibid., 4: '. . . ipsam quoque uxorem non tibi suffecisse, sed concubinarum nescio quarum commixtione pollutum loquentur homines et forsitan mentiuntur.'
[7] For which see Pauly-Wissowa, N.B., 5te Halbbd. (1897), 698–9, art. 'Bonifatius'.
[8] Aug., *Ep.* 220, 7.

was sent against him under three commanders, whom he duly defeated and killed. A second force was then dispatched under the Goth, Count Sigisvult, which appears to have been more successful. Carthage and Hippo were occupied[1] and Boniface reduced to a critical situation.[2]

It was then that Count Boniface, according to a tradition which is more than a little suspect,[3] decided to redress the balance by calling the Vandals to his assistance. Whether he did so or not is really of little consequence. Africa, a green and fertile province, had long exercised an attraction for the Germans[4] and the opportunity provided by a civil war was too good to miss. To the confusion caused by the internecine strife of Roman armies were added the chronic incursions of Berber tribes from beyond the frontiers, the same tribes which Boniface had failed so signally to subdue. A foreign invader might expect little opposition, and no one would be better aware of this than Gaiseric, king of the Vandals and the Alans, an able ruler, intelligent, treacherous, and inspired with a hatred of Rome and things Roman. Accordingly, in May 429 the nations of the Vandals and the Alans embarked and, crossing the Straits of Gibraltar, advanced eastward across Africa, massacring and burning as they went. According to Victor Vitensis, the Vandal population numbered eighty thousand souls,[5] which means that the fighting men can hardly have exceeded some fifteen thousand[6]—not a very formidable force with which to invade a province like Africa, had there been any adequate resistance. In the event, however, there was none; and the methods of frightfulness which the Vandals employed took the heart out of any local resistance.[7]

Too late it dawned on the Roman government and on Boniface that, if Africa were to be saved, they must unite against the common enemy. A court official of the highest rank, an *illustris* named Darius, was sent to Africa, and a peace was patched up. Darius even seems to have concluded a truce with the Vandals,[8] but this was of short duration, for Gaiseric was

---

[1] See the remark of the Arian bishop, Maximinus, *Collatio cum Maximino*, 1: 'Maximinus dixit: Ego non ob istam causam in hanc civitatem adveni, ut altercationem proponam cum Religione tua, sed missus a comite Sigisvulto contemplatione pacis adveni.'

[2] For the background to the revolt of Boniface, see Bury, *Later Roman Empire*, i, 244ff.; Julien, *Histoire de l'Afrique du Nord*, 2e éd., i, 234-5.

[3] See Julien, op. cit., i, 235. The two authorities for the story are Procopius and Jordanes, both of whom wrote a century after the incidents they record. Prosper, *Chronicon*, subanno 427 says: 'a concertantibus in auxilium vocantur', which would imply that both Boniface and Sigisvult called in Gaiseric. Bury, op. cit., i, 245 n^6, because of the evidence of Procopius, interprets 'concertantibus' as being Boniface.

[4] See Bury, op. cit., i, 185, 202.

[5] Victor Vitensis, *Historia Persecutionis*, I, 1. *CSEL* vii, 3.

[6] The calculation of Bury, op. cit., i, 246.   [7] Possidius, *Vita*, 28.

[8] Aug., *Ep.* 229, 2: '. . . ipsa bella verba occidere'; *Ep.* 230, 3: 'si non extinximus [sc. Darius] bella, certe distulimus.' See Bury, op. cit., i, 247 n^5.

determined to pillage, even if he could not conquer, the rich eastern provinces of Africa. Fighting broke out afresh and Boniface was defeated. He retreated into Hippo, which was soon invested by the Vandal forces.

For Augustine no more tragic disaster could have darkened his old age. Only his trust in God sustained him in these calamities, and calmly he prepared to meet the end. Three or four years earlier, in late 425 or early 426, he had prepared a literary testament for posterity called the *Retractationes*, in which he passed in review his writings to that date, and where he had modified or changed his opinion, gave his reasons for so doing. The desire to carry out such a revision had been in his mind since at least 412,[1] but it was not until his old age, when he was seventy-two, that he was able to put it into effect.[2] The result was a precious catalogue of Augustine's works,[3] which contains valuable information regarding certain books now lost, and which serves as a monument to the humility and care for veracity of the author, who was anxious that his 'second thoughts' might be made clear to posterity.[4]

The siege of Hippo lasted fourteen months, but Augustine lived to see only three of them. During the advance of the Vandals he showed an almost Stoic calm and was heard to say: 'He will not be great who thinks it a great matter that wood or stones fall and mortals die',[5] but in his heart he was bitterly grieved. He had been joined in Hippo by certain of his friends who had been driven from their sees, among them Possidius, and on one occasion, sitting at table with them, he remarked: 'You know, in

[1] Aug., *Ep.* 143, 2: 'Si enim mihi deus, quod volo, praestiterit, ut omnium librorum meorum quaecumque mihi rectissime displicent, opere aliquo ad hoc ipsum instituto colligam atque demonstrem, tunc videbunt homines, quam non sim acceptor personae meae.'

[2] Possidius, *Vita*, 28: 'Ante proximum vero diem obitus sui a se dictatos et editos libros recensuit, sive eos quos primo tempore suae conversionis adhuc laicus, sive quos presbyter, sive quos episcopus dictaverat, et quaecunque in his recognovit aliter quam sese habet ecclesiastica regula a se fuisse dictata et scripta, cum adhuc ecclesiasticum usum minus sciret minusque sapuisset, a semetipso et reprehensa et correcta sunt. Unde etiam duo conscripsit volumina, quorumest titulus *De Recensione Librorum*.' It will be noticed that the title given by Possidius has not prevailed against the traditional title.

[3] To which must be added Possidius' *Elenchus*, of which a critical text by André Wilmart will be found in *Miscellanea Agostiniana*, ii, 149–233.

[4] On the *Retractationes*, see P. M. J. Lagrange, 'Les Retractations éxégetiques de saint Augustin', in *Misc. Agost.*, ii, 373–95; John Burnaby, 'The "Retractationes" of St Augustine: Self-criticism or Apologia?' in *Augustinus Magister*, i, 85–92. Burnaby shows that there is a considerable apologetic strain in the *Retractationes*: '. . . the proportion of *defensio* to *reprehensio* is (approximately) as 40% to 60%—a much larger proportion of *defensio* than either the author's original plan or the terms of his Prologue would lead us to expect' (p. 83). Burnaby emphasizes, however (p. 92), that Augustine never desired to be regarded as the 'infallible master'.

[5] Possidius, *Vita*, 28: 'Et se inter haec mala cuiusdam sapientis sententia consolabatur: "Non erit magnus magnum putans quod cadunt ligna et lapides, et moriuntur mortales."' For the origin of this phrase (which comes from Plotinus, *Enn.*, I, iv, 7) see Michele Pellegrino, *Possidio, Vita di s. Agostino*, Edizioni Paoline, 1955, 226 n[14].

the time of this calamity of ours, I have only one prayer to God: either that He will deign to free this city from its enemies or, if He decrees otherwise, that He will make His servants strong to bear His will or at least take me to Himself out of this world.'[1] The words impressed his hearers. They had hitherto been lamenting the calamities which had overtaken them; now they joined Augustine in offering up the same prayer.[2]

The presence of savage enemies around the city wall did not alter Augustine's way of life. Until he fell ill with his last sickness, he continued to preach to the people,[3] and with the Vandals at the gate, he continued writing the great reply to Julian of Eclanum, the last and most formidable of the Pelagian controversialists, which remained unfinished at his death. He had no concern with regard to the provision of a successor as bishop, if he should die. Four years before, on 26 September 426, he had recommended to his people the presbyter Heraclius and they had enthusiastically accepted Augustine's candidate.[4] Now all that remained to do was to await the issue of the siege. Augustine held strongly to the traditional African view that it was the duty of a bishop to remain among his flock for as long as anyone had need of him. Before the Vandal army had landed in Africa,[5] when the Berber tribes from beyond the frontier were raiding the province, a number of bishops had appealed to him, with regard to the proper conduct of a bishop in the event of hostile attack. One of them, Honoratus, quoted the words of the Gospel: *When they persecute you in this city, flee to another* (Matt. 10.23) to justify flight in the face of persecution. In a long letter[6] Augustine conceded that there were circumstances when flight was justified: when, as in the case of St Athanasius, the bishop was the sole object of attack and his sacred ministry could be discharged by others, or if all the inhabitants of a spot had fled, so that there was nothing to be gained by the clergy remaining. But if the laity remain, and the danger to clergy and laity is the same, then the laity must not be deserted in their time of need.[7] Did not Christ warn us of the hireling, who flees because he is a hireling and does not care for the sheep?[8] With the approach of the enemy, people will flock to the churches, some seeking to be baptized, some to be reconciled, others to be absolved. If the clergy have gone, they will depart unregenerate and unabsolved.[9] Accordingly,

---

[1] Possidius. *Vita*, 29.   [2] Ibid., 28, 29.
[3] Ibid., 31: 'Verbum Dei usque ad ipsam suam extremam aegritudinem impraetermisse, alacriter et fortiter, sana menta sanoque consilio in ecclesia praedicavit.'
[4] The proceedings are recorded by Aug., *Ep.* 213. See Van der Meer, op. cit., i, 410–414. It is unlikely that Heraclius was ever consecrated.
[5] I assume that it was before the Vandal invasion, though Possidius in his narrative quotes the letter after the siege had begun.   [6] Aug., *Ep.* 228, quoted by Possidius, *Vita*, 30.
[7] Aug., *Ep.* 228, 2, 6.   [8] Ibid., 6.   [9] Ibid., 8.

the clergy must remain. If their blood is shed, they will have their reward like the martyrs, for having laid down their life for the people committed to their charge.[1]

In the third month of the siege of Hippo, Augustine fell sick with fever and took to his bed.[2] He had always held that no baptized Christian, not even a bishop of saintly life, ought to leave this world without showing worthy and ample penitence. He therefore caused the seven penitential psalms[3] to be written on leaves of vellum and hung on the wall by his bed, so that he could study them continually with many tears. Ten days before he died, he asked his friends to visit him only when the physician came or when food was brought, so that he might spend his whole time in prayer. He made no will, since he had abandoned all his possessions to God but, with the love of books and letters which had characterized him throughout his life, he gave special instructions that the library of the church of Hippo should be preserved for posterity. (Alas! it was to perish with so much else at the Arab conquest.) His church, with its ornaments and revenues, was entrusted to the priest responsible for its care. And so, with all worldly cares laid aside, Augustine calmly awaited the end, sick in body, but with his sight and hearing and all his other physical faculties unimpaired.[4] He died on 28 August 430,[5] fortified by the presence and prayers of his friends, in the seventy-sixth year of his age and approaching the fortieth since his ordination. He was buried by his friends and the Holy Sacrifice offered on his behalf.[6]

Augustine's prayer had been heard and he was spared the anguish of

[1] *Ep.*, 3: '. . . qui vero propterea patiuntur, quia fratres, qui eis ad Christianam salutem indigebant, deserere noluerunt, sine dubio suas animas pro fratribus ponunt.'

[2] Possidius, *Vita*, 29: 'Et ecce tertio illius obsidionis mense decubuit febribus, et illa ultima exercebatur aegritudine.' It must be to the onset of this illness that Victor Vitensis refers when he says: 'Tunc illud eloquentiae, quod ubertim per omnes campos ecclesiae decurrebat, ipso metu siccatum est flumen' (*Hist. Persecut.*, I, i, 3. *CSEL* vii, 6), since we know from Possidius, *Vita*, 31 that Augustine continued to preach up to the time of his illness.

[3] '. . . psalmos Daviticos, qui sunt paucissimi, de paenitentia', Possidius, *Vita*, 31. Are these the seven penitential psalms of the Middle Ages and modern times (Pss. 6; 31 [32]; 37 [38]; 50 [51]; 101 [102]; 129 [130]; 142 [143])? We do not know, and Possidius does not tell us the number; but Cassiodorus, writing in the next century, refers in his *Exposition on the Psalms* to the penitential psalms (*Expos. in Ps.* 6. *MPL* lxx, 60), and they are the same as those of today. See V. Leroquais, *Les Livres d'Heures manuscrits de la Bibliothèque Nationale*, Tom. I, Paris, 1927, xx–xxi. In view of this, it seems likely that the psalms mentioned by Possidius are the traditional seven penitential psalms.

[4] Possidius, *Vita*, 31.

[5] Prosper, *Chronicon*: 'Theodosio XIII et Valentiniano III Coss. Aurelius Augustinus episcopus per omnia excellentissimus moritur v Kal. Septembris, libris Iuliani inter impetus obsidentium Wandalorum, in ipso dierum suorum fine respondens et gloriose in defensione Christianae gratiae perseverans.' *M.G.H. Auctores Antiquissimi*, ix, *Chronica Minora*, ed. Th. Mommsen, i (1892), 473.

[6] Possidius, *Vita*, 31.

seeing the ruin of his city. In July 431 Gaiseric raised the siege. The Vandals were not good engineers, and walled cities like Hippo, Cirta (the
modern Constantine) and Carthage were beyond their capacity to master.
The rest of the country, however, was in their hands. Meanwhile, fresh
forces arrived from Italy and Constantinople under the command of Aspar,
the general of the eastern emperor, Theodosius II. Aspar and Boniface
united their armies and engaged Gaiseric in open battle, in which they
were totally defeated and rendered incapable of offering further resistance
to the invader. Hippo fell soon afterwards, and the Vandals entered the
city, which was looted but not utterly destroyed.[1] Gaiseric established his
court there, and it was at Hippo that peace was concluded with the Roman
government on 11 February 435, by which the Vandals entered the service
of the Roman Empire as *foederati*, paying a small tribute and sending an
annual draft of hostages to Ravenna as surety for their loyalty.[2] In return
for this, they were permitted to occupy the three regions of Mauretania
and part of Numidia, including Possidius' see of Calama. Gaiseric, for his
part, had no intention of regarding this settlement as anything more than a
truce, by which he organized his conquests and prepared for fresh offen-
sives. Four years after the Convention of Hippo, this thoroughgoing
exponent of *Realpolitik* suddenly set it aside and occupied Carthage on 19
October 439, almost without striking a blow. Ten years after his landing in
Africa, the province was his, and nearly six centuries of Roman dominance
came to an end.

So ended the earthly career of the theologian who, according to Victor
of Vita, had in his lifetime written two hundred and thirty-two books,
excluding his letters and sermons.[3] A few weeks after Augustine's death,
an envoy of the Emperor Valentinian III arrived at Carthage with an
invitation to him to take his seat at the Ecumenical Council which was to
be held at Ephesus at Whitsuntide 431 to deal with the dispute between
St Cyril of Alexandria and the Patriarch Nestorius of Constantinople
regarding the union of the two Natures in the incarnate Christ.[4] It was a
last, and fitting, tribute to the great Doctor of the Latin Church.

---

[1] See Marec, *Hippone: Antique Hippo Regius*, 28.   [2] See Julien, op. cit., i, 237.
[3] Victor Vitensis, *Hist. Persecut.*, I, i, 3: 'Usque ad illud tempus ducentos iam triginta
et duo confecerat libros, exceptis innumerabilibus epistulis vel expositione totius
psalterii et evangeliorum atque tractatibus popularibus, quas Graeci omelias vocant,
quorum numerum conprehendere satis inpossibile est.' *CSEL* vii, 6.
[4] Liberatus Carthaginensis, *Brevarium*, 5: 'Scripsit imperator sacram et beato
Augustino Hipponiregiensi episcopo per Ebagnium [Evagnium] magistrianum, ut ipse
concilio praestaret sui praesentiam. Qui Ebagnius veniens Carthaginem magnam, audivit a
Capreolo, ipsius urbis antistite, beatum Augustinum ex hoc mundo migrasse ad Dominum, acceptisque ab eo ad imperatorem litteris loquentibus de obitu beati Augustini
Constantinopolim, unde venerat, rediit.' *MPL* lxviii, 977.

4

The Manichaean Religion

*Let us seal our mouth that we may find the Father, and seal our hands that
we may find the Son, and guard our purity that we may find the holy Spirit.
Glory to our Lord Mani through the Father, honour to his Elect through
the Son, blessing to his Catechumens through the holy Spirit. Victory and
Salvation may there be through them to the soul of the blessed Mary.*
    Manichaean Psalm to the Trinity, translated
    from the Coptic by C. R. C. ALBERRY

THE MANICHAEAN faith, in which Augustine passed more than nine of
the formative years of his life, which he was afterwards, as a Catholic
Christian, to attack, but from whose influence—or so his enemies alleged
—he never wholly freed his imagination, must be reckoned among the
strangest and most bizarre of the many strange and bizarre fantasies which
the human mind has conceived. Nevertheless, it merits some consideration,
and not only because of the influence which it exercised upon Augustine.
A religious movement which lasted for twelve centuries and which,
during that period, was to be found to a greater or a lesser degree throughout the land-mass which stretches from the European shores of the Atlantic to the coast of the Chinese Empire, is of the most profound interest to
the student of religions. If, however, we add to this longevity and wide
diffusion the historical consideration that twice in its career, under the
Roman Empire and during the Middle Ages, without any state support it
constituted a serious menace to the Christian Church, we shall find ourselves marvelling, not so much at the system itself, as at the manner in
which it has been eclipsed and become forgotten in the present age. It
resembles those lost cities of the desert wastes, whose very existence is
known only to the traveller and the antiquarian, but which were once the
homes of princes. The religion which attracted the young rhetorician of
Carthage was an impressive one, and remains impressive even in its ruin.

It is not easy for the modern reader to feel for Manichaeism that sympathy which every religion demands if it is to be understood. Its ways of
thought and principles are alien to ours, its morality too extreme and its
doctrine too fantastic. Only a very austere heart can fail to find some
fellow-feeling for the religions of the classical world. The long-continued
tradition of the study of Greek and Latin and, even more, the influence of

those literatures on poets and thinkers in modern languages, on a Keats, a Chénier, or a Goethe, have made us familiar with the gods of Greece and Rome and induced an instinctive sympathy for their worshippers. It is difficult not to be touched by the great gods of Olympus and Latium and even more by the lesser deities, the little, friendly gods of field and fountain, the ancestral gods, the *Lares domestici* and the *Penates familiares*, homely Vesta flickering on the hearth, yellow Ceres garlanded with cornears, and even the gross Priapus with his sickle. The emotion which we feel may, indeed, be a literary and conventional one, a nostalgic yearning for another and simpler age and very far removed from the harsh realities of life in a world lacking all but the simplest domestic comforts and the scantiest aids to agriculture. Nevertheless, such an emotion at least makes us ready to sympathize with the pagan religion, and it is not without distaste that we read some of Augustine's more embittered diatribes against it in the *De Civitate Dei*. Now this sympathy, which can so readily be given to the classical religions, is wholly lacking for Manichaeism. It appears to us, in the language of one of its most profound students, as a 'barren, inhuman, and absurd religion and also, without doubt, in certain aspects puerile'.[1] Nevertheless, as Professor Puech proceeds to point out, a study of the Manichaean writings themselves reveals grandeur and fervour, profound faith, moving lyricism, and art of delicate beauty. A faith which proclaimed the existence of evil in the world but which offered the hope of liberation to myriads of men and women, which inculcated a moral discipline and a respect for life often sadly lacking in those who denounced and persecuted it, and which could inspire its children to face torture and martyrdom uncomplaining, deserves better at the hands of the Christian theologian or Church historian than it sometimes receives, and

---

[1] Henri Charles Puech, *Le Manichéisme: son fondateur; sa doctrine*, Paris, 1949, 91. This magisterial work is by far the most comprehensive study of Manichaeism available at the present time, and my description of Manichaean history and doctrine is based largely upon it. Alfred Adam, *Texte zum Manichäismus* (Kleine Texte für Vorlesungen und Übungen, Nr. 175), Berlin, 1954 is a useful collection of excerpts from primary sources. F. C. Baur, *Das Manichäische Religionssystem*, Tübingen, 1831 (photographically reproduced 1928) is still valuable. O'Meara, *The Young Augustine*, 61–79 is based largely upon Puech. Sir Steven Runciman, *The Medieval Manichee*, 2nd ed., Cambridge, 1955, 12–18, draws upon F. C. Burkitt, *The Religion of the Manichees*, Cambridge, 1925 (now outdated in certain respects) and A. V. Williams Jackson, *Researches in Manichaeism*, New York, 1932. For practical purposes, the student of Augustine can turn to Puech for his information, supplementing him by P. Alfaric, *L'evolution intellectuelle de saint Augustin*, I, Paris, 1918 and, by the same author, *Les écritures manichéennes*, 2 vols., Paris, 1918. Joseph Rickaby, *The Manichees as St Augustine saw them*, London, 1925, is a useful collection of extracts from Augustine's writings, linked by an explanatory essay; but the author's utter contempt for the Manichees detracts from the value of his study. More balanced is A. Anthony Moon, *The De Natura Boni of Saint Augustine* (Catholic University of America Patristic Studies, Vol. 88), Washington, D.C., 1955.

the present account seeks to present its doctrines in the best possible light.

The founder of the sect, Mani (known to the Greeks and Romans under the forms of Manes, Manikhaïos, and Manichaeus), was born in Babylonia on 14 April 216,[1] being of Persian stock and of aristocratic lineage. He was lame, a fact which may shed some light upon his subsequent horror of the body and its operations. His father, Patek, as a result of a heavenly revelation, joined a baptizing Gnostic sect, in which Mani probably passed some of his youth, and which may have helped to develop his ascetic inclinations. According to his own account, he was twice the recipient of revelations from heaven, the first occasion being when he was twelve or thirteen years old, the second at the age of about twenty-four. The result of these two revelations was to convince Mani that he was the last of the prophets of God, bearing the whole and final truth, of which previous religions had been but partial manifestations. He claimed indeed to be the apostle[2] of Jesus Christ while, to his followers, he was more, being the very Paraclete whom Christ had promised to send.[3] He inaugurated his apostolate by a short visit to India, perhaps with the intention of acquiring knowledge of Buddhist doctrine or, possibly, to gain converts from among the Christian communities already established there. On the accession of Shâhpuhr I to the throne of Persia, Mani returned, managed to secure an interview with the new sovereign—probably on 9 April 243[4]—and made such an impression that his religion was accorded full liberty of preaching throughout the Persian Empire. Throughout the reign of the formidable Shâhpuhr—it was he who defeated and captured the Emperor Valerian in AD 260 in the most humiliating disaster suffered by a Roman army in the east since the defeat of Crassus at Carrhae—Mani seems to have enjoyed freedom for his missionary activities and on Shâhpuhr's death (probably in April 273) he succeeded in obtaining a renewal of letters of protection granted by him from his son and successor, Hôrmizd. Unfortunately for the prophet, Hôrmizd only reigned a year, being succeeded by his brother, Bahrâm I, in 274. Under the new sovereign, the priests of the fire-worshippers, who constituted the official religion of Persia, launched a campaign against Mani, as one who was ruining the state religion and stealing the king's subjects from their proper religious duties. Summoned before the king and menaced with torture and death, Mani showed courage and preserved his dignity. He was dragged away to prison, loaded with chains in such a

[1] For the date, see Puech, op. cit., pp. 32–33.
[2] C. Ep. Fund., v, 6; vi, 7; viii, 9; C. Faust, XIII, iv.
[3] De Haeres., 46; De Util. Cred., iii, 7.
[4] Puech, op. cit., p. 46, considers this dating of S. H. Taqizadeh preferable to the previously accepted one of 20 or 21 March 242.

manner as to preclude all movement of his head or limbs and, in this condition, survived from 31 January to 26 February 277.[1] At last he died, worn out by his sufferings. His followers were accustomed to speak of these twenty-six days' suffering as his crucifixion—a term evidently borrowed from orthodox Christianity.[2] After death, the corpse was decapitated and dismembered, the head being exhibited over the gate of the capital city of Gundêshâhpuhr and the members scattered abroad. His followers saved what they could of the body and the remnants were afterwards buried at Ctesiphon.

Mani was dead, but the faith which he proclaimed not only lived on but grew and expanded. Missionaries carried it beyond the borders of the Persian Empire into that of Rome. Within twenty years of its founder's death, Manichaeism was established in North Africa and, on 31 March 297, in response to complaints which had reached him the previous year, Diocletian issued an imperial rescript, ordering the burning of Manichees and magicians together with their sacred books,[3] thereby inaugurating the series of persecutions which the unhappy sect was to suffer in the Roman Empire, and not only at the hands of a heathen emperor. Nevertheless, despite imperial legislation, which may not have been very rigorously applied, Manichaeism continued to spread. In Africa, by the fourth century, it appears to have won over and superseded the various Gnostic sects which had flourished there in the late second and early third centuries, and against which Tertullian had fulminated. No doubt many persons attracted to Gnosticism would have found in Manichaeism the last and finest flowering of Gnostic speculation and adopted it accordingly, so that we may very reasonably speak of a Gnostic-Manichaean African tradition.[4] But what-

---

[1] For these dates, see Puech, op. cit., pp. 52–53.

[2] This is misunderstood by O'Meara, *The Young Augustine*, 62, who says that Mani was literally crucified. For a discussion of the term 'crucifixion' see Puech, op. cit., p. 107 n^{64}, and for a list of the various forms in which the prophet's death is said to have taken place, p. 21.

[3] Text in *Codex Gregorianus*, xv, 3 (ed. P. Krüger, *Collatio libr. iuris anteiustin.*, iii, 1890, 187–8; Adam, *Texte zum Manichäismus*, 82–83. See M. Besnier, *L'Empire romain de l'avènement des Sévères*, Paris, 1937, 324; W. Seston, 'Sur l'authenticité et la date de l'édit de Dioclétien contre de Manichéisme', in *Mélanges de philologie, de littérature et d'histoire anciennes offerts à Alfred Ernout*, Paris, 1940, 345–54 and *Dioclétien et la Tétrarchie*, Paris, 1946, 122.

[4] See W. H. C. Frend, 'The Gnostic-Manichaean Tradition in Roman North Africa', in *JEH* iv, 1953, 13–26, who speaks (p. 15) of 'the existence of historical continuity between the Gnostics and the Manichees in Africa. The Gnostics fade out at the time of the Great Persecution and their place is immediately taken by the Manichees.' Less plausible is Frend's suggestion that there was in African Christianity a tradition of exaggerated respect for the Epistles of St Paul to which the Manichees, who also held the Apostle of the Gentiles in the highest esteem, were able to appeal (pp. 22–23). Frend's views are cited by O'Meara, *The Young Augustine*, 63 and criticized by Gerald Bonner, 'The Scillitan Saints and the Pauline Epistles', *JEH* vii (1956) 141–6.

ever the reason, by the second half of the fourth century, Manichaeism was an established tradition in Roman North Africa, where its doctrines made a particular appeal to intellectuals like the young Augustine and his friend Alypius. The nature of these doctrines must now be investigated.

The religion founded by Mani was essentially eclectic, drawing upon elements from at least three great religions. From the Zoroastrianism of Mani's native Persia came the Dualism which is the foundation of his doctrine; from Buddhism, belief in reincarnation and, perhaps, the rule of life imposed on the Manichaean Elect; finally, from Christianity came reverence for the name of Jesus, whose apostle Mani claimed to be. The importance of the rôle assigned to Jesus by Mani certainly justifies the attitude of those Fathers of the Church who regarded Manichaeism as a Christian heresy,[1] though the Jesus of Mani's system is very different from the Word made flesh of Christian devotion and dogma. Rather, he is a transcendent being, the manifestation of the Saving Intellect or *Nous*.[2] This conception, indeed, gives the clue to the real nature of Manichaeism; it is less an example of religious syncretism than a manifestation—the last and the greatest—of Gnosticism. This movement, which flourished in the second and third centuries AD, was composed of various sects, differing in details but united by a tendency to amalgamate Christian doctrine with pagan Hellenistic ideas regarding an intermediate world of superhuman beings between the One supreme God and the world of man, and by a doctrine of Man which sees the human soul as some part of the Divine which has fallen into the prison of matter and from which it may be delivered by an illuminating knowledge (*gnōsis*) to which each Gnostic sect declared that it alone had the key. In this, Manichaeism faithfully followed its predecessors. It offered to its followers knowledge of God and of the nature of Man; a knowledge which is concealed from the unenlightened soul, weighed down by the defiling bonds of matter. Self-knowledge was the great gift which Manichaeism claimed to bestow upon its adherents. In the words of Professor Puech, *gnōsis* is *epignōsis*,[3] acquaintance with oneself and God. For this reason, the Manichees claimed that theirs was a religion founded upon reason and it was, indeed, precisely this claim which attracted the young Augustine to them. 'I persuaded myself that belief was more to be accorded to those who taught than to those who gave orders,'

---

[1] See E. Waldschmidt and W. Lentz, *Die Stellung Jesus im Manichäismus*, Berlin, 1926 (Abhandlungen der Preussischen Akademie der Wissenschaften, 1926, No. 4). Cf. the remarks of F. C. Burkitt, 'Manichaica', in *JTS* xxxv (1934), 185–6.

[2] Puech, op. cit., pp. 81–82.

[3] Ibid., p. 71.

F

he says of his own conversion to Manichaeism,[1] and elsewhere speaks of the Manichaean boast that, while the Catholics gave their people doctrines which were to be believed on the authority of the Church, they themselves persuaded men to believe only by force of argument and demonstration.[2]

In fact, however, this appearance of rationalism was wholly misleading and Manichaeism, despite its grandiose claims, a piece of mythology more fantastic than anything to be found in the Arabian Nights. The basic theme of the myth was the struggle of the soul, fallen from heaven into the prison of the flesh, to escape and return to its proper country by the aid of Saving Intelligence, or *Nous*. If this basic theme is borne in mind, it is possible to make some sense of the complicated pattern of Manichaean doctrine.

The foundation of Mani's system was Dualism, the belief in two co-equal and co-eternal powers of Good and Evil. From all eternity these two have existed side by side: Light and Darkness, Good and Evil, God and Matter. Neither can destroy the other, and the only superiority which Good can claim over Evil is in the moral order and in the fact that, at the last, when this world, the product of an attack by the forces of Evil upon the Good, is finally dissolved and Good separated from Evil, there will be no further admixture nor possibility of the powers of Darkness renewing their offensive against the realm of Light. Such a superiority of Good over Evil hardly implies any inequality.

In the beginning, the two principles of Good and Evil existed in two wholly separate kingdoms. Over the one ruled the Father of Greatness, with his five dwellings—or attributes—of Sense, Reason, Thought, Imagination, and Intention,[3] and served by innumerable angels. Over the other, the Prince of Darkness held sway. The kingdom of Evil consists of five gulfs—the number five has a peculiar significance in Manichaean thought—which, in descending order, are the realms of Evil Smoke (or Mist); Devouring Fire; Evil Air (or Destructive Wind); Water (or Slime); and Darkness. Each is presided over by a monstrous ruler, in the shape, respectively, of a demon, a lion, an eagle, a fish, and a serpent. Each is the

---

[1] *De Beata Vita*, i, 4: 'mihique persuasi docentibus potius quam iubentibus esse credendum.'

[2] *De Utilitate Credendi*, i, 2: '. . . se autem nullum premere ad fidem nisi prius discussa et enodata veritate.' Cf. *De Moribus*, I, ii, 3: 'nihilque aliud maxime dicunt [Manichaei], nisi rationem prius esse reddendam.'

[3] The names of the dwellings are so translated by Burkitt, *The Religion of the Manichees*, 19, 33. Puech, op. cit., p. 75 renders them as Intelligence, Raison, Pensée, Réflexion, Volonté. Cf. Jackson, op. cit., p. 233 (Intelligence or Mind; Knowledge; Reason; Thought; Deliberation).

home of a species of living creature: of demons or bipeds; of quadrupeds; of birds; of fish; and of serpents.[1]

Before the creation of the world, the two kingdoms were not only distinct but separate.[2] Nevertheless, they were not by nature preserved from the possibility of contact for, while they were both infinite, the Kingdom of Light extended to the North, the East, and to the West, but the Kingdom of Darkness to the South alone, so that there was a point of contact, where the Kingdom of Darkness pierced like a wedge into the realms of Light.[3] It was this point of contact, an enclave of Darkness in the world of Light, which made possible the intermingling which we see in the present world, where good and evil are mixed. For while in the Kingdom of Good all was calm and peaceful, the Kingdom of the Prince of Darkness was a scene of endless turmoil, internecine war, lust, and mutual destruction by its evil inhabitants. It was a consequence of this restlessness that a vague, unregulated desire[4] took hold of the dark ruler and his subjects to invade the Kingdom of Light and possess it for themselves. It was this movement of demonic concupiscence which brought this world, with all its miseries, into existence.

Precisely because of its calm and pacific nature, the Kingdom of Light had no natural defences to repel an assault such as was now delivered upon it.[5] Accordingly, the Father of Greatness decided not to call upon his angels to resist the attack of the powers of Darkness but to fight the enemy himself. He therefore evoked (it should be noticed that Mani avoids using a word which would suggest sexual generation) a first emanation, the Mother of Life, who, in turn, evoked another being, Primal Man (not to be confused with Adam who, according to the Manichees, was the fruit of a diabolical union). Primal Man, clothed in the Five Bright Elements: Air;[6]

[1] De Haer., 46; C. Ep. Fund., xv, 19; xxvi, 28. References in Augustine to the two kingdoms collected by P. Alfaric, L'évolution intellectuelle de saint Augustin, 99–101. See also Puech, pp. 75, 164 n^{298}.

[2] See Aug., C. Fortun., 14, 18–20; De Haer., 46.

[3] See Augustine, C. Ep. Fund., xx, 22–xxiii, 25. This is the significance of the remark in Conf., V, x, 20: 'Et quia deum bonum nullam malam naturam creasse qualiscumque me pietas credere cogebat, constituebam ex adverso sibi duas moles utramque infinitam, sed malam angustius, bonam grandius, et ex hoc initio pestilentioso me cetera sacrilegia sequebantur.' The Good is infinite grandius because it extends north, east, and west; Evil angustius, because it extends only to the south.

[4] 'Here, as elsewhere in many ancient religions, a conception which has its true root in human nature is expressed and believed in as a cosmological happening, for I cannot doubt that Mani's point is, that the beginning of Evil is unregulated desire.' (Burkitt, Religion of the Manichees, 20–21.)

[5] See Augustine, De Moribus, II, xii, 25; C. Faust., V, iv: '. . . cum et ipsum deum gentis adversae tumultu perterritum'; De Vera Relig., ix, 16. Burkitt, op. cit., 22; Jackson, op. cit., p. 224.

[6] This element is also called Breeze, Aether, and Hyle (ὕλη). See Burkitt, op. cit., 24–25; Jackson, op. cit., p. 225 n^{11}.

Wind; Light; Water; and Fire, which formed his armour or his soul, descended to the frontier of the Kingdoms of Light and Darkness and engaged the enemy armies in combat. Here he was defeated and left lying senseless on the field, while the Five Bright Elements were devoured by the princes of Darkness, the infernal Archons.

This was the Fall, as the Manichees conceived it; and yet the descent and defeat of Primal Man was, in fact, the beginning of salvation and the restoration of the harmony which the invasion of Light by Darkness had disrupted. The Bright Elements which the evil Archons had devoured were the soul of Primal Man, the Son of God, who was himself an hypostasis of the soul of his Father. In consequence, the dark Archons had, within their own entrails, a portion of the substance of God, which is poison to demonic natures. Thus, the defeat of Primal Man could be regarded as a stratagem[1] or as a voluntary sacrifice for the defeat of evil.[2] Whichever might be the case, the forces of evil were now at a disadvantage and measures for their destruction could be taken in hand.

When Primal Man recovered consciousness, having fallen into the depths of the infernal abyss, he addressed to the Father of Greatness a cry for help, which he repeated seven times. God therefore evoked a new series of emanations; first, the Friend of the Luminaries who, in turn, evoked the Great Ban ('the Great Architect'), who evoked the Living Spirit. This last, accompanied by his five sons, the Custody of Splendour, called in the west Splenditens; the King of Honour; Adamas; the King of Glory; and Omophoros (otherwise Atlas) who sustains the worlds on his shoulders, descended to the frontier of the region of Darkness and there uttered a piercing cry, the prototype of the call to salvation which was to be uttered by the prophet Mani.[3] To this cry, Primal Man gave answer. This Call and Answer became two divinities, *Xhrôshtag* and *Padvâχtag*,[4] who ascended together to the Living Spirit and to the Mother of Life, who reassumed them, the Living Spirit assuming the Call and the Mother of Life the Answer. Now the Living Spirit descended once more accompanied by the Mother of Life into the very depth of the Kingdom of Dark-

---

[1] See Theodore van Khoni on Mani, tr. by Dr Abraham Yohannan in Jackson, *Researches*, 226: 'Thereupon the Primal Man gave himself and his Five Sons as food to the Five Sons of Darkness, just as a man who has an enemy mixes deadly poison in a cake and gives it to him.'

[2] For a discussion of the voluntary nature of the defeat of Primal Man, see Puech, op. cit., p. 168 n^{309}.

[3] Jackson, op. cit., p. 228 and n^{22}; Puech, op. cit., p. 78. Puech renders the title of the son of the Living Spirit, called here the Custody of Splendour, as 'L'Ornement de la Splendeur', thereby following Pognon and Cumont. See Jackson, pp. 296-7 n^3.

[4] See F. C. Burkitt, 'χröϑtaγ and ραϑνχātaγ, Call and Answer', in *JTS* xxxvi (1935), 180-1. Cf. Jackson, op. cit., p. 231 n^{36}.

ness. He extended his hand to Primal Man, who grasped it and was drawn out of the place of his captivity. In the company of the two divinities who had delivered him, Primal Man ascended into the Paradise of Lights, his heavenly country. The first martyr, he had become the first of the redeemed, the archetype of the humiliation and trials of humanity, but also of its deliverance.[1]

Nevertheless, although Primal Man had been delivered, the Five Bright Elements were still mingled with darkness in the entrails of the evil Archons, and it was necessary that they too should be delivered. Their deliverance was the sole purpose of the construction of the world.[2] Accordingly, the Living Spirit accompanied by his five sons[3] once more descended, this time to do battle with the forces of Evil. The evil Archons were defeated, killed, and flayed. From their skins the heavens were created, the mountains from their bones, and the earth from their flesh and excrements.[4] The universe so formed consists of ten firmaments, which the Custody of Splendour sustains aloft, and eight earths, borne on the shoulders of Omophoros or Atlas. Then the Living Spirit (significantly called the Demiurge in Greek versions of the myth) began a primary liberation of Light by dividing into three portions the mixture of Light and Darkness which composes the universe. The portion of Light which had not suffered from its contact with Darkness was formed into the Sun and the Moon; the portion only lightly contaminated made the stars. The remaining portion, which composes the world, being heavily defiled required more complicated treatment.[5] In response to the prayers of the Mother of Life, Primal Man and the Living Spirit, the Father of Greatness proceeded to evoke a third evocation, whose principal hypostasis is the Messenger or the Third Envoy, who is himself the father of the twelve Virgins of Light, who correspond to the twelve signs of the zodiac. To the Messenger fell the task of organizing the world into a vast machine to draw out, refine,

[1] On Primal Man, see A. V. W. Jackson, *Researches*, 255–70, 'Notes on the Rescue of Primal Man'. Puech, op. cit., 76–78.

[2] See A. V. W. Jackson, op. cit., pp. 314–20, 'Allusions to the Ten Heavens and Eight Earths and the Legend about their Formation'.

[3] See Jackson, op. cit., pp. 296–313, 'The Five Sons of the Living Spirit'.

[4] For the construction of the universe, see Jackson, op. cit., pp. 22–73, 314–20.

[5] The Manichaean account of the creation of the universe from the bodies of the defeated Archons may well be inspired by the Babylonian legend of the creation of the world by the god Marduk from the corpse of the monster Tiamat (for which see J. V. Kinnier Wilson, 'The Epic of Creation', in *Documents from Old Testament Times*, ed. D. Winton Thomas, London, 1958, 10–11). The conception of the creation of the world from the body of a fallen enemy is not, of course, peculiar to the Near East. Another example is to be found in the Scandinavian Poetic Edda, where the gods fashion the world from the corpse of the dead giant, Ymir (see *The Lay of Vaftruthnir*, st. 21 and *The Lay of Grunnir*, st. 40, 41 in *The Poetic Edda*, translated with an introduction and explanatory notes by Lee M. Hollander, University of Texas Press, Austin, Texas, 1928, 52, 70).

and restore the imprisoned Light to its proper home. The wheels of this cosmic machine are Wind, Water, and Fire, which are turned by the King of Glory, one of the five sons of the Living Spirit and supremely, the Sun and the Moon. It is to this last, during the first half of the month, that liberated fragments of Light are transferred, causing it to swell and become full. Then, during the second half of the month, the Light is transferred from the Moon, which accordingly wanes, to the Sun, whence they are finally transmitted to the Kingdom of Light.[1] But in addition to this mechanical method, the Messenger employed other means of securing the liberation of Light particles. He appeared in the Sun, sometimes in a female form before the male demons and sometimes as a male before the females, thereby inflaming their concupiscence and provoking an emission of their seed, in which Light was confined. The seed fell upon the earth. From the moist part was engendered a sea-monster, which Adamas the warrior, one of the sons of the Living Spirit, struck with his lance and slew. From the dry element sprang five trees, from which grew the vegetable kingdom.[2] The female demons, made pregnant by their very nature and affected by the rotation of the zodiac where they are bound, gave birth to abortions which, falling to the earth, devoured the buds of the trees, so that they assimilated part of the Light contained in them and then, being seized by concupiscence, united together and gave birth to a demon progeny, which is the origin of the animal kingdom, rated by Mani lower in the hierarchy of values than the vegetable.[3] So the Light which had been imprisoned in the bodies of the demons was transferred to the earth; but it still remains bound in the plants and in the bodies of animals.

Meanwhile, the King of Darkness, alarmed by the appearance of the Messenger and desiring to ensure that he should not be compelled to disgorge the Light which he had secured for his kingdom, engendered two demons, a male called Ashaqloun and a female called Namraël, and sent them into the world to frustrate the purposes of the powers of Light.[4] Ashaqloun devoured all the abortions of the female demons, in order to concentrate the maximum of captive Light in himself, and then united with Namraël, to engender the first two human beings, Adam and Eve. In Adam, the first born of the pair, was the greater part of the Light; Eve, for her part, is predominantly a creature of Darkness.[5] The human race, then,

[1] Puech, op. cit., pp. 79–80.
[2] Alfaric, *L'évolution intellectuelle de saint Augustin*, 111–15 gives references to the creation of vegetables and animals from Augustine's writings.
[3] Puech, op. cit., p. 80.
[4] See Jackson, op. cit., pp. 106–8, 251 n^{134}.
[5] See Alfaric, *L'évolution intellectuelle de saint Augustin*, 119 nn^3 and [4].

is sprung of demonic parents, as is witnessed by its body, which is the same form as that of the demons, and by its sexuality, which urges it to couple and reproduce, thus continuing to imprison particles of Light in the flesh. Nevertheless, because of the presence of some particles of Light, man is not wholly a diabolic creature; a good nature exists in him and he can, if he strives to do so by hearing the words of the prophets and pre-eminently the prophet Mani, free himself from his fleshly bonds, and ascend to the Paradise of Light.[1]

After his birth, Adam lay upon the ground, weighed down by his infernal flesh, senseless, and forgetful of his heavenly origins. To rouse him from his sleep came the Saviour, Jesus, sent from the powers of heaven. He is the being whom the Manichees adored as *Yishô' Zîwâ*, Jesus the Splendour, Jesus the Luminous, and whose name, used, as Augustine says, as a sort of glue by the Manichees to entrap the unwary, proved one of the strongest inducements to bring the future bishop of Hippo into the ranks of the Manichaean Auditors.[2] Nevertheless, the being called Christ whom the Manichees adored was very different from the Child born at Bethlehem and laid in a manger because there was no room for Him at the inn. For the Manichees the very suggestion of the Incarnation was unthinkable, since it involved the descent of the pure Spirit of God into the foul prison of the flesh. 'Christ was not a prophet,' wrote Faustus the Manichee, 'nor was He a prophet like Moses, for Moses was a man and Christ was God; Moses was a sinner, Christ was holy; Moses was born of human coition, and Christ of a Virgin, according to you or, as I hold, not born even of a virgin; Moses, when he angered God, was slain in the mountain, Christ, who is well-pleasing to the Father, suffers of His own free will.'[3] Christ, indeed, only seemed to be in the likeness of sinful flesh during His appearance on earth and therefore, as His flesh was not true flesh, so His Passion was a mere pretence and His Resurrection a fable.[4] As a Manichaean Auditor, Augustine was surprised by the fact that the Manichees made a great ceremony of their feast of the *Bêma*, the day on which Mani died, but ignored the festival of Easter. He was told that while Mani

---

[1] See Fr. Cumont, *La cosmogonie manichéenne* (*Recherches sur le Manichéisme*, I), Brussels, 1908, 42–49 and Ernesto Buonaiuti, 'La prima coppia umana nel systema Manichaeo' in *Saggi sul cristianesimo primitivo*, Città di Castello, 1923, 150–70. Note Augustine's comment on Adam, *De Moribus*, II, xix, 73: 'Adam dicitis sic a parentibus suis genitum, abortivis illis principibus tenebrarum, ut maximam partem lucis haberet in anima et perexiguam gentis adversae.'

[2] *Conf.*, III, vi, 10.

[3] *C. Faust.*, XVI, iv. Cf. *C. Ep. Fund.*, vii, 8.

[4] Aug., *Ep.* 236, 2: '. . . negantes scilicet Christum natum esse de virgine nec eius carnem veram confitentes fuisse sed falsum ac per hoc et falsam eius passionem et nullam resurrectionem fuisse contendunt.'

was really and truly martyred, Christ, since He was not true flesh, only appeared to die on the Cross, and so His fictitious Passion should not be celebrated.[1] Clearly then, the shining being who appeared to Adam as he lay on the ground and roused him from his deadly sleep was far removed from the Second Person of the Christian Trinity. In fact, he is Illumination, the *Nous* or Saving Intellect.[2] He awoke Adam, opened his eyes, and revealed to him the circumstances of his creation, the infernal origin of his body, and the *gnōsis*, the divine knowledge of things, by which he might escape from this world and return to the heavenly realm, to which he rightly belonged in virtue of his soul. In the Manichaean theology, it is Jesus and not the serpent who persuades Adam to taste of the Tree of Knowledge. Having tasted, Adam became aware of the truth and resolved to abstain from intercourse with his wife, since by the generation of new human beings the particles of Light continue to be passed from one body to another and so remain longer bound in their prison of the flesh. Unfortunately Eve, a weaker creature than Adam, with only a little Light and much Darkness in her being, was unable to observe the requirements of the heavenly plan which had been unfolded to them. She tempted Adam and, as a result of their union, the human race grew and expanded, with the result that the process of the liberation of Light from Darkness has been delayed.[3]

In his mission to Adam, we have seen one aspect of the Manichaean Jesus, the active power of the intellect revealing to mankind the way of escape from the predicament in which it finds itself. There was, however, another aspect, the aspect of the 'suffering Jesus', who typifies the anguish of the human soul in its bondage to matter. The portions of Light which are imprisoned in this world are consubstantial with God, particles of Him bound up in matter. Now this Light is particularly present in the vegetable kingdom, in the fruit which is man's food, and it was, therefore, the custom of the Manichees to see in the fruit of trees a symbol of the person of *Jesus Patibilis*—'Suffering Jesus'—the 'pathetic aspect of the transcendent Jesus, the unhappy part needing salvation of *Yishô' Zîwâ*, the Saviour inasmuch as he is pure Light'.[4] The Manichaean concept of the suffering Jesus was, in some sense, a psychological equivalent of the Catholic doctrine of the human nature of Christ which endured the Passion and the

---

[1] *C. Ep. Fund.*, viii, 9: '. . . Christum autem, qui natus non esset, neque veram, sed simulatam carnem humanis oculis ostendisset, non pertulisse, sed finxisse passionem.'

[2] Puech, op. cit., p. 82.

[3] Burkitt, *Religion of the Manichees*, 31–33. Alfaric, *L'évolution intellectuelle*, 122–3, with references to appropriate passages in Augustine's writings.

[4] Puech, op. cit., p. 82. Cf. Burkitt, *Religion of the Manichees*, 31.

Crucifixion; but dogmatically it was poles apart for, as the Manichaean Faustus declared in the work to which St Augustine wrote a lengthy reply, 'Suffering Jesus' was not a divine man, but the fruit which is man's food. In this sense, said Faustus, 'Suffering Jesus, who is the life and salvation of men, is suspended from every tree.'[1] Such an approach universalized the action of the Crucifixion, but at the price of turning it into pantheism. Like Pascal, the Manichees believed that Jesus will be in agony to the end of the world,[2] but they understood by this phrase something utterly different.[3]

The machine for the separation of Light from Darkness had been established and through the ages, according to Mani, it continued the work for which it was designed. Gradually the particles of Light were disengaged from the carnal mass; the souls of the Elect, after death, were gathered into the 'Column of Glory' from which they were transferred, by means of the Moon and of the Sun, to the Paradise of their origin.[4] But this process of liberation is impeded by the sins of men, of whom the great majority choose to cling to the mixture and, in defiance of the advice of Jesus to Adam, to bring children into the world and so prolong the captivity of Light in Matter. But in the end, when the doctrines of Mani have been preached and adopted, will come the Last Days. First will come a series of apocalyptic trials, called by the Manichees the Great War; these will end in the triumph of the Manichaean Church and the last opportunity for the conversion of those men who have hitherto remained plunged in error. There will follow the Last Judgement before the *bêma* or tribunal of Christ, the separation of Good and Evil, and a short reign by Jesus and the Elect, after which the world will be burnt in a great fire to last for 1,468 years. This is the last act of purification; after it is over, such particles of Light as remain will be gathered together in a Statue, which will ascend to heaven; while the damned and the demons will be gathered together in a lump, the *bôlos*, and will be buried in a deep pit, which will be covered by a huge stone. This is the last act of the cosmic drama; Light and Darkness are once again separate, as they were in the beginning, and the powers of Evil

---

[1] *C. Faust.*, XX, ii: '. . . patibilem Iesum, qui est vita ac salus hominum, omni suspensus ex ligno.'

[2] *Pensées*, No. 553: 'Jésus sera en agonie jusqu'à la fin du monde: il ne faut pas dormir pendant ce temps-là.'

[3] In the words of Faustus, *C. Faust.*, XXXII, vii: 'Credimus cetera, praeterea crucis eius mysticam fixionem, qua nostrae animae passionis monstrantur vulnera.' Cited by Puech, op. cit., p. 83.

[4] Puech, op. cit., p. 83. Alfaric, *L'évolution intellectuelle de saint Augustin*, 109–11 and Burkitt, *Religion of the Manichees*, 43, give a different order: Cosmic machine—Moon—Sun—Column of Glory, which is adopted by Runciman, *The Medieval Manichee*, 14–15. For these two alternative orders, see Puech, op. cit., pp. 176–7, n^{349}.

will never again be able to invade the Kingdom of Light, being confined by the walls built by the Great Ban, to keep them in their own place.[1]

Some difference of opinion prevailed among the Manichees as to whether all the Light which was originally devoured by the Dark Archons would finally be recovered. Some believed that a total separation would be achieved but others, more pessimistic, held that certain souls, by reason of their sins, would be so intimately bound to the Darkness that they would become inseparable, and the Father of Greatness would never be able to restore them to his substance. In consequence, after the Last Judgement, they would share the eternal prison of Evil. Thus the victory of Light although final would not be complete; some part of the substance of Light would remain for ever in the power of Darkness.[2]

Such, in outline, was the dogma of the church founded by Mani. It remains to examine the organization of that church and the morals which were the consequence of the dogma.

Professor Puech has noted three traits which characterize the Manichaean religion. First, it was a universal creed, the fulfilment of all revelations which had gone before and destined, in the thought of its founder, to inherit the earth.[3] Secondly, it was a missionary religion, which certainly fulfilled its destiny, inasmuch as its missionaries carried its message from its Iranian cradle to the eastern shores of the Atlantic and to the eastern shores of the Chinese Empire.[4] Finally, it was a religion of the Book. Mani considered that the weakness of the religious systems which had preceded his, apart from the sustained assaults launched upon them by the powers of Darkness, had been the failure of their founders to record their revelations personally. He, at least, made no mistake on this issue; with his own hand, he composed a canon of scripture: the *Shâbuhragân*, dedicated to King Shâhpuhr; the *Living Gospel*; the *Treasure of Life*; the *Pragmateia*—known in the Latin west as the *Epistle of the Foundation*; the *Book of Mysteries* (or *Secrets*); the *Book of the Giants*, and his *Letters*.[5] This definitive canon did not prevent the appearance of a flood of apocrypha, but the basic object of the prophet was secured: Manichaean dogma was, in essentials, well established and the Church of the Holy Spirit, as its

[1] Puech, op. cit., pp. 84–85.

[2] Aug., *Ep.* 236, 2: '... et quod purgari de ipsa dei parte non potuerit, in fine saeculi aeterno ac poenali vinculo conligari, ut non solum violabilis et corruptibilis et contaminabilis credatur deus, cuius pars potuit ad mala tanta perduci, sed non possit saltem totus a tanta coinquinatione et immunditia et miseria vel in saeculi fine purgari.'

[3] Puech, op. cit., pp. 61–63.

[4] Ibid., pp. 63–66.

[5] List in Puech, op. cit., p. 67; O'Meara, *The Young Augustine*, 62. On these works, see Alfaric, *Les écritures manichéennes*, esp. II, 3–137. Extracts in Adam, *Texte zum Manichäismus*, 1–26.

adherents called themselves, was singularly free from heresies and schisms. This is the more remarkable in view of the widely differing areas in which it was established and the many languages into which its sacred book were rendered. But dogmatic uniformity was only one aspect of Manichaeism; with faith, there went a code of conduct and a discipline inspired by that faith; both must be studied if we are to understand the nature of the Manichaean church.

The theological principles of Mani's doctrine reveal a world in which Light is mingled with Darkness and promise salvation through the dissolution of this unnatural union. To effect this dissolution, it is necessary for every man to struggle in his own life by means of a rigid ascetic discipline. Revelation has come through Jesus and His apostle Mani, men's souls have been enlightened with wisdom from on high, but it is necessary for them to work out their salvation by detaching themselves from the flesh and by living after the spirit. Then, after death, the purified soul may attain to the Kingdom of Light, its natural homeland. If, on the other hand it fails to respond to the message from heaven it will, after death, be reborn in another body, for Mani accepted the doctrine of transmigration.[1]

The discipline demanded for the liberation of the soul from the body was a hard one. We must kill within ourselves all that partakes of matter, all the lusts and concupiscences of the flesh, which continue to hold the spirit in bondage. Carried to its logical conclusion such a discipline would involve suicide by starvation, such as was actually practised by the Albigensian heretics of twelfth- and thirteenth-century Provence in their rite called the *Endura*, in which some devotee would deliberately starve himself to death amid the rejoicing of his fellows.[2] We do not know whether the Manichees of the fourth century practised anything similar to the *Endura*—it was not frequent among the Albigenses. Nevertheless, suicide apart, the Manichee who wished to fulfil all the demands of his religion was expected to live a life of extreme severity. He might not eat meat or drink wine, own property or till the soil. One meal a day must suffice him, and his single garment had to last for a year. He might not engage in any worldly occupation; in particular, he must avoid not only marriage but any sort of sexual relations. He fasted often, and for long periods. His life had to be spent in perpetual pilgrimage. Such a life, it was believed, enabled the devotee to become an instrument in the great machine of cosmic regeneration. The food that he ate was transformed, by the natural

---

[1] See A. V. W. Jackson, 'The Doctrine of Metempsychosis in Manichaeism', in the *Journal of the American Oriental Society*, xlv (1925), 246–68.
[2] For the *Endura* see Runciman, *The Medieval Manichee*, 158–9.

processes of metabolism, so that particles of Light imprisoned therein lodged in his body and, after his death, were released, to return to the original mass in the Kingdom of Light. Further than this, it was thought that particles of Light were released by the action of his digestion and breathed out during his prayers, 'breathing out angels—no, rather portions of God! groaning in prayer and belching', was Augustine's crude and rather brutal description of the process after he had ceased to be a Manichee.[1]

It is obvious that, if every Manichee had been required to observe the full rigour of his religion, the sect would have had few adherents and would have died out within a single generation. In practice, the full Manichaean life was lived by only a minority, a religious élite known, appropriately enough, as the Elect. The bulk of the Manichees were found in the grade of Auditor—'Hearers' or catechumens. On them a milder way of life was imposed. They were bound to a code of ten commandments, which included prohibitions of idolatry and witchcraft, coveteousness, killing and adultery, lying, effeminacy, and neglect of their religious duty. They were required to confess to God and to the Elect, and to observe certain fasts for fifty days in the year. Within these limits, they were permitted to live ordinary lives in the world; they might own property, be farmers, artisans or merchants, eat meat and drink wine, marry or keep a mistress and have children, though every inducement was offered to them to refrain as far as possible from procreation which, by continuing to confine the soul in flesh, hindered the separation of Good and Evil and the dissolution of the world. The concessions made to them with regard to owning property and making money were of particular importance, for their primary religious duty was to minister to the needs of the Elect, who were not permitted to fend for themselves but who required another to pluck and prepare the fruit and vegetables which constituted their lawful food. The reason for this curious prohibition becomes clear if we understand the Manichaean attitude to the material world, which they regarded, not as an insensate mass of minerals, but as a living creature, capable of being wounded and hurt by a thoughtless action. Thus, everything that we do may either constitute a defilement, by bringing us into contact with matter, or a sacrilege, by offering violence to the Light confined within that matter. Hence the Manichees believed that the fig-tree suffered and shed tears when its fruit was plucked;[2] that the plough-share wounded the

---

[1] *Conf.*, III, x, 18: 'Quam tamen ficum si comedisset aliquis sanctus alieno sane, non suo scelere decerptam, misceret visceribus et anhelaret de illa angelos, immo vero particulas dei gemendo in oratione atque ructando: quae particulae summi et veri dei ligatae fuissent in illo pomo, nisi electi sancti dente ac ventre solverentur.'
[2] Ibid.

earth; that the air moaned with pain at the blow that whistled through it; and that the water in which a man bathed was defiled by his bathing. Such actions were crimes, hardly less than the killing of an animal or a man, though less, indeed, than that supreme sin, fornication.[1]

For this reason the Elect, who were required to observe to the letter the prohibitions of the Manichaean religious code, could not themselves pluck fruit from the trees, cook vegetables, or bake bread, in order to eat. This had to be done for them by some devoted Auditor, who brought the food to the saint to whom it was his privilege to minister. The latter, having first ritually cursed the bearer of his repast for having perpetrated the crime by which he was to be fed and expressly dissociated himself from the transaction, would then absolve his guilty benefactor and give him the benefit of his prayers.[2] By actions such as this the Auditor, provided that he observed the requirements of his grade, might hope after death to be reborn as one of the Elect and so ultimately attain to the joys of Paradise. Failure in his duties would result in rebirth as one of the lower animals.[3]

The essential difference in the Manichaean hierarchy was between the grades of Elect and Auditor. The Elect were the spiritual élite; to them the Auditors paid reverence and confessed. Nevertheless, there was a Manichaean clergy, consisting of presbyters, bishops, and a higher order, *Magister*. According to Augustine, there were seventy-two bishops and twelve *Magistri*, over whom was placed a supreme pontiff, the successor of Mani.[4] The presbyters were ordained by the bishops who themselves were consecrated by the *Magistri*.[5] Augustine also speaks of Manichaean deacons.[6] The Manichaean clergy played, by Christian standards, only a minor part in the life of the church. This was, however, not surprising, for any sort of sacramental life, as understood in traditional Christianity, was lacking in the Manichaean system. They did not baptize; to do so would be to defile the water in which the candidate would be dipped, though they used the word to describe the formal imposition of hands by which a convert joined the sect or, being a member, was raised to a superior

---

[1] Puech, op. cit., pp. 87–88.

[2] Puech, op. cit., p. 90. For the formula of abjuration used by the Elect, see C. H. Roberts, *Catalogue of the Greek and Latin Papyri of the John Rylands Library*, III, Manchester, 1938, 42–43.

[3] Puech, op. cit., p. 86.

[4] *De haeres.*, 46: 'Nam ex electis suis habent duodecim, quos appellant magistros, et tertium decimum principem ipsorum: episcopos autem septuaginta duos, qui ordinantur a magistris; et presbyteros, qui ordinantur ab episcopis.'

[5] Ibid. For the Manichaean hierarchy, see Burkitt, *The Religion of the Manichees*, Appendix II, 105–7.

[6] Ibid.: 'Habent etiam episcopi diaconos.' Aug., *Ep.* 236, 2: 'Sed ipsi auditores ante electos genua figunt, ut eis manus supplicibus inponantur non a solis presbyteris vel episcopis aut diaconibus eorum sed a quibuslibet electis.'

grade. They had no Eucharist, although they applied the word to the ritual meals of the Elect.[1] These omissions are hardly surprising. The sacramental system of Catholic Christianity depends upon the belief that matter, which is God's creation and therefore good, can be used by Him for bestowing Grace by means of an appropriate formula. 'The word comes to the element and the sacrament is made', as Augustine succinctly expresses it.[2] To the Manichees, such an idea would have been abhorrent. Their ambition was to separate the Light from matter, not to bring it into matter; while the very conception of Christ voluntarily making bread and wine into His Body and Blood shocked them. Sacramentalism, by its very nature, was foreign to the Manichees. Their worship was one of prayers, psalms, and fasts; their faith one of the Book. The function of the clergy was to preach and call to repentance; theirs was essentially a ministry of the Word which might equally well be performed by the Elect.[3] The central note of Manichaeism was the call to salvation, the proclamation of the means and the response of the enlightened, who became part of the machine working for the liberation of Light from matter. Since in order to be a part of the cosmic machine, the Manichaean Elect had to discipline himself to feats of endurance far beyond the power of the ordinary adherent, he was therefore entitled to, and received, the highest honours for his devotion. Here again we see a significant and characteristic feature of Manichaeism: the prophet enlightened, but it was upon the will of the individual that the response depended. Grace, in the Catholic sense, played no part. Indeed, by a rather curious irony, the Manichees might in this be said to come very near to a Christian sect which most vehemently denounced them and all their works. In the course of the Pelagian controversy, Augustine was furiously attacked by Julian of Eclanum and his allies for his doctrine of Original Sin which, they declared, arose from a Manichaean hatred of the body and human sexuality which he had never discarded during his years as a Catholic bishop. Yet the Pelagian doctrine, which sees Grace as being essentially an illumination,[4] which shows men

[1] Puech, op. cit., p. 87.

[2] *In Iohannis Evang.*, *Tr.* 80, 3: 'Detrahe verbum, et quid est aqua nisi aqua? Accedit verbum ad elementum, et fit Sacramentum, etiam ipsum tanquam visibile verbum.' Cf. St Ambrose, *De Sacramentis*, IV, iv, 14: 'Sed panis iste panis est ante verba sacramentorum; ubi accesserit consecratio, de pane fit caro Christi.' *CSEL* lxxiii, 51–2.

[3] *De haeres.*, 46: 'Habent etiam episcopi diaconos. Iam caeteri tantummodo Electi vocantur: sed mittuntur etiam ipsi qui videntur idonei, ad hunc errorem, vel ubi est, sustentandum et augendum; vel, ubi non est, etiam seminandum.'

[4] See the quotation from Pelagius, preserved by Augustine in *De Gratia Christi*, vii, 8: ' "Adiuvat enim nos deus", inquit [Pelagius], "per doctrinam et revelationem suam, dum cordis nostri oculos aperit; dum nobis, ne praesentibus occupemur, futura demonstrat; dum diaboli pandit insidias; dum nos multiformi et ineffabili dono gratiae caelestis illuminat." '

the way to salvation and then imposes upon them a severe discipline to obtain it, is not very different in its psychological approach from that of the Manichees. Both attribute too much to the power of human will and assume that once the wise man has been shown the proper course of action, he will be both willing and able to follow it. In practice, of course, the Manichees recognized that very few men had either the inclination or the power to live to the full the life they extolled and that was why their Elect received, while yet living, the honours paid among the Catholics to the saints. In outward appearance, the Manichaean Elect, unkempt and unbathed, in his one garment, penniless, and nourished only by bread, vegetables, and fruit, was not strikingly different from a monk from the deserts of Egypt or Syria; but in spirit the two were utterly opposed. For the monk, the sense of his sins and the need to seek the forgiveness of God were primary, and pride the last, and greatest, temptation. For the Elect, this sense of humility was lacking; in a certain fashion, the Manichaean Elect was not merely the servant of God but was actively aiding God who needed such help for His liberation.[1] Indeed, it might be said that, in one sense, the Elect was God, for in his pure body was the greatest concentration of Light that can be found on earth.

In view of the very evil reputation which the Manichees enjoyed in the mind of orthodox Christians, so that their name during the Middle Ages was applied to every Dualistic sect, Paulicians, Bogomils, and Albigenses, who were themselves suspected of being guilty of loathsome practices,[2] it may be asked what relation the actual standards of the Manichees bore to their theoretical morality. The question is not an easy one to answer. All our evidence against them comes from hostile sources, naturally inclined to believe the worst about an enemy. Moreover, the fact that the Manichees were an illegal religion in the Roman Empire compelled them, to a greater or lesser degree, to preserve a certain discretion in their doings,[3] with the inevitable consequence that suspicions about them were intensified. This however proves nothing; the early Christians, living under conditions not very different, were accused of the most horrifying crimes: incest, infanticide, and Thyestian banquets. Memories of this fact should

[1] This point is well brought out by Burkitt, *The Religion of the Manichees*, 46–47: 'It is not for nothing that "mourner" is one of the Syriac technical terms for a Christian monk. The Manichee Elect does not appear to have been a "mourner". He was indeed fenced about with tabus—"touch not, taste not, handle not"—but by virtue of his profession he was already Righteous, and he was called *Zaddīkā*, i.e. "the righteous", by his co-religionists.' Cf. the remarks of Puech, op. cit., p. 91.
[2] See Runciman, *The Medieval Manichee*, 175–7.
[3] See Augustine's remark about the Roman Manichees, when he arrived there in 383, in *Conf.*, V, x, 19: 'plures enim eos Roma occultabat'. The expression gave great offence to the Manichees when the *Confessions* appeared. See Courcelle, *Recherches*, 236.

be a warning against paying attention to rumours. Furthermore, it was not only rival religions like Christianity and, later, Islam which disliked the Manichees. Secular governments, even if only lukewarm in their religious duties, refused to tolerate Manichaeism or its later Dualistic manifestations. The ideal of the Manichaean Elect: non-violence, celibacy, and holy idleness, was and is intolerable to every secular government. If the Manichees had had their way, the human race would have died out, and this is a possibility which appals ordinary men or women even if, as is usually the case, they have no clear conception of why they consider the human race ought to persist. In consequence, the Manichees were as hateful to the state as to their religious rivals and earned the bad opinion of everybody.[1]

Nevertheless, there are certain considerations which may explain, if not wholly justify, the evil reputation enjoyed by the Manichees down the ages. They apply, principally, to the Auditors, who constituted by far the largest element of the Manichees, and the one least strictly disciplined.

The Manichaean Auditor, as we have seen, was in theory subjected to a code of conduct which, if far less exacting than that imposed upon the Elect, was nevertheless a strict one. It was generally summed up by the code of the 'Three Seals': the seal of the mouth, forbidding blasphemy, lying, and similar offences; the seal of the hand, which prohibited murder, theft, and any action whereby injury might be offered to the Light imprisoned in the material creation; and, lastly, the seal of the bosom, which, in the case of the Elect, meant an absolute abstention from all sexual experiences and, in the case of the Auditors, forbade fornication, adultery, and similar sins of the flesh.[2] The degree to which these rules of conduct would be observed no doubt depended very much upon the individual Manichee, and some must have fallen as far short of their ideal as any Catholic Christian from his. Thus, in theory, the military profession was closed to a Manichee, since he was not allowed to take life. In practice, however, we know of at least one high-ranking Roman officer who was a Manichaean Auditor, the Count Sebastian, who was killed at the battle of Adrianople in 378, after having been the commander of the army of Egypt, where he showed himself as the bitter enemy of St Athanasius, and as a

[1] It will be recalled that Augustine's conversion to Manichaeism was the only occasion when his mother refused to allow him to live at her house or eat at her table, *Conf.*, III, xi, 19: '. . . eam [Monnicam] consolatus es, [Domine], et vivere mecum cederet et habere mecum eandem mensam in domo. Quod nolle coeperat aversans et detestans blasphemias erroris mei.' It is significant that the mere possession of a mistress had not had such an effect on Monica's attitude to her son.
[2] On the Three Seals, see Augustine, *De Moribus*, II, x, 19; xi, 20–xviii, 66. Jackson, *Researches*, 334–6 gives allusions in Pahlavi and Turkish Manichaean texts.

brutal persecutor of the Catholics.[1] To what degree Sebastian was an isolated phenomenon in Manichaean history we cannot tell; but unless St Athanasius is in error—and there is no reason why he should have been misinformed on the point; Manichaeism was well established in Egypt—we have the phenomenon of a Manichee occupying one of the highest posts in the Roman army, in flat violation of the principles of conduct of his sect. Admittedly, from the Christian point of view, military service was not, in itself, a sin (though the more austere elements in the Church always remained doubtful as to whether it could be rightly undertaken by a servant of Christ); but Manichaean principles did not admit of any possibility of rendering to Caesar his due, and if it were possible to overlook them in this particular, it would be possible to disregard them in other matters.

Furthermore, certain of the rules of conduct for Manichaean Auditors were, in themselves, calculated to make the sect unpopular, notably those relating to charity. It was not merely desirable but definitely required in a Manichaean Auditor that he should furnish alms, that is, food, to the Elect; but he was forbidden to supply food to any non-Manichaean since that would result in a continued imprisonment of particles of Light in matter, although there was no objection to giving money.[2] Inevitably, the Manichees were accused of inhumanity; 'There is no compassion among Manichees,' observes St Athanasius, 'charity to the poor is a stranger among them.'[3] The accusation was unfair; but it probably accurately expresses the feeling of an age in which the lavish distribution of charity was one of the most highly esteemed marks of the devout man.

But the charges commonly levelled against the Manichees were of another, and darker, kind. It was rumoured that their alleged asceticism was merely a cloak for hideous and obscene practices founded upon, and justified by, the methods employed by the powers of Light for liberating the particles of Light imprisoned in the bodies of the princes of Darkness by the stimulation of their concupiscence. Tales were told that the ritual meals of the Elect, to which the Manichees applied the name of the Eucharist, were the occasion for the consumption of disgusting food, taken in conformity with the belief that Light was purged in their entrails. This

[1] For details of the outrages committed by Sebastian's soldiery on the Catholics of Egypt, see Athanasius, De Fug., 6 (MPG xxv, 652), and Hist. Ar., 55, 59, 61 (MPG xxv, 760, 764, 768); for his military exploits, see Ammianus Marcellinus, 23, iii, 5; 25, viii, 7, 16; 26, vi, 2; 27, x, 6; 30, v, 13; x, 3; 31, xi, 1; 2; xii, 1, 6; xiii, 18. An outline in his career will be found in Pauly-Wissowa, Real-Encyclopädie, 2te Reihe, 3ter Halbbd. (Stuttgart, 1921), 954. Against the naturally dark picture of his nature painted by St Athanasius may be set the comment of Ammianus Marcellinus (who knew him personally): 'quietum quidem virum et placidum sed militari favore sublatum' (30, x, 3).
[2] See Puech, Le Manichéisme, 187–8 n[378].
[3] Athanasius, Hist. Ar., 61 (MPG xxv, 768 A–B). Cf. Aug., De Moribus, II, xv, 36.

belief was commonly held by the enemies of the Manichees and Augustine himself ultimately came to accept it. At the present day, when passion has been spent and Manichaeism is merely an episode in the religious history of humanity, the historian will wish to decide, so far as he is able, how much credence should be given to this accusation.

Augustine is obviously an important witness, in that he spent more than nine years in the Manichaean religion and should have had ample opportunity to discover discreditable features in the lives of its adherents. Inevitably, in any religious community, scandals would arise; Augustine discovered a number of the Elect at Carthage whose lives fell short of the standard required of them and, to his disgust, no action was taken against them by the Manichaean hierarchy, from fear that the guilty men would betray them to the secular authority as a revenge.[1] Again, while Augustine was at Rome before he secured his appointment at Milan, an unpleasant scandal occurred in the Manichaean community, in the sudden death of a boy who was being trained with a view to becoming one of the Elect himself.[2] Yet again, while he was at Milan, Augustine learned of the failure of the attempt of a certain Constantius, who afterwards himself became a Catholic, to establish a Manichaean monastery at Rome, where the rules of conduct enjoined by Mani would be strictly observed. In practice the attempt failed because of the frailty of the would-be holy men.[3] All these incidents, however, merely indicate what might be expected in a religion of exaggerated austerity: that certain of its adherents were incapable of observing the precepts of their faith. This does not prove any widespread or abnormal depravity, still less the existence of deliberately obscene rituals. Furthermore, we have Augustine's own admission that, as a Manichaean Auditor, he saw nothing scandalous at any Manichaean service.[4]

Such a testimony ought to dispel any serious doubts as to the integrity of the Manichees if it were not for the fact that, as Augustine grew older, his suspicions regarding Manichaean morality increased, apparently in the light of fresh evidence. In his book *On the Morals of the Manichees*, which he wrote at Rome in 388, he speaks of the rumour of obscene banquets and declares that it is confirmed by the Manichaean hatred of con-

---

[1] *De Moribus*, II, xix, 68–69.
[2] Ibid., xiv, 52.
[3] *De Moribus*, II, xx, 74; *C. Faust.*, V, v, vii. See Courcelle, *Recherches*, 179 n[1], 228.
[4] *C. Fortun.*, 3: 'De moribus autem vestris plene scire possunt, qui electi vestri sunt. nostis autem me non electum vestrum, sed auditorem fuisse. itaque quamvis et orationi vestrae interfuerim, ut interrogasti, utrum separatim vobiscum habeatis aliquam orationem, deus solus potest nosse et vos. ego tamen in oratione, in qua interfui, nihil turpe fieri vidi, sed solum contra fidem animadverti. quam postea didici et probavi, quod contra solem facitis orationem. praeter hoc in illa oratione vestra nihil novi comperi.'

ception and their teaching that Light is liberated from its fleshly prison in the meals of the Elect.[1] In his dispute with the Manichee Fortunatus, held in 392, Augustine, while admitting that he himself saw nothing unfitting at Manichaean services as an Auditor, remarks that he does not know what is done at the Eucharists of the Elect.[2] By the time that he came to write his treatise *On the Nature of Good* in 405, the saint had (or thought that he had) evidence confirming the charges commonly levelled against the Manichees:

> Let those who are grievously deceived and poisoned with this deadly error notice this. They profess that part of God can be released and purged by eating. But if it is bound by the intercourse of male and female, by necessity this horrible error compels them to release it not only from bread, vegetables and apples, which are the only things they appear in public to accept; but they must also release and purge the part of God by sexual intercourse, if it has been conceived in the womb, and can be bound there. Some are said to have confessed in a public tribunal that they have done this, not only in Paphlagonia but even in Gaul, as I heard from a Catholic Christian at Rome. When they are asked by what written authority they do these things, I hear they produce the passage from the *Thesaurus* which I quoted a moment ago. When this charge is made against them they are accustomed to reply that one of their number, that is one of the Elect, broke away and made a schism and founded this foul heresy. So it is quite clear that though some of them may not behave in that way, those who do, get the idea from their books. Let them then throw away these books if they abhor the crime, which they are urged to commit if they retain the books. If they do not commit it they try to live cleanly, contrary to the teaching of the books.[3]

This seems minute and circumstantial confirmation of the charges brought against the Manichees, unless we doubt the veracity of the Catholic Christian who, during Augustine's second stay at Rome which lasted from the summer of 387 to that of 388, gave him this information concerning Manichaean enormities which had taken place in Gaul. But a serious doubt arises as to whether, in fact, the alleged enormities in Gaul have any connection with the Manichees at all. In the autumn of 386 a

---

[1] *De Moribus*, II, xviii, 66: 'Iamvero, cum vehementer satagitis, ne per concubitum anima ligetur in carne, et vehementer asseritis, per sanctorum cibum animam de seminibus liberari, nonne confirmatis, o miseri, quod de vobis homines suspicantur? Cur enim de tritico, et de faba, et de lenticula aliisque seminibus, cum his vescimini, liberare vos velle animam creditur, de animalium seminibus non creditur? . . . Quae si non facitis, quod utinam ita sit, videtis tamen quantae suspicioni vestra superstitio pateat, et quam non sit hominibus succensendum id opinantibus, quod de vestra professione colligitur, cum vos animas per escam et potum, de corporibus et sensibus liberare praedicatis.'

[2] *C. Fortun.*, 3: 'quid autem inter vos agatis, qui electi estis, ego scire non possum. nam et eucharistiam audivi a vobis saepe quod accipiatis; tempus autem accipiendi cum me lateret, quid accipiatis unde nosse potui?'

[3] *De Nat. Boni*, 47. Tr. by Burleigh, p. 347.

series of executions took place at Trèves, in which perished Priscillian, an ascetic Spanish layman who, with a group of his disciples, had been accused of sorcery—a capital offence in the Roman Empire. The Priscillianists were regarded by many Catholics as being a Manichaean sect and it is likely that obscenities alleged against the Manichees of Gaul by Augustine's Roman informant were, in fact, those with which Priscillian had been charged a year or so earlier.[1]

If this is indeed the case, it is apparent that the evidence of this passage cannot be used against the Manichees, and is significant only as bearing witness to the growing suspicion in Augustine's mind that there was definite substance in the popular reports regarding Manichaean practices. Otherwise, it is difficult to see why he should have failed to make use of this story at an earlier date. By 428, however, when he came to write his treatise *On Heresies* for Quodvultdeus, suspicion had hardened into certainty:

> On this account or, rather, by a certain necessity of this execrable superstition, their Elect are compelled to consume a pseudo-eucharist sprinkled with human seed, so that the divine substance may also be purified from that, as from other food which they receive. But they themselves deny that they do this, and affirm that this is the practice of others under the name of Manichees. However, they were discovered in the Church of Carthage (as you know, for you were a deacon at the time) by the activity of Ursus the tribune, who was then an official of the imperial household. Some of them were brought forward, and a girl called Margarita disclosed this most wicked shame, and said that she had been defiled on account of this criminal mystery, when she was not yet twelve years old. Ursus then compelled with difficulty a certain Eusebia, a sort of Manichaean nun, to confess that she too had suffered the same. At first, she declared that she was a virgin and demanded to be inspected by a midwife; but on being examined and found not to be so, she revealed the whole revolting crime, in which flour is strewn below a man and the woman in copulation to receive and mingle with the seed, using terms similar to Margarita, whom she had not heard, for she was not present when the girl gave evidence. More recently, as the episcopal records which you sent me show, some were detected and led to the church and, under a searching interrogation, confessed that sacrament —not a sacrament, indeed, but an abhorrent sacrilege. One of whom, Viator by name, declared that those who do these things should properly be called *Catharistae*. He reported that other parts of the Manichaean

---

[1] See E. Ch. Babut, *Priscillien et le priscillianisme* (Bibliothèque de l'École des Hautes-Études, Fasc. CLXIX), Paris, 1909, 14 n^2 and 179 n^2; J. A. Davids, *De Orosio et sancto Augustino Priscillianistarum adversariis commentatio historica et philologica*, The Hague, 1930, 258–61; and Courcelle, *Recherches*, 218 n^5. For the date of Priscillian's execution, see Adhémar d'Alès, *Priscillien et l'Espagne chrétienne à la fin du IVe siècle*, Paris, 1936, Appendice II, 167–73.

sect were divided into Matarii and, specifically, Manichees; but he was unable to deny that all three forms have sprung from one founder and are generally styled Manichees. And, certainly, there is no doubt that the Manichaean scriptures are common to all of them, in which are recorded these monstrosities concerning the change from male to female and from the female to the male form, to enflame and, by concupiscence, to dissolve the rulers of Darkness of each sex, so that the divine substance held captive in them may be set free and escape, from which this shameful conduct follows, let them deny it as they may.[1]

This is Augustine's final judgement of his former co-religionists delivered only two years before his death and fortified with circumstantial evidence. But does it really amount to very much ? Two scandals concerning the Manichees have come to light, in both of which confessions have been made confirming the worst accusations brought against them. But it should be remembered that, in the case of the interrogations presided over by the imperial official Ursus, torture was probably applied and certainly threatened. In such circumstances, even an innocent person might well hasten to supply the inquisitor with the information which he desired. The melancholy history of the witch-trials of Europe, not to speak of more recent and more terrible legal processes, bears witness to the power of physical pain and prolonged interrogation to persuade the victim to confess to any number of enormities.[2] The Manichaean religious, Eusebia, was only constrained to confess with difficulty and it is improbable that she would have demanded a physical examination if she had not herself believed that she was a virgin.[3] Nor can the result of the examination be regarded as a decisive factor. 'I find the tryal of the Pucellage and virginity of Women, which God ordained the Jews, is very fallible', wrote Sir Thomas Browne,[4] and modern medicine is even less inclined to attach undue weight to mere anatomical virtue. Indeed, Augustine himself was fully aware of the limitations of such evidence, when it concerned Catholic religious.[5] Finally, we have to reckon with the Manichees' statement that

[1] De Haeres., 46.
[2] Augustine, in his famous letter to Marcellinus (Ep. 133), refers to the normal instruments of Roman judicial investigation—the rack, the hooks, and the fire. The saint, it will be remembered, commends Marcellinus for not having employed these during the course of his inquiry, and congratulates him for securing confession by a judicious use of the rod, 'a sanction used by schoolmasters, by parents, and often even by bishops in their ecclesiastical judgements'!
[3] One can just conceive of a very brazen effrontery, which bargained upon the unwillingness of the authorities to take up the challenge; but Eusebia would have had no grounds for supposing that they would decline to do so.
[4] Religio Medici, I, x.
[5] dCD, I, xviii: 'Obstetrix virginis cuiusdam integritatem manu velut explorans sive malevolentia sive inscitia sive casu, dum inspicit, perdidit. Non opinor quemquam tam stulte sapere, ut huic perisse aliquid existimet etiam de ipsius corporis sanctitate, quamvis membri illius integritate iam perdita.'

these practices were not the work of their own adherents, but of a schismatic faction. In short, of the three instances which Augustine adduces as evidence of alleged Manichaean obscenities, the first probably refers to another sect altogether, while the two others rest upon evidence which is decidedly suspect, in the light of the appalling evidence which is all too richly available, regarding the ability of innocent persons to supply damning evidence against themselves under pressure from a hostile judiciary.

If, however, we decline to accept Augustine's evidence at its face value, we have still to answer the question why it was that the Manichees and their spiritual descendants of the later Middle Ages acquired such an evil reputation. Such a question is entirely legitimate, and cannot be shrugged aside on the grounds of general Manichaean unpopularity.

One obvious factor in the growth and consolidation of the legend was the fact that the Manichaean scriptures were indisputably full of obscene material. It is no accident that Augustine constantly returns to the episode in *The Treasure* concerning the stimulation of the concupiscence of the male and female demons, to secure the release of the particles of Light imprisoned in their bodies. Since such myths were, in the eyes of the Manichees, the record of actual events in the redemption of the world, it is not to be wondered at that the non-Manichee, particularly if hostile to the sect, came to believe that they could serve as a pattern of conduct for the Manichaean believer. Such an assumption may not have been logical but it was understandable, especially when we remember that the Manichees themselves argued that Catholic veneration of the Old Testament necessarily involved approbation of the vices of various men recorded therein.[1]

Secondly, and very important, is the Manichaean attitude to sexuality. In theory, as we have seen, their ideal was one of absolute continence, and this was, in practice, imposed upon the Elect, who were the only Manichees fully living the way of life declared by the Apostle of Jesus Christ. Such a discipline was, clearly, too much for the ordinary Auditor[2] and

---

[1] *C. Faustum*, XXII, lxii: 'Quod ita nobis Faustus vel ipsa Manichaea perversitas arbitratur adversum, quasi nobis in illius scripturae veneratione dignoque praeconio vitia hominum, quae illa commemorat, necesse sit adprobare; quin potius necesse est, ut, quanto illam religiosius accipimus, tanto fidentius illa culpemus, quae per eius veritatem certius culpanda didicimus.'

[2] Ibid., XXX, vi: 'Denique vos eum praecipue concubitum detestamini, qui solus honestus et coniugalis est et quem matrimoniales quoque tabulae prae se gerunt, liberorum procreandorum causa: unde vere non tam concumbere quam nubere prohibetis. concumbitur enim etiam causa libidinum, nubitur autem nonnisi filiorum. nec ideo nos dicatis non prohibere, quia multos vestros auditores in hoc oboedire nolentes vel non valentes salva amicitia toleratis.'

provision had to be made for human frailty. In practice, the Manichees permitted marriage to their Auditors but discouraged them, so far as might be possible, from having children.[1] Sexual desire might indeed proceed from the promptings of the powers of Darkness, but it was by conception that the divine substance was bound in the flesh. For that reason, the lusts of the flesh might be excused provided that they did not lead to pro-creation. The Manichaean teachers were, apparently, prepared to offer advice as to how pregnancy might be avoided[2] and some of their tech-niques appear to have been effective. In Augustine's own case, it is signifi-cant that his son, Adeodatus, was born before he became a Manichee; during the whole period in which he was a member of the sect, no more children were born to him, although he remained faithful to his concubine.[3] There is no reason to doubt that Augustine made strenuous efforts to con-form to the highest Manichaean ideals[4] but he failed, as the squalid sequel to his mother's arrival in Milan and the dismissal of his concubine as an

[1] Ibid., XXII, xxx: 'Sicut enim lex illa aeterna, id est voluntas dei creaturarum omnium conditoris conservando naturali ordini consulens, non ut satiandae libidini serviatur, sed ut saluti generis prospiciatur, ad prolem tantummodo propagandam mortalis carnis delectationem dominatu rationis in concubitu relaxari sinit: sic e contrario perversa lex Manichaeorum, ne deus eorum, quem ligatum in omnibus seminibus plan-gunt, in conceptu feminae artius conligetur, prolem ante omnia devitari a concumbenti-bus iubet, ut deus eorum turpi lapsu potius effundatur quam crudeli nexu vinciatur. non igitur Abraham prolis habendae insana cupiditate flagrabat, sed Manichaeus prolis devitandae insana vanitate delirabat. proinde ille naturae ordinem servans nihil humano concubitu agebat, nisi ut homo nasceretur; iste perversitatem fabulae observans nihil in quolibet concubitu timebat, nisi ne deus captivaretur.' C. Secund., 21: 'novi, unde veniat indignatio tua; non enim tibi tam fornicaria displicet in fornicatione, quam quod in matrimonium commutata est et conversa ad pudicitiam coniugalem, ubi deum creditis vestrum in procreando filios artioribus carnis vinculis conligari: cui putatis parcere meretrices, quia dant operam, ne concipiant, ut ab officio pariendi liberae libidini ser-viant. feminae quippe conceptus apud vos carcer est et vinculum dei.'

[2] De Moribus, II, xviii, 65: 'Quae cum magna voce et magna indignatione dixeritis, ego vos lenius interrogabo ad hunc modum: nonne vos estis qui filios gignere, eo quod animae ligentur in carne, gravius putatis esse peccatum, quam ipsum concubitum? Nonne vos estis qui nos solebatis monere, ut quantum fieri posset, observaremus tempus, quo ad conceptum mulier post genitalium viscerum purgationem apta esset, eoque tem-pore a concubitu temperaremus, ne carni anima implicaretur?'

[3] Conf., IV, ii, 2. Note his reference to the 'pact of lustful love, where children are born against our will, although once born, they compel us to love them.' See Alfaric, L'évolution intellectuelle, 151 n[3], and Courcelle, Recherches, 71 and nn. Augustine does not say what other contraceptive devices, if any, were used by the Manichees, other than that mentioned in De Moribus, II, xviii, 65 (see previous note). This is the tempus ageneseos of modern moral theologians. Other methods were certainly known in the ancient world; see the reference in C. Secund., 21 to 'meretrices . . . [quae] dant operam, ne concipiant, ut ab officio pariendi liberae libidini serviant'. Another reference to contraception may be in C. Faustum, XXII, xxx: 'prolem ante omnia devitari a concum-bentibus iubet, ut deus eorum turpi lapsu potius effundatur quam crudeli nexu vincia-tur.' This would seem to be coitus interruptus.

[4] Courcelle, Recherches, 71 n[3], draws attention to Conf., VIII, vii, 17 in this connection. Cf. Augustine's admission in Conf., VIII, i, 2: 'Iam enim me illa [sc. saecularia gaudia] non delectabant prae dulcedine tua et decore domus tuae, quam dilexi, sed adhuc tenaciter conligabar ex femina.'

obstacle to his projected marriage was to reveal.[1] Unless, however, we are
to assume that Augustine was unusually incontinent (and we have no
reason to do so), it is probable that many other Manichaean Auditors were
in a condition similar to his and were tolerated, so long as they took steps
to avoid having children. Since, however, all sexual relations were in
essence sinful, it is likely that the Manichaean hierarchy would tolerate a
wide range of sexual experience among their Auditors, so long as they
remained infertile. In such circumstances, it would not be surprising if
certain of the weaker members of the sect took advantage of toleration to
indulge in considerable licence. It is significant that during the later
Middle Ages the Albigenses, whose superior caste, the Perfects, lived a
life as fully ascetic as the Manichaean Elect, were alleged by the Catholics
to hold that matrimony was no more than prostitution and that there was
no salvation for the man begetting sons and daughters.[2] In consequence,
the Believers (credentes) of the sect—the Albigensian equivalent of the
Manichaean Auditors—were suspected of debauchery and unnatural
orgies. They were thought to hold the comforting belief that it was not
possible to sin with any part of the body below the navel and to say that
incestuous union with a mother or a sister was no more sinful than with
any other woman.[3] No doubt they were maligned to a certain degree; and
no doubt Augustine's own writings played a part in influencing their
enemies, since Catholic apologists were quick to identify any Dualist
opponents with the Manichees of Augustine's day. So Guibert of Nogent,
writing about an heretical sect which gathered round a peasant called
Clementius at Bucy-le-long near Soissons in 1125 who denied the sacrament of the Eucharist and taught that marriage and generation were crimes,
tells a lurid story about the promiscuous orgies in which these heretics
were believed to indulge at their meetings after the lights had been extinguished—so lurid, indeed, as to remind the reader that precisely the same
accusations were levelled against the early Christians in their assemblies—
particularly when our author adds that babies conceived at these orgies were
burnt as soon as born and their ashes used for making a species of communion bread.[4] The significant point, however, is Guibert's remark that

[1] Conf., VI, xv, 25.
[2] Pierre de Vaulx-Cernay, Hystoria Albigensis, ed. P. Guébin and E. Lyon, Paris, 1926,
i, 13: 'sacrum matrimonium meretricium esse nec aliquem in ipso salvari posse predica-
bant filios et filias generando.'
[3] Ibid., p. 17: 'Non credimus autem silendum quod et quidam heretici dicebant quod
nullus peccare poterat ab umbilico et inferius. . . . item dicebant quod non peccabat quis
gravius dormiendo cum matre vel sorore sua quam cum qualibet alia.'
[4] Guibert de Nogent, Monodiarum sive de vita sua, ed. Bourgin, Paris, 1907, iii, 213.
Cf. Tertullian, Apologeticus, 7–9, and note his argument (cc. 7, 14–8, 4) that natural

of all the heretics listed by Augustine this sect most closely resembles the Manichees,[1] which may mean that he looked at them with the eyes of a student of Augustine and indulged in a certain amount of wishful thinking with regard to their beliefs. What at least is clear, both with regard to the heretics of Soissons of the twelfth century and the Albigenses of thirteenth-century Provence, is that both stressed the sinful nature of marriage and generation. Since, however, all sexual relations were sinful, and since the supreme crime was to bring a child into the world, it is not unlikely that the ordinary Believer of the medieval heretical sect might have been urged to 'sin strongly', provided that no child resulted from his actions.[2] (It is significant that both these movements were accused of tolerating sodomy.) It is reasonable to assume that the Manichees were in a condition very similar to that of their later imitators. Any ascetic movement which sets its face against the normal manifestations of sexuality and especially against procreation, is likely to be accused of secret enormities by its enemies, whose suspicions will be intensified by evidence of frailties among weaker members and camp-followers. That there were scandals in the Manichaean community at Carthage need not be doubted; that these were the result of a deliberate policy, as Augustine came to believe, is more open to question. At a later date, when the evidence is so scanty and furnished only by enemies, it is reasonable as well as charitable to receive it with caution, especially when we remember that Augustine did not discover any gross abnormalities so long as he remained a Manichaean Auditor.

We may, therefore, acquit the Manichees of the more extreme charges of immorality which have been brought against them. It would be agreeable if we could also speak with respect of their intellectual qualities, but even with the most sympathetic examination, their thought remains bizarre and, in Puech's words, puerile. Thus, although it is permissible to speak of the Manichaean theology as one in which the theme is the struggle

instinct, in the case of a large body of persons, can be relied upon to revolt against practices of such a nature: '. . . ut fidem naturae ipsius appellem adversus eos, qui talia credenda esse praesumunt. Ecce proponimus horum facinorum mercedem: vitam aeternam repromittunt. Credite interim! De hoc enim quaero, an et qui credideris tanti habeas, ad eam tali conscientia pervenire. Veni, demerge ferrum in infantem nullius inimicum, nullius reum, omnium filium; vel, si alterius officium est, tu modo adsiste morienti homini, antequam vixit; fugientem animam novam exspecta, excipe rudem sanguinem, eo panem tuum satia, vescere libenter. Interea discumbens dinumera loca, ubi mater, ubi soror; nota diligenter, ut, cum tenebrae ceciderint caninae, non erres! Piaculum enim admiseris, nisi incestum feceris. Talia initiatus et consignatus vivis in aevum. Cupio respondeas, si tanti aeternitas; aut si non, ideo nec credenda. Etiamsi credideris, nego te velle; etiamsi volueris, nego te posse.' *CSEL* lxix, 21.

[1] Guibert de Nogent, op. cit., p. 213: 'Si relegas haereses ab Augustino digestas, nulli magis quam Manicheorum reperies convenire.'

[2] This is the view of Runciman, *The Medieval Manichee*, 152.

between spirit and matter, it would be a mistake to assume that, for the Manichee, spirit was non-material, in the sense in which two and a half millennia of the influence of Greek metaphysics have made us understand the word. On the contrary, both Light and Darkness, Spirit and Matter, are material, but the one is more fine and tenuous than the other. Augustine, it will be recalled, was perplexed by precisely this difficulty when he was at Rome, still nominally adhering to the Manichaean sect, but already dissatisfied and disillusioned by the failure of his meeting with Faustus. He was unable to conceive of God except in terms of a corporeal mass[1] and, even after his arrival at Milan, when the sermons of Ambrose had convinced him that many of the objections which the Manichees levelled against the Catholic faith and, in particular, their claim that the Catholics had an anthropomorphic conception of God were unfounded, he still had no conception of how there might be any spiritual substance,[2] and had to wait until he had access to the writings of the Neo-Platonists to be able to form such a conception.[3] It would be unjust to judge the Manichees too severely on this account. The Stoics never rose above a material conception of God as a fiery mind[4] or as a breath (*pneuma*)[5] interpenetrating all things, even the ugly and the loathsome. In the case of the Manichees, however, the situation is complicated by their dualism. If, on the one hand, they could not conceive of any existent being which was not, in some sense, material, they were in this no different from the majority of

[1] *Conf.*, V, x, 19–20: 'Et quoniam cum de deo meo cogitare vellem, cogitare nisi moles corporum non noveram—neque enim videbatur mihi esse quicquam, quod tale non esset —ea maxima et prope sola causa erat inevitabilis erroris mei. [20] Hinc enim et mali substantiam quandam credebam esse talem et habere suam molem tetram et deformem, sive crassam, quam terram dicebant, sive tenuem atque subtilem, sicut est aeris corpus: quam malignam mentem per illam terram repentem imaginantur. Et quia deum bonum nullam malam naturam creasse qualiscumque me pietas credere cogebat, constituebam ex adverso sibi duas moles, utramque infinitam, sed malam angustius, bonam grandius, et ex hoc initio pestilentioso me cetera sacrilegia sequebantur.'

[2] *Ibid.*, VI, iii, 4: 'Ubi vero etiam conperi *ad imaginem tuam hominem a te factum* ab spiritalibus filiis tuis, quos de matre catholica per gratiam regenerasti, non sic intellegi, ut humani corporis forma determinatum crederent atque cogitarent, quamquam quomodo se haberet spiritalis substantia, ne quidem tenuiter atque in aenigmate suspicabar, tamen gaudens erubui non me tot annos adversus catholicam fidem, sed contra carnalium cogitationum figmenta latrasse.'

[3] See his admission, *Conf.*, VII, i, 1: 'Clamabat violenter cor meum adversus omnia phantasmata mea et hoc uno ictu conabar abigere circumvolantem turbam inmunditiae ab acie mentis meae: et vix dimota, *in ictu oculi* ecce conglobata rursus aderat et inruebat in aspectum meum et obnubilabat eum, ut quamvis non forma humani corporis, corporeum tamen aliquid cogitare cogerer per spatia locorum sive infusum mundo sive etiam extra mundum per infinita diffusum, etiam ipsum incorruptibile et inviolabile et inconmutabile.'

[4] *Stoicorum Veterum Fragments*, ed. H. von Arnim, i, frag. 157.

[5] Ibid., frag. 159. The Stoic *pneuma* must not be confused with the Christian use of the term in John 4.24: 'God is a spirit (*pneuma*)', which has behind it, not Greek philosophy, but the Hebrew Scriptures. See Edwyn Bevan, *Later Greek Religion*, London, 1927, 2 n[2].

men in any age; but unfortunately for themselves, with this practical materialism went the belief expressed in the whole of their ascetic system, that matter, simply as matter, was something evil. Indeed the Manichees, or at least those of the Graeco-Roman world, in their anxiety to explain that their dualism did not commit them to polytheism, were led to adopt the word *hyle* (ὕλη), the formless, passive Matter of Aristotelian and other Greek philosophies which only becomes actual by the imposition of Form, and to bestow it upon the principle of evil. 'Is there one God or two?' asked the Manichee, Faustus, indignantly, 'clearly one. How then do you claim that we say two? The name of two gods has certainly never been heard in our assertions',[1] and he proceeded to explain that his sect taught that there were two principles of Good and Evil, God and *Hyle*, and identified the latter with the demon of Catholic Christianity.[2] In fact, of course, the Manichees had adopted the word and not the philosophical concept, as Augustine was not slow to point out. 'Not even matter which the ancients called "Hyle" is to be called evil. I do not mean what Manes in his stupid vanity ignorantly calls "Hyle", that is to say the power that forms bodies. He is rightly said to be introducing a second god. . . . By "Hyle" I mean matter completely without form and quality, out of which are formed the qualities we perceive, as the ancients said. Hence wood is called "Hyle" in Greek, because it is suitable material for workmen, not that it makes anything but that something may be made out of it. That "Hyle" is not to be called evil. It has no form by which we can perceive it. Indeed, it can hardly be conceived because it is so utterly without form. But it has the capacity to receive form.'[3] The Manichaean *Hyle*, the active principle of Evil, co-equal and co-eternal with the Father of Greatness, is clearly far removed from the formless, passive *hyle* of Greek philosophy. Nevertheless, the use of the term is significant, and affords an example of the sort of logical dilemma which the Manichaean religion could impose upon its more thoughtful members. They hated matter, but could conceive of no non-material existence. Of a similar nature was the problem which Nebridius had proposed to them at Carthage, during Augustine's period in the sect: What could the powers of Darkness have done to the Father of Greatness, if he had refused to fight with them? If they could have injured him, then clearly, the Manichees' assertion that he was incorruptible and inviolable was untrue. If, on the other hand, they could have done him no

---

[1] *C. Faust.*, XXI, i: 'Faustus dixit: Unus deus est, an duo? plane unus. quomodo ergo vos duos adseritis? numquam in nostris quidem adsertionibus duorum deorum auditum est nomen.'
[2] Ibid.: '...duo principia confitemur, sed unum ex his deum vocamus, alteram hylen, aut, ut communiter et usitate dixerim, daemonem.' [3] *De Nat. Boni*, 18. Tr. by Burleigh, p. 331.

injury, then what conceivable benefit could he have gained from a combat in which a part of his pure substance should have fallen into the foul bondage of the forces of Darkness?[1] From the Manichaean side came no effective reply; nor, indeed, could any have come. Shackled to a monstrous cosmogony and destitute of any metaphysical sytem, it was little wonder that Manichaeism provided Augustine, as a Catholic apologist, with some of the easiest of his controversial victims.

The question inevitably arises why, in the face of such obvious weakness, did Manichaeism originally impress Augustine as an intellectual force, as it clearly did. The answer is probably to be found in two factors, the one positive, the other negative. On the positive side, the sheer massive structure of the system must have seemed very imposing, with each detail of the world provided for and suitably explained. The cosmic machine, established by the forces of Light for the liberation of the world and supposedly in harmony with astronomical theory, was calculated to impress the inquirer, especially one like Augustine, whose education had been in literature and whose scientific knowledge was of the scantiest. Secondly, on the negative side, the fact that the Manichees had developed their technique for attacking the Catholic Scriptures into a fine art clearly carried much weight, as the hostile application of the Higher Criticism invariably does. Unfortunately, as Augustine was to discover, the negative power of the Manichees as critics was not matched by any comparable ability as apologists. The allegorical method of scriptural interpretation countered their attacks on the Old Testament; but their fundamentalism where their own scriptures were concerned prevented them from employing it themselves, when the incompatibility of Mani's cosmology with the accepted astronomy of the day was revealed, and Faustus of Milevis, the great savant, at whose coming, or so his admirers declared, all Augustine's doubts would be resolved, modestly confessed his inability to meet the problems which were presented to him. In this simple honesty we see the nemesis of Manichaean intellectual pretensions.

It was not, however, from its intellectual qualities that Manichaeism derived its power but, rather, from its moral note and the hope that it held out to its adherents of liberation from an unhappy and defiled existence. Sir Steven Runciman has observed of the last manifestation of Christian dualism that 'it was not an ignoble religion. It taught the value of the fundamental virtues; it faced with courage the anxious question of evil. But it was a religion of pessimism. It held out no hope for individual men and their salvation. Mankind should die out, that the imprisoned fragments

---

[1] *Conf.*, VII, ii, 3.

of Godhead should return to their home. It was a religion without hope, and such a religion cannot survive unless it be helped artificially. For Hope is a necessary part of religion. Faith and Charity alone are not enough.'[1] Much of this could equally well be applied to the Manichees of the fourth century as to the Albigenses of the thirteenth, though one may question whether the pessimism which found expression in the belief that the human race should die out was really, in practice, very different from the outlook of a saint like St Jerome, who so enthusiastically commended virginity and who has provided the Manichees with an unsuspected and wholly unsolicited testimonial, by recording that it was the custom of the worldly population of Rome, when they saw a woman in the garb of a consecrated virgin, to call her a 'wretched solitary and a Manichee'.[2] No doubt the Manichaean Elect, like St Jerome, preached celibacy while being fully aware that only a small number would adopt it. This is not to suggest that the theology behind these attitudes was the same. On the contrary, it was utterly different; but it would be a mistake to assume that every Manichee of Augustine's day was in a state of gloom and despair. He could see, beyond the miseries and injustices of this world, the glories of the Kingdom of Light, and knew that Mani, the Apostle of Jesus Christ, had come from the land of Babel to utter the great call to salvation, which was to resound across the world. Salvation was offered to the man who would take it. Why should the faithful believer be dismayed?

Our information regarding the eventual fate of Manichaeism in Africa is tantalizingly scanty. To what degree Augustine's onslaughts, delivered after he had become a Catholic, discredited it in the eyes of its adherents cannot adequately be judged; but it seems reasonable to suppose that the outcome of debates like those against Fortunatus and Felix, especially when the latter was crowned by the conversion of Augustine's opponent to Catholic Christianity, must have had a considerable effect, both upon Catholic waverers, attracted to Manichaeism, and upon Manichees who, like Augustine when he left Africa for Rome, were becoming disillusioned with their religion. Again, the hostility of the secular authorities was clearly unfavourable to the spread of the religion; the Manichee was forced to lead an underground existence, which may establish an *esprit de corps* among the bolder spirits, but which has a depressing effect upon more

---

[1] *The Medieval Manichee*, 179–80.
[2] Hieron., *Ep.* 22, 13: 'Istae sunt, quae solent dicere: "*omnia munda mundis.* sufficit mihi conscientia mea. cor mundum desiderat deus. cur me abstineam a cibis, quos deus creavit ad utendum?" et si quando lepidae et festivae volunt videri et se mero ingurgitaverint, ebretiati sacrilegium copulantes aiunt: "absit, ut ego me a Christi sanguine abstineam." et quam viderint tristem atque pallentem, miseram et monacham et Manicheam vocant, et consequenter; tali enim proposito ieiunium heresis est.' *CSEL* liv, 160–1.

ordinary souls. However, the will to survive on the part of the Manichees was remarkable, and in the face of every difficulty and danger they maintained themselves in Africa until the coming of the Vandals. For them, as for the Donatists, this event brought only a change of masters and they suffered, with the Catholics and Donatists, from the religious intolerance and frank cruelty of the Arian conqueror. Many of them fled to Rome,[1] and were discovered there by pope Leo the Great in 443, when the confessions of those who had been arrested led to the discovery of a great number of their co-religionists,[2] and to the uncovering, to the satisfaction of Leo at least, of their obscene rites and practices.[3] Towards the end of the year, the Elect of both sexes were brought before an assembly presided over by the pope.[4] As a result of this tribunal, many Manichees were persuaded to recant, to anathematize Mani and his doctrine publicly in church, and to sign an act of abjuration. Those who remained obstinate were condemned to perpetual exile.[5] Nevertheless, Manichees continued to hide at Rome, and St Leo found it necessary to exhort his flock to denounce those whom they knew to be Manichees to the clergy,[6] and to warn those who remained silent that they would have to answer for it at the judgement seat of Christ.[7]

Meanwhile, the Manichees who remained in Africa contrived to hold their ground and even to make converts from among the Arian Vandals, particularly among their clergy. However, with the succession of Hunneric, a ferocious Arian, in 477, a savage persecution began, and many Manichees were burned alive or sent into exile overseas.[8] The discovery

---

[1] Leo, *Serm.* 16, 5: '. . . quos aliarum regionum perturbatio nobis intulit crebriores.' *MPL* liv, 179A.

[2] Prosper, *Chronicon*, sub anno 443: 'Hoc tempore plurimos Manicheos intra urbem latere diligentia papae Leonis| innotuit, qui eos de secretis suis erutos et oculis totius ecclesiae publicatos omnes dogmatis sui turpitudines et damnare fecit et prodere incensis eorum codicibus, quorum magnae moles fuerant interceptae. quae cura viro sancto divinitus, ut apparuit, inspirata, non solum Romanae urbi, sed etiam universo orbi plurimum profuit. . . . multique Orientalium partium sacerdotes industriam apostolici rectoris imitati sunt.' *MGH*, Auctores Antiquissimi, ix, *Chronica Minora*, ed. Th. Mommsen, i, 1892, 479.   [3] Leo, *Serm.* 16, 4–5. *MPL* liv, 178–9.

[4] Ibid., 16, 4: 'Residentibus itaque mecum episcopis ac presbyteris, ac in eundem consessum Christianis viris ac nobilibus congregatis, Electos et Electas eorum iussimus presentari.'

[5] Leo, *Ep.* 7, 1: 'per publicos iudices perpetuo sunt exsilio relegati'. *MPL* liv, 621A.

[6] *Serm.* 9, 4. *MPL* liv, 163A–C.

[7] *Serm.* 16, 5: '. . . et qui tales non prodendos putant, in iudicio Christi inveniantur rei de silentio.' *MPL* liv, 179B.

[8] Victor Vitensis, *Historia Persecutionis Africanae Provinciae*, II, i, 1: 'Mortuo igitur Geiserico Huniricus maior filius patri succedit. Qui in primordia regni, ut habet subtilitas barbarorum, coepit mitius et moderatius agere, et maxime circa religionem nostram; ut etiam ubi antea sub rege Geiserico praeiudicatum fuerat, ne spiritales fierent conventus, conventicula concurrerent populorum. Et ut se religiosum ostenderet, statuit sollicitius requirendos hereticos Manicheos; ex quibus multos incendit, plurimos autem distraxit navibus transmarinis.' *CSEL* vii, 24.

that many Arian clergy were, in secret, Manichees, spurred the Vandal king to yet greater efforts.[1] What the precise effect of these were, we do not know. Undoubtedly, the Manichees must have suffered fearfully,[2] and for them, the Byzantine reconquest would bring no amelioration of their lot. Nevertheless, Manichaeism was too profoundly rooted in Africa for it to be totally extinguished. Fulgentius, bishop of Ruspe in Byzacena (468–533), the bright light of African theology under the Vandal domination, mentions the case of an alleged Catholic who held that flies, scorpions, and other obnoxious creatures were the creation of the devil.[3] At the end of the sixth century Pope Gregory the Great, among his many other preoccupations, found it necessary to write to the deacon Cyprian, bailiff of the papal patrimony in Sicily, to remind him to pursue the Manichees, and bring them back to the Catholic faith[4] and to caution the bishop of Scyllaceum, in Bruttium, against any unconsidered ordination of Africans, who might be Manichees or Donatists.[5] Gregory the Great's words were repeated by Gregory II in 723,[6] and were afterwards employed by Gerbert, archbishop of Capua, in a diploma of 978;[7] by Athenulph, archbishop of Capua in 1032;[8] by pope Nicholas II in 1060;[9] and by Alfanus, archbishop of Salerno, in 1066.[10] The repetition of this formula until the eleventh

---

[1] Ibid., 1–2: 'Quos paene omnes Manicheos suae religionis invenit et praecipue presbyteros et diaconos Arrianae hereseos; unde magis erubescens amplius in illis exarsit. De quibus repertus est unus, nomine Clementianus, monachus illorum, scriptum habens in femore: Manicheus discipulus Christi Iesu.' *CSEL* vii, 24.

[2] Which led Albert Dufourcq, *De Manichaeismo apud Latinos quinto sextoque saeculo*, Paris, 1900, 50–1, to assume that the Manichees were wiped out: 'Temporibus illis peractis [sc. Augustini], monimenta rarissima fiunt: Hunericum, Vandalorum regem (477–84) Manichaeos inquiri iussisse Victor Vitensis refert eosque Arianos fieri coegisse. Quae Manichaeorum Africanorum mentio ultima exstat; nec mirum: cum a Catholicis primum, ab Arianis deinde vexarentur, eorum ecclesias esse lapsas intelleges.' Dufourcq was wrong in assuming that Victor Vitensis is the last reference to African Manichaeism; but he may well be right in thinking that the Vandalic persecution was the effective death blow to the Manichees in the province of Africa.

[3] *De Incarnatione*, 32–33. *MPL* lxv, 591–2. Cf. *Ad Trasimundum*, I, v (col. 229); *Serm.* 4, 10 (col. 736); and *De Veritate Praedestinationis*, III, xxi, 34 (col. 668). Fulgentius' references to Manichaeism are all rather formal, and give no real information as to the state of the sect in Africa in his day.

[4] Greg., *Ep.* V, 8: 'De Manichaeis qui in possessionibus nostris sunt, frequenter dilectionem tuam admonui, ut eos persequi summopere debeas, atque ad fidem catholicam revocare.' *MPL* lxxvii, 729B.

[5] Ibid., II, 37: 'Afros passim vel incognitos peregrinos, ad ecclesiasticos ordines tendentes, nulla ratione suscipias quia Afri quidam Manichaei, aliqui rebaptizati.' *MPL* lxxvii, 575C.

[6] Greg. II, *Ep.* 4: 'Afros passim ad ecclesiasticos ordines praetendentes nulla ratione suscipiat, quia aliqui eorum Manichaei, aliqui rebaptizati saepius sunt probati.' *MPL* lxxxix, 502; Mansi, *Concilia*, xii, 239.

[7] Ferdinando Ughelli, *Italia Sacra*, 2nd ed., vol. vi, Venice, 1720, 442.

[8] Ibid., p. 536.

[9] *Ep.* 25 (ad Clerum Sistaricensem). *MPL* cxliii, 1347A.

[10] Ughelli, *Italia Sacra*, vol. vii, 1721, 571.

century, that is, until the final extinction of Christianity in North Africa, has led to the suggestion that the province which saw the greatest triumphs of Manichaeism in the Latin part of the Empire, was also its last stronghold in the west.[1] Against this view it may be urged that the mere fact that a formula is employed is sufficient to raise doubts as to its value as evidence of contemporary conditions.[2] The most that can be said with safety is that African Manichaeism managed to survive until the eighth century, when Gregory II wrote against it.[3] After this, it vanishes from history. Like their rivals, the Catholics and the Donatists, the African Manichees bequeathed no descendants to posterity. Like the Donatists, who detested them, we are forced to form our estimate of them from the testimony of their sworn enemies. It would be wise to bear this continually in mind, and think of them accordingly.

[1] Ém. de Stoop, *Essai sur la diffusion du Manichéisme dans l'empire romain* (Université de Gand: Recueil de travaux publiés par la faculté de philosophie et lettres, fasc. 38), Ghent, 1909, 119.
[2] See J. C. L. Gieseler, *Lehrbuch der Kirchengeschichte*, 3te Aufl., 2te Bd., 1te Abt., Bonn, 1831, 354: 'Ob aber diese Formel für alle die Zeiten, in denen sie gebraucht worden ist, beweise, lässt sich eben wegen ihres formulärischen Characters bezweifeln.'
[3] This is the view of Puech, *Le Manichéisme*, 64: 'Il y avait encore des Manichéens en Afrique au VIIIᵉ siècle.'

5

Augustine's Polemic against the Manichees

'Did you say the stars were worlds, Tess?'
'Yes.'
'All like ours?'
'I don't know; but I think so. They sometimes seem to be like the apples on our stubbard-tree. Most of them splendid and sound—a few blighted.'
'Which do we live on—a splendid one or a blighted one?'
'A blighted one.'

THOMAS HARDY, *Tess of the d'Urbervilles*

Viditque Deus cuncta quae fecerat: et erant valde bona.

GENESIS 1.31

IT MIGHT very plausibly be assumed that, of all Augustine's writings, those directed against the Manichees were least likely to have any enduring value. The study of the refutation of a system so alien and apparently irrelevant to modern thought would appear to pertain to the realm of literary archaeology rather than to problems of perennial interest and to be of greater value as a monument to the range of Augustine's thought than as a guide to Christian doctrine. Such an assumption would be very wide of the mark. Certain aspects of Augustine's polemic, those which are specifically directed against details of Manichaean belief, are not likely to engage the reader's attention today unless he happens to have an interest in the history of religions; but the larger issues are as relevant in the twentieth century as they were in the fourth and fifth and are likely to remain so for as long as Christians engage in controversy with enemies of the faith or attempt to explain those questions which any inquiring mind, however firm its faith, is likely to ask in a world which clearly falls short of the best of all possible worlds that we can imagine.

Augustine's years as a Manichee and his subsequent career as a Catholic apologist raised in his mind three basic problems to which it was necessary to find an answer. The first was the problem of evil: where does it come from and why does it persist? Secondly there was the problem of the Scriptures. How are they to be understood, when many apparent contradictions exist between the Old Testament and the New? And if we are

G

taught—as we are certainly taught by Christian tradition—that certain passages in the Old Testament, notably those dealing with ritual purity and the observance of the Law, are no longer literally binding upon baptized Christians, how are we to decide what these passages may be? Finally, and arising from this, is the whole question of understanding the Bible. In many matters the Church tells us to believe, even though our intellect remains dissatisfied. What then is the relationship between authority and reason? The question ushers in the vaster one of the nature of the Church and her authority over her members.

All these questions, among the most profound and important which can be asked, were involved in Augustine's disputes with the Manichees and prepare the way for his treatment of similar issues in later controversies. Thus, writing against the Donatists, the saint again found himself discussing the nature of the Church and arguing how certain passages of Scripture are to be interpreted. In the Pelagian controversy, it might be said that all the questions raised: Grace and Free Will; Predestination and Reprobation; Original Sin and the Fall, spring from the problems which he had discussed in his writings against the Manichees. So it is that Augustine's anti-Manichaean polemic, far from being an isolated element in his works, is a highly important preparation for theological discussions which were not envisaged at the time when he wrote.

The problem of evil, which is, perhaps, the most profound of those which were involved in the dispute between the Catholics and the Manichees, was one that had haunted Augustine from his earliest days. In his later life, he was to recognize it as one of the principal factors in his youthful conversion to Manichaeism. In the book *On Free Will* he makes Evodius say: 'Since you force me to agree that we are not taught to do evil, tell me the cause why we do evil?' and replies: 'That is a question that gave me great trouble when I was a young man. It wearied me and drove me into the arms of heretics. By that accident I was so afflicted and overwhelmed with such masses of vain fables that, had not my love of finding the truth obtained divine aid, I should never have found my way out or breathed the pure air of free inquiry.'[1] It is possible, indeed, that

---

[1] *De Lib. Arb.*, I, ii, 4: 'Ev.: Age iam . . . dic mihi unde malum faciamus. A.: Eam quaestionem moves, quae me admodum adulescentem vehementer exercuit et fatigatum in hereticos impulit atque deiecit. Quo casu ita sum adflictus et tantis obrutus acervis inanium fabularum, ut, nisi mihi amor inveniendi veri opem divinam impetravisset, emergere inde atque in ipsam primam quaerendi libertatem respirare non possem.' Tr. Burleigh, p. 114. Cited by Régis Jolivet, *Le problème du mal d'après saint Augustin*, 2e éd., 10—a work to be consulted on this subject. See also M. F. Sciacca, *Saint Augustin et le Néoplatonisme*, 13–19. On evil, in the wider setting of its relation to *dolor*, anguish, see Luigi Macali, *Il problema del dolore secondo s. Agostino*, Rome, 1943.

the problem of evil first presented itself to Augustine in his childhood, in his unhappy school-days, when his elders laughed at the beatings that he suffered 'though the strokes I received were a great and heavy evil (*malum*) to me'.[1] The spectacle of the bishop of Hippo recalling and lamenting his schoolboy whippings is calculated to amuse the reader, rather than to impress him but, as is the case with all Augustine's reminiscences, the reference is not without a purpose. The saint is concerned to show that, from our earliest childhood, we are faced with the fact of evil and with the experience of anguish, which is the state in which our being finds itself when it has come into contact with evil.[2] Furthermore, the problem of evil is not the less if we have not personally experienced any but minor manifestations. The great disasters of humanity: wars, massacres, and the like, present the problem on the grand scale, but in everyday experience minor events—the treachery of a friend whom we had trusted; actions of apparently pointless selfishness or unkindness in others or, more disconcertingly, in ourselves; or even (though here the problem is not quite the same) the sudden and agonizing death of one whom we love—bring us face to face with the fact of evil in a world which, we are told, was created by a good and loving God. In such circumstances, human nature demands an explanation, which it is the task of the theologian to supply, so far as he is able. This is what Augustine attempted to do in his writings against the Manichees, and not without success. It should however be remembered, with all due deference to a great thinker and Christian teacher, that no merely rational explanation of evil however cogently argued is satisfactory. Ultimately, for the Christian, the answer to the problem of evil lies, not in theological argument but in a fact—a wooden cross on which there hangs a Man, naked and dead:

Regnavit a ligno Deus—

God reigned from the tree and by His death destroyed Death. Much harm can be done by the Christian apologist who, confident in his own belief and impatient of the questioning of those who do not enjoy the grace of faith, shows a lack of sympathy with their difficulties and even implies that they are fools to be troubled. It is wiser and more Christian to recognize frankly that the origin of evil is a mystery, and one which is not to be explained but, rather, to be seen in the light of the Incarnation: in the poor stable, where the child who was God lay, because there was no room at the inn;

[1] *Conf.*, I, ix, 14.
[2] See Macali, *Il problema del dolore*, 19: 'Il dolore è lo stato nel quale viene a trovarsi il nostro essere quando è a contatto con il male.' Cf. Aug., *De Lib. Arb.*, III, xxiii, 69: 'Quid est enim aliud dolor nisi sensuo divisionis vel corruptionis inpatiens?'

in the tears which He shed by the grave of Lazarus; in the garden, where He prayed that the cup might pass from Him so vehemently that His sweat was like drops of blood; and, at the last, in the scourging, the spitting, the crown of thorns and that awful and unfathomable cry: 'My God, my God, why hast Thou forsaken me?' Meditation of the Cross and Passion is a surer answer to the problem of evil than intellectual argument.

Nevertheless, it may be necessary, and in Augustine's own case certainly was necessary, to attempt to find some rational explanation of evil, if only because there will always exist persons who, because of their particular intellectual outlook are incapable of finding the answer to their difficulties by an act of faith. For them, a philosophical examination of the problem is a necessity, and this was the motive which led Augustine to devote so much attention to the nature of evil in his writings.

We have already seen that, from a very early period of his life, Augustine was haunted by the problem of evil.

And I kept seeking for an answer to the question, Whence is evil? And I sought it in an evil way, and I did not see the evil in my very search. . . . Thus I conceived Thy creation itself to be finite, and filled by Thee, the infinite. And I said, 'Behold God, and behold what God hath created!' God is good, yea, most mightily and incomparably better than all His works. But yet He who is good has created them good; behold how He encircles and fills them. Where, then, is evil, and whence does it come and how has it crept in? What is its root and what is its seed? Has it no being at all? Why, then, do we fear and shun what has no being? Or if we fear it needlessly, then surely that fear is evil by which the heart is unnecessarily stabbed and tortured—and indeed a greater evil since we have nothing real to fear, and yet do fear. Therefore, either that is evil which we fear, or the act of fearing is in itself evil. But, then, whence does it come, since God who is good has made all these things good? Indeed, He is the greatest and chiefest good, and hath created these lesser goods; but both Creator and created are all good. Whence then is evil?[1]

Augustine thus summarizes the problem of evil as it presents itself to the theist who believes that God is good and the creator of the world. If we deny the existence of God or hold, like Lucretius, that the gods, although they exist, are remote and unconcerned with humanity; still more, if we conceive of them, in Thomas Hardy's word, as making 'sport' with helpless men, then there is no problem and we can, at best, only curse 'whatever brute and blackguard made the world'. But if we are none of these and believe that God is good, how are we to reconcile this belief with the undoubted fact that the world, as it exists, falls far short of what we would wish?

[1] *Conf.*, VII, v, 7. Tr. by Outler, pp. 138–9.

To this question the Manichees, like other Dualists, had a ready answer. In their doctrine, the two principles of Light and Darkness are, in this world, intermingled. All that is evil is the work of Darkness, whose baneful influence affects even man himself, whose evil actions are not his own responsibility but the working of the dark power within him. Man is a being endowed with two souls, one good and one evil, and his evil impulses come from the latter.[1] The cause of evil in the world is Evil itself, and God is concerned with nullifying the effect of that Evil by the purgation of the Light which is imprisoned in matter. Sin is simply the operation of the evil element which naturally exists in human nature.

The dualistic explanation appears, superficially, to give an adequate reply; but upon examination it becomes apparent that, like many other simple explanations, it raises as many problems as it resolves. In the first place, the Manichees were faced by the difficulty that, although their theology was dualistic, they nevertheless desired to maintain the doctrine of one God. Faustus of Milevis protested indignantly against the accusation that he and his fellows believed in two gods, and assured the Catholics that the principle of Evil, commonly called Hyle, was not a god but the devil.[2] This might seem to be merely a difference of name, but it was, in fact, more fundamental than this, for the Manichees—no doubt because they were at heart Christians even if heretical Christians—were unable to remain pure Dualists but were, in the last resort, Monarchians, recognizing that the Father of Greatness is, in a certain sense, the supreme ruler against whom the powers of Darkness are rebels rather than equal and independent enemies.[3] It is true that the Manichaean God is not omnipotent. He may restore Light and Darkness to their original state of

---

[1] C. Faust., VI, viii: 'Deinde cum duas animas esse in uno animantis corpore adfirmant, unam bonam de gente lucis, alteram malam de gente tenebrarum, numquid, cum occiditur animal, bona anima fugit et mala remanet? . . . cum ergo in morte cuiuslibet animalis utraque anima, et bona et mala, deserat carnem, cur immunda caro dicitur, quasi a sola bona anima deseratur?' Cf. De Duabus Animabus, passim; De Vera Religione, ix, 16; Retract., i, 14[15].

[2] C. Faust., XXI, i: 'Faustus dixit: Unus deus est, an duo? plane unus. quomodo ergo vos duos adseritis? numquam in nostris quidem adscrtionibus duorum deorum auditum est nomen. sed tu unde hoc suspicaris, cupio scire. quia bonorum et malorum duo principia traditis? est quidem, quod duo principia confitemur, sed unum ex his deum vocamus, alterum hylen, aut, ut communiter et usitate dixerim, daemonem.' Ibid., iv: '[Augustinus dixit:] Nam cito videtur Faustus se defendisse, cum ait: non dicimus duos deos, sed deum et hylen. porro autem cum quaesieris, quam dicat hylen, audies plane describi alterum deum. si enim materies informis corporalium formarum capax ab eis hyle appellaretur, quae appellata est ab antiquis, nemo eam nostrum coargueret dici deum. nunc vero quantus error est, quanta dementia vel materiem corporum dicere opificem corporum vel opificem corporum negare deum?'

[3] For the distinction between Monarchianism (not to be confused with a term commonly, and perhaps misleadingly, applied to the Patripassian heresies of the third century AD) and pure Dualism, see Runciman, The Medieval Manichee, ch. vii, 'The Dualist

separation, but he was unable to prevent their admixture when the forces of Darkness made their attack on his realm. Nor is he incorruptible. Particles of himself were devoured by the dark Archons, and are now being distilled from the materials of which this world is composed; while the existence of the sinister *bôlos*, the great clod in which are to be confined the souls of Light which have become too defiled by Darkness to be cleansed and released, makes it clear that a certain part of God will remain in the power of Darkness for ever. But this was theory. In practice the Manichees —those of Africa at least—were not prepared to admit that God could be defiled. God, they held, was incorruptible—a fact which Augustine was able to put to good use in his successful debate with Felix the Manichee who, because of his unwillingness to assert that God was corruptible, was ultimately persuaded to anathematize Mani and become a Catholic Christian.[1] This reluctance on the part of the Manichees to carry their theological premises to a logical conclusion left them helpless in the face of Nebridius' question: what would the force of Darkness have done if God had declined its challenge to battle?

> If they replied that it could have hurt Thee, they would then have made Thee violable and corruptible. If, on the other hand, the dark could have done Thee no harm, then there was no cause for any battle at all; there was less cause for a battle in which a part of Thee, one of Thy members, a child of Thy own substance, should be mixed up with opposing powers, not of Thy creation; and should be corrupted and deteriorated

Tradition' and particularly pp. 171–5. Runciman appears to regard Manichaean as Dualistic, rather than Monarchian (see his remark, p. 174: 'The one [of the two streams in Christian Dualism] the more strictly Dualist or, if you will, the more Manichaean, lingered in Armenia and travelled with Armenian colonists to the Balkans'); but against this should be set his comment (p. 12): 'It is fashionable nowadays to regard Mani as lying outside the pale of Christianity. . . . But he always carefully called himself Mani, Apostle of Jesus Christ.'

[1] *C. Felice*, II, xx: 'FEL. dixit: Manichaeus dicit quia polluta est pars Dei; et Christus dicit quia polluta est anima, et venit liberare illam de pollutione. AUG. dixit: Sed anima non est pars Dei. Nam tu iam confessus es quia Manichaeus dixit pollutam partem Dei; nos autem pollutam dicimus animam ex voluntate peccati; non esse autem animam partem Dei, non de Deo genitam, sed a Deo factam. Sic ergo dicitur anima ex Deo, quomodo dicitur aliquod opus fabri ex artificio eius, vel ex ipso factum, non tamen de ipso genitum, sicut filius eius. Tu ergo quia iam confessus es Manichaeum dixisse pollui partem Dei, et iamdudum dixisti anathemandum qui dicit corruptibilem vel contaminabilem Deum vel naturam eius; iam anathemasti, quod non vis fateri. Hoc enim quod dixisti, quia polluitur et quia mundatur, hoc ipso quod dicis, Mundatur, expressisti quia polluitur; et non habes unde evadas: et Manichaeus, et tu dixisti quia polluitur pars Dei. Anathema ergo Manichaeum, aut anathemandus es cum Manichaeo.
FEL. dixit: Ego non a Manichaeo didici quia polluta est pars Dei; sed a Christo didici quia propter animam venit quae polluta erat.
AUG. dixit: A Christo non didicisti quia anima pars Dei est.
FEL. dixit: A Christo didici quia anima ex Deo est.
AUG. dixit: Et nos didicimus quia animo ex Deo est, sed non est pars Dei. Sic est enim anima ex Deo, quomodo factura ex artifice; non de Deo, sicut Filius de Patre.'

and changed by them from happiness into misery, so that it could not be delivered and cleansed without Thy help. This offspring of Thy substance was supposed to be the human soul to which Thy Word—free, pure, and entire—could bring help when it was being enslaved, contaminated, and corrupted. But on their hypothesis that Word was itself corruptible because it is one and the same substance as the soul. And therefore if they admitted that Thy nature—whatsoever Thou art—is incorruptible, then all these assertions of theirs are false and should be rejected with horror. But if Thy substance is corruptible, then this is self-evidently false and should be abhorred at first utterance. This line of argument, then, was enough against those deceivers who ought to be cast forth from a surfeited stomach—for out of this dilemma they could find no way of escape without dreadful sacrilege of mind and tongue, when they think and speak such things about Thee.[1]

Thus Manichaean doctrine confronted its adherents with a logical paradox resembling the notorious problem of the consequences of an encounter between an irresistible force and an immovable object, a dilemma from which it is possible to escape only by denying the truth of one or the other of the two predicates. Augustine, since he refused to deny the incorruptibility of God, was forced to seek for some explanation of evil other than the Manichaean. The key to this explanation he found suggested in the writings of the Neo-Platonists, though in adopting it for his own use, Augustine subjected it to a fundamental modification in conformity with Christian dogma.

As a first step to his inquiry, Augustine asks: What is evil?[2] The question is a necessary one, for we cannot begin to discuss where a thing comes from before we have first established what it is. The Manichaean explanation of evil as a substance has been rejected, because it conflicts with our beliefs about the nature of God. There is however another reason for rejecting it: the Manichaean account of the realm and substance of evil, in its own terms, is inadequate, for in the Kingdom of Absolute Evil, so called, it is not hard to discover features which are not evil at all. The dark lord, Hyle, enjoyed health and well-being in his rule; nourishment existed for his myrmidons; fecundity of offspring was to be found in the Kingdom of Darkness as well as in the realms of Light and so too was the enjoyment of pleasures. Yet the Manichees ask men to believe that, quite apart from being evil to the Light, the Kingdom of Darkness was an evil

---

[1] *Conf.*, VII, ii, 3. Trans. by Outler, pp. 136–7.
[2] *De Moribus*, II, ii, 2: 'Percunctamini me unde sit malum; at ego vicissim percunctor vos quid sit malum. Cuius est iustior inquisitio? eorumne qui quaerunt unde sit, quod quid sit ignorant; an eius qui prius putat esse quaerendum quid sit, ut non ignotae rei (quod absurdissimum est) origo quaeratur?' See Jolivet, op. cit., pp. 19ff.

in itself![1] On the contrary, we are concerned, not with two kingdoms, one good and one evil, but with two kingdoms, both good, but one better than the other. The Manichees may reply that the Kingdom of Darkness is full of discord and internecine strife. Granted; and for that reason we can say that the Kingdom of Light is better; but the Kingdom of Darkness cannot be wholly bad, or how can we account for the fecundity of its peoples?[2] The fact is, whether the Manichees like it or not, that their Kingdom of Darkness is not a place of pure evil at all, and so their definition falls to the ground and we must seek another.

What then is evil? It cannot be a substance, as the Manichees believe, since a substance is either incorruptible or corruptible. If it is the former, then the question of evil does not arise; if, on the other hand, it is corruptible and becomes corrupted, it is clear that it was originally good. Evil, then, is not a substance,[3] but rather something which is not a substance, a lack, a privation.[4] This gives us the clue to the true definition of evil. Evil is not a substance; it is not a thing at all. It is, literally, nothing. Evil is simply a privation of good.[5]

[1] *C. Faust.*, XXI, xiv: 'Cur non ergo haec aut duo bona dicitis aut duo mala, vel magis et duo bona et duo mala, duo bona apud se, duo mala in alterutrum? postea, si opus fuerit, quaeremus, quid horum sit melius aut peius. interim quia duo bona erant apud se, ita consideratur: regnabat deus in terra sua, regnabat et hyle in sua; sanitas regnantium et ibi et hic; copia fructuum et ibi et hic; fecunditas prolis utrobique; suavitas propriarum voluptatum apud utrosque. sed illa gens, inquiunt, excepto eo, quod vicinae luci mala erat, et apud se ipsam mala erat.'

[2] Ibid.: 'Interim bona eius [sc. regni tenebrarum] multa iam dixi; si et vos mala eius potueritis ostendere, erunt duo regna bona, sed illud melius, ubi nullum erat malum. quaenam ergo huius mala dicitis fuisse? vastabant se, inquit, invicem laedebant, occidebant, absumebant. si ad hoc solum ibi vacaretur, quomodo ibi tanta agmina gignerentur, nutrirentur, perficerentur? erat ibi ergo et quies et pax. verumtamen fateamur illud fuisse melius regnum, ubi nulla discordia; duo tamen bona ista multo accommodatius dixerim quam unum bonum et alterum malum, ut illud sit melius, ubi nec singuli sibimet ipsis nocebant nec invicem; hoc autem inferius bonum, ubi quamvis invicem adversarentur, unumquodque tamen animal suam salutem, incolumitatem, naturamque tuebatur.'

[3] *Conf.*, VII, xii, 18: 'Et manifesttaum est mihi, quoniam bona sunt, quae corrumpuntur, quae neque si summa bona essent, corrumpi possent, neque nisi bona essent, corrumpi possent, quia, si summa bona essent, incorruptibilia essent, si autem nulla bona essent, quid in eis corrumperetur, non esset. Nocet enim corruptio et, nisi bonum minueret, non noceret.'

[4] Ibid.: 'Aut igitur nihil nocet corruptio, quod fieri non potest, aut, quod certissimum est, omnia quae corrumpuntur, privantur bono. Si autem omni bono privabuntur, omnino non erunt.'

[5] *dCD*, XI, ix: 'Mali enim nulla natura est; sed amissio boni mali nomen accepit.' *Enchir.*, iii, 11: 'Quid est autem aliud quod malum dicitur, nisi privatio boni?' *C. Adver. Legis*, I, v, 7: 'Non est ergo malum nisi privatio boni. Ac per hoc nusquam est nisi in re aliqua bona.' *De Moribus*, II, v, 7: 'Quaeram ergo tertio quid sit malum. Respondebitis fortasse, Corruptio. Quis et hoc negaverit generale malum esse? Nam hoc est contra naturam, hoc est quod nocet. Sed corruptio non est in seipsa, sed in aliqua substantia quam corrumpit: non enim substantia est ipsa corruptio. Ea igitur res quam corrumpit, corruptio non est, malum non est. Quod enim corrumpitur, integritate et sinceritate privatur.'

This anhypostatic conception of evil[1] is to be found throughout Augustine's writings and it affords the key to the problem of a Creator who is wholly good and a world which falls far short of perfection, and hence of the fact of sin, its origin and its remedy. All created things are of God; but evil is not a created thing, but a corruption, a deterioration of what is created, and hence cannot be assigned to God, except inasmuch as He permits it. Evil does not come from God, although without His will it would not be and is used by Him for His own good purposes.

Augustine owed to the Neo-Platonists the discovery that evil is a privation of good, but it is important not to over-emphasize his debt to them for, on this issue, there is a great gulf fixed between Neo-Platonism and Christian doctrine,[2] a gulf determined by the basic opposition between the Christian doctrine of creation out of nothing and the dualism which seems to be inherent, if not in the writings of Plato himself,[3] at least in the thought of his later followers. Thus Plotinus, while firmly relegating Evil to the realm of Non-Being, never arrives at the Augustinian position of Evil as simply a privation of Good:

> If such be the Nature of Beings and of That which transcends all the realm of Being [sc. The Good], Evil cannot have place among Beings or in the Beyond-Being; these are good.
> There remains, only, if Evil exist at all, that it be situate in the realm of Non-Being, that it be some mode, as it were, of the Non-Being, that it have its seat in something in touch with Non-Being or to a certain degree communicate in Non-Being.
> By this Non-Being, of course, we are not to understand something that simply does not exist, but only something of an utterly different order from Authentic-Being: there is no question here of movement or position with regard to Being; the Non-Being we are thinking of is, rather, an image of Being or perhaps something still further removed than even an image.[4]

In this passage, we see what it was in Neo-Platonist teaching which gave Augustine the inspiration to reject the Manichaean idea that Evil was

---

[1] De Divers. Quaest. LXXXIII, q. 6: 'Omne quod est, aut est corporeum, aut incorporeum. Corporeum sensibili, incorporeum autem intelligibili specie continetur. Omne igitur quod est, sine aliqua specie non est. Ubi autem aliqua species, necessario est aliquis modus, et modus aliquid boni est. Summum ergo malum nullum modum habet; caret omni bono. Non est igitur; quia nulla specie continetur, totumque hoc nomen mali de speciei privatione repertum est.'

[2] For the contrast between Augustine's doctrine of evil and that of Plotinus, see Régis Jolivet, Le problème du mal, 131–62, and M. F. Sciacca, Saint Augustin et le Néoplatonisme, 13–19.

[3] See the denial of A. E. Taylor, Plato: the Man and his Work, London, ed. of 1960, 443 and n[2].

[4] Enneads, I, viii, 3. Tr. by Stephen Mackenna, Plotinus: The Ethical Treatises, i, London, 1917, 94.

a material substance, equal and opposite to Good. At the same time, we can also see that Augustine went beyond Platonism in his own theory. For him, Evil is nothing—a mere lack of Good. Plotinus does not go so far. For him, Evil exists as an image of being, even though it be an attenuated image, belonging to an utterly different order from Authentic Being. The door, indeed, is left open for a reintroduction of Evil as a self-existing reality and this is precisely what Plotinus proceeds to do. Evil is the contrary of The Good; and The Good he defines as 'that on which all else depends, towards which all Existences aspire as to their source and their need, while Itself is without need, sufficient to Itself, aspiring to no other, the measure and Term of all.'[1] Evil, on the other hand, is lack of measure and of all else beside:

> Some conception of [Evil] would be reached by thinking of measurelessness as opposed to measure, of the unbounded against bound, the unshaped against a principle of shape, the ever-needy against the self-sufficing: think of the ever-defined, the never at rest, the all-accepting but never sated, utter dearth; and make all this character not mere accident in it but its equivalent for essential-being, so that, whatsoever fragment of it be taken, that part is all lawless void, while whatever participates in it and resembles it becomes evil, though not of course to the point of being, as itself is, Evil-Absolute.[2]

Plotinus proceeds to argue that Evil must have an existence independently of Good:

> Does not Measure exist apart from unmeasured things? Precisely as there is Measure apart from anything measured, so there is Unmeasure apart from the unmeasured. If Unmeasure could not exist independently, it must exist either in an unmeasured object or in something measured; but the unmeasured could not need Unmeasure and the measured could not contain it.
>
> There must, then, be some Undetermination-Absolute, some Absolute Formlessness; all the qualities cited as characterising the Nature of Evil must be summed under an Absolute Evil; and every evil thing outside of this must either contain this Absolute by saturation or have taken the character of evil and become a cause of evil by consecration to this Absolute.[3]

By this reasoning, Plotinus has restored Evil to an equal place with Good in the sensible world. Moreover, and from the Christian point of view, more alarmingly, he identifies Evil with Matter ($\H{\upsilon}\lambda\eta$). We must be careful at this point not to misrepresent him. $\H{Y}\lambda\eta$, in his terminology, has

---

[1] I, viii, 2. Mackenna, p. 93.
[2] I, viii, 3. Mackenna, p. 94.
[3] Ibid. Mackenna, p. 95.

none of the solid qualities which the English word Matter conveys. It is a mere abstraction; potentiality without any potency; a bare receptacle of Form. 'Matter', says Plotinus, 'is incorporeal, because Body exists only after it; Body is a composite of which Matter is an element.'[1] Nevertheless, when all allowance has been made, the fact remains that the Plotinian Evil is not the simple privation of Augustine's doctrine.

> Evil is not in any and every lack; it is in absolute lack. What falls in some degree short of the Good is not Evil; considered in its own kind it might even be perfect, but where there is utter dearth, there we have Essential Evil, void of all share in Good; this is the case with Matter.
>
> Matter has not even existence whereby to have some part in Good: Being is attributed to it by an accident of words: the truth would be that it has Non-Being.
>
> Mere lack brings merely Not-Goodness: Evil demands the absolute lack—though, of course, any very considerable shortcoming makes the ultimate fall possible and is already, in itself, an evil.
>
> In fine we are not to think of Evil as some particular bad thing—injustice, for example, or any other evil trait—but as a principle distinct from any of the particular forms in which, by the addition of certain elements, it becomes manifest. Thus there may be wickedness in the Soul; the forms this general wickedness is to take will be determined by the environing Matter, by the faculties of the Soul that operate and by the nature of their operation, whether seeing, acting, or merely admitting impression.[2]

Finally, to complete his picture of Evil, Plotinus assures us that it is inevitable:

> But why does the existence of the Principle of Good necessarily comport the existence of the Principle of Evil? Is it because the All necessarily comports the existence of Matter? Yes: for necessarily this All is made up of contraries: it could not exist if Matter did not. The Nature of this Kosmos is, therefore, a blend; it is blended from the Intellectual-Principle and Necessity: what comes into it from God is good; evil is from the Ancient Kind which, we read, is the underlying Matter not yet brought into order by the Ideal-Form. . . . There is another consideration establishing the necessary existence of Evil.
>
> Given that The Good is not the only existent thing, it is inevitable that, by the outgoing from it or, if the phrase be preferred, the continuous down-going or away-going from it, there should be produced a Last, something after which nothing more can be produced: this will be Evil.
>
> As necessarily as there is Something after the First, so necessarily

---

[1] *Enneads*, III, vi, 7: ἔστι μὲν οὖν ἀσώματος, ἐπείπερ τὸ σῶμα ὕστερον καὶ σύνθετον καὶ αὐτὴ μετ' ἄλλου ποιεῖ σῶμα.

[2] I, viii, 5. Mackenna, p. 97.

there is a Last: this last is Matter, the thing which has no residue of good in it: here is the necessity of Evil.[1]

This Neo-Platonist view of the necessity of Evil, which is identified with Matter, is wholly alien to the Christian doctrine expressed in the account of the creation given in Genesis: 'In the beginning God created the heaven and the earth. . . . And God saw every thing that He had made, and behold, it was very good',[2] and Augustine accordingly rejects it in a passage which, though directed against the Manichees, is equally effective against Plotinus.

> We Catholic Christians worship God, from whom are all good things, great or small, all measure great or small, all form great or small, all order great or small. All things are good; better in proportion as they are better measured, formed and ordered, less good where there is less of measure, form and order. These three things, measure, form and order, not to mention other things which demonstrably belong to them, are as it were generic good things to be found in all that God has created, whether spirit or body. God transcends all measure, form and order in His creatures, not in spatial locality but by His unique and ineffable power from which come all measure, form and order. Where these three things are present in a high degree there are great goods. Where they are present in a low degree there are small goods. And where they are absent there is no goodness. Moreover, where these three things are present in a high degree there are things great by nature. Where they are present in a low degree there are things small by nature. Where they are absent there is no natural thing at all. Therefore, every natural existent is good.[3]

Thus Augustine has taken from the Neo-Platonists a certain conception of Evil, which he has modified and developed in the light of Christian dogma in order to provide an effective weapon for demolishing the arguments of the Manichees. Created things are good; there can be a hierarchy of created things, some more and some less good, without necessarily involving any existence of Evil. Evil arises from the corruption of a nature which is essentially good. What is called evil is good corrupted; if it were not corrupted, it would be wholly good; but even when it is corrupted, it is good in so far as it remains a natural thing, and bad only in so far as it is corrupted.[4]

'Nevertheless,' a critic might reply, 'the problem of Evil still remains

---

[1] I, viii, 7. Mackenna, pp. 100-1. For an examination of the notion of Matter in Plotinus, see W. R. Inge, *The Philosophy of Plotinus*, 3rd ed., i, 128-31.
[2] Gen. 1.1, 31.   [3] *De Nat. Boni*, 3. Tr. by Burleigh, p. 327.
[4] Ibid., 4: 'Proinde cum quaeritur, unde sit malum, prius quaerendum est, quid sit malum. quod nihil aliud est quam corruptio vel modi, vel speciei vel ordinis naturalis. mala itaque natura dicitur, quae corrupta est; nam incorrupta utique bona est. sed etiam ipsa corrupta, in quantum natura est, bona est; in quantum corrupta est, mala est.'

unsolved. Granted that by your definition certain difficulties inherent in Manichaeism have been removed, notably the logical absurdity of something which is "purely evil". But to conceive of Evil as something negative, as a corruption of what is good by nature, does not explain how such a corruption came about. Furthermore, even if we accept, for the purposes of discussion, the notion that Evil has no positive existence, it is abundantly clear that Evil, as we experience it in the world, is something disagreeably positive. It is not the fact that the world, as we know it, is not the best that we can conceive that shocks us; we do not complain of the fact that we are not like angels. What does appal us is the train of calamities which pursues man from the cradle to the grave; the ills of both body and spirit which assail him; the misery which apparently afflicts the animal world as well as the human race. To say that Evil is merely corruption does not explain how this came to be, especially if you postulate, as you do, a Creator who is the Highest Good. Indeed, the situation of the world would certainly seem to suggest a positive force of Evil, like the prince of Darkness in whom the Manichees believe, rather than a good Creator who, for some mysterious reason, has permitted what He has made to decay.'

Such an argument is perfectly valid and deserves consideration, for it is certainly true that, when the Manichaean doctrine of positive Evil has been banished from the stage and replaced by the anhypostatic conception of Evil, the problem of the origin of this Evil not only remains, but demands an explanation with an increased urgency. To it, Augustine made two replies, which will be considered in turn.

The first line of argument which Augustine follows may, without frivolity, be termed that of the 'whole picture' or the 'long-term view'.[1] This springs from the Augustinian sense of due measure and harmony in the whole order of created things. Each individual thing which God has created is good, but the goodness of the whole is greater than the goodness of the mere sum of the parts. In the description of the creation of the world in the book of Genesis it is said that each individual created thing was good; but when God looked upon all that He had made, behold, it was very good.[2] If we, situated as we are in a small part of the universe and

---

[1] For what follows, see Jolivet, op. cit., pp. 44–63.
[2] Conf., XIII, xxviii, 43: 'Et vidisti, deus, omnia quae fecisti, et ecce bona valde, quia et nos videmus ea, et ecce omnia bona valde. In singulis generibus operum tuorum, cum dixisses, ut fierent, et facta essent, illud atque illud vidisti quia bonum est. Septiens numeravi scriptum esse te vidisse, quia bonum est quod fecisti; et hoc octavum est, quia vidisti omnia quae fecisti, et ecce non solum bona sed etiam valde bona tamquam simul omnia. Nam singula tantum bona erant, simul autem omnia et bona et valde. Hoc dicunt etiam quaeque pulchra corpora, quia longe multo pulchrius est corpus, quod ex membris pulchris omnibus constat, quam ipsa membra singula, quorum ordinatissimo conventu conpletur universum, quamvis et illa singillatim pulchra sint.'

unable to see, in this life at least, the whole grand design, are displeased
with some detail, this is an inevitable consequence of our limitations as
created beings. We resemble the man who looked at one square of a
mosaic and accused the artist of having violated the laws of harmony of
colour because he was unable to see the overall pattern.[1] If however we
are on our guard against such a misunderstanding, we may see the har-
monious operations of God even in those things which might seem to be
evidence against them. In a classical exposition of this view in the nineteenth book of the *City of God*, Augustine points out that if a man be suspended head downwards on a rope, he feels pain because his soul, being at
peace with his body, urges it to return to a state of equilibrium. If this is
not possible, the natural order asserts itself: the man dies, his soul departs
to its assigned place and the body remains on the rope, bearing down
towards the earth, where it ought to rest. If corruption is not prevented by
the processes of embalming, the corpse dissolves to its natural elements
and the peace and order of nature is still preserved. This is Augustine's
exposition at its most philosophical; but it may be better appreciated in its
extremest form in a passage in the *De Natura Boni*:

> Even the eternal fire which is to torment the impious is not an evil thing.
> It has its own measure, form and order, debased by no iniquity. But
> torment is evil to the damned for whose sins it is the due reward. Nor is
> light an evil thing because it hurts the weak-eyed.[2]

It is not necessary to linger over the first of Augustine's explanations of
the cause of evil. It serves a useful purpose in that it warns us against a
purely subjective approach to the problem and provides an answer to the
Manichee who thought to demonstrate the positive existence of evil by
inviting his opponent to take hold of a live scorpion: 'If he did that, he
would be convinced not by words but by brute fact that evil is a substance.'[3] Clearly, the scorpion's poison is not an evil to the scorpion but
only to his enemies. It is not an evil to his nature, but only to humanity.[4]

---

[1] *De Ordine*, I, i, 2: 'Sed hoc pacto, si quis tam minutum cerneret, ut in vermiculato
pavimento nihil ultra unius tessellae modullum acies eius valeret ambire, vituperaret
artificem velut ordinationis et compositionis ignarum eo, quod varietatem lapillorum per-
turbatam putaret, a quo illa emblemata in unius pulchritudinis faciem congruentia simul
cerni conlustrarique non possent. nihil enim aliud minus eruditis hominibus accidit,
qui universam rerum coaptationem atque conceptum inbecilla mente conplecti et con-
siderare non valentes, si quid eos offenderit, quia suae cogitationi magnum est, magnam
rebus putant inhaerere foeditatem.'

[2] *De Nat. Boni*, 38. Tr. by Burleigh, p. 338. Cf. *dCD*, XII, iv.

[3] *De Moribus*, II, viii, 11: '. . . "Vellem scorpionem in manu hominis ponere, ac videre
utrum non subtraheret manum; quod si faceret, non verbis, sed re ipsa convinceretur
aliquam substantiam malum esse."'

[4] Ibid.: 'Quis enim meliuscule imbutus et eruditus, non videat per inconvenientiam
corporalis temperationis haec laedere, ac rursus per convenientiam non laedere, saepe

But the process of reasoning behind this argument is one which can only appeal to the disinterested mind, which is prepared to see God as the great artist who alone sees the total effect of the picture which He is painting. The God of the Christian religion is not, however, primarily the great artist but the God of Love; and the 'long-term view', although it may remove Evil from the totality of the creation, does not remove it from the individual creature. Rather, it lays itself open to the objection of Malebranche: if shadows are necessary for the beauty of a picture, or discords for the beauty of a musical composition, is it therefore necessary for pregnant women to miscarry and give birth to monstrosities?[1]—a question to which Antoine Arnauld, an uncompromising exponent of Augustinian theory but lacking his master's largeness of mind, said in effect: yes.[2]

It is clear, then, that Augustine's first line of argument needs developing, and that it is necessary to probe more deeply into the origin of Evil. We recognize that God is the creator of good things only and that Evil is a corruption. We admit the fact that there is much in the world as we experience it which must be accounted corruption and therefore evil. But we maintain that the cause of this corruption is not to be sought in God, but in the rebellious will of Man. Evil is essentially moral evil and is the result of sin, which is the abuse of Man's free will. Sin, befittingly, draws upon itself a condign penalty, which is physical evil.[3]

According to the Manichees, Adam was a being composed of two hostile natures, the one good and the other evil.[4] According to Augustine, Adam, like all other created things, was created good but liable to corruption from the mere fact of being created.[5] The Manichees held that sin in

etiam commoda non parva conferre? Nam si illud venenum per seipsum malum esset, eumdem scorpionem magis priusque perimeret. . . . Erit ergo eadem res et bonum et malum? Nullo modo, sed malum est quod contra naturam est.'

[1] Nicolas Malebranche, *3e Lettre en réponse au livre Ier des Réflexions*, 264, cited by Jolivet, op. cit., p. 54.

[2] Arnauld, *Réflexions sur le livre des vraies et des fausses idées*, I, cap. 2, cited by Jolivet, op. cit., pp. 52–53.

[3] *C. Adimantum*, 26: 'Dupliciter enim appellatur malum: unum quod homo facit, alterum quod patitur; quod facit, peccatum est; quod patitur, poena.' *De Vera Rel.*, xii, 23: 'Hoc est totum quod dicitur malum, id est, peccatum et poena peccati'; *De Gen. ad Lit. Lib. Imp.*, i, 3: 'Ecce autem omnia quae fecit deus bona valde: mala vero non esse naturalia; sed omne quod dicitur malum aut peccatum esse aut poenam peccati.'

[4] *De Moribus*, II, xix, 73: 'Adam dicitis sic a parentibus suis genitum, abortivis illis principibus tenebrarum, ut maximam partem lucis haberet in anima, et perexiguam gentis adversae.' *De Nat. Boni*, 46: 'Nam et a quibusdam principibus gentis tenebrarum sic dicunt Adam primum hominem creatum, ut lumen ab eis ne fugeret teneretur.'

[5] *Enchir.*, iv, 12: 'Naturae igitur omnes, quoniam naturarum prorsus omnium Conditor summe bonus est, bonae sunt: sed quia non sicut earum Conditor summe atque incommutabiliter bonae sunt, ideo in eis et minui bonum et augeri potest.' Cf. *De Nat. Boni*, 3, 10; *C. Ep. Fundamenti*, 38–39; *dCD*, XIV, xi.

Adam was the operation of the Evil principle.[1] For Augustine it was the turning away of a will which was itself good from its Creator to lesser goods.[2] Does this therefore make God the author of sin?[3] By no means. God made man morally upright and man's good will was the creation of God. His evil will must be regarded as a defect, a movement from being to not being.[4] But how did it come about? This is a question to which Augustine frankly admits that he has no answer:

> We cannot doubt that that movement of the will, that turning away from the Lord God is sin; but surely we cannot say that God is the author of sin? God, then, will not be the cause of that movement; but what will be its cause? If you ask this, and I answer that I do not know, probably you will be saddened. And yet that would be a true answer. That which is nothing cannot be known. Only hold fast to your pious opinion that no good thing can happen to you, to your senses or to your intelligence or to your thought which does not come from God. Nothing of any kind can happen which is not of God. . . . All good is from God. Hence there is no natural existence which is not from God. Now that movement of 'aversion', which we admit is sin, is a defective movement; and all defect comes from nothing. Observe where it belongs and you will have no doubt that it does not belong to God. Because that defective movement is voluntary, it is placed within our power. If you fear it, all you have to do is simply not to will it. If you do not will it, it will not exist. What can be more secure than to live a life where nothing can happen to you which you do not will? But since man cannot rise by his own free will as he fell by his own will spontaneously, let us hold with steadfast faith the right hand of God stretched out to us from above, even our Lord Jesus Christ.[5]

[1] *C. Faustum*, XXI, iii: 'Vos autem non valentes discernere, quid faciat Deus beneficio, quid iudicio, quia et a corde et ab ore vestro longe est psalterium nostrum, ubi dicitur: *misericordiam et iudicium cantabo tibi, domine* [Ps. 100.1 (101.1)], quicquid vos pro infirmitate humanae mortalitatis offenderit, alienatis omnino ab arbitrio et iudicio Dei veri videlicet habentes paratum alterum deum malum, quem vobis non veritas ostendit, sed vanitas fingit, cui tribuatis non solum quicquid facitis iniuste, verum etiam quicquid patimini iuste.'

[2] *Enchir.*, viii, 23: '. . . nequaquam dubitare debemus, rerum quae ad nos pertinent bonarum causam non esse nisi bonitatem Dei; malarum vero ab immutabili bono deficientem boni mutabilis voluntatem, prius angeli, hominis postea.'

[3] *De Lib. Arb.*, II, xx, 54: 'Sed tu fortasse quaesiturus es, quoniam movetur voluntas cum se avertit ab incommutabili bono ad mutabile bonum, unde iste motus existat. Qui profecto malus est, tametsi voluntas libera, quia sine illa nec recte vivi potest, in bonis numeranda sit. Si enim motus iste, id est aversio voluntatis a domino deo, sine dubitatione peccatum est, num possumus auctorem peccati deum dicere?'

[4] *dCD*, XIV, xi: 'Fecit itaque Deus, sicut scriptum est, hominem rectum ac per hoc voluntatis bonae. Non enim rectus esset bonam non habens voluntatem. Bona igitur voluntas opus est Dei; cum ea quippe ab illo factus est homo. Mala vero voluntas prima, quoniam omnia opera mala praecessit in homine, defectus potius fuit quidam ab opere Dei ad sua opera quam opus ullum, et ideo mala opera, quia secundum se, non secundum Deum; ut eorum operum tamquam fructuum malorum voluntas ipsa esset velut arbor mala aut ipse homo in quantum malae voluntatis.'

[5] *De Lib. Arb.*, II, xx, 54. Tr. by Burleigh, pp. 168–9.

Three points arise from the consideration of this passage from the conclusion of the second book of Augustine's great anti-Manichaean treatise *On Free Will*. First, that he recognizes that the final answer to the question 'Why did Man fall?' is unanswerable, at least in this life. Secondly, that while admitting this, he declares unequivocally that whatever the cause of the Fall, the responsibility for it rests with Man and not with God, since the essence of the Fall is a defective movement, a turning away from God, and nothing positive. Finally—and this fact is important, in view of accusations that he subsequently modified his opinions on Free Will—he makes it abundantly clear that, though it was within the power of the first man to sin by himself, it is not within the power of his descendants to return to the place from which Adam fell without the Grace of Christ. In this passage, probably written at Rome at the very beginning of his Christian life,[1] we have the pattern of Augustine's subsequent thought on the origin of sin and the need for Grace.

The cause of Evil is sin, and the responsibility for sin is man's. Sin was not due to God, who created all things good;[2] it was not due to the mysterious fruit of the forbidden tree (which even in the fourth century was beginning to be thought of as an apple); and it was certainly not due to the possession of Free Will, for Free Will is itself a good, although an intermediate good, which can either cleave to God, the unchangeable good, or be directed to other lower goods.[3] Man's sin was the misdirection of this intermediate good,[4] and for this misdirection he alone must bear the responsibility. Augustine returns to the voluntary nature of the Fall again and again:

If the defect which we call sin overtook a man against his will, like a fever, the penalty which follows the sinner and is called condemnation would rightly seem to be unjust. But in fact sin is so much a voluntary evil that it is not sin at all unless it is voluntary. This is so obvious that no one denies it, either of the handful of the learned or of the mass of the unlearned.[5] . . . Every evil man is the author of his evil deeds. If you wonder how that is, consider what we have just said: evil deeds are punished by the justice of God. They would not be justly punished

---

[1] In the *Retractationes*, i, 8 [9], Augustine says that he wrote the first two books of the *De Libero Arbitrio* at Rome, during his enforced stay in the later months of 387 and the spring and summer of 388, and the final book at Hippo, after being ordained a presbyter, i.e. between 391 and 395. This passage would, therefore, seem to have been written 387/388; but we cannot rule out the possibility of later revisions and insertions while the third book was being composed.   [2] *De Nat. Boni*, 34.

[3] *De Lib. Arb.*, II, xix, 52: 'Voluntas ergo, quae medium bonum est . . .'; ibid., 53: 'Voluntas ergo adherens communi atque incommutabili bono impetrat prima et magna hominis bona, cum ipsa sit medium quoddam bonum.'

[4] Ibid., 53: 'Voluntas autem aversa ab incommutabili et communi bono et conversa ad proprium bonum aut ad exterius aut ad inferius, peccat.'   [5] *De Vera Rel.*, xiv, 27.

unless they were done voluntarily.[1] . . . To his most excellent creatures, that is to rational spirits, God has given the power not to be corrupted if they do not will to be; but remain obedient under the Lord their God and cleave to His incorruptible beauty. But if they will not remain obedient and are willingly corrupted by sin, they are unwillingly corrupted by penalties.[2] . . . God indeed, the author of natures, and certainly not of vices, created man upright; but he, being by his own will depraved, and justly condemned, begot depraved and condemned offspring.[3]

This last sentence gives the key to the Augustinian explanation of the cause of Evil in the world. Man of his own free will has sinned, and drawn upon himself the punishment due to the divine justice:

Who can doubt that his is a penal state? Every just penalty is the penalty of sin and is called punishment. If the penalty is unjust, there is no doubt that it is, in fact, penalty, but it has been imposed on man by some unjust power that lords it over him. But it is mad to have any doubt about the omnipotence or the justice of God. Therefore man's penalty is just and is recompense for sin.[4]

Augustine is here speaking primarily of the penalty due for sin which is seen in the present weakness of the human will to command itself, even when it wishes to serve God; but he does not limit the penalty merely to inadequate powers of volition. In the work *On True Religion* he declares: 'The human body was perfect of its kind before man sinned, but after he had sinned it became weak and mortal',[5] while in his later writings, especially under the stimulus provided by the Pelagian controversy, he was to emphasize that the whole train of human woes: death, spiritual and physical, disease, the weakness of our bodies and their disobedience to our commands, and all the many other ills that flesh is heir to, are the consequence and penalty of that act of voluntary disobedience of our progenitor in which, in some mysterious fashion, all humanity shared.[6]

It will be observed that Augustine's explanation of the origin of Evil in the world deals exclusively with man. He says very little about that other problem which has perplexed and tormented many sensitive souls, of why animals who have not apparently fallen should suffer as they do, and why

---

[1] *De Lib. Arb.*, I, i, 1. Cf. III, xv, 46.   [2] *De Nat. Boni*, 7.
[3] *dCD*, XIII, xiv.   [4] *De Lib. Arb.*, III, xviii, 51. Tr. Burleigh, p. 201.
[5] *De Vera Rel.*, xv, 29. Tr. Burleigh, p. 238.
[6] E.g. *dCD*, XIII, xiii: 'Iam quippe anima libertate in perversum propria delectata et Deo dedignata servire pristino corporis servitio destituebatur, et quia superiorem dominum suo arbitrio deseruerat, inferiorem famulum ad suum arbitrium non tenebat, nec omni modo habebat subditam carnem, sicut semper habere potuisset, si Deo subdita ipsa mansisset. Tunc ergo coepit caro concupiscere adversus spiritum, cum qua controversia nati sumus, trahentes originem mortis et in membris nostris vitiataque natura contentionem eius sive victoriam de prima praevaricatione gestantes.'

the world of living things should be a battleground and a charnel-house.[1] One does not find in Augustine St Paul's sense of cosmic suffering and yearning for relief, expressed in the famous reference to the 'whole creation' which 'groaneth and travaileth with pain'[2] while it awaits its redemption by Christ. This lack of feeling on Augustine's part is a curious one, and it is perhaps a little facile to ascribe it to African brutality,[3] though he undoubtedly had his share of this unattractive quality. No doubt we may see in St Paul a particular largeness of mind which made him the Apostle of the Gentiles; but it would be a mistake to ascribe Augustine's silence simply to insensitivity.[4] More plausibly, it may be referred to the circumstances of his writing. Against the Manichaean view that Evil was a positive being he had to maintain that it was merely a defect and a corruption of God's creation which arises from the misuse of man's free will. God had to be exculpated from any charge of evil and the responsibility of created beings asserted. In this connection, Augustine repeatedly refers to the fact that, even before the sin of Adam, there had been a fall among angelic natures,[5] and it is possible to look for the cause of suffering in the lower orders of creation to the activities of the devil who is permitted, for a season, to trouble the earth.

Augustine's emphasis on the power and responsibility of human will, for the proof of which he was willing to refer the Manichees to their own experience,[6] was later to be used by the Pelagians as evidence for their contention that man's salvation is in his own power, when once he has been enlightened by divine Grace and cleansed by baptism. In his reply, Augustine

[1] He does, however, say in *dCD*, XII, iv that the faults of beasts and trees and other unreasonable, senseless or lifeless creatures whereby their natures are destroyed are not to be condemned, but to be ascribed to the Divine plan to perfect the inferior beauty of the universe by successive alteration of created things (cf. *De Lib. Arb.*, III, xxiii, 69). He is also clear that living animals feel (*De Vera Rel.*, xxix, 53). But he does not seem to have been led by this to consider the problems raised by animal suffering.

[2] Rom. 8.22. [3] As does T. A. Lacey, *Nature, Miracle and Sin*, 8–9, 111–12.

[4] There is always a danger, when discussing the feeling and suffering of the lower animals, to fall into anthropomorphic conceptions. When dealing with animals, our own feelings ought, no doubt, to be our rough practical guide; but it is a mistake to assume that the problem of animal suffering is identical with that of human suffering. It is possible that much of what we imagine to be suffering, e.g. the sensations of a bird in a cat's mouth, may be devoid of the anguish that a human being would endure in a parallel situation.

[5] *De Lib. Arb.*, III, xxv, 75–76; *De Nat. Boni*, 33; *De Catech. Rud.*, xviii, 30; *dCD*, XII, vi; etc.

[6] *Cum Felice*, II, iii: 'Ecce autem liberum arbitrium, atque inde quemque peccare si velit, non peccare si nolit, non solum in divinis scripturis, quas non intelligetis, sed etiam in verbis ipsius Manichaei vestri probo. Circumclusus enim videt potentiam veritatis, contra quam conatus fuerat aliam naturam quam non fecit deus, inducere contra deum, non solida veritate, sed inani phantasmate: tamen ad confitendum verum de libero arbitrio, plus in eo valuit natura humana in qua eum deus efficit, quam fabula sacrilega quam sibi ipse confinxit.'

so dwelt upon the need for Grace as a power to act, and not merely as
an illumination, and on the fact of divine Prescience and Predestination, as
to cause many of his contemporaries, and not a few modern critics, to
regard him as having abandoned his earlier voluntarism and returned,
paradoxically, to the Manichaean determinism of his youth, with the
omnipotent will of God replacing the impulse of the two souls of Manichaeism. Augustine was very conscious of this accusation and in the *Retractations* makes a special point of controverting it. His arguments have not
convinced all his readers, but they are not, in themselves, unreasonable. In
dealing with the Manichees, he remarks, he did not speak of the Grace of
God, because it was not then under discussion.[1] Nevertheless, it is to be
remembered that he begins his work *On Free Will* with an acknowledgement of the divine aid (*ops divina*) which brought him from the fables of
the Manichees to the truth,[2] and that the third book, completed between
four and eight years later, contains an exposition of the characteristic
Augustinian view of all humanity sinning in Adam, though expressed in
more optimistic language than he was in the habit of using in his later
writings.[3] Furthermore, Augustine never withdrew what he said on the
subject of free will when he wrote against the Manichees. In the third book
On Free Will he says to Evodius:

> You could not imagine that 'having in our power' means anything else
> than 'being able to do what we will'. Therefore there is nothing so much
> in our power as is the will itself. For as soon as we will [*volumus*] im-
> mediately will [*voluntas*] is there.[4] We can say rightly that we do not
> grow old voluntarily but necessarily, or that we do not die voluntarily

[1] *Retract.*, i, 8 [9], 4: 'In his atque huius modi verbis meis, quia gratia dei commemorata non est, de qua tunc non agebatur, putant Pelagiani vel putare possunt suam
nos tenuisse sententiam.'   [2] *De Lib. Arb.*, I, ii, 4. Quoted above, p. 194.
[3] Ibid., III, xx, 55: 'Ut autem de illo primo coniugio et cum ignorantia et cum difficultate et cum mortalitate nascamur, quoniam illi cum peccavissent et in errorem et in
erumnam et in mortem praecipitati sunt, rerum moderatori deo iustissime placuit, ut et in
ortum hominis originaliter appareret iustitia punientis et in provectu misericordia liberantis. Non enim damnato primo homini sic adempta est beatitudo ut etiam fecunditas
adimeretur; poterat enim et de prole eius quamvis carnali et mortali aliquod in suo genere
fieri decus ornamentumque terrarum. Iam vero ut meliores gigneret quam ipse esset non
erat aequitatis. Sed ex conversione ad deum ut vinceret quisque supplicium quod origo
eius ex aversione meruerat, non solum volentem non prohiberi sed etiam adiuvari
oportebat. Etiam sic enim rerum creator ostendit quanta facilitate potuisset homo, si
voluisset, retinere quod factus est, cum proles eius potuit etiam superare quod nata est.'
[4] Augustine here plays upon the sense of *volo* in a way which is impossible in English,
with our distinction between *wish* and *will*. Cf. I, xii, 25: '[A.] Nam quaero abs te, sitne
aliqua nobis voluntas? E. Nescio. A. Visne hoc scire? E. Et hoc nescio. A. Nihil ergo
deinceps me interroges. E. Quare? A. Quia roganti tibi respondere non debeo nisi
volenti scire quod rogas. Deinde nisi velis ad sapientiam pervenire, sermo tecum de
huiuscemodi rebus non est habendus. Postremo amicus meus esse non poteris nisi velis
ut bene sit mihi. Iam vero de te tu ipse videris, utrum tibi voluntas nulla sit beatae vitae
tuae. E. Fateor, negari non potest habere nos voluntatem.' See Lacey, *Nature, Miracle,
and Sin*, 50–51.

but from necessity, and so with other similar things. But who but a raving fool would say that it is not voluntarily that we will?[1]

It is significant that this declaration, which immediately precedes an assertion that God's foreknowledge does not remove the voluntary character of our actions,[2] was not disowned by Augustine when he came to write the *Retractitions*. On the contrary, he reaffirmed what he had previously stated:

> Wherefore, do not let the Pelagians exult as if I had been pleading their cause, because in these books I said much in favour of free will, which was necessary for the purpose I had in view in that discussion. For the Pelagians are a new brand of heretics who assert the freedom of the will in such a way as to leave no room for the grace of God, since they say that it is given to us according to our merits. I have said, it is true, in the First Book, that evil-doing is punished by God. And I added: 'It would not be justly punished unless it were done voluntarily.'[3]

Finally, in the treatise *On Grace and Free Will*, written towards the end of Augustine's life in 426 or 427, when the zeal with which he had asserted the absolute necessity of the Grace of God for every good thought and deed had caused some of his hearers to suppose that he denied free will,[4] the saint reaffirms it as vigorously as in the early writings against the Manichees. He founds it upon Scripture,[5] and supports it with a chain of references;[6] but he warns his readers against trying to separate it from the Grace of God, as do those who trust in their own powers.[7] Free will is not

---

[1] *De Lib. Arb.*, III, iii, 7. Tr. by Burleigh, pp. 174–5.

[2] Ibid.: 'Quam ob rem, quamvis praesciat deus nostras voluntates futuras, non ex eo tamen conficitur, ut non voluntate aliquid velimus. . . . [8] Attende enim, quaeso, quanta caecitate dicatur: "Si praescivit deus futuram voluntatem meam, quoniam nihil potest aliter fieri quam praescivit, necesse est ut velim quod ille praescivit; si autem necesse est, non iam voluntate, sed necessitate id me velle fatendum est." O stultitiam singularem! Quo modo ergo non potest aliud fieri quam praescivit deus, si voluntas non erit, quam voluntatem futuram ille praesciverit.'   [3] *Retract.*, i, 8 [9], 3. Tr. Burleigh, p. 103.

[4] *De Grat. et Lib. Arb.*, i, 1: 'Propter eos qui hominis liberum arbitrium sic praedicant et defendunt, ut Dei gratiam qua vocamur ad eum et a nostris malis meritis liberamur, et per quam bona merita comparamus quibus ad vitam perveniamus aeternam, negare audeant et conentur auferre, multa iam disseruimus, litterisque mandavimus, quantum nobis Dominus donare dignatus est. Sed quoniam sunt quidam, qui sic gratiam Dei defendunt, ut negent hominis liberum arbitrium; aut quando gratia defenditur, negari existimant liberum arbitrium; hinc aliquid scribere ad vestram Charitatem, Valentine frater, et caeteri qui simul Deo servitis, conpellente mutua charitate curavi.'

[5] Ibid., ii, 2: 'Revelavit autem nobis per Scripturas suas sanctas, esse in homine liberum arbitrium.'   [6] Ibid., ii, 2–iii, 5.

[7] Ibid., iv, 6: 'Sed metuendum est ne ista omnia divina testimonia, et quaecunque alia sunt, quae sine dubitatione sunt plurima, in defensione liberi arbitrii, sic intelligantur, ut ad vitam piam et bonam conversationem, cui merces aeternas debetur, adiutorio et gratiae Dei locus non relinquatur; et audeat miser homo, quando bene vivit et bene operatur, vel potius bene vivere et bene operari sibi videtur, in se ipso, non in Domino gloriari, et spem recte vivendi in se ipso ponere, ut sequatur eum maledictum Ieremiae prophetae dicentis, *Maledictus homo qui spem habet in homine, et firmat carnem brachii sui, et a Domino discedit cor eius* (Ierem. 17.5).'

sufficient unless aided by Grace;[1] but the fact that it is God which work-eth in man both to will and to do does not deprive man of his freedom.[2] Our will is always free, but it is not always good;[3] we can indeed keep the divine commandments but, since *the will is prepared by the Lord*,[4] we must ask Him for such strength as is required to enable us to perform them.[5] Our free will is not taken away by Grace, but is changed from evil to good and, when good, is aided.[6]

In the light of such assertions, the suggestion that Augustine abandoned his earlier views can hardly be sustained. The old bishop defended human freedom and human responsibility for action as strongly as did the young convert. The change, if change is to be sought, lies rather in his outlook. There is, in the Augustine of the early anti-Manichaean treatises, an optimism which is lacking in the older man who wrote against the Pelagians, and there is in the catechumen a certain breadth of mind which we miss in the mature Christian. The enthusiasm for Plato and the Platonists, the excitement at the discovery that Christianity is the reality for which the philosophers of old were seeking, all this was to be replaced by a sterner and more critical attitude to human wisdom and to the pagan world. But what Augustine's mind lost in breadth during his growth in the faith, it gained in depth. If the passage of time made him less confident in man, it taught him to know God; and thus, however much we may regret certain features in his mature mind which seem to look to the power rather than to the love of God, we cannot but feel that the overall change was for the better. Plato was no answer to the Pelagians; St Paul was.

We now turn to the second of the problems which faced Augustine in

[1] Ibid., iv, 9: 'Non autem intrat [homo] in tentationem, si voluntate bona vincat con-cupiscentiam malam. Nec tamen sufficit arbitrium voluntatis humanae, nisi a Domino victoria concedatur oranti, ne intret in tentationem. . . . Homo ergo gratia iuvatur, ne sine causa voluntati eius iubeatur.'

[2] Ibid., ix, 21: 'Non enim, quia dixit, *Deus est enim qui operatur in vobis et velle et operari, pro bona voluntate* (Philipp. 2.13), ideo liberum arbitrium abstulisse putandus est'; ibid., x, 22: 'Itaque, fratres, debetis quidem per liberum arbitrium non facere mala, et facere bona; hoc enim nobis lex Dei praecipit in Libris sanctis, sive veteribus, sive novis; sed legamus et adiuvante Domino intelligamus Apostolum dicentem; *Quia non iustificabitur ex lege omnis caro coram illo. Per legem enim cognitio peccati* (Rom. 3.20). *Cognitio* dixit; non, Consumptio. Quando autem cognoscit homo peccatum, si non adiuvat gratia ut cognitum caveatur, sine dubio lex iram operatur.'

[3] Ibid., xv, 31: 'Ne autem putetur, nihil ibi facere ipsos homines per liberum arbitrium, ideo in psalmo dicitur, *Nolite obdurare corda vestra*. . . . Semper est autem in nobis voluntas libera, sed non semper est bona.'

[4] Prov. 8.35 (LXX): ἑτοιμάζεται θέλησις παρὰ Κυρίου.

[5] *De Grat. et Lib. Arb.*, xvi, 32: 'Certum est enim nos mandata servare, si volumus: sed quia *praeparatur voluntas a Domino*, ab illo petendum est ut tantum velimus, quantum sufficit ut volendo faciamus.'

[6] Ibid., xx, 41: 'Satis me disputasse arbitror adversus eos qui gratiam Dei vehementer oppugnant, qua voluntas humana non tollitur, sed ex mala mutatur in bonam, et cum bona fuerit adiuvatur.'

his writings against the Manichees: how to defend the Scriptures, and especially the Old Testament, against their attacks.[1]

The most compelling reason for the Manichees to reject the Old Testament was simple enough: it was wholly irreconcilable with the revelation delivered to them by Mani. The God of the Hebrew Scriptures, the Creator and ruler of the material world who looked upon what He had made and saw that it was very good, was utterly removed from the Father of Greatness, ruling in the Kingdom of Light. Nevertheless besides the authority of Mani his followers, whose boast it was that they appealed to the reason and did not command men to believe without due demonstration, sought to discredit the Old Testament on two grounds, which Faustus of Milevis, the theological spokesman of the African Manichees, developed at length in the book against the Catholics, to which Augustine was afterwards to reply. In the first place, Faustus declared, to accept the Old Testament is to bind oneself to Jewish ceremonial observance—like most controversialists, Faustus did not hesitate to inform his opponents how they ought to believe their own faith—and since the Catholics did not do so, it was dishonest of them to claim to receive the Old Testament into their canon.[2] Secondly, Faustus pointed to the many scandals recorded in the Old Testament about the lives of the patriarchs. If these are true, he wondered how the Catholics could venerate them as holy men. If on the other hand they are untrue—and he added generously that he was quite prepared to believe the Old Testament writers to have been liars on this matter, judging from the lies which they told about God—then these writers should be punished, their books condemned, and the good name of the patriarchs cleared from such scandals. In any case, the books of the Old Testament, as they exist at present, are not worthy of acceptance.[3]

It had been problems of precisely this character which facilitated Augustine's adherence to the Manichees in his youth,[4] and he was therefore

---

[1] See Rickaby, *The Manichees as St Augustine saw Them*, 27–48.
[2] *C. Faust.*, VI, i: 'Faustus dixit: Accipis vetus testamentum? quomodo, cuius praecepta non servo? puto quidem, quia nec tu; nam peritomen ego ut pudendam despui, ac, si non fallor, et tu; cessationem sabbatorum ut supervacuam, credo, quod et tu; sacrificia ut idolatriam, non dubito, quod et tu; porcina certe non ego sola abstineo, tu item non solam comedis. ego quidem, quia omnem carnem inmundam existimem, tu vero, quia nihil immundum: quo utroquo ab utroque nostrum vetus destruitur testamentum', etc.
[3] Ibid., XXII, iii: '. . . damnamus enim detestati actus iniquos, quos ultro de se nec interrogati confessi sunt rei; aut si haec per invidiam scriptorum adversus eos malignitas finxit, puniantur scriptores, damnentur eorum libri, purgetur propheticum nomen indigna fama, gravitati atque censurae suae patriarcharum reddatur auctoritas. [iv] Et sane fieri potuit, ut quemadmodum de deo inpudenter idem tanta finxerunt. . . . fieri, inquam, potuit, ut et de dei hominibus mentirentur, qui de deo ipso tanta protervitate mentiti sunt. sed vos consentite nobiscum, ut portent scriptores crimen, si vultis eodem liberari prophetas.' [4] *Conf.*, III, vii, 12–13.

peculiarly well equipped to answer Faustus on this issue. He did this in a massive work of thirty-three books, the *Contra Faustum*, his *magnum opus* against Manichaeism, written in AD 400; but the outlines of his argument had already appeared some nine years earlier in his essay *On the Usefulness of Belief*, addressed to his friend, Honoratus, whom Augustine had himself persuaded to become a Manichee, and whom he was now anxious to lead to the Catholic faith.

A modern Christian apologist, engaged upon the refutation of the sort of arguments which the Manichees brought against the Old Testament, would probably base his defence upon the conception of a progressive revelation of God to His chosen people, beginning with the covenant with Abraham and leading to the Incarnation, when the veil was finally lifted and Himself revealed in the person of Jesus Christ. As regards the alleged scandals of the Old Testament: the cruel massacres perpetrated by the Israelites; the polygamy of many of the Patriarchs; and the like, he would argue that these reflected primitive conditions, stages through which even the Chosen People had to go in order to acquire the religious education which was to be the education of the world. This method owes something to the popular versions of Darwinian evolution and a great deal to the historical and critical attitude among biblical scholars which has been steadily developing since the seventeenth century and with particular speed since the nineteenth. Augustine, of course, did not have the methods of the modern apologist at his disposal; but he was able to arrive at somewhat similar conclusions by adapting the method of allegorical interpretation of Scripture, which he had learned from St Ambrose at Milan, according to which *the letter killeth, but the Spirit giveth life*.

Accordingly, Augustine tells Honoratus that the Old Testament Scripture is transmitted in a fourfold sense: historical; aetiological; analogical; and allegorical.[1] In the historical sense, we are told what was written or done, or what was not done but only written about as if it were. In the aetiological sense, we are told the cause by which a thing was written or done. In the analogical sense, we are shown that there is no opposition between the Old and the New Testaments; and in the allegorical sense, we learn that some things are not to be taken literally, but understood in a figurative manner.[2]

---

[1] *De Util. Cred.*, iii, 5: 'Omnis igitur scriptura, quae testamentum vetus vocatur, diligenter eam nosse cupientibus quadrifariam traditur: secundum historiam, secundum aetiologiam, secundum analogiam, secundum allegoriam. ne me ineptum putes graecis nominibus utentem. primum quia sic accepi nec tibi hoc aliter audeo intimare quam accepi.'
[2] Ibid.: 'Secundum historiam ergo traditur, cum docetur, quid scriptum aut quid gestum sit; quid non gestum, sed tantummodo scriptum quasi gestum sit. secundum aetiolo-

All these senses of Scripture were employed by our Lord and His apostles. Thus, Christ's answer to those who criticized His disciples for plucking ears of corn on the Sabbath (Matt. 12.3–4), was an example of the historical, and His explanation of the origin of the bill of divorcement— *Moses because of the hardness of your hearts suffered you to put away your wives* (Matt. 19.8)—of the aetiological.[1] Examples of the analogical sense require no enumeration, but Augustine speaks with scorn of the Manichaean tactics, when confronted with them, of claiming that the New Testament has been corrupted by interpolations made by Judaizing Christians.[2] Finally, there is the allegorical sense, the sense in which St Paul speaks of Abraham's two children, the one by a bond-maid, the other by a free-woman, which is an allegory of the two covenants, the one from Mount Sinai, and the other from above.[3]

Here these wicked men, while they try to make the Law of none effect, at the same time compel us to approve of these Scriptures. They pay attention where it is said that those are in servitude who are under the Law, and above other passages brandish this decisive one: *You who are justified by the Law are banished from Christ. You have fallen from grace.*[4] Now we admit that all this is true. We do not say the Law is necessary save for those for whom servitude is profitable. It was profitably laid down because men, who could not be won from their sins by reason, had to be coerced by threats and terrors of penalties which even fools can understand. When the grace of Christ sets men free from such threats and penalties it does not condemn the Law but invites us now to submit to His love and not to be slaves to fear. Grace is a benefaction conferred by God, which those do not understand who desire to continue under the bondage of the Law. Paul rightly calls them unbelievers, reproachfully, who do not believe that they are now set free by our Lord Jesus from a servitude to which they had been subjected by the just judgement of God. Hence this other saying of the same apostle: *The Law was our pedagogue in Christ.*[5] God, thus, gave men a pedagogue whom they might fear, and later gave them a master whom they might love. But in these precepts and mandates of the Law which Christians may not now lawfully obey, such as the Sabbath, circumcision, sacrifice and the like, there are contained such mysteries that every pious man may understand there is nothing more pernicious than to take whatever is there literally, and nothing more wholesome than to let the truth be revealed by the spirit. For this reason: *The Letter killeth but the Spirit quickeneth.*[6] And again: *The same vail remains in the reading of the Old*

giam, cum ostenditur, quid qua de causa vel factum vel dictum sit. secundum analogiam, cum demonstratur non sibi sit adversari duo testamenta, vetus et novum. secundum allegoriam, cum docetur non ad litteram esse accipienda quaedam, quae scripta sunt, sed figurate intellegenda.'

[1] Ibid., iii, 6.   [2] Ibid., iii, 7.   [3] Gal. 4.22–26.
[4] Gal. 5.4.   [5] Gal. 3.24.   [6] II Cor. 3.6.

Testament and there is no revelation, for in Christ the vail is done away.[1] It is not the Old Testament that is done away in Christ but the concealing vail, so that it may be understood through Christ. That is, as it were, laid bare, which without Christ is obscure and hidden. The same apostle adds immediately: *When thou shalt turn to Christ the vail will be taken away.*[2] He does not say: The Law or the Old Testament *will be taken away.* It is not the case, therefore, that by the grace of the Lord that which was covered has been abolished as useless; rather, the covering has been removed which concealed useful truth. This is what happens to those who earnestly and piously, not proudly and wickedly, seek the sense of the Scriptures. To them is carefully demonstrated the order of events, the reasons for deeds and words, and the agreement of the Old Testament with the New, so that not a point remains where there is not complete harmony; and such secret truths are conveyed in figures that when they are brought to light by interpretation they compel those who wished to condemn rather than to learn, to confess their discomfiture.[3]

This chapter summarizes Augustine's case against the Manichaean condemnation of the Old Testament. The ceremonial requirements of the Law were, in their day, of value in that they applied profitable coercion to sinners who could not be persuaded by reason. They are not, however, any longer binding for those who have been set free from sin by the Grace of Christ. Nevertheless, the Scripture is not thereby abolished, because these ceremonial requirements were types and shadows of greater mysteries which were revealed in Christ, by whose coming the vail has been taken away, so that the faithful may understand the 'secret truths which are conveyed in figures', and accept them as part of the Christian revelation. There is no doubt of Augustine's conviction on this matter. 'I call my conscience to witness, Honoratus,' he declares, 'I call God who dwells in pure souls to witness, that I am convinced there is nothing more wise, more chaste, more religious than those Scriptures which the Catholic Church accepts under the name of the Old Testament',[4] and he later suggests that some of the less apparently edifying passages may have been introduced to exercise the intellect of the reader in seeking another and more suitable interpretation, referring—not very happily, from the point of view of a modern critic—to the less decent passages in the classical authors, which generations of scholars had sought to understand in an edifying and improving sense.[5]

[1] II Cor. 3.14.   [2] II Cor. 3.16.
[3] *De Util. Cred.*, iii, 9. Tr. by Burleigh, pp. 297–8.
[4] Ibid., iv, 13. Burleigh, p. 301.
[5] Ibid., vii, 17: 'Quid? si illa, quae nonnullos inperitos in eisdem scripturis videntur offendere, eo sunt ita posita, ut cum res abhorrentes a sensu qualiumcumque hominum, nedum prudentium atque sanctorum, legerentur, secretam significationem multo studio-

It was from this position that Augustine answered Faustus of Milevis' attack upon the Old Testament. Faustus asserted that the only way in which the Old Testament could be accepted was by the practice of the Mosaic Law and that, in any event, it was discredited by the scandals recorded within it. Augustine replied by emphasizing the fact that the objections are removed if the allegorical interpretation is properly applied. It was not only the words of the men of the Old Testament which were prophetic, but their very lives. Indeed, in a sense, the whole people of Israel was a great prophet, since it prefigured in its history the great things which were to come.[1] It is, however, important to examine the sense of Scripture carefully, and decide what is to be taken literally, and what figuratively. The precepts of the Mosaic Law fall into two classes: precepts of life relating to conduct (*praecepta vitae agendae*), namely the Decalogue, which is still in force; and precepts of life with a signification (*praecepta vitae significandae*), namely, the ceremonial requirements of the Law, which prefigured the New Covenant and which have been abrogated by it.

I have spoken above [says Augustine, in the *Contra Faustum*] of how and why the Old Testament is to be received by the heirs of the New; but since Faustus was just now concerned with the promises of the Old Testament, but now wants to deal with its precepts, I reply that the Manichees completely fail to understand the difference between precepts of life relating to conduct, and precepts of life having a signification. For example: *Thou shalt not covet* is a precept of life relating to conduct; *Thou shalt circumcise every male on the eighth day* is a precept of life having a signification. Out of ignorance the Manichees and all others who are displeased by the letter of the Old Testament, not understanding that what God commanded the ancient people to celebrate was a shadow of what was to come, but noting that it is not observed in that manner in the present, condemn these things, which were certainly suited to past time, when those things which are now manifested were signified as coming in the future.[2]

In this particular context, Augustine remarks that the command to

sius quaereremus? nonne cernis, ut Catamitum bucolicorum, cui pastor durus effluxit, conentur homines interpretari et Alexim puerum, in quem Plato etiam carnem amatorium fecisse dicitur, nescio quid magnum significare, sed inperitorum iudicium fugere adfirment, cum sine ullo sacrilegio poeta uberrimus videri possit libidinosas cantiunculas edidisse?'
[1] *C. Faust.*, XXII, xxiv: 'Qua in re hoc primum dico illorum hominum non tantum linguam, verum etiam vitam fuisse propheticam totumque illud regnum gentis Hebraeorum magnum quendam, quia et magni cuiusdam, fuisse prophetam. quocirca, quod ad eos quidem adtinet, qui illic erant eruditi corde in sapientia dei, non solum in his, quae dicebant, sed etiam in his, quae faciebant, quod autem ad ceteros ac simul omnes illius gentis homines, in his, quae in illis vel de illis divinitus fiebant, prophetia venturi Christi et ecclesiae perscrutanda est. omnia enim illa, sicut dicit apostolus, *figurae nostrae fuerunt* (I Cor. 10.6).
[2] *C. Faust.*, VI, ii.

circumcise the flesh of the foreskin was very apt, 'for in what member could the stripping away of carnal and mortal concupiscence be more aptly figured, than in that from which carnal and mortal offspring takes its origin?'[1]

In the same spirit in which he had declared to Honoratus that the Law

was profitably laid down because men, who could not be won from their sins by reason, had to be coerced by threats and terrors of penalties which even fools can understand,[2]

Augustine answered Faustus with regard to the Mosaic Law:

On account of its stony heart, the Jewish people received many precepts, appropriate rather than good in themselves, by which future things were prefigured and prophesied, although they were celebrated by those who did not understand. When however these things came to pass, and what they signified was revealed, the precepts are not now ordered to be performed, but to be read and to be understood.[3]

A similar principle governs Augustine's reply to Manichaean charges of immorality recorded in the Old Testament. He makes it clear that to defend the Old Testament and to respect the patriarchs is not to approve of sins committed by them. 'We are defending the Holy Scriptures and not the sins of men', he says, and emphasizes the fact that the record of a wrong action does not imply divine approbation of it.[4] On the contrary, the more religiously a Catholic Christian accepts Holy Scripture, the more he must censure actions which he has learnt from the same Scripture to deserve censure.[5] Accordingly, since fornication and all illicit sexual intercourse is condemned in Scripture whenever it is recorded, it is presented to us for condemnation and not for praise. Or again, whoever supposed that the cruelty of Herod, when he ordered the Innocents to be massacred on the occasion of Christ's nativity, deserved anything other than detestation? But the Gospel merely records the fact without comment. Augustine recognizes that this particular example may not impress

[1] Ibid., VI, iii: 'In quo enim membro congruentius expoliatio carnalis et mortalis concupiscentiae figuratur, quam unde carnalis et mortalis fetus exoritur?'
[2] De Util. Cred., iii, 9.
[3] C. Faust., XVIII, iv.
[4] Ibid., XXII, xlv: 'Nos tamen scripturas sanctas, non hominum peccata defendimus, sic autem de huius facti purgatione satagimus, quasi hoc deus noster aut fieri iusserit aut factum adprobaverit aut ita iusti homines in illis libris appellentur, ut si voluerint peccare, non possint. cum ergo in litteris, quas isti reprehendunt, deus huic facto nullum iustitiae testimonium perhibuerit.'
[5] Ibid., XXII, lxii: 'Quod ita nobis Faustus vel ipsa Manichaea perversitas arbitratur adversum, quasi nobis in illius scripturae veneratione dignoque praeconio vitia hominum, quae illa commemorat, necesse sit adprobare; quin potius necesse est, ut, quanto illam religiosius accipimus, tanto fidentius illa culpemus, quae per eius veritatem certius culpanda didicimus.'

the Manichees, who denied the Incarnation, but refers them to the Old Testament, where similar examples of Jewish wickedness and blindness are related without condemnation, but are nevertheless detested by all readers.[1] Nevertheless, a man who is recorded as being guilty of an offence against the divine law, may well have a symbolic value in his own person. The Manichees asked how it was that Judas,[2] the son of Jacob, who lay with his daughter-in-law,[3] was numbered among the twelve patriarchs, while Judas Iscariot was cast out of the number of the twelve apostles. If Judas Iscariot were condemned why was Judas the son of Jacob, after he had committed so great a crime, blessed by his father with all his other brethren?[4] Augustine replies that Jacob's prophecy does not refer to Judas, but to his descendant, Christ; and for that reason, Holy Scripture must not be silent about Judas' great wickedness, just as it must not be silent about the words of his father, spoken after the commission of the offence of which the father was ignorant, which refer to another person.[5]

However, Augustine protests, very much in the manner in which a modern scholar might do, against any too facile denunciation of the actions of the men of the Old Testament, particularly in the field of sexual morality. For obvious reasons, the Manichees made much of such matters in which, they argued, the patriarchs fell far short of their own high moral standards. 'I have rejected silver and gold,' said Faustus of Milevis, 'I carry no copper coin in my purse, being content with my daily bread and taking no thought for the morrow whence my belly shall be filled or my body clothed, and you ask me whether I accept the Gospel. You see in me Christ's beatitudes which make the Gospel and you ask whether I accept it. You see a man poor and mild, a peaceful man of pure heart, mourning, hungering and thirsting, persecuted and hated for righteousness' sake, and you doubt whether I accept the Gospel!'[6] To such self-confidence, the virtue of the patriarchs seemed a poor thing. Augustine, however, refused to admit that the standards of conduct of his own age were an infallible guide to those of the past. He makes a distinction between the eternal law of God, which remains unchanged for every age and nation, and the habits

---

[1] Ibid.: 'ibi enim fornicatio et omnis inlicitus concubitus divino iure damnatur, ac per hoc, cum talia quorundam facta commemorat, de quibus eo loco suam taceat sententiam, iudicanda nobis permittit, non laudanda praescribit. quis enim nostrum in ipso evangelio non detestatur Herodis crudelitatem, cum de Christi nativitate sollicitus tot infantes iussit occidi? at hoc factum ibi non vituperatur, sed tantum narratur. sed ne hoc Manichaei vesana inpudentia falsum esse contendant, quia et ipsam Christi nativitatem, qua Herodes perturbatus est, negant, ipsorum Iudaeorum inmanitatem et caecitatem legant, quemadmodum illic tantummodo narretur, non vituperetur, et tamen ab omnibus detestetur.'   [2] Called Judah in the A.V.
[3] Gen. 38.1–30.   [4] Gen. 49.8–12.
[5] C. Faust., XXII, lxiii.   [6] Ibid., V, i.

and customs of particular peoples in particular situations. A sin is anything
which is done or said against the eternal law of God, which law is the
Divine Reason or Will of God commanding the natural order of things to
be preserved and forbidding it to be troubled.[1] But it does not follow that
the same action is at every time or in every situation against this law. In the
case of Abraham, whose decision to have offspring by the Egyptian Hagar
after the Lord had promised him a seed as numerous as the stars of heaven
had been the subject of some caustic comment by Faustus, Augustine
declared that the intention of Abraham was to conserve the natural order
of things by begetting children and not out of an absurd desire for offspring, or the impulse of lust.[2] A similar case was that of Jacob:

> When [polygamy] was the custom, it was no crime; it is now a crime
> because it is not the custom. For some sins are against nature, some
> against custom, some against precept. If you consult nature, it was not
> for lustfulness that Jacob used those women [i.e. Leah and Rachel and
> the two handmaids] but for the sake of having children. If you consult
> custom at that time and in those lands, the thing was constantly done. If
> you consult precept, it was forbidden by no law. Why is it a crime now
> for any one to act so, except because the thing itself is not allowed by
> custom and law?[3]

This conception of a fixed moral law which regulates the essentials of
conduct and which never changes, as opposed to local precepts and customs suitable for their day and age, is Augustine's great argument against
Manichaean attacks on Old Testament morality and must be accounted
one of his major discoveries. He had no inkling of it in his youth. As he
himself says in the *Confessions*:

> I was entirely ignorant as to what is that principle within us by which we
> are like God, and which is rightly said in Scripture to be made *after
> God's image*. Nor did I know that true inner righteousness—which does
> not judge according to custom but by the measure of the most perfect
> law of God Almighty—by which the customs of various places and times

[1] *C. Faust.*, XXII, xxvii: 'Ergo peccatum est factum vel dictum vel concupitum aliquid
contra aeternam legem. lex vero aeterna est ratio divina vel voluntas dei ordinem
naturalem conservari iubens, perturbari vetans.'
[2] Ibid., XXII, xxx: 'Aeterna ergo lege consulta, quae ordinem naturalem conservari
iubet, perturbari vetat, videamus quid peccaverit, id est, quid contra istam legem fecerit
pater Abraham in his, quae velut magna crimina Faustus obiecit. *habendae*, inquit, *prolis
insana flagrans cupidine et deo, qui id iam sibi de Sara coniuge promiserat, minime credens,
cum pelice volutatus sit.* insana vero iste Faustus criminandi cupiditate caecatus et
haeresis suae nefas prodidit et Abrahae concubitum nesciens erransque laudavit. sicut
enim lex illa aeterna, id est voluntas dei creaturarum omnium conditoris conservando
naturali ordini consulens, non ut satiandae libidini serviatur, sed ut saluti generis
prospiciatur, ad prolem tantummodo propagandam mortalis carnis delectationem
dominatu rationis in concubitu relaxari sinit.'
[3] Ibid. XXII, xlvii. Tr. by Rickaby, op. cit., p. 38. Cf. *dCD*, XV, xvi.

were adapted to those places and times (though the law itself is the same always and everywhere, not one thing in one place and another in another). By this inner righteousness Abraham and Isaac, and Jacob and Moses and David, and all those commended by the mouth of God were righteous and were judged unrighteous only by foolish men who were judging by human judgement and gauging their judgement of the customs of the whole human race by the narrow norms of their own customs. It is as if a man in an armoury, not knowing what piece goes on what part of the body, should put a greave on his head and a helmet on his shin and then complain that they did not fit. Or as if, on some holiday when afternoon business was forbidden, one were to grumble at not being allowed to go on selling as it had been lawful for him to do in the forenoon. Or, again, as if in a house, he sees a servant handle something that the butler is not permitted to touch, or when something is done in the stable that would be prohibited in a dining-room, and then a person should be indignant that in one house and one family the same things are not allowed to every member of the household. Such is the case with those who cannot endure to hear that something was lawful for righteous men in former times that is not so now; or that God, for certain temporal reasons, commanded then one thing to them and another now to these; yet both would be serving the same righteous will. These people should see that in one man, one day, and one house, different things are fit for different members; and a thing that was formerly lawful may become, after a time, unlawful—and something allowed or commanded in one place that is justly prohibited and punished in another. Is justice, then, variable and changeable? No, but the times over which she presides are not all alike because they are different times. But men, whose days upon the earth are few, cannot by their own perception harmonize the causes of former ages and other nations, of which they have no experience, and compare them with those of which they do have experience; although in one and the same body, or day, or family, they can readily see that what is suitable for each member, season, part, and person may differ. To the one they take exception; to the other they submit.[1]

In his defence of the Old Testament, Augustine suggested an approach and provided a method which met the Manichaean objections, if it failed to convince hardened Manichees like Faustus. But discussions of the interpretation of Scripture inevitably lead to the fundamental question: How are we to accept Scripture? Where does authority reside to enable us to understand it? And how are we to use our reason when we approach it, especially in the face of authority?

This is, perhaps, the crucial intellectual problem in Augustine's dealings with his former co-religionists, since the Manichees claimed that theirs was a rational religion appealing to the intellect. 'What else compelled me

[1] *Conf.*, III, vii, 12–13. Tr. by Outler, pp. 69–70.

for nearly nine years to spurn the religion implanted in me as a boy by my parents, to follow those men and listen diligently to them, than that they said we were overawed by superstition and were bidden to believe rather than to reason, while they pressed no one to believe until the truth had been discussed and elucidated ?'[1] Absurd as the idea seems to us today, Manichaeism represented itself as a reasonable faith, as reasonable as anything that the eighteenth century produced, and held that it was the Catholics who were the irrational authoritarians. On the other hand Augustine, while he came, as a Catholic Christian, to recognize the need for authority to direct the human understanding, did not therefore reject, as some converts do, the God-given power of reason. In the great mysteries of the faith, he was capable as a bishop of urging a correspondent to cherish the intellect, 'for the Holy Scriptures themselves which persuade us to have faith in great matters before we understand them, cannot be useful to you unless you rightly understand them'.[2] Where Augustine differed from the Manichees, and from all other alleged rationalists in religion, was in his frank recognition that there comes a point when the human mind fails. In the words of Pascal: 'The last stage of reason is to recognize that there is an infinity of things which surpass it. Reason is but feeble if it does not go so far as to know that.'[3] Where reason fails, the revelation of God supplies the Christian with the light which he could not have of himself; but this illumination does not relieve him from the responsibility of using his intellect, both before and after illumination.

Discussion of the relationship between reason and authority occurs frequently in Augustine's works, but may very conveniently be studied by once more turning to the book *On the Usefulness of Belief*, written shortly after he had been ordained a presbyter in 391. This work, it will be remembered, was addressed to Honoratus, a friend of Augustine's student days, a pagan whom Augustine had himself converted to Manichaeism.[4] Honora-

---

[1] *De Util. Cred.*, i, 2. Burleigh, p. 292.

[2] *Ep.* 120, iii, 13: 'Intellectum vero valde ama, quia et ipsae scripturae sanctae, quae magnarum rerum ante intellegentiam suadent fidem, nisi eas recte intellegas, utiles tibi esse non possunt.'

[3] *Pensées*, No. 267: 'La dernière démarche de la raison est de reconnaître qu'il y a une infinité de choses qui la surpassent; elle n'est que faible, si elle ne va jusqu'à connaître cela.' Cf. No. 270: 'Saint Augustin: la raison ne se soumettrait jamais, si elle ne jugeait qu'il y a des occasions où elle se doit soumettre. Il est donc juste qu'elle se soumettre, quand elle juge qu'elle se doit soumettre.'

[4] *De Util. Cred.*, i, 2: 'Tu nondum christianus, qui hortatu meo, cum eos vehementer execrareris, vix adductus es, ut audiendi tibi atque explorandi viderentur, qua, quaeso, alia re delectatus es, recordare, obsecro te, nisi magna quadam praesumptione ac pollicitatione rationum? sed quia diu multumque de inperitorum erroribus latissime ac vehementissime disputabant—quod cuivis mediocriter erudito esse facillimum sero didici—si quid etiam suorum nobis inserebant, necessitate retinendum, cum alia non ocurrerent, in quibus adquiesceremus, arbitrabamur.'

tus had, however, retained his independence of mind. Like Augustine, he found the Manichaean theory that the Old Testament passages in the New were interpolations made by Judaizing Christians quite unconvincing.[1] It was to this independence of mind that Augustine now addressed himself, in an effort to persuade Honoratus to leave the Manichees and to join the Catholic Church, and it was essential to show that the appeal to authority did not imply a rejection of the intellect as the Manichees asserted.[2]

Augustine recognizes that Honoratus will want an explanation of why, in being taught, it is necessary to begin with faith and not with reason.[3] No doubt one objection to belief is that it is a characteristic of credulous persons. Augustine replies that we must be careful about how we use the word credulous, for just as there is a wide difference between the man who is studious and the man who is merely curious; between the man who is interested in things which concern him, and the man who is a mere collector of trifling information; so there is a similar difference between a believer and a credulous person.[4] However, the sceptic may reply that, even if we admit the distinction between belief and credulity, it does not follow that one is good and the other evil. Perhaps they are merely different degrees of the same vice, like being occasionally and habitually drunk. Augustine retorts that this sort of reasoning, if applied to human relationships, would make friendship impossible, for without belief in a friend, it is impossible to speak of friendship.[5] Honoratus may perhaps reply that although it may be granted that all belief is not wrong, it is nevertheless wrong, where religion is concerned, to accept it on trust before one knows. Augustine then confronts him with this question: which is worse, to hand on religion to one who is unworthy and comes with a deceitful heart, or to believe the man who hands it on? He assumes that Honoratus will not hesitate to agree that it is worse to hand it on to the unworthy. Very well; if Honoratus is in the presence of a man who is going to give him religious

---

[1] *De Util. Cred.*, iii, 7: 'Quae vox mihi semper quidem, etiam cum eos audirem, invalidissima visa est: nec mihi soli, sed etiam tibi—nam bene memini—et nobis omnibus, qui paulo maiorem diligentiam in iudicando habere conabamur quam turba credentium.'

[2] Ibid., ix, 21: '[Haeretici] catholicam maxime criminantur quod illis, qui ad eam veniunt, praecipitur, ut credant, se autem non iugum credendi inponere, sed docendi fontem aperire gloriantur.'

[3] Ibid., ix, 22: 'Sed quaeris fortasse vel de hoc ipso aliquam accipere rationem, qua tibi persuadeatur non prius ratione quam fide te esse docendum.'

[4] Ibid.: 'Itaque ut inter studentem alicuius rei et omnino studiosum rursumque inter curam habentem atque curiosum, ita inter credentem et inter credulum plurimum interest.'

[5] Ibid., x, 23: 'Quid? si enim et credere et credulum esse vitiosum est, quemadmodum et ebrium et ebriosum esse? quod qui certum existimat, nullum mihi habere posse amicum videtur. si enim turpe est aliquid credere, aut turpiter facit, qui amico credit, aut nihil amico credens quomodo amicum vel ipsum vel se appellet, non video.'

H

instruction and is asked: is your conscience clear? he will expect the questioner to believe his reply. In that case, he surely cannot complain if the instructor says: I believe you; but would it not only be fair for you to believe me, seeing that if I possess any truth, you are going to receive a benefit and I am going to bestow one? The only possible reply to such a question must be: Yes, I ought to believe you.[1]

> But you say: would it not have been better to have given me a reason so that I might follow where he led without any rashness? Perhaps it would. But it is a difficult matter for you to know God by reason. Do you think that all men are fitted to grasp the reasons by which the human mind is drawn to the knowledge of God? Or are a good many so fitted or only a few? I think only a few, you say. Do you believe you are of their number? That is not for me to say, you reply. Do you think, then, that your religious teacher ought to believe this of you? Suppose he does so. Then remember that he has twice believed you when you said things he could not be certain of; but you were unwilling to believe him even once when he was speaking about religion. Granted then that you approach religion with a true mind, and that you belong to the small number of those who are able to grasp the reasons by which divine power leads to certain knowledge, do you think that religion is to be denied to other men who are not endowed with so clear a mind? Are they not to be brought to the inmost sanctuary step by step? You see what is obviously the more religious thing to do; for you cannot think that any man who desires so great a possession ought to be abandoned or rejected. But don't you think that he will not attain real truth otherwise than by first believing that he will reach his goal; then by presenting his mind as a suppliant; finally by purifying his life by action in obedience to certain great and necessary precepts? Of course you do.[2]

Augustine distinguishes between knowledge, which we owe to reason, and belief, which we have by authority,[3] and distinguishes between the truly blessed who believe the very truth, and those studious lovers of truth who believe upon authority.[4] He points out that the idea that nothing should be believed which is not known is, in fact, refuted by the experiences of everyday life. How can children show the dutifulness which they owe to their parents unless they believe them to be such? And how can this be known by reason? We have to accept the word of the mother, stating that

---

[1] *De Util. Cred.*, x, 23.
[2] Ibid., x, 24. Tr. by Burleigh, p. 310.
[3] Ibid., xi, 25: 'Quod intellegimus igitur, debemus rationi, quod credimus, auctoritati, quod opinamur, errori. sed intellegens omnis etiam credit, credit omnis et qui opinatur; non omnis qui credit intellegit; nullus qui opinatur intellegit.'
[4] Ibid.: 'haec ergo tria si ad illa quinque hominum genera, quae paulo ante commemorarimus, referantur, id est duo probanda, quae priora posuimus, et tria reliqua vitiosa: invenimus primum beatorum genus ipsi veritati credere, secundum autem studiosorum amatorumque veritatis auctoritati. in quibus duobus generibus laudabiliter creditur.'

her husband is the father of the child, and of the midwife and nurses that she was indeed delivered of such a child. And even here, the possibility of error is not ruled out, for the mother may herself be deceived by having her real son stolen and another infant put in his place. But in practice, nobody raises objections of this sort and indulges in methodical doubt which, once admitted, would result in the collapse of all that we understand by the sacred bond of the family.[1]

Again, it is manifest in our earthly life that foolish persons live better and more useful lives if they obey the precepts of the wise.[2] But how can a foolish person decide who is wise? for so long as he remains foolish, his decision of this point will be valueless.[3] And when religion, a far more important matter than anything in our earthly lives, is the object of our search, God alone can supply the solution to this great difficulty. But we ought not to be seeking true religion unless we believe that God exists and that He brings help to human minds; for what is the point in engaging in long and laborious search, or devoting oneself with all the thought and care to the matter which the matter deserves, unless one believes that the object of inquiry actually exists? 'Rightly therefore and in full accord with the majesty of the Catholic discipline, it is insisted that those who come to religion must be asked to have faith before anything else.[4]

But whose is the authority behind this Catholic discipline, by which we are commanded to believe? Christ's. 'I confess that I have come to believe in Christ, and to hold what He said is true, though supported by no reason.'[5] Certainly, says Augustine, I did not see Christ with my own eyes as it was His will to be seen by men like me, as recorded in the Scriptures.

From whom did I derive my faith in Him? . . . I see that I owe my faith to opinion and report widely spread and firmly established among the peoples and nations of the earth, and that those peoples everywhere observe the mysteries of the Catholic Church. Why, then, should I not rather ask most diligently of them what Christ taught, seeing that I was brought by their authority to believe that what He taught was profitable?[6]

Augustine, then, appeals to antiquity, to the *consensio gentium*, the general consent of mankind.[7] But supposing the heretic produces the Scriptures to support his case?

---

[1] *De Util. Cred.*, xii, 26.
[2] Ibid., xii, 27: 'quis mediocriter intellegens non plane viderit stultis utilius atque salubrius esse praeceptis obtemperare sapientium quam suo iudicio vitam degere?'
[3] Ibid., xiii, 28.   [4] Ibid., xiii, 29.
[5] Ibid., xiv, 31.   [6] Ibid. Tr. by Burleigh, p. 316.
[7] Ibid.: 'hoc ergo credidi, ut dixi, famae celebritate, consensione, vetustate roboratae.'
Cf. *C. Ep. Fund.*, iv, 5: '. . . tenet consensio populorum atque gentium.'

If any new or unheard-of writing is produced or commended by a handful of people without reasonable confirmation, we believe not it but those who produce it. Wherefore if you, being so few and unknown, produce Scriptures, we are unwilling to believe. And at the same time you are acting contrary to your promise in demanding faith rather than giving a reason. You will appeal again to tradition and general consent. At long last restrain your obstinacy and your wild lust to propagate your sect, and advise me rather to consult the leaders of the great mass of believers. This I shall do most diligently and with the greatest possible efforts, so as to learn something about these Scriptures from men apart from whom I should not know that there was anything to learn.[1]

The passage just quoted would seem to suggest that Augustine ranked the visible Church above the Scriptures and, although in this particular instance he is probably referring not to the canonical Scriptures at all but to the many Manichaean sacred writings,[2] the matter requires some discussion. Augustine has often been accused of having exalted institutional Christianity unduly, carried away by the majesty of the organization into which he had been brought.[3] In particular, one famous declaration has been quoted time and time again: 'Indeed, I should not have believed the Gospel, if the authority of the Catholic Church had not moved me thereto'[4] —a phrase stigmatized by the Rev. Dr Farrar as 'the memorable but not very happy assertion that Augustine would not have believed the Gospel had he not been moved thereto by the authority of the Church. He here shows himself', continued the future Dean of Canterbury, 'far less wise than Luther, who placed the Church as far below Christ as the creature is below the creator.'[5] With the merits or demerits of Luther's theological views we are fortunately not here concerned; but it is important to be clear about Augustine's.

Now there is no question of Augustine's love and veneration for the Church of Christ nor of the powerful impression which the spectacle of the Church militant made upon his imagination.[6] But two points should be

---

[1] Ibid. Burleigh, p. 317.   [2] See above, p. 170.
[3] Cf. Reuter, *Augustinische Studien*, 98–99.
[4] *C. Ep. Fund.*, v, 6: 'ego vero evangelio non crederem, nisi me catholicae ecclesiae conmoveret auctoritas.'   [5] F. W. Farrar, *Lives of the Fathers*, ii, 510.
[6] See, for example, the reasons for adhering to the Catholic Church in *C. Ep. Fund.*, iv, 5: 'multa sunt alia, quae in eius gremio me iustissime teneant. tenet consensio populorum atque gentium; tenet auctoritas miraculis inchoata, spe nutrita, caritate aucta, vetustate firmata; tenet ab ipsa sede Petri apostoli, cui pascendas oves suas post resurrectionem dominus commendavit, usque ad praesentem episcopatum successio sacerdotum; tenet postremo ipsum catholicae nomen, quod non sine causa inter tam multas haereses sic ista ecclesia sola obtinuit, ut cum omnes haeretici se catholicos dici velint, quaerenti tamen alicui peregrino, ubi ad catholicam conveniatur, nullus haereticorum vel basilicam suam vel domum audeat ostendere. ista ergo tot at tanta nominis christiani carissima vincula recte hominem tenent credentem in catholica ecclesia, etiamsi propter nostrae intellegentiae tarditatem vel vitae meritum veritas nondum se apertissime ostendat.'

remembered. In the first place, Augustine thinks of the Church as having authority because it is the instrument of divine providence. Thus, he points out for the benefit of Honoratus the many changes which Christianity has introduced into the moral life of society—asceticism; liberality; the contempt of hardship and death[1]—and continues:

> All this has divine providence accomplished through the predictions of the prophets, through the Incarnation and teaching of Christ, through the journeys of the apostles, through the reproaches, crosses, blood and deaths of the martyrs, through the laudable lives of the saints, and in every case through miracles worthy of such achievements and virtues, and suitable to the various times. When, therefore, we see such fruit progressively realized by God's aid, shall we hesitate to place ourselves in the bosom of His Church? For it has reached the highest pinnacle of authority, having brought about the conversion of the human race by the instrumentality of the Apostolic See and the successions of bishops. Meantime heretics have barked around it in vain, and have been condemned partly by the judgement of the common people, partly by the weighty judgement of Councils, partly also by the majesty of miracles. To be unwilling to give it the first place is assuredly the mark of consummate impiety or of heady arrogance.[2]

The emphasis in this passage is on the unity and continuity of the Church. It is not to the visible Church of his age as such to which Augustine appeals but to the Church spread out through time and rooted in eternity, proclaimed in the prophets, established in the Incarnation and teaching of Christ, and today to be seen in the universal Church. There is here no sense of division between Christ and His Church; rather, there is in this passage an expression of the doctrine of the Mystical Body, which Augustine found expressed in the Donatist theologian Tyconius whose writings he later commended to his Catholic brethren as an aid to the understanding of Scripture.[3]

Again, it is important to observe that when Augustine declared that he would not have believed the Gospel if he had not been moved thereto by the authority of the Catholic Church, he was speaking in a controversial situation. The Manichees are supposed, in effect, to say: 'Here is the Gospel. We will now demonstrate to you the truth of our religion', to which the Catholic replies: 'I believe in the Gospel, because the Church tells me to do so. The Church with the same authority tells me not to believe in

---

[1] De Util. Cred., xvii, 35. Cf. De Vera Rel., iii, 5.

[2] De Util. Cred., xvii, 35. Burleigh, p. 321.

[3] De Doctr. Christ., III, xxxi, 44: 'Prima [regula] de Domino et eius corpore est; in qua scientes aliquando capitis et corporis, id est, Christi et Ecclesiae unam personam nobis intimari, . . . non haesitemus quando a capite ad corpus, vel a corpore transitur ad caput, et tamen non receditur ab una eademque persona.'

Manichaeism.'[1] And we may note that even in this context, Augustine does not say: 'I would not have believed Christ' but, 'I would not have believed the Gospel'; and there is a difference between the two.

Furthermore, we must allow for the exaggeration produced by controversy, for Augustine elsewhere maintains that the Scriptures are the first rule of authority for the Church.[2] 'Who but Thou, our God, didst make for us that firmament of the authority of Thy divine Scripture to be over us? . . . Thy divine Scripture is of more sublime authority now that those mortal men through whom Thou didst dispense it to us have departed this life.'[3] We are not permitted to doubt the truth of Holy Scripture;[4] it is the authority which God has placed first in His Church.[5] It prepares the way for the Incarnation, as letters which announce the coming of a king.[6] In controverting heretics who will not accept the authority of the Church, it is possible to appeal to Scripture alone.[7]

Nevertheless, for Augustine Scripture is not the only rule of faith; for the language used by the holy books is not always clear, and the exegete must have recourse to the Rule of Faith,[8] which is to be found expressed in the baptismal creeds[9] and in the tradition of the Church, received from the Apostolic doctrine by the Apostolic succession and so passed by one generation of Catholic Christians to another[10]—the custom of the universal Church.[11] It is in this sense that Augustine would not have received the Gospel unless he had been moved by the authority of the Church. No derogation of Scripture is implied in this phrase, but merely a recognition

[1] See Pierre Batiffol, *Le catholicisme de saint Augustin*, 5e éd., Paris, 1930, i, 25–26.
[2] See Batiffol, op. cit., i, 21ff.; Pontet, *L'exégèse de s. Augustin prédicateur*, 111–48.
[3] *Conf.*, XIII, xv, 16. Tr. Outler, p. 308.
[4] *C. Faust.*, XI, v: 'in illa vero canonica eminentia sacrarum litterarum . . . non licet dubitare quod verum sit.'
[5] *Enar. in Ps.* 103, i, 8: 'Hanc auctoritatem primo posuit Deus in Ecclesia sua.'
[6] *Enar. in Ps.* 90, ii, 1: 'De illa civitate unde peregrinamur, litterae nobis venerunt: ipsae sunt Scripturae, quae nos hortantur ut bene vivamus. Quid dicam venisse litteras? Ipse rex descendit.'   [7] See Batiffol, op. cit., i, 26 *n*[2].
[8] *De Doctrina Christ.*, III, ii, 2: 'Cum ergo adhibita intentio incertum esse perviderit quomodo distinguendum aut quomodo pronuntiandum sit, consulat regulam fidei, quam de Scripturarum planioribus locis et Ecclesiae auctoritate percepit.'
[9] *De Fide et Symbolo*, 1: 'Est autem catholica fides in symbolo nota fidelibus memoriaeque mandata quanta res passa est brevitate sermonis: ut incipientibus atque lactantibus eis, qui in Christo renati sunt, nondum scripturarum divinarum diligentissima et spiritali tractatione atque cognitione roboratis paucis verbis credendum constitueretur, quod multis verbis exponendum esset proficientibus et ad divinam doctrinam certa humilitatis atque caritatis firmitate surgentibus.'
[10] *In Iohan. Evang.*, Tr. 37, 6: 'Nos, id est, catholica fides veniens de doctrina Apostolorum, plantata in nobis, per seriem successionis accepta, sana ad posteros transmittenda, inter utrosque, id est inter utrumque errorem tenuit veritatem.'
[11] Cf. *De Baptismo*, II, vii, 12: 'saluberrimam consuetudinem tenebat ecclesia . . . quam consuetudinem—credo ex apostolica traditione venientem, sicut multa non inveniuntur in litteris eorum neque in conciliis posterorum et tamen, quia per universam custodiuntur ecclesiam, non nisi ab ipsis tradita et commendata creduntur.'

of the very obvious fact that, unless a reader claims for himself the ability to decide what is to be admitted to the canon of Scripture and how the text is to be interpreted, he must look for some direction in his study.

Finally, we may note the actual wording used in the much-criticized sentence. It is always dangerous for the historian to attempt to discuss the finer shades of meaning of a sentence in a language not his own, centuries after it was uttered; but it is important to notice the phrase Augustine uses: *nisi me catholicae ecclesiae commoveret auctoritas*—'unless the authority of the Catholic Church moved me thereto'. The verb used— *commoveo*—is a fairly strong one; we might perhaps render it 'constrain' in the context; but it is significant that what constrains is *auctoritas*— authority—a word which, in the political theory of the later Roman Empire, had a peculiar meaning, very different from the coercive power— *potestas*—of the Roman emperor.[1] Authority—*auctoritas*—for the Roman is a non-coercive force, founded upon tradition and social position, the sort of influence which, in pagan days, the Board of Pontiffs (*collegium pontificum*) might have exercised, an essentially moral influence, but not to be compared in everyday life with the *imperium*, the executive power of the consuls and, later, of the emperors. 'The ethical prestige of *auctoritas* was higher than that of *potestas*, but effective power lay with the *potestas*.'[2]

If we may assume that Augustine was acquainted with this peculiar sense of *auctoritas* and that he did not simply choose his words at random, then the expression he uses is perfectly intelligible. It is not the case of an arbitrary and dictatorial body which merely says: believe! but, rather, of a majestic and venerable institution, which already commands his respect and love and so urges him to the acceptance of her doctrines. It is as if the Church were to say: 'You do not yet understand; but trust me, and you will come in time to know what you now believe by faith', just as God had spoken to Augustine's imagination at Milan: 'I am the food of the full-grown: grow, and you shall feed upon Me.'[3]

It seems then that the celebrated assertion which has been discussed in some detail is by no means so sweeping as has sometimes been supposed but is, indeed, no more than the expression of what must be the attitude of any thoughtful Christian who cares to ask himself upon what authority he receives the Scriptures. It is possible that in the twentieth century many persons will feel that the defence which has been offered need be addressed only to a small and steadily dwindling band of Protestant Fundamentalists

[1] See F. Dvornik, 'Pope Gelasius and Emperor Anastasius I', in *Byzantinische Zeitschrift*, xliv (1951), 111–16.
[2] Dvornik, art. cit., p. 113.
[3] *Conf.*, VII, x, 16: 'Cibus sum grandium: cresce et manducabis me.'

who will, in any event, be immune to any attempt at rational persuasion. Nevertheless, the defence is worth making, if only because of the many people who have spoken of Augustine rather as if he were a Gregory VII or a Boniface VIII, born out of due time. We shall have occasion to say more of this later in this book, when we examine the manner in which Augustine applied his theological views to the problems which arise in the fact that the Church Militant lives and works within the earthly state, and that her members are also citizens of secular societies. At this stage, however, it will suffice to say only this: that it is a mistake to read into the age of the Fathers or, indeed, into much post-patristic theology, the idea which occurs to many western Christians today, both Catholic and Protestant, of a sort of opposition between the Church and the Bible, as if a man were forced to say: I take my stand upon the Church, or, I take my stand upon the Bible, rather than saying: I take my stand upon the Church and upon the Bible, since neither of these can be considered in isolation from the other. The apparent antinomy, Church or Bible—one of the disastrous legacies of the Reformation—is fast vanishing among instructed Christians of all communions; and it will find no support from Augustine or, indeed, from any of the Fathers, Greek or Latin. The only way in which the patristic writers can be said to subordinate the Scriptures to the Church is in a frank recognition that the unaided human intellect, weakened and darkened by the Fall, is not sufficient to come to a clear understanding of the Bible, unless it be aided by the tradition which has come down through the ages from Christ and His Apostles and from the illumination which it pleases God to give to the Saints and to Councils of the Church for the fuller understanding of revealed truth.

It would, of course, be absurd and in flat contradiction of the facts to imply, in the picture we have tried to present of Augustine's attitude to the Church, that he did not recognize that the Church's authority includes a coercive discipline over her members. How else, indeed, would heretics be denounced and wrongdoers penanced? The saint recognizes clearly enough that the Church has certain powers of physical compulsion; there is that famous remark, almost an aside, in his letter to Count Marcellinus, when he congratulates that official on securing confessions with remarkable mildness, not with the tortures usually employed in Roman courts, but by the judicious use of the rod, a sanction used by schoolmasters, by parents, and even by bishops in their ecclesiastical courts![1] Further than this, we know that Augustine in his later life came to approve the results obtained

---

[1] Aug., *Ep.* 133, 2: '. . . qui modus cohercitionis et a magistris artium liberalium et ab ipsis parentibus et saepe etiam in iudiciis solet ab episcopis haberi.'

by the intervention of the civil power against the violence of the Donatist extremists; though here we shall see that the view which represents him as the forerunner of the Inquisition and its attendant horrors is very wide of the mark.[1] Nevertheless, when all is admitted, there is no reason to depart from the picture we have drawn of the Catholic Church of Augustine's theology exercising *auctoritas* rather than a coercive *potestas*, and constraining, where it does constrain, in order that the Christian may believe with faith where he cannot enter by reason. Adolf von Harnack, a scholar not much inclined to be dazzled by any vision of the majesty of the Church, was aware of this when he wrote: 'Even where [Augustine] assigned an imperious power to the authority of the Church, he only did so in the end in order to give the individual soul an assurance which it could not attain by any exertion or any individual act of pardon.'[2]

Against the Manichaean claim that the appeal of religion should be to the reason and not to faith, Augustine defended the Catholic doctrine that belief must precede reason in accepting the Faith. But Augustine was the last person to hold that, once acceptance of dogma has been made, the Christian may allow his intellect to be idle. In his later years, it is true, he came to regret his earlier enthusiasm for philosophy and for implying that only the philosopher could be a perfect Christian, since he had discovered that many very holy men had had no learning,[3] but this did not imply that the learned man must forget his learning on becoming a Christian. The sort of attitude which praises holy simplicity and approves of the simple and child-like faith of clever men who make no attempt to understand the doctrines of their religion would receive little encouragement from Augustine, who firmly believed that the human intellect was given to men to be used and not to be neglected. 'Entering by faith into the sanctuary of God, you enter by believing, you learn by understanding.'[4] Augustine is too profound a student of religious pyschology to imagine that one can make a rigid distinction between believing and understanding. His great text is that of Isaiah in the Septuagint version: *Except ye believe, ye shall not understand,*[5] but he adds that the reward which Christ promises to believers: *This is life eternal that they may know Thee, the only true God, and Jesus*

[1] See below, pp. 294-311.
[2] Harnack, *Lehrbuch der Dogmengeschichte*, 4te Aufl., Tübingen, 1910, iii, 65. Tr. from third German ed. by James Millar, *History of Dogma*, London, 1898, v, 65.
[3] *Retract.*, i, 3: 'Verum et his libris [sc. *De Ordine*] displicet mihi . . . quod multum tribui liberalibus disciplinis, quas multi sancti multum nesciunt, quidam etiam sciunt et sancti non sunt.'
[4] Aug., *Serm.* 48, v, 7: 'sic intrans fide in sanctuarium Dei, intrans credendo, discis intelligendo.'
[5] Isa. 7.9: Nisi credideritis, non intellegetis. Vulg.: Si non credideritis, non permanebitis. A.V.: If ye will not believe, surely ye shall not be established.

Christ whom Thou hast sent,[1] is a reward of knowledge, not of mere belief, while to those who already believed, our Lord said: *Seek and ye shall find*.[2] 'He cannot be said to have found, who merely believes what he does not know. And no one is fit to find God, who does not first believe what he will afterwards learn to know.'[3] Furthermore, although in the context of the inner understanding of revealed truths faith precedes reason—the matter under discussion when Augustine wrote against Manichaean rationalism—there is another perfectly legitimate sense in which reason has to precede faith,[4] as Augustine was well aware, from his spiritual pilgrimage from Manichaeism to Catholic Christianity. Before we can make the act of faith, we must by rational processes satisfy ourselves about the veracity of the witness, the claim which he makes to be believed. 'The treatment of the soul, which God's providence and ineffable lovingkindness administers, is most beautiful in its steps and stages. There are two different methods, authority and reason. Authority demands belief and prepares man for reason. Reason leads to understanding and knowledge. But reason is not entirely absent from authority, for we have got to consider whom we have to believe, and the highest authority belongs to truth when it is clearly known. . . . It is our duty to consider what men or what books we are to believe in order that we may rightly worship God, wherein lies our sole salvation. Here the first decision must be this: Are we to believe those who summon us to the worship of many gods or those who summon us to worship one God? Who can doubt that we ought rather to follow those who summon us to worship one God, especially since the worshippers of many gods agree that there is one God who rules all things?'[5] These are the arguments of the book *On True Religion*, written in 389-90. At the end of his life, in 428, Augustine reaffirms the same truths in the treatise *On the Predestination of the Saints*. 'Who does not see that thought precedes belief? for no one believes anything unless he first thinks that it should be believed.'[6] And when by reasoning we have come

---

[1] Iohan. 17.3.   [2] Matt. 7.7.
[3] *De Lib. Arb.*, II, ii, 6: 'Nisi enim et aliud esset credere, aliud intellegere et primo credendum esset quod magnum et divinum intellegere cuperemus, frustra propheta dixisset: *Nisi credideritis, non intellegetis*. Ipse quoque dominus noster et dictis et factis ad credendum primo hortatus est quos ad salutem vocavit, sed postea cum de ipso dono loqueretur quod erat daturus credentibus non ait: *Haec est autem vita aeterna ut credant*, sed: *Haec est*, inquit, *vita aeterna ut cognoscant te verum deum et quem misisti Iesum Christum*. Deinde iam credentibus dicit: *Quaerite et invenietis*; nam neque inventum dici potest quod incognitum creditur neque quisquam inveniendo deo fit idoneus, nisi ante crediderit quod est postea cogniturus.'
[4] Well brought out by Portalié, *DTC*, art. 'Augustin', 2337-40 (ET, 114-18).
[5] *De Vera Rel.*, xxiv, 45, xxv, 46. Tr. by Burleigh, p. 247.
[6] *De Praedest. Sanct.*, ii, 5: 'Quis enim non videat, prius esse cogitare quam credere? Nullus quippe credit aliquid, nisi prius cogitaverit esse credendum.'

to make the act of faith, our mind is set free for further processes of reasoning and understanding, as we advance to the happy consummation, when we shall know God. 'He who believes thinks; for by believing he thinks, and by thinking he believes.'[1] In the letter written in 410 to Consentius, the Catholic layman who wished virtually to exclude reason from the discussion of divine things which, he held, are only to be perceived by faith,[2] Augustine affirms that both faith and reason have their function, and advises his correspondent to use his intellect to understand by reason what he holds by faith,[3] for God does not endow us with reason without intending it to be used.[4] Moreover, Augustine draws the attention of Consentius to the fact that, if it is reasonable that faith should precede reason for the deeper truths which cannot be grasped, it is a matter of undoubted fact that the process of reasoning which leads to this conclusion must itself precede faith.[5]

Of all Augustine's religious opponents, the Manichees were, perhaps, the easiest victims. They suffered in argument because, although they claimed to be rationalists, they were, in practice, shackled to a complicated cosmology which, even in the not very scientifically minded thought world of the later Roman Empire, could not long stand up against critical examination. They were, moreover, at a disadvantage because, in a certain sense, their instincts were too Christian to permit them to defend their more specifically Manichaean formulas adequately. The Manichee Felix, when hard-pressed, found himself unable to maintain, as a rigorous interpretation of his creed required, that a part of God had been polluted in the attack by the powers of Darkness upon the powers of Light,[6] and was ultimately forced by Augustine's arguments publicly to anathematize Mani and to join the Catholic Church. Finally, the fact that the Manichees were a proscribed sect and one commonly supposed to be given to secret enormities, gave Augustine an excellent debating weapon, which the language of the Manichees did nothing to blunt.[7]

[1] Ibid.: 'Non enim omnis qui cogitat, credit; cum ideo cogitent plerique, ne credant: sed cogitat omnis qui credit, et credendo cogitat, et cogitando credit.'
[2] Inter Aug., *Ep.* 119, 1: '. . . non tam ratio requirenda de deo quam auctoritas est sequenda sanctorum.'
[3] Aug., *Ep.* 120, i, 2: 'Si a me vel a quolibet doctore non inrationabiliter flagitas [rationem], ut, quod credis, intellegas, corrige definitionem tuam, non ut fidem respuas, sed ut ea, quae fidei firmitate iam tenes, etiam rationis luce conspicias.'
[4] Ibid., i, 3: 'Absit namque, ut hoc in nobis deus oderit, in quo nos reliquio animantibus excellentiores creavit. absit, inquam, ut ideo credamus, ne rationem accipiamus sive quaeramus, cum etiam credere non possemus, nisi rationales animas haberemus.'
[5] Ibid.: 'si igitur rationabile est, ut magnam quandam, quae capi nondum potest, fides antecedat rationem, procul dubio quantulacumque ratio, qua hoc persuadet, etiam ipsa antecedit fidem.'
[6] *De Actis cum Felice*, II, xx.   [7] See above, pp. 160, 177ff.

It may be held then that, from the purely controversial point of view, Augustine's anti-Manichaean polemics were the most successful of all that he wrote. His case against the Donatists was, perhaps, quite as well prepared and delivered; but the Donatists were tougher adversaries in every sense than were the Manichees and were not inclined to be convinced by mere fact. They had their theories and, if facts did not fit, so much the worse for fact. The Pelagians were an altogether different proposition. In facing them, Augustine encountered for the first time opponents really worthy of his steel, who were as capable as he of giving hard knocks and of scoring controversial points. Beside them the Manichees were easy victims.

Nevertheless, the writings against the Manichees are of importance, not only in that they prepared Augustine's technique for later struggles against more formidable adversaries, but because they forced him to examine, for the benefit of Christian posterity, some of the intellectual difficulties which had hindered his acceptance of Catholic Christianity in his youth, notably the problem of evil and the problems raised by the acceptance of the Old Testament by the heirs of the New. By his writings on these matters, Augustine left a permanent legacy to western theologians, which is still of value to the Christian philosopher and exegete.

6

Augustine and Donatism

Adulterari non potest sponsa Christi, incorrupta est et pudica. Unam domum novit, unius cubiculi sanctitatem casto pudore custodit. Haec nos Deo servat, haec filios regno quos generavit adsignat. Quisque ab ecclesia segregatus adulterae iungitur a promissis ecclesiae separatur, nec perveniet ad Christi praemia qui reliquit ecclesiam Christi. Alienus est, profanus est, hostis est. Habere non potest Deum patrem qui ecclesiam non habet matrem.

SAINT CYPRIAN

WHEN AUGUSTINE returned to Africa in 388, it was to a church divided, with brother ranged against brother, and altar set up against altar. The Donatist Church, born of the disputes which followed the Diocletianic persecution regarding the validity of sacraments conferred by those alleged to have been gulity of the sin of *traditio*, but with a lineage extending back to the days of St Cyprian and reflecting only too well the stormy African temperament, had, in three-quarters of a century, grown and expanded until it more than equalled the Catholic as the church of Africa.[1] Its power lay, not so much in the cities—though even here, it had many supporters[2]—but rather on the high plains of Numidia, never so thoroughly Romanized as the coastline, where the indigenous population, Berber-speaking peasants, often ignorant of Latin,[3] stubbornly refused to be transformed into subjects of the Roman Empire in anything but name. African national feeling, which is to be found strongly expressed in the attitude of a thinker as Roman as Augustine (as witness the famous letter to the pagan grammarian, Maximus of Madauros, in which the saint rebukes the grammarian for his cultured contempt for the uncouth names of the Christian martyrs),[4] resisted the appeal of Latin as it later resisted that of Arabic so that, in the mid-twentieth century, a respectable proportion of the population of central Algeria speaks Berber, as did their fathers

---

[1] For the history of Donatism, see W. H. C. Frend, *The Donatist Church*, and for the doctrinal issues involved, G. G. Willis, *Saint Augustine and the Donatist Controversy*, London, 1950.

[2] See Augustine, *Ep.* 93, v, 17, where the saint records the successful conversion of Thagaste, 'quae cum tota esset in parte Donati', to the Catholic faith through the application of the penal laws and refers to other examples of which he had heard.

[3] See Frend, op. cit., pp. 57–58.

[4] Aug., *Ep.* 17. See the comments of Frend, op. cit., p. 231.

before them.[1] To this fierce, independent cast of mind the Donatist Church made an unquestionable appeal. Whereas the Catholics were indissolubly linked in the eyes of the African peasant with the Roman state, the pagan oppressor, the Donatists were the sons of the martyrs, members of a church which had never compromised with the godless tyrant but had retained that spirit of defiance, implicit in the fulminations of Tertullian and expressed in the life and death of the great Cyprian, the hero of all Africans, to whom Catholic and Donatist alike looked as the doctor of the African Church.

A distinguished authority has called Donatism 'a movement of protest in Roman North Africa'[2] and this aspect ought always to be remembered in studying its history. While the theological issues involved were real enough they were, in the last resort, only the expression and not the cause of an attitude of mind which led many Africans into schism in the early fourth century and kept them hostile to Catholic Christianity long after their historical claims had been proved baseless and their theological arguments controverted. Ultimately, as Augustine was to discover, the best weapon against the Donatists was neither eloquence nor intellectual argument but coercion by the secular authority. It is not desirable at this stage to discuss Augustine's attitude towards the employment of the resources of the state in religious disputes; but it is to be observed that, when he came in the end to approve the use of force to bring back the recalcitrant to the fold, he hovered on the brink of discovering why his dialectic, which had proved so devastating against the Manichees, appeared to have relatively little effect upon the Donatists. For them, historical fact and theological dogma did not, in the long run, matter. Let it be proved that the Catholic hierarchy did not descend from the *traditores* while many of their own bishops probably did; let it be argued that, in either case, the validity of the sacraments administered by them was not affected, since the grace of God works through unworthy ministers; let it be shown that they themselves were frequently inconsistent in the application of their own principles—all this might be, but the fiery core of Donatism remained untouched. The weak might yield, but the sons of the martyrs remained defiant to the last and death itself could not shake their constancy. The unbending spirit of Donatism is typified in the dramatic interview between Augustine and Emeritus of Caesarea. In September 418, seven years after the Conference of Carthage which had seen the condemnation of Donatism

---

[1] See C. H. Julien, *Histoire de l'Afrique du nord*, 2e éd., 50, and bibliography.
[2] Frend: this is the sub-title of *The Donatist Church*. See particularly his final summing up, pp. 315–36. Note, however, Marrou's comment on the work in *S. Augustin et l'augustinisme*, 189: 'brillant, partial (très pro-donatiste et anti-augustinien)'.

and the deployment of the resources of the state to bring the heretics back into the unity of the Church, Augustine visited Caesarea, the capital of Mauretania Caesariensis (the modern Cherchel, in Algeria), on business entrusted to him by pope Zosimus.[1] He met Emeritus in the street on 18 September, and exchanged greetings with him. A certain pathos must have attached to this man, one of the leading bishops of his church, now abandoned by many of his flock who had made their peace with the Catholics and himself exposed to the penalties imposed by law on heretics. The meeting between the two protagonists of Catholicism and Donatism was relatively cordial, and something in Emeritus' manner led Augustine to hope that he might be persuaded to make his peace. He therefore invited him to come to the Catholic basilica. The Donatist accepted the invitation with the cryptic observation: 'I cannot refuse what you will, but I can will what I will'—a remark which suggested to Augustine that Emeritus might agree to be reconciled. Accordingly he led him to the church and there, in the presence of an interested crowd of spectators, preached a sermon, in which he begged Emeritus with great earnestness not to delay, but to be reconciled and to embrace the bond of unity. Moved by his words, the congregation broke into cries of: 'Here or nowhere!' Emeritus, however, remained silent and made no response to this appeal. He agreed, nevertheless, to come to another, and more formal, conference two days later on 20 September, to be held in the presence of the Catholic bishop of Caesarea, Deuterius.

On the day appointed a huge congregation assembled, including many former Donatists and some who remained Donatists at heart. Augustine was supported by his friends, Alypius and Possidius, together with three Mauretanian bishops, and all present fully realized the critical nature of the discussion and the triumph which the Catholics would enjoy in the conversion of Emeritus. But such a triumph was not to be granted. The spirit of the old Donatist had hardened in the intervening days and he refused to speak, in spite of requests from Augustine that he should at least explain his motives for coming, in view of his uncompromising silence. For Augustine, the disappointment was bitter indeed; the vision of the reconciliation of the two rival bishops, Deuterius and Emeritus, must have been constantly before his eyes and now the promise was denied. In vain he asked Emeritus to argue his case and to justify the Donatist assertion that Count Marcellinus, the imperial commissioner at the Conference of Carthage, had been corrupted; there was no reply. In vain Augustine urged every weakness in the Donatist cause; his powers of persuasion

[1] Possidius, *Vita*, 14; Aug., *Epp.* 190, i, 1; 193, i, 1; *Retract.*, ii, 77 [51].

failed to move the stony silence of his rival. At the last, Emeritus left the church unconverted. Thereafter, he vanishes from history. We do not know what motives prevailed to quench his hesitant gesture in the direction of reunion; it is enough that, in the moment of decision, devotion to his tradition proved stronger than all other considerations. The Catholic Church and the Roman Empire had alike failed to shake him.[1]

If a man like Emeritus exemplified the stubborn endurance of the Donatist leaders, the physical violence and suicidal fanaticism which equally characterized the movement were expressed by the Circumcellions. The shock-troops of Donatism derived their name from the fact that they lived *circum cellas*[2]—'around the shrines' of the martyrs, from which they received their food.[3] Devotion to the cult of the martyrs was a feature of Donatism, but to the Circumcellions it was a way of life and an inspiration, for they desired to attain to the palm of martyrdom by every means, not excluding suicide. Their war-cry—a sound of terror in peaceful ears—was *Deo Laudes!*—'Praise to God!'[4] Their favourite weapons were clubs called 'Israels',[5] since they were forbidden in the Gospel to carry a sword —a piece of self-denial recalling the scruples of the martial bishop Odo at the battle of Hastings—but later they were to supplement these clubs with more conventional weapons: slings, axes, stones, lances, and even swords.[6] The name of Circumcellions, sometimes contracted to Circellions,

[1] The debate with Emeritus is described in Augustine's treatises *De Gestis cum Emerito* and *Sermo ad Caesariensis Ecclesiae plebem*; further details in *C. Gaudentium*, I, xiv, 15. Frend, op. cit., p. 295 n^4, compares Emeritus with Cranmer in 1556; but there is a world of difference between Cranmer's exhortation to his hearers to 'love altogether like brethren and sisters', and his advice to the rich to minister to those in need 'for if they ever had occasion to shew their charity, they have it now at this present, the poore people being so many, and victuals so deere', and Emeritus' sullen silence. Moreover, it should be observed that the temptation 'to deny their life's work for the sake of personal security' to which Frend alludes, was vastly different in the cases of these two men. Cranmer was in danger of his life, recanted in the hope that he would be reprieved, and subsequently discovered that, whatever he did, he was to be burned. Emeritus was in no personal danger; the worst that was likely to befall him was exile. As Augustine very fairly says of his behaviour at the second conference, 'dilatus perseveravit, convictus obmutuit, in-laesus abscessit' (*C. Gaud.*, I, xiv, 15). In the circumstances, a comparison seems an undeserved compliment to Emeritus.
[2] *Enar. in Ps.* 132, 3: 'Nam circumcelliones dicti sunt, quia circum cellas vagantur'; *C. Gaudentium*, I, xxviii, 32: 'genus hominum . . . victus sui causa cellas circumiens rusticanas.'
[3] See Frend, op. cit., p. 73; T. Büttner and E. Werner, *Circumcellionen und Adamiten*, Berlin, 1959, 41ff. For the use of *cella* as a martyr's shrine, see *CIL* viii, 9585. An illustration of this important inscription will be found in Stéphane Gsell, *Cherchel: Antique Iol-Caesarea*, revised by M. Leglay and E. S. Colosier, Algiers, 1952, 29. The old explanation of the name of Circumcellions as meaning 'around the farm-houses', although retained in Julian, op. cit., i, 216, seems no longer tenable.
[4] Aug., *Ep.* 108, v, 14; *Enar. in Ps.* 132, 6; *C. Litt. Petil.*, II, lxv, 146; lxxxiv, 186.
[5] *Enar. in Ps.* 10, 5; *Psalmus c. partem Donati*, ed. Anastasi, 161: 'Fustes Israheles vocant.'
[6] *C. Epist. Parm.*, I, xi, 17; *C. Litt. Petil.*, II, lxxxviii, 195; xcvi, 222.

was bestowed upon them by the Catholics; they called themselves 'soldiers of Christ' and 'Agonistici'—*agon* being the technical name for the martyr's struggle[1]—and it is possible that they adopted some form of monastic habit,[2] although they rejected the name of monk,[3] while their way of life was very far removed from the worst monks to be found in the west[4] and surpassed even those ferocious ascetics from the Egyptian deserts, whom the patriarchs of Alexandria were accustomed to summon to their support and who formed, in the words of N. H. Baynes, 'the patriarch's fanatic bodyguard'. Indeed, as Augustine remarked, they 'lived like brigands, died as Circumcellions, and then were honoured as martyrs.'[5] For martyrdom was the goal of the Circumcellion, though preferably preceded by the slaughter of an enemy of the faith. They raged against the pagan with the same fury that they raged against the Catholics.[6] Some of the more death-determined would stop travellers and require them to deliver the fatal stroke.[7] If the traveller refused, he was threatened with murder himself; and it is not without satisfaction that one reads of a certain young man who, having fallen into the hands of the Circumcellions and been given the choice of the two grisly alternatives, managed to persuade his captors to allow him to bind their hands to facilitate execution. Unwisely, they agreed; and the young man, having duly secured them, administered a sound thrashing, before he departed, unscathed and undefiled by their blood.[8] Failing to find someone willing to kill him, the Circumcellion would achieve a pseudo-martyrdom by a direct act of suicide, by hurling himself from a rock—a very popular method—or by

---

[1] *Enar. in Ps.* 132, 6. See Paul Monceaux, 'L'epigraphie donatiste', *Revue de philologie*, xxxiii (1909), 151–2.

[2] Isidore, *De Officiis Ecclesiasticis*, II, xvi, 7 (*MPL* lxxxiii, 796–7), which is based on Augustine, *De Opere Monachorum*, xxviii, 36. Augustine, however, does not there use the term Circumcellion, but speaks of 'milites Christi' who could be Catholic monks.

[3] *Enar. in Ps.* 132, 3; 6. For the hatred felt by many Africans for monks, see Salvian, *De Gubernatione Dei*, VIII, iv, 19–22 (*MGH* Auc. antiquis., I, i, 106–7), and cf. Augustine's account of the sight of monks at Carthage, *Enar. in Ps.* 147, 8: 'Aliquando, dimisso theatro aut amphitheatro, cum coeperit ex illa cavea evomi turba perditorum, aliquando tenentes in animo phantasias vanitatis suae, et memoriam suam pascentes rebus non solum inutilibus, sed et perniciosis, gaudentes in eis tanquam in dulcibus, sed pestiferis; vident plurumque, ut fit, transire servos Dei, cognoscunt ipso habitu vel vestis vel capitis, vel fronte notos habent, et dicunt apud semetipsos et secum: O miseros istos, quid perdunt.'

[4] The 'Gyrovagi' who lived by wandering from place to place, staying for only three or four days at a time in any one spot, and given over to their own pleasures and to gluttony, 'of whose most wretched life', says St Benedict, 'it is better to keep silent than to speak' (*Regula*, i, 13. *CSEL* lxxv, 19).

[5] Aug., *Ep.* 88, 8: 'vivunt ut latrones, moriuntur ut Circumcelliones, honorantur ut martyres.'

[6] *C. Epist. Parm.*, I, x, 16. Cf. Aug., *Ep.* 185, iii, 12. See J. H. Baxter, 'The Martyrs of Madaura', *JTS* xxvi (Oct. 1924), 21–37.   [7] *De Haeres.*, 69.

[8] Theodoret, *Haereticarum Fabularum Compendium*, IV, 6. *MPG* lxxxiii, 424.

precipitating himself into a river or into a fire.[1] Due announcement would
be made to the intending suicide's friends, who assembled at the place
of sacrifice and brought supplies of food for the delectation of the victim
before his self-immolation.[2]

In some matters, the Donatists employed techniques worthy of a later
age, as when they took to throwing acid mixed with quicklime into the
eyes of their victims to blind them.[3] Furthermore—a tendency of great
interest to the modern social historian—their hatred was directed, not only
against their religious opponents but against the landowners and the
moneyed classes. They were themselves peasants, *agrestes*,[4] who had given
up their holdings, to whom the landlord and the money-lender were the
natural enemy. St Optatus of Milevis, writing of the earlier period of
Donatism before Augustine's birth, makes it clear that their grievances
were economic, as well as religious; in their neighbourhood the landlord
could not rest easy in his possessions nor had the creditor any hope of
exacting payment for his debt.[5] Such an aspect of Donatism will cause no
surprise; the miserable conditions of life in the later Roman Empire were
well calculated to encourage revolts in the unprivileged classes of society.
In Gaul, for example, we have the movement known as the Bagaudae, of
which our authorities tell us little but of which we can gather two facts
from entries in a Gallic chronicle: that in 435, under the leadership of a
certain Tibatto, practically the entire slave population of Armorica, an
area far exceeding in extent the modern Brittany and consisting of a vast
stretch of land between the mouth of the Garonne and that of the Seine,
including the provinces of Poitou, Brittany, Anjou, and Normandy, rose in
rebellion against the Empire and succeeded for the space of two years of
establishing an independent state before they were crushed in 437.[6] In

[1] Optatus Milevitanus, *De Schismate Donatistarum*, iii, 4. *CSEL* xxvi, 83. Aug., *Epp.*
43, viii, 24; 173; 185, iii, 12; 204, 2; *C. Litt. Petil.*, I, xxiv, 26; *De Haeres.*, 69.
[2] Theodoret, *Haeret. Fabul. Comp.*, iv, 6. This practice perhaps looks back to the days
of the persecutions, when the faithful would bring supplies of food for the imprisoned
confessors. A similar archaizing tendency may be noticed in the fact that the Circumcellion, searching for a victim who might be terrorized into killing him, was particularly
delighted if he could secure a magistrate. Aug., *Ep.* 185, iii, 12: 'Nonnumquam et a
iudicibus transeuntibus extorquebant violenter, ut a carnificibus vel ab officio ferirentur.'
[3] *C. Cresc.*, III, xlii, 46.
[4] *C. Gaud.*, I, xxviii, 32: 'Quis enim nescit hoc genus hominum in horrendis facinori-
bus inquietum, ab utilibus operibus otiosum, crudelissimum in mortibus alienis,
vilissimum in suis, maxime in agris territans, ab agris vacans, et victus sui causa cellas
circumiens rusticanas, unde et Circumcellionum nomen accepit, universo mundo
pene famosissimum Africani erroris opprobrium.' See Büttner and Werner, op. cit., 44–45.
[5] Optatus, iii, 4: '. . . nulli licuit securum esse in possessionibus suis; debitorum
chirographa amiserant vires, nullus creditor illo tempore exigendi habuit libertatem.'
CSEL xxvi, 82. Cf. Aug., *Ep.* 185, iv, 15: 'quis, quod illi noluissent, exactor exegit . . .?'
[6] For a brief outline of the history of the Bagaudae (sometimes called Bacaudae) see
E. A. Thompson, *A History of Attila and the Huns*, 68–70.

certain respects Donatism as a movement resembles the Bagaudae, but with a strong religious doctrine as well as a sentiment of social discontent. In this movement, the Circumcellions played a decisive part, and exemplified the spirit which animated the whole.[1]

From the point of view of the Donatist higher clergy, the intellectual leaders of the schism, the Circumcellions were both an asset and an embarrassment. Clearly, it was a great advantage to have at their disposal bodies of men ready to kill and be killed and unhindered by any scruples. On the other hand, there was a very real danger that such forces might get out of control and refuse to submit to the discipline of their spiritual pastors. Thus from one point of view, their value as a private army was demonstrated in 347 when Donatus, bishop of Bagai (always a stronghold of Donatism), called upon them to resist the troops of the imperial commissioners, Paul and Macarius, who had been sent to Africa to resolve the dispute and who had acquired a reputation for partiality in the interest of the Catholics. A bloody battle ensued, in which the Circumcellions were massacred and the bishop himself taken and afterwards killed.[2] This attempt at resistance had turned out disastrously, and it was probably folly on the part of Donatus to attempt a formal engagement with regular troops, but the episode is significant as showing both the spirit of the Circumcellions and the state of affairs in the mid-fourth century, when a bishop could openly defy the imperial authorities by force of arms. So far, so good; but the Circumcellions could prove a liability to their leaders. Like most irregular troops lacking the restraint of formal military discipline, they were apt to get out of hand. Indeed, on occasion, the Donatist bishops found it necessary to disown the Circumcellions[3] and even appeal to the secular authorities to deal with the terrifying forces which they had called up but, like the sorcerer's apprentice, now found themselves unable to control.[4]

Thus, the Donatist Church reposed securely on a basis of popular devotion on the part of the indigenous peasantry, buttressed by the powerful,

[1] For the social aspect of the Circumcellions, see K. von Nathusius, *Zur Charakteristik der Circumcellionem*, Greifswald, 1900; F. Martroye, 'Une tentative de revolution sociale en Afrique', in *Revue des questions historiques*, lxxvi (1904), 353–416; lxxvii (1905), 1–53; and Büttner and Werner, op. cit., pp. 1–72 (a summary of modern researches from the Communist point of view).

[2] Optatus, iii, 4. *CSEL* xxvi, 83–84. Cf. Optatus' comments upon the Donatist bishops, ii, 18: 'Episcopis uestris iubentibus et praesentibus supra altare catholici diaconi occisi sunt.' Ibid., p. 52.

[3] *C. Epist. Parm.*, I, xi, 17; *C. Litt. Petiliani*, I, xxiv, 26; *Gesta Coll. Carth.*, iii, 297: 'Ubi dicunt Donatistae quod circumcelliones faciunt ad sacerdotes minime pertinere.' *MPL* xi, 1248.

[4] Optatus, iii, 4—the appeal to Count Taurinus, the Roman military commander, for his help against the Circumcellions, Fasir and Axido, *duces sanctorum* and their men. *CSEL* xxvi, 82.

if unpredictable, influence of the Circumcellions. These factors in themselves would have made it a formidable rival to the Catholics, but it enjoyed a further advantage in the possession of a series of able leaders and thinkers among its higher clergy from the time of Donatus the Great onwards. Parmenian, Donatist bishop of Carthage from 363 to 391, was both an administrator and an able polemical writer; Optatus of Thamugadi, whose episcopate lasted from his consecration in 388 to his death in prison ten years later, was an arrogant, masterful pontiff, who for a whole decade dominated southern Numidia and kept almost royal state in his great basilica at Timgad, until he was foolish enough to join the rebel, Count Gildo, in his bid for supreme power in Africa and perished, disowned by his colleagues; Emeritus of Caesarea; Petilian of Constantine; and Primian of Carthage—all these were able men, and 'most obstinate defenders of a very bad cause'.[1] The leaders, unlike the ordinary Donatist, were Latin-speaking, well educated by any ecclesiastical standard, and able to employ their pens to good effect in controversy. Vitellius, who wrote the treatise *De eo quod odio sint mundo servi Dei* about the middle of the fourth century, was judged by Gennadius worthy of inclusion in his collection of ecclesiastical writers;[2] the great Parmenian himself found time, among his many commitments, to write the work in five books to which St Optatus of Milevis replied on behalf of the Catholics; while his letter against his fellow sectarian Tyconius had so great an influence that Augustine found it necessary to reply to it in his *Contra Epistulam Parmeniani* written in 398, when Parmenian had been dead for seven years or more. But the greatest, and most original, genius among the Donatist writers was not a cleric but a layman: Tyconius—the same Tyconius whom Parmenian denounced and excommunicated. Much of his work has, unfortunately, been lost; but enough has survived for us to be able to form an idea of his very remarkable mind, which makes him both the most interesting and the least typical of Donatist writers.[3]

---

[1] Inter Opera Aug., *Ad Catholicos Epistola*, i, 1: 'tam malae causae pertinacissimi defensores.' *CSEL* lii, 231. See Frend, op. cit., pp. 247–8.

[2] Gennadius, *De Script. Ecclesiast.*, 4: 'Vitellius Afer, Donatianorum schisma defendens, scripsit "De eo quod odio sint mundo servi Dei". In quo si tacuisset de nostro velut persecutorum nomine, egregiam doctrinam ediderat.' *MPL* lviii, 1063.

[3] Gennadius, *De Script. Ecclesiast.*, 18: 'Tichonius natione Afer, in divinis litteris eruditus, iuxta historiam sufficienter, et in saecularibus non ignarus fuit; in ecclesiasticis quoque negotiis studiosus. Scripsit *De Bello intestino* libros tres et *Expositiones diversarum causarum*, in quibus ob suorum defensionem, antiquarum meminet synodorum. E quibus omnibus agnoscitur Donatianae partis fuisse. Composuit et Regulas ad investigandam et inveniendam intelligentiam Scripturarum, septem, quas in uno volumine conclusit. Exposuit et Apocalypsin Ioannis ex integro, nihil in ea carnale, sed totum intelligens spiritale. . . . Floruit hic vir aetate qua iam memoratus Ruffinus, Theodosio et filio eius regnantibus.' *MPL* lviii, 1071, 1072.

Two of Tyconius' works have perished, the *De Bello Intestino* and the *Expositiones Diversarum Causarum*. The *Liber Regularum*—'Book of the Rules'[1]—has survived and laid the foundation of western allegorical interpretation of Holy Scripture, since it aroused the admiration of the author's contemporaries including Augustine himself, who commended it enthusiastically in the *De Doctrina Christiana*.[2] Finally, considerable fragments of Tyconius' Commentary on the Apocalypse have survived, preserved for us in the commentary of the Spaniard, Beatus of Labiena, who wrote in the eighth century.[3] From this, and from some of Augustine's references to Tyconius' writings, we can reconstruct the outlines of his thought. He was loyal to the Church in which he had been brought up, but his honesty and independence of mind led him to demonstrate weaknesses in the Donatist position to such effect that it seemed to Augustine that his decision to remain a Donatist must have been due to madness.[4] Tyconius accepted the Donatist view of the Church of the Martyrs, tried and proved by persecution; but he remembered the evangelical injunction that the tares should grow with the wheat until the end of the world, and this led him to ask whether faithful Christians ought to separate themselves from the wicked. Ought they not rather to remain in the world, fortified by the sacraments which they receive? Here, Tyconius conceived an idea which was to be taken over by Augustine and developed in one of his most famous and influential works. The real division, said Tyconius, is not a division of churches but of two supernatural societies: the city of God and the city of the devil, each of which is made up of individuals governed by contrary wills.[5] From this it follows that the Donatist principle of separation is mistaken. Hypocrites and sinners may be found even in the Church. But Tyconius went further. He was not prepared to un-church foreign churches which remained in communion with the African Catholics. The Church is universal and not confined to the relatively small band of the faithful comprised in the Donatist communion in North Africa.[6]

---

[1] Edited by F. C. Burkitt, *The Book of Rules of Tyconius* (*Cambridge Texts and Studies*, iii, 1), 1894. [2] *De Doct. Christ.*, III, xxx, 42. Cf. *Ep.* 41, 2.

[3] Ed. by H. Florez, Madrid, 1770 and re-edited by H. A. Sanders, *Beati in Apocalypsin libri duodecim*, American Academy of Rome, 1930. Unfortunately, Sanders does not indicate which portions of the Beatus commentary are taken from Tyconius, so the edition is of little use in the study of the latter. See W. Neuss, *Die Apocalypse des hl. Johannes in der althispanischen und altchristlichen Bibel-Illustration. Der Problem der Beatus-Handschriften*, Munster, 1931.

[4] *De Doct. Christ.*, III, xxx, 42: 'Tichonius quidam qui contra Donatistas invictissime scripsit, cum fuerit donatista, et illic invenitur absurdissimi cordis, ubi eos non omni ex parte relinquere voluit.'

[5] See T. Hahn, *Tyconius-Studien. Ein Beitrag zur Kirche- und Dogmengeschichte des vierten Jahrhunderts*, Leipzig, 1900, 23–30 (gives references).

[6] Tyconius, *apud* Aug., *C. Epist. Parm.*, I, ii, 2.

Such an outlook was intolerable to the average Donatist and was attacked by Parmenian in the letter written about 378. In this, Parmenian denounced Tyconius' assertion that the Church is universal in her extension. The overseas churches, he held, forfeited their claim to catholicity by remaining in communion with the African *traditores* and therefore lacked that holiness which characterizes the true Catholic Church.[1] Moreover, during the persecutions there had been *traditores* in every country, but only in Africa had the Catholic [i.e. the Donatist] Church broken off relations with them.[2] So Holy Church, which was formerly spread throughout the world, is now reduced to the pure church of Africa. Tyconius was not convinced by this rejoinder and continued to maintain his views until, in about 385, Parmenian summoned a council and excommunicated him.[3] Disowned by his fellows, he appears never to have joined the Catholics, and by rejecting him, the Donatists threw away the most brilliant and original thinker who had appeared among them.

The case of Tyconius deserves attention because it stands as an example of the essentially sterile and restricted outlook of Donatism and goes far to explain why, though it had remarkable powers of resistance, it lacked the vitality which enabled churches like the Nestorian and the Monophysite to maintain themselves, even in the face of the triumphant advance of Islam. The Donatist Church looked formidable at the beginning of the last decade of the fourth century; it had numbers, enthusiasm, and a remarkable career of success behind it; yet, within twenty years, it was to be broken and humiliated, though not finally crushed. The causes of this change of fortune are worth considering.

To begin with, there was a change in leadership of both the Catholics and the Donatists. Parmenian and his Catholic rival, Genethlius, both died about 391–2 and in the elections which followed the Catholic bishop of Carthage, Aurelius, was the better choice. Since Augustine is so plainly the dominating figure in the Donatist controversy on the Catholic side, it is only just that Aurelius should be given credit for the important, perhaps decisive, part which he played in the struggle for unity during the next twenty years. His talents were those of the organizer, the good committee man. He was neither a scholar nor a theologian and his literary remains amount to no more than official correspondence. Nevertheless, he was worthily to fulfil his duties as a successor of St Cyprian in what had become, in effect, the metropolitical see of Africa. Aurelius not only led the African Church through the later stages of the Donatist controversy, but was its leader and director in the struggle to secure the condemnation of

---

[1] *C. Epist. Parm.*, I, i, 2.   [2] Ibid., I, iii, 4–5.   [3] Ibid., I, i, 1; Aug., *Ep.* 93, x, 44.

Pelagianism. He survived until the eve of the Vandal invasion, leaving behind him the reputation of a great prelate and organizer.

By way of contrast, the new Donatist bishop of Carthage, Primian, was a man of violence rather than a leader or a diplomat. In consequence, it was not long after his election that a party of opposition began to form, led by one of his deacons named Maximian, said to be a kinsman of Donatus the Great.[1] The Maximianists began to show the all too familiar marks of a formidable schism of a type to which Donatism was but too prone. Being by nature sectarian and exclusive, it possessed to the full those fissiparous tendencies to which exclusive sects are liable. It is, one might say, the fate of schismatic bodies to become divided in themselves and Donatism was no exception. Already, in Parmenian's day, Rogatus of Cartenna and nine colleagues, disgusted by the excesses of the Circumcellions, had decided to break away from the main body of the Donatist Church[2] and this movement, although oppressed by Firmus during his revolt of 372,[3] managed to maintain itself until Augustine's time.[4] Again, Claudian, the Donatist bishop of Rome, who had proved a serious nuisance to pope Damasus and had been expelled from the city some time after 378, contrived, on his return to Carthage, to quarrel with his co-religionists there and broke away to form his own party, the Claudianists.[5] With such inspiring examples, the Maximianists could hardly fail to prosper. They appear to have had the support of the richer and more respectable members of the Donatist community at Carthage.[6]

Primian excommunicated Maximian, while the latter was ill and unable to speak in his own defence,[7] and then embarked upon a rake's progress, readmitting Claudianist schismatics to communion, together with persons guilty of incest.[8] At the same time, he indulged in various acts of violence, causing a deacon, who had baptized the sick, presumably without the bishop's authority, to be thrown into a sewer.[9] Opposition against Primian hardened. A letter of complaint against his misdeeds was sent to the Donatist episcopate, and in a short time, towards the end of 392, a council of forty-three bishops assembled at Carthage to hear the charges brought against him. Primian refused to recognize its authority and was fortunate in having the local authorities and the bulk of the townspeople on his side. These broke up the council and drove its members in flight from the town. It reassembled in a house in the suburbs and passed an

[1] Aug., *Ep.* 43, ix, 26: '. . . qui dicitur esse Donati propinquus.'
[2] Aug., *Ep.* 93, iii, 11. [3] *C. Epist. Parm.*, I, x, 16; *C. Litt. Petil.*, II, lxxxiii, 184.
[4] Aug., *Ep.* 93, viii, 24. [5] *Enar. in Ps.* 36, ii, 20.
[6] Ibid., 19; Aug., *Ep.* 43, ix, 26. [7] *Enar. in Ps.* 36, ii, 20.
[8] Ibid. [9] Ibid.

unfavourable judgement on Primian, which was communicated by its members to their colleagues throughout Africa.[1] A more formal gathering assembled on 24 June 393 at Cabarsussi in Byzacena, the most easterly of the African dioceses, composed largely of bishops of the eastern areas,[2] precisely those parts where Catholicism was strongest and Latin influence most marked. The language of this Council was one of studied moderation,[3] but Primian's outrages had been too flagrant to be ignored. He was condemned, and clergy and laity alike were ordered to break off communion with him. Maximian was consecrated bishop of Carthage in his stead.

Unfortunately for the moderate men who assembled at Cabarsussi, they had to reckon with their fellow bishops of Numidia and Mauretania, the home of the Circumcellions and the pure faith of Donatism. These strenuous prelates were not prepared to see the unity of their church shattered merely to gratify the middle-class prejudices of the better citizens of Carthage. Primian's treatment of his flock had been in the best traditions of Donatist rule. A universal council of the Donatist Church was summoned to Bagai, in southern Numidia, and met on 24 April 394. Three hundred and ten bishops, mainly from Numidia and Mauretania, assembled under Gamalius, Primate of Numidia, with Primian in the place of honour. Fearful was the denunciation of the Maximianists; they were declared to be schismatics and threatened with the fate of the Egyptian armies, overwhelmed in the Red Sea, or of Dathan, Korah and Abiram, whom the earth swallowed up.[4] The condemnation of Primian was reversed; Maximian and twelve of his consecrators, together with the dissenting Carthaginian clergy, were excommunicated, and all involved in the schism were required to return to the bosom of the Church.[5]

Armed with this formidable pronouncement, Primian lost no time in taking action against his rivals, and he enjoyed the support of the civil authorities. The rule of Count Gildo from 395 to 397, advised by the ruffianly bishop Optatus of Thamugadi, enabled more intensive pressure to be brought against the unlucky Maximianists and many returned to communion. These happy days came to an end in 398 with the defeat and death of Gildo, but by then, the back of Maximianist opposition had been broken and, at the time of the great conference of 411, many had rejoined the mother church.

To the Catholics, the Maximianist schism was a heaven-sent opportunity for controversial purposes, and they did not fail to make use of it,

---

[1] *Enar. in Ps.* 36, ii, 20.   [2] Aug., *Ep.* 93, viii, 24; *Ad Catholicos Ep.*, iii, 6.
[3] Text reconstructed in *MPL* xi, 1185–9.   [4] Aug., *De Gestis cum Emerito*, 10.
[5] *De Gestis cum Emerito*, 11; *C. Cresconium*, IV, xxxv, 42. Given in full, *MPL* xi, 1189–91.

particularly stressing the fact that the Donatist leaders had been willing to receive Maximianists into communion without rebaptism, despite the ferocious nature of the denunciations delivered at Bagai.[1] The Donatists themselves, for obvious reasons, made light of it, affecting to regard it as simply a domestic affair, without any of the implications which had caused them to separate themselves from the *traditores*. In one sense they were right, since there is no evidence of any tendency on the part of the Maximianists to look to the Catholics for allies, any more than did Tyconius after his excommunication. What the affair of Maximian showed, in the same fashion but on a larger scale than that of Tyconius, was the violent and narrow mind of Donatism. No breadth of vision or considerations of the elementary requirements of conduct were to be allowed to affect the unity of the Church and both prophet and reformer were alike to be savagely repressed. By such action, it became clear that the essence of Donatism was a despotism, enunciated by the bishops, applauded by the mob, and enforced, in the last resort, by the violence of the Circumcellions. But even these did not prevent internal schism; and it might well seem, to a shrewd observer, that, if some sort of security were given to deserters, such as might be afforded by the official proscription of Donatism, many of the more lukewarm of its adherents would be well content to return to the quieter fold of the Catholic Church. It was this consideration which powerfully affected the development of Augustine's opinion of the lawfulness of coercion by the state. Many persons actually claimed to welcome it, since it gave them a pretext for leaving an unsatisfactory church and ensured them the protection of the secular arm against any reprisals of their former brethren.

Again, it was a weakness of Donatism, in the last resort, that it persistently allied itself with unsuccessful rebellious movements in Africa and so drew upon itself the wrath of established authority. That Donatism should be hostile to the Roman Empire might be thought to follow logically from its first principles: what has the Church to do with Caesar, the persecutor? In practice, however, the Donatists did not take this line. At the very beginning of the schism they appealed to the Emperor Constantine, as one sprung of righteous stock whose father had never persecuted the faith, to send Gallic judges to settle the dispute.[2] Only after their claims

---

[1] Aug., *C. Epist. Parm.*, III, vi, 29. In his debate with Emeritus, Augustine dwelt upon this episode of Donatist history, and the part played by Emeritus therein. *Gesta cum Emer.*, 8–12.

[2] Optatus, i, 22. See Jones, *Constantine the Great and the Conversion of Europe*, 104, who draws attention to the fact that in this petition of 15 April 313 the Donatists did not appeal to Constantine as being a Christian himself—'perhaps this startling fact had not yet won credence in Africa'.

had been rejected by two councils, the one summoned by Pope Miltiades in 313 and the larger gathering which assembled at Arles in the following year, and the 'excellent emperor', as they had called him, had taken steps to enforce the conciliar decisions, did the Donatists adopt a hostile attitude to the state.[1] From then onwards, their practice was to throw in with any movement which seemed likely to give them what they wanted. Their former appeal to the emperor was, for the time, forgotten. Then, about the year 346, Donatus approached the Emperor Constans for recognition as the sole bishop of Carthage;[2] but with the arrival of two imperial officials, Paul and Macarius, probably in the spring of 347, the situation altered. The commissioners showed themselves to be sympathetic to the Catholics, and this proved too much for Donatus. When they tried to approach him he rebuffed them angrily with the words: 'Quid imperatori cum ecclesia ?—What has the emperor to do with the Church?' and forbade his people to accept any of the alms which were being distributed to both parties indifferently.[3] The imperial commission proved a failure. Negotiations broke down and hostilities ensued. The Donatists were defeated, their leader exiled and, for a time, the Catholics seemed restored to power. The anti-Catholic policy of Julian the Apostate and the abilities of Parmenian saved Donatism. During the revolt of Firmus in 372, the Donatists lent him their support. On the collapse of his rebellion three years later, they suffered the inevitable repression at the hands of the imperial general Theodosius, but his execution in 377 on a charge of treason left as senior official in Africa the *vicarius*, Flavian, who sympathized with the Donatist cause.[4] A few years later in 397, the smouldering embers of discontent burst out afresh when Count Gildo, a younger brother of Firmus, who had remained faithful to the emperor during his brother's revolt and been rewarded with the command of the African army, now rebelled on his own account, with a view to transferring Africa to the eastern part of the Empire. For ten years his friend and ally, Optatus of Thamugadi, had terrorized the Catholics of Numidia, and now Donatism made a bid for supremacy in Africa. The venture failed, and from then onwards the command and administration of Africa was in the hands of Catholic officials. It must have been clear to all who could read

[1] Frend, p. 165, gives 316 as the turning-point in their attitude.

[2] Optatus, ii, 12: '[Donatus] Carthaginis, qui provocavit, ut unitas proximo tempore fieri temptaretur'; iii, 3: '[Donatus] cuius veneficio videtur unitatis negotium esse commotum.' *CSEL* xxvi, 68, 73.

[3] Ibid., iii, 3. *CSEL* xxvi, 73.

[4] Aug., *Ep*. 87, 8: 'vos Flaviano quondam vicario, partis vestrae homini, quia legibus serviens nocentes, quos invenerat, occidebat, non communicastis ?'

the signs of the times that, if the Catholics could once bring the Donatists to debate, they could rely on the sympathy and support of the imperial authorities. Indeed, considering the record of Donatism, the moderation of the government is surprising.

Finally, it was a disastrous weakness of Donatism that it never contrived to build up a body of support in the Empire outside Africa.[1] A small Donatist community had been established at Rome in the early days of the schism whose members, for lack of a more suitable place, met for worship in a cave, a practice which earned them the name of *Montenses*— Mountaineers—among the citizens of Rome.[2] Their first bishop was Victor of Garba, followed in order by Boniface, Encolpius, Macrobius and Lucian, whose successor, Claudian, was able to take advantage of the struggle between pope Damasus and the anti-pope Ursinus to conduct an active and apparently successful campaign among the poorer classes of Rome, many of whom came forward to be rebaptized.[3] His success, however, was of short duration. Damasus, having disposed of Ursinus, was able to turn his attention to Claudian, and an appeal to the Emperor Gratian procured the expulsion of his rival from Rome. A certain number of his followers continued to maintain themselves there and in November 407 we find the penal laws, already operating in Africa, being applied to them.[4] Four years later, at the Conference of Carthage of 411, the Donatists produced a certain Felix who, they claimed, was bishop of Rome—a claim which was immediately challenged by Aurelius of Carthage and upon which they did not attempt to lay any great emphasis.[5] The fact is hardly surprising. Claudian's failure had marked the collapse of the only serious attempt of Donatism to establish itself outside Africa, and henceforth it was to be a peculiarly African movement. This fact caused little concern to the Donatists; rather, it was a source of pride that only in Africa had the Lord preserved a very small remnant, free from the taint of *traditio*. But for this view they paid the inevitable price and gave Augustine the obvious weapon of ridiculing the sectarian assumption that they alone were pure and all the rest of the world in error. 'The untroubled globe of the world', he wrote in a famous phrase, 'judges those men not to

---

[1] See F. Martroye, 'Une tentative de révolution sociale en Afrique', in *Revue des questions historiques*, lxxvi (1904), 389–90.

[2] *De Haeresibus*, 69: 'Isti haeretici in urbe Roma Montenses vocantur, quibus hinc ex Africa solent episcopum mittere: aut hinc illuc Afri episcopi eorum pergere, si forte ibi eum ordinare placuisset.'

[3] See letter of Roman council 378/9 in Mansi, *Concilia*, iii, 626.

[4] *Cod. Theod.*, XVI, v, 43.

[5] *Gesta Coll. Carth.*, i, 157–62. *MPL* xi, 1321–2.

be good, who separate themselves from the whole world, in a particular part of the world.'[1] He was able to remind the Donatists that there was no prophecy in Holy Writ that sanctity should depart from the world and remain only in Africa,[2] and ridicule the picture of the Rogatist bishop of Cartenna, a minister of a schism within a schism, who maintained none the less that, although the Gospel has been preached to the Indians and the Persians, they cannot be cleansed from their sins unless they come to Cartenna to receive the only true baptism of the 'Catholic' church![3] Tyconius had evolved an answer to such arguments with his theory of Afro-Catholicism, but the Donatists had rejected Tyconius. Intellectually sterile, they had no constructive answers to argument; only unlimited powers of resistance, based upon hatred and exclusiveness.

It is therefore apparent that, by the end of the fourth century, a number of forces were operating which were calculated to weaken the imposing structure of Donatism and, ultimately, to undermine it. To say this, however, is not to detract in any way from Augustine's own personal contribution to the campaign against Donatism. For almost thirty years of his life, from his ordination in 391 until 420, when his last anti-Donatist work, the *Contra Gaudentium Donatistarum Episcopum Libri II* appeared, he was constantly engaged in controversy, writing, speaking, and organizing. He was soon recognized by the Donatists as their great enemy and the Circumcellions on one occasion paid him the compliment of laying an ambush for him, into which he would have fallen if he had not, by a happy

---

[1] *C. Epist. Parm.*, III, iv, 24: 'Quapropter securus iudicat orbis terrarum bonos non esse, qui se dividunt ab orbe terrarum in quacumque parte terrarum.' It was the phrase 'securus iudicat orbis terrarum', quoted by Wiseman in his article in the *Dublin Review* of 1839, which was to have such a profound effect upon Newman: 'Hardly had I brought my course of reading to a close, when the *Dublin Review* of that same August was put into my hands, by friends who were more favourable to the cause of Rome than I was myself. There was an article in it on the "Anglican Claim" by Dr Wiseman. This was about the middle of September. It was on the Donatists, with an application to Anglicanism. I read it, and did not see much in it. The Donatist controversy was known to me for some years, as has appeared already. The case was not parallel to that of the Anglican Church. St. Augustine in Africa wrote against the Donatists in Africa. They were a furious party who made a schism within the African Church, and not beyond its limits. It was a case of Altar against Altar, of two occupants of the same See, as that between the Non-jurors in England and the Established Church; not the case of one Church against another, as of Rome against the Oriental Monophysites. But my friend [Robert Williams], an anxiously religious man, now, as then, very dear to me, a Protestant still, pointed out the palmary words of St Augustine, which were contained in one of the extracts made in the *Review*, and which had escaped my observation. "Securus iudicat orbis terrarum." He repeated these words again and again, and, when he was gone, they kept ringing in my ears. "Securus iudicat orbis terrarum." ' *Apologia*, ed. of 1865, 116–17.

[2] *Ep.* 129, 3: 'Non autem invenerunt aliquod testimonium divinorum eloquiorum, ubi dictum est eam perituram de ceteris partibus mundi et in sola Africa Donati parte mansuram.'

[3] *Ep.* 93, vii, 22.

accident, taken the wrong turning at a road junction and so escaped their clutches.[1]

From the time of his conversion until his ordination, Augustine had been concerned partly with philosophical writings, inspired by the conversations at Cassiciacum, and partly with polemical works against the Manichees. It was after his ordination that he set himself to combat the Donatist menace and in about 394 he produced his first anti-Donatist work the *Psalmus abecedarius* or *Psalmus contra Partem Donati*. The *Abecedarius* is unique among the writings of Augustine in that it is the only one of any length written in verse (poetry it is not). 'Augustine', says Professor Beare, acidly, 'was no unlettered or ungifted fanatic, but a scholar, an ardent reader of classical poetry, and a master of prose. Yet his Psalm stands beside the works of Commodian as a monument of the decay of quantitive verse'[2]—and it must be confessed that not even the most devoted of the saint's admirers is likely to make any great claim for the *Psalmus* as a work of literature. But the creation of a work of literature was no part of Augustine's intention when writing it. On the contrary, his plan was to present the Catholic case to the widest possible audience and to provide the faithful with a convenient résumé of the facts which they could commit to memory and so equip themselves with a ready answer to Donatist arguments. 'Wishing to bring the facts of the Donatist affair to the notice of the humblest and most ignorant and uneducated people,' he wrote, 'and to fix them in their memory to the best of my ability, I wrote a psalm for them to sing, going through the Latin alphabet to the letter V. Such works are called *abecedarian*. I omitted the last three letters of the alphabet and added in their place a sort of epilogue, as though their mother the Church were addressing them.'[3] The construction of the psalm is, then, as follows: a proemium of five lines, introduced by the hypopsalma or refrain of the work: 'Vos qui gaudetis de pace   modo verum iudicate'—

---

[1] Possidius, *Vita Augustini*, 12; Aug., *Enchir.*, v, 17: 'Nam nobis ipsis accidit ut in quodam bivio falleremur, et non iremus per eum locum ubi opperiens transitum nostrum Donatistarum manus armata subsederat: atque ita factum est ut eo quo tendebamus, per devium circuitum veniremus; cognitisque insidiis illorum, nos gratularemur errasse, atque inde gratias ageremus Deo.'

[2] William Beare, *Latin Verse and European Song*, London, 1957, 248.

[3] *Retract.*, i, 19 [20]. For a discussion of the psalm see Beare, op. cit., pp. 248–50; H. J. Rose, 'Saint Augustine as a forerunner of medieval hymnology', in *JTS* xxviii (July 1927), 383ff.; P. Monceaux, *Histoire littéraire*, vii, 1923, 81–85; H. F. Muller and P. Taylor, *A Chrestomathy of Vulgar Latin*, New York, 1932, 120–4; F. J. E. Raby, *A History of Christian Latin Poetry*, 2nd ed., Oxford, 1953, 20–22; H. Vroom, *Le psaume abécédaire de saint Augustin et la poésie latine rythmique*, Nijmegen, 1933. Critical editions of the psalm have been published by Dom D. C. Lambot in the *Revue Bénédictine*, xlvii (1935), 318–28; W. Bulst, *Hymni latini antiquissimi LXXV Psalmi III*, Heidelberg [1956], 139–46, 169–70, 197–8; and Rosario Anastasi, *Aurelii Augustini Psalmus contra Partem Donati*, Padua, 1957 (the edition used here).

'You who rejoice in peace now judge what is the truth'; then a series of twenty twelve-line strophes with the initial letters of the first line of each strophe succeeding one another in alphabetical order (hence the name abecedarian) and the strophes separated by the hypopsalma. The alphabetical succession of the stanzas goes up to the letter V and the last three letters of the alphabet are omitted. In their place, after the last occurrence of the refrain follows a passage of thirty lines not in alphabetical order— the epilogue to which Augustine refers.

The verses themselves are not constructed in the manner of the classical poetry which Augustine had loved so passionately in his youth since the saint feared that the use of such metres would compel him to employ words which were not in common use among the members of his congregation.[1] On the other hand, to call the metre accentual[2] and to describe it as a trochaic acatalectic tetrameter[3] is, as Professor Beare has argued,[4] not really a very good description. In fact, the verse structure of the psalm is much simpler. Each line consists, generally, of sixteen syllables, divided equally by a caesura, with a regular accent falling on the penultimate syllable in each half-line. To obtain the sixteen syllables, elision must be observed as a general, but not invariable, rule and in certain cases two adjoining vowels may be allowed to run together, though even so, a number of nine-syllabled and seven-syllabled lines remain. The metrical scheme, then, is decidedly rough, but sufficient for an uncultured audience to memorize:[5] a syllabic structure, with one fixed accent in each

---

[1] *Retract.*, i, 19 [20]: 'ideo autem non aliquo carminis genere id fieri volui, ne me necessitas metrica ad aliqua verba, quae vulgo minus sunt usitata, conpelleret.'

[2] As does Willis, op. cit., p. 37 following Rose, art. cit.

[3] Muller and Taylor, op. cit., pp. 120–1: '. . . as the rhythm is a faulty trochaic, it can be compared to a trochaic acatalectic tetrameter. The rhythm is based on accent with one rhyme for the whole poem.'

[4] Op. cit., p. 249: 'In general it may be said that a trochaic cadence is observed; in most cases this might be called quantitative as well as accentual, in a few it is accentual only. In the rest of the half-line accent, as well as quantity, seems to be disregarded: cf. line 196 [203 of Rosario's ed.]:

Quid vóbis ad haec vidétur? Secúnda méssis ecclésiae

where the accent clashes with the supposed trochaic rhythm throughout, except in the cadences.' Beare points out (p. 248), that 'the accent almost always falls on the second-last syllable of the half-line; endings like *veniat, iudicio* must be read with synizesis of the *i, venyat, iudicyo*, if we are to get the number of syllables right; they will then conform with the general rhythm of the cadence, which is accentually trochaic'.

[5] Cf. Monceaux's comment on the resemblance of the *Psalmus* to later romance poetry, op. cit., p. 85: 'On remarquera la frappante analogie de ce vers latin avec le vers roman, qui de même a pour éléments fondamentaux l'isosyllabie, la césure regulière, la rime ou l'assonance, l'accent fixe à l'hémistiche et à la fin. Cette versification nouvelle est-elle une création du génie d'Augustin? On ne peut affirmer. Mais elle apparait pour la première fois dans le *Psalmus contra Partem Donati*, elle ne se trouve que là dans l'antiquité, et elle marque la plus importante des étapes dans l'évolution rythmique qui aboutit à notre versification moderne.'

half-line.[1] Furthermore, there is an elementary rhyme scheme, for each
line ends on the vowel e or occasionally on the diphthong ae. The rhyme,
like the alphabetical arrangement of the strophes, is an ornament, not a
structural principle, and both features are designed to make it easier to
remember the words. It would be a mistake to regard Augustine as a
pioneer in the use of rhyming verse; on the contrary, though he was
familiar with the use of rhyme, it is in his prose that we find it most
effectively employed.[2]

The opening stanzas of the poem will make its form clear:[3]

     Vos qui gaudetis de pace,   modo verum iudicate.

     Foeda est res causam audire   et personas accipere.
     Omnes iniusti non possunt   regnum dei possidere.
     Vestem alienam conscindas   nemo potest tolerare:
5   quanto magis pacem Christi   qui conscindit dignus [est] morte?
     Et quis est ista qui fecit   quaeramus hoc sine errore.

     Vos qui gaudetis de pace,   modo verum iudicate.

     Abundantia peccatorum   solet fratres conturbare.
     Propter hoc dominus noster   voluit nos praemonere
10   comparans regnum caelorum   reticulo misso in mare.
     Congregavit multos pisces   omnes genus hinc et inde,
     quos cum traxissent ad litus,   tunc coeperunt separare:
     bonos in vasa miserunt,   reliquos malos in mare.
     Quisquis novit evangelium,   recognoscat cum timore.
15   Videt reticulum ecclesiam,   videt hoc saeculum mare;
     genus autem mixtum piscis   iustus est cum peccatore;
     saeculi finis est litus: tunc est tempus separare;
     qui modo retia ruperunt,   multum dilexerunt mare;
     vasa sunt sedes sanctorum,   quo non possunt pervenire.

20   Vos qui gaudetis de pace,   modo verum iudicate.

     Bonus auditor fortasse   quaerit qui ruperunt rete.
     Homines multum superbi,   qui se iustos dicunt esse.
     Sic fecerunt conscissuram   et altare contra altare.
     Diabolo se tradiderunt,   cum pugnant de traditione
25   et crimen quos commiserunt   in alios volunt transferre.
     Ipsi tradiderunt libros   et nos audent accusare,
     ut peius committant scelus   quam quod commiserunt ante,
     quia possint causam librorum   excusare de timore,

---

[1] 'It seems that Augustine is as indifferent to accent as to quantity in the first six syllables of the half-line' (Beare, op. cit., p. 250).

[2] For examples, see Marie Comeau, *La rhétorique de saint Augustin*, Paris, 1930, esp. pp. 48–50, 55–57.

[3] I quote from Rosario's edition.

quo Petrus Christum negavit   dum terreretur de morte.
30   Modo quo pacto excusabunt   factum altare contra altare?
Et pace Christi conscissa   ut spem ponant in homine,
Quod persecutio non fecit,   ipsi fecerunt in pace.

Vos qui gaudetis de pace,   modo verum iudicate.

Custos noster, deus magne,   tu nos potes liberare
35   a pseudoprophetis istis,   qui nos quaerunt devorare.
Maledictum cor lupinum   contegunt ovina pelle.
Nomen iusti ovina pellis,   schisma est in lupino corde.
Qui non noverunt scripturas,   hos solent circumvenire;
audiunt enim traditores   et nesciunt quid gestum est ante.
40   Quibus si dicam probate,   non habent quid respondere.[1]
Suis se dicunt credidisse: dico ego mentitos esse;
quia et nos credidimus nostris,   qui vos dicunt tradidisse.
Vis nosse qui dicant verum?   Qui manserunt in radice.
Vis nosse qui dicant falsum?   Qui non sint in unitate.
45   Olim causa iam finita est.   Quid vos non statis in pace?

Vos qui gaudetis de pace,   modo verum iudicate.

You who rejoice in peace now judge what is the truth!

It is a shameful thing to hear a contested suit and not judge impartially. Those who are unjust cannot possess the kingdom of God. No one will tolerate it if you rend another man's garment; much more is he who rends the peace of Christ worthy of death. And who is the man who does such things? Let us inquire without any error who it may be.

You who rejoice in peace now judge what is the truth!

The multitude of sinners is wont to trouble the brethren and on this account our Lord wished to warn us beforehand, comparing the kingdom of heaven to a net cast into the sea which gathered fishes of every kind from every place. When they had dragged the net to the shore, the fishermen began to separate the fish, putting the good ones into jars and throwing the bad ones back into the sea. Let him who understands the Gospel consider this with fear. He sees that the net is the Church and this world is the sea. The mixed draught of fishes is the admixture of the righteous with sinners. The shore is the end of the world, and then comes the time of separation. Those who first broke the net loved the world over-much. The jars are the thrones of the saints, where they can never win.

You who rejoice in peace now judge what is the truth!

Perhaps one of the good men who hear this will ask: who broke the net? Men of over-weening pride who declared themselves to be righteous.

---

[1] Muller and Taylor, op. cit., p. 123 *n*[3], draw attention to the fact that the phrase 'non habent quid respondere' anticipates the Romance syntax 'Ils n'ont (ils ne savent) que répondre' instead of the classical 'responderent'.

So they made a schism and set up altar against altar. They yielded themselves to the devil and quarrel about *traditio*, trying to impute to others the crime which they themselves committed. For they it was who surrendered the Scriptures, and they dare to accuse us, that they may commit a greater wickedness than they did before. For the surrender of the Scriptures might be excused by fear, through which Peter denied Christ, when he was afraid of death. But by what argument will they justify altar set against altar and Christ's peace broken so that they might put their trust in man? What persecution did not do, they did themselves in time of peace.

You who rejoice in peace now judge what is the truth!

O great God our guardian, Thou canst free us from these false prophets who seek to devour us. They have the accursed heart of the wolf in sheep's clothing. For they have a sheepskin of the name of righteousness and schism in their hearts. They are accustomed to deceive those ignorant of the Scriptures; for these hear the word *traditores* and do not know what actually happened in the past. But if I say: 'Prove it!' they have no answer, but say they have believed their leaders. Now I say that those leaders have lied. We believe our own authorities who say that it is you who are the *traditores*. Do you want to know who tell the truth? Those who have remained in the root [i.e. in the vine]. Do you want to know who lie? Those who are not in unity. The whole affair was settled long ago. Why do you not remain in the peace of the Church?

You who rejoice in peace now judge what is the truth!

The *Psalmus* gives an account of the rise and progress of Donatism (*Erant quidam traditores   librorum de sancte lege / episcopi de Numidia*), of Donatus the Great's appeal to the emperor:

> Nam Donatus tunc volebat   Africam totam obtinere;
> tunc iudices transmarinos   petiit ab imperatore.
> Sed haec tam iusta petitio   non erat de caritate.

Donatus wished to dominate the whole of Africa, so he petitioned the emperor to send judges from overseas; but this appeal, quite just in itself, did not come from charity—

and of the Donatist refusal to accept the judgement of these same judges when it proved unfavourable to their cause. It passes to contemporary affairs: 'You talk of the Macarian persecution. If Macarius persecuted you, we regret this as much as you. But this was in the past; today, it is we who suffer the atrocities of your Circumcellions for which there is no

I

excuse.'[1] Finally comes the epilogue, in which the Church herself is made to appeal to the schismatics, begging them to return to unity and cease to rend her in two.[2]

The composition of the *Psalmus* showed that Augustine had grasped an essential feature of the dispute: that the Catholic laity must be encouraged and instructed and provided with an answer to the challenge of Donatist propaganda. Indeed, one might go further, and say that the appeal to the mass of the population was the key to the issue and it is a measure of the failure of Augustine's policy that, in the long run, he never persuaded the hard core of the Donatist faithful by his efforts. It has been said—and it is probably true—that Augustine saved Catholicism in Africa;[3] but his goal, the total destruction of Donatism and the unfeigned conversion of the whole body of its supporters to the Catholic Church, was never accomplished.

The instruction of the laity was, however, only a part of Augustine's campaign. Popularization was one thing; but it was also necessary to meet the Donatist intellectuals on their own ground, to disprove their historical arguments and to refute their theological principles. Hitherto, the literary side of the battle had been to the advantage of the Donatists; only one Catholic writer had come forward to oppose them, St Optatus of Milevis.[4] Now, however, a new and very formidable champion appeared on the Catholic side, whose ability as a controversialist was calculated to drive his Donatist opponents to fury.[5]

It will be necessary to give a brief account of the course of the campaign against Donatism, from the time of Augustine's ordination until its official condemnation at Carthage in 411, before passing to a consideration of the effect of his anti-Donatist polemic on the saint's theology. Since we are concerned with Augustine and not with the history of Donatism as such, only an outline need be given; but such an outline is essential if we are to understand the development of the saint's thought, particularly in the field of the relation of Church and state.

About the same time that he wrote the *Psalmus*, Augustine produced a

---

[1] *Psalmus*, 144–65, esp. 164–5:

> Nolite nobis iam, fratres,   tempus Macharii imputare
> Si crudeles erant illi,   et nobis displicent valde.

[2] Ibid., 268–97.

[3] Possidius, *Vita*, 7: 'Atque Dei dono levare in Africa ecclesia catholica exorsa est caput, quae multo tempore illis convalescentibus haereticis, praecipueque rebaptizante Donati parte maiorem multitudinem Afrorum, seducta et pressa et oppressa iacebat.'

[4] To be distinguished from his namesake, the Donatist bishop of Thamugadi.

[5] See, for example, the violent outburst of Petilian, recorded by Augustine in *C. Litt. Petil.*, II, xvii, 38: 'vere diaboli filius es, dum moribus indicas patrem.'

controversial treatise, the *Contra Epistulam Donati haeretici*, now lost. In it, he disputed the claim expressed by the founder of Donatism, Donatus the Great, in a letter which was still circulating at the time, that true baptism could be found only in his communion.[1] In addition, Augustine attacked the Donatists in his sermons[2] and in his correspondence. Already, as a newly ordained priest, he had written to Maximinus, the Donatist bishop of Sinitum, protesting about his action in rebaptizing a Catholic deacon, and begging him most earnestly not to continue to rend the seamless robe of Christ.[3] The tone of the letter is one of studied moderation and compares with that of another written soon after Augustine's consecration, to Proculeianus, his Donatist rival in the see of Hippo.[4] At this stage of the controversy, Augustine's desire was to avoid all bitterness and recrimination. He was dominated by the idea, which was to haunt him throughout the dispute, that if once the rival parties were brought together in a conference and could discuss the issues involved rationally, the whole matter could be easily resolved. Unfortunately, as he was to find, the Donatist mind was remarkably impervious to argument.

After his consecration as bishop of Hippo in 395, Augustine increased his efforts against the schismatics, thus exposing himself to the sort of reprisals favoured by the Circumcellions, so that he was on more than one occasion in danger of his life. The early years of his episcopate coincided with the period when Donatism came nearest to securing the domination of Africa, and Optatus of Thamugadi ruled southern Numidia from his great cathedral and waged relentless war upon Catholic and Maximianist alike, secure in the favour of Count Gildo, the military commander in Africa. Under the inspiration of Optatus, the Circumcellions increased their activity[5] and improved their equipment.[6] This period of Donatist triumph came to an end with the collapse of Gildo's bid for power which was followed by his death and that of his henchman, and involved the Donatists in the repression which inevitably followed the failure of the revolt.[7] In the meantime, the Catholics had not been idle. In 397 and perhaps again in 398, Augustine had visited Thubursicum Numidarum (the modern Khamissa) to hold conferences with the Donatist bishop,

---

[1] *Retract.*, i, 20 [21].
[2] *Enar. in Ps.* 54, 26.
[3] *Ep.* 23. Maximinus later became a Catholic (Aug., *Ep.* 105, ii, 4; *dCD*, XXII, viii: 'Forte accidit, ut ego *et collega tunc meus, episcopus Sinitensis ecclesiae Maximinus*, in proximo essemus; ut veniremus rogavit, et venimus.'
[4] Aug., *Ep.* 33.   [5] *C. Litt. Petil.*, I, xxiv, 26.
[6] *C. Epist. Parm.*, I, xi, 17.
[7] *Cod. Theod.*, VII, viii, 7, 9; IX, xxxix, 3; xl, 19; xlii, 16, 19.

Fortunius.[1] On 1 September 397,[2] while Gildo was still in power, the third Council of Carthage decreed that the sons and daughters of bishops and clergy should not be permitted to marry schismatics or heretics[3]—an anti-Donatist measure—but decided that the question of whether converts from Donatism who had been baptized in their infancy should be allowed to proceed to holy orders should be referred to the bishops of Rome and Milan for their views.[4] This represented an attempt to facilitate the return of Donatists to unity. Hitherto, the custom had been to deny them the right to become ordained or, if they were already clergy, to exercise their sacerdotal functions in the Church. But as early as 393 at the Council of Hippo the question of Donatist clergy who submitted had been raised and it had been decided, as a matter of expediency, that if the person concerned had not baptized converts to Donatism or if he brought his congregation over with him, he should be allowed to continue to exercise his clerical functions.[5] There was, clearly, some doubt about the decision; hence the embassy of 397 to Rome and Milan. The Italian bishops apparently disapproved of the plan, and the matter was raised afresh in June 401.[6] The reply of the Italian council which considered the proposal was still negative and the final decision of the Africans, reached at Carthage in the following September, was that while ex-Donatist clergy were, in principle, to be reduced to the status of laymen, a Catholic bishop could make exception in his own diocese if the need for clerical assistance were urgent.[7]

Augustine, meanwhile, continued to write. In the De Agone Christiano, written about 396 or 397, he warned his readers against certain heretics, among whom he includes the Donatists,[8] following this a little later by a work of two books, no longer extant, entitled Contra Partem Donati.[9] Some time after this, between 398 and 400, he produced the first of his great dogmatic works against Donatism—the three books of the Contra

---

[1] Aug., Ep. 44.

[2] The date given for this council varies from 28 August to 1 September. See Hefele-Leclercq, Histoire des conciles, II, i, 100–1 n[3].

[3] Canon xii: 'Item placuit, ut filii vel filiae episcoporum vel quorumlibet clericorum gentibus vel haereticis aut schismaticis matrimonio non iungantur.' Text in E. J. Jonkers, Acta et Symbola Conciliorum quae saeculo quarto habita sunt (Textus Minores, vol. xix), Leiden, 1954, 124.

[4] Canon xlvii: 'De Donatistis placuit, ut consulamus fratres et consacerdotes nostros Siricium et Simplicianum de solis infantibus, qui baptizantur penes eosdem, ne quod suo non fecerunt iudicio, cum ad ecclesiam Dei salubri proposito fuerint conversi, parentum illos error impediat, ne provehantur sacri altaris ministri.' In Jonkers, op. cit., p. 136.

[5] Canon xli. Printed in MPL xi, 1185. See Hefele-Leclercq, Histoire des conciles, II, i, 89.

[6] MPL xi, 1195–7. Hefele-Leclercq, II, i, 126.

[7] MPL xi, 1197–9. Hefele-Leclercq, II, i, 127.

[8] De Agon. Christ., xxix, 31.

[9] Retract., ii, 31 [5].

Epistulam Parmeniani. The letter of Parmenian which Augustine attacked was the one denouncing the theories of Tyconius, which still enjoyed a wide popularity among the Donatists, even though Parmenian had been seven years or more in his grave. In the *Contra Epistulam Parmeniani,* Augustine concerned himself with defending Tyconius' view and re-counting the history of the schism to prove that Caecilian was innocent. In the second book, he announced that he would devote another to the question of baptism,[1] and he fulfilled this promise some time later in the seven volumes of the *De Baptismo contra Donatistas,* one of the longest of his works on the theological issues involved by rebaptism and, perhaps, the most important of his anti-Donatist writings. In this, the saint argues that baptism can certainly be administered outside the Catholic Church by heretics and schismatics, since the sacrament is not their gift but Christ's, but that it cannot avail for the spiritual profit of the recipient until he returns to the fold of the One True Church. Furthermore, Augustine denies the Donatist claim that in their theology they followed the authority of St Cyprian, asserting that St Cyprian, rightly understood, does not support the Donatist case but condemns it.

Thus, the period from his consecration until the fourth Council of Carthage of 401 was, for Augustine, a time of intense literary activity, especially when it is remembered that, in addition to his formal treatises, he produced a number of letters, some long enough to be reckoned minor pamphlets in themselves.[2] For the Catholic Church, it was a time when her fortunes began to improve. Gildo's defeat marked a decisive point in the history of the two rival churches; from now onwards, the emperors were increasingly disposed to identify the Donatists with other religious dissidents proscribed by the law. On 25 June 399, an imperial rescript was addressed to the *vicarius* of Africa confirming to the Catholic Church her privileges and imposing a fine on those who should violate or neglect them.[3] About the same time, a lawsuit occurred which augured ill for Donatism in the future. A Catholic claimed the reversion of property, left by his Donatist sister to certain of her fellow sectarians, among whom a Donatist bishop named Augustine was the principal beneficiary. The brother appealed to the law. Judgement was given in his favour on the ground that no heretic could benefit from a legacy, and specific provision was made for action against the Circumcellions if they should attempt to prevent him from obtaining possession. Hitherto, the laws against heretics

[1] *C. Epist. Parm.,* II, xiv, 32.
[2] *Epp.* 33; 34; 35; 43; 44; 51; 53; perhaps also 49, 52, 56, 57, which cannot be accurately dated.
[3] *Cod. Theod.,* XVI, ii, 34.

had not been applied to the Donatists; now conditions were changing, and very much for the worse from their point of view.[1]

By 401 the situation was such that the Council which met at Carthage on 13 September decided to send representatives into the Donatist-dominated areas of Africa to preach on the history of the controversy and particularly on the Maximianist schism.[2] The result of this decision was increased violence from the Circumcellions,[3] who appeared, once again, to be beyond the control of their leaders.[4] Donatist clergy who were converted ran the risk of having their tongues cut out, or being blinded with the lime and acid which formed so horrible a part of the Circumcellion armoury.[5] One such priest was abducted, savagely beaten, flung into a ditch, clothed in a garment of rushes, and then held captive for twelve days before he was released.[6] The Catholics, for their part, began to take hostages.[7] Violence increased, and by 403 it became obvious that something must be done to moderate the prevailing conditions. On 24 August of that year, another council was held at Carthage, at which a manifesto was drawn up, probably with the assistance of Augustine, inviting the Donatists to a conference, though the language used, with its talk of Catholic authority and the need for the 'correction' of Donatist errors, was not, perhaps, very well suited to secure its objective.[8] Possibly this consideration was perceptible to the Catholics; for shortly after, on 13 September, they approached the Proconsul, Septimius, requesting that the Donatists should first be gently admonished and afterwards summoned before the municipal courts, that they might discuss their beliefs with the Catholics in public.[9] To be summoned by the secular authority to appear before local magistrates, many of whom would be pagans, was an outrage to all that the Donatists held sacred and they not surprisingly rejected the appeal.[10]

At some time between 400 and 403, Augustine wrote the third of his four great theological works on Donatism which have come down to us: the three books of the *Contra Litteras Petiliani*. Petilian, perhaps the ablest of the Donatist leaders, had been born about 365 and had been trained for the bar. He was the son of Catholic parents but, when he was approaching the age of thirty, he was seized by the Donatists, rebaptized,

---

[1] Details of the case are given in Aug., *C. Epist. Parm.*, I, xii, 19.
[2] See *MPL* xi, 1199.   [3] See *Ad Catholicos Epistolam*, xix, 50; xx, 54.
[4] *Contra Cresconium*, III, xlv, 49.   [5] Ibid., III, xlii, 46.
[6] Ibid., III, xlviii, 53; *Epp.* 88, 6; 105, ii, 3.
[7] *C. Litt. Pet.*, II, lxxxiii, 184; *Ad Cath. Epist.*, xx, 55.
[8] *MPL* xi, 1200–1. See Monceaux, *Histoire littéraire*, vi, 128–31.
[9] *MPL* xi, 1201–2.
[10] *Ad Donatistas post Coll.*, i, 1; *Brev. Coll.*, III, iv, 4.

and ordained. He seems to have considered this forcible conversion as an act of God, and thereafter placed his considerable abilities at the service of his new Church. About 400, he wrote a letter against the Catholics, addressed to the Donatist clergy, to which Augustine felt it necessary to reply. He did so in three books, the first addressed to his own congregation, the other two directed to Petilian himself, answering him point by point Barely had the second book of the *Contra Litteras Petiliani* been published, when another appeared, under the name of Augustine, entitled *Ad Catholicos Epistula contra Donatistas*, often referred to as the treatise *On the Unity of the Church* (*De Unitate Ecclesiae*).[1] In this, the saint mentioned that he has written a personal appeal to Petilian but had, as yet, received no reply. The reply was soon forthcoming and included a good deal of personal invective, directed against Augustine, based upon information gratuitously supplied by the *Confessions*, which had appeared some five years before. The third book against Petilian, written in answer to it, brought into the fray the Donatist layman Cresconius, a grammarian of ability, who defended Petilian in a letter to Augustine. For some reason, Augustine's reply to this was delayed and did not appear until after 405 (probably in 406 or 407). Then, however, he answered Cresconius in detail, in four books—the fourth of his major works on Donatism.

In the winter of 403/4, when the Catholic bishops returned to their dioceses after the September council, Augustine and his friend Possidius of Calama attempted to put into effect the request made to and granted by the Proconsul Septiminus, that Donatist bishops should be summoned before the local magistrates to debate their cause with the Catholics. They therefore summoned their respective rivals, Augustine Proculeianus and Possidius Crispinus. The Donatist bishops, however, declined to appear until they had consulted a council of their own Church and, when a reply had been received forbidding them to appear, they refused to discuss the matter further.[2] Possidius thereupon decided to take action on his own account and began a vigorous campaign in his diocese,[3] with the result that he was soon assaulted by a band of Circumcellions and was fortunate to escape with his life.[4] To the Catholics, this seemed an admirable opportunity for seeing if the laws against heretics could be applied. The Circumcellion band had been led by a presbyter, who came under the jurisdiction of Crispinus, the Donatist bishop of Calama. The bishop, then,

---

[1] There are considerable doubts about the authenticity of this treatise. Altaner, *Patrologie*, 5te Aufl., 1958, 391: 'nicht sicher echt'. The work was certainly written at Hippo, and it seems likely that it was written by one of Augustine's clergy, assisted by the master.   [2] *C. Cresconium*, III, xlvi, 50. *Ep.* 88, 7.
[3] Aug., *Ep.* 105, ii, 4.   [4] *C. Cresconium*, III, xlvi, 50.

could be held responsible for the action of the priest and a legal action was duly brought against him. If it could be argued that he was a heretic he would be liable to a fine of ten pounds of gold. He was, accordingly, cited to appear before the local magistrates, who referred the case to the court of the proconsul at Carthage. Here, the accused denied the charge of heresy, asserting that the issue between his Church and the Catholic was one of schism, not heresy. His argument proved convincing and he was acquitted.[1] This was a terrible blow to the Catholic leaders; the case had excited much interest and it would be disastrous if the Donatists should be able to establish for themselves an immunity from the law relating to heresy. The Catholics therefore appealed against the decision and the proconsul reversed his previous acquittal. Crispinus was pronounced a heretic and duly sentenced to be fined ten pounds of gold, in accordance with the law.[2] Augustine and Possidius, however, intervened to save him from having to pay. The principle was what mattered to them; they had no desire to give their opponents a further opportunity of representing themselves as martyrs and the Catholics as persecutors. Crispinus, who clearly recognized the danger to which his conviction exposed, not merely himself, but the whole Donatist Church, hastily set out for Ravenna to appeal before the imperial court. The result of his appeal was even more disastrous than he could have anticipated. Not only was the fine reimposed, but the proconsul and his court were reprimanded and fined for neglect of duty. Once again, the Catholics intervened, to prevent the fine from actually being exacted, for as Augustine remarked: 'Martyrem non facit poena sed causa'—'It is not the penalty but the cause which makes a martyr.'[3]

The assault on Possidius, however, was but one among many which were occurring throughout Africa, and when the next Catholic council assembled at Carthage on 16 June 404, it was decided to appeal to the state for the active repression of the Donatists. The bishops Theasius and Evodius, who bore the petition of the council to the emperor, were instructed to request for military protection of Catholic churches and property, and for the enforcement of the imperial laws against heretics in respect of the Donatists.[4] On their arrival, however, the envoys found that

---

[1] Possidius, *Vita*, 12: 'Qui [Crispinus] resultans legibus praesentatus cum apud proconsulem se negaret haereticum, oborta est necessitas, ut illi, recedente ecclesiae defensore, a catholico episcopo resisteretur et convinceretur eum esse quod se fuisse negaverat.'
[2] *C. Cresconium*, III, xlvii, 51.
[3] *C. Cresconium*, III, xlvii, 51; Aug., *Ep*. 88, 7 and Possidius, *Vita*, 12, for details of the case of Cresconius. It is to be observed that, on a previous occasion, Augustine had protested to him for his action in rebaptizing his tenants, and had threatened him with the ten-pound fine. See *Ep*. 66 and cf. *C. Litt. Pet.*, II, lxxxiii, 184.
[4] *MPL* xi, 1202-4. Hefele-Leclercq, II, i, 155-6.

the imperial court had already made up its mind to take action against the Donatists.[1] Maximian of Bagai, a former Donatist bishop, who had been converted to the Catholic Church and had retained his see, had been a victim, like so many others, of Circumcellion violence (in his case, not unprovoked) and had been driven from his city to Ravenna, where he laid his case before the emperor.[2] His still recent scars horrified the court; action was resolved upon and, in the months of February and March, a series of decrees issued from the Imperial Chancery, designed to suppress the turbulent schismatics. The Donatists were equated with the Manichees— always the most inauspicious of neighbours in any Roman imperial legislation;[3] their property confiscated for the benefit of the Catholic Church; their meetings prohibited and their clergy menaced with exile. They were deprived of the right of bequeathing or receiving legacies or of making contracts. Rebaptism was sternly and repeatedly forbidden, and slaves of Donatists who were able to flee from such ceremonies were to be rewarded with their freedom; indeed, by the fact that they rebaptized, the Donatists, in the eyes of the emperor, had destroyed their own argument that they were schismatics and not heretics by insulting the sacrament. Resistance was to be regarded as sedition and suppressed accordingly. Judges who failed to carry out the decree were to be heavily fined. In theory, at least, the government had decided that the Donatist Church must cease to be.[4]

There was, however, in the later Roman Empire a tendency for fact to differ markedly from theory, and it was by no means certain that imperial fulminations would necessarily mean the destruction of Donatism. But one thing at least was clear: that the Catholic episcopate would do its utmost to see that the law did not remain a dead letter. On the day of the promulgation of the imperial decree in Carthage, Primian, Petilian, and a number of other prominent Donatists set out for Ravenna to appeal to the emperor,[5] and many of their humbler followers soon began to come over to the Catholic Church. On 23 August 405 the tenth Council of Carthage

[1] Aug., *Ep.* 88, 7: 'Sed sic cum legati Romam venerunt, iam cicatrices episcopi catholici Bagaitani horrendae ac recentissimae imperatorem commoverant, ut leges tales mitterentur, quales et missae sunt.'
[2] *C. Cresconium*, III, xliii, 47; *Ep.* 185, vii, 26–28.
[3] Cod. Theod., XVI, v, 38: 'Nemo Manichaeum, nemo Donatistam, qui praecipue (ut conperimus) furere non desistunt, in memoriam revocet.'
[4] The decrees against Donatism are *Cod. Theod.*, XVI, v, 37; 38; 39; 41; 43; 44; 46; 51; 52; 54; 55; 56. These are specifically directed against the schism. In addition, the following decrees are directed against rebaptism: XVI, vi, 1; 2; 3; 4; 5; 6; 7. The general decree of Theodosius I against heresy is XVI, v, 21 (15 June 392). Helpful is William K. Boyd, *The Ecclesiastical Edicts of the Theodosian Code*, 54–57, but marred by certain inaccuracies, e.g. it dates XVI, v, 37 to 398 instead of 405.
[5] Aug., *Ep.* 88, 10.

sent a message of thanks to the emperor for his action, at the same time dispatching letters to local magistrates, urging them to speed the work of unification.[1] Augustine himself lost no time in bringing the law to bear in Hippo, to evict his rival, Proculeianus, in whose confiscated cathedral Augustine, with the same sense of the value of publicity which had inspired the *Psalmus contra Partem Donati*, exhibited a copy of one of his own anti-Donatist works.[2] But this triumph was short-lived; Proculeianus returned,[3] and the Circumcellions continued to be active.[4] Indeed, after the death of Proculeianus his successor, Macrobius, was able to make a triumphal entry into Hippo, escorted by a band of armed Circumcellions. However, he was rash enough to preach a sermon denouncing violence, and upon this they incontinently departed.[5] Events in Hippo were representative of the province as a whole; the Catholics gained ground in certain places and it is likely that the sum total of their gains was numerically impressive, but their successes were not uniform for the entire country. In some areas of Numidia, the Donatists not only maintained themselves but even had successes.[6]

Meanwhile Primian and his companions were on their way to Ravenna to appeal to the emperor. Like Crispinus in 404, they were well aware of the serious consequences which the Edict of Unity would have for their Church. They arrived at the imperial court in January 406 and found the African Catholic bishop Valentinus already there to anticipate them. They offered to debate the issues of the dispute with him in the presence of the Praetorian Prefect who could act as an assessor.[7] This proposal was refused; but they appear to have so far succeeded in their appeal that they were permitted to return to Africa. Next year, on 15 November 407, the government decided to extend the operation of its anti-Donatist laws to the community which still survived at Rome—the only place outside Africa where Donatism had secured a foothold.[8] In 408 the fall and execution of Count Stilicho,[9] the Vandal soldier who, since the death of the Emperor Theodosius the Great in 395, had been the virtual ruler of the western half of the Empire, inspired the Donatists with the hope that there might be a change of policy towards them, since it was widely believed that the policy of the government had hitherto been that of the all-powerful German minister and not that of the emperor. Hope stirred

[1] *MPL* xi, 1211–12. Hefele-Leclercq, II, i, 156.   [2] *Retract.*, ii, 53 [27].
[3] *Ep.* 88, 6.   [4] *C. Cresconium*, III, xliii, 47; xlvii, 51; *Ep.* 88, 1, 8.
[5] *Ep.* 108, v, 14.   [6] See Frend, op. cit., p. 267.
[7] *Gesta Coll. Carth.*, iii, 141. *MPL* xi, 1388. Aug., *Ep.* 88, 10. Seeck, *Gesch. des Untergangs der antiken Welt*, iii, 364.   [8] *Cod. Theod.*, XVI, v, 43.
[9] For an account of his régime, see J. B. Bury, *History of the Later Roman Empire*, i, 106–73.

afresh and assaults were renewed on Catholic clergy and converts. These were the brave days when Macrobius of Hippo was able to make his triumphant entry into the town, attended by a Circumcellion bodyguard,[1] and the old guard which had supported Gildo began to lift up its head.[2] The Catholics, however, were quick to take action. A delegation was sent to Ravenna, asking the emperor to confirm the anti-Donatist laws,[3] while Augustine lost no time in getting into touch with Olympius, Master of the Offices, who had been the agent of Stilicho's fall and murder and who had now succeeded him as chief minister in the west.[4] These measures succeeded in producing a fresh crop of constitutions directed against the schism. On 11 November 408 the first of these proscribed the partisans of Gildo;[5] another, of 24 November, was aimed at those who disturbed Catholic services;[6] a third, of 27 November, forbade all assemblies of heretics.[7] 13 January 409 saw a decree laying down penalties for those who pillaged churches,[8] while further decrees of 15 January and 26 June 409[9] reminded imperial officials of the consequences of failure to enforce the law. In fact, the African proconsul Donatus needed no exhortations to perform his duties, and we find Augustine writing to him, asking him to inflict some penalty less than death.[10]

The elevation to the purple of the Urban Prefect of Rome, Attalus, backed by the threats of the Gothic leader, Alaric, on 3 November 409, was followed by an attempt by the usurper to seize Africa, which was held for the Emperor Honorius by Count Heraclian, the executioner of Stilicho. Attalus dispatched a force under a Roman aristocrat called Constans to displace Heraclian, but the expedition proved a failure and Constans perished. Honorius demonstrated his gratitude for the loyalty of the Africans by remitting all arrears of taxation[11] and by some sort of edict of toleration, whose text has not been preserved, but which gave great offence to the Catholics. A council met at Carthage to consider the situation on 14 June and a delegation was dispatched to the emperor protesting against this action.[12] Despite his difficulties—he had at one time been on the point of taking ship for Constantinople—Honorius listened to their protests and agreed to their request. A rescript was sent to Heraclian on 25 August 410 (the day following the sack of Rome, which Honorius is stated to have

[1] Aug., *Ep.* 108, v, 14.
[2] *Ep.* 105, ii, 6 (a reference to a Donatist rumour that, with the death of Stilicho, all legislation against them would be repealed).
[3] Mansi, *Concilia*, iii, 810. Hefele-Leclercq, II, i, 158-9.   [4] *Epp.* 96, 97.
[5] *Cod. Theod.*, IX, xl, 19.   [6] Ibid., XVI, v, 44; Aug., *Ep.* 100, 2.
[7] Ibid., XVI, v, 45.   [8] Ibid., XVI, ii, 31.
[9] Ibid., XVI, v, 46, 47.   [10] Aug., *Ep.* 100, 2.
[11] *Cod. Theod.*, XI, xxviii, 6.   [12] Mansi, *Concilia*, iii, 810. Hefele-Leclercq, II, i, 159.

borne with the greatest sang-froid, when the news reached him in his fastness at Ravenna[1]) ordering him to put down heresy by rigorous means.[2] A few weeks later, another edict announced that Count Marcellinus, a high official of the Imperial Chancery, was to go to Africa, to convoke and preside at a conference, to discuss the whole matter of the schism.[3] At last the Donatists were to have the discussion which had been denied them five years earlier at Ravenna; but the fact that Marcellinus was a personal friend of Augustine and that the decree appointing him spoke ominously about the 'removal of superstition' was calculated to modify their satisfaction considerably. Their one hope was to prove that it was they, and not their rivals, who were the Catholic Church of Africa; and it must have been clear that in the circumstances under which the conference would be held this would be an extremely difficult operation, with the odds heavily weighted on the side of the Catholics.

The Conference of Carthage, which lasted from 25 May to the evening of 8 June, with two adjournments, was an epic climax to the years of dispute and recrimination which had elapsed since the fateful appeal of the Donatist bishops to the Emperor Constantine ninety-eight years earlier. Two hundred and eighty-six Catholic bishops were ranged against two hundred and eighty-four Donatists. The proceedings of the conference, which were taken down at the time in shorthand, have been partly lost, but enough has survived to fill one hundred and ninety columns of Migne's *Patrologia Latina*[4] and to present a vivid picture of the encounter whose outcome could hardly be in doubt, from the moment when Marcellinus read the imperial rescript convening the conference and the Donatists heard themselves denounced as spreaders of vain error and needless dissension.[5] Marcellinus discharged his duties as adjudicator with remarkable impartiality, given the specified limits of the imperial rescript, and the Donatists did their cause no good by needless arrogance when they refused to sit down, first on the ground that Christ had stood before His judge and later because they declined to sit with the ungodly, and so kept

---

[1] Procopius, *De Bello Vandalico*, i, 2. Honorius, it is said, was much devoted to the breeding of chickens. To him came the eunuch responsible for the imperial aviary, with the awful news: 'Your majesty, Rome has perished!' 'Rome perished!' exclaimed the imperial chicken fancier, 'but she was feeding out of my hand only just now!' He referred to an exceptionally choice fowl, which he had named Rome. When the eunuch made the situation clear, the emperor seems to have been much relieved. 'My dear fellow,' he replied, 'I thought you were talking about the chicken!'

[2] *Cod. Theod.*, XVI, v, 51.   [3] Ibid., XVI, xi, 3.

[4] *MPL* xi, 1231–1420.

[5] *Gesta Coll. Carth.*, i, 4: '[Donatistae] qui Africam, hoc est, regni nostri maximam partem, et saecularibus officiis fideliter servientem, vano errore et dissensione superflua decolorant.' *MPL* xi, 1260. Note the Christian emperor's complaint against those who disturb the social order and prevent the payment of taxes.

the conference on its feet throughout the three sessions;[1] or by the care-
lessness with which they prepared their brief, so that they appealed to the
history of Optatus of Milevis to confirm a point of fact, only to discover
that the evidence given was precisely contrary to what they hoped to
prove.[2]

Nevertheless, even if they had shown discretion and the profoundest
legal ability, it is difficult to see how the Conference could have ended
otherwise than it did. The general strategy of the Donatists was to present
themselves as the true Catholic Church of Africa,[3] 'the Church which is
persecuted but does not persecute'.[4] If they could succeed in this, they
would not have to concern themselves with the churches outside Africa.
Unfortunately, it was hardly possible for the imperial commissioner to
accept such an argument. He was bound, by first principles, to regard as
Catholic the Church which was actually in communion with other churches
overseas.[5] The burden of proof to the contrary lay upon the Donatists, and
the argument turned upon historical fact. Here, the Catholics had an
enormous advantage. Facts and documents were too unmistakably on their
side, and the climax was reached when Marcellinus asked the Donatists
whether they had any documents to counter those produced by the
Catholics to show that Caecilian and his consecrator, Felix of Apthungi,
had been declared innocent of the charge of *traditio*, only to be told that
some of the evidence had been destroyed.[6] There is no doubt that the
honours of the debate were with the Catholics and that they amply
succeeded in proving their case. Marcellinus pronounced his decision in
their favour and, on 26 June, proclaimed it throughout the African
provinces.[7] All persons in positions of authority were required to assist in
the suppression of Donatist assemblies and the confiscation of Donatist
property. The Donatists, meanwhile, appealed to the emperor;[8] but they
must have realized from past experience that their appeal would carry
little weight. Honorius was still, at the time, in grave difficulties; although
Alaric was dead, his armies remained in Italy, while in Gaul the fall of the
usurper Constantine (executed in September 411) was soon followed by

---

[1] Ibid., i, 144–5; ii, 4; *MPL* xi, 1319–20, 1354. Aug., *Brev. Coll.*, II, i; *Serm.*, 99, viii,
8; *Ad Donatistas post Coll.*, v, 7. The reference is to Ps. 25.5 [26.5]: Odivi ecclesiam
malignantium: et cum impiis non sedebo. Cf. *C. Epist. Parm.*, III, v, 26.
[2] *Gesta Coll. Carth.*, iii, 530–8. *MPL* xi, 1256. *Brev. Coll.*, III, xx, 38; *Ad Don. post
Coll.*, xxxi, 54; Aug., *Ep.* 141, 9.
[3] See the speech of Emeritus of Caesarea, *Gesta Coll. Carth.*, iii, 99. *MPL* xi, 1380–1.
[4] See the Donatist letter to Marcellinus of 7 June. *Gesta Coll. Carth.*, iii, 258. *MPL* xi,
1408.
[5] *Gesta Coll. Carth.*, iii, 92, 103. *MPL* xi, 1379, 1382.
[6] Ibid., iii, 584. *MPL* xi, 1258.   [7] *MPL* xi, 1418.
[8] Possidius, *Vita*, 13; Aug., *Ad Donatistas post Coll.*, xii, 16.

the elevation of a new tyrant; but nothing would induce the western emperor to abandon the Church to which he was attached. Honorius received Marcellinus' report and acted upon it. On 30 January 412 an edict was issued proscribing Donatism. To profess it was a crime to be punished by a scale of fines, ranging from fifty pounds of gold in the case of an *illus-tris*—the highest rank in the aristocracy—to five pounds for a plebeian. Circumcellions were to be fined ten pounds of silver, while peasants and slaves were to be flogged. Donatist clergy were to be exiled to remote corners of the Empire and all Donatist property surrendered to the state.[1] The full weight of the law was to be brought into operation; only the sanction of capital punishment was omitted.

The Conference of Carthage was a personal triumph for Augustine and he lost no time in exploiting it. In the years immediately preceding it, his pen had been continually engaged. He completed his four books against Cresconius; he published the lost work *Probationum et Testimoniorum contra Donatistas Liber*—this was the work which he affixed to the wall of the Donatist basilica at Hippo, when he took possession of it in 406 after the proclamation of the Edict of Unity—and another, also lost, *Contra Donatistam nescio quem.*[2] This, like the *Probationum et Testimoniorum Liber*, apparently dealt with the history of the schism and the case of Caecilian. Yet another lost book, the *Admonitio Donatistarum de Maximianistis*, was written in 409 and treated of the Maximianist schism.[3] In 410 appeared the one surviving work of this period, *De Unico Baptismo contra Petilianum*, written to answer a pamphlet of Petilian's, *De Unico Baptismo.*[4] In this, Augustine once more asserted the doctrine that baptism is the gift of Christ and not of the man by whom it is administered, who may well be a sinner. The dispute between pope Stephen and Cyprian is discussed, and Cyprian is shown to have been wrong on a point of doctrine although, as Augustine triumphantly reminded his antagonist, his great charity prevented him from going into schism, even upon an issue so vital. About the same time, another lost book, the *De Maximianistis contra Donatistis*, gave the Maximianist schism more detailed treatment than had been possible in a work designed for the general reader like the *Admonitio.*[5] In addition to these treatises, Augustine wrote a large number of letters on Donatism,[6] including the long and important letter to Vincent, Rogatist bishop of Cartenna,

[1] *Cod. Theod.*, XVI, v, 52.
[2] *Retract.*, ii, 54 [28].
[3] Ibid., ii, 55 [29].
[4] Ibid., ii, 60 [34].
[5] Ibid., ii, 61 [35]: 'non brevissimum, sicut antea, sed grandem multo diligentius.'
[6] Aug., *Epp.* 87; 88; 89; 93; 97; 100; 105; 108; 112.

probably written in 408,[1] and another to Macrobius, his Donatist rival in Hippo, to be dated between late in 409 and August 410.[2]

The results of the Conference of Carthage spurred Augustine to fresh efforts. Realizing that few people would be inclined to study the lengthy official record of the proceedings, he produced a summary, suitable for the purposes of propaganda, the *Breviculus Collationis*—'Summary of the Conference'.[3] This appeared at the end of 411 and was followed, in 412, by yet another appeal, 'To the Donatists after the Conference' (*Ad Donatistas post Collationem*),[4] a long and careful work intended to cover every aspect of the controversy and to prevent any further misrepresentations by the Donatist leaders. It concluded with an eloquent appeal, addressed to the generous instincts of his readers:

> We know how many of you—and perhaps all, or almost all—are accustomed to say: 'Oh, if they could only come together! if they could only have a discussion sometime and the truth emerge from their debate!' Well, it happened. Falsehood was found guilty and truth revealed. Why then is unity still shunned and charity scorned? Why must we still be divided by the names of men? God is One who created us. Christ is One who redeemed us. The Spirit is One, who ought to bring us together. Let the name of the Lord now be honoured and let it manifest itself to you in joyfulness, that you may know your brethren in the unity of the name. The error which separated us has already been vanquished in the meetings with your bishops. May the time come when the devil in your hearts may be vanquished and Christ be favourable to His flock, gathered in peace as He has commanded.[5]

The earnest tone of this appeal suggests that, even with the full force of the state directed against them, the Donatists were not returning to unity in the numbers which the Catholics had anticipated. In the towns converts were coming in, but in the country on the high plains of Numidia, always a stronghold of Donatism, the situation was otherwise. A council of Catholic Numidians met at Constantine on 14 June 412 and warned the Donatists not to delay reconciliation with the Universal Church,[6] but it may be wondered how much effect this warning had. Indeed, the decision reached at Carthage drove some of the more moderate elements among the Donatists into the extremist camp. Thus Macrobius, Donatist bishop of Hippo, who had once counselled moderation and been deserted by his Circumcellion bodyguard for his pains, now became a Circumcellion commander himself.[7]

---

[1] *Ep.* 93. See Goldbacher, *CSEL* lviii, 28–29.
[2] *Ep.* 108. Goldbacher, p. 32.
[3] *Brev. Coll.*, praef.; *Retract.*, ii, 65 [39].
[4] *Retract.*, ii, 66 [40].
[5] *Ad Don. post Coll.*, xxxv, 58.
[6] Aug., *Ep.* 141.
[7] Aug., *Ep.* 139, 2.

In 413 it seemed as if there was a possibility of one more of those changes in fortune which had marked the progress of the struggle between Catholic and Donatist. Count Heraclian, in the past a loyal servant of Honorius, decided to make a bid for imperial power. Since most of the regular forces of Italy were being employed in Gaul, he seemed to have a good hope of success. Accordingly, he set sail for Italy in the summer, with a large fleet and army. But Heraclian's plans miscarried. Defeated, he fled to Africa, where he was pursued by his conqueror, Count Marinus, arrested at Carthage and beheaded. His fate had been deserved; but tragically, it involved others who had had no share in his venture: Count Marcellinus, who had presided over the Conference of 411, and his brother, Apringius. Both were suddenly arrested and, despite the intervention of the Catholic bishops, they were executed on 13 September.[1] It was a personal blow to Augustine, who had a great affection for Marcellinus as a man, and potentially an ominous development for the Catholic cause. The Donatists were suspected of having denounced Marcellinus as a means of getting rid of a hated enemy,[2] though there is no direct proof of their guilt and the motives for his execution must remain a mystery. However, the death of the imperial commissioner did not mean any reversal of the policy introduced on his recommendation. Two rescripts to the Proconsul of Africa, Julian, dated 17 June and 30 August 414 respectively,[3] reaffirmed the anti-heretical legislation of previous years, and a third of 25 August 415 again ordered the enforcement of the Edict of Unity against the schismatics.[4] The Catholics, for their part, did not fail to take advantage of the facilities afforded to them by the intervention of the state. The council which met at Carthage on 1 May 418 to denounce Pelagianism in the face of pope Zosimus' delay in condemning Pelagius and Caelestius, drew up elaborate provisions for the integration of Catholic and Donatist communities of the same cities, and for the employment of Donatist bishops who had come over to the Catholic faith. At the same time, it urged its members not to delay in taking over Donatist communities within their dioceses.[5] Another Carthaginian council, which met a year later on 25 May 419, confirmed the previously enacted canons of African councils, including those directed against the Donatists.[6]

It was in 418 that Augustine had his dramatic, but unsuccessful, inter-

[1] Aug., *Ep.* 151, 6.
[2] Ibid., 3–9; Orosius, *Historiae adversus Paganos*, vii, 42. *CSEL* v, 558–9; Hieron. *Adversus Pelagianos*, III, 19. *MPL* xxiii, 588–9.
[3] *Cod. Theod.*, XVI, v, 54 and 55.
[4] Ibid., XVI, v, 56.
[5] *Canones*, ed. Bruns, Can. 121, 123, 124. Hefele-Leclercq, II, i, 194.
[6] Hefele-Leclercq, II, i, 201 and n^2 for references.

view with Emeritus of Caesarea. Two years later appeared his last anti-Donatist work, the *Contra Gaudentium*, directed against the Donatist bishop, Gaudentius of Thamugadi, a violent fanatic and a worthy successor to the infamous Optatus. Gaudentius had refused to hand over his basilica to the imperial officials in conformity with the law, and threatened to burn down the building, with himself and his congregation, if any attempt were made to take possession by force. Dulcitius, the tribune and notary responsible for taking action in the matter, forwarded to Augustine two letters which he had received from the Donatist bishop with a request that he would reply to them. Augustine duly took up the challenge and wrote the first of his books against Gaudentius. In it, he covered familiar ground afresh, defending state coercion in spiritual matters, denouncing the Donatist tendency to suicide, and reiterating the arguments drawn from the Donatist treatment of the Maximianists. A letter was received from Gaudentius in reply, and once again Augustine wrote in answer to it. The outcome of the affair is not known;[1] but in the writings which it provoked we have what is virtually Augustine's last word on the subject of Donatism.[2] He had been working and writing against Donatism for more than a quarter of a century. All possible arguments had been deployed and any fresh work could only be a repetition of what had already been said many times. New controversies crowded upon him, which were to preoccupy his mind during the remaining ten years of his life. Soon after the Conference of Carthage he wrote the first of his books against the Pelagians, the *De Peccatorum Meritis et Remissione*, and so embarked upon the dispute which was to overshadow the rest of his career and in which he was to find opponents of greater ability than any the Donatists had managed to produce. In 413 he began work on the *De Civitate Dei*, the massive piece of Christian apologetic which was to occupy thirteen years and not to be completed until 426. He was still to find work for his pen in works on Bible criticism and treatises directed against the Arian heresy. And,

---

[1] 'Some traces of burning were found over the cathedral area, but these may well belong to the sixth century and not to the period of Gaudentius' (Frend, op. cit., p. 296 *n*[5]) and as we have the statements of Procopius that Thamugadi was destroyed by the Mauri of the Aurès during the Vandal epoch (*De Bello Vandalico*, ii, 13: ἀλλὰ καὶ πόλιν Ταμουγαδιν ... ἔρημον ἀνθρώπων οἱ Μαυρούσιοι ποιησάμενοι ἐς ἔδαφος καθεῖλον, ὅπως μὴ ἐνταῦθα ᾖ δυνατὰ ἐνστρατοπεδεύσασθαι τοῖς πολεμίοις, ἀλλὰ μηδὲ κατὰ πρόφασιν τῆς πόλεως ἄγχι ἐς τὸ ὄρος ἰέναι. *CSHB* ii, vol. i, 466) it seems reasonable to associate such traces of burning with a later date (late fifth to early sixth century) rather than with the age of Augustine.

[2] There are occasional references to Donatism in his anti-Pelagian writings. Thus, in *De Anima et eius Origine*, III, ii, 2, he remonstrates with Vincentius Victor, a convert from the Rogatist schism, on retaining the name of Vincentius, which was that of the successor of Rogatus. In *Contra Iulianum*, he refers to the case of Caecilian and the judgement of pope Miltiades (I, iii, 7) and justifies an appeal to the secular arm by instancing the Conference of Carthage (III, i, 5).

finally, he had begun to realize the hopelessness of arguing with Donatism; and this realization found expression in a steadily increasing tendency to approve coercion by the secular arm, which seemed to be so effective where reasoned argument failed.

It would, however, be wrong to assume that by 420 the struggle with Donatism was virtually over. This may have been generally true of the town, and we have no direct evidence for the country, though it is possible that the letter of bishop Honoratus, written to Augustine in 428, two years before the latter's death, asking what was to be done in the event of a barbarian invasion, may point to a continuation of Donatist activity.[1] All we can say is, that after the exchange of letters between Augustine and Gaudentius in 420, we have very little information about Donatism in Africa. With the coming of the Arian Vandals, it is likely that Catholic and Donatist suffered equally as *Homousiani*, believers in the consubstantiality of the Son with the Father in the Holy Trinity. The Donatists play no part in African history during the period of Vandal domination nor do they reappear at the Byzantine reconquest. Then, at the end of the sixth century, they suddenly emerge in the correspondence of pope Gregory the Great.[2] The pope is alarmed at the survival of Donatism in Numidia, and writes first to the Byzantine general, Gennadius, Exarch of Africa, and then, when his appeal goes unheeded, to his own legates, Columbus and Hilarius. In 593 we find him addressing Gennadius' Praetorian Prefect, Pantaleo; but his repeated appeals, both to the Byzantine administration and to the African episcopate, do not appear to have been successful. Finally, in August 596 a papal letter is dispatched to Constantinople to the Emperor Mauricius himself.[3] Whether this final appeal succeeded or not we do not know, but in any case the days of Christianity in Africa were numbered. Gregory the Great died in 604. Less than forty years later, the first Arab raiders appeared. The hostile attitude of the Berber tribesmen towards the Arabs delayed the permanent occupation of the country until the end of the century; but with the Berbers once won over to Islam, the situation was altered. The African domination of Rome had been based on the coastal cities; that of Islam drew its strength from the Moorish inhabitants of the interior. From thence emerged a flood of warriors who swept down to the coast, driving out the Byzantine forces and ultimately spreading across the sea to Spain and Sicily. The fall of Carthage in 698 marked the

[1] Such is the opinion of Frend, op. cit., p. 298. Honoratus' letter was answered by Aug., *Ep.* 228.

[2] See Holmes Dudden, *Gregory the Great*, London, 1905, 298, 414–28, and Frend, op. cit., pp. 309–14.

[3] Gregorius, *Ep.* VI, 65. *MPL* lxxvii, 848–9.

decisive victory for Islam. Certain Christian communities lingered on until the eleventh century and some Roman memories lingered in the name of 'Afri' or 'Afarec', given by the Moslems to the descendants of the last Christian converts to Islam but, after a few centuries, even these vanished.[1] No romance language survived in North Africa, nothing Roman was preserved in its institutions and no Christian body maintained itself, as happened in other Muslim countries such as Egypt and Syria. The violent disputes of the fourth and fifth centuries, the oppression of the Vandal domination and the Byzantine reconquest, had proved too much. Weakened as much by internal dissension as by external attack, the once flourishing African Church perished and Christianity proved to have been only an episode in the history of the Berber peoples. Today, the muzzein calls to prayer where once were heard the war-cries of opposing Christian factions: 'Deo laudes!' and 'Deo gratias!' The church of Tertullian, of Cyprian, and of Augustine survives in the noble monuments which the spade of the archaeologist continues to uncover and in the manuscripts of the writings of its doctors, which fill the great libraries of Europe. But there are no Christians in North Africa who descend from that church and the Christian historian, considering both the grandeur of the past and its utter extinction, may well marvel at the workings of divine providence and call to mind a phrase of Scripture that came very readily to Augustine's lips: *How unsearchable are His judgements and His ways past finding out!*

[1] For the last centuries of Christianity in Barbary, see William Seston, 'Sur les derniers temps du Christianisme en Afrique', in *Mélanges d'archéologie et d'histoire* (École française de Rome), liii (1936), 101–24; W. C. Frend, 'North Africa and Europe in the early Middle Ages', *Transactions of the Royal Historical Society*, fifth series, V (1955), 61–80; Julien, *Histoire de l'Afrique du Nord*, i, 277–9; and J. F. P. Hopkins, *Medieval Muslim Government in Barbary*, London, 1958, 62–70.

7

The Theology of the Donatist Controversy

Dic Christi Veritas,
dic cara raritas,
dic rara Caritas,
ubi nunc habitas?

ANON., from the *Carmina Burana*

THE THEOLOGICAL issues of the Donatist controversy are dominated by the majestic figure of St Cyprian. Both parties claimed him as their father and their inspiration; both appealed to his life and writings to confirm their own doctrine. To depart from his teaching was a step of the utmost gravity, requiring a careful defence. To the mass of the people, Cyprian was the great hero, the martyr-bishop of Carthage, to whom the highest honour and veneration were due. His reputation was not confined to Africa. Rome honoured him, and his name is mentioned to this day in the canon of the Roman Mass. More surprisingly, his cult spread to the Christian east. Gregory Nazianzen delivered an eloquent encomium upon him, marred only by the fact that St Gregory really knew very little about his hero's life and confused him with another Cyprian, a converted magician of Antioch. Today, the Greeks celebrate his feast on 31 August (and, in a rather pleasing fashion, keep that of his adversary, pope Stephen of Rome, who has been almost wholly neglected in the west, on 2 August). Famous abroad, Cyprian was unrivalled at home. During Augustine's lifetime, African devotion was very ready to celebrate the anniversary of his martyrdom with dances around his tomb.[1] Nor did his cult lapse during the period of Vandal domination. As an ante-Nicene martyr, he was as acceptable to the Arians as to the Catholics and when the Vandal king, Hunneric, confiscated the Catholic churches in 484, the great basilica of St Cyprian by the harbour of Carthage was taken over by the Arians for their own worship. Half a century later, in the autumn of 532, the Byzantine army under Belisarius approached the city on the eve of the festival called the Cypriana. The Vandal clergy had decorated the church for the solemnity

---

[1] Aug., *Serm.* 311, v, 5.

and the Catholics watched with disgust the preparations of the hated German heretics. A report went abroad that Cyprian had appeared in a dream to many of the faithful, uttering words of comfort and promising that a time was at hand when he would avenge the injury offered to himself, and the Catholics eagerly awaited the fulfilment of the pledge. Then came the news of the defeat of the Vandals at the battle of Ad Decimum. Their priests fled in panic and the citizens of Carthage entered the church, lighted the lamps, and celebrated the Cypriana according to the Catholic rite. Their patron had not forgotten them.[1]

The reason for St Cyprian's influence on the theological discussions between Catholic and Donatist is to be found, not so much in his writing, as in his personality and the circumstances of his life and death. Intellectually, he cannot compare with Tertullian, not to speak of Augustine; but intellect is not the only nor indeed the primary test of a Christian teacher, and if Cyprian lacked the originality of the first great African Christian writer, he had a depth of character and sense of responsibility wholly lacking in Tertullian—a fact which may explain why the one lived a bishop and died a martyr while the other, after hurling defiance at the Roman Empire, lived to an extreme old age to die outside the communion of the Catholic Church. Cyprian's culture may have been a narrow one; he nourished himself primarily on the Bible and the works of Tertullian, though it is possible to over-emphasize the limitations of his mental horizon. Indeed, there is reason to think that he had a wider erudition than was formerly supposed, and a not inconsiderable acquaintance with Greek theology.[2] His strength lies, however, in his concern with the practical application of theological principles, rather than with speculation, so that one may say that though St Cyprian is an African of the Africans, he is also, to a remarkable degree, an embodiment of the 'antique Roman'. Throughout his life, his bearing is that of the aristocrat. At his trial before the proconsular court, he shows the dignity of the high-born gentleman, and the proconsul accepts him as such.[3] In dealing with his African colleagues, he invariably showed exquisite courtesy and tact, since it was a cardinal point of his doctrine of the episcopate that all bishops are equal in office; but he nevertheless succeeded in establishing himself as the

---

[1] Procopius, De Bello Vandalico, i, 21.

[2] See Hugo Koch, 'I rapporti di Cipriano con Ireno ed altri scrittori greci', in Ricerci religiosi, v (1929), 137–63.

[3] See the Acta Proconsularia in CSEL iii (1), Appendix, cx–cxiv. Cyprian is arrested by two senior officers (c. 2), and spends the night in the house of one of them. The proconsul, although not admitting any delay in the trial, is considerate: 'consule tibi', to which Cyprian gives the proud answer: 'Fac quod tibi praeceptum est. In se tam iusta nulla est consultatio' (c. 3).

leader of the African bishops, while always insisting that he was only one among many.[1] Within his own lifetime, he was already being consulted on issues affecting the Church in Gaul[2] and in Spain.[3] During his dispute with Stephen of Rome, he was able to secure the support of eastern bishops like Firmilian of Caesarea[4] and Dionysius of Alexandria.[5] Indeed, as Paul Monceaux very justly remarked of the dispute between Stephen and Cyprian, 'while the bishop of Rome claimed to command everyone, and remained alone, the bishop of Carthage, who proclaimed the independence of the churches, obtained the unanimous assent of the African communities, and the approbation of the Christian East'.[6] Such was Cyprian in his life. His martyr's death consolidated his influence.

The theological issues of the Donatist controversy may be grouped under three main headings: (i) The nature of the Church; (ii) the Sacraments and their validity; and (iii) the relationship between Church and state with regard to the employment of state coercion of schismatic and heretical Christians.[7] It is necessary, as a preliminary, to consider the teaching of St Cyprian with regard to the first two of these. With regard to the third, for obvious reasons, he has little to say.

Cyprian's doctrine of the Church may conveniently be studied in his treatise *On the Unity of the Catholic Church* written in 251.[8] The circumstances which led to its composition anticipate, in a remarkable way, those which gave rise to Donatism; and the fact is hardly surprising, since Donatism stood in a theological tradition which looks back to the age of Cyprian and beyond, to the earliest days of Christianity in Africa. We have already described in the Introduction how, during the Decian persecution of 250 to 251, many Christians lapsed, either by offering sacrifice or procuring by various means certificates of conformity without actually sacrificing. Afterwards some were seized with remorse and wished to return to the Church of the Christ whom they had denied. Among the faithful there were two extreme schools of thought on this matter: those who held that the lapsed could never, in this life, be readmitted to communion but

---

[1] See, for example, his remarks at the Council of 1 September 258, *Sent. episcoporum num. lxxxvi de haeret. baptizandis*, Proem. *CSEL* iii (1), 435–6.
[2] *Ep.* 68. See Jalland, *The Church and the Papacy*, 169.
[3] *Ep.* 67. See Jalland, op. cit., p. 172.
[4] *Ep.* 75. See Jalland, op. cit., 167–78.
[5] See F. C. Conybeare, 'Newly discovered letters of Dionysius of Alexandria to the popes Stephen and Xystus', in *EHR* xxv (1910), 111–14.
[6] *Histoire littéraire de l'Afrique chrétienne*, ii, 230.
[7] These are dealt with, in the order (i), (iii), (ii), by Willis, *Saint Augustine and the Donatist Controversy*, 93–168.
[8] For the date of the *De Unitate*, see Maurice Bévenot, *St Cyprian's De Unitate, Chap. 4 in the light of the manuscripts*, Rome, 1937, 66–77.

could only pass their days in lifelong penance in the hope that, at the last, God would give them the pardon that His Church dared not pronounce; and those who believed that the intercession of the confessors, who had defied all the attempts of the persecutors to make them sacrifice but who had not, for some reason, been executed, would avail for the weakness of those who fell. Cyprian admitted neither of these two views. He regarded apostasy as one of the gravest of sins and, in his treatise *On the lapsed*, recounts some grim stories of the fate of apostate Christians who attempted to receive the sacrament without having been reconciled with the Church. On the other hand, he rejected the rigorist view that absolution could never be given in this life, regarding it as calculated to drive the penitent to despair.[1] His policy was that the penitent should be readmitted to communion after a suitable period, so that he should not depart this life deprived of the sacraments of the Church.[2]

This policy displeased the extremists of both parties. At Carthage, a movement was formed against Cyprian under the leadership of a deacon, Felicissimus, which set up a church of its own in which the lapsed were received back to Communion without any delay.[3] More serious was the rigorist schism formed at Rome under the ascetic Novatian, who contrived to get himself consecrated anti-pope in opposition to pope Cornelius, and founded a schismatic church which was destined to have a long career spreading to the east where it survived until the fifth century. It was against schismatics such as these that Cyprian wrote the *De Unitate Ecclesiae*.[4]

---

[1] Cyprian, *Ep.* 55, 17: 'Sed quoniam est in illis [lapsis] quod paenitentia sequente revalescat ad fidem et ad virtutem de paenitentia robur armatur—quod armari non poterit, si quis desperatione deficiat, si ab ecclesia dure et crudeliter segregatus ad gentiles se vias et saecularia opera convertat vel ad haereticos et schismaticos reiectus ab ecclesia transeat, ubi etsi occisus propter nomen postmodum fuerit extra ecclesiam constitutus et ab unitate adque a caritate divisus coronari in morte non poterit—et ideo placuit frater carissime, examinatis causis singulorum libellaticos interim admitti, sacrificatis in exitu subveniri, quia exomologesis apud inferos non est nec ad paenitentiam quis a nobis conpelli potest, si fructus paenitentiae subtrahatur. si proelium prius venerit, corroboratus a nobis invenietur [armatus] ad proelium: si vero ante proelium infirmitas urserit, cum solacio pacis et communicationis abscedit.' *CSEL* iii (2), 635–6.

[2] Ibid.

[3] *Epp.* 41 and 43. *CSEL* iii (2), 587–9, 590–7.

[4] The *De Unitate*, and more particularly its famous fourth chapter, has been a subject of the liveliest controversy since the Reformation, with regard to the evidence which it gives, or may give, regarding the primacy of the see of Peter, and St Cyprian's views concerning that primacy. It is beyond the scope of this study to enter into a discussion of the matter. I have taken for my text of the *De Unitate* the 'received text' of the *CSEL*, whose attribution to Cyprian has never been in doubt. A general survey of the matter is given by Willis, op. cit., pp. 110–12, to whose bibliography may be added A. d'Alès, *La théologie de saint Cyprien*, Paris, 1922, 97–140. Willis is not entirely fair in his remarks about Bévenot, *Saint Cyprian's* De Unitate, *Chap. 4 in the light of the manuscripts* and it may be noted that when he records that Chapman and Bévenot 'differ from one another,

It was probably against the Novatianists that the *De Unitate* was directed and its argument is dominated by the thought: *One* Holy Catholic Church. Cyprian addresses himself to those whom God has destined to be the salt of the earth[1] and warns them against the wiles of the enemy, the old serpent who, discomfited by Christ's coming in the flesh and held in check by the spread of the Gospel, has found new ways to deceive men with heresies and schisms, by which he overturns faith, corrupts truth and divides unity. This he is able to do when men do not turn to the source of truth or seek their Head or preserve the doctrine of the heavenly rule.[2] But recourse to the fountain head is easy, and Cyprian bases his argument on two of our Lord's injunctions; the first being the promise to Peter: *On this Rock I will build my Church* (Matt. 16.18); and the second being the power communicated, after the Resurrection, to all the Apostles: *Receive ye the Holy Ghost; whose soever sins ye remit, they are remitted unto them, and whose soever sins ye retain, they are retained* (John 20.21, 22). By these, an equal partnership in honour and power was bestowed upon all the Apostles but to Peter first, in order that the Church of Christ might be shown to be one, as is written in the Song of Songs: *My dove, my undefiled is but one; she is the only one of her mother, she is the choice of her that bare her.* St Paul likewise urges this unity: *There is one body, and one Spirit, one hope of your calling, one Lord, one faith, one baptism, one God.*[3] Every Christian ought to hold firmly to unity but especially bishops, who should demonstrate it in a one and undivided episcopate; for the episcopate is one and its power is held by the bishops *in solidum*, as a body, so that each enjoys the power without having an exclusive title.[4] Nor is unity impaired by the fact that there are many bishops; for there is but one sun although many rays of light proceed from it; a tree may have many branches but these branches have one root; many streams flow from the same spring but their unity is preserved in the source of their origin. Take a ray from the sun and it gives no light; break a branch from the tree and it bears no fruit; cut the stream from its source and it will dry up. So it is with the Church of God. She extends her beams through the whole world, but there is only one light which is diffused everywhere. She spreads her branches in all lands and flows widely with many streams, 'but there is one Head, one origin, one

---

the former holding that the *textus receptus* is prior, and the interpolation later, the latter the reverse', he omits to mention that there is evidence that Chapman had, before his death, accepted the view promulgated by Bévenot and intended to have written an article on the subject (Bévenot, op. cit., pp. 12–13). A useful summary of Cyprian's views about the Roman see will be found in H. Burn-Murdoch, *The Development of the Papacy*, London, 1954, 125–34.

[1] *De Unit.*, 1. *CSEL* iii (1), 209.
[2] Ibid., 3. *CSEL* iii (1), 211–12.
[3] Ibid., 4. *CSEL* iii (1), 212–13.
[4] See A. d'Alès, op. cit., pp. 130–6.

mother prolific with offspring; of her are we born, by her milk we are nourished, by her spirit we are quickened'.[1] The Church is the chaste bride of Christ and bears sons for Him alone.

> Whoever, having been cut off from the Church, is joined with an adultress, is separated from the promises of the Church. Nor will he come to the rewards of Christ who leaves the Church of Christ. He is a stranger, a profane person, an enemy. None can have God for a father who has not the Church for a mother. If any had been able to escape outside the ark of Noah, there might have been a way of escape for him who is outside the Church. The Lord warns us and says: *He who is not with Me is against Me, and he who gathereth not with Me scattereth.* He who breaks the peace and concord of Christ is against Christ and he who gathers outside the Church of Christ scatters the Church of Christ.[2]

The mystery of the unity of the Church of Christ is to be found in various passages of Scripture. It is like the seamless garment which could not be divided because it was woven from the top throughout; like the one kingdom of David which was afterwards rent asunder, because of Solomon's sin; like the one flock of the Good Shepherd; like the house of the harlot Rahab, undestroyed in the ruin of Jericho; like the house wherein the paschal lamb must be eaten; the house of the psalmist, where God makes men of one mind to dwell;[3] and like the Spirit in the form of a dove, a mild animal whose character the Church must bear and very different from wolves, dogs and serpents who, by their cruel instincts, represent heresy.[4] Heresies must come, to reveal which is the true grain, and which the chaff[5] that Christ has already condemned by His prophet.[6] The baptism of heretics and schismatics defiles the recipient. From it are born not sons of God but children of the devil. It is useless for schismatics to appeal to Christ's words: *Where two or three are gathered together in My name, there am I in the midst* (Matt. 18.20), for they falsify the Gospel by omitting the condition set by the Lord for his presence; the union of hearts in peace (Matt. 18.19). Here, St Cyprian has a special word for Confessors who desert the Church. A schismatic may be put to death for the name of Christ but he cannot be regarded as a martyr, for he has violated the first principle of martyrdom, by not maintaining fraternal charity and, as St Paul says, *though I give my body to be burned, and have not charity, it*

---

[1] *De Unit.*, 5: 'unum tamen caput est et origo una et una mater fecunditatis successibus copiosa: illius fetu nascimur, illius lacte nutrimur; spiritu eius animamur.' *CSEL* iii (1), 214.

[2] Ibid., 6. *CSEL* iii (1), 214–15.

[3] Ps. 67.7 [68.6]. St Cyprian quotes from the Old Latin version of the psalm: 'Deus qui inhabitare facit unanimes in domo.' The Vulgate renders it: 'Deus qui inhabitare facit unius moris in domo.' [4] *De Unitate*, 7–10. *CSEL* iii (1), 215–18.

[5] Ibid., 10. *CSEL* iii (1), 218–19. [6] Ibid., 11. *CSEL* iii (1), 219.

profiteth me nothing (I Cor. 13.3). 'Such a man can be killed, but he cannot be crowned.'[1] Indeed, he is worse than the man who has lapsed and now repents, for one laments his crime and seeks to be reconciled, while the other glories in his sin and draws other souls after him.[2]

The note of unity sounds so clearly and persistently in the *De Unitate* and indeed throughout the whole of Cyprian's writings, that it seems incredible that he could ever have been invoked as the patron of a schismatic church. There is, however, a particular declaration which defines the theological doctrine on which Donatism was to be founded: that the baptism of those outside the Church is a defilement which begets, not sons for God but children for the devil.[3] This particular assertion stems directly from the Cyprianic view of the Church. Strictly speaking, his doctrine does not recognize any possibility of schism, since the schismatic, by his own action, passes outside the Church, where alone can valid sacraments be administered.[4] St Cyprian invests the Christian bishop with the powers of the Jewish high priest under the old dispensation. Hence, a lapsed or schismatic bishop is deprived of all ability to administer valid sacraments by the Mosaic statute against uncleanness[5] and is moreover exposed to the punishment of the schismatics of the Old Testament, Korah, Dathan, and Abiram, whom the earth swallowed up alive.[6] This is the foundation of the Cyprianic view of the invalidity of sacraments administered by heretics: by passing outside the Church they have become spiritually dead. It is a simple doctrine and, inasmuch as it centres all the Christian life upon fellowship within the Church, wholly admirable. Its weakness is twofold. On the practical level, it works well for as long as bishops agree among themselves, since the bishop is the focal point for the faithful of his diocese. It does not, however, adequately provide for the problems raised by disagreement, when the disputants lack St Cyprian's largeness of mind which triumphed over the limitations of his theory. More serious is the

---

[1] Ibid., 14: 'occidi talis potest, coronari non potest.' *CSEL* iii (1), 223. Cf. *Epp.* 55, 17; 60, 4. *CSEL* iii (2), 636, 694.

[2] Ibid., 19. *CSEL* iii (1), 227.

[3] Ibid., 11: 'quando aliud baptisma praeter unum esse non possit, baptizare se opinantur: vitae fonte deserto vitalis et salutaris aquae gratiam pollicentur. non abluuntur illic homines sed potius sordidantur, nec purgantur delicta sed immo cumulantur. non Deo nativitas illa, sed diabolo filios generat.' *CSEL* iii (1), 219.

[4] 'Schism does not indeed divide the Church, which is essentially indivisible, but it separates its authors from the Church, and puts them in the position of apostates. These are natural and inevitable judgements according to the rigid view of unity held by St. Cyprian' (Willis, op. cit., pp. 100–1).

[5] *Epp.* 65, 2; 67, 1, 9. *CSEL* iii (2), 723, 735–6, 742–3. See Willis, op. cit., p. 103.

[6] *De Unit.*, 18; *Ep.* 73, 8. *CSEL* iii (1), 226; (2), 784. It will be remembered that this same view was repeated by the Donatists, in their denunciations of the Maximianists at Bagai, *De Gestis Cum Emerito*, 10.

narrow nature of the view taken of the sacraments—a tendency, if one dare to say so, to limit the operation of God's grace and to take no account of the overflowing of the divine mercy, which operates even beyond the bounds which God visibly sets for Himself in the economy of His Holy Church.[1]

It will be clear that both Donatist and Catholic theology represented a possible interpretation of the thought of St Cyprian. The Donatists on their side took their stand upon his theory of the sacraments. They asserted that the Catholic bishops descended from *traditores*. By the act of *traditio*, the predecessors of the Catholics had passed outside the Church. In consequence, none of the sacraments administered by them had any validity and it was therefore necessary to rebaptize any Catholic returning to the unity of the true Church which was, in their eyes, that of Donatus the Great.

The Catholics, no less than the Donatists, claimed St Cyprian as their master, but for them the starting-point was his charity and hatred of schism. They denied the allegation that their ancestors had been *traditores* and were able to bring forward much evidence to support that denial. But they equally grounded their argument on another factor: the wickedness of the Donatists in making a schism, even if their accusations had been justified. St Optatus of Milevis, the only apologist whom the Catholics produced before Augustine, speaks of the conduct of the schismatics in the same language of St Cyprian. He likens them to branches broken from the tree, shoots cut from the vine, or a spring severed from its source.[2] He denounces them, in the words of Jeremiah, for having forsaken the fountain of living waters and hewed for themselves broken cisterns which can hold no water.[3] Optatus, too, employs words drawn from the Song of Solomon: 'My beloved is one; one is my bride, and one my dove.'[4]

St Augustine was also ready to appeal to the authority of St Cyprian, for whom he had the deepest love and veneration. He calls him 'the blessed Cyprian, whom holy Mother Church counts among those few and rare

---

[1] Newman expresses this with great felicity in his poem 'Schism':

> What though their fathers sinned, and lost the grace
>   Which seals the Holy Apostolic Line?
> Christ's love o'erflows the bounds His Prophets trace
>   In His revealed design.

[2] Optatus, ii, 9: 'Intellegite vel sero vos esse filios inpios, vos esse fractos ramos ab arbore, vos esse abscisos palmites a vite, vos rivum conscisum a fonte. non enim potest origo esse rivus, qui parvus est et non de se nascitur, aut arbor a ramo concidi, cum arbor fundata suis radicibus gaudeat et ramus, si fuerit exsectus, arescat.' *CSEL* xxvi, 45. Cf. St Cyprian, *De Unit.*, 5. *CSEL* iii (1), 214.
[3] Optatus, iv, 9: 'Dereliquerunt fontem aquae vivae, et effossos ac detritos sibi fecerunt lacus.' *CSEL* xxvi, 116. Cf. *De Unit.*, 11. *CSEL* iii (1), 219.
[4] Optatus, ii, 13. *CSEL* xxvi, 48. Cf. *De Unit.*, 4. *CSEL* iii (1), 213.

men of most excellent grace'.[1] 'I will learn,' he says, 'if I can, from Cyprian's writings, if my sins do not hamper me and assisted by his prayers, the peace and consolation with which the Lord governed his Church through him.'[2] But he did not, on that account, hesitate to refute the Cyprianic doctrine of the invalidity of the sacraments of heretics. 'The authority of Cyprian does not frighten me,' he declares, 'because the humility of Cyprian restores me.'[3] Augustine bases his argument on the fact that Cyprian, despite his views on heretical baptism, refused to break the bond of unity with Stephen of Rome even when the pope threatened him with excommunication[4] and speaks indignantly of the self-deception of the Donatists who appeal, after the flesh, to Cyprian's authority, when they are refuted, after the spirit, by his charity.[5]

Nevertheless, the fact that St Cyprian's teaching was quoted by the Donatists in defence of their schism made it necessary for Augustine to examine closely the Cyprianic doctrine of the Church and the sacraments, and to put forward, not new doctrine, for he would certainly have denied that he was in any way an innovator, nor even corrected doctrine, for he would equally certainly have disclaimed any intention to set himself up as the judge of the doyen of African theologians; but, rather, a new interpretation of doctrine, an interpretation demanded by the changed conditions which the schism in the African Church had brought about.

What is the nature of the Church of Christ? According to the Donatists, it is a congregation of the saints, on earth as in heaven, and for that reason it will always be a tiny remnant.[6] At the time of the Diocletianic persecution there were *traditores* in every part of the world, but in Africa alone had the Church broken off relations with them. Thus, in every other part of the world the Church had become infected with the guilt of *traditio* and had thus ceased to be the Church.[7] Such a doctrine was simple and super-

---

[1] *De Bapt.*, VI, ii, 3.   [2] Ibid., V, xvii, 23.
[3] Ibid., II, i, 2: 'Non me terret auctoritas Cypriani, quia reficit humilitas Cypriani.'
[4] *De Unico Baptismo*, xiv, 23: 'Cum ergo Stephanus non solum non rebaptizaret haereticos, verum etiam hoc facientes vel ut fieret decernentes excommunicandos esse censeret, sicut et aliorum episcoporum et ipsius Cypriani litterae ostendunt, tamen Cyprianus cum eo in unitatis pace permansit.'
[5] *De Baptismo*, I, xviii, 28: '. . . de cuius sibi auctoritate isti carnaliter blandiuntur, cum eius caritate spiritaliter perimantur.'
[6] *C. Cresconium*, IV, liii, 63: '*In paucis*, inquis, *frequenter est veritas, errare multorum est*, non intellegens, quomodo a domino dictum sit paucos intrare per angustam portam, cum et multos dixerit ab oriente et occidente recubiteros cum Abraham, Isaac, et Jacob et in Apocalypsi demonstrentur ex omni gente et tribu et lingua milia candidatorum, quae nemo numerare possit. . . . noli ergo in conparatione multitudinis gentium catholicarum de vestra paucitate gloriari, sicut non vis, ut Maximianenses in conparatione multitudinis vestrae de sua paucitate glorientur.'
[7] *C. Epist. Parm.*, II, i, 2: 'Et quid tenebrosius praesumptionibus hominum, qui propter temere obiecta et numquam probata crimina traditorum, quae si vera essent, num-

ficially coherent; but it was, in fact, a thoroughly muddle-headed piece of argument, worthy of the men who formulated it. In the first place, it was inaccurate as regards fact. There was no evidence for the charge that the Catholic hierarchy descended from *traditores* and much to suggest that the founders of Donatism had committed the very crime of which they accused others. Augustine, from the composition of the *Psalmus contra Partem Donati* to the Conference of Carthage, constantly repeats that the Donatist account of the cause of the schism is untrue and that the facts which can be established from available records are quite otherwise. He does not, however, seek to base his argument on historical fact alone. On the contrary, he maintains that, even if the Donatist contention were true and the African Catholics had fallen into sin, it would not justify the Donatists in remaining in separation.

Parmenian, in his Epistle against Tyconius, had declared that the Christians of Gaul and Spain and Italy by association with the crimes of the *traditores* of Africa had become like them.[1] In Africa alone had there been the necessary separation of peoples.[2] Augustine denounces this suggestion. If it is true, what becomes of the promise to Abraham,[3] *In thy seed shall all the nations of the earth be blessed*?[4] The Donatists quoted St Paul in defence of their view: *Not only they who do these things, but also those who agree with them so doing.*[5] Did it seem a small matter to them to condemn so many great Christian peoples unheard, unless they could also dare to adduce the Apostle's words, but not his sense, against himself?[6] There is no prophecy in Scripture that sanctity should depart from the earth, and remain only in Africa,[7] and how could the Donatists dare to rebaptize a Christian coming, say, from Mesopotamia and utterly ignorant of the names both of Caecilian and Donatus?[8]

---

quam deo praeiudicarent quominus quod promisit impleret, perisse dicunt christianum nomen de tot gentibus in orbe terrarum et in sola Africa remansisse?' Cf. *C. Cresc.*, II, xxxvii, 46.

[1] *C. Epist. Parm.*, I, ii, 2: '. . . Gallos et Hispanos et Italos et eorum socios, quos utique totum orbem vult intellegi, traditoribus Africanis commercio scelerum et societate criminum dicit [Parmenianus] esse consimiles.'

[2] Ibid., I, iii, 4: 'Dicit etiam Parmenianus hinc probari consceleratum fuisse orbem terrarum criminibus traditionis et aliorum sacrilegiorum, quia, cum multa talia fuerint tempore persecutionis admissa, nulla propterea facta est in ipsis provinciis separatio populorum. [3] Gen. 22.18. [4] *C. Epist. Parm.*, I, ii, 2.

[5] Rom. 1.32: Non solum qui faciunt ea, sed etiam qui consentiunt facientibus.

[6] *C. Epist. Parm.*, I, iii, 5: 'Parum enim fuit tot et tantos populos christianos damnare inauditos, nisi etiam contra ipsum apostolum eius quidem verba, sed non eius intellectum depromere auderent?' [7] Aug., *Ep.* 129, 3.

[8] *Enar. in Ps.* 10, 5: 'Quod si nec te nec me polluit quod nescimus, quae causa est ut rebaptizes eos qui tempora traditionis et Macarianae invidiae non noverunt? Quae causa est ut christianos de Mesopotamia venientes, qui Caeciliani et Donati nec nomen audierunt, rebaptizare audeas, et neges esse christianos?'

Augustine lays stress upon the fact of universal extension as the mark of the Catholic Church. To the Donatist Petilian, who claimed for his own communion the style of Catholic and sought to interpret the word 'catholic' as meaning 'only' or 'whole' (*unicum sive totum*), Augustine replied with heavy irony: 'Of course, I have learned very little Greek, almost none in fact; but at least I can say without impertinence that I know that ὅλον does not mean "one" but "the whole", and καθ' ὅλου "universal".'[1] The verdict of the whole world condemns schismatics,[2] and for this reason Augustine urges the Donatists to return to the one true fold[3] and to the unity which is declared by communion with the Apostolic See,[4] and with the seven Churches of Asia addressed by St John the Divine in the Apocalypse and the recipients of the Pauline epistles.[5]

The Church of Christ, however, is not only One and Catholic; she is also Holy. To the question: In what sense are we to say that the Church here on earth is holy? the Donatists had a ready answer. The Church is holy by virtue of the holiness of her members. She is a congregation of the saints and it was for this reason that Majorinus and Donatus the Great called the faithful from communion with renegades and apostates. Many Donatists went further still. They did not merely claim to be a congregation of the saints but denied the name of Christian to anyone else. They were in the habit of saying to a Catholic whom they hoped to persuade to join them: 'You'd be a good man if you weren't a *traditor*. Think things over and become a Christian!'[6] Seldom in the history of the Christian Church has sectarian arrogance paraded its claims so blatantly.

Augustine flatly rejected this claim. In the first place, it fails the test of simple and observable fact: many Donatists did not live the lives of saints. Drunkenness was all too common among them,[7] the morals of many of their adherents were decidedly questionable,[8] the violence of the Circumcellions, with their clubs and their acid-throwing, was a byword and, finally, there was the life of Optatus of Thamugadi, Gildo's henchman of

---

[1] *C. Litt. Pet.*, II, xxxviii, 91.

[2] *C. Epist. Parm.*, III, iv, 24: 'quapropter securus iudicat orbis terrarum bonos non esse, qui se dividunt ab orbe terrarum in quacumque parte terrarum.'

[3] *C. Litt. Pet.*, II, xcvii, 224: 'Obsecramus vos: corrigimini, redite ad hanc evidentissimam totius orbis unitatem.'   [4] Aug., *Ep.* 53, i, 2.

[5] *C. Cresc.*, II, xxxvii, 46; IV, xxv, 32; *C. Litt. Pet.*, II, i, 3.

[6] *De Baptismo*, II, vii, 10: 'Bonus homo, si non esses traditor; consule animae tuae, esto christianus!'

[7] *C. Cresc.*, IV, lxiii, 77: 'negas eas quas dixi tyrannicas vestrorum in fundis alienis dominationes et bacchationes ebrietatum.' *C. Litt. Pet.*, I, xxiv, 26: 'bacchationes ebrietatum.'

[8] *C. Ep. Parm.*, II, ix, 19: 'an cum moechis particulam suam forte non ponunt, qui greges ebrios sanctimonalium suarum cum gregibus ebriis circumcellionum die noctuque permixtos vagari turpiter sinunt?'

evil memory.[1] In his criminal career was incarnate the refutation of the Donatist claim to exclusive sanctity. But this refutation by observed and observable fact was not the essential element in the charge which Augustine brought against the Donatists. In the spirit of St Cyprian he urged that, even if their claims had been substantiated by holiness of living, such holiness would have been nullified by the sin of schism.[2] Schism is a worse sin than *traditio*[3]—we remember St Cyprian's warning to the schismatic confessor, that his guilt is worse than that of the man who has lapsed, and now repents[4]—and even the high virtue of dedicated virginity will avail nothing to one who has deserted the Church.[5] The schismatic is as one waging civil war against his brothers and must inevitably lack the Holy Spirit, which is the spirit of charity.[6] Therefore it will avail him nothing, even if he should be burned alive for the faith.[7] Schism is an 'abominable separation'[8] and a 'devilish division'.[9] How different was the attitude of the great Cyprian, whom the Donatists profess to venerate and to follow![10]

To this Donatist dream of the church of the saints, Augustine opposes another: the Universal Church, spread throughout the world and containing within itself both good and evil until the final separation of the Last Day. It is the vision of Tyconius,[11] promised by God to Abraham[12] and

[1] C. Epist. Parm., II, i, 2: 'Insuper adversus nos facta sua clamant dicentes: *vae his qui ponunt lucem tenebras et tenebras lucem.* itane lux erat Optatus, et eum tota Africa tenebras appellabat? . . . facilius unus Optatus partem Donati in una Africa notissimus et apertissimus maculavit quam quilibet Afer traditor tot gentes per orbem terrarum etsi non dicam falsis criminibus accusatus, tamen, quod impudentissime negatur, ignotus.'

[2] C. Litt. Pet., I, xxiv, 26: 'Vestros autem fructus si consideremus, omitto tyrannicas in civitatibus et maxime in fundis alienis dominationes, omitto furorem circumcellionum et praecipitatorum ultro cadaverum cultus sacrilegos et profanos, bacchationes ebrietatum, et sub uno Optato Gildoniano decennalem totius Africae gemitum; omitto ista, quia sunt in vobis quidam qui haec sibi displicere ac semper displicuisse proclament. sed ea se dicunt, quia comprimere non possunt, pro pace tolerare; ubi se iudicio suo condemnant, quia, si amarent pacem, non discinderent unitatem!' Ibid., II, xcvi, 221.

[3] De Baptismo, III, ii, 3: 'cum etiam si vera crimina obicerent multo sunt maiora scelera haeresum et schismatum. . . .'

[4] Cyprian, De Unitate, 20. CSEL iii (1), 227–8.

[5] Aug., Ep. 208, 7 (ad Feliciam): 'Si enim de isto saeculo exires separata ab unitate corporis Christi, nihil tibi prodesset servata integritas corporis tui.' The virgin Felicia, to whom Augustine wrote, had been distressed by scandals in the Church and was tempted to go over to the Donatists.

[6] Aug., Ep. 185, x, 46: 'Apostolus Petrus quando salvatorem negavit et flevit et apostolus mansit, nondum acceperat promissum spiritum sanctum; sed multo magis isti eum non acceperunt, ubi a corporis compage divisi, quod solum corpus vivificat spiritus sanctus, extra ecclesiam et contra ecclesiam sacramenta tenuerunt et tamquam civili bello nostris contra nos erectis signis armisque pugnarunt.'

[7] Aug., Ep. 173, 6: 'Foris autem ab ecclesia constitutus et separatus a compage unitatis et vinculo caritatis aeterno supplicio punireris, etiamsi pro Christi nomine vivus incendereris.' Cf. Cyprian, De Unitate, 14: 'occidi talis potest, coronari non potest.'

[8] Aug., Ep. 43, viii, 21.   [9] De Bapt., V, ii, 2.

[10] De Bapt., IV, viii, 11; V, ii, 2; C. Cresc., II, xxxi, 39.   [11] C. Epist. Parm., I, i, 1.

[12] Ibid., I, ii, 2: 'quid dictum est ad Abraham? *In semine tuo benedicentur omnes gentes.*'

declared to us in the parables of the draught of fishes[1] and of the tares
which were sown among the wheat and which must grow there until the
final harvest.[2] If the communion of evil and good were destructive of the
good as the Donatists claimed, then the Church would have perished long
ago in the time of Cyprian himself.[3] Indeed, on this principle Cyprian
should not have remained in communion with Stephen of Rome, lest he
should have incurred the infection of a sinner; and by failing to do so he
ensured that the whole mass of the unity became corrupt, long before the
days of Majorinus and Donatus.[4]

The Church however was not destroyed in the past by the admixture of
good and bad among its members, nor does it perish now. The separation
will come at the Judgement and not before, for 'the field is the world, and
not Africa; and the harvest the end of the age and not the time of Donatus'.[5] The holiness of the Church is the holiness of Christ and not of man.
The Donatists quoted the text from Ecclesiasticus in defence of their
view: *As the judge of the people is himself, so are his ministers: and as the
ruler of the city, so are they that dwell in it*,[6] but, says Augustine, they
utterly fail to understand the meaning of the text.

> Let them understand that the one prince of the city is our Lord Jesus
> Christ, whose ministers are good. He is the ruler of His city Jerusalem,
> whose citizens accord with the dignity of the ruler, not to equality but
> according to His measure who said to them, *Ye shall be holy since I am
> holy*,[7] that is, according to a certain likeness, into which we are changed
> *from glory unto glory as by the Spirit of God*,[8] the gift of Him who makes
> us to be *conformed to the image of His Son*.[9] But the devil is the prince of
> the other evil people and the ruler of the city which in an allegory is
> called Babylon—a prince who, with his angels, is called by the Apostle
> Paul *ruler of this darkness*[10] that is, of sinners. And the devil's ministers
> are like him because they *transform themselves into ministers of righteous-
> ness* even as he *transforms himself into an angel of light*,[11] and the citizens

[1] *Psalmus c. Partem Don.*, 8–19. *C. Epist. Parm.*, III, iii, 19.

[2] Aug., *Epp.* 76, 2; 93, iv, 15; *De Unico Baptismo*, xvii, 31; *C. Cresc.*, II, xxxv, 44;
xxxvi, 45; III, l, 55; IV, xxvi, 33; lvi, 67; *C. Gaud.*, I, xxiv, 27.

[3] *De Baptist.*, II, vi, 8: 'Si ergo tali communione malorum pereunt iusti, iam ecclesia
temporibus Cypriani perierat. Unde igitur extitit origo Donati, ubi catechizatus est, ubi
baptizatus, ubi ordinatus, quando iam ecclesiam contagio communionis extinxerat? si
autem erat ecclesia, nihil obesse mali bonis in una communione potuerunt. quare vos
separastis?'

[4] *De Unico Baptismo*, xiv, 24: 'debuit ergo Cyprianus ab huius [sc. Stephani] communione discedere, ne cum fure concurreret, ne peccatis communicaret alienis, ne contagione inquinaretur inmundi, ne pollutus fieret tangendo pollutum, ne fermento
corrumperetur aliorum. Hoc ergo quoniam non fecit, sed cum eis in unitate permansit
tota ipsius unitatis tunc massa corrupta est nec perseveravit ecclesia, quae postea sanctos
istorum Maiorinum pareret et Donatum.'

[5] *C. Litt. Petil.*, III, ii, 3.   [6] Ecclus. 10.2.   [7] Lev. 19.2.
[8] II Cor. 3.18.   [9] Rom. 8.29.   [10] Eph. 6.12.
[11] II Cor. 11.15, 14.

of Babylon conform to their most evil ruler by deeds resembling his. But the manifest separation of these two peoples and two cities will be when the harvest is winnowed; until which times love bears with every part of the crop, lest while those who are the grain too hastily flee from the chaff, they impiously separate themselves from others of the grain.[1]

So, under the image of the two cities, which he had learned from Tyconius and was later to develop in the *City of God*, Augustine defines the holiness of the Church. It is not that she is a congregation of the saints —indeed, she cannot be in this world, for all her members are stained with the sin which they draw from Adam, and dare not say that they are free of all sin[2]—but she is sanctified by her ruler, who alone is the priest without sin, who has entered into the Holy of Holies.[3]

From the consideration of the nature of the Church, we pass to the doctrine of the sacraments, and especially baptism. Here, the Donatist case was based securely upon the teaching and example of St Cyprian. He had held that sacraments given outside the Church are not merely value-less but actively harmful.[4] The reason for his belief that a schismatic can-not administer valid sacraments springs as we have seen from his doctrine of the Church: heresy and schism put a man outside the Church com-pletely, as also, in the case of an ordained person, does serious sin, which renders him incapable of exercising a valid ministry because of the Levi-tical statutes about uncleanness. This was a dogma which the Donatists accepted. In defence of their view they quoted from Isaiah: *The transgressor that sacrifices a calf to me, is as he that kills a dog; and he that offers fine flour, as one that offers swine's blood; he that gives frankincense for a memorial, is as a blasphemer;*[5] from Exodus: *Let the priests that draw nigh to the Lord God be sanctified, lest perchance the Lord abandon them; when the ministers approach the altar let them not bring a sin in themselves, lest they die;*[6] and from Leviticus: *The man who has a blemish or defect, let him not approach to offer gifts to God.*[7] The validity of the sacraments depends on

---

[1] *C. Epist. Parm.*, II, iv, 9.

[2] Ibid., II, vii, 14: 'quamvis enim, in quantum ex deo nati sumus, non peccemus, inest tamen adhuc etiam quod ex Adam sumus, quia *nondum est absorpta mors in victoriam* (I Cor. 15.54), quod etiam in corporum resurrectione promittitur, ut omni modo beati et immaculati et incorrupti simus qui iam secundum fidem *filii Dei sumus*, sed secundum speciem *nondum apparuit quod erimus* (I Iohan. 3.2). nondum enim re, sed *spe salvi facti sumus. sees autem quae videtur, non est spes. quod enim videt quis, quid sperat? si autem quod non videmus speramus, per patientiam exspectamus.* quamdiu autem per patientiam exspectamus *redemptionem corporis nostri* (Rom. 8.23–25), non audeamus nos dicere carere omni vitio, ne ipsa superbia sit immanissimum vitium.'

[3] Ibid.

[4] Cyprian, *De Unitate*, 11: 'Non abluuntur illic homines sed potius sordidantur, nec purgantur delicta sed immo cumulantur.' Cf. *C. Litt. Pet.*, II, ii, 4.

[5] Isa. 66.3, LXX. Quoted *C. Epist. Parm.*, II, v, 10.

[6] Ex. 19.22; 30.20, 21. *C. Epist. Parm.*, II, vii, 12.   [7] Lev. 21.17. Ibid.

the worthiness of the minister, and Petilian of Constantine expresses this in
the most uncompromising fashion:

> What we look for is the conscience of the giver, giving in holiness, to
> cleanse that of the recipient. For he who knowingly receives faith from
> the faithless receives not faith but guilt. For everything consists of an
> origin and root, and if it have not something for a head, it is nothing, nor
> does anything well receive second birth, unless it is born again of a good
> seed.[1]

This was the Donatist doctrine and it was one, it must be emphasized,
which reflected a very ancient attitude in the Church, held by such great
figures as Cyprian of Carthage and Firmilian of Caesarea. It would have
been possible for Augustine to have argued along these lines himself and
to have turned the tables upon his antagonists by maintaining that, while
the charges which they had brought against the Catholics were unproved,
the fact of their own schism was undeniable and, on their own terms, invalidated their sacraments. Augustine, however, did not argue in this
fashion; partly, no doubt, because of his desire to bring the Donatist
masses into the fold of the Church,[2] but even more because the Roman
custom of not rebaptizing converted heretics—the same custom over which
Stephen had threatened to excommunicate Cyprian—had prevailed. You
cannot appeal to the *orbis terrarum* and, at the same time, disregard the
custom of the *orbis terrarum*. Moreover Augustine had, not merely a
greater range of vision than his opponents, but also an infinitely deeper
spiritual understanding of the operation of God through the sacraments.[3]
It is unjust to him to regard his theology as being largely shaped by
expediency;[4] he never disguises his horror of the crime of schism and dis-
approves of the action of episcopal colleagues who allow converts from
Donatism who have been rebaptized or who have been Donatist ministers
to exercise clerical office in the Catholic Church.[5] He was not, however,

---

[1] *C. Litt. Pet.*, III, xx, 23. Cf. I, i, 2–3 and II, iii, 6–v, 10, where, however, the words
'sancte'—'in holiness' and 'sciens'—'knowingly' are omitted, an omission which
caused Petilian to accuse Augustine of deliberate misrepresentation (III, xvii, 20).
Augustine retorted that this made no difference to his argument: 'Si *conscientia sancte
dantis attenditur quae abluat accipientis* et *qui fidem sciens a perfido sumpserit non fidem
percipit sed reatum*, unde abluitur accipientis conscientia, cum maculosam dantis ignorat
et cum fidem nesciens sumit a perfido? rogo, unde abluitur?' (ibid., III, xx, 23). On the
significance of Petilian's accusation, see Pierre Courcelle, *Recherches sur les* Confessions
de saint Augustin, 238–45, esp. 241.
[2] On this, see Willis, op. cit., pp. 152–4.
[3] See the comments of Frend, op. cit., p. 324.
[4] As Willis appears to do, op. cit., p. 153.
[5] *De Unico Baptismo*, xii, 20: 'nec ad clericatum admittantur, sive ab haereticis rebaptizati sint sive prius suscepti ad illos redierint sive apud illos clerici sive laici fuerint et
qui haec nostrorum neglegenter agunt et eos forte clericos in catholica faciunt vel esse
permittunt, quamvis a diligentioribus fraterno iure culpentur, tamen nec ipsi eis

prepared to have his own theology conditioned by that of his antagonists, but followed what he believed to be the truth without consideration of the consequences.

In the first place, on the historical level, he argued that the practice of rebaptism was not, and had not been, the custom of the universal Church, nor had it been known in Africa until the days of Agrippinus, Cyprian's predecessor in the see of Carthage.[1] It had been confirmed by Cyprian and his colleagues at the Council of 258[2] in opposition to pope Stephen; but afterwards the judgement of the universal Church had approved the practice of the Roman church.[3] The Donatists cling to the error of Cyprian while they disregard his virtues[4] and turn the human error of rebaptizing heretics into the diabolical presumption of rebaptizing Catholics.[5]

It is not only the facts of the past and the judgement of the universal Church which condemn Donatist theory. They have not been consistent to their own principles, as was shown in the case of the Maximianist schism. This, in Augustine's view, was a sign given by God to settle the controversy, so that the Donatists might be compelled to confess from their own actions what they refused to do when charity urged them.[6] Indeed, the condemnation of the Maximianists at Bagai and the subsequent reception of many of them back into the Donatist Church together with those whom they had baptized while in schism without any rebaptism, removed all possible pretext for argument.[7] Augustine urged his fellow

clericatum deferendum putant, nisi quos ab illis malis vel noverunt emendatos esse vel credunt.' This is the view of Augustine in 410; it is in accordance with the decision of the Council of Carthage of September 401 (see *MPL* xi, 1197–9).

[1] *De Baptismo*, II, vii, 12: 'Hanc ergo saluberrimam consuetudinem per Agrippinum prodecessorem suum dicit sanctus Cyprianus quasi coepisse corrigi; sed sicut diligentius inquisita veritas docuit, quae post magnos dubitationis fluctus ad plenarii concilii confirmationem perducta est, verius creditur per Agrippinum corrumpi coepisse, non corrigi.'

[2] Ibid., I, xviii, 28: 'Extant beati martyris Cypriani in eius litteris magna documenta, ut ad illum iam veniam de cuius sibi auctoritate isti carnaliter blandiuntur, cum eius caritate spiritaliter perimantur. nam illis temporibus, antequam plenarii concilii sententia quid in hac re sequendum esset totius ecclesiae consensio confirmaret, visum est ei cum ferme octoginta coepiscopis suis Africanarum ecclesiarum omnem hominem, qui extra ecclesiae catholicae communionem baptizatus fuisset, oportere ad ecclesiam venientem denuo baptizari.' [3] Ibid.

[4] *De Unico Baptismo*, xiii, 22: 'nam illud quod adiungit de episcopo Carthaginensi Agrippino, de inclito martyre Cypriano, de septuaginta praecessoribus Cypriani, quia hoc fecerunt et fieri praeceperunt, o quam detestandus error est hominum, qui clarorum virorum quaedam non recte facta laudabiliter se imitari putant, a quorum virtutibus alieni sunt!'

[5] Ibid.: 'ego autem ut quod de hac re sentio breviter dicam: rebaptizare haereticos, quod illi fecisse dicuntur, tunc fuit humani erroris, rebaptizare autem catholicos, quod adhuc isti faciunt, semper est diabolicae praesumptionis.'

[6] *De Baptismo*, I, vi, 8: 'Voluit enim Deus per Maximianistas eam [causam] finiri, ut quod caritate suadente nolebant exemplo suo cogente fateantur.'

[7] Ibid., I, v, 7. *C. Litt. Pet.*, I, xxviii, 29.

Catholics to keep the facts of the Maximianists in their mind as the most obvious, and most effective, argument against Donatist claims.[1] Their own actions refute the principles upon which they have built their case.

Augustine's view of the sacraments is based upon the conception of Christ, the high priest without sin,[2] who is the sole giver of sacramental grace because to Him alone belongs the power of conferring it, but who administers it by human agents.[3] What these administer is the baptism of Christ, whose sanctity cannot be corrupted by unworthy ministers, any more than the light of the sun is corrupted by shining through a sewer.[4] A little consideration will demonstrate this, since we are well aware that the materials with which the sacraments are administered—water, wine, bread, and the like—are corruptible, but the grace which they convey is not corruptible. So it is with human ministers; good or bad, their character does not affect the validity of the sacrament.[5] The *validity*, it must be emphasized, for its effect will depend on the recipient. The man who receives the sacraments in a state of sin receives them validly enough but they operate, not to his salvation but to his condemnation.[6] Nevertheless, if he repents and is reconciled with the Church, the sacraments begin to be effective for his salvation and there must be no question of repeating them. The Donatist attempt to defend rebaptism by the example of St Paul at Ephesus, who caused certain men who had been baptized with the baptism of John to be baptized with the baptism of Christ,[7] is wholly misleading, since the Apostle did not reiterate the baptism of John but gave the baptism of Christ to those who lacked it.[8] The schismatic and the heretic are in a quite different situation. The baptism they receive is the

---

[1] *C. Litt. Pet.*, I, xxvi, 29.   [2] *C. Epist. Parm.*, II, vii, 14.

[3] *In Iohan, Evang. Tr.*, 5, 6: 'Aliud est enim baptizare per ministrium, aliud baptizare per potestatem. Baptisma enim tale est, qualis est ille in cuius potestate datur; non qualis est ille per cuius ministrium datur.'

[4] *De Baptismo*, III, x, 15: 'Baptismus vero Christi verbis evangelicis consecratus et per adulteros et in adulteris sanctus est, quamvis illi sint inpudici et immundi, quia ipsa eius sanctitas pollui non potest et sacramento suo divina virtus adsistit sive ad salutem bene utentium sive ad perniciem male utentium. an vero solis vel etiam lucernae lux, cum per caenosa diffunditur, nihil inde sordium contrahit, et baptismus Christi potest cuiusquam sceleribus inquinari?'

[5] Ibid.: 'si enim ad ipsas res visibiles quibus sacramenta tractantur, animum conferamus, quis nesciat eas esse corruptibiles? Si autem ad id quod per illas agitur, quis non videat non posse corrumpi, quamvis homines per quos agitur pro suis moribus vel praemia percipiant vel poenas luant?'

[6] *De Unico Baptismo*, vi, 8: 'Quamobrem sicut nihil eis proderat ad salutem, qui verum deum ignorantes eum tamen colebant, immo et oberat ad perniciem, quod falsos deos simul colentes eidem vero deo sacrilegam iniuriam faciebant, sic nihil prodest haereticis ad salutem, quod extra ecclesiam verum baptismum per ignorantiam et tradunt et tenent, immo et obest ad damnationem, quod in sacrilega iniquitate erroris humani etiam divini sacramenti non per quam mundentur, sed per quam severius iudicentur, detinent veritatem.'

[7] Acts 19.1–5.   [8] *De Unico Baptismo*, vii, 11.

baptism of Christ, and it is not the Christian sacraments which they receive which make them heretical but their wicked separation.[1] For this reason, Augustine does not command the Donatists to cease to give the sacraments, but to cease to give them in separation; nor does he forbid their lay people to cease to receive, but to cease to receive in separation.[2] Indeed, he lays it down as a principle that, in a case of extreme necessity, a Catholic catechumen who cannot find a Catholic priest may receive baptism from a Donatist, so long as he guard in his heart the Catholic peace. If he should then die, the Catholic Church will reckon him among her members; and if he should survive and return to a Catholic congregation, his action will not merely not be condemned but will be applauded.[3] If the Donatists should ask: Since you accept our baptism, what are we supposed to lack, that you should think it necessary to urge us to join your communion? the answer is: It is not your baptism we accept, for the baptism which you confer is not yours, but the baptism of God and the Church, wherever it shall be found and by whomsoever it has been conferred.[4]

This is the kernel of Augustine's doctrine of the administration of the sacraments in general and of baptism in particular. The sacrament of a baptized person and the sacrament of giving baptism of an ordained person abide in them even if they depart from the unity of the Church. No harm can be done to either sacrament; and just as that baptism is accepted which cannot be lost by departing from the unity, so likewise must that baptism be accepted which has been conferred by a schismatic priest, who did not lose the power to administer the sacrament when he deserted the Church.[5] Certainly, the sacraments so administered have no salutary effect so long as the recipient remains outside the Church—Augustine likens

[1] Aug., *Ep.* 93, xi, 46: 'cum autem transitis ad nos, prius utique relinquitis, quod eratis, ne ad nos haeretici transeatis. "baptiza ergo me", inquis. facerem, si baptizatus non esses, aut si Donati vel Rogati, non Christi baptismo baptizatus esses. non sacramenta Christiana te faciunt haereticum sed prava dissensio.'

[2] *De Baptismo*, I, ii, 3: 'Non eis [schismaticis] itaque dicimus: "nolite dare", sed: "nolite in schismate dare", nec eis quos videntur baptizaturi dicimus: "nolite accipere", sed: "nolite in schismate accipere".' [3] Ibid.

[4] Ibid., I, xiv, 22: 'Frustra ergo nobis dicunt: "si baptismum nostrum acceptatis, quid minus habemus, ut nobis de vestra communione consulendum putetis?" respondemus enim: non baptismum vestrum acceptamus, quia non est baptismus ille schismaticorum vel haereticorum, sed dei et ecclesiae, ubicumque fuerit inventum et quocumque translatum.'

[5] Ibid., I, i, 2: 'Sacramentum enim baptismi est quod habet qui baptizatur, et sacramentum dandi baptismi est quod habet qui ordinatur. sicut autem baptizatus, si ab unitate recesserit, sacramentum baptismi non amittit, sic etiam ordinatus, si ab unitate recesserit, sacramentum dandi baptismi non amittit. nulli enim sacramento iniuria facienda est: si discedit a malis, utrumque discedit, si permanet in malis, utrumque permanet. sicut ergo acceptatur baptismus, quam non potuit amittere qui ab unitate discesserat, sic acceptandus est baptismus, quem dedit ille qui sacramentum dandi cum discederet non amiserat.'

them to health-giving medicines given to a man afflicted by a mortal
wound, the wound of schism, which must be cured before they can be of
any value[1]—but they cannot be destroyed and resemble the military
mark, the *nota militaris*, which can be borne and received by deserters,
but which ought not to be borne or received outside the army and yet
which must not be changed or reimposed when the deserter returns to
military duty.[2] Thus Augustine makes a clear distinction between baptism
and the right of conferring baptism. 'The right of conferring baptism
reposes only in the Church, as the Body of Christ; and only when so conferred and received can it have its full value. Yet where it exists among
schismatics, it is not to be rejected, but completed by the imposition of
hands for reconciliation, to make a man able in the fold of the Church
to enjoy all the blessings of the Holy Spirit.'[3] A fitting summary of Augustine's may be found in his fourth book against the Donatist Cresconius:

> Notwithstanding, we deal with these matters lest the unity of the har-
> vest should be deserted on account of evil dispensers of the sacraments—
> not their own, but the Lord's—who must, of necessity, be mixed among
> us, until the winnowing of the Lord's field. Now to make a schism from
> the unity of Christ, or to be in schism, is indeed an evil and a great evil,
> nor is it in any way possible that Christ should give to the schismatic
> what he has—not faith, but a sacrilegious error; or that a schismatic
> should cleave, in Christ, to the root; or that Christ should be the
> fountain head to the schismatic. And yet, if he give the Baptism of
> Christ, it shall have been given and if he receive, it shall have been
> received, not to eternal life but to eternal damnation if he shall per-
> severe in sacrilege, not by turning a good thing into evil but by having a
> good thing to his evil, so long as he has it being evil.[4]

From the doctrinal considerations of the Church and of the sacraments,
we turn to the third great topic which engaged Augustine's attention
during the Donatist controversy: the relation between Church and state
with regard to the coercion of religious dissidents. Augustine's views on

---

[1] *De Baptismo*, I, vii, 11: 'Quid ergo prodest homini vel sana fides vel sanum fortasse
solum fidei sacramentum, ubi letali vulnere schismatis perempta est sanitas caritatis, per
cuius solius peremptionem etiam illa integra trahuntur ad mortem?'
[2] Ibid., I, iv, 5: 'Intueantur etiam similitudinem notae militaris, quia extra militiam a
desertoribus et haberi et accipi potest, sed tamen extra militiam nec habenda nec accipienda est et reducto vel perducto ad militiam nec mutanda nec iteranda est.' Cf. *De
Symbolo*, viii, 16: 'Sed haereticis Baptismum non mutamus. Quare? quia sic habent
Baptismum, quomodo desertor habet characterem: ita et isti habent Baptismum; habent,
sed unde damnentur, non unde coronentur. Et tamen si desertor ipse correctus incipiat
militare, numquid audet quisquam et characterem mutare?' *C. Gaudentium*, I, xii, 13:
'In eis autem, qui hoc Sacramentum non ad auxilium, sed ad iudicium foris accipiunt,
quia nec in desertore violamus characterem regium, fit illud quod scriptum est, *caritas
cooperit multitudinem peccatorum*.'
[3] Willis, op. cit., 159–60.   [4] *C. Cresc.*, IV, xxi, 26.

this subject have been the source of much discussion and not a little condemnation, some of it extravagant. To avoid any misunderstanding, it may be said that, while some of his admirers may regret that he abandoned his earlier views, it is an exaggeration to speak of him as taking his place 'in the line of development which leads to the tortures and burnings of the Inquisition'.[1] The worst feature of Augustine's attitude to coercion is that he defended it on the ground of expediency, because it seemed to succeed in bringing about conversion where argument and exhortation failed; but instead of committing ourselves to denunciation, it is more useful to examine the change of circumstances and the development of his thought which led to those final conclusions which have been so often and so loudly deplored.

In the first place, certain general considerations are to be borne in mind, regarding the attitude of the Church to the state in the first three centuries, before the conversion of Constantine the Great and the promise which it gave of an entirely new order in the Roman world. During the first three centuries of its career, the Christian religion was the object of fierce, though spasmodic, persecutions, which were calculated by their very nature to bring out and throw into relief all those elements which were most hostile to secular authority. Nevertheless, with the obvious and famous exception of the Apocalypse of St John the Divine, with its amazing vision of Babylon the Great, mother of harlots and abominations and drunken with the blood of the saints and of the martyrs of Jesus—an exception produced by particular circumstances—the general attitude of the Christian Church was not one of hostility to the Roman state and the Roman order. Where the Faith was concerned, the Church was adamant; but in other matters she heeded the injunction of the Apostle, that every soul should be in subjection to the higher powers, which are ordained of God. Even in a writer like Tertullian, whom one might reasonably suppose to have an *a priori* dislike of the Empire, we find indeed a different view. In the treatise which he addressed in 212 or 213 to the proconsul, Scapula, who had broken the peace which the Church had enjoyed under his predecessors and begun a savage persecution, Tertullian is at pains to affirm the loyalty of the Christians: 'The Christian is an enemy of no man,

---

[1] As does W. Montgomery, *St Augustine*, 242. Cf. the very just observation of W. J. Sparrow-Simpson, *The Letters of St Augustine*, 113–14: 'It would be difficult to be more unhistoric and more unjust than to represent Augustine as a Torquemada born before his time. That his unhappy misinterpretation of the Scripture words formed a deadly precedent, and led to appalling consequences, is indeed only too painfully true. But Augustine is not the only great thinker who failed to anticipate the consequences of his teaching: consequences from which, it may be safely said, no man would have recoiled more completely.'

still less of the emperor; and since he knows him to be ordained of his God, it is necessary that he should love, revere, and honour the emperor, and wish for his safety and that of the whole Roman empire for as long as the world endure; for so long will the empire endure.'[1] The most diehard Roman patriot could hardly ask for a more loyal declaration. Elsewhere, Tertullian speaks of the emperor as being necessary for the stability of the age[2] and even maintains that it is the continued existence of the Roman Empire which prevents the coming of Anti-Christ.[3] Other Christian writers express a similar view. Melito of Sardis, in his Apology directed to Marcus Aurelius, promises that emperor happiness, if he will protect 'the philosophy', i.e. Christianity, which has grown up in the Roman Empire since the time of Augustus, from which time the power of Rome became great and splendid.[4] But, on a practical level, the Church was prepared to go even further than this, as was shown by the case of Paul of Samosata. Paul, after being deposed from the patriarchate of Antioch in 269, refused to surrender the bishop's house, which he continued to occupy until 272, when an appeal was made to the Emperor Aurelian when he occupied the city in the course of his first campaign against Palmyra. Aurelian's judgement, declaring the ownership of the house to pertain to the bishop recognized by the bishops of Italy and Rome, is of the greatest significance for many reasons; but the fact which must be stressed here is, that though the emperor was, in a strict sense, only giving judgement in a civil action regarding the ownership of a house, the issues involved were far wider, and the Christian community cheerfully accepted the ruling of a pagan emperor with regard to the definition of the lawful bishop of Antioch.[5]

With such a background, it is not difficult to recognize that the conversion of Constantine only accentuated the sense of the Church working within the Empire, and of a divine mission of the latter as well as of the former. The surprise sometimes expressed at the speed with which Christianity assumed the rôle of the official religion of the Roman Empire, dispossessing and finally outlawing her pagan predecessor and rival,

---

[1] *Ad Scapulam*, 2: 'Christianus nullius est hostis, nedum Imperatoris; quem sciens a Deo suo constitui, necesse est ut et ipsum diligat, et revereatur, et honoret, et salvum velit, cum toto romano imperio, quousque saeculum stabit. Tamdiu enim stabit.' *MPL* i, 700.
[2] *Apologeticus*, 21, 24: '. . . sed et Caesares credidissent super Christo, si aut Caesares non essent necessarii saeculo, aut si et Christiani potuissent esse Caesares.' *CSEL* lxix, 58–59.
[3] *De Carnis Res.*, 24: 'Quis, nisi Romanus status, cuius abscessio in decem reges dispersa antichristi superducet?' *CSEL* xlvii, 60.
[4] Melito, *apud* Euseb., *HE* IV, xxvi, 7.
[5] The episode is described by Eusebius, *HE* VII, xxx, 19, who remarks that the emperor adjudicated in the affair 'most justly' (αἰσιώτατα).

becomes less intelligible if the outlook of the past is remembered, and the raptures of Eusebius of Caesarea over the Emperor Constantine, the new David of the Messianic kingdom of Isaiah fulfilled in the Christian Empire, are readily explicable.[1] Indeed, only an austere spirit could fail to feel some sympathy with Eusebius as he rejoices in the spectacle of the emperor taking his place among the bishops at the Council of Nicaea and refusing to be seated until they gave their consent, in contrast to the imperial consistory where the courtiers stood in their master's presence. The triumph of Christianity after three centuries of hostility could hardly fail at the time to move the heart of any believer, even if today it is only too easy to see the dangers which such an alliance of Church and state held in store. But, rightly or wrongly, the events of Constantine's reign made it clear that he did not regard the Empire and the Church as two separate entities, but was fully prepared to intervene in the affairs of the latter; and further, that many Christians saw nothing objectionable in such imperial intervention.

Furthermore, so far as the Donatist dispute was concerned, both sides were willing to appeal to the secular arm, and to enlist its services when they could. At the last, it was the Catholics who succeeded in securing the favour of the state and the help of its officials in putting down their rivals; but it was the party of Donatus which first appealed to the Emperor Constantine,[2] and it was only when their appeal had been rejected that they began to express the sentiments of Donatus' remark to the imperial notaries: 'What has the emperor to do with the Church?'[3] But the passage of time altered their views, and the close of the year 361 (or, possibly, the beginning of 362) saw their exiled leaders appealing to the Emperor Julian for permission to return to Africa. The language of the petitioner is apt to be highly coloured and to bear little resemblance to the character of the ruler addressed; but by any standards, the phraseology of the Donatist bishops was fulsome in the extreme, if we may judge from the words, fatal to their cause from a controversial point of view: 'since with thee, justice

---

[1] This is not, of course, to deny the existence of another element in early Christian writing, which is expressed by Tertullian in *De Corona* and still more in the verses of Commodian, and which were to find reiteration in some of Augustine's references to the state. Such an ambivalence is, however, inevitable in a religion like Christianity, and does not seem to me to outweigh the positive attitude to the Empire which is generally to be found.

[2] Augustine dwells upon this in the *Psalmus c. Partem Donati*, ed. Anastasi, 101–3:

> Nam Donatus tunc volebat   Africam totam obtinere;
> tunc iudices transmarinos   petiit ab imperatore.
> Sed haec tam iusta petitio   non erat de caritate.

[3] Optatus, iii, 3. *CSEL* xxvi, 73.

alone holds sway',[1] which provided Augustine with a debating point which he was quick to seize, and to which he frequently returned.[2] It was not merely that the legal title of the Donatists to the churches which they occupied depended on the edict of the apostate emperor;[3] but it was the fact that they had publicly proclaimed, in effect, either that Christian sanctity, which had no place with Julian, was not justice, or else that the worship of demons was,[4] which destroyed their claim to be the Church of the Saints as surely as it demolishes that of being independent of the state.

But this was not all. The Donatists had had no scruples in employing the secular arm against their own schismatics, the Maximianists,[5] nor did they protest against the legislation against pagan sacrifices[6] but were, on the contrary, prepared to take the law into their own hands in their zeal for the suppression of the heathen.[7] Indeed, the picture which the Donatists spread about themselves, and which modern readers may be led to accept in discussing them, is utterly unlike the reality. Far from disdaining to appeal to the state, the Donatists were only too ready to do so, if they thought that they could gain any advantage. Primian, Petilian, and their allies did not hesitate to proceed to the imperial court to protest against the anti-Donatist edicts of 405 and even offered to debate the issue

---

[1] Aug., *Ep.* 105, ii, 9: 'Quibus [sc. filiis Constantini] succedens Iulianus, desertor Christi et inimicus, supplicantibus vestris Rogatiano et Pontio libertatem perditioni parti Donati permisit: denique tunc reddidit basilicas haereticis, quando templa daemoniis, eo modo putans Christianum nomen posse perire de terris, si unitati ecclesiae, de qua lapsus fuerat, invideret et sacrilegas dissensiones liberas esse permitteret. haec erat eius praedicanda iustitia, quam supplicantes Rogatianus et Pontius laudaverunt dicentes homini apostatae, quod apud eum sola iustitia haberet locum.'

[2] *Enar. in Ps.* 36, ii, 18; *C. Epist. Parm.*, I, xii, 19; *Ep.* 93, iv, 12; *C. Litt. Petil.*, II, xcii, 203; xcvii, 224.

[3] *C. Epist. Parm.*, I, xii, 19: 'Nec pro eis [sc. Donatistis] aliquid promulgasse invenitur nisi apostata Iulianus, cui pax et unitas christiana nimium displicebat. . . . aliorum autem imperatorum leges quam vehementes adversus eos latae sint quis ignorat?'

[4] Ibid.: '. . . dixerunt enim, quod aput eum sola iustitia locum haberet. quid ergo aliud dixisse reperiuntur nisi vel christianam sanctitatem non esse iustitiam, quae aput illum nullum haberet locum, aut honorem daemonum esse iustitiam?' *Ep.* 93, iv, 12: 'sed tamen nondum ab eis [Donatistis] separati eratis [Rogatistae], quando Iuliano imperatori in sua petitione dixerunt, quod apud eum sola iustitia locum haberet; quem certe apostatam noverant, et idololatriis deditum sic videbant, ut aut iustitiam esse idolatriam faterentur, aut se scelerate mentitos negare non possent, ut apud eum dicerent solam locum habere iustitiam, apud quem magnum locum cernerent habere idolatriam.' *C. Litt. Petil.*, II, xcii, 203: 'quibus verbis . . . et idololatria Iuliani et apostasia iustitia est appellata.'

[5] *C. Epist. Parm.*, I, x, 16: '. . . ita caeci et insani, ut, cum schismaticos suos Maximianistas per potestates a catholicis imperatoribus missas de basilicis excluserint et vi magna iussionum et auxiliorum cedere sibi compulerint, arguant catholicam, si pro ea catholici principes tale aliquid fieri praeceperint.' Cf. Aug., *Ep.* 93, iv, 12.

[6] Aug., *Ep.* 93, iii, 10: 'Quis enim nostrum, quis vestrum, non laudat leges ab imperatoribus datas adversus sacrificia paganorum?'

[7] *C. Epist. Parm.*, I, x, 16: 'Cur ergo ipsi [Donatistae] ubi possunt templa [pagana] subvertunt et per furores circumcellionum talia facere aut vindicare non cessant? an iustior est privata violentia quam regia diligentia?'

between themselves and the Catholics in the presence of the Praetorian Prefect.[1] This offer was refused; but it is a further demonstration of the fact that the Donatist leaders were willing, on occasion, to accept the intervention and the adjudication of the civil authority.[2]

Finally, there is a third consideration, which affects any estimate which we may make on the subject of state coercion in the Donatist controversy, and that is the attitude of the state itself. Here again, it is easy for the ecclesiastical historian and still more for the theologian with only an incidental interest in the historical background, to assume too readily that the policies of Church and state were identical, and that the former had only to call and the latter would hasten to obey. Such an attitude would probably be wide of the mark in most periods of European history; but it would be wholly erroneous in respect of the later Roman Empire. The Roman state was an institution with a policy of its own; it had existed before the adoption of Christianity, and no emperor, however convinced a Christian he might be, was prepared to regard himself merely as an earthly executive of the Church Militant. On the contrary, he was an autocrat, the embodiment of the will of the Roman people, elected by the army and the Senate and not appointed by the Church. It is significant that, in the eastern part of the Empire, although the emperor was usually crowned by the Patriarch of Constantinople, this was not constitutionally essential because 'the consent of the Church was not formally necessary to the inauguration of a sovran'.[3] Indeed, when St Optatus of Milevis remarked that the state is not in the Church, but the Church is in the state,[4] he was enunciating what would appear to be merely a truism to any constitutionally minded Roman citizen, however devoutly Christian.

Now the attitude of the Roman state towards the Donatists was not exactly identical with that of the Catholics. Certainly, successive Roman emperors from Constantine to Honorius were anxious to bring the schism to an end and there is no reason to doubt their sincerity as Christians in this matter, but they had another consideration as rulers: that of attempting to maintain the peace and good order of a province whose importance, as a source of supply to Italy, could not be overrated. For this reason, official policy with regard to the Donatists was frequently restrained by the desire to avoid alienating a large section of the population, and repeated efforts were made, from the mission of Paul and Macarius in 347 to that of

---

[1] *Gesta Coll. Carth.*, iii, 141. *MPL* xi, 1388.   [2] See Frend, op. cit., p. 268 and *n*[3].
[3] Bury, *History of the Later Roman Empire*, i, 11. The whole chapter is of interest in this connection.
[4] Optatus, iii, 3: 'non enim respublica est in ecclesia, sed ecclesia in republica, id est in imperio Romano,' *CSEL* xxvi, 74.

Count Marcellinus in 411, to bring about reconciliation between the rival churches. These attempts alternated with periods of repression, like Constantine's measures from 317 to 321, or the days of the Macarian persecution, 348 to 361, when the authorities' patience had been tried to the uttermost. But the Macarian persecution was brought to an end by the accession of Julian the Apostate, whose short reign gave the Donatists an opportunity to recover their strength, an opportunity which was to stand them in good stead for many years afterwards. Furthermore, from the reign of Julian until the Edict of Unity of 405, they were in a strong position, since it was not easy to proceed against them legally except on a charge of violence. The only general law which could be invoked was that of Theodosius the Great against heresy,[1] but the charge was not one which could easily be established when the Donatists claimed that they were a schism and not a heresy and when it was difficult to adduce any doctrinal issue on which they were demonstrably unorthodox. Hence the importance of legal actions, like the one recorded by Augustine in the *Contra Epistulam Parmeniani*[2] or that brought against Crispinus,[3] to establish the fact that Donatism was as reprehensible as Manichaeism or Arianism. Fortunately for the Catholics, the imperial authorities were already coming to the same conclusion; but it was not until the Edict of Unity of 405 that the emperor definitely decided that Donatism must be ended at all costs, and until that year, the only real instrument in the hands of the Catholic, apart from the general law against heresy, were the edicts against rebaptism,[4] which clearly only applied in a limited number of cases.

Furthermore, if we regard 405 as the turning-point in the attitude of the emperors towards Donatism, it is significant that the decision was made, not as a result of the appeal by the Council of Carthage of 404 but because of the assault made on Maximian of Bagai. It was his scars, and not the arguments of the Catholic delegates, which decided the emperor to take action.[5] Hitherto the government, despite general fulmination against heresies, had shown remarkable restraint in dealing with the African schism. What really changed its policy was the revelation that events in Africa were not simply a doctrinal controversy but social disorders consti-

---

[1] *Cod. Theod.*, XVI, v, 21, the *lex generalis* of *C. Epist. Parm.*, I, xii, 19. *Cod. Theod.*, XVI, v, 37, though dated 400, is to be assigned to 405. See ed. of Mommsen and Meyer, I, 2, Berlin, 1905, 89, note to II, viii, 24.
[2] *C. Epist. Parm.*, I, xii, 19.
[3] *C. Cresconium*, III, xlvii, 51; Aug., *Ep.* 88, 7; Possidius, *Vita*, 12.
[4] *Cod. Theod.*, XVI, vi, 1 (20 February 373); vi, 2 (17 October 377). It was under these laws that Augustine threatened Crispinus in 402 for the compulsory rebaptism of his tenants. Aug., *Ep.* 56.
[5] Aug., *Ep.* 88, 7.

tuting a serious menace to the stability of an important province.[1] From then onward, the policy of the state was one of ever-increasing coercion, intermitted only with a brief gesture of toleration after the crisis of the usurpation of Attalus.[2] In 410, the threat of capital punishment was added to the existing penalties[3] and it was repeated in 414.[4] We have, however, no satisfactory evidence as to the frequency with which it was inflicted. It is at least clear that Donatist bishops like Emeritus[5] and Petilian[6] were able to continue to operate.

From the foregoing, it will appear that the conditions under which Augustine expressed and modified his views regarding religious persecution were a great deal more complicated than have sometimes been supposed and that any picture which shows him as an isolated thinker, converted from a belief in toleration to an enthusiasm for persecution and bringing the Church with him must be rejected. Too many factors are involved for such a simple analysis. Moreover, the change in Augustine's views was neither so abrupt nor so thoroughgoing as may at first sight appear. It has already been shown that there was nothing in the tradition of the Church which would cause Augustine to reject, on first principles, the possibility of the state intervening in support of the Church. Nevertheless, at the beginning of his anti-Donatist polemic he was opposed to the use of force and preferred to rely on the power of argument. This was the weapon which had proved so effective against the Manichees and would, he hoped, prove equally effective against the Donatists. In 397, in an anti-Manichaean treatise, he had written:

> It was our part to choose the better course, that we might find a way to your correction, not by contention, strife, and persecutions, but by mild consolation, friendly exhortation, and quiet discussion, as it is written: *The servant of the Lord must not strive, but be mild towards all men, apt to teach, patient, in meekness correcting those that think otherwise.*[7]

In such an excellent frame of mind Augustine turned his attention to the Donatists. In his earlier correspondence with them, he is at pains to

---

[1] Cf. the comment of Boyd, *The Ecclesiastical Edicts of the Theodosian Code*, 55: 'The social aspects of the Donatist schism also made it a subject of legislation in the later fourth and early fifth centuries. The emperors from Constantine to Honorius, with the exception of Constans, permitted the Donatists to remain unmolested. The edicts of Gratian and Valentinian which mentioned them were not enforced outside of Italy. But finally when the schism broadened from an ecclesiastical quarrel to a source of civil disorder, persecution was resorted to.'

[2] Mansi, *Concilia*, iii, 810: 'Legationem susceperunt contra Donatistas Florentius, Possidius, Praesidius et Benenatus episcopi, eo tempore quo lex data est, ut libera voluntate quisquis cultum christianitatis exciperet.'   [3] *Cod. Theod.*, XVI, v, 51.

[4] Ibid., XVI, v, 54.   [5] *C. Gaudentium*, I, xiv, 15.

[6] Ibid., I, xxxvii, 47.   [7] *C. Epist. Fund.*, i, 1 (II Tim. 2.24, 25, Old Latin version).

emphasize that he has no wish for any man to be coerced into the Catholic communion; rather, his policy is to try to bring his opponents to discussion, where the facts can be made clear without rancour. He assures the Donatists that he does not regard them as heretics:

> But though the doctrine which men hold be false and perverse, if they do not maintain it with passionate obstinacy—especially when they have not devised it with the rashness of their own presumption but have accepted it from parents who had been misguided and had fallen into error—and if they are with anxiety seeking the truth and are prepared to be set right when they have found it, such men are not to be counted heretics.[1]

Unhappily for such sentiments, debate did not, in fact, bring the results which Augustine had anticipated. He himself comments gloomily upon the unsatisfactory attitude of the people who attended his debate with the Donatist bishop, Fortunius, held towards the end of 397 or the beginning of 398,[2] and he was early made aware that his persuasive oratory was of little avail against the dour fanaticism of his adversaries.

What changed Augustine from opposition to support of persecution, and when did it occur? Was it a dramatic *volte-face*? Such questions are, in fact, badly put, and misleading. Augustine has supplied us with his own account of the reason for his conversion, in the letter written in 408 to Vincent, the Rogatist bishop of Cartenna:

> I yielded to these opinions which my colleagues urged. For my original view was nothing else than this: that no one should be compelled to the unity of Christ, but we must employ words, fight by disputation, and conquer by reasoning, lest we should have feigned Catholics whom we knew to be avowed heretics. But this opinion was overcome, not by the arguments of those who opposed me, but by the examples which they adduced. For first, there was the case of my own city which, when it was wholly Donatist, was brought to Catholic unity by fear of the imperial laws, and which we now see hating your disastrous opinions, so that it would never be believed that Donatism had ever existed within it. And so it was with many others, whose names they brought to my notice, that by these facts I should know to be rightly able to be understood what is written: *Give occasion to a wise man, and he will be wiser.*[3] For how many, as we surely know, were already touched by the truth most clearly revealed, and even then wished to be Catholics, but put it off from day to day, fearing the enmity of their own people! How many were bound by heavy fetters, not of truth, which you never presumed to urge, but by long-established custom, so that in them was fulfilled that divine decree :*A stubborn servant will not be reproved with words; for*

---

[1] Aug., *Ep.* 43, 1. Tr. by W. J. Sparrow-Simpson.
[2] Aug., *Ep.* 44, i, 1. [3] Prov. 9.9. Old Latin version

even if he understand, still he will not obey![1] How many for that reason thought the true Church to be that of Donatus, because security made them sluggish, disdainful, and indolent! How many had the way to us barred by the rumours of slanderers, who noised it abroad that we offered some strange thing at God's altar![2] How many believed that it was of no account in what sect a Christian might be, and therefore remained in the Donatist party, because they had been born there, and no one compelled them to depart from thence and to transfer to the Catholics![3]

This passage is of great importance in clarifying Augustine's view about coercion by the secular authority. Originally he rejected it, because he had been afraid that it would only bring about hypocritical conversions. Such a view is a reasonable and laudable one but not strikingly enlightened or humane, and certainly not a liberal one by any standards.[4] The outlook is a higher utilitarianism, which would be changed if it could be shown that persecution did effect sincere conversions. Moreover, it does not consider the question of the right of the secular authority to intervene to suppress heresy. So far as Augustine was concerned at the beginning of his career, this consideration was a purely academic one in which he was not particularly interested. His concern was with the Church, not the state. So in the lost work, the *Contra Partem Donati*, where he considered only to reject the possibility of the intervention of the state, he did so, he afterwards declared, because he was not then aware either of the extremes of violence to which the Donatists were prepared to go or of the beneficial effects of coercion.[5] But this view was not shared by many of his colleagues; and at the Council of Carthage of 404 there was a strong party in favour of a petition to the emperor for more rigorous action against the Donatists, which urged its case by pointing to the results which had been obtained where it had been applied.[6] Augustine, however, was still opposed to this

---

[1] Prov. 29.19. Old Latin version.

[2] Perhaps a reference to Donatist accusation of Manichaean orgies among Catholics.

[3] Aug., *Ep.* 93, v, 17.

[4] 'Schon diese Stelle zeigt, dass Augustins Stellungnahme zu dieser Frage nur durch Opportunitätsgrunde bestimmt war.' M. Zepf, 'Zur Chronologie der antidonatistischen Schriften Augustins' in *Zeitschrift für die Neutestamentliche Wissenschaft*, viii (1929), 54. This article is most helpful in establishing Augustine's thought in the matter of state coercion of heretics.

[5] *Retract.*, ii, 31 [5]: 'Quorum in primo libro dixi *non mihi placere ullius saecularis potestatis inpetu scismaticos ad communionem vehementer artari.* et vere mihi tunc non placebat, quoniam nondum expertus eram, vel quantum mali eorum auderet inpunitas vel quantum eis in melius mutandis conferre posset diligentia disciplinae.'

[6] Aug., *Ep.* 185, vii, 27: 'Ita enim existimabamus eis territis et nihil tale facere audentibus posse libere doceri et teneri catholicam veritatem, ut ad eam cogeretur nemo, sed eam, qui vellet, sine formidine sequeretur, ne falsos et simulatores catholicos haberemus. et quamvis aliis fratribus aliud videretur iam aetate gravioribus vel multarum civitatum et locorum exempla curantibus, ubi firmam et veram catholicam videbamus,

plan. His sole concession was that a deputation should be sent asking for the enforcement of existing laws, in order that the Donatists might be dissuaded from terrorizing those who were willing to become Catholics of their own volition.[1] In fact, by the time the emissaries arrived at Rome, the government had already made up its mind to take action, and far more drastic action than that requested by the African episcopate.[2] As we have seen the imperial decision, however gratifying it might be to certain elements among the African Catholics, was made quite independently of their petition.

These facts enable us to establish fairly closely the date of Augustine's conversion from an opponent of state action to an apologist for it. In 404 he was opposed to it; by 408 he is defending it. The crucial period came during the application of the Edict of Unity of 405, when Augustine could see for himself the success of compulsion. In this respect, it is important not to misunderstand the passages of the Contra Epistulam Parmeniani[3] and the Contra Litteras Petiliani, which seem to suggest that he was advocating coercion at an earlier date.[4] The Contra Epistulam Parmeniani was written when Parmenian had already been dead for several years and in answering it Augustine had to deal with arguments which referred to events of an earlier period. Indeed, since Parmenian died about 391/2,[5] it is clear that his letter could hardly have dealt with the edict of Theodosius the Great against heresy, which was not issued until 15 June 392,[6] but could only have envisaged the legislation against rebaptism[7] and the repressive measures of Macarius, which were still fresh in the minds of his followers. But the fact that he referred to these matters, dwelling with characteristic Donatist unction on the theme of 'the Church persecuted for righteousness' sake',[8] meant that Augustine had to answer; and he did so, by arguing that, if the state has power to punish the works of the flesh enumerated by the Apostle and offences such as poisoning and idolatry, why should it not restrain heretics and impious dissensions? And why should the Donatists complain of this, when they themselves let loose the furies of the Circumcellions against the temples of the pagans, availed

quae tamen ibi talibus beneficiis dei constituta esset atque firmata, dum per priorum imperatorum leges ad communionem homines catholicam cogerentur, obtinuimus tamen, ut illud potius, quod dixi, ab imperatoribus peteretur. decretum est in concilio nostro, legati ad comitatum missi sunt.'

[1] Aug., Ep. 185, ii, 25.

[2] Ep. 88, 7: 'Sed sic cum legati Romam venerunt, iam cicatrices episcopi catholici Bagaitani horrendae ac recentissimae imperatorem commoverant, ut leges tales mitterentur, quales et missae sunt.'

[3] As does Willis, op. cit., pp. 128–9.

[4] See Zepf, op. cit., pp. 53–56

[5] Monceaux, Histoire littéraire, iv, 53.

[6] Cod. Theod., XVI, v, 21.

[7] Ibid., XVI, vi, 1 (373); XVI, vi, 2 (377).

[8] C. Epist. Parm., I, ix, 15.

themselves of the aid of the secular authority in their campaign against the Maximianists,[1] and appealed to the apostate Julian as one, in their own words, with whom justice alone held sway?[2] Similarly, against Petilian, Augustine defends the lawfulness of an appeal to the state to expel the Donatists from churches which have been unjustly usurped[3] and once more draws a parallel between such action by the Catholics against the Donatists and their own proceedings against the Maximianists.[4] Nevertheless, although action of this sort may be lawful, it must not exceed the limits of Christian mildness[5] and Augustine does not personally identify himself with this particular point of view.[6] He writes as an apologist for the Catholics, not as a private theologian.

After 405 the situation has altered. Augustine saw, or thought he saw, that the arguments of his colleagues had been right and his own view mistaken. Conversions took place, and he was satisfied that they were genuine.

Some now say: Even then we wanted to become Catholics. Thanks be to God, who gave us occasion for doing it and cut short our hesitant delaying! Others say: We knew what the truth was, but some habit or other held us. Thanks be to God, who has broken our chains, and brought us to the bond of peace! Others say: We did not know this was the Truth nor did we wish to learn; but fear made us attentive, since we were afraid that we should perhaps suffer the loss of temporal goods without any gain of eternal things. Thanks be to God, who has stirred us from our negligence with the goad of terror, that by being anxious we should, at the very least, consider these matters which, being secure, we should never concern ourselves to know! Others say: We were afraid to enter because of false rumours, which we should not have known to be false if we had not entered, and would not have entered unless we had been compelled. Thanks be to God, who has driven away our fear with His rod and taught us by experience what empty vanities lying rumour spread abroad about His Church! So it comes that we now believe that those things also are false which the authors of this heresy alleged, when their posterity fabricates such worse lies. Others say: We thought it was of no account where we held the faith of Christ; but thanks be to God, who has gathered us in from division and shown us that it befits the One God that He should be worshipped in unity![7]

---

[1] C. Epist. Parm., I, x, 16.   [2] Ibid., I, xii, 19.

[3] C. Litt. Petil., II, xix, 43: 'Cur non etiam hoc fieri potest, ut per ordinatas et legitimas potestates de sedibus, quae inlicite usurpantur vel ad iniuriam dei retinentur, pius expellat impium et iustus iniustum?' Cf. C. Cresc., III, xliii, 47.   [4] Ibid., II, xx, 45.

[5] C. Epist. Parm., I, xiii, 20: 'Postremo, si quid forte aliquando immoderatius in eos factum est, ut christianum excederet lenitatem, displicet omnibus frumentis messis dominicae, id est in Christo laudabilibus christianis.'

[6] C. Litt. Petil., II, xxiii, 53: 'nam neque occido te nec probas te ab aliquo occidi nec, si probes, ad me pertinet quicumque te occiderit, sive secundum potestatem legitime sibi a domino datam iuste fecerit sive sicut messis dominicae palea cupiditate aliqua mala scelus admiserit.'   [7] Aug., Ep. 93, v, 18.

Augustine's enthusiastic tone will probably fail to rouse the same emotion in the breast of the modern reader, who may feel that such a declaration would carry more conviction coming from an ex-Donatist rather than from a representative of the party in whose interest pressure was being applied. There is however no reason to suppose that Augustine himself had any misgivings, in the case of the types of converts whom he had specified; and it seems probable that converts who were willing to become Catholics but who hesitated to do so without the stimulus of compulsion, through fear of Circumcellion reprisals, may have been fairly numerous.[1] At all events, there is no doubt that by 408 the success of the imperial measures against Donatism had done its work in convincing him that his previous attitude had been mistaken. We now see him as an apologist for coercion, and the unfortunate text *Compel them to come in* is pressed into service.[2] But even here, we should beware of laying upon it an emphasis which it does not deserve in the context. One of the most important occasions upon which Augustine uses it was in the letter written in 417 to Count Boniface, the Roman officer who was afterwards to play a tragic and somewhat ambiguous rôle in African affairs during the last years of Augustine's life. Boniface, a simple soldier by almost any standards, had written to Augustine for guidance on religious affairs, desiring to know what the difference might be between a Donatist and an Arian. (Augustine's answer seems to have done little good for the recipient, since Boniface, after professions of orthodox zeal and insincere yearnings for a monastic life, was later to take an Arian for his second wife.) In the letter sent in answer to the Count's question Augustine, after distinguishing between the two heresies, gives the general an account of the rise and progress of the Donatist movement, painting a grim picture of the Circumcellions, their fanaticism, and of the helplessness of the Catholics in the face of their violence.[3] Hence arose the necessity of appealing to the emperors. If it is objected that the Apostles did not desire coercive legislation against their opponents, Augustine replies that times are changed. Before the Roman Empire became Christian men saw the exemplification of the words of the Psalmist: *The kings of the earth stand up and the rulers*

---

[1] Similar statements have been heard in the twentieth century coming from the lips of persons of Western Democratic sentiments. Certain utterances by the British in Malaya, during the emergency there in the 40's and 50's, are of the same pattern as those of Augustine during the later stages of the Donatist controversy. In each case, actions of a decidedly unliberal character are defended (perhaps justly) on the ground of their long-term results. It is hardly logical to defend the one and condemn the other, unless one holds that terrorism under the pretext of religion deserves an immunity not accorded to that practised for political ends.

[2] Aug., *Ep.* 185, vi, 24. Cf. *C. Gaud.*, I, xxv, 28.

[3] Aug., *Ep.* 185, iii, 12–iv, 18.

take counsel together against the Lord and against his anointed;[1] but since the conversion of Constantine, the true picture is in the words of the same psalm: *And now, ye kings, understand; be learned ye that are judges of the earth. Serve the Lord with fear and rejoice unto him with reverence*,[2] that is, repress irreligion with due severity.[3]

> What prudent man could say to kings: 'Do not care by whom the Church of your Lord in your realm is constrained or oppressed; it is no concern of yours who in your kingdom wishes to be religious or sacrilegious', when you cannot say to them: 'It is no concern of yours who is chaste or who unchaste in your kingdom.' Why then, when man is given free will by God, should adultery be punished and sacrilege permitted? Is it a less weighty matter that the soul should not keep faith with God than that a woman should be faithless to her husband? or if those things are to be punished more mildly which are done, not out of contempt but from ignorance of religion, are they, for that reason, to be ignored?[4]

Augustine recognizes that it is better for men to be led to the worship of God than to be compelled by force. It may, however, be necessary; and though we begin by fear perfect love will, in the end, cast out fear.[5] Why then should not the Church compel her lost sons to return if the lost sons compel others to go to perdition?[6] And so we have the injunction: *Compel them to come in.*

This was Augustine's final attitude; but it did not, as we have tried to show, represent the total reversal of his opinions as many critics have claimed. His earlier view had been more opportunist and his later position more reasonable than has usually been recognized. When all allowance has been made, it is difficult to see how any state could have tolerated Donatism in the form in which it expressed itself, or that the Church is to be condemned for welcoming the action of the state in putting down a movement in which savage violence was so prominent a characteristic. Indeed, if Augustine had been content merely to accept and to apply the legislation against the Donatists, he would have escaped a good deal of the odium which has been heaped upon his name by scholars who never knew the nature of a life lived under the threat of the terrorist or experienced any conditions other than those procured by the existence of a well-drilled police force. Unfortunately for himself Augustine, with characteristic honesty, admitted that he had changed his mind—a change which no one, in the circumstances, could condemn—but then proceeded to rationalize

---

[1] Ps. 2.2.   [2] Ps. 2.10–11.   [3] Aug., *Ep.* 185, v, 19.
[4] Ibid., v, 20.   [5] Ibid., vi, 21.
[6] Ibid., vi, 23: 'Cur ergo non cogeret ecclesia perditos filios, ut redirent, si perditi filii coegerunt alios, ut perirent?'

his outlook, thereby providing ammunition both for those who wished to justify persecution on religious grounds, and for those who wished to denounce it in the person of the man to whom the persecutors appealed. In this, he has had an unfortunate destiny and the Donatists have proved better propagandists than they knew.

It is to be hoped that it is possible today to take a more balanced view of Augustine's teaching about the repression of Donatism than was possible a few generations ago. It is clear that we cannot judge him by the standards of nineteenth-century Liberalism, which have not worn well; nor is it just to make him the father of subsequent defenders of persecution, with whom he would have had no sympathy whatsoever. Furthermore, some allowance must be made for the conditions of his age and particularly those prevailing in North Africa in his lifetime. Most of us would probably agree with an Oxford historian who, writing of the attitude of the English bishops towards the followers of Wycliffe, remarked: 'That a man should be burnt for a refusal to accept the church's teaching as authoritative, we may all now agree, is monstrous. But it was possible to think differently in 1401 without being a monster.'[1] What is true of fifteenth-century England is even more true of fifth-century Africa, where there was no question of anyone being burnt, unless it were Gaudentius of Thamugadi and his companions, with their threats of suicide by incineration. Augustine, during the years in which he had struggled with Donatism, had been tried to the uttermost, and towards the end, the strain began to tell. Such seems to be the case of the celebrated passage in his work against Gaudentius in which, replying to the Donatist bishop's contention that the effects of official repression were driving numbers of Donatists to suicide, Augustine, after rehearsing the long and depressing list of crimes perpetrated upon Catholics by Donatist violence, declares abruptly that it is better for a few abandoned men to perish than that innumerable souls, whose way to salvation they impede, should burn with them for ever in Hell.[2] The declaration shocks us; but we should bear in mind the past history of the controversy.

That the lessons learned from the struggle with Donatism lingered in Augustine's mind and coloured his subsequent thought cannot be denied. During the Pelagian controversy, when pope Zosimus appeared to have been misled by the defence of Pelagius and Caelestius, the African episcopate had no hesitation in appealing from him to the emperor and Augus-

---

[1] K. B. McFarlane, *John Wycliffe and the Beginnings of English Nonconformity*, London, 1952, 187.
[2] *C. Gaud.*, I, xxii, 25: 'Tolerabilius enim longe pauciores pertinacissimi vestri suis praecipitiis vel submersionibus vel ignibus pereunt, quam innumerabiles populi illis eorum salutem impedientibus incendio cum illis aeterni ignis ardebunt.'

tine was ready to defend such an appeal in his writings against Julian of Eclanum.[1] Two considerations should, however, be remembered. At the end of his career, in the controversy with Julian, Augustine reaffirmed the fact (which he repeated in his *Retractations*) that it was the violence of the Circumcellions which had first turned him to approve the idea of action by the secular arm.[2] Secondly, it is important to distinguish between Augustine's theory and his practice. Even when he had come to regard the use of force as justifiable in order to bring recalcitrant Donatists into the fold, he disapproved of brutality and set his face against the death penalty, even for the gravest offences. In a letter written in 412 to his friend, Count Marcellinus, the imperial commissioner who had presided at the Conference of Carthage of the previous year and who was now entrusted with the task of enforcing the imperial decrees, Augustine appeals for leniency to be shown to a party of Circumcellions who had murdered one Catholic priest and cruelly mutilated another. He is disturbed by the possibility that Marcellinus may decide to punish the offence by the full rigour of the law, and writes to abjure him, by his faith in Christ, and by the mercy of Christ, not to proceed to extreme measures. The Church does not desire that criminals should be punished on the principle of an eye for an eye and a tooth for a tooth; rather, she prefers that they should be deprived of the opportunity to work evil by imprisonment or that their energies should be given an outlet by useful labour without the loss of life or limb.

> Christian judge, fulfil the duty of a tender father; in your anger against the crime, remember to consider the claims of humanity, and when you punish the crimes of wicked men, do not yourself give way to lust for vengeance but rather direct your will to heal the wounds of the sinners. Do not renounce the fatherly zeal which you showed in conducting the interrogation, when you secured a confession of atrocious crimes, not by the rack, the irons, or the fire, but by the use of the rod—a form of correction employed by teachers of the liberal arts, by parents, and often even by bishops in their ecclesiastical judgements. [This last observation sheds a rather lurid light on the discipline of an episcopal court in Augustine's day; but it must be remembered that it was usual in the criminal courts of that time to employ torture to secure a confession, and the Emperor Valentinian had even caused it to be applied to senators, in cases of high treason, in the previous century.] You showed leniency

---

[1] *Op. Imp. c. Iul.*, i, 10: 'Absit a christianis potestatibus terrenae reipublicae, ut de antiqua catholica fide dubitent, et ob hoc oppugnatoribus eius locum et tempus examinis praebeant: ac non potius in ea certi atque fundati, talibus, quales vos estis, inimicis eius disciplinam coercitionis imponant. Quod enim propter Donatistas factum est, eorum violentissimae turbae fieri coegerunt, ignorantes quid ante sit gestum, quod eis fuerat ostendendum: quales vos turbas Deus avertat ut habeatis; Deo tamen propitio non habetis,'
[2] *Retract.*, ii, 31 [5].

in discovering the crime; do not be more cruel in punishing it; for it is more important and necessary to discover crime, than to punish it. . . . Do not let the power to punish make you harsh, whose gentleness was not shaken by the need to investigate. Do not send for the executioner now that the crime has been proved, when you were not willing to employ the torturer to discover it.[1]

Marcellinus was not the only recipient of such letters. Augustine addressed another, about the same time, to his brother, the proconsul Apringius,[2] while two years later the African *vicarius*, Count Macedonius, was the object of yet another such request, which he granted in a courteous letter containing, however, a tactfully expressed suggestion that life would be easier if the bishop of Hippo could manage to keep to his proper sphere,[3] only to receive in reply a letter explaining that, while Augustine abhorred the crime and did not desire that it should go unpunished, he pitied the sinner and desired his conversion. 'It is only too easy to hate bad men because they are bad; it is less common, but it is religious, to love them because they are men.'[4] He argues that bishops ought to intercede for the guilty for fear lest having been condemned in this world they may die in such a manner that they suffer for ever in the next.[5] He refers Macedonius to an occasion when the count himself interceded in the church of Carthage on behalf of a cleric with whom the bishop was angry. If it were right for Macedonius to attempt to mitigate the rigours of ecclesiastical discipline, it must equally be right for a bishop to attempt to soften the severity of secular discipline, particularly when the life of the accused is at stake. He reminds Macedonius that all men are sinners[6] and urges the bishop's right to intercede.[7] The effect of this lengthy letter upon Macedonius must have been very gratifying for the author, for the count replied in a short, but very complimentary letter,[8] which Augustine acknowledged in his turn, disclaiming the wisdom which Macedonius had ascribed to him,[9] but rejoicing to find him an ardent seeker after truth and urging him to love and serve God. Seldom have Church and state debated together so fruitfully and, withal, so graciously.

---

[1] Aug., *Ep.* 133, 2.   [2] Aug., *Ep.* 134.
[3] Aug., *Ep.* 152, 2: 'pro his quoque interveniendum putat sacerdotium vestrum, de quibus adeo futuri spes nulla est, ut etiam in praesenti eadem criminis ratio perseveret.'
[4] Aug., *Ep.* 153, i, 3: 'facile est enim atque proclive malos odisse, quia mali sunt, rarum autem et pium eosdem ipsos diligere, quia homines sunt.'
[5] Ibid: 'ideo compellimur humani generis caritate intervenire pro reis, ne istam vitam sic finiant per supplicium, ut ea finita non possint finire supplicium.'
[6] Ibid., iv, 10–v, 14.   [7] Ibid., vi, 17–19.
[8] *Apud* Aug., *Ep.* 154.
[9] Aug., *Ep.* 155, i, 1: 'Quamvis sapientiam, quam mihi tribuis, in me non agnoscam. . . .'

In these letters we see a different Augustine from the one which certain of his critics have conjured up. Here, instead of the great persecutor and the apologist for persecution, we see the servant of Christ, anxious to mitigate the harshness of the law and, in its place, to extend the charity without which all other virtues are vain by reminding those in authority that, since we are all sinners, we must never let our horror of the crime overcome our love for the sinner. In fact, of course, the division between these two Augustines is an imaginary one based upon a distorted picture of the saint's views upon the function of the state when it deals with the affairs of the Church. What these views were, in the matter of dealing with religious dissidents like the Donatists, it has been the task of this chapter to try to establish. The wider issues of Church and state in the disposings of the Divine Providence were, at a later date, to be developed by Augustine in the most influential of his writings, the *City of God*.

8

The Pelagian Controversy: the Course

Reniement de saint Pierre. Dire au Christ: je te resterai fidèle, c'était déjà
le renier, car c'était supposer en soi et non dans la grâce la source de
la fidélité. Heureusement, comme il était élu, ce reniement est devenu
manifeste pour tous et pour lui. Chez combien d'autres de telles vantardises
s'accomplissent—et ils ne comprennent jamais.

SIMONE WEIL

Batter my heart, three person'd God . . .
                                        for I,
Except you'enthrall mee, never shall be free,
Nor ever chast, except you ravish mee.

JOHN DONNE

THE PELAGIAN controversy, with the discussion of the nature of Grace
and of Predestination to which it gave rise, is, apart from the literary
interest of the *Confessions* and of the *City of God*, the aspect of St Augustine's life and thought which has most impressed posterity. The very title
accorded to him, 'the Doctor of Grace', proclaims it. This is not to suggest
that the views which he expressed have always commanded universal
support. They would never fulfil the requirements of the so-called Vin-
centian canon as doctrine received 'always, everywhere, and by all'—
though it remains a debatable point as to how much Christian doctrine
would survive that somewhat exacting test. And it may be added that it is
easier to hold strong, and especially hostile, views on Augustinian teaching
than to devote time and thought to the examination of what he actually
said and the circumstances in which he said it. It is, of course, always
easier to oppose and denounce than to understand; and it may be admitted
that Augustine has not been altogether fortunate in his disciples. Any
author who numbers Gottschalk, Calvin, and Cornelius Jansen among his
expositors is much to be pitied. The connection generally held to exist
between Calvinism and the teaching of the bishop of Hippo is likely to
prejudice many modern readers at the outset. As long ago as 1880 William
Bright, Regius Professor of Ecclesiastical History in the University of
Oxford, could write: 'In our time, too, the recoil from Calvinism has been
singularly vehement and destructive; and students who come fresh to St
Augustine's Anti-Pelagian writings will probably be more "offended"

than their predecessors of two or three centuries back at some extreme statements on Grace and the Fall into which he is led by his controversial intensity.'[1] The recoil of which Bright spoke is likely still to be operative in the second half of the twentieth century, even though the optimism which characterized so much of the Liberal Theology of the beginning of that century is no more. Many persons who would indignantly repudiate any suggestion that they held liberal opinions in theology find aspects of Augustine's teaching a scandal and a stumbling-block. Such sentiments are understandable and may be reconciled with perfect orthodoxy. Nevertheless, it would be a mistake to allow a repulsion inspired by certain features of the saint's thought to blind the student to the depth and profound truth of Augustine's religious thought. Furthermore, we must beware of any mental attitude which promises to explain Augustine away in the light of a preconceived notion of the development of his thought, such as may be found in the violent, and not always accurate, little book by Thomas Allin, published posthumously in 1911. In this work, Allin maintained that there were two distinct theologies in Augustine's writings: an earlier, or 'catholic' doctrine; and a later one, produced 'by the maturer workings of his mind'—the theology of the writings against Pelagius. 'Unfortunately,' he went on, 'whenever these later tendencies of Augustine's teaching are pointed out in our own days, there are to be found writers of a certain class who point us to the earlier and better teachings of his Catholic period, altogether forgetting the fact that in his later days he had given them up completely. One would hardly attempt to defend the later absolutism of Pio Nono by quoting his early liberalism. Nor would one strive to prove Dr Pusey to be a lover of German theology in his later years by pointing to an early book of his in praise of German thought.'[2] It may be questioned whether the parallels which Allin suggested are really fair ones; but the arbitrary division of Augustine's thought into earlier and later periods, with a suggestion of progress (or regress, if the word be preferred), is one which must not be accepted without question, but subjected to careful examination and scrutiny. That Augustine changed his opinion on some matters no one will deny, and we have his own evidence in the *Retractations*, published towards the end of his life, in which he put on record the circumstances which had led to the composition of his various books and indicated points on which he had changed his mind. He does not, however, consider himself seriously to have altered his opinions regarding Grace and Free Will; and there is, therefore, no justification for

---

[1] William Bright, *Select Anti-Pelagian Treatises of St Augustine*, xiii.
[2] Allin, *The Augustinian Revolution in Theology*, London, 1911, 108–9.

an *a priori* contrast between Augustine's earlier and later writings in the fashion of Allin. Rather, we should consider the fact that Augustine saw the corpus of his writings as a cohering whole with each part supporting the rest and recognize that we cannot dismiss any part of his writings out of hand, as views abandoned with the passage of the years, but must rather compare such views with other works, to see if they are really as contradictory as some would have us believe. One consideration at least ought continually to be borne in mind: whether he was an innovator or not, Augustine did not regard himself as bringing fresh doctrine into the Church but as defending the accepted faith; and the support which he found suggests that many other Catholic Christians of his day were of the same opinion.

Before beginning an account of the events of the Pelagian controversy, it would be well to remind ourselves of a significant fact with regard to Grace and to Predestination, namely, that while they are closely connected, the former is a peculiarly Christian doctrine in a way that the latter is not.[1] Grace, to use Augustine's language, is a help or an aid, without which we cannot love and serve either God or our neighbour. Christ's sayings declare this again and again. *Without Me, ye can do nothing.*[2] *Ye have not chosen Me, but I have chosen you.*[3] *No man can come unto Me, except the Father, which sent Me, draw him.*[4] *And I, if I be lifted up from the earth, will draw all men unto Me.*[5] By definition, Grace is gratuitous; it is given by God and undeserved by men. The labourers in the vineyard who had borne the burden and heat received no greater wages than those who were hired at the eleventh hour;[6] and in the parable of the great supper, when the invited guests made excuse, the master of the house sent his servants out into the highways and the hedges to compel passers-by to come in.[7]

Examples such as these of the Divine initiative are confirmed by others which reveal another element: that of Divine prescience. When Simon Peter vehemently protested his devotion and loyalty, Christ replied with a warning of the approaching denial.[8] More terrible are the sayings regarding Judas Iscariot: *the Son of Man goes as it is written of Him; but woe unto*

---

[1] Seeck, bitterly hostile to Augustine, performs a useful service by drawing attention to the non-Christian philosophical background of Predestination, *Geschichte des Untergangs der antiken Welt*, vi (1920), 20: 'Denn wenn er auch die Prädestination als erster in die rechtgläubige Theologie eingeführt hat, so war sie doch nicht nur in der griechischen Philosophie schon seit Jahrhunderten vorgebildet, sondern auch der Donatist Tyconius hatte ganz Ähnliches gelehrt.'   [2] Iohan. 15.5.
[3] Ibid., 15.16.   [4] Ibid., 6.44.
[5] Ibid., 12.32.   [6] Matt. 20.1–16.
[7] Luc. 14.23.   [8] Matt. 26.34; Marc. 14.30; Luc. 22.34; Iohan. 13.38.

him by whom the Son of Man is betrayed : it had been good for that man if he had not been born,[1] and the declaration that offences must come, *but woe to that man by whom the offence cometh.*[2] And there is a hint, not merely of prescience but of Predestination—a hint which Augustine was powerfully to develop—in Christ's saying that the mighty works which were done in Chorazin and Bethsaida and left them unmoved, would have converted Tyre and Sidon to whom they were not vouchsafed.[3] It is not necessary to turn to St Paul to find the doctrine of Grace and a declaration of Divine foreknowledge and the ensuing possibility of Predestination. The words of Christ Himself are sufficient.

Nevertheless, there is much in the Gospels which may be quoted as proclaiming the freedom of man's choice, and placing upon the individual the responsibility for his actions. The would-be disciple is told to take up his cross and follow the Master.[4] Judgement is declared because light has come into the world, and men preferred the darkness, because their deeds were evil.[5] The servant who buried his talent is condemned,[6] while the virgins who took no oil for their lamps are excluded from the marriage feast.[7] Christ denounces those who hear His sayings but fail to do them, and likens them to the man who built upon sand.[8]

It is apparent, then, that an appeal may be made to the Gospels and not only to St Paul to establish the doctrines of Grace, Predestination, and Free Will. All have their place in Christian doctrine; but the emphasis laid upon them in the daily life of the faithful will be determined by the particular circumstances. A teacher or spiritual director without any intention of detracting from the primacy of prevenient Grace may, nevertheless, tend to lay stress on the need for personal effort. It must be altogether rare for a man to be suffered to remain in a state of deliberate sin on the strength of a plea that he has not yet received the gift of Grace which would enable him to abandon it. This is hardly to be wondered at. The Christian teacher will reply that Grace is not lacking, but the sinner has failed to respond to the gift of Grace through the exercise of his free will. There is, however, a danger that the Christian moralist, particularly if he has himself been preserved from the fiercest temptations, may lay undue stress upon the power of the will, forgetting the words of Christ, *Without Me ye can do nothing.* It is not a matter for wonder that the greatest saints, with that deep spiritual understanding of dogma which is one of the marks

---

[1] Matt. 26.24, 25; Marc. 14.21.   [2] Matt. 18.7; Luc. 17.1.
[3] Matt. 11.21; Luc. 10.13.
[4] Matt. 10.38; 16.24; Marc. 8.34; 10.21; Luc. 9.23; 14.27.
[5] Iohan. 3.19.   [6] Matt. 25.24–28.
[7] Matt. 25.1–13.   [8] Matt. 7.26–29; Luc. 6.49.

of sanctity, have not only been more conscious of their sins than other men but have always proclaimed their own helplessness: *Not I, but the Grace of God which was with me*,[1] and declared, as the Lord commanded: *We are unprofitable servants; we have done that which was our duty to do.*[2]

The monk Pelagius, whose name, perhaps unjustly, has become indelibly associated with the heresy which minimizes the need for Grace, was by nature an ascetic and a moralist.[3] A native of the British Isles, he was a well-educated man with a profound knowledge of the Bible and a respectable familiarity with the classical authors and the Christian Fathers. The date of his birth is uncertain, and may fall anywhere between AD 350 and 380. He was a layman and was often called a monk, although there is no evidence that he was ever formally associated with a religious community —a fact which would not inspire the same surprise in the fifth century as it would in the fifteenth or the twentieth. It is usual, in writing of him, to record that his life, so far as is known, was innocent of scandal, although it is not easy to see, given his particular views, how he could have commanded attention if he had ostentatiously failed to practise what he preached. However, it is only just to emphasize his reputation for virtue. He was a friend of the saintly Paulinus, bishop of Nola,[4] and Augustine himself always spoke of Pelagius' personal character with respect. His motives for leaving Britain are not known and have been the subject of conjecture;[5] but there is good reason to think that he had been resident in the city of Rome for many years before he left it in 409,[6] in the face of the threat to the city by the army of Alaric the Goth.

The very evil reputation which has clouded the name of Pelagius for centuries has, in late years, been somewhat modified by the labours of scholars,[7] so that today he has been, if not exactly rehabilitated, at least cleared of some of the more extravagant charges which have been levelled against him. It is possible that the pendulum has swung too far and that the heresiarch now enjoys a more favourable reputation than he deserves; but we are at least better able to understand his mentality and motives than were our predecessors. We can no longer think of him as a rationalist and his system as fundamentally godless. Such accusations may possibly

---

[1] I Cor. 15.10.   [2] Luc. 17.10.

[3] The best general modern study of the life and career of Pelagius is Georges de Plinval, *Pélage : ses écrits, sa vie et sa réforme*, Lausanne, 1943. In English, the most recent work is John Ferguson, *Pelagius : A Historical and Theological Study*, Cambridge, 1956.

[4] Aug., *Ep.* 186, i, 1.

[5] See Plinval, op. cit., pp. 63–71; Ferguson, op. cit., pp. 42–44.

[6] Aug., *Ep.* 177, 2: 'in urbe Roma, ubi ille diu vixit'; *De Pecc. Orig.*, xxi, 24: 'in urbe Roma, ubi diutissime vitam duxerat.'

[7] Notably Alexander Souter. See Torgny Bohlin, *Die Theologie des Pelagius und ihre Genesis*, Uppsala/Wiesbaden, 1957, 1ff.

be brought against his followers and expositors and we can still speak of the heresy of Pelagianism; but Pelagius himself is less heterodox than the system to which he has given his name. He certainly did not deny the need for Grace, and the essential nature of baptism looms large in his writings.[1] If we are to understand Pelagius and his thought, we must recognize the nature of the opposition against which he fought: Manichaeism.[2] It was against the determinism which was implicit in the Manichaean doctrine of the evil character of Matter and the idea of the Two Souls that Pelagius directed his polemic[3] and asserted the power of man's free will. He seems himself to have been endowed with a temperament singularly free from the storms and stresses of temptation, and this would tend to make him intolerant of excuses which appealed to the frailty of human nature. Such a man would inevitably be repelled by the very different experiences of Augustine, as was revealed by a famous episode which occurred at Rome in 405, when a certain bishop quoted, in Pelagius' hearing, the passage in the tenth book of the *Confessions*, in which Augustine, having terminated the autobiographical element of the work, turns to the contemplation of the mercy of God, which had brought him from the temptations and sins of his youth to the freedom of the yoke of Christ:

> My whole hope is in Thy exceeding great mercy and that alone. Give what Thou commandest and command what Thou wilt. Thou commandest continence from us, and when I knew, as it is said, that no one could be continent unless God gave it to him, even this was a point of wisdom, to know whose gift it was. For by continence we are bound up and brought back together in the One, whereas before we were scattered abroad among the many. For he loves Thee too little who loves along with Thee anything else which he does not love for Thy sake, O Love, who dost burn forever and art never quenched. O Love, O my God, enkindle me! Thou commandest continence; give what Thou commandest, and command what Thou wilt.[4]

These words provoked a furious reaction from Pelagius. Here in the words of one of the leading luminaries of western Christendom was expressed all that he found most intolerable in the excuses of the slothful. The repetition of the phrase: *Da quod iubes, et iube quod vis!*— 'Give what Thou commandest, and command what Thou wilt!' proved too

[1] Bohlin, op. cit., pp. 15–45. The researches of Herr Bohlin confirm the traditional view that Grace meant little more for Pelagius than man's natural endowment, the enlightenment of his darkened mind, and the remission of sins in baptism.

[2] And also Arianism. See Bohlin, pp. 10–15.

[3] Cf. the comment of Plinval, op. cit., p. 217: 'Une philosophie simple et ingénieusement présentée complète les règles practiques: elle est surtout de tendance anti-manichéenne et anti-prédestinationiste.'

[4] *Conf.*, X, xxix, 40. Tr. Outler, p. 225.

much. He cried out: 'I cannot bear it!' and a violent altercation with the bishop was barely averted.[1] In this, the first recorded encounter between the views of the protagonists in the Pelagian controversy, we seem to have what is virtually an epitome of their respective temperaments: the Doctor of Grace, conscious of his utter dependence on divine aid; and the preacher and spiritual director, well aware of the readiness of human nature to find excuses for avoiding spiritual responsibility. But such a contrast, although dramatic, is misleading. Augustine had far more practical experience of the difficulties of parochial ministry than Pelagius and it is easy, in following the course of the controversy, to forget that Augustine the theologian was writing, not from a chair of Moral Theology, but from the day-to-day pre-occupations of administering a diocese containing as many sinners, with as many excuses and explanations, as his adversary ever encountered. It is a possible view that Augustine so concerned himself with theory that he forgot practical facts; it is certain that he was never preserved from the daily contemplation of these same facts.

It would seem that, about this time, the conceptions which have come to be regarded as characteristically Pelagian were taking shape in the mind of their founder. These were, first, a conception of Grace as being either a natural faculty or, at best, a form of illumination and cleansing from sin by baptism. This found expression in a letter to St Paulinus of Nola, written in 405 or 406,[2] to which Pelagius afterwards appealed as a proof of the orthodoxy of his views. Augustine, however, when he read it, found Grace barely mentioned, and then in the sense of the natural powers of human nature bestowed by God, rather than in the specifically theological con-notation. Indeed, this theological Grace appeared to be inserted briefly, as if the writer were afraid that its absence would be noticed; but even then in a form which made it impossible to say whether Pelagius meant the remission of sins, the teaching and example of Christ, or the aid to human nature and doctrine given by the inspiration of burning and illuminating charity.[3] Secondly, and closely connected with the theory of Grace, went a

---

[1] *De Dono Persever.*, xx, 53: 'Quid autem meorum opusculorum frequentius et delectabilius innotescere potuit, quam libri *Confessionum* mearum? Cum et ipsos ediderim antequam Pelagiana haeresis exstitisset; in eis certe dixi Deo nostro, et saepe dixi: "Da quod iubes, et iube quod vis!" Quae mea verba Pelagius Romae, cum a quodam fratre et coepiscopo meo fuissent eo praesente commemorata, ferre non potuit, et contradicens aliquanto commotius, pene cum eo qui illa commemoraverat litigavit.'

[2] See Plinval, op. cit., pp. 226–7.

[3] *De Grat. Christ.*, xxxv, 38: 'Hanc ergo epistulam legi et inveni eum paene per totam non immorari nisi in facultate et possibilitate naturae, et paene ibi tantum dei gratiam constituere; christianam vero gratiam tanta brevitate sola nominis commemoratione perstringit, ut nihil aliud videatur quam eam tacere timuisse. utrum tamen eam in remissione peccatorum velit intellegi an etiam in doctrina Christi, ubi est et conver-sationis eius exemplum, quod aliquot locis suorum opusculorum facit, an credat aliquod

particular doctrine of the Fall. Pelagius denied that Adam's sin injured his descendants, or that there was any transmission of his fault in consequence of his transgression. The primal innocence of our first ancestor is renewed in each of his descendants and thus any doctrine of Original Sin is ruled out at the very beginning. Nor is physical death a penalty and a result of the Fall, but a natural consequence of human life. Adam's death was, however, a personal punishment, inflicted upon him for having disobeyed God's command.[1] This was a view which was to be developed later by Julian of Eclanum with the argument that there would have been no need for marriage and the commandment to increase and multiply if there had been no death.

Both Augustine and Pelagius were to accuse the other of innovation; but in fact, each could quote traditional support for his views. Augustine could point to his old teacher, St Ambrose, for support in his doctrine of Original Sin,[2] and it is with obvious delight that he quotes St Cyprian for the benefit of an African congregation.[3] On the other hand, Pelagius' views about Original Sin would not have seemed strange to Tertullian who, though he was the first Latin writer to use the term *vitium originis* to describe the blemish which man's nature has suffered since the Fall,[4] nevertheless urged delay in administering baptism, on the ground that there was no need for innocent children to hurry to the remission of sins,[5] while Pelagius' general theory of the nature of man and his condition after

adiutorium bene agendi adiunctum naturae atque doctrinae per inspirationem flagrantissimae et luminosissimae caritatis non apparet omnino.' Cf. Aug., *Ep.* 186, i, 1: 'Quo libro id continetur et multipliciter atque abundanter adseritur, quod etiam quibusdam litteris agit ad tuam venerationem datis, ubi dicit non se existimari sine gratia dei defendere liberum arbitrium, cum possibilitatem volendi atque operandi . . . a creatore nobis naturaliter insitam diceret.'

[1] Texts in Plinval, op. cit., pp. 32–33, 150 *nn.*, 179, 236.

[2] Ambrose, *De Exc. Sat.*, ii, 6: 'Lapsus sum in Adam, de paradiso eiectus in Adam, mortuus in Adam; quomodo revocet, nisi me in Adam invenerit, ut in illo culpae obnoxium, morti debitum, ita in Christo iustificatum.' *MPL* xvi, 1317. *De Poenit.*, I, iii, 13: 'Omnes homines sub peccato nascimur, quorum ipse ortus in vitio est, sicut habes lectum, dicente David, *Ecce enim in iniquitatibus conceptus sum, et in delictis peperit me mater mea.* Ideo Pauli caro corpus mortis erat, sicut ipse ait: *Quis me liberabit de corpore mortis huius?* Christi autem caro damnavit peccatum, quod nascendo non sensit, quod moriendo crucifixit; ut in carne nostra esset iustificatio per gratiam, ubi erat ante colluvio per culpam.' *MPL* xvi, 470. *In Evang. sec. Luc.*, ii, 56: 'Non enim virilis coitus vulvae virginalis secreta reseravit: sed immaculatum semen inviolabili utero Spiritus sanctus infudit: solus enim per omnia ex natis de femina sanctus Domnius Iesus, qui terrenae contagia corruptelae immaculati partus novitate non senserit, et coelesti maiestate depulerit.' *MPL* xv, 1572–3. Quoted by Augustine, *De Pecc. Orig.*, xli, 47. Other quotations from Ambrose in *C. duas Epist. Pel.*, IV, xi, 29–31.

[3] Aug., *Serm.* 294, xx, 19.

[4] Text., *De Anima*, 41. See J. F. Bethune-Baker, *An Introduction to the Early History of Christian Doctrine*, ed. of 1954, 306.

[5] *De Baptismo*, 18: 'Quid festinat innocens aetas ad remissionem peccatorum?' *MPL* i, 1221.

Adam's sins found support in the East, particularly in Theodore of Mopsuestia, of whose writings he may have had some knowledge.

For a time, we hear little of Pelagius after 405. About the year 409, when Alaric the Goth menaced Rome, he left Italy, and came to Sicily, together with his friend and disciple, Caelestius. The latter, to whom must be assigned as much responsibility for the spread and development of Pelagianism as to Pelagius himself, was a lawyer, of noble birth and endowed with considerable dialectical skill. Even before encountering Pelagius he seems to have had an inclination towards the ascetic life, and his meeting with the heresiarch led him to forsake a legal career and turn his thoughts wholly to religion. Once converted to Pelagius' opinions, Caelestius devoted himself to propagating them. Indeed, it may be doubted whether Pelagianism, as the term is understood today, would ever have been known but for his activities.

Pelagius and Caelestius remained in Sicily probably until the news came of the sack of Rome and then crossed to Africa. They landed at Hippo when Augustine happened to be absent and spent only a short time there before moving on to Carthage. Augustine would have liked to have met Pelagius and was disappointed to find, on his return, that he had already left Hippo, though relieved to learn that he had not expressed the views generally imputed to him.[1] In 411, at the Conference of Carthage, he saw him occasionally, but they did not speak together.[2] Augustine heard persons declare in conversation that what infants gained from baptism was not remission of sins but sanctification;[3] but though startled by this novel assertion, he had no opportunity of contradicting it. Pelagius then departed for Palestine and the chance of any discussion was ended. Caelestius, however, remained in Africa and devoted himself to propagating the ideas of himself and his master. He spoke and apparently wrote a book,[4] and seems to have made a considerable impression among the Christians of Carthage.[5] He even seems to have entertained hopes of ordination,[6] when he was accused of heresy by Paulinus, a deacon of Milan, who was at that time visiting Africa in order to collect material for

[1] *De Gest. Pel.*, xxii, 46: 'Postea vero quam in Africam venit, me absente nostro, id est Hipponensi litore exceptus est, ubi omnino, sicut comperi a nostris, nihil ab illo huius modi auditum est, quia et citius, quam putabatur, inde profectus est.'
[2] Ibid.
[3] *De Pecc. Mer. et Rem.*, III, vi, 12: 'Nam ante parvum tempus a quibusdam transitorie conloquentibus cursim mihi aures perstrictae sunt, cum illic apud Carthaginem essemus, "non ideo parvulos baptizari, ut remissionem accipiant peccatorum, sed ut sanctificentur in Christo".'
[4] Ibid., I, xxxiv, 64.   [5] *De Gest. Pel.*, xxxv, 62.
[6] Aug., *Ep.* 157, iii, 22: 'Nam unus eorum nomine Caelestius in eiusdem civitatis ͟Carthaginis͡ ecclesia iam ad presbyterii honorem subrepere coeperat.'

his biography of St Ambrose.[1] A charge was drawn up on seven counts asserting that Caelestius not only taught, but employed others to teach throughout the province the following propositions: that Adam was created mortal and would have died even if he had not sinned; that his sin injured only himself and not the human race; that infants at the time of their birth are in the same state that Adam was in before the Fall; that mankind as a whole did not die through Adam's death or transgression, nor would it rise again through Christ's resurrection; that the Law had the same effect as the Gospel in bringing men into the Kingdom of Heaven; and that even before the coming of Christ there had been sinless men.

The charge was heard before Aurelius, bishop of Carthage, and Caelestius defended himself stoutly in a manner which did credit to his legal training. Augustine has left an account of part of the proceedings in his treatise *On Original Sin*:

Bishop Aurelius said: 'Let what follows be read', and it was read out: 'That the sin of Adam injured himself alone and not the human race.' When it had been read, Caelestius said: 'I said I was doubtful about the transmission, but in such a way that I would agree with him to whom God had given the grace of knowledge, since I have heard various opinions from those who have yet been ordained priests in the Catholic Church.' Paulinus the Deacon: 'Name them!' Caelestius: 'The holy priest Rufinus, who resided at Rome with the holy Pammachius. I heard him say there is no transmission of sin.' Paulinus: 'Is there anyone else?' Caelestius: 'I have heard many people say the same thing.' Paulinus: 'Name them!' Caelestius: 'Isn't one priest enough for you?' A little later, at another point, Bishop Aurelius said: 'Let the rest of the charge be read', and it was read out: 'That new-born infants are in that state that Adam was in before the Fall', to the end. Bishop Aurelius: 'Caelestius, did you ever teach, as Deacon Paulinus asserts, that new-born infants are in the state that Adam was in before the Fall?' Caelestius: 'Let him explain his expression "before the Fall".' Paulinus: 'No, do you rather deny that you taught this. [To the court] I give him two alternatives: either let him deny that he taught this in the past or let him condemn it at the present.' Caelestius: 'I have just said, let Paulinus explain what he meant by "before the Fall".' Paulinus: 'Deny that you taught this!' Bishop Aurelius: 'I should like to know what I am to infer from this objection. I personally say that Adam was placed in Paradise and is said to have been originally created immortal, but afterwards through the Fall was made corruptible. Do you say this, brother Paulinus?' Paulinus: 'Yes, my Lord.' Aurelius: 'What is the state of unbaptized infants today? Is it the same as that of Adam before the Fall or does it carry with it the guilt of the Fall from the same origin of sin from

L

which it is born? That is what Deacon Paulinus wishes to hear.' Paulinus: 'Let him deny whether he taught this or not!' Caelestius: 'I have
told you that as regards the transmission of sin I have heard various
people within the Catholic Church deny it and others assert it. It therefore follows that the affair is a matter of opinion, not of heresy. I have
always said that infants need baptism, and ought to be baptized. What
more does he want from me?'[1]

So the unedifying wrangle dragged on with Paulinus as prosecuting
counsel behaving in the manner of his tribe and reducing the whole affair
to the time-honoured formula: Answer yes or no! while Caelestius, equally
determined, steadily refused to give the answer required, while agreeing
that children ought to be baptized. For his accusers, as Augustine was
later to remark,[2] the question was not about the need for baptism, which
nobody disputed, but the nature of its effects: did it cleanse from Original
Sin or did it not? Caelestius had indeed admitted in his book that infants
needed baptism to share in the common regeneration of humanity.[3] This
might appear to be an admission that baptism was necessary for the remission of sins, even of infants—an admission that Caelestius did, in fact,
subsequently make[4] but understanding thereby that children were capable
of sin from the very moment of their birth.[5] At all events, the Carthaginian
synod was not prepared to accept his protestations but demanded that he
should condemn the various propositions which he was accused of holding. He refused to do this and was excommunicated. He considered an
appeal to Rome but decided otherwise and left Carthage for Ephesus.[6]

It was at this point that Augustine entered upon the scene. He had not
been present at the synod of Carthage, but soon informed himself of the
views of Caelestius and his adherents and began to denounce them in his
sermons. Then, at the request of his friend Count Marcellinus, he produced the first of his anti-Pelagian writings, the treatise *De Peccatorum
Meritis et Remissione et de Baptismo Parvulorum*. Marcellinus, on reading
this, found difficulty in the assertion that it was possible, with Grace, for a

---

[1] *De Pecc. Orig.*, iii–iv, 3.
[2] Ibid., xix, 21: 'Sed non inde quaestio est; de purgatione originalis peccati in parvulis
quaestio est.'
[3] Ibid.: 'Nam et Caelestius apud Carthaginem in libello suo redemptionem confessus
est parvulorum et tamen noluit confiteri ex Adam in eos transisse peccatum.' Cf. *De Pecc.
Mer. et Rem.*, I, xxxiv, 63: 'Proinde quod adtinet ad baptismum parvulorum, ut eis sit
necessarius, redemptionem etiam ipsis opus esse concedunt, sicut cuiusdam eorum
[Caelestii?] libello brevissimo continetur, qui tamen ibi remissionem alicuius peccati
apertius exprimere noluit.'
[4] *De Pecc. Mer. et Rem.*, II, xxxvi, 58.
[5] Ibid., I, xxxiv, 63: 'Non tamen originaliter, inquiunt, sed in vita iam propria, postea-
quam nati sunt, peccatum habere coeperunt.'
[6] Marius Mercator, *Commonitorium*, I, i, 2. *MPL* xlviii, 71–73.

man to live without sin although in fact no man had ever done so except Christ. To answer this difficulty, Augustine composed another work, *De Spiritu et Littera* (*On the Spirit and the Letter*) in which, without excluding the application of the text to the allegorical interpretation of Holy Scripture, which he had first learned from St Ambrose,[1] he now read in the light of the context, and explained *the letter which killeth* as the Mosaic Law, which declares what ought to be done but gives no strength to perform it, and *the Spirit which giveth life* as the Life-giving Paraclete, by whose presence the will is lifted up and the Law of God written upon the hearts of men. This treatise, 'which, perhaps, next to the *Confessions*, tells us most of the thoughts of that "rich, profound, and affectionate mind", on the soul's relation to its God',[2] is undoubtedly one of the outstanding writings produced by Augustine during the Pelagian controversy and deserves attentive study.[3]

Despite Augustine's denunciations, Pelagianism continued to spread in Africa, and the disciples of Caelestius began to become aggressive. To the charge of innovation they responded with a counter-charge, and it was against this that Augustine delivered a famous sermon,[4] preached in the great church of Carthage,[5] on 27 June 413. At the close of his address the preacher, taking a copy of the letters of St Cyprian, the great African martyr and former bishop of Carthage, read the passage in which the saint emphatically asserts that children should be baptized as soon as possible after their birth, to free them 'from the infection of the ancient death drawn from their first birth',[6] and to secure remission 'not of their own sins but of another's'. There could be no doubt about the influence of a quotation of their great patron upon a Carthaginian congregation and Augustine was drawing on experience of controversial method gained from his encounters with the Donatists. But he had another, and no doubt equally compelling, reason for appealing to St Cyprian. From a remark of Augustine's in connection with this sermon,[7] it would appear that the Pelagians

---

[1] *Conf.*, V, xiv, 24.
[2] Bright, *Anti-Pelagian Treatises*, xxi.
[3] There is a translation in Burnaby, *Augustine: Later Works*, 195–250.
[4] Aug., *Serm.* 294.
[5] *De Gest. Pel.*, xi, 25: 'in basilica Maiorum'.
[6] Cyprian, *Ep.* 64, 5: 'Si etiam gravissimis delictoribus . . . remissa peccatorum datur et a baptismo atque gratia nemo prohibetur, quanto magis prohiberi non debet infans qui recens natus nihil peccavit, nisi quod secundum Adam carnaliter natus contagium mortis antiquae prima nativitate contraxit, qui ad remissam peccatorum accipiendam hoc ipso facilius accedit quod illi remittuntur non propria sed aliena peccata.' *CSEL* iii (2), 720.
[7] *De Gest. Pel.*, xi, 25: 'Haec sunt, quae nonnullis fratribus quidam talia sentientes ita persuadere conabantur, ut de orientalibus comminarentur ecclesiis quod, nisi qui haec tenerent, earum possent iudicio condemnari.'

were beginning to appeal to the eastern churches which were inclined, perhaps as a result of the legacy of Greek philosophy, to take a more optimistic view of humanity than commended itself to the west, and to threaten their opponents with the censure of those churches. If this form of argument had become at all general, Augustine had a powerful reason for appealing to the teaching of St Cyprian who, outstandingly among the saints of the west, commanded the esteem and admiration of the Greeks.[1] If this hero of oriental piety could be quoted as supporting the views of the opponents of Pelagianism, they had little to fear from the intervention of the Greek-speaking churches, and could successfully represent themselves as standing in the way of orthodoxy proclaimed by the great Carthaginian martyr.

Despite his strenuous opposition to Pelagian doctrine, Augustine remained on good terms with Pelagius himself, writing to him with every expression of esteem and without reference to theological differences[2]— an act of courtesy which was later to be ill repaid, when Pelagius employed the letter, with its affectionate phraseology, to suggest that Augustine was sympathetic to his opinions.[3]

Augustine's efforts seem to have had some effect in reclaiming certain African Pelagians, but he was well aware that the evil was not dead. In the following year, 414, hearing from a correspondent named Hilary of Pelagianizing tendencies in Sicily, he wrote him a long letter on the subject.[4] He also discovered that Pelagius had so influenced two young men, Timasius and James, that he had induced them to give up all hopes of worldly advancement in favour of the ascetic life and to adopt his theories.[5] They were, however, beginning to entertain doubts, and now decided to confide those doubts in Augustine, sending him a copy of a work of Pelagius *On Nature* with the request that he would refute it.[6] In this work, Pelagius spoke of Grace, but in the sense of the natural faculties and without reference to the supernatural quality.[7] Indeed, Augustine was later to describe the treatise as a defence of human nature against the Grace of God

---

[1] St Gregory Nazianzen devotes a sermon to the praise of St Cyprian, and after declaring that 'the name that was formerly great among the Carthaginians now belongs to the world', sums him up by declaring: 'the very memory of the man is sanctification'. (*Or.* 24, 6, 7. *MPG* xxxv, 1176, 1177.) It is clear, however, that St Gregory had very little knowledge of the real Cyprian, whom he confuses with Cyprian of Antioch, a very different character.

[2] Aug., *Ep.* 146. He uses terms such as 'dominus dilectissimus'; 'desideratissimus frater'; 'tua benignitas'.

[3] *De Gest. Pel.*, xxvi, 51–xxix, 53.

[4] Aug., *Ep.* 157.

[5] Ibid., *Epp.* 177, 6; 179, 2.

[6] *De Gest. Pel.*, xxiii, 47, xxiv, 48. See Plinval, op. cit., p. 239.

[7] *De Nat. et Grat.*, x, 11–xi, 12.

by every available means.[1] Pelagius contended, not that any sinless man necessarily existed, but that it was possible for one to do so. 'Our discussion', he remarked, 'is concerned with possibility alone',[2] and he regarded the establishment of the possibility of sinlessness as the important point of the controversy.[3] This done, he argued that a man can be sinless through his natural endowments, though he employed the word 'Grace', but in the sense which Augustine declared to be wholly insufficient.[4] Augustine reviewed and replied to Pelagius in his book *On Nature and Grace*, published early in 415. The tone of the work was friendly and he refrained from mentioning Pelagius by name. The theme of his argument was that human nature, though created in a sound state, has been corrupted by sin, and that only by the Grace of Christ, which is given freely and without any regard to merits, can an infant or a human being of any age be saved. Two short chapters virtually sum up Augustine's thought on the subject of Grace and afford an admirable summary of his doctrine.

> The nature of man was certainly first created blameless and without any vice; but the human nature by which each one of us is now born of Adam requires a physician, because it is not healthy. All the good things, indeed, which it has by its conception, life, senses, and mind, it has from the highest God, its creator and artificer. But the vice which darkens and disables these good natural qualities, so that nature has need of enlightenment and healing, did not come from the blameless maker but from Original Sin, which was committed by free will. For this reason our guilty nature draws upon itself a most just penalty. For if we are now *in Christ a new creature*,[5] we were yet *by nature sons of wrath, even as the rest; but God, who is rich in mercy, on account of the great love with which He loved us, even when we were dead through our trespasses, raised us up to life with Christ, by whose grace we are saved.*[6] But this Grace of Christ, without which neither infants nor grown persons can be saved, is not bestowed as a reward for merits, but is given gratis, whence it is called Grace. *Being justified*, says Paul, *freely [gratis] through His blood.*[7] Whence it is that those who are not made free by that blood, whether because they have not been able to hear, or because they were not willing to obey, or were not able to hear on account of their youth, and have not received the bath of regeneration which they might have done and through which they might have been saved, are most justly condemned because they are not without sin, whether it be that which they drew

[1] *Retract.*, ii, 68 [42]: 'Venit etiam in tunc manus meas quidam liber Pelagii, ubi hominis naturam contra dei gratiam, qua iustificatur inpius et qua Christiani sumus, quanta potuit argumentatione defendit.'

[2] *De Nat. et Grat.*, vii, 8: ' "Nos," inquit [Pelagius], "de sola possibilitate tractamus; de qua nisi quid certum constiterit, transgredi ad aliud gravissimum esse atque extra ordinem ducimus." '   [3] *Ibid.*, x, 11.   [4] *Ibid.*, xi, 12; li, 59.

[5] II Cor. 5.17.   [6] Eph. 2.3–5.   [7] Rom. 3.24.

from their origin or that which they have added by evil practices. *For all have sinned*, whether in Adam or in themselves, *and come short of the glory of God*.[1]

Two incidental features of the *De Natura et Gratia* have exercised considerable influence upon later Christian thought. The first is the employment of a word which has come to have a sinister significance in Augustinian theology: *massa*—a mass or lump, used to describe the total of unregenerate humanity from whom God, with inscrutable mercy and regardless of merit, chooses His elect, who are to be delivered from the eternal pains which they have most justly deserved.[2] This is not, indeed, the first time that Augustine employs the word. Its first recorded use by him is in the treatise *On various questions*, sent to Simplicianus bishop of Milan in 397, in which, commenting on Romans 9.21, he wrote:

> From Adam has sprung one mass of sinners and godless men, in which both Jews and Gentiles belong to one lump, apart from the Grace of God. If the potter out of one lump of clay makes one vessel unto honour and another unto dishonour, it is manifest that God has made of the Jews some vessels unto honour and others unto dishonour, and similarly of the Gentiles. It follows that all must be understood to belong to one lump.[3]

Seven years later in 404 Augustine employed the word and the conception in his dispute with Felix the Manichee—an interesting fact, because it showed that he had no fear that the Manichees would attempt to identify the mass of sin with the *bôlos* or clod of light mixed with darkness which, at the end of the world, would have to be discarded as incapable of purgation.[4]

Accordingly, by the time the Pelagian controversy began, the idea of the *massa* was clearly defined in the mind of Augustine; and in the *De Natura et Gratia* he expresses it in a few, terrible words:

> The whole mass deserves punishment; and if due punishment of damnation should be inflicted upon all it would, without doubt, be awarded not unjustly. Those therefore who are liberated from thence through Grace are named, not vessels of their own merits but vessels of mercy.

[1] Rom. 3.23. *De Nat. et Grat.*, iii, 3–iv, 4.
[2] Newman brought the term into English poetry in *The Dream of Gerontius*, lines 686–9:

> And ages, opening out, divide
> The precious and the base,
> And from the hard and sullen mass
> Mature the heirs of grace.

[3] *De Div. Quaest. ad Simplic.*, I, q. 2, 19. Tr. by Burleigh, p. 402.
[4] *C. Felice*, II, 11: 'Quia enim Adam peccaverat et omnis illa massa et propago peccati maledicta erat, dominus autem carnem de ipsa massa suscipere voluit, ut suscipiendo mortalitatem, quae de poena venerat, solveret mortem, quod de gratia veniebat.'

Of whose mercy, save of Him who sent Christ Jesus into this world to save sinners, whom He foreknew and predestined and called and justified and glorified? What man, therefore, rages to such a degree of madness as not to offer ineffable thanks to the mercy of God, liberating whom He willed, when he could in no way rightly complain against God's justice, if He should condemn the whole of humanity?[1]

The second detail to be noted deserves mention for its importance in another field of theology: the sinlessness of the Mother of God. Pelagius had drawn up a list of just persons, men and women who, he affirmed, were recorded as having lived without sin, among whom was the Virgin Mary 'whom it is necessary that piety confess to be without sin'. Augustine's comment is as follows: 'The holy Virgin Mary excepted—since, in a discussion of sin, I do not want to make any mention whatever of her for the honour of the Lord, for whence do we know what extra measure of Grace was accorded to her to vanquish sin in every way, who deserved to conceive and bear Him who, it is certain, had no sin? the holy Virgin Mary excepted then, if we had been able to assemble all those holy men and women when they lived here, and had asked them whether they were without sin, what do we think they would have replied? What our author [Pelagius] says, or what the Apostle John says? I put it to you: whatever degree of excellence they had while in this body, if they had been able to be asked this, would they not have replied with one voice: *If we say that we have no sin, we deceive ourselves and the truth is not in us*?[2] Or would they have made this reply more out of humility than from truth? but in this connection, it is well said: "Do not put the praise of humility into some degree of falsehood." And so, if they should declare the truth, they would admit to having sin; and because they confessed it humbly, truth would be in them; but if they should lie in this matter, they would none the less have sin, because truth would not be in them.'[3]

[1] *De Nat. et Grat.*, v, 5: 'Universa igitur massa poenas debet et si omnibus debitum damnationis supplicium redderetur, non iniuste procul dubio redderetur. qui ergo inde per gratiam liberantur, non vasa meritorum suorum, sed vasa misericordiae nominantur. cuius misericordiae nisi illius, qui Christum Iesum misit in hunc mundum peccatores salvos facere, quos praescivit et praedestinavit et vocavit et iustificavit et glorificavit? quis igitur usque adeo dementissime insaniat, ut non agat ineffabiles gratias misericordiae quos voluit liberantis, qui recte nullo modo posset culpare iustitiam universos omnino damnantis.'   [2] I Iohan. 1.6.
[3] *De Nat. et Grat.*, xxxvi, 42: 'Excepta itaque sancta virgine Maria, de qua propter honorem domini nullam prorsus, cum de peccatis agitur, haberi volo quaestionem; unde enim scimus quid ei plus gratiae conlatum fuerit ad vincendum omni ex parte peccatum, quae concipere ac parere meruit, quem constat nullum habuisse peccatum? hac ergo virgine excepta, si omnes illos sanctos et sanctas, cum hic viverent, congregare possemus et interrogare, utrum essent sine peccato, quid fuisse responsuros putamus? utrum hoc quod iste dicit, an quod Iohannes apostolus? rogo vos. quantalibet fuerint in hoc corpore excellentia sanctitatis, si hoc interrogari potuissent, una voce clamassent: *si dixerimus quia peccatum non habemus, nos ipsos decipimus et veritas in nobis non est.* an id humilius

Augustine, it will be noticed, is careful in his affirmation of universal human sinlessness to give Mary a place apart. It is not so much that he declares her personal sinlessness, as that he absolutely refuses to discuss the matter *propter honorem Domini*, for the honour of the Lord. This specific reference to the Mother of God—and the total number of such references is not very large in the great bulk of Augustine's writings—is evidence of the particular place which Mary enjoyed in the eyes of Christians by the beginning of the fifth century, not only in the Greek east but in the traditionally conservative Latin west.[1]

In 415, about the same time that he was writing the *De Natura et Gratia*, Augustine received an anonymous document which had been circulating among the Christians of Sicily, and which was now forwarded to him for refutation by two bishops, Eutropius and Paul. It was generally believed that the pamphlet came from the pen of Caelestius, and the style in which it was written lent substance to that opinion. It consisted of sixteen arguments or heads of considerations (*ratiocinationes*), designed to reduce the anti-Pelagian position to an absurdity by presenting its adherents with a series of paradoxes apparently involved in their doctrine. The general tone is not a happy one, and suggests a desire to gain a cheap dialectical triumph rather than to debate profound issues with a sincere desire to arrive at the truth. An example of the style may be quoted from the third of the arguments.

Again it must be asked: what is sin? a natural quality or an accidental? If it is natural it is not sin; but if, on the other hand, it is an accidental, it can disappear; and what can disappear can be avoided; and what can be avoided, a man is able to be without.

Augustine's replies are short and to the point:

Answer: sin is not natural; but the power of the will is inadequate to nature, and especially to corrupted nature whereby we are made children of wrath, to avoid sin unless it is aided and healed by the Grace of God through Jesus Christ our Lord.[2]

---

responderent fortasse quam verius? sed huic iam placet et recte placet, "laudem humilitatis in parte non ponere falsitatis." ita hoc si verum dicerent, haberent peccatum; quod humiliter quia faterentur, veritas in eis esset; si autem hoc mentirentur, nihilominus haberent peccatum, quia veritas in eis non esset.'

[1] Augustine's Mariology is well summed up by Altaner (who also provides an excellent bibliography), *Patrologie*, 5te Aufl., 404: 'Ganz klar lehrt Augustinus die stete Jungfräulichkeit Marias, auch in partu (*Sermo* 186, 1; 215, 3), und ebenso bezeugt er den Glauben an ihre persöhnliche Sündenlosigkeit (*Nat. Grat.*, xxxvi, 52); dagegen ist die vielberufene Stelle im *Op. Imp. c. Iul.*, iv, 122 kein Beweis dafür, dass Augustinus bereits die Unbefleckte Empfängnis Marias gelehrt hat.' It may be remarked in this connection that the Greek Orthodox Church, which comes no whit behind the Roman in its devotion to the Godbearer, does not profess the doctrine of the Immaculate Conception.

[2] *De Perf. Iust. Hom.*, ii, 3.

The anonymous pamphleteer did not, however, confine himself solely to enunciating logical paradoxes, but followed his display of dialectic by a collection of scriptural texts which enjoin sinlessness and which appear to assume the possibility of fulfilling this injunction.[1] Then, with remarkable frankness, he quotes others which seem to be hostile to his thesis,[2] but makes no attempt to harmonize apparent contradictions. He ends on his initial theme: can a sinless man exist? Answer, if God wills it, he can. But He does will it. Therefore he exists.[3]

Augustine replied to this work in his essay *De Perfectione Iustitiae Hominis*, which appeared probably in early 415.[4] Throughout this work he insisted that, while a means exists to a life without sin, which is indeed possible, that means is the Grace of God. He meets the texts which Caelestius—or the author of the treatise, if it were not he—had quoted and harmonizes them with his own doctrine. Finally, at the end, he adduced the petition of the Lord's Prayer: *Forgive us our debts*, as a proof of the universal fact of sin, since a sinless man would only have to pray: *Lead us not into temptation but deliver us from evil.*[5]

The pace of the story now quickens, and action succeeds to literary polemic. Pelagius had departed to Palestine, where he found many who sympathized with his outlook: Ctesiphon, Anianus, and John, then bishop of Jerusalem. But he found also an adversary as formidable as Augustine, though very different from him in personality, in St Jerome. Jerome had been living at Bethlehem since 386 when he, and a little band of friends and disciples, had established a nunnery there, under the rule of his devoted admirer Paula, and a monastery, presided over by the saint himself. Asceticism, scholarship, and controversy had hitherto occupied Jerome's life, and he was fully prepared to cross swords with another antagonist.

It is difficult to come to a satisfactory conclusion about Jerome's character, though very easy to form a most unfavourable opinion. In his nature we find a variety of apparently contradictory tendencies which, combined with his scholarship and his impetuous language, make him seem larger than life, a comic exaggeration of the traditional holy man. By far the most erudite of the Latin, or perhaps of any of the Fathers, and endowed with a deep love of classical literature, he was never free from the haunting fear

---

[1] *De Perf. Iust. Hom.*, ix, 20. [2] Ibid., xi, 23. [3] Ibid., xx, 43.
[4] 418 is the *terminus ante quem*, since it was in that year that the Council of Carthage condemned the proposition that there were sinless men before the coming of Christ while Augustine, in *De Perf. Iust. Hom.*, xxi, 44, says that he does not dare to condemn persons holding this opinion, though he is not able to defend them. Ferguson, op. cit., p. 65, argues for the date 415. [5] *De Perf. Iust. Hom.*, xxi, 44.

that there was some sinful element in his appreciation of pagan eloquence.[1] He had a capacity for great enthusiasms and for friendships which all too readily might change into violent enmities. The unrestrained language in which he expressed his disapproval has not helped posterity to judge him favourably. A ferocious ascetic who had spent three years mortifying his flesh in the wilderness, he openly proclaimed that he praised marriage as a means of producing virgins.[2] In so saying, he agreed with the sentiments of the Fathers and with Christian tradition, but it was characteristic of him that he expressed his views with a peculiar brutality.

Some one will say: 'Do you dare to disparage wedlock, a state which God has blessed?' It is not disparaging wedlock to prefer virginity. No one can make a comparison between two things if one is good and the other evil. Let married women take their pride in coming next after virgins. 'Be fruitful,' God said, 'and multiply and replenish the earth.' Let him then be fruitful and multiply who intends to replenish the earth; but your company is in heaven. The command to increase and multiply is fulfilled after the expulsion from Paradise, after the recognition of nakedness, after the putting on of the fig leaves which augured the approach of marital desire. Let them marry and be given in marriage who eat their bread in the sweat of their brow, whose land brings forth thorns and thistles, and whose crops are choked with brambles. My seed produces fruit a hundredfold.[3]

It might be thought that so determined a celibate would hardly be popular with women; but in spite of—or perhaps because of—his uncompromising views, Jerome was never without a train of female admirers, pious women who hung upon his words and were delighted to turn to him for advice and instruction, which he ungrudgingly gave. During his years at Rome, from 381 to 385, he had inspired the noble young widow, Blesilla, the daughter of his friend Paula, with such enthusiasm for asceticism that her sudden death was ascribed by the Roman mob to the fasting and self-neglect enjoined by her austere director.[4] His letter to the virgin Eustochium,[5] the sister of Blesilla, which contained many strictures on the morals of the Romans, gave great offence, but did not discourage the master nor deter his female disciples. Lack of confidence in his own

---

[1] The limitations which this consideration imposed upon his Greek studies are well brought out by Courcelle, *Les lettres grecques en Occident*, 2e éd., esp. pp. 111–15.

[2] Hieron., *Ep.* 22, 20: 'Laudo nuptias, laudo coniugium, sed quia mihi virgines generant: lego de spinis rosas, de terra aurum, de conca margaritum. numquid, qui arat, tota die arabit? nonne et laboris sui fruge laetabitur? plus honorantur nuptiae, quando, quod de illis nascitur, plus amatur.' *CSEL* liv, 170.

[3] Ibid., 22, 19. *CSEL* liv, 168. Trans. by F. A. Wright in the Loeb edition, *Select Letters of St. Jerome*, 91–93; but Wright's 'approach of nuptial desire' is a courteous understatement of Jerome's 'pruriginem nuptiarum'!

[4] *Epp.* 38; 39.   [5] *Ep.* 22.

abilities was never a failing in Jerome, and he was capable of writing a lengthy treatise on the education of a little girl, undismayed by the fact that his knowledge on the topic of female education was purely theoretical.[1]

Nevertheless, when all this is recognized, there remain other considerations, which suggest that Jerome had other and more amiable qualities than might be deduced from what has been said. It is, perhaps, rash to compare him with Samuel Johnson, but there are certain Johnsonian characteristics about him. It is clear that despite his ferocity, his prejudices, and his quarrelsome nature, there were many men and women who could love and esteem him. Fierce as he was, he practised what he preached, and his denunciation of the lax moral standards of Roman society was justified. He was capable of sympathy, and generous sympathy; he was willing, at the request of a friend, to write to an unknown woman and her daughter, who were estranged from one another, to beg them to be reconciled.[2] After an inauspicious beginning, for which he was not to blame, he was a loyal and appreciative friend of Augustine, in whom he recognized a genius for speculation as great as, or greater than, his own in the field of textual scholarship. His loyalty and devotion to the Church and the services which he rendered to her by his assiduous labour in biblical studies in the face of much ignorant and prejudiced opposition are beyond praise. He appreciated his own merits and had little patience with fools, in this again reminiscent of Johnson. There is much that is attractive in him; he is, indeed, a profoundly human personality, despite his violence and exaggeration. He resembles Johnson; but for the medievalist, there is another figure whom he recalls yet more strongly: St Peter Damiani. In both we see the same combination of asceticism, scholarship, suspicion of that scholarship, and a capacity for the most violent denunciation of what they deemed to be wrong. But Jerome is a more independent and less sensitive figure than Damiani. One cannot imagine Jerome succumbing, as Damiani did, to the spell of Hildebrand.[3]

---

[1] *Ep.* 107.   [2] *Ep.* 117.
[3] The violence of Jerome's invective and, in particular, the language he used after the death of his former friend Rufinus are very distasteful at the present day. Certainly, Jerome's remarks about the dead Rufinus: 'The scorpion lies beneath the earth between Enceladus and Porphyrion; the many-headed hydra has at last ceased to hiss against me' (*Praef. in Ezechiel*, Lib. I. *MPL* xxv, 16–17) are not what we desire that one Christian should write about another. On the other hand, allowance must be made for the conventions of the age. The employment of what Professor Baynes has called 'ecclesiastical Billingsgate' was all too common in the patristic age, and we may quote what Baynes said in respect of the violent language of Athanasius: 'This is in the tradition of ancient advocacy: Demosthenes and Cicero would have comprehended Athanasius better than many modern commentators' (*Byzantine Studies*, 368). As regards Jerome, it is necessary to recall the strength of the rhetorical tradition in his writing. See the comments of Labriolle, *Hist. de la litt. latine chrétienne*, 3e éd., i, 10: 'Villemain s'indignait fort d'un

At the time of Pelagius' arrival in the east, Jerome was living in his monastery at Bethlehem, devoting himself to study and asceticism. Characteristically he was on bad terms with his bishop, John of Jerusalem, and the fact that the bishop was a friend and patron of Pelagius was no recommendation of the latter in the eyes of Jerome. In 414 both he and Pelagius addressed letters to the noble virgin Demetrias on the occasion of her taking the veil, and Jerome's warning to her against the followers of Origen might be interpreted as a warning against Pelagius and his teaching.[1] Indeed, it is possible that the two men had already clashed at an earlier date in 394, during Jerome's controversy with Jovinian.[2] Now, however, the contest was to be greatly embittered, and an attempt by Pelagius to bring about a reconciliation was rejected by Jerome.[3]

About the middle of the year 415, not long after the appearance of Augustine's *De Perfectione Iustitiae Hominis* if we have dated that work correctly, there arrived in Palestine the man who was to be the most bitter and violent enemy of Pelagius and his supporters. Paul Orosius was a Spanish priest, a native of Tarragona, and was at that time about thirty years old. In the early part of 415 he had come to Africa to consult Augustine about the spread of the heresies of Origen and Priscillian[4] in Spain. In Orosius, a burning zeal for the Faith was united with a narrow and ungenerous nature, and the whole allied to an impetuous temperament, and a remarkable naïvety, which was later to have full rein in his *History against the Pagans*. He impressed Augustine, who answered his questions and then advised him to go on to Palestine to consult Jerome for further instruction, making him the bearer of letters concerning the Pelagian dispute. Orosius arrived in Bethlehem and installed himself in Jerome's monastery, whence he was summoned on 28 July to attend a diocesan synod at Jerusalem. Jerome himself was not present; the strained relations between him and the bishop would have made his presence an embarrassment. On the way to the synod, Orosius apparently encountered Pelagius and had some conversation with him.[5] At the synod, bishop John asked Orosius to

passage de la fameuse lettre de saint Jérôme à Hélidore: "Si [s'opposant à ta vocation] ton père se couche sur le seuil de ta porte pour te retenir, passe pardessus le corps de ton père" (*per calcatum perge patrem*). [*Ep.* 14, 2.] "Férocité religieuse!" s'écriait Villemain. Pure rhétorique, répondrons-nous.' Labriolle draws attention to a similar counsel in the *Controversiae* of Seneca, I, viii, 15.
[1] Hieron., *Ep.* 130, 16. *CSEL* lvi, 196. See Ferguson, op. cit., p. 59.
[2] See Plinval, op. cit., pp. 50–55.   [3] Hieron., *Ep.* 133. *CSEL* lvi, 241–60.
[4] For Priscillianism, see Adhémar d'Alès, *Priscillien et l'Espagne chrétienne à la fin du IVe siècle*. There is a good short sketch, markedly favourable to Priscillian, in F. Holmes Dudden, *The Life and Times of St Ambrose*, i, 217–40.
[5] Orosius, *Apol.*, 4: 'Ego autem vobis annuentibus dixi: "Pelagius mihi dixit docere se, hominem posse esse sine peccato et mandata Dei facile custodire, si velit."' *CSEL* v, 608.

tell them what he could about Pelagius and Caelestius. Reports of the happenings in Africa had reached Palestine and these, combined with the dispute between Jerome and Pelagius, had decided the eastern clergy that the matter required investigation. Orosius, newly arrived from the west, was an obvious source of information. Orosius told of the trial and condemnation of Caelestius, produced and read the letter of Augustine to Hilary refuting the Pelagian pamphlet, and announced that the bishop of Hippo was, at that moment, at work on a treatise refuting the opinions of Pelagius. Bishop John decided that Pelagius should be summoned, in order that he might have the opportunity of replying to the charges brought against him. Accordingly, he came into the assembly. When asked whether he had indeed taught the doctrines attacked by Augustine, he replied, with some hauteur: 'What is Augustine to me?'—a rejoinder which shocked the majority of those present, to whom the name and reputation of Augustine were well known, as the man who had restored unity to the African Church, torn by the Donatist schism. The bishop of Jerusalem was not, however, disposed to allow the matter to be settled out of hand by an appeal to the authority of a foreign bishop, however distinguished. It was not the habit of Greek bishops to go to the Latins to learn theology, and there was the further consideration of the authority of a bishop within his own diocese. 'It is I who am Augustine here', he observed, to which Orosius, with a lack of finesse which all too frequently marked his writing and speaking, retorted: 'If you represent Augustine's person, follow his faith!' a remark which at least ensured that Pelagius would receive a fair hearing before the indignant bishop John.

Accordingly, although only a layman, Pelagius was invited to take his place in the synod and Orosius was asked to state his charges. The latter, who was supported by two priests named Posserius and Avitus, declared that Pelagius had affirmed that a man could, if he willed, live without sin and easily keep God's commandments. Pelagius acknowledged that such was his teaching. Orosius thereupon denounced it as condemned by the Council of Carthage, by Augustine, and by Jerome. Bishop John asked him if he and his friends were prepared to act as accusers and it became clear to the anti-Pelagian faction that the decision of the African council, which they regarded as final, carried in itself no weight in an assembly of eastern clerics.[1] Furthermore, the fact that Orosius spoke no Greek and had to address the synod through an interpreter did not make his task of

---

[1] *Apol.*, 5: 'Porro autem episcopus Iohannes nihil horum audiens a nobis exigere conabatur, ut accusatores nos ipso iudice fateremur. responsum saepissime est ab universis: "nos accusatores huius non sumus".' *CSEL* v, 609.

denunciation any easier. However, he persevered, and asserted that Pelagius held that a man could, if he would, be without sin, and that such a belief was heretical. Pelagius, on being asked to explain this, replied: 'I did not mean that human nature is naturally endowed with sinlessness; but if a man is prepared to toil and struggle to avoid sin and to walk in the commandments of God for his salvation, he has from God the possibility of doing so.' The declaration was greeted by a murmur of protest. It was inadequate; it gave no place to the Grace of God. Pelagius quoted Scripture to prove the necessity for Grace, and when this did not quell the protests against him, he anathematized anyone who should say that a man could advance in virtue without such help.[1] Bishop John approved and asked Orosius and his supporters whether this admission were not satisfactory: 'or do you deny the necessity for God's help?'[2] Now the tables were turned with a vengeance, and Orosius had no alternative but to accept Pelagius' anathema. He realized, however, that he must at all costs prevent the synod from coming to a decision which might involve a condemnation of the Council of Carthage, and therefore declared that the whole question was of Latin origin and best understood by Latins, and should therefore be referred to Innocent, the bishop of Rome.[3] This suggestion was agreed to, and the synod broke up, without having taken any minutes.[4] Orosius seemed to have gained at least part of his case, but he was to have a rude awakening. When on 12 September he presented himself at the Church of the Resurrection at Jerusalem to assist the bishop at the annual festival of the dedication, bishop John turned on him and violently denounced him as one who held that it was impossible for a man to live without sin, even with the help of God. Orosius indignantly denied the charge and wrote an *Apology*, addressed to the clergy of Jerusalem, in order to clear himself. Pelagius' opponents had been discomfited by bishop John's action but they were in no mood to let the matter drop. Two Gallican bishops, Heros of Arles and Lazarus of Aix, who had been driven from their sees for their

---

[1] *De Gest. Pel.*, xxx, 54; xiv, 37.

[2] Orosius, *Apol.*, 6: 'Si sine adiutorio Dei hoc hominem posse diceret [Pelagius], pessimum et damnabile erat; nunc autem cum adiciat, posse hominem esse sine peccato non sine adiutorio Dei, vos quid dicitis? an forte vos Dei adiutorium denegatis?' *CSEL* v, 610.

[3] Ibid., 6: 'Dein cum . . . clamaremus, Latinum esse haereticum, nos Latinos, haeresim Latinis magis partibus notam Latinis iudicibus disserendam . . . novissimam sententiam protulit [episcopus], confirmans tandem postulationem intentionemque nostram, ut ad beatum Innocentium, papam Romanum, fratres et epistulae mitterentur, universis quod ille decerneret secuturis.' *CSEL* v, 610-11.

[4] *De Gest. Pel.*, xvi, 39: 'Praesertim quia non [in] gestis agebatur, quae improbi ne mentiantur, boni autem ne aliquid obliviscantur utiliter instituta sunt.' The failure to take minutes of the proceedings, a common practice in the Roman world where stenographers abounded, was a curious omission, and capable of a sinister interpretation.

support of the usurper, Constantine III, had found refuge in Palestine. They had studied Pelagius' writings and the anonymous tract believed to be the work of Caelestius and were horrified by what they found. They therefore drew up a *libellus*, or formal charge, which they presented to Eulogius of Caesarea, the primate of Palestine, who summoned thirteen bishops, including John of Jerusalem,[1] to meet in council at Diospolis (Lydda) at the end of December. The council duly assembled; but both the accusers were absent. One was sick, and the other declined to be present alone.[2] Pelagius therefore had the field to himself and made good use of his opportunities. He read various letters which he had received from bishops of high repute, including the letters which Augustine had written to him two years before.[3] The council was properly impressed, and then commanded that the *libellus* should be read in Greek translation, asking Pelagius to reply to each separate article of accusation. Seven charges were levelled against him drawn from his writings. He was alleged to have affirmed that no man can be without sin, unless he have knowledge of the Law; that all men are ruled by their wills; that in the Day of Judgement, no mercy will be shown to the wicked and to sinners, but they must be burned in eternal fires; that evil does not enter the thought; that the Kingdom of Heaven is promised in the Old Testament as well as in the New; that a man can, if he will, be without sin (this was supported by three quotations, drawn from an adulatory letter to a widow); and that the Church here below is without spot or wrinkle (a charge which sought to accuse Pelagius of Donatist leanings).[4]

To these charges, Pelagius replied through an interpreter—a circumstance which goes far to explain the result of the investigation. His conduct has been unkindly described as equivocation; more lenient critics have seen in it an attempt to satisfy orthodox views without abandoning his own position. A sample of his method may be given from his treatment of the first article of accusation. When asked if he had, indeed, declared that no man can be without sin unless he have knowledge of the Law, he replied: 'Certainly I did, but not in the way that my accusers think. I did not say, a man cannot sin who has knowledge of the Law but, he is helped to avoid sin by knowledge of the Law as it is written, *He has given the Law for a help*.'[5] Much edified by this declaration, the synod declared that such a view was not alien to the Church which, as Augustine was later to observe, it is not, only in Pelagius' writings the words have been used in a

---

[1] Names in *C. Iul.*, I, v, 19; vii, 32.
[2] *De Gest. Pel.*, i, 2; xxxv, 62.   [3] Ibid., xxi, 45; xxvi, 51–xxix, 53.
[4] The charges in *De Gest. Pel.*, i, 2; iii, 5; iii, 9; iv, 12; v, 13; vi, 16; xii, 27. Listed in Ferguson, op. cit., p. 87.   [5] Isai. 8.20 LXX.

quite different connotation.[1] However, from the point of the synod, Greek bishops by no means anxious to plumb the depths of Latin anthropology, the reply of the accused, maintaining his adherence to the Catholic faith, was wholly welcome. Their desire was to compose a dispute, not to prolong it.

It was thus possible for Pelagius, by judicious explanation, to meet the various articles urged against him. In reply to the second he declared that he merely asserted free will, since 'God aids the man choosing good, but the man who sins is himself at fault, on account of free will.'[2] Once again the synod could applaud the orthodoxy of the accused. The third article was significant, since it illustrates the attitude of the Greek Church of that time towards the universalism of Origen, who had asserted the salvation of all, even of the devil. Thus it was easy for Pelagius to say that by sinners he meant those who would be condemned as such at the Last Day and to add that anyone who denied this would be guilty of Origenism.[3] The fourth charge relating to evil entering the thought, he stated to be a misrepresentation of what he had actually said.[4] The fifth, 'that the Kingdom of Heaven is also promised in the Old Testament', he explained as a simple scriptural reference to the Old Testament, and not implying that it was promised in the dispensation of Mount Sinai.[5] To the sixth charge of maintaining that a man could, if he chose, live without sin, which was buttressed by three other alleged quotations from his writings, he replied by disowning these three and recognizing only the one included in the allegation, which he explained by adding the important qualification that sinlessness was possible only by a combination of the Grace of God with man's efforts. Pelagius added that he had never said that any human being from infancy to old age had ever been wholly free from sin.[6] Finally, he answered the last article objected against him, that he had declared that the Church below was without spot or wrinkle, by saying that she is wholly cleansed by the baptismal laver and that the Lord wishes her to remain so.[7] This statement, like the others, satisfied the synod.

[1] *De Gest. Pel.*, i, 2: '. . . recitata sunt obiecta Pelagio, illud est primum, quod in libro suo quodam scribit "non posse esse sine peccato nisi qui scientiam legis habuerit." quo recitato synodus dixit: "tu haec edidisti, Pelagi?" at ille respondit: "ego quidem dixi, sed non sicut illi intellegunt. non dixi non posse peccare qui scientiam legis habuerit, sed adiuvari per legis scientiam ad non peccandum, sicut scriptum est: *legem in adiutorium dedit illis.*" hoc audito synodus dixit: "non sunt aliena ab ecclesia, quae dicta sunt a Pelagio!" plane aliena non sunt quae respondit; illud vero quod de libro eius prolatum est aliud sonat. sed hoc episcopi, Graeci homines et ea verba per interpretem audientes, discutere non curarunt, hoc tantum intuentes, quid ille qui interrogabatur sensisse se diceret, non quibus verbis eadem sententia in eius libro scripta diceretur.'

[2] Ibid., iii, 5. See Plinval, op. cit., p. 287. [3] Ibid., iii, 9–11.
[4] Ibid., iv, 12. [5] Ibid., v, 13–15.
[6] Ibid., vi, 16–xi, 26. Plinval, p. 287. [7] Ibid., xii, 27.

Pelagius was then questioned about the propositions brought against Caelestius at Carthage in 412 and the views held by his Sicilian followers. 'I spoke earlier about the possibility of a man being without sin', he answered. 'As regards the charge that there were sinless men before the advent of Christ, I say so because according to Holy Scriptures certain men lived just and holy lives before His coming. The remaining statements are not mine, as my accusers themselves admit, and I am therefore not required to answer for them. However, to satisfy this holy synod, I anathematize those who hold such views or held them at any time.'[1] To another charge, based on a quotation from a book ascribed to Caelestius, which the accusers admitted was not verbally accurate but more according to the sense than to the actual words,[2] that we do more than is commanded in the Law and the Gospel, Pelagius replied by denying the authorship of the passage and saying that his own reference had been to the words of St Paul: *Concerning virgins I have no commandment of the Lord*.[3] This explanation once more satisfied the synod. Then another series of propositions was brought forward, 'capital charges', says Augustine, 'which must without doubt be condemned and by which Pelagius would certainly have been condemned had he not anathematized them'.[4] In one of these, Caelestius was stated to have written that the Grace and help of God was not given for individual actions, but was to be found in free will or in the Law and teaching. In another, it was affirmed that the Grace of God was given 'according to our merits, since if God gave it to sinners, He would seem to be unjust', and the argument was developed by asserting that if we do all things by Grace, then every time we are conquered by sin the defeat is not ours but of the Grace of God, who wishes to help us but is unable to do so. This reasoning led again to the final conclusion: 'if Grace is of God when we conquer sins, He Himself is therefore at fault when we are conquered by sin, because He is either unable to help us or unwilling to do so'.[5] To this Pelagius replied shortly that whether Caelestius held these opinions or not was no affair of his, and for his own part he anathematized those who held them.[6] The delighted synod accepted his statements by which, indeed, he would appear to have accepted the orthodox doctrine of Grace, if it were not for the fact that he forthwith proceeded to use language which implied that all graces had been given to the Apostle Paul as a matter of

---

[1] *De Gest. Pel.*, xi, 24.
[2] Ibid., xiii, 29: 'magis secundum sensum quam secundum verba.'
[3] I Cor. 7.25.   [4] *De Gest. Pel.*, xiv, 30.
[5] Ibid.: 'si gratia dei est, quando vincimus peccata, ergo ipse est in culpa, quando a peccato vincimur, quia omnino custodire nos aut non potuit aut noluit.'
[6] Ibid.

desert.¹ Finally, seven other propositions from Caelestius' book were read, asserting that the title 'Sons of God' implied that we had been made sinless; that forgetfulness and ignorance could not be accounted sin; that the will cannot be free if it needs the help of God, since each of us has it in his own power to act or to refrain from acting; that our victory comes from our wills; that the victory is ours, since we take up arms of our own free wills; that since St Peter says we are *partakers of the divine nature*,² it follows that if the soul cannot be free from sin, God cannot be free either;³ and that pardon is not given to penitents by the grace and mercy of God but according to the merits and works of the penitent.⁴ These the synod solemnly condemned in the name of the Holy Catholic Church of God and asked Pelagius what he had to say. In his reply he repeated his previous contention that these views were not his and that he ought not to have to answer for them. His own doctrines he declared to be orthodox; those quoted were not his, and he rejected them according to the judgement of Holy Church and anthematized anyone who opposed and contradicted her teaching. 'I believe in the Trinity of one substance and all things according to the teaching of the Holy Catholic Church; and if anyone understand other than this, let him be anathema.'⁵ Satisfied with this declaration, the synod declared Pelagius to be of the communion of the Catholic Church.⁶

The synod of Diospolis represents the zenith of Pelagius' fortunes and he was not unnaturally disposed to make the most of the verdict of his judges. A letter, said to be his, came into the hands of Augustine, and impressed him unfavourably by its tone: 'a carnal letter of swelling elation'.⁷ The writer rejoiced in the verdict of the fourteen bishops, which had brought the blush to the cheek of accusation and scattered the whole evil band of conspiracy.⁸ But the writer of the letter went further. At Diospolis Pelagius had been accused of holding that a man could, if he chose, live without sin, and had defended himself by declaring that a man

¹ Ibid., xiv, 32: 'Pelagius respondit, . . . "non enim auferimus gratiarum diversitatem, sed dicimus donare deum ei qui fuerit dignus accipere omnes gratias, sicut Paulo apostolo donavit".' This language made Augustine uneasy: 'Cum ergo [Pelagius] non ait donare deum cui voluerit, sed ait, "donare deum ei, qui fuerit dignus accipere, omnes gratias", non potui, cum legerem, non esse suspiciosus. ipsum quippe gratiae nomen et eius nominis intellectus aufertur, si non gratis datur sed eam qui dignus est accipit' (ibid., 33).
² II Peter 1.4.   ³ This seems to be a distortion of what was actually said.
⁴ *De Gest. Pel.*, xviii, 42; xxxv, 65.   ⁵ Ibid., xix, 43; xxxiii, 58.
⁶ Ibid., xx, 44.   ⁷ Ibid., xxx, 55.
⁸ Ibid., xxx, 54: ' "Quatuordecim episcoporum sententia definitio nostra comprobata est, qua diximus posse hominem sine peccato esse et dei mandata facile custodiri, si velit. quae sententia", inquit, "contradictionis os confusione perfudit et omnem in malum conspirantem societatem ab invicem separavit." '

could so live with the help of God and Grace.[1] The writer of the letter was to improve on this and declare that a man could live without sin and *easily* keep the commandments of God, without ever mentioning the important qualification of the need for divine help and Grace.[2] Nor was this all. A Palestinian deacon named Charus, by birth a native of Hippo, brought Augustine an account of the synod of Diospolis, apparently from Pelagius and purporting to give an account of the charges brought and of his answers.[3] Certain clerics of Hippo who read the report claimed that they had in their possession a work, believed to be by Pelagius, addressed to a certain widow and expressing the very sentiments which he had disowned at Diospolis. The book was produced and read; and Augustine, for his part, was left wondering whether Pelagius had lied to the synod or whether the treatise to the widow was wrongly ascribed to him, in a fashion which had once happened to Augustine himself.[4] Whether Pelagius was innocent or not, discrepancies were later found between Pelagius' version of the proceedings at Diospolis and the official minutes.

In the meantime, Pelagius' pen was not idle. He produced a *Defence of Free Will* in four books, which Augustine later attacked in his own work *On the Grace of Christ and Original Sin*. Pelagius' position seemed to be a strong one; acquitted by the synod, he was winning support at Jerusalem where his patron, bishop John, saw to it that he was able to expound his views with confidence. Then, suddenly, a series of disasters descended upon him.

The first was a raid launched by a group of malcontents upon Jerome's religious community at Bethlehem in the course of the year 416. The use of violence was an all too frequent feature in the history of the Church in the fourth and fifth centuries and the attack on Jerome's monastery, where a deacon was murdered, buildings set on fire and the religious brutally handled, seemed to be an act of revenge for the old scholar's opposition to Pelagius and his doctrines.[5] Pelagius himself may be acquitted of responsibility; but like many another leader, he was held answerable for the actions of those believed to be his followers.

Secondly, there came the news of his excommunication by pope Innocent I, by letters dated 27 January 417. The moving force behind this

---

[1] *De Gest. Pel.*, vi, 16: 'Pelagius respondens ait: "posse quidem hominem esse sine peccato et dei mandata custodire, si velit, diximus; hanc enim possibilitatem deus illi dedit. non autem diximus quod inveniatur aliquis ab infantia usque ad senectam qui nunquam peccaverit, sed quoniam a peccatis conversus proprio labore et dei gratia possit esse sine peccato, nec per hoc tamen in posterum inconversibilis."'

[2] Ibid., xxx, 54: 'posse hominem sine peccato esse et dei mandata facile custodire.'

[3] Ibid., i, 1; xxxii, 57–xxxiii, 58.

[4] Ibid., vi, 19.

[5] Ibid., xxxv, 66.

condemnation was the African episcopate, determined not to let the acquittal by the synod of Diospolis shield Pelagius from further attacks. Early in 416, the indignant Orosius had left Palestine for Africa, bringing with him two letters, one from Jerome to Augustine[1] and the other from Heros and Lazarus, which was read to an African provincial synod which assembled at Carthage in the middle of 416.[2] This letter, together with the testimony of Orosius, caused the synod to decide that both Caelestius, who had recently secured ordination at Ephesus, and Pelagius should be anathematized, unless they themselves anathematized the errors imputed to them. A letter was dispatched to pope Innocent I requesting him to add the anathema of the apostolic see to that of Africa signed by Aurelius of Carthage and sixty-seven other bishops.[3] The bishops of Numidia, Augustine among them, met shortly after at Milevum and wrote to Innocent in a similar strain. Their letter bore fifty-nine signatures.[4] In addition to these two letters, Aurelius, Augustine, Alypius, Evodius and Possidius wrote to the pope a personal letter, describing the Pelagian misuse of the word grace and enclosing a copy of the treatise which had provoked Augustine to write his reply, *On Nature and Grace*.[5] The letter was not specifically aimed at Pelagius; indeed, it admitted that he might have changed his views and expressed the pious hope that this might indeed be the case,[6] but it urged the need for prompt action by summoning him to Rome[7] or at the very least by demanding that he anathematize the various errors which were urged against him.[8] The body of the African episcopate was determined for action against a heresy which had now begun to assume formidable proportions.

Innocent showed no undue precipitation in acting on the African bishops' letter. He seems, from his own account, not to have heard of any Pelagians at Rome[9] and was not prepared to overestimate the danger.[10] However, the reading of the Pelagian treatise sent to him from Africa filled him with horror, and on 27 January 417 he solemnly pronounced Pelagius and Caelestius excommunicate, until they should give satisfaction.[11] With regard to the synod of Diospolis, he declared that he had received a document professing to be a record of the proceedings, but he was not sure of its authenticity and could therefore neither confirm nor condemn them.[12] He was thus spared a direct clash with the Greeks.

[1] Hieron., *Ep.* 134 (inter Aug., *Ep.* 172). *CSEL* lvi, 261–3.   [2] Aug., *Ep.* 175, 1.
[3] Ibid.   [4] Ibid., *Ep.* 176.   [5] *Ep.* 177.
[6] Ibid., 3: 'Non agitur de uno Pelagio, quia iam fortasse correctus est, quod utinam ita sit . . .'   [7] Ibid.   [8] Ibid., 15.
[9] *Ep.* 183, 2: 'seu hic illi in urbe sunt, quod nescientes nec manifestare possumus nec negare.'
[10] See Plinval, op. cit., p. 305.   [11] Aug., *Epp.* 181, 8; 182, 6.   [12] *Ep.* 183, 3, 4.

Barely had Innocent launched his excommunication against Pelagius when the news reached him of the assault on Jerome's monastery and angered him still more. Unpopular as Jerome might be in the east he was, in the eyes of the Latins, one of the great luminaries of the Church and an attack upon him filled them with horror. The outrage appeared the greater in view of the aristocratic connections of his friend Eustochium and the other high-born ladies who occupied the nunnery at Bethlehem. The imperial court as well as the papacy was scandalized at an assault on such noble persons. Augustine, who was just completing an account of Pelagius' doings in Palestine for the information of his friend Aurelius of Carthage, added a horrified postscript,[1] while pope Innocent dispatched furious letters to Jerome, regretting that he had made no formal accusation against Pelagius,[2] and a very severe one to John of Jerusalem, accusing him of negligence and incompetence.[3]

The news of Innocent's condemnation was a terrible blow for Pelagius, the more so because his friend and patron John of Jerusalem was nearing the end of his life and he could not be sure that he would continue to enjoy the favour of his successor. He therefore decided to withdraw temporarily from Jerusalem, much to the satisfaction of Jerome, who expressed his feelings with characteristic forcefulness.[4] Pelagius' fears, however, proved groundless. John's successor, Praylius, proved as sympathetic as John himself and Pelagius was soon back in Jerusalem, at work on a declaration of faith to be submitted to Innocent.[5]

Innocent however was already dead, having expired on 12 March 417 forty-four days after excommunicating the two leading Pelagians, and had been succeeded by Zosimus, a pontiff whose Greek name may help to explain the sympathetic treatment he accorded to Pelagius and Caelestius in the early days of his reign. The new pope was soon visited by Caelestius, who had tried to establish himself at Constantinople and been expelled by the patriarch, Atticus.[6] Caelestius presented Zosimus with a written profession of faith, in which he declared himself ready, if he had erred on points of right belief, to be guided by the judgement of the pope.[7] Zosimus convened a Roman synod, which assembled in the basilica of St Clement on the Caelian hill, to the south-east of the city. Caelestius made a good impression. He was personally examined by the pope and, while declining

---

[1] De Gest. Pel., xxxv, 66.   [2] Hieron., Ep. 136.
[3] Hieron., Ep. 137.
[4] Hieron., Ep. 138, who apparently indicates Pelagius under the soubriquet of Catiline. CSEL lvi, 265–6.
[5] De Grat. Christ., xxx, 32.   [6] Mercator, Commonit., I, i, 3. MPL xlviii, 73–75.
[7] De Pecc. Orig., vi, 6; xxiii, 26.

to condemn the statements imputed to him at the synod of Carthage, declared that he was ready to abide by the letters of the late pope Innocent.[1] His defence impressed Zosimus, who decided not to take any precipitate action, but postponed his decision for two months, requiring Caelestius' accusers to present themselves within that time, to urge their case against him. In contrast to the caution which he showed in dealing with Caelestius, he did not delay to excommunicate Heros and Lazarus as troublemakers. In the letter in which he communicated these decisions to the African episcopate, he reproached them for the undue precipitancy which, he declared, they had shown in the whole matter.[2]

Shortly after writing this letter, Zosimus dispatched another,[3] in which he informed the Africans of the decision he had taken in the matter of Pelagius. He had received a copy of the defence which the latter had drawn up for the dead pope Innocent together with a covering letter from bishop Praylius of Jerusalem, recommending Pelagius in the warmest terms. The support of Praylius and the language of Pelagius impressed the solemn assembly of the Roman church to which it was read. It was agreed that such a man could not be unorthodox. Accordingly, he was solemnly acquitted, and Zosimus communicated the news to the Africans in a strongly worded letter of 21 September, which he was to live to regret.[4] In it he spoke with particular bitterness of Heros and Lazarus, whom he regarded as having been turbulent and vicious throughout their careers, and whose very accusation implied a strong probability of the accused being innocent.

While Zosimus' letter was on its way to Africa, Augustine preached a sermon at Carthage. Disquieting rumours that all was not well had already reached him and so, when on Sunday, 23 September, he preached in the great Carthaginian basilica of St Cyprian, he took as his theme the Pelagian controversy, employing language to emphasize the fact that, in the opinion of the African bishops, the whole affair was already settled. 'My brethren,' he concluded, 'refute those who contradict and bring to us those who resist. Two councils have already sent letters to the apostolic see, and

---

[1] De Pecc. Orig., vii, 8; C. duas Ep. Pel., II, iii, 5.
[2] Zosimus, Ep. de causa Caelestii, 'Magnum pondus'. MPL xlv, 1719–21.
[3] 'Qui, sans doute fut portée aux évêques d'Afrique par le même messager', Plinval, op. cit., p. 315.
[4] Zosimus, Ep. de causa Pelagii, 'Postquam a nobis'. MPL xlv, 1721–3. The question of papal infallibility does not arise in respect of Zosimus and his handling of the Pelagian controversy, since he erred on a point of fact, as to whether certain persons held particular views, and not on a point of faith or morals. For a convenient summary see Burn-Murdoch, The Development of the Papacy, 212–20. His comment is: 'The mistake of Pope Zosimus as to the sincerity of Coelestius and Pelagius did not involve any question of the infallibility of his teaching when given ex cathedra' (p. 216).

rescripts have already come from there. The matter is concluded; oh that the error may now end!'[1]

The arrival of the pope's letter on 2 November seemed to give Augustine's words the lie, but the African episcopate had no intention of treating the affair in any way except on the assumption that it was concluded. Letters were sent to Rome in which a respectful style of address in no way derogated from the fixed determination to abide by the decision of pope Innocent.[2] From Palestine Jerome wrote, offering encouragement to the anti-Pelagian forces.[3] Furthermore—and it may be that this was the decisive factor in the struggle—the judgement of the pope was not shared by all his Roman flock. A hard core of opposition remained. Among its

[1] Aug., *Serm.* 131, x, 10: 'Redarguite contradicentes, et resistentes ad nos perducite. Iam enim de hac causa duo concilia missa sunt ad Sedem Apostolicam: inde etiam rescripta venerunt. Causa finita est: utinam aliquando finiatur error!' This is the famous passage often misquoted as 'Roma locuta est, causa finita est.' William Bright, *The Roman See in the Early Church*, London, 1896, 130 *n.*, pointed out that twenty-four years earlier Augustine had said to the Donatists: 'Olim causa iam finita est. Quid vos non statis in pace?' (*Psalmus c. Partem Donati*, ed. Anastasi, 45); while at a later date, not noticed by Bright, after the Conference of Carthage of 411, he had written: 'Nocte causa finita est, sed ut nox fineretur erroris' (*Ad Donat. post Coll.*, xxxv, 58). See also *C. Iul.*, III, i, 5: 'Vestra vero apud competens iudicium communium episcoporum modo causa finita est'; ibid., III, xxi, 45: 'Causa itaque nostra finita est.' Clearly, the formula 'causa finita est'— 'it's all settled!' appealed to Augustine, and too much stress should not be laid upon it. There are, however, certain scholars, e.g. Luke Rivington, *The Primitive Church and the See of St. Peter*, London, 1894, 291 and Abbot John Chapman, *Studies in the Early Papacy*, London, 1925, 156, who consider that Augustine's words are epitomized in the misquotation.

[2] *C. duas Epist. Pel.*, II, iii, 5: 'Tot enim et tantis inter apostolicam sedem et afros episcopos currentibus et recurrentibus scriptis ecclesiasticis, etiam gestis de hac causa apud illam sedem Caelestio praesente et respondente confectis.' Zosimus, in his letter of 21 March 418, refers to two letters from the African bishops. MPL xlv, 1726. 'L'histoire de cette période,' observe the authors of Fliche and Martin, *Histoire de l'Église*, iv, Paris, 1937, 108 *n*[4], 'a été compliquée à plaisir par Garnier (*PL* xlviii, 319–78), et Quesnel (*PL* lvi, 959–1006), qui ont supposé un premier grand concile d'Afrique, tenu au printemps (ou en automne, Quesnel, xiv, 971), et, entre cet hypothétique concile "de 214 évêques" et celui "de 224 (ou 226) évêques" du 1er mai 418, au moins deux conciles intermédiaires en novembre 417 et février–mars 418, et encore un autre, le 17 juin 418, où l'on aurait adopté "les canons" (d'après une phrase probablement mal interprétée d'Augustin, *Epist.* 200, 2).' Ferguson, p. 108 echoes this view, referring to the 'perverted ingenuity of some church historians who fashion Councils almost at will'. As examples of such historians he gives, in a footnote, the names of Garnier and Quesnel. 'It may be', he continues, 'that there was a semi-official synod hurriedly summoned in November; it may be that Aurelius, like Ambrose on another occasion, took it upon himself to act in the name of those who had subscribed to the decisions of the full synod in 416, perhaps confirming his actions by correspondence.' The obvious objection to the multiplication of hypothetical councils is one which will occur to anyone who has ever tried to convene an extraordinary meeting of a body as small and as concentrated spatially as a parochial church council: people are busy and simply cannot spare the time continually to attend meetings especially if, as was the case with the African bishops, many had to make long journeys. Certainly, the Africans had a taste for councils; but it should be remembered that the decision of the Council of Hippo of 393 for annual councils proved unworkable, and so the eleventh Council of Carthage of 407 had to set the decision aside and decree that councils should only be summoned when required (Hefele-Leclercq, II, i, 157).

[3] Hieron., *Ep.* 141. *CSEL* lvi, 290–1 (Inter Aug., *Ep.* 195).

members and perhaps the leading spirit was Marius Mercator, who was later to play his part as the translator into Latin of the events in the east which led to the condemnation of Nestorius at Ephesus in 431 and who wrote two works, now lost, against Pelagius and Caelestius.[1] On the other side stood Caelestius, uncondemned, and supported by Julian, bishop of Eclanum, a vigorous controversialist, destined to become the last and probably the most formidable of all the antagonists with whom Augustine crossed swords in a lifetime of polemical writing. The debate was waged with increasing bitterness and, at the last, broke out into open violence, when the Pelagian party assaulted one of its opponents, Constantius.[2] Once again, as in the assault on Jerome's monastery in 416, the use of force proved a disaster for those who employed it. The degree to which the defenders of orthodoxy were involved in the appeal to the emperor which was to ruin the Pelagian cause is not clear; but there can be little doubt that whatever pressure was brought to bear from Africa, the imperial government could not remain indifferent to a religious dispute which gave rise to civic disturbances. Only seven years had elapsed since the decree for the suppression of Donatism had been issued and the resources of the state brought to bear on the African dissidents. It was not likely that outbreaks which recalled the methods of the Circumcellions would be tolerated in Italy.

Meanwhile Zosimus himself was beginning to entertain doubts about the soundness of Caelestius' opinions. In a letter of 21 March 418 addressed to the African churches he reaffirmed all his claims for the authority of the apostolic see but added that no final decision had been taken in the case before him; he neither approved Caelestius wholly nor condemned him utterly.[3] It was the beginning of the end. On 30 April the Emperor Honorius, from the fastnesses of Ravenna where his perception of the need to preserve the imperial person from danger had long since taken him, issued a rescript condemning those who denied the Fall and demanding that Pelagius and Caelestius, both of whom he assumed to be at Rome, should be banished.[4] The next day, 1 May, a general council of over two hundred African bishops[5] assembled at Carthage and passed a series of

[1] See Aug., *Ep.* 193. For an outline of Mercator's writings see Labriolle, *Hist. de la litt. lat. chrét.*, 3e éd., ii, 661–2; Altaner, *Patrologie*, 413–14. It has been suggested that one of Mercator's lost treatises is the *Hypomnesticon contra Pelagianos et Caelestianos. MPL* xlv, 1611–64.

[2] Prosper, *Chronicon*, sub anno 418. *MGH Chronica Minora*, ed. Th. Mommsen, Berlin, i, 1892, 468.

[3] Zosimus, *Ep. ad Afros*, 'Quamvis Patrum'. *MPL* xlv, 1725–6.

[4] *MPL* xlv, 1726–8; ibid., xlviii, 379–386; Mansi, iv, 444.

[5] Prosper, *Contra Collat.*, 5 says 214; Photius, *Bibl.* 53 says 226; while Mansi, *Sacr. Conc.*, iv, 377 estimated the number as 203.

nine canons against Pelagianism.[1] These affirmed the connection of human mortality with the Fall; the relation of infant baptism to Original Sin and the impossibility of the salvation of unbaptized infants; insisted that Grace was more than forgiveness of sins or illumination and that it did not merely assist obedience; and declared that even the holiest persons had sins for which they must entreat God's pardon.[2] The combination of the imperial edict with the intransigence of the Carthaginian Council may well have played its part in bringing Zosimus to a decision; but it would be ungenerous to assume that his subsequent action was dictated by pressure, either of the court or of the African bishops. It is more likely that he was affected by the conduct of the Pelagians at Rome and the strength of the hostility shown to them. Moreover he seems, about this time, to have read Pelagius' commentary on Romans and to have been shocked by the doctrine which he found in it. He therefore ordered Caelestius to appear before him; but the accused ignored the summons and precipitately departed from the city.[3] His flight appeared to be an admission of guilt and he stood self-condemned. Zosimus thereupon issued a lengthy document, now lost, known as the Epistola Tractoria,[4] in which he condemned and excommunicated both Pelagius and Caelestius and affirmed the doctrines of Grace, Original Sin, and the efficacy of baptism for every age and state. A copy of the letter was sent to Constantinople; emperor and pope were alike arrayed against Pelagianism. Subscription to the Tractoria was enforced in Italy by imperial authority, but eighteen bishops, led by Julian of Eclanum, refused to sign. Julian appealed to a general council of the Church, but his appeal was rejected and he himself deposed. Nothing however could quench his enthusiasm, and he was to remain an active and embittered enemy of Augustine until the saint's death.

For Pelagius, Zosimus' decision was the ruin of all his hopes. To some friends of Augustine living in Palestine, Pinianus, his wife Melania and her mother Albina, he protested his orthodoxy, anathematizing those who denied that the Grace of God, by which Christ came into the world to save sinners, was necessary, not only every hour or every moment, but for

---

[1] There is no reason to see any direct correlation between the issue of the imperial rescript and the meeting of this Council.

[2] Prosper, Contra Collat., 5, 3. MPL li, 227. Printed in MPL xlv, 1728–30.

[3] It would greatly help our evaluation of Zosimus' conduct if we could be certain of the date of the summons in relation to the imperial edict. Was Caelestius' flight due to panic, and despair of maintaining his theological position, or was it merely in anticipation of action by the secular arm. See Plinval, p. 323 n[1].

[4] Mercator, Commonitorium, i, 5; iii, 1 (MPL xlviii, 77–83, 90–95). Fragments in Aug., Ep. 190, 23; Prosper, Contra Collat., 5, 3 (MPL li, 228); Coelestinus, Epist. ad Galliarum Episcopos (MPL xlv, 1758).

each individual action of our lives.[1] Augustine, however, replied that he had never found any satisfactory recognition of the nature of Grace in the writings of Pelagius[2] and declined to accept his declaration of faith. By now the tide of hostility was rising fast against the unhappy moralist. Condemned by a synod presided over by Theodotus of Antioch and abandoned by his former patron Praylius, he was expelled from Jerusalem and departed, probably for Egypt.[3] Hereafter, he vanishes from history. It is to be hoped that, at the last, he found the peace which the storms of seven years of controversy had denied him, and the truth for which he sought. His fate deserves our pity, if his views cannot command our approbation.

Caelestius, characteristically and appropriately, enjoyed a more dramatic fate. In 423, after the death of Zosimus, he reappeared in Rome, hoping to satisfy pope Boniface as to the orthodoxy of his views. He failed, and only succeeded in getting himself expelled from Italy.[4] In 429 he is to be found in Constantinople, where he joined Julian of Eclanum and other deposed Pelagian bishops. Nestorius, the patriarch of Constantinople, had spoken vigorously enough against those who denied the transmission of Adam's sin; but it was hoped that he might prove more generous as a man than his predecessor, Atticus. The belief proved a tragic miscalculation on the part of the Pelagian party. Nestorius, indeed, heard their protestations sympathetically and wrote to Rome for further information; but unluckily for them, his own reputation was already compromised by his dispute with St Cyril of Alexandria regarding Nestorius' denunciation of the use of the word theotokos—God-bearer—to describe the Virgin Mary. Nestorius was condemned at the Council of Ephesus in 431 and in the shipwreck of his fortunes the Pelagian cause finally floundered. His generosity had proved more damaging than the hostility of others and the names of Caelestius, Pelagius and Julian were among those who were condemned by the Council.[5] Augustine had triumphed, but did not live to see the final victory. He had been among the bishops summoned to the Council of Ephesus, but he never arrived there, dying in the beleaguered city of Hippo in circumstances which seemed to proclaim, at least by worldly standards, the ruin of his life's work. In the twelve years of life which remained to him after the events of 418, Pelagianism, and the discussions to which it gave rise, were far from being a dead issue. Condemned alike by Church and state, the heresy found a powerful defender in Julian of Eclanum, while the increasing intransigence which marked Augustine's later writings caused

[1] De Grat. Christ., ii, 2.   [2] Ibid., xxxv, 38–xxxvii, 41.
[3] For the last years of Pelagius, see Plinval, op. cit., p. 330; and Ferguson, op. cit., p. 114.   [4] Prosper, Contra Collat., 21, 2. MPL li, 271.
[5] Mansi, iv, 1338; Schwartz, Act. Conc. Œc., I, i, 3, p. 9.

alarm and opposition among men who were not, in principle, sympathetic to Pelagius and his opinions.

Julian, bishop of Eclanum, the son of a bishop and by reason of his talents marked out from an early age for the episcopate, is one of the tragic figures of the Pelagianism controversy. But for the zeal with which he embraced and defended the views of Pelagius, he might have ended his days as an honoured figure in the Church. Instead, his participation in the dispute failed to enhance its dignity, while the polemical writings which passed between him and Augustine were neither edifying nor conducive to the establishment of truth. The character of Julian has appealed to many historians but it is not easy to see why. It is to his credit that he held firmly to the doctrine of the goodness of all created things, including marriage, which he considered to have been impugned by the Augustinian theory of the transmission of Original Sin; but since he was himself married, this is hardly a matter for surprise. Married clergy are apt to be sensitive on the point, particularly in an age when popular sentiment favours asceticism and where the monk is the great hero of the religiously minded. More impressive in such an environment is an attitude like that of the aged Paphnutius, a monk and an ascetic famous for his chastity who, at the Council of Nicaea, when it was proposed that married clergy should be required to abstain from intercourse with their wives, strongly opposed the suggestion, declaring that no man should be separated from the wife whom he had married before ordination.[1] Moreover, there is to be seen in Julian's character an arrogance of a most unattractive nature. He showed no respect for Augustine, a man thirty years his senior and a friend of his family, but sneeringly termed him the 'Punic Aristotle'; nor did he make any attempt to conceal his scorn for the simple people who, his vanity assured him, made up the Catholic party. Augustine retorted by calling Julian an overconfident youth, and the tone of the debate was, from the first, unedifying.[2] One could wish indeed that the whole episode had been omitted from the history of the Church. It achieved nothing and led only to an increasingly rigorous reiteration of Augustine's predestinarian theory.

From the exposition of this theory arose the dispute which was to mark a new development in Augustine's writings on Grace—the campaign which he waged against the so-called Semi-Pelagians.[3] In a letter written in

[1] Socrates, *HE* i, 11, ed. Bright, p. 30.

[2] *Op. Imp. c. Iul.*, i, 7: 'tractator Poenus'; iii, 199: 'Aristoteles Poenorum'; v, 11: 'philosophaster Poenorum'. For his contempt of the *simplices*, see *C. Iul.*, II, x, 37. For Augustine's retort, see *C. Iul.*, II, viii, 30: 'iuvenis confidentissimus'.

[3] For a general description of the dispute, see Mary Alphonsine Lesousky, *The* De Dono Perseverantiae *of St Augustine* (Catholic University of America Patristic Studies, vol. 91), Washington, D.C., 1956, 1–101.

418 to the Roman presbyter Sixtus[1] (later pope Sixtus III), the saint had expressed his doctrine of Predestination in the starkest terms. Eight or nine years later Florus, a monk of Hadrumetum in Byzacena, while absent from his monastery on a visit to Uzala, his former home, came upon a copy of this letter, admired it, and sent a copy back to his monastery for the edification of the brethren. When it was read, however, it caused violent disagreement among the monks, some of whom asserted that it destroyed the freedom of the will.[2] It was necessary to send two of the community, hostile to Augustine's teaching, to Hippo (where they were subsequently joined by a third, favourable to his views) to hear the bishop's explanations from his own lips.[3] They returned, bearing two letters of explanation from Augustine,[4] who subsequently composed a treatise *On Grace and Free Will* for the benefit of the abbot of Hadrumetum and his community.[5] In this the saint declared that the doctrine of free will must be maintained, but in such a fashion as to provoke the comment that, according to Augustine's argument, we ought not to rebuke a man for not keeping God's commandments but only to pray that he might keep them.[6] On hearing of this comment, Augustine composed another work *On Rebuke and Grace*, in which he contended that while rebuke is justified in the case of a Christian who had fallen into sin, it would only be effective if he were one of the elect. This sort of argument did nothing to allay the suspicion which his teaching inspired in certain quarters among persons who had no sympathy with the views of the Pelagian party. From Provence, Augustine's friend and admirer, Prosper, wrote a lengthy letter[7] telling him of the difficulty which his doctrine was causing many servants of God in Marseilles. They thought it contrary to the traditions of the Fathers and the interpretation of the Church. They themselves believed in the possible salvation of all human beings, holding that the idea of the election of some and the reprobation of the rest led to fatalism. Another letter to the same effect came from a certain Hilary. If men's fates were determined by predestination, what was the use of warning or correction? If the Grace conferred on the first man did not ensure his perseverance, but the Grace conferred on his

---

[1] Aug., *Ep.* 194.
[2] *Ep.* 216, 2, 3. For the date, see Goldbacher, *CSEL* lviii, 57.
[3] *Ep.* 214, 1.
[4] *Epp.* 214; 215. The second was composed after the arrival at Hippo of the third monk, Felix.
[5] *Retract.*, ii, 92 [66].
[6] Ibid., ii, 93 [67]: 'Rursus ad eosdem [monachos Adrumetinos] scripsi alterum librum, quem de correptione et gratia praenotavi, cum mihi nuntiatum esset dixisse ibi quendam neminem corripiendum, si dei praecepta non facit, sed pro illo, ut faciat, tantummodo orandum.'
[7] Aug., *Ep.* 225, written in 429. See Goldbacher, *CSEL* lviii, 60–61.

predestined successors did, then their treatment is unequal. The writer made it clear that he did not himself share the doubts of the brethren on whose behalf the letter was written.[1]

Augustine replied to these letters in two more treatises *On the Predestination of the Saints* and *On the Gift of Perseverance*. No hint of compromise tempers these works. Predestination is declared to be independent of any foreseen piety, and no man will be judged according to what he might have done had circumstances been different.[2] Men are chosen in order that they may believe and not because they believe.[3] Perseverance is the gift of God by which we persevere to the end, in Christ.[4] The Grace of God is not given according to merits, because God is merciful; nor is it given to all, because He is just.[5] To the question why, in the case of two infants both equally bound by Original Sin, one should be taken and the other left, or of two adult sinners, why one should be called and follow, while the other is either not called or not so called that he will follow, Augustine gives no answer except to affirm that the judgements of God are inscrutable.[6] Predestination to life or rejection to reprobation are alike absolute.[7] If we say that faith begins of ourselves and by that beginning we deserve to receive other gifts of God, we come to the Pelagian view, abhorrent to the Catholic faith, that Grace is given according to our merits.[8] Augustine, although he realizes the difficulty caused by his doctrine for simple souls, nevertheless maintains that, because it is true, it must not be suppressed.[9] It should, however, be expounded discreetly, so that a congregation is not continually reminded that the elect among them are certainly saved and the reprobate certainly lost.[10]

Such tact in no way reconciled his opponents. His friend, Prosper of Aquitaine, threw himself unreservedly into the struggle and violently attacked those who rejected the teachings of his hero. Among them were men of distinction like John Cassian, the saintly abbot of St Victor of

[1] *Ep.* 226, written in 429. Goldbacher, pp. 60–61.
[2] *De Praed. Sanct.*, xii, 24.
[3] Ibid., xvii, 34: 'Intelligamus ergo vocationem qua fiunt electi: non qui eliguntur quia crediderunt, sed qui eliguntur ut credant.'
[4] *De Dono Persev.*, i, 1: 'Asserimus ergo donum Dei esse perseverantiam, qua usque in finem perseveratur in Christo.' [5] Ibid.,viii, 16.
[6] Ibid., ix, 21: 'Ex duobus itaque parvulis originali peccato pariter obstrictis, cur iste assumatur, ille relinquatur: et ex duobus aetate iam grandibus impiis, cur iste ita vocetur, ut vocantem sequatur, ille autem aut non vocetur, aut non ita vocetur; inscrutabilia sunt iudicia Dei.'
[7] Ibid., xii, 30; xiv, 35. [8] Ibid., xxi, 54.
[9] Ibid., xvi, 40: 'Dicatur ergo verum, maxime ubi aliqua quaestio ut dicatur impellit; et capiant qui possunt: ne forte cum tacetur propter eos qui capere non possunt, non solum veritate fraudentur, verum etiam falsitate capiantur, qui verum capere, quo caveatur falsitas, possunt.'
[10] Ibid., xxii, 57–61, esp. 58.

Marseilles,[1] and Euladius, the bishop of Arles.[2] It has become customary to refer to them as Semi-Pelagians, and it seems improbable that the name will be superseded, though it is, in fact, a misleading one. Nor is the title of Anti-Augustinians, which some modern historians have suggested as an alternative, much happier. The opposition forces of southern Gaul did not in any way subscribe to Pelagius' views, nor did they reject Augustine's except in the matter of his predestinarian teaching which, they held, led to a denial of freedom. Furthermore they were shocked by the suggestion that God does not wish all men to be saved but only some and by Augustine's attempts to explain away the Pauline declaration that God *will have all men to be saved*.[3] They admired and cited Augustine's earlier writings; but they refused to accept a doctrine which seemed to them to reduce the individual human soul to the condition of a mere puppet in the divine plan. Christ had wept over Jerusalem and had cried: *How often would I have gathered thy children together, even as a hen gathers her chickens, and ye would not!*[4] Without Grace a man can do no good thing; but he must be allowed the freedom of desiring Grace, for Grace is not irresistible. The Saviour died for all; and nothing that Augustine could say availed to alter their opinion.

The dispute continued long after Augustine's death, with his friend and disciple, Prosper of Aquitaine, continuing to defend Augustinian doctrine. During the saint's lifetime, the language of controversy had become steadily more bitter and now tempers were roused and vituperation increased. Prosper was not always a fair controversialist, while his opponents did not shrink from uttering statements of what they declared to be predestinarian teaching which misrepresented Augustine in a very unsavoury manner. To his discredit, Vincent of Lerins, the author of the famous *Commonitorium against the Profane Novelties of all Heretics*, entered the lists and compiled a scurrilous list of alleged deductions from Augustine's writings, designed to exhibit them in the worst possible light.[5]

It has been necessary to dwell upon the events of the Pelagian controversy in some detail, in order to give a background to the discussion of the theology of Augustine's writing on the subject. That theology has to be deduced from the series of controversial pamphlets produced in a particular situa-

---

[1] For the rôle of Cassian in the Pelagian controversy, see Léon Cristiani, *Jean Cassien*, ii, 237–68.

[2] Not Hilary, as the majority of MSS. read. See Owen Chadwick, 'Euladius of Arles', in *JTS* xlvi (1945), 200–5. Chadwick's arguments are accepted by Elie Griffe, *La Gaule chrétienne à l'époque romaine*, ii, 191–3.

[3] I Tim. 2.4. See below, p. 389.   [4] Matt. 23.37.

[5] *Capitula obiectionum Vincentianarum*, refuted by Prosper of Aquitaine. *MPL* li, 177–190. See H. Koch, *Vincent von Lérins und Gennadius (Texte und Untersuchungen zur altchristlichen Litteratur*, xxxi), 1907, 2.

tion. The historian's task is accordingly the harder, since he has to decide what emphasis is to be placed upon a sentence or on a remark made in the course of controversy which may be one of those unconsidered utterances which debate is apt to engender. Hence there is a wide divergence of views among scholars as to the precise nature of Augustinian thought. Some are pessimistic, and paint his system in the darkest colours; others take a more cheerful view and feel that his more extreme statements can be explained in the light of a particular situation, and do not represent the best and most enduring features of his work. It is possible that neither of these extremes is the true verdict on Augustine; but in view of the importance of the issues involved we dare not simply assume that the truth must automatically be found somewhere between them. Nothing is gained, either by underestimating the depth and profundity of the instinct which led Augustine to fight so fiercely and continuously in defence of the Grace of God or by minimizing the terrible conclusions to which he was driven by the inexorable logic of his theory of predestination. The subject is too great and too profound to admit of any facile explanation. It may be that Augustine would have been wise to heed those words of St Paul which he himself quoted in a famous sermon: *O the depth of the riches both of the wisdom and knowledge of God! how unsearchable are His ways past finding out!*[1] Since however he chose, or was constrained, to discuss the topic, the historian must be ready to examine the matter without preconceptions, prepared to understand before he seeks to criticize. On the controversy as a whole, it would be well to bear in mind the words of a great secular historian who viewed the battle from afar without any of the personal feelings of the theologian:

> Augustine, the fiery man of action, knew more about the human will than Pelagius the reserved and dreaming wanderer. It was the ineffective, unpractical man who insisted on the freedom of the will; the strong man knew that such insistence was the unconscious betrayal of inner weakness. Augustine was right: a determinism of the kind which he preached is indispensable to sound ethical doctrine. . . . Augustine's thought, still today dominating civilization like a colossus, expressed the demonic energy of the early Christian mind, conscious of itself as drawing on stores of energy that were not finite, like the human personality, but infinite.[2]

[1] Rom. 11.33, quoted by Aug., *Serm.* 26, xii, 13.
[2] R. G. Collingwood in Collingwood and Myres, *Roman Britain and the English Settlements*, 2nd ed., Oxford, 1949, 309.

9

The Pelagian Controversy: the Issues

Adam sinned, and *I* suffer; I *forfeited* before I had any *possession* or could claime any *Interest*; I had a *Punishment*, before I had a *being*, And *God* was displeased with *me* before *I* was *I*; I was built up scarse 50 years ago, in my Mothers womb, and I was cast down, almost 6000 years agoe, in *Adams* loynes; I was *borne* in the last *Age* of the world, and *dyed* in the first. How and how justly do we cry out against a Man, that hath sold a *Towne*, or sold an *Army*. And *Adam* sold the *World*.

JOHN DONNE

De parentis protoplasti fraude factor condolens
quando pomi noxialis morte morsu corruit,
ipse lignum tunc notavit, damna ligni ut solveret.

VENANTIUS FORTUNATUS

IN ANY discussion of the Pelagian heresy, it is desirable to keep in mind certain considerations which influenced its formulators and disseminators. In justice to Pelagius, who has probably been the victim of a good deal of misrepresentation both in his own lifetime and in the succeeding centuries, it should be emphasized that he did not formulate Pelagianism out of sheer wilfulness and then proclaim it out of vainglory. On the contrary, he seems to have shunned publicity and to have avoided controversy for as long as he could. Again, too much stress ought not to be laid upon the intellectual background to Pelagianism. Certain affinities may indeed be seen with Stoicism; while the Pelagians were able to evolve a simple and apparently coherent doctrine of Man which, when expounded by accomplished casuists like Caelestius or Julian of Eclanum, had the air of a well-reasoned theological system, from which a code of behaviour naturally follows. But to approach the first great purely Latin heresy in such a frame of mind is to miss the point and, at the same time, to be unfair to its exponents. For Pelagianism, dangerous as its thought was and disastrous as its triumph would undoubtedly have been for Christian devotion and dogma, sprang from principles which were, in themselves, generous and even noble. We must not think of it as a comfortable, optimistic philosophy. with a supreme faith in man and an inability to see sin in the world, Rather, it must be understood as a reforming movement, which failed owing to a faulty appreciation of human nature, arising from a false understanding of the nature of sin—not the fact; the Pelagians were well enough aware of that—and the nature of the Redemption. If we may use a medical analogy, we can say that the Pelagians saw that the patient was ill, but made a faulty diagnosis, from which they prescribed an inadequate, and dangerous, treatment. Augustine had the merit of understanding the nature of the complaint to a much better degree, so that his prescription was efficacious, though certain aspects of his diagnosis were, perhaps, mistaken. But it is certain that Pelagius never fell into the error of supposing a sick world to be well.

Pelagianism was a reforming movement in the corrupt world of the later Roman Empire. It was born in an age of active cruelty, passive selfishness, and unbridled lust and avarice.[1] While the machine of government pressed more and more heavily upon the shoulders of its subjects, the burden was unequally borne, so that it was the peasant and the little man who bore the weight of taxation, from which the rich were virtually immune. Moreover, while there was everywhere corruption in everyday life, there was also deterioration in the standards of the Church. Although the notion of a kind of golden age in the first Christian centuries will not bear investigation, since it is clear that, from Apostolic times, the Church has had many members whose conduct was unworthy of their profession, there is not a little to be said for the view that the triumph of Christianity under Constantine and his successors was, in a certain sense, a tragedy for the Church. The great age of the martyrs had passed; Christianity, from the worldly point of view, had succeeded, with inevitable consequences. If it were no longer heroic to be a Christian, it was at any rate respectable, and a profession of Christianity need not necessarily imply a radical change in the convert's life. Augustine deemed it desirable to warn his fellow Christians against the belief that liberal almsgiving could redeem deadly sin.[2] Jerome, in a letter of 413, writes with burning words of the selfishness which characterized the death-agony of the western part of the Empire:

Shame on us, the world is falling in ruins, but our sins still flourish. . . . We live as though we were doomed to death on the morrow, but we build houses as though we were going to live for ever in this world. Our

---

[1] For a picture of the age, see Sir Samuel Dill, *Roman Society in the last Century of the Western Empire*, 2nd ed., London, 1899—a mass of detail; also Ferdinand Lot, *La fin du monde antique et le début du Moyen Age*, Paris, 1927, esp. cap. X: 'Corruption de l'esprit publique'.

[2] *Enchir.*, xix, 70: 'Sane cavendum est ne quisquam existimet infanda illa crimina, qualia qui agunt, regnum Dei non possidebant, cotidie perpetranda, et eleemosynis cotidie redimenda. In melius quippe est vita mutanda, et per eleemosynas de peccatis praeteritis est propitiandus Deus; non ad hoc emendus quodam modo, ut ea semper liceat impune committere.'

M

walls glitter with gold, gold gleams upon our ceilings and upon the capitals of our pillars: yet Christ is dying at our doors in the persons of His poor, naked and hungry.[1]

In his younger days, Jerome was roused to indignation by the worldliness and luxury of the Christians of Rome, and his vehement denunciations are among the most lively part of his fascinating correspondence, while the zeal with which he set about to reclaim the Romans from their unworthy lives aroused passionate hostility to him. Nor were these abuses confined to the Latin part of the Empire; the East rivalled and surpassed the West, and John Chrysostom devoted all the power of his matchless oratory, first at Antioch and later at Constantinople, to attacking the sins of his flock until he became, in the words of his biographer, 'as intolerable to worldly Christians as a lamp to sore eyes'.[2] Unhappily, it was not merely greed and vanity which disfigured the name of Christian; cruelty to slaves of a kind— though not to the degree—which Juvenal had denounced three centuries earlier was familiar enough in many avowedly Christian households.[3] St Paul's letter to Philemon had made little impression on these stony hearts.

Furthermore, among the mass of the Christian populace, there were many to whom Christianity was simply a way to salvation, a miraculous rite which guaranteed safety in the next world, without any suggestion that it might influence conduct in this. Superstition and optimism coloured their thought; Augustine remarked that in Africa there were many who did not believe in the eternal punishment of the damned.[4] Others attempted to combine Christianity with an observance of pagan convention, and frequented both Christian churches and pagan theatres,[5] while

[1] Hieron., *Ep.* 128, 5. *CSEL* lvi, 161. Tr. by F. A. Wright, Loeb ed., p. 479.

[2] Palladius, *Vita Chrysostomi*, 18: βαρὺς γὰρ αὐτοῖς ἦν καὶ φαινόμενος, καθάπερ λύχνος λημιῶσιν ὄμμασιν. *MPG* xlvii, 62.

[3] Cf. Chrysostom, *Hom. in Epist. ad Ephes.*, 15, 3–4, where the saint describes the flogging of a slave-girl for some trivial offence with Juvenal, *Satire* VI, 490ff. J. B. Bury, *History of the Later Roman Empire*, i, 138–42, draws attention to Chrysostom's homily, but points out that there were masters who took the deepest interest in the well-being of their slaves. It should be noted that Chrysostom does not condemn all corporal punishment of slaves: Τί οὖν, οὐ χρὴ τύπτειν; οὐ τοῦτο λέγω· δεῖ μὲν γὰρ, ἀλλὰ μήτε συνεχῶς, μήτε ἀμέτρως, μήτε ὑπὲρ τῶν οἰκείων ἀδικημάτων, ὅπερ ἀεὶ φημι, μήτε τῆς ὑπηρεσίας ἄν τι ἐλλείπῃ, ἀλλ' εἰ τὴν ἑαυτῆς βλάπτει ψυχήν· ἄν ὑπὲρ τοιαύτης τύπτῃς αἰτίας, ἐπαινέσονται πάντες, καὶ ὁ ἐγκαλέσων οὐδείς· ἄν δὲ ὑπὲρ τῶν σῶν, ὠμότητα πάντες καταγνώσονται καὶ ἀπήνειαν. *MPG* lxii, 109. The preacher reminds his hearers that a Christian slave is a sister in the faith: Ἀδελφή σοῦ γέγονεν, ἄν ᾖ πιστή. See Aimé Puech, *St Jean Chrysostom et les mœurs de son temps*, Paris, 1891, 143–56.

[4] *Enchir.*, xxix, 112: 'Frustra itaque nonnulli, immo quam plurimi, aeternam damnatorum poenam et cruciatus sine intermissione perpetuos humano miserantur affectu, atque ita futurum esse non credunt.' Cf. *dCD*, XXI, xxiv, xxvii.

[5] *De Catech. Rud.*, xxv, 48: 'Animadversurus etiam quod illae turbae impleant ecclesias per dies festos Christianorum, quae implent et theatra per dies sollemnes paganorum.' *dCD*, I, xxxv: 'Qui [sc. quidam Christiani] etiam cum ipsis inimicis adversus Deum, cuius sacramentum gerunt, murmurare non dubitant, modo cum illis theatra, modo ecclesias nobiscum replentes.'

there was even the case in Augustine's own diocese of a sub-deacon who was a Manichaean Auditor for years, continuing all the time to minister to a Catholic congregation.[1] It has been observed—and surely rightly—that the mass of educated opinion in the fourth and fifth centuries is neither Christian nor pagan but 'an elegant pedantry, a vague liberalism, a watery humanity, a fluid pantheism, and above all, a vast superstition, creeping up from the lower classes as rationalism decayed'.[2] This was the atmosphere in which Pelagianism developed.

It was against this laxity that Pelagius and his followers protested, and it was this protest which influenced their theology and the expression of it. Hence we have Pelagius' celebrated assertion that, in the day of judgement, no mercy will be shown to sinners but they will be burned in eternal fires.[3] As a calculated theological statement it is as merciless and terrifying as any of those assertions of Augustine which have distressed charitable souls; but it is not so much a calculated theological statement as the exclamation of a preacher seeking to rouse his hearers from the slumber of sin. There was, in Pelagianism, a great potential missionary fervour, and it is a tragedy that it was not possible to employ that fervour in the service of the Church.

Having said this, however, it must be emphasized that, beside the potential fervour, there was an actual danger, in a sense of self-sufficiency springing from an inadequate understanding of human character. This is admirably expressed by Pelagius' discussion of the nature of human action in his book, *De Libero Arbitrio*, preserved for us in Augustine's treatise *De Gratia Christi*, written in answer to it. In any action, according to Pelagius, and *a fortiori*, in any moral action, three elements are to be seen. First, we must be able to do it; secondly, we must be willing to do it; and, finally, the action must be carried out.[4] The words Pelagius uses are

---

[1] Aug., *Ep.* 236.   [2] Moss, *The Birth of the Middle Ages*, 32.

[3] *De Gestis Pel.*, iii, 9: 'Item recitatum est quod in libro suo Pelagius posuit: "In die iudicii iniquis et peccatoribus non esse parcendum, sed aeternis eos ignibus exurendos."' Hieron., *Dialogus adversus Pelagianos*, i, 28: 'In die iudicii iniquis et peccatoribus non parcendum, sed aeternis eos ignibus exurendos. . . . Scriptum est [enim] in centesimo tertio psalmo: *Deficiant peccatores a terra et iniqui, ita ut non sint* (Ps. 103.35 [104.35]). Et in Isaia: *Comburentur iniqui et peccatores simul, et qui relinquunt Deum, consumabuntur* (Isai. 1.28 LXX).' *MPL* xxiii, 520–1. Pelagius' book referred to was the *Liber Eulogiarum*.

[4] *De Grat. Christ.*, iv, 5: ' "Nos," inquit [Pelagius], "sic tria ista distinguimus et certum velut in ordinem digesta partimur. primo loco posse statuimus, secundo velle, tertio esse; posse in natura, velle in arbitrio, esse in effectu locamus. primum illud, id est posse ad deum proprie pertinet, qui illud creaturae suae contulit, duo vero reliqua, hoc est velle et esse ad hominem referenda sunt, quia de arbitrii fonte descendunt. ergo in voluntate et opere bono laus hominis est, immo et hominis et dei, qui ipsius voluntatis et operis possibilitatem dedit quique ipsam possibilitatem gratiae suae adiuvat semper auxilio; quod vero potest homo velle bonum atque perficere, solius dei est. potest itaque illud unum esse, etiamsi duo ista non fuerint, ista vero sine illo esse non possunt." '

356 ST AUGUSTINE OF HIPPO

posse, velle and *esse*, but it is simpler to use the words employed by Augustine to describe the Pelagian analysis: possibility; will; and action.[1] Of these three, possibility comes from the natural endowment which every creature has from God, and is of Him alone; but the will which brings about the action, and the action itself, must be assigned to man, since they arise from free choice. And so, reasoned Pelagius, 'in the Will and in good work there is praise for man or, rather, for man and God, who has given the possibility of will and work, and who always assists that possibility with the help of His grace. For it certainly is of God alone that man is able to will a good thing and bring it to completion; and this one quality, possibility, is able to exist without the other two, will and action; but these two latter cannot exist without the first.'[2]

Pelagius did not fail to emphasize the divine contribution: a man is free not to have a good will and not to perform a good action, but he cannot lose his capacity for doing good.[3] As an example, he instances the physical fact of sight. That I can see is not under my control; but the use I make of my sight is. And what is true of sight is true of our other endowments. God has given us the power to act, to speak, and to think, and helps us to do so; but whether we act, speak, or think rightly depends upon ourselves. We can turn these gifts to evil uses; but this does not alter the fact that the original endowment was of God. Possibility depends on Him, and on Him alone.[4]

The weakness of such a discussion of the nature of our actions is only too clear, and the example chosen singularly unfortunate since, as Augustine pointed out, the psalmist cried: *Turn away mine eyes lest they behold vanity*[5]—a petition which has no meaning if the use we make of sight depends upon our will.[6] Most men, however, do not need to turn to Holy Scripture to have Pelagius' theory disproved. We know only too well, from our own experience, that our behaviour does not involve the simple factors that he suggests. Right action is not merely a matter of decision, *for the good which I would I do not; but the evil which I would not, that I*

---

[1] Ibid., iii, 4: 'Nam cum tria constituat atque distinguat, quibus divina mandata dicit impleri: possibilitatem, voluntatem, actionem—possibilitatem scilicet, qua potest homo esse iustus, voluntatem, qua vult esse iustus, actionem, qua iustus est—horum trium primum, id est possibilitatem datam confitetur a creatore naturae nec esse in nostra potestate, sed eam nos habere, etiamsi nolimus, duo vero reliqua, id est, voluntatem et actionem nostra esse asserit atque ita nobis tribuit, ut nonnisi a nobis esse contendat.'
[2] Ibid., iv, 5. Cited above, p. 355 n^4.
[3] Ibid.: ' "Itaque liberum mihi est nec voluntatem bonam habere nec actionem, nullo autem modo possum non habere possibilitatem boni; inest mihi, etiamsi noluero, nec otium sui aliquando in hoc natura recipit." '   [4] Ibid.
[5] Ps. 118.37 [119.37].
[6] *De Grat. Christ.*, xv, 16.

practise.[1] St Paul's admission has been echoed by generations of Christians, and by none more sincerely than the bishop of Hippo, for Augustine could remember the cry of his youth: 'Give me chastity and continence, but not yet.'[2] It would be easy to smile at this naïve prayer if the experience were not such a familiar one in the life of anyone who attempts to live the Christian life at all seriously. The besetting sin need not be incontinence, it may be any one of the other six deadly sins; but whatever it is, there is a struggle between a sincere desire to be rid of it and the lurking feeling that the sacrifice is too great, that we need a little longer, just a few days more, before making the effort lest having God we may have naught beside. Augustine, when he prayed for chastity but with the famous mental reservation, was not being hypocritical; rather, he entertained simultaneously two contradictory desires and his will was divided against itself, in a fashion which defies the neat categories of Pelagius' system.

For to go along that road and indeed to reach the goal is nothing else but the will to go. But it must be a strong and single will, not staggering and swaying about this way and that—a changeable, twisting, fluctuating will, wrestling with itself while one part falls as another rises. Finally, in the very fever of my indecision, I made many motions with my body; like men do when they will to act but cannot, either because they do not have the limbs or because their limbs are bound or weakened by disease, or incapacitated in some other way. Thus if I tore my hair, struck my forehead, or, entwining my fingers, clasped my knee, these I did because I willed it. But I might have willed it and still not have done it, if the nerves had not obeyed my will. Many things then I did, in which the will and power to do were not the same. Yet I did not do that one thing which seemed to me infinitely more desirable, which before long I should have power to will because shortly when I willed, I would will with a single will. For in this, the power of willing is the power of doing; and as yet I could not do it. Thus my body more readily obeyed the slightest wish of the soul in moving its limbs at the order of my mind than my soul obeyed itself to accomplish in the will alone its great resolve. How can there be such a strange anomaly? . . . The mind commands the body, and the body obeys. The mind commands itself and is resisted. The mind commands the hand to be moved and there is such readiness that the command is scarcely distinguished from the obedience in act. Yet the mind is mind, and the hand is body. The mind commands the mind to will, and yet though it be itself it does not obey itself. Whence this strange anomaly and why should it be? I repeat: The will commands itself to will, and could not give the command unless it wills; yet what is commanded is not done. But actually the will does not will entirely; therefore it does not command entirely. For as far as it wills, it commands. And as far as it does not will, the

[1] Rom. 7.19. [2] *Conf.*, VIII, vii, 17.

thing commanded is not done. For the will commands that there be an act of will—not another, but itself. But it does not command entirely. Therefore, what is commanded does not happen; for if the will were whole and entire, it would not even command it to be, because it would already be. It is, therefore, no strange anomaly partly to will and partly to be unwilling. This is actually an infirmity of mind, which cannot wholly rise, while pressed down by habit, even though it is supported by the truth. And so there are two wills, because one of them is not whole, and what is present in this one is lacking in the other.[1]

In this description of the mental turmoil which preceded his conversion, Augustine has provided a refutation of the Pelagian theory of the nature of volition before it was ever formulated. Our will is not the simple, single and complete faculty which Pelagius assumes but is built up out of numerous conflicting impulses.[2] Hence it is that a man can only strengthen and direct his will by coming or, rather, by being brought under another external influence—the Grace of God.

It has been necessary to dwell upon, even to labour, the difference between Augustine and Pelagius in their attitude to the will, since it is hardly an exaggeration to say that from this difference springs the fundamental cleavage between their respective theologies. The facts of Augustine's life, his own bitter experience, taught him man's utter dependence upon divine grace. Thus the great prayer which so outraged Pelagius: 'Give what Thou commandest and order what Thou wilt!'[1] is the answer to that other pathetic intercession: 'Give me chastity and continence—but not yet!' That is why the mind of Augustine is dominated by the sense of utter dependence on the grace of God. *Without Me, ye can do nothing*[3] is one of his favourite texts, as are, also, the words of St Paul: *O Man, who art thou that repliest against God? Shall the thing formed say unto Him that formed it, Why hast Thou made me thus?*[4] Accordingly, Augustine holds, as the basis of his doctrine of man, that while the fact of the Fall has made the grace accorded to man stronger and more wonderful, it has not made it more necessary.[5] Adam in Paradise before he sinned had every possible good of body and soul,[6] he was free from the stresses and temptations

---

[1] *Conf.*, VIII, viii, 19–ix, 21. Tr. by Outler, pp. 170–1.
[2] See William Temple, 'The Divinity of Christ', in *Foundations*, ed. by B. H. Streeter, London, 1913, 235–7, where the passage from the *Confessions* given above is quoted.
[3] Iohan. 15.5.   [4] Rom. 9.20.
[5] See Abercrombie, *The Origins of Jansenism*, 1ff.
[6] *dCD*, XIV, xxvi: 'Vivebat itaque homo in paradiso sicut volebat, quamdiu hoc volebat quod Deus iusserat; vivebat fruens Deo, ex quo bono erat bonus; vivebat sine ulla egestate, ita semper vivere habens in potestate. Cibus aderat ne esuriret, potus ne sitiret, lignum vitae ne illum senecta dissolueret. Nihil corruptionis in corpore vel ex corpore ullas molestias ullis eius sensibus ingerebat. Nullus intrinsecus morbus, nullus ictus metuebatur extrinsecus. Summa in carne sanitas, in animo tota tranquillitas.'

which have afflicted his descendants since the Fall,[1] yet for all this he had need of an aid, an *adiutorium*, without which, having the gift of free will, he could not avoid falling into sin[2] but which, having free will, he could if he chose abandon.[3] As a matter of historical fact, Adam did abandon the *adiutorium* and fell; but without it he could never have even hoped to persevere, since free will suffices for evil but is not sufficient for good, unless aided by the omnipotent Goodness which is God.[4] Why free will, which Augustine elsewhere refers to as a *media vis*, a midway power capable of being turned to faith or turned away to unbelief,[5] should here be regarded as having in itself a tendency to evil is not easy to decide, unless it springs from the inevitable imperfection of created things, inevitable from the very fact of their being created, which makes them tend to not-being unless they are conserved by the power of God.[6] The point which Augustine regards as fundamental, however, is that not even before the Fall could man be righteous without Grace.

> Man lived in Paradise as he wished, so long as he wished what God had ordered; he lived enjoying God, from whom, the Good, man also was good; and he lived without lacking anything, having it in his power to live thus for ever.[7]

[1] *De Corr. et Grat.*, xi, 29: 'Quid ergo? Adam non habuit Dei gratiam? Imo vero habuit magnam, sed disparem. Ille in bonis erat, quae de bonitate sui Conditoris acceperat: neque enim ea bona et ille suis meritis comparaverat, in quibus prorsus nullum patiebatur malum. Sancti vero in hac vita, ad quos pertinet liberationis haec gratia, in malis sunt, ex quibus clamant ad Deum, *Libera nos a malo* (Matt. 6.13). Ille in illis bonis Christi morte non eguit: istos a reatu et haereditario et proprio, illius Agni sanguis absolvit. Ille non opus habebat eo adiutorio, quod implorant isti cum dicunt: *Video aliam legem in membris meis* (Rom. 7.23). . . . Quoniam in eis *caro concupiscit adversus spiritum, et spiritus adversus carnem* (Gal. 5.17), atque in tali certamine laborantes ac periclitantes dari sibi pugnandi vicendique virtutem per Christi gratiam poscunt. Ille vero nulla tali rixa de se ipso adversus se ipsum tentatus atque turbatus, in illo beatitudinis loco sua secum pace fruebatur.'

[2] Ibid., xi, 31: 'Istam gratiam non habuit homo prius, qua nunquam vellet esse malus: sed sane habuit, in qua si permanere vellet, nunquam malus esset, et sine qua etiam cum libero arbitrio bonus esse non posset, sed eam tamen per liberum arbitrium deserere posset.'

[3] Ibid.

[4] Ibid.: 'Nec ipsum [sc. Adam] ergo Deus esse voluit sine sua gratia, quam reliquit in eius libero arbitrio. Quoniam liberum arbitrium ad malum sufficit, ad bonum autem parum est, nisi adiuvetur ab omnipotenti bono.'

[5] *De Spir. et Litt.*, xxxiii, 58: 'Prius igitur illud dicamus et videamus utrum huic satisfaciat quaestioni, quod liberum arbitrium naturaliter adtributum a creatore animae rationali illi media vis est, quae vel intendi ad fidem vel inclinari ad infidelitatem potest.'

[6] Cf. *Enchir.*, iv, 12: 'Naturae igitur omnes, quoniam naturarum prorsus omnium conditor summe bonus est, bonae sunt; sed quia non sicut earum conditor summe atque incommutabiliter bonae sunt, ideo in eis et minui bonum et augeri potest.'

[7] *dCD*, XIV, xxvi: 'Vivebat itaque homo in paradiso sicut volebat, quamdiu hoc volebat quod Deus iusserat; vivebat fruens Deo, ex quo bono erat bonus; vivebat sine ulla egestate, ita semper vivere habens in potestate.'

And yet he had need of Grace, if he were to persevere in that blessed condition![1]

Man did not persevere. He sinned and fell of his own free will and left to his descendants a legacy of sin and weakness. To conquer that sin and to restore the lost power, the Word was made flesh. Christ, by His death upon the Cross and by His rising from the dead, has borne our sins and freed us from the power of death and hell. To aid our weakness, He gives us, beside Grace such as Adam had, another and a stronger Grace:[2]

Neither knowledge of the divine Law, nor our nature, nor the remission of sins alone constitute Grace; but it is given to us by our Lord Jesus Christ, so that, by it, the Law may be accomplished, nature delivered, and sin vanquished.[3]

Grace is not only the endowment given to us as created beings made in the image of God, but it is the ministration of the Holy Spirit, assisting our wills and actions.[4] In the words of Augustine's prayer:

The house of my soul is too narrow for Thee to come in to me; let it be enlarged by Thee. It is in ruins; do Thou restore it. There is much about it which must offend Thy eyes; I confess and know it. But who

---

[1] *De Corr. et Grat.*, xi, 32: 'Tunc ergo dederat homini Deus bonam voluntatem; in illa quippe eum fecerat qui fecerat rectum: dederat adiutorium, sine quo in ea non posset permanere si vellet; ut autem vellet, in eius libero reliquit arbitrio. Posset ergo permanere si vellet: quia non deerat adiutorium per quod posset, et sine quo non posset perseveranter bonum tenere quod vellet.'

[2] *De Nat. et Grat.*, liii, 62: 'Quando enim istis rectissime dicitur: "quare sine adiutorio gratiae dei dicitis hominem posse esse sine peccato?" non tunc de illa gratia quaestio est, qua est homo conditus; sed de ista, qua fit salvus per Iesum Christum dominum nostrum.' *De Corr. et Grat.*, xi, 29: 'Quid ergo? Adam non habuit Dei gratiam? Imo vero habuit magnam, sed disparem.' *Ibid.*, xi, 30: 'Proinde etsi non interim laetiore nunc; verumtamen potentiore gratia indigent isti: et quae potentior quam Dei unigenitus Filius, aequalis Patri et coaeternus, pro eis homo factus, et sine suo ullo vel originali vel proprio peccato ab hominibus peccatoribus crucifixus?'

[3] *De Grat. et Lib. Arb.*, xiv, 27.

[4] *De Spir. et Litt.*, iii, 5: 'Nos autem dicimus humanam voluntatem sic divinitus adiuvari ad faciendam iustitiam, ut praeter quod creatus est homo cum libero arbitrio praeterque doctrinam qua ei praecipitur quemadmodum vivere debeat accipiat spiritum sanctum, quo fiat in animo eius delectatio dilectioque summi illius atque incommutabilis boni, quod deus est, etiam nunc cum per fidem ambulatur, nondum per speciem, ut hac sibi sicut arra data gratuiti muneris inardescat inhaerere creatori atque inflammetur accedere ad participationem illius veri luminis, ut ex illo ei bene sit, a quo habet ut sit.' *Ibid.*, v, 7: '. . . bene vivere donum esse divinum non tantum quia homini deus dedit liberum arbitrium, sine quo nec male nec bene vivitur, nec tantum quia praeceptum dedit, quo doceat quemadmodum sit vivendum, sed quia per spiritum sanctum diffundit caritatem in cordibus eorum quos praescivit ut praedestinaret, praedestinavi ut vocaret, vocavit ut iustificaret, iustificavit ut glorificaret.' *De Grat. Christ.*, xxxiv, 37: 'Illos etiam, quos in eisdem litteris, quas [Pelagius] misit ad sanctae memoriae papam Innocentium, libros suos vel scripta commemorat, legi praeter unam epistulam, quam se brevem misisse ad sanctum Constantium episcopum dicit, nec alicubi potui reperire hanc eum gratiam confiteri, qua non solum possibilitas naturalis voluntatis et actionis, quam dicit nos habere etiamsi nec volumus nec agimus bonum, sed ipsa etiam voluntas et actio subministratione sancti spiritus adiuvatur.'

will cleanse it? or to whom shall I cry but to Thee? *Cleanse Thou me from my secret faults, O Lord, and keep back Thy servant from strange sins.*[1] *I believe, and therefore do I speak.*[2] But Thou, O Lord, Thou knowest. *Have I not confessed my transgressions unto Thee, O my God; and hast Thou not put away the iniquity of my heart?*[3] I do not contend in judgement with Thee, who are Truth itself; and I would not deceive myself, lest my iniquity lie even to itself. I do not, therefore, contend in judgement with Thee for *if Thou, Lord, shouldst mark iniquities, O Lord, who shall stand?*[4]

The Pelagians also had a doctrine of Grace. It must be remembered that they were Christians, and regarded themselves as orthodox Christians, standing in the traditions of the Catholic faith. Nevertheless, they were prevented by their particular theory about the will and man's power over it from ever entertaining the sort of approach which had been forced upon Augustine by the experiences of his life. From the Pelagian point of view, the freedom which man was supposed to enjoy by reason of free will made unthinkable the Augustinian conception of Grace as an aid by which man is able to will.[5] Julian of Eclanum did not hesitate to speak of man as 'emancipated from God' by the possession of free will,[6] while Caelestius asserted that the will could not be free if it needed the help of God, since each of us has it in his own power either to act or to refrain from acting.[7] Pelagius, in his letter to the virgin Demetrias, wrote:

We say: 'It is hard! It is difficult! We cannot, we are but men, compassed about by the fragile flesh!' Blind folly and profane rashness! We accuse the God of knowledge of a twofold ignorance, so that He seems to be ignorant of what He has done or what He has commanded—as if, unmindful of human frailty, whose author He Himself is, He has imposed commands upon man which man is not able to bear.[8]

At the Synod of Diospolis, Pelagius was accused of having written that 'all men are ruled by their own wills', an accusation which he met by explaining that he was referring to free will, since God helps the man who chooses

---

[1] Ps. 18.13, 14 [19.12, 13].
[2] Ps. 115.10 [116.10].
[3] Ps. 31.5 [32.5].
[4] Ps. 129.3 [130.3]. *Conf.*, I, v, 6. Tr. by Outler, p. 34.
[5] *De Spir. et Litt.*, xxxiv, 60: 'Adtendat et videat non ideo tantum istam voluntatem divino muneri tribuendam, quia ex libero arbitrio est, quod nobis naturaliter concreatum est, verum etiam quod visorum suasionibus agit deus, ut velimus et ut credamus.'
[6] *Op. Imp. c. Iul.*, i, 78: 'Libertas arbitrii, qua a Deo emancipatus homo est, in admittendi peccati et abstinendi a peccati possibilitate consistit.'
[7] *De Gest. Pel.*, xviii, 42: 'In decimo capitulo [Caelestii libri positum objectum est] "non esse liberum arbitrium, si dei indigeat auxilio, quoniam in propria voluntate habet unusquisque aut facere aliquid aut non facere".'
[8] Pelagius, *Epist. ad Demetriaden*, 16. *MPL* xxxiii, 1110.

good, while the sinner must bear the responsibility for his own actions.[1]

With this particular assumption of the freedom of the will, the Pelagian doctrine of Grace was likely to be very different from the Augustinian. The Pelagians spoke about Grace, it is true, and Pelagius was justifiably indignant when persons hinted otherwise;[2] but what he, and still more his followers, meant by Grace fell short of the essential *adiutorium* of Augustine's thought. The careful analysis of Pelagius' doctrine of Grace which has been made by Herr Torgny Bohlin,[3] basing his work on the Pauline commentaries made by Pelagius before he became involved in controversy, serves only to confirm the accuracy of Augustine's judgement about his thought.[4] In his approach to human nature, Pelagius was dominated by the sense of the need to refute the Manichaean doctrine of the two souls in man, the one good and the other evil, and their belief that matter and the human body are evil. In consequence, he emphasized the anhypostatic conception of evil: evil is not a substance but a privation, and all that exists is good. Accordingly, he found it impossible to believe that something non-material could have any real effect upon human nature, something essentially good and created by God. Hence, the Pelagian conception of Grace was a fluctuating one, and not easily established. Initially, Pelagius applies it to man's natural qualities, which are good because they are created by a good Creator. This is the Grace of creation.[5] So in his treatise *De Natura*, Pelagius defended the assertion that a man could, if he chose, be without sin, by proclaiming that this was done by Grace; but he immediately explained this away by saying that Grace was something that man enjoyed as a part of his nature. 'For if I said: a man can argue, a bird can fly, or a hare can run, and should not mention the means whereby these actions are performed (namely tongue, wings and feet) should I have denied the means of these actions, when I have admitted the actions themselves?'[6] Such a definition of Grace is clearly not what the New Testament understands by the word, as Augustine was not slow to point out.[7] Indeed, it was

---

[1] *De Gest. Pel.*, iii, 5: 'Adiecit enim episcopalis synodus et ait: "legatur et aliud capitulum". et lectum est in eodem libro suo posuisse Pelagium "omnes voluntate propria regi". quo lecto Pelagius respondit: "et hoc dixi propter liberum arbitrium, cui deus adiutor est eligenti bona; homo vero peccans ipse in culpa est quasi liberi arbitrii". quo audito episcopi dixerunt: "neque hoc alienum est ab ecclesiastica doctrina".'

[2] *De Grat. Christ.*, xxxv, 38: ' "Legant," inquit [Pelagius], "illam epistulam, quam ad sanctum virum Paulinum episcopum ante duodecim fere annos scripsimus, quae trecentis forte versibus nihil aliud quam dei gratiam et auxilium confitetur nosque nihil omnino boni facere posse sine Deo." '

[3] *Die Theologie des Pelagius und ihre Genesis*, esp. pp. 15–46.

[4] See above, p. 317 *n*[1].

[5] *Schöpfungsgnade*. See Bohlin, op. cit., pp. 15–22.   [6] *De Nat. et Grat.*, xi, 12.

[7] Ibid.: 'Videtur certe haec eum commemorasse, quae natura valent; creata sunt enim haec membra huiusmodi naturis, lingua, alae, pedes, non tale aliquid posuit, quale de

simply the Pelagian conception of 'possibility' under the name of Grace. Secondly, Pelagius spoke of Grace in terms of enlightenment.[1] Our will is fundamentally sound but our mind is clouded and needs to be shown what it ought to do. Hence the importance assigned by the Pelagians to the Law in the Old Testament and to the teaching of Christ in the New. Caelestius was accused at Carthage in 412 of teaching that the Law had the same effect as the Gospel in introducing men into the kingdom of heaven. Pelagius himself at the Synod of Diospolis was faced with a quotation from his own writings that the kingdom of heaven is promised in the Old Testament as well as in the New—a quotation which he explained as referring to the promise in the book of Daniel that *the saints of the Most High shall receive the kingdom*,[2] though his accusers believed that he had a very different doctrine in mind.[3] No doubt Pelagius was sincere in his disavowal of an interpretation placed upon his words by his enemies; and we may well believe that he did not regard the Law as doing more than assist men to virtue;[4] but it is significant that at no point in the controversy did he make an unambiguous declaration that Grace was more than redemption from past sin by Christ and thereafter the help given by Law and doctrine.[5] This, indeed, is the third aspect of his doctrine of Grace: remission of sins through baptism.[6] This is certainly part of the Catholic doctrine of Grace; but Pelagius seems to think in terms of remission of sins to be followed by illumination, enabling man to lead the Christian life, and not of the continual help of the indwelling of the Holy Spirit. Thus, in the letter to Demetrias, in which he prided himself that he gave full place to the Grace of God,[7] his conception of Grace was simply the formula: redemption from sin by Christ followed by the inspiration of the example of Christ stirring us to perfection of justice.[8] In the stress of

gratia intellegi volumus, sine qua homo non iustificatur, ubi de sanandis, non de instituendis naturis agitur.'
[1] *Offenbarungsgnade*. Bohlin, op. cit., pp. 22–29.   [2] Dan. 7.18.
[3] For Caelestius, see *De Gest. Pel.*, xi, 23; *De Pecc. Orig.*, xi, 12. For Pelagius, *De Gest. Pel.*, v, 13.   [4] Cf. Ferguson, *Pelagius*, 177.
[5] *De Grat. Christ.*, xli, 45: 'Sed in his etiam quatuor libris [de Libero Arbitrio] quaecumque pro gratia videtur dicere, qua iuvamur, ut declinemus a malo bonumque faciamus, ita dicit, ut nullo modo a verborum ambiguitate discedat, quam discipulis sic possit exponere, ut nullum auxilium gratiae credant, qua naturae possibilitas adiuvetur, nisi in lege atque doctrina.'   [6] *Vergebungsgnade*. Bohlin, op. cit., pp. 29–45.
[7] *De Grat. Christ.*, xxxvii, 40: ' "Legant," inquit, "etiam quam ad sacram Christi virginem Demetriadem in Oriente conscripsimus, et invenient nos ita hominis laudare naturam, ut dei semper gratiae addamus auxilium." '
[8] *Epist. ad Demetriaden*, 8: 'Nam si etiam ante Legem, ut diximus, et multo ante Domini nostri Salvatoris adventum iuste quidam vixisse et sancte referantur; quanto magis post illustrationem adventus eius, nos id posse credendum est, qui instructi per Christi gratiam et in meliorem hominem renati sumus; qui sanguine eius expiati atque mundati, illiusque exemplo ad perfectam iustitiam incitati, meliores illis esse debemus, qui ante Legem fuerunt.' *MPL* xxxiii, 1105.

controversy after his condemnation by pope Zosimus, Pelagius could anathematize those who thought or said that the Grace of God, by which
Christ came into this world to save sinners, was not necessary, not only for
every moment, but for each individual action of our lives;[1] but even here,
it is difficult to see that he implied more than that the Grace of God by
which our sins are remitted should be borne in mind continually to strengthen our resolution and that Christ, by His life and teaching, has left us an
example, which encourages us to avoid sin.[2] At one point indeed Pelagius
did speak of the 'multiform and ineffable gift of heavenly Grace'—an
expression which caused one scholar to hold that Pelagius did, in fact,
admit internal Grace in the orthodox sense;[3] but even here, it is significant
that he spoke of this gift as 'illuminating' and not aiding us. Moreover, the
words form only one of four dependent clauses in a sentence where the
whole tone is to speak of Grace in terms of enlightenment. 'God helps us',
wrote Pelagius, 'through His doctrine and revelation, while He opens the
eyes of our heart; while He shows us future things, lest we should be concerned with present matters; while He reveals the snares of the devil; and
while He illuminates us with the multiform and ineffable gift of heavenly
Grace. Does the man who says this seem to you to deny Grace? Or does he
not, rather, confess the free will of man and the Grace of God?'[4] The
answer to this rhetorical question can hardly be other than Augustine
actually gave: 'This is to place the Grace of God in the Law and in doctrine.'[5]

    The same reasons which prevented the Pelagians from having any satis-
factory theory of Grace conditioned their thinking about the primal sin, so
that they never formulated any doctrine of the Fall as Augustine and later
theologians understood the term. Since their system of morality was one
based upon the unfettered exercise of the will and because they insisted
that it was always possible for a man to discharge his moral obligations,
they were compelled to deny that Adam's sin had in any way affected his

---

[1] De Grat. Christ., ii, 2. Cf. Libellus Fidei, 13. MPL xlv, 1718; De Gest. Pel., xiv, 30.

[2] De Grat. Christ., ii, 2: 'Quia, etsi gratiam dei, qua Christus venit in mundum peccatores salvos facere, in sola peccatorum remissione constituat, potest huic sensui verba
ista coaptare dicens ideo eam per singulas horas, per singula momenta et per actus
singulos necessariam, ut semper in memoria retinentes et reminiscentes dimissa nobis
esse peccata non peccemus ulterius adiuti non aliqua subministratione virtutis, sed
viribus propriae voluntatis quid sibi remissione peccatorum praestitum fuerit per actus
singulos recordantis.'

[3] J. B. Mozley, A Treatise on the Augustinian Doctrine of Predestination, 2nd ed., London, 1878, 50.

[4] De Grat. Christ., vii, 8.

[5] Ibid.: 'Denique dei adiutorium multipliciter insinuandum putavit commemorando
doctrinam et revelationem et oculorum cordis adapertionem et demonstrationem
futurorum et apertionem diabolicarum insidiarum et multiformi atque ineffabili dono
gratiae caelestis illuminationem, ad hoc utique, ut divina praecepta et promissa discamus.
hoc est ergo gratiam dei ponere in lege atque doctrina.'

descendants except by evil example. In any case, the attitude to religion of Pelagians like Caelestius and Julian of Eclanum seems to have been essentially moral and intellectual. They had little sense of mystery, and the Genesis narrative of the Garden of Eden and the forbidden tree did not excite their wonder. Rather, their approach was a rationalistic one. Adam, they held, was mortal and would have died even if he had not sinned,[1] since otherwise the command to increase and multiply would have been superfluous.[2] He was not exempt from the ills of the flesh which afflict his descendants, and Augustine was able to indulge in some rather heavy-footed humour in his polemic against Julian of Eclanum, by dwelling on the miseries which our first parents must have suffered in Paradise, according to the Pelagian view.[3] Certainly, the Pelagians had no very high opinion of the unfallen Adam. 'Raw, inexperienced, rash, without experience of fear or example of virtue, he stole the food whose sweetness and beauty had ensnared him at the suggestion of the woman.'[4] Nor was the first sin of any outstanding significance. The sin of Adam in Eden was less than that of Cain the fratricide or the unnatural offences of the Sodomites, said Julian of Eclanum; why should God be thought to punish it with a quite disproportionate penalty?[5] On the contrary, Adam's sin injured only himself and not his descendants, and infants are today born in the same state as that of Adam before the Fall.[6] Everyone, in fact, 'starts fair', and even before the coming of Christ there had been sinless men. Pelagius compiled a whole list of Old Testament worthies whom he declared to have been sinless,[7] and both he and Julian spoke with admiration of the actions of virtuous pagans.[8] Pelagius argued, also, against the view that human nature has been corrupted by sin, on the grounds that sin is an action, not a substance, and a non-substantial thing, a mere name, cannot weaken or change our nature.[9] This logical ingenuity was not very

---

[1] De Pecc. Mer. et Rem., I, ii, 2: 'Qui dicunt "Adam sic creatum, ut etiam sine peccati merito moreretur non poena culpae, sed necessitate naturae", profecto illud, quod in lege dictum est: *Qua die ederitis, morte moriemini* (Gen. 2.17), non ad mortem corporis, sed ad mortem animae, quae in peccato fit, referre conantur.' Op. Imp. c. Iul., i, 79: 'Factum est enim animal rationale, mortale, capax virtutis et vitii, quod posset ex concessa sibi possibilitate vel servare Dei mandata, vel transgredi, vel magisterio naturali conservare ius humanae societatis, liberumque haberet alterutram velle partem, in quo peccati et iustitiae summa est.'
[2] Op. Imp. c. Iul., vi, 30.   [3] Ibid., iii, 147, 154.   [4] Ibid., vi, 23.
[5] Ibid.   [6] De Gest. Pel., xi, 23, 24.   [7] De Nat. et Grat., xxxvi, 42.
[8] Pelagius, Epist. ad Demetriaden, 3. MPL xxxiii, 1101. C. Iul., IV, iii, 30–32.
[9] De Nat. et Grat., xix, 21: ' "Primo," inquit, "de eo disputandum est, quod per peccatum debilitata dicitur et immutata natura. unde ante omnia quaerendum puto," inquit, "quid sit peccatum: substantia aliqua an omnino substantia carens nomen, quo non res, non existentia, non corpus aliquod, sed perperam facti actus exprimitur." deinde adiungit: "Credo, ita est. et si ita est," inquit, "quomodo potuit humanam debilitare vel mutare naturam, quod substantia caret?" '

convincing even to the Pelagians themselves in the face of universal and repeated sinfulness,[1] and they were forced to admit to a darkening of the minds of men, both as a race and as individuals, by repeated sins.[2] Hence they were able to find in the necessity of custom a sort of psychological substitute for Original Sin,[3] just as the conception of the long use of sinning performed the functions of the Fall in Catholic theology. But even here they approached the matter from an intellectual standpoint; men's minds were darkened and needed the 'file of the Law' to remove the rust. The grace of Christ illuminated the dark mind and showed what should be done; but men's wills were adequate for the task, if they were once shown the way.

The characteristic feature of the Pelagian attitude to Paradise and the Fall is its reasonableness and enlightenment, and beside it the view promulgated by Augustine has an extravagant air. In the first place, he entirely rejects the view of an Adam of low intellectual attainments though of high moral character. Adam in Paradise, according to Augustine, was in a condition highly removed from that of his descendants since the Fall. He was exempt from the physical disabilities which the Pelagians imagined. Certainly he had an animal body; but the animal body was so created that if Adam had not sinned, he would have been turned into a spiritual being without tasting death.[4] But this did not mean that he was not intended to beget offspring. In his earlier years, Augustine had been inclined to the view, common among Greek theologians, that the command to Adam and Eve to be fruitful and multiply referred to a spiritual union productive of good works to the praise of God, and that biological reproduction was only known after the Fall;[5] but as he progressed in the Christian life, he changed his views. Adam's mutation into a spiritual being would have taken place *post genitos filios*, after he had begotten sons.[6] Meanwhile he enjoyed every possible good of body and mind: immortality conditional

---

[1] *De Grat. Christi*, x, 11: '[Pelagius] adiunxit: "operatur in nobis velle quod bonum est, velle quod sanctum est, dum nos terrenis cupiditatibus deditos et mutorum more animalium tantummodo praesentia diligentes futurae gloriae magnitudine et praemiorum pollicitatione succendit; dum revelatione sapientiae in desiderium dei stupentem suscitat voluntatem; dum nobis"—quod tu alibi negare non metuis—"suadet omne quod bonum est".'   [2] *Ad Demet.*, 8. *MPL* xxxiii, 1104–5.
[3] Augustine calls it 'necessitas consuetudinis', *Op. Imp. c. Iul.*, iv, 103. See Abercrombie, *The Origins of Jansenism*, 22.
[4] *De Pecc. Mer. et Rem.*, I, ii, 2: 'Quamvis enim secundum corpus terra esset et corpus in quo creatus est animale gestaret, tamen, si non pecasset, in corpus fuerat spiritale mutandus et in illam incorruptionem, quae fidelibus et sanctis promittitur, sine mortis supplicio transiturus.'
[5] See M. Müller, *Die Lehre des hl. Augustinus von der Paradiesesehe und ihre Auswirkung in der Sexualethik des 12. und 13. Jahrhunderts bis Thomas von Aquin*, Regensburg, 1954, 20–22.   [6] *Enchir.*, xxviii, 104.

upon obedience,[1] perfect health and a mind untroubled by passion,[2] and an intellect which far exceeded that of the most brilliant genius among his descendants.[3] Proof of this is afforded by his ability to name the animals; a proof which may amuse the modern scholar,[4] but which was supported by a saying, ascribed to Pythagoras, that he who gave names to things must be reputed not only the wisest but the most ancient of sages.[5] To these physical and mental goods were added others of a spiritual nature. No hard laws were laid upon Adam save the one simple command of obedience;[6] and while, because of the need to obey and the limitations of his created nature, he could not do all things, he had yet the gift that he desired to do only what was in his power and so did whatever he would.[7] He was, however, no mere puppet, for he had the gift of free will and also, as we have seen, an aid or help, to safeguard him against the risk of abusing that gift.

Therefore man lived in Paradise as he desired, whilst he only desired what God commanded. He enjoyed God, from whence was his good. He lived without need, and had life eternal in his power. He had meat for hunger, drink for thirst, the tree of life to keep off age. He was free from all bodily corruption and feeling of molestation. He feared neither disease within nor violence without. Height of health was in his flesh, and fulness of peace in his soul; and as Paradise was neither fiery nor frosty, no more was the inhabitants' good will offended either with desire or fear. There was no true sorrow, nor vain joy. Their joy continued by God's mercy, whom they loved with a pure good conscience and an unfeigned faith.[8]

In such conditions was our progenitor created and it was in his power to persevere therein until God, as a reward, and without any necessity of death, should bring him to a yet better state, in which he would not only be unable to sin but would also be unable to entertain any desire to sin[9]

[1] *De Gen. ad Litt.*, VI, xxv, 36.   [2] *dCD*, XIV, xxvi.
[3] *Op. Imp. c. Iul.*, v, 1.
[4] N. P. Williams, *The Idea of the Fall and Original Sin*, London, 1927, 361-2, who speaks of this 'curious contention'.
[5] Cf. the Pseudo-Clementine *Eclogae Propheticae*, ed. Stählin, Leipzig, 1909, 146-7. The thought behind this saying is presumably inspired by the belief, widely held in all ages, and in all parts of the world, that an intimate connection exists between the essence of a thing and its name. Hence the reluctance in early Judaism, to utter the ineffable name YHWH and—on a very different level—the important consequences which may ensue in a fairy story from the hero or the heroine learning the name of some fairy or goblin.   [6] *dCD*, XIV, xv.   [7] Ibid.
[8] *dCD*, XIV, xxvi (John Healey's translation).
[9] *Enchir.*, xxvii, 104: 'Quapropter etiam primum hominem Deus in ea salute in qua conditus erat, custodire voluisset, eumque opportuno tempore post genitos filios sine interpositione mortis ad meliora perducere, ubi iam non solum peccatum non committere, sed nec voluntatem posset habere peccandi, si ad permanendum sine peccato, sicut factus erat, perpetuam voluntatem habiturum esse praescisset.'

or, by the abuse of free will, cast all the enjoyment of present and future good away, and bring himself and all his issue into death, both physical and spiritual, from which, but for the mercy of God, there is no deliverance.[1]

Adam sinned and fell, and his fall was a disaster for the whole human race. Augustine leaves us in no doubt as to the importance of Adam's sin as an event in human history but never gives a thoroughly satisfactory explanation of the reason for Adam's disobedience. Given the fact that Adam was left with free will, a gift capable of being abused, nothing was left undone which might have prevented him from falling. Indeed, it was precisely the ease with which God's commandment might have been observed which made Adam's transgression so heinous.[2] Every man who has sinned since the Fall has laboured under the burden of a wounded and disabled will, which makes him prone to seek lesser created goods instead of the supreme goodness of God; but Adam suffered from no such weakness. It is this freedom from any outside pressure which made the eating of the forbidden fruit, in itself a trivial action, the supreme act of treason and defiance to God on the part of a human being, *for Adam*, says the Apostle, *was not seduced; but the woman was seduced*.[3] She thought the serpent's words were true but her husband, knowing that they were false, sinned with her by a kind of social necessity, being unwilling to break fellowship with his partner, even though this meant defying God.[4]

St Augustine rightly emphasizes that man was made morally upright, possessed of good will, and that the first evil will, which was antecedent to all evil deeds, was a defection by man from the original act of God to acts of his own, rather than anything positive;[5] but true though this may be, it leaves unanswered the question: why did man fall, a being created morally upright, without any natural tendency to evil, endowed with free will which is, in itself, a natural quality and, in this case, safeguarded by a special grace? The problem remains, whether or not we regard the account

---

[1] *dCD*, XIII, xiv.   [2] Ibid., XIV, xii.
[3] I Tim. 2.14.   [4] *dCD*, XIV, xi.

[5] Ibid., XIV, xi: 'Fecit itaque Deus, sicut scriptum est, hominem rectum ac per hoc voluntatis bonae. Non enim rectus esset bonam non habens voluntatem. Bona igitur voluntas opus est Dei; cum ea quippe ab illo factus est homo. Mala vero voluntas prima, quoniam omnia opera mala praecessit in homine, defectus potius fuit quidam ab opere Dei ad sua opera quam opus ullum, et ideo mala opera, quia secundum se, non secundum Deum; ut eorum operum tamquam fructuum malorum voluntas ipsa esset velut arbor mala aut ipse homo in quantum malae voluntatis. Porro mala voluntas quamvis non sit secundum naturam, sed contra naturam, quia vitium est, tamen eius naturae est, cuius est vitium, quod nisi in natura non potest esse; sed in ea, quam creavit ex nihilo, non quam genuit Creator de semet ipso, sicut genuit Verbum, per quod facta sunt omnia: quia, etsi de terrae pulvere Deus finxit hominem, eadem terra omnisque terrena materies omnino de nihilo est, animamque de nihilo factam dedit corpori, cum factus est homo.'

of the Fall, as given in Genesis, as literal history, and has probably never been better expressed, in non-theological terms, than by Bishop Butler, in his youthful correspondence with Dr Samuel Clarke.

Since it may be said, as you hint, that this stronger disposition to be influenced by vicious motives may have been contracted by repeated acts of wickedness, we will pitch upon the first vicious action anyone is guilty of. No man would have committed this first vicious action if he had not had a stronger (at least as strong) disposition in him to be influenced by the motives of the vicious action, than by the motives of the contrary virtuous action; from whence I infallibly conclude, that since every man has committed some first vice, every man had, antecedent to the commission of it, a stronger disposition to be influenced by the vicious than by the virtuous motive. My difficulty upon this is, that a stronger natural disposition to be influenced by the vicious than the virtuous motive (which every one has antecedent to his first vice), seems . . . to put the man in the same condition as though he was indifferent to the virtuous motive; and since an indifferency to the virtuous motive would have incapacitated a man from being a moral agent, or contracting guilt, is not a stronger disposition to be influenced by the vicious motive as great an incapacity?[1]

To this problem, Augustine gives no effective answer. He definitely asserts in the treatise *On Continence* that God, if He had chosen, could have created a man incapable of sinning;[2] and he elsewhere observes that every being capable of sinning is a being created *ex nihilo*, out of nothing, which suggests that the reason for man's sin may be sought in the fact of the radical weakness of a being created out of nothing.[3] No doubt the problem of the primal sin is indissoluble, at least in this world, and no practical benefit can be derived from investigating it. Such, at least, was Augustine's opinion, in the third book of his work *On Free Will*:

What need is there, therefore, to seek the origin of the movement whereby the will turns from the unchangeable to the changeable good? We acknowledge that it is a movement of the soul, that it is voluntary and therefore culpable. And all useful learning in this matter has its object and value in teaching us to condemn and restrain that movement, and to convert our wills from falling into temporal delights to the enjoyment of the eternal good.[4]

[1] Joseph Butler, *Letters to Clarke*, 8 [2], in *The Works of Bishop Butler*, ed. J. H. Bernard, i, London, 1900, 336.
[2] *De Continentia*, vi, 16: 'Non autem potestas deo defuit talem facere hominem, qui peccare non posset.'
[3] *Op. Imp. c. Iul.*, v, 39: 'Non igitur mihi proferantur alia, quae de nihilo facta sunt, et peccare non possunt: quoniam non dico, Omne quod ex nihilo factum est, peccare potest; sed dico, Omne quod peccare potest, ex nihilo factum est.'
[4] *De Lib. Arb.*, III, i, 2. Tr. Burleigh, p. 171. On the question of Augustine's teaching about the primal sin, see Jolivet, *Le problème du mal*, 82–92.

Whatever the causes of the Fall, the consequences for Adam and his descendants are, in Augustine's view, as manifold as they are disastrous. They are, first, death: death of the body and, more awfully, death of the soul—a punishment inflicted justly upon all of Adam's seed save upon those whom it pleases God, out of His infinite mercy and entirely without any consideration of merit, to elect to salvation. Secondly, it means a clouding and weakening of all man's faculties. His body becomes liable to disease in a regrettable and familiar way; but, in a far more distressing way, he loses control over his body so that, even when he is well, his will cannot fully control it and has to confess its impotence to rule the body which, the philosophers are all agreed, should be subservient to the soul. But even this is not enough. The body has not only become a rebel, but the mind has become darkened and weakened by sin. The power of the will of vitiated nature is inadequate to avoid sin, unless it has a special aid—the Grace of Christ.[1] Not that human nature is utterly corrupt; it still retains some trace of the divine image,[2] some little spark remains of the reason whereby man was made in the image of God.[3] Indeed, Augustine is prevented by his basic principle that evil is merely a privation from ever entertaining any doctrine of total corruption. Evil is a corruption of good, and evil can only be as long as there is some good to be corrupted. A wholly evil thing is a contradiction in terms: by definition it is non-existent.[4]

It is necessary to analyse rather closely Augustine's view of the nature and transmission of Original Sin, since it is hardly an exaggeration to say that it dominates his whole conception of human nature since the Fall, so that all human activity must be seen in the light of our disastrous heritage from the first Adam, from which we are delivered only by the sacrificial death of the Second, if we are among the elect of God. But what is Original Sin? 'Nothing', answers Augustine, 'is better known when the preacher declares it, nothing is more secret when we try to understand it.'[5] This may, indeed, have been true enough of an African congregation of the fourth or fifth century; but the passage of fifteen centuries or more has seen a wonderful decline in our understanding of theological doctrine, and even among those who are theologians there are differing theories, among which the Augustinian is but one of several. It is, therefore, of the utmost

---

[1] De Perf. Iust. Hom., ii, 3.
[2] De Spir. et Litt., xxviii, 48.
[3] dCD, XXII, xxiv: 'non in eo tamen penitus extincta est quaedam velut scintilla rationis, in qua factus est ad imaginem Dei.'
[4] De Vera Rel., xx, 38; De Nat. Boni, 4–6; Enchir., iv, 12; etc.
[5] De Moribus, I, xxii, 40: 'Nihil est ad praedicandum notius, nihil ad intelligendum secretius.'

importance that we should try to establish clearly what the saint means when he talks about Original Sin.

If we admit that the sin of Adam had a certain effect upon his descendants—and we deny this only at the cost of ranging ourselves in the ranks of the Pelagians—we can consider that effect in three ways. First, we can regard it primarily from what may be called the medical aspect, and think of Original Sin in terms of an hereditary disease, which weakens and enfeebles our nature, making us spiritually sick and in need of the Divine Physician, by whose stripes we are healed. This is the view which has most largely commended itself to the Christian east, and which probably commends itself to many Christians, both eastern and western, today. Secondly, we may regard Original Sin from a juridical point of view. In his sin, Adam involved the whole human race which, in some fashion, shared his guilt. This aspect is characteristically western and Latin—Sir Henry Maine pointed out long ago that it had an obvious appeal to a culture whose highest intellectual achievement was in the realm of law[1]—and it has had a fascination for Latin theologians, leading at times to some curious theories, including the famous one rejected by St Anselm in his *Cur Deus Homo*, that by sin man had voluntarily withdrawn himself from God and committed himself to the service of the devil, from whose dominion he could only be released by some abuse by his infernal master of the power which he had quite lawfully acquired—an abuse which was, in fact, committed at the Crucifixion, when the devil failed to recognize the Divinity of Christ beneath the human form, and so laid hands unjustly on One who had never submitted Himself to the rule of Satan.[2] Thirdly, these two views can be combined so that we think of Original Sin both as an inherited disease and as inherited guilt—this latter concept unfamiliar today, but familiar enough to the Jews of the Old Testament (to go no further afield), who knew that the Lord was a jealous God, who visited the sins of the fathers upon the children unto the third and fourth generations.

It is this third view which is adopted by Augustine: Original Sin is both a disease and a crime. We all sinned in Adam, and share both the guilt and the penalty of his Fall.

How did we sin in Adam? *Omnes enim fuimus in illo uno, quando omnes fuimus ille unus*—'In that one man were we all, when we were all that one man.'[3] Augustine's theory is that of the seminal identity of the human race

---

[1] H. S. Maine, *Ancient Law*, 1st ed., London, 1861, 356–9; ed. by Sir Frederic Pollock, London, 1920, 364–8.

[2] On the importance of St Anselm's rejection of this venerable theory, see R. W. Southern, *The Making of the Middle Ages*, London, 1953, 234–7.

[3] *dCD*, XIII, xiv.

with Adam. Since all future generations were, in one sense, present in our progenitor's loins at the time of the Fall, so all mankind participated, in some mysterious fashion, in the sin, and drew upon itself condign punishment.

The doctrine is a subtle one and not easily understood, since it is by no means clear how we can be thought of as existing, except potentially, in the seed in the body of Adam before Eve conceived by him, and to hold us responsible for our actions, in such a shadowy and inchoative existence, seems to be wholly unreasonable by any standard of ethics. Augustine tended to lay stress upon the Latin translation of Romans 5.12: *Propterea sicut per unum hominem in hunc mundum peccatum intravit, et per peccatum mors, et ita in omnes homines mors transivit, in quo omnes peccaverunt*— 'Therefore, just as sin entered this world by one man and through sin, death; so death passed into all men, in whom all sinned.' The crux of this passage turns on the last four words: *in quo omnes peccaverunt*—'in whom [that is, in Adam] all men sinned'.

On a first reading of the Latin, this is a possible, if not the obvious, translation. But does it represent the thought of St Paul? If we turn to the Greek, we find that it does not and cannot bear the interpretation which Augustine wishes to place upon it, for the Greek is ἐφ' ᾧ πάντες ἥμαρτον, and not ἐν ᾧ, which Augustine's interpretation requires. This is a disconcerting—perhaps one should say a reassuring—discovery; but nothing is to be gained by laughing at or bemoaning Augustine's reliance on a faulty translation.[1] It is more important to try to establish the reason for his error. Although never a finished scholar he was, in his later years, quite familiar with the Greek Bible and well accustomed to verifying points in dispute by reference to Greek manuscripts. Why he failed to do so in this case, when so much depended upon the precise meaning of St Paul, is something of a mystery, especially in view of the fact that some of the Pelagians rendered the Greek more accurately as *quia* or *propter quod*— 'because all have sinned'.[2] It is, of course, conceivable that he did so, and was misled by a faulty reading; but we have no evidence that anything of this nature happened. Rather, it is more likely that Augustine was so absorbed by his theory that he did not give it the critical examination which it required. In any case, the theory of seminal identity, though

---

[1] As does Allin, *Augustinian Revolution in Theology*, 140: 'We begin with a truly amazing fact—Augustine's theory of original sin starts from a false rendering. The Greek phrase ἐν τῷ [*sic*] was by the Latin versions rendered as *in quo*, and St Paul was thus made to say *in quo omnes peccaverunt* (in whom all sinned), instead of "*because* (in that) all sinned".'

[2] Pelagius however in his Commentary on Romans renders it as *in quo*.

clearly buttressed by the false rendering of Romans 5.12—a rendering retained, incidentally, by St Jerome in the Latin Vulgate—does not depend upon it. What it demands of a supporter is a belief that the biblical account of the Fall is literal history combined with the ability to ignore the problem of how moral responsibility can be incurred by a being which exists, as yet, only in potentiality—a belief which, as we have noticed, could be readily accorded in the ancient world, accustomed to the idea of divine retribution to the third and fourth generations.

Furthermore, the faulty rendering of the phrase in Romans, although much employed by Augustine, was not his own original interpretation but was already familiar to Latin theologians before the Pelagian controversy. Particularly important in this respect is the contribution of Ambrosiaster, the fourth-century Roman commentator on the Pauline epistles, whose writings long circulated under the famous name of St Ambrose, but whose identity remains a mystery, despite all the learned and ingenious suggestions which have been propounded.[1] Ambrosiaster, in commenting on *in quo omnes peccaverunt*, had asserted that the words *in quo* referred to Adam and had added: 'It is clear that all have sinned in Adam as in a lump (*quasi in massa*); for since he was corrupted by sin, all whom he begot have been born under sin.'[2] Here we have the foundation of Augustine's doctrine, including the word *massa*, a lump, which he was to repeat again and again, always in a derogatory sense, when he described fallen humanity. Augustine was familiar with Ambrosiaster's commentaries, though he ascribed them mistakenly to St Hilary of Poitiers, citing the passage just mentioned in the fourth book of the work *Contra duas Epistolas Pelagianorum*.[3]

---

[1] Notably by Dom Germain Morin who has put forward as candidates Isaac the Jew; Decimus Hilarianus Hilarius; Evagrius of Antioch; and Nammius Aemilianus Dexter. For details and references see P. de Labriolle, *Histoire de la littérature latine chrétienne*, i, 417–21.

[2] Ambrosiaster, *Commentarius in Epist. ad Rom.*, v, 12: '*In quo*, id est, in Adam, omnes peccaverunt. Ideo dixit, *in quo*, cum de muliere loquatur, quia non ad speciem retulit, sed ad genus. Manifestum itaque est in Adam omnes peccasse quasi in massa; ipse enim per peccatum corruptus, quos genuit, omnes nati sunt sub peccato. Ex eo igitur cuncti peccatores, quia ex eo ipso sumus omnes; hic enim beneficium Dei perdidit, dum praevaricavit, indignus factus edere de arbore vitae, ut moreretur. Mors autem dissolutio corporis est, cum anima a corpore separatur.' *MPL* xvii, 92. Ambrosiaster, however, regards damnation as the consequence of actual, rather than Original, sin. 'Est et alia mors, quae secunda dicitur, in gehenna, quam non peccato Adae patimur, sed eius occasione propriis peccatis acquiritur: a quo boni immunes sunt, tantum quod in inferno erant, sed superiori, quasi in libera, qui ad caelos ascendere non poterant; sententia enim tenebantur data in Adam, quod chirographum in decretis morte Christi deletum est (Colos. 2.14). Sententia autem decreti fuit, ut unius hominis corpus solveretur super terram: anima vero vinculis detenta exitia pateretur' (*MPL* xvii, 92–93). Cf. his comment on the just men of the Old Testament, *ad Rom.*, v, 14 (col. 95): 'In quos autem [mors] non regnavit, quia non peccaverunt in similitudinem praevaricationis Adam, sub spe reservati sunt adventui Salvatoris in libera, sicut legitur de Abraham.'

[3] Aug., *C. duas Epist. Pel.*, IV, iv, 7.

Based upon Ambrosiaster, and finding further support for his theories in the writings of St Cyprian[1] and his old master St Ambrose,[2] Augustine seems never to have entertained any doubt that his interpretation of St Paul was anything other than the right one. And even if he had done so and realized that the translation 'in whom all sinned' was inaccurate, it is doubtful if he would have felt any need to revise his general theory which, as we have seen, does not depend upon the meaning of a single verse from Romans, however important it might appear.

So far, we have considered the doctrine of seminal identity, which treats Original Sin in a juridical fashion, so that it is equated with what may be called original guilt—Augustine actually uses the term *originalis reatus* to describe it;[3] but mixed with this universal guilt is another element, the vice (*vitium*) or sickness caused by the Fall. This weakness both dominates our lives and determines the way in which we inherit the guilt of Adam. The key to the understanding of it lies in that element of human nature which Augustine calls concupiscence.

Among the privileges enjoyed by Adam in Paradise before the Fall were, as we have seen, perfect health and freedom from passion. Reason and will exercised perfect dominion over the actions of his body.[4] But Adam did not enjoy this enviable state through his own powers; his rule over himself depended on obedience to God, and disobedience to his creator drew upon itself as an inevitable consequence a loss of power to control his own body.[5] This loss of power is particularly evident in human sexuality. Our sexual appetite and ability are not directly under our will at all, and with this weakness—perhaps because of it—there exists a sense of shame, the sense of sexual shame which came upon Adam and Eve after the Fall, when their eyes were opened and they perceived their nakedness.[6] This shame Augustine associates with the loss of control which he regards as the punishment of the disobedience of the Fall, and in so doing he is probably right; but the conclusion which he drew from this, that in Paradise man had the same control over his sexual organs that he has today over his hand or foot, is based upon a defective knowledge of physiology.[7]

[1] Cyprian, *Ep.* 64, quoted by Aug., *De Pecc. Mer. et Rem.*, III, v, 10. See other examples in *C. duas Epist. Pel.*, IV, viii, 20–x, 28.
[2] *De Exc. Sat.*, ii, 6; *De Poenit.*, I, iii, 13, quoted by Aug., *De Pecc. Orig.*, xli, 47. See also *C. duas Epist. Pel.*, IV, xi, 29–31.
[3] *De diversis Quaest. ad Simplic.*, i, q. 2, 20.   [4] *Op. Imp. c. Iul.*, v, 1.
[5] *dCD*, XIV, xv; *Op. Imp. c. Iul.*, vi, 22.
[6] *De Pecc. Mer. et Rem.*, I, xvi, 21: 'Tunc ille extitit bestialis motus pudendus hominibus, quem in sua erubuit nuditate.' For the discussion which follows, see Müller, op. cit., pp. 24–26.
[7] See L. Ruland, *Grenzfragen der Naturwissenschaften und Theologie*, Munich, 1930, 14–17; cited by Müller, op. cit., p. 25.

Nor can this objection be met by postulating a change in our basic physiological structure consequent upon the Fall. Indeed, Augustine himself assures us that male and female were ordained in the beginning as we see them today in the sexes.[1] Thus, all we can say is that Augustine was misled by the defective medical science of his age into formulating a theory which is scientifically untenable, so far as it assumes that the loss of control caused by the Fall is demonstrated by sexual physiology.[2] The conclusion is regrettable, but unavoidable.

On a foundation of physiological fact, erroneously explained, and a sense of shame accurately observed and probably rightly associated with the physiological fact, Augustine rears the structure of his theory of the transmission of Original Sin. Because of the disobedience of our members and the fact of shame, an element has come into human sexuality since the Fall which is both a consequence and a cause of sin. That element is concupiscence or lust.[3]

The difficulty which confronts the modern reader who tries to understand the Augustinian conception of concupiscence lies in the fact that, for Augustine, concupiscence is present even in the legitimate sexuality of Christian marriage. It has been pointed out that a nineteenth-century Englishman felt that the same passion—romantic love—could be either virtuous or vicious according as it was directed towards marriage or not;[4] and no doubt many people would today still hold the same opinion; but it is quite alien to Augustine's temper. Concupiscence, the passionate, uncontrolled element in sexuality, exists in lawful wedlock, where it can be excused if its aim is procreation and the discharge of the marriage debt. But why is it vicious? a question which may particularly be asked today, when a vast quantity of literature, of varying degrees of respectability, has grown up on the topic of the importance of physical satisfaction in marital relationships. Is the pleasure afforded by sexual intercourse in itself any more reprehensible than that given, say, by the enjoyment of good food? Why should one particular pleasure be singled out for rebuke?

Augustine's answer turns upon the notion of the disobedience of our appetites to the will.

Although therefore there are many lusts, yet when the word lust is spoken without any mention of the object, we commonly understand by

---

[1] *dCD*, XIV, xxii: 'Certum est igitur masculum et feminam ita primitus institutos, ut nunc homines duos diversi sexus videmus et novimus.'

[2] For Augustine's interest in medical and scientific matters, see Cunningham, *St Austin*, 137–41; Pope, *St Augustine of Hippo*, 228–53.

[3] *Concupiscentia* or *libido carnalis*. See Appendix C: '*Concupiscentia* and *Libido*'.

[4] C. S. Lewis, *The Allegory of Love*, London, 1946, 13–14.

it sexual desire by which the generative parts are excited. For this holds sway not only in the whole body, nor externally, but also dominates within, moving the whole man with such a mixture of sexual emotion and carnal appetite that the bodily pleasure so produced is the highest of them all, so that in the very moment of consummation it overwhelms almost all the light and power of cogitation.[1]

It will be noticed that what is condemned in concupiscence is precisely that element which the romantic lover and, *a fortiori*, the modern sexologist regard as its greatest recommendation; but it must be remembered that, in the case of the romantic lover at least, he and Augustine are talking about different emotions. The idea of romantic love as an emotion which may, in certain circumstances, be inspiring and even ennobling, was unknown to Augustine as it was unknown to Thomas Aquinas.[2] What Augustine would have said if he had been confronted with the reconciliation between erotic passion and Christianity effected by Dante in the *Divine Comedy* we do not know. The romantic vision, which Charles Williams has finely called the 'Beatrician moment . . . of revelation and communication by means of a girl',[3] was outside the categories of his thought. Dante met Beatrice in the streets of Florence and saw in her the first foreshadowings of the vision of the love which moves the sun and the other stars. Of this first meeting he wrote: 'Incipit vita nova.'[4] Augustine came to the vision of God after a youth of vanity and sin and his cry was: 'Sero te amavi!'—'Late have I loved Thee, O beauty, so old and so new, late have I loved Thee.'[5] Some have seen in Augustine's teaching about sexuality the remorse and disgust of the former rake; but quite apart from the fact that such a view grossly exaggerates the sensuality of his youth, it is clear from his language that when he appeals to a sense of shame in sexuality very generally felt and therefore good evidence for the accuracy of his theories, he expects that his appeal will be accepted by the majority of his readers, whether Christian or pagan, without much argument.[6] In an age when

[1] *dCD*, XIV, xvi.
[2] See Lewis, op. cit., pp. 16–17. One should perhaps mention the comment of Sir Maurice Powicke, *King Henry III and the Lord Edward*, Oxford, 1947, i, 157 *n*[1]: 'Historians tend to be cynical and slapdash when they discuss this matter [married love in the Middle Ages]. In one of his sermons preached in England (1229) Jordan of Saxony says: "aliquando est iuvenis ardens in amore puelle et est continens pro eius amore quia credit ipsam accipere in uxorem . . ."; *EHR* liv (1939), 14. In his fine book *The Allegory of Love*, which is neither cynical nor slapdash, C. S. Lewis has overlooked evidence of this kind.'   [3] Charles Williams, *The Figure of Beatrice*, London, 1953, 123.
[4] *La vita nuova*, i: 'In quella parte del libro della mia memoria, dinanzi alla quale poco si potrebbe leggere, si trova una rubrica, la quale dice: *Incipit Vita Nova.*'
[5] *Conf.*, X, xxvii, 38.
[6] *dCD*, XIV, xvii: 'Quod itaque adversus damnatam culpa inoboedientiae voluntatem libido inoboedienter movebat, verecundia pudenter tegebat. Ex hoc omnes gentes, quoniam ab illa stirpe procreatae sunt, usque adeo tenent insitum pudenda velare, ut

ascetism was growing among serious-minded Christians, and was also to be found among pagans like Plotinus and Julian the Apostate, a theory like Augustine's would not seem so unreasonable as it does today. Certainly there were objectors like Helvidius and Julian of Eclanum; but in this context it is clear that what Julian meant by concupiscence was little more than the pleasure afforded by the operations of a healthy body.[1] Thus he did not shrink from maintaining that concupiscence, in his sense, existed in the body of our Lord, a contention which shocked Augustine.[2] Julian's attitude has an element of common sense which is refreshing; but it does not seem prudish to suggest that, in his discussion of the matter, he passed beyond the bounds of Christian good taste in speaking about the Incarnate Lord, so that the sympathy which he gains by his candour he forfeits by his coarseness. His discussion with Augustine on this matter is among the least edifying of their depressing controversy.

Concupiscence, then, is that element of lust which is inseparable from fallen sexuality, even in Christian marriage. Augustine does not in any sense disparage matrimony. As a state of life, he ranks it below dedicated virginity and chaste widowhood; but in so doing, he merely follows the doctrine of the Fathers and Christian tradition. He emphasizes that marriage is instituted by God for the purpose of filling up the number of the elect in the kingdom of Heaven[3] and that sexual intercourse, undertaken with that end in view, is not only permitted but useful and honest[4] and, to a certain extent, praiseworthy.[5] But the good of marriage must be distinguished from the sickness of concupiscence in which men who know not God love their wives,[6] and this sickness is present in Christian marriage, though it is there directed into the good use of procreation.[7] Thus two things are simultaneously propagated: nature, which is good; and the vice of nature, which is evil.[8] It is from, and by, concupiscence that the

---

quidam barbari illas corporis partes nec in balneis nudas habeant, sed cum earum tegementis lavent. Per opacas quoque Indiae solitudines, cum quidam nudi philosophentur, unde gymnosophistae nominantur, adhibent tamen genitalibus tegmina, quibus per cetera membrorum carent.'

[1] *Op. Imp. c. Iul.*, v, 11: 'Ipsa ergo . . . virilitas, in genitalium et viscerum compage ac sanitate consistens, quae et appetentiae et efficientiae vires ministrat, vis a me voluptatis et concupiscentiae nominata est. Ideo enim non voluptatem simpliciter, sed vim voluptatis appellare malui, ut universum illum ardorem, qui et ante opus, et in opere sentitur, ostenderem.'

[2] Ibid., iv, 48–54.

[3] *De Bono Coniugali*, ix, 9. For Augustine's teaching on marriage, see Bernard Alves Pereira, *La doctrine du marriage selon saint Augustin*, 2e éd., Paris, 1930.

[4] *De Pecc. Orig.*, xxxiv, 39.

[5] *De Serm. Dom. in Monte*, I, xv, 42. See Pereira, op. cit., p. 88 n².

[6] *De Pecc. Orig.*, xxxiii, 38.   [7] Ibid., xxxvii, 42.

[8] Ibid., xxxiii, 38: 'Simul autem utrumque propagatur, et natura et naturae vitium, quorum est unum bonum, alterum malum.'

378 ST AUGUSTINE OF HIPPO

guilt of Original Sin is conveyed from the parents to the child.[1] Concupiscence itself is not Original Sin; it is a wound and a vice of human nature, making it a slave to the devil;[2] can be the occasion of sin, even in the baptized;[3] and is the means whereby Original Sin is transmitted. It is an infection which conveys an inherited legal liability. It is cleansed by baptism, but its effects are not removed, and it is for that reason that the children of baptized parents are themselves in need of the laver of regeneration.[4]

Because of their inherited guilt, all men who are born by human generation form a lump of sin, a *massa peccati, luti, perditionis*,[5] justly deserving damnation, even if they commit no sins to add to the guilt which they

[1] Ibid., xxxvii, 42: 'Hinc est, quod infantes etiam qui peccare non possunt, non tamen sine peccati contagione nascuntur, non ex hoc quod licet, sed ex eo quod dedecet. nam ex hoc quod licet natura nascitur, ex illo quod dedecet vitium. naturae nascentis est auctor deus, qui hominem condidit et qui virum et feminam nuptiali iure coniunxit, vitii vero auctor est diaboli decipientis calliditas et hominis consentientis voluntas.'

[2] *De Nuptiis et Concupiscentia*, I, xxiii, 26: 'Hoc generi humano inflictum vulnus a diabolo quidquid per illud nascitur cogit esse sub diabolo, tamquam de suo fructice fructum iure decerpat, non quod ab illo sit natura humana, quae non est nisi ex deo, sed vitium, quod non est ex deo. non enim propter se ipsam, quae laudabilis est, quia opus dei est, sed propter damnabile vitium, quo vitiata est, natura humana damnatur. et propter quod damnatur, propter hoc et damnabili diabolo subiugatur.'

[3] *C. duas Epist. Pel.*, I, xiii, 27: 'Sed de ista concupiscentia carnis falli eos credo vel fallere, cum qua necesse est ut etiam baptizatus—et hoc si diligentissime proficit et spiritu dei agitur—pia mente confligat. sed haec etiamsi vocatur peccatum, non utique quia peccatum est, sed quia peccato facta est, sic vocatur, sicut scriptura manus cuiusque dicitur, quod manus eam fecerit'; *De Bono Coniug.*, vi, 6: 'Iam in ipsa quoque inmoderata exactione debiti carnalis, quam eis non secundum imperium praecepit, sed secundum veniam concedit apostolus, ut etiam praeter causam procreandi sibi misceantur, etsi eos pravi mores ad talem concubitum impellunt, nuptiae tamen ab adulterio seu fornicatione defendunt'; *C. Iul.*, V, xii, 46: 'Si enim aliter posset, et tamen concumberent coniuges, apertissime libidini cederent, atque illo malo uterentur male: cum vero propter quod sexus ambo sunt instituti, nisi eorum commixtione non nascitur homo; propter hoc mixti coniuges illo malo utuntur bene: si autem de libidine quaerunt etiam voluptatem, venialiter male.'

[4] *De Pecc. Orig.*, xxxix, 44: 'Obesset ista carnis concupiscentia etiam tantummodo quod inesset, nisi peccatorum remissio sic prodesset, ut quae in eis est, et nato et renato, nato quidem et inesse et obesse, renato autem inesse quidem, sed non obesse possit. in tantum autem obest natis, ut, nisi renascantur, nihil possit prodesse, si nati sunt de renatis. manet quippe in prole, ita ut ream faciat originis vitium, etiam si in parente reatus eiusdem vitii remissione ablutus est peccatorum, donec omne vitium, cui consentiendo peccatur, regeneratione novissima consumatur, id est ipsius etiam renovatione carnis, quae in eius resurrectione futura promittitur, ubi non solum nulla peccata faciamus, sed nec habeamus ulla desideria vitiosa, quibus consentiendo peccemus, ad quam beatam perfectionem huius quod nunc datur sancti lavacri gratia pervenitur.' Augustine illustrates the fact that the children of baptized parents need the grace of baptism by the example of the cultivated olive, which produces the wild olive (see *C. duas Epist. Pel.*, I, vi, 11; *De Nupt. et Concup.*, I, xxxii, 37); and by the fact that the son of a circumcised father is himself in need of circumcision (*C. Iul.*, VI, vii, 18).

[5] See the famous catalogue compiled by Dom Odilo Rottmanner, *Der Augustinismus. Eine dogmengeschichtliche Studie*, Munich, 1892, 8, where the list of derogatory epithets: *Massa luti, peccati, peccatorum, iniquitatis, irae, mortis, perditionis, damnationis*, etc., is given with copious references.

inherit by being born at all, unless they are cleansed by the saving waters of baptism. In the case of unbaptized infants, Augustine holds that theirs will be the mildest penalty; but this is hardly an encouraging reassurance.[1] Christ alone, who was born of the Virgin Mary by the overshadowing of the Holy Spirit, is free from the fatal legacy and could therefore be offered as a sacrifice for the sins of others.[2] By His death was the ransom paid and the human race delivered from the power of Death and Hell. Is every man, therefore, to be saved? Alas! for Augustine the answer was a decided no. Nothing in the Catholic faith is more certain than the fact that not all men are to be saved.[3] A common damnation has come upon us as a consequence of Adam's sin, from which no one is ever freed except by the mercy of God, who makes a separation of mankind to show in some the power of grace and, in others, the vengeance of divine justice. If all men had been damned, there would have been no place for God's mercy; if all had been saved, none for His justice;[4] and it must be added that the number of the damned exceeds that of the redeemed, so that the elect may praise the wonderful mercy which has set them free.[5] This mercy is utterly gratuitous. God is no acceptor of persons, and chooses His vessels of mercy without regard to preceding merits. Hence the elect have every reason to be thankful, but the reprobate have no cause to complain; they have received their just reward, for there is no iniquity with God.[6] If it is asked why, in the case of two

---

[1] *De Pec. Mer. et Rem.*, I, xvi, 21: 'Potest proinde recte dici parvulos sine baptismo de corpore exeuntes in damnatione omnium mitissima futuros'; *Enchir.*, xxiii, 93: 'Mitissima sane omnium poena erit eorum qui praeter peccatum quod originale traxerunt, nullum insuper addiderunt; et in caeteris qui addiderunt, tanto quisque tolerabiliorem ibi habebit damnationem, quanto hic minorem habuit iniquitatem'; *Ep.* 184A, i, 2: 'In illa damnatione minima poena, non tamen nulla.' See also *Ep.* 186, iv, 12; *C. Iul.*, V, xi, 44.

[2] *Enchir.*, xiii, 41: 'Nulla igitur voluptate carnalis concupiscentiae seminatus sive conceptus, et ideo nullum peccatum originaliter trahens; Dei quoque gratia Verbo Patris unigenito, non gratia Filio, sed natura, in unitate personae modo mirabili et ineffabili adiunctus atque concretus, et ideo nullum peccatum et ipse committens; tamen propter similitudinem carnis peccati in qua venerat, dictus est et ipse peccatum, sacrificandus ad diluenda peccata.'

[3] A fact which Pelagius employed at the synod of Diospolis to explain his statement that in the day of judgement no mercy will be shown to sinners, but they will be burned in eternal fires, by declaring that anyone who believed otherwise would be a supporter of Origen's universalism. *De Gest. Pel.*, iii, 9-11; cf. *dCD*, XXI, xvii.

[4] *dCD*, XXI, xii.

[5] *De Corrept. et Grat.*, x, 28: 'Quod ergo pauci in comparatione pereuntium, in suo vero numero multi liberantur'; *dCD*, XXI, xii.

[6] *Ad Simplic.*, i, q. 2, 22: 'Debitum si non reddis, habes quod gratuleris; si reddis, non habes quod quaeraris'; *Ep.* 194, ii, 4: 'Quod autem personarum acceptorem Deum se credere existimant, si credant quod sine ullis praecedentibus meritis, cuius vult miseretur, et quos dignatur, vocat, et quem vult religiosum facit; parum attendunt quod debita reddatur poena damnato, indebita gratia liberato, ut nec ille se indignum queratur, nec dignum se iste glorietur. atque ibi potius acceptionem nullam fieri personarum, ubi una eademque massa damnationis et offensionis involvit, ut liberatus de non liberato discat

little children, perhaps twins, both equally bound to the mass of perdition by reason of their origin, one should be taken and the other left, Augustine has no reply. The judgements of God are inscrutable and the clay must not say to the potter, Why hast thou made me thus? In his contemplation of the divine decrees, Augustine loses himself in awe, an awe which gives a sombre eloquence to his terrible words:

There was one lump of perdition out of Adam to which only punishment was due; thence are made *vessels unto honour*[1] out of the same lump. For *the potter hath power over the clay of the same lump*[2]—of what lump? for it had already perished, just damnation was assuredly already due to that lump. Give grateful thanks that you have escaped. You have escaped the death certainly due and found life, which was not due. *The potter hath power over the clay of the same lump to make one vessel unto honour and another unto dishonour.* But, you say, why has He made me to honour and another to dishonour? What shall I answer? Will you hear Augustine, who have not heard the Apostle saying, *O man, who art thou, who repliest against God?*[3] Two little children are born. If you ask what is due, they both cleave to the lump of perdition. But why does its mother carry the one to grace, while the other is suffocated by its mother in her sleep? Will you tell me what that one deserved which was borne to grace, and what that one deserved whom its sleeping mother suffocated? Both have deserved nothing of good but *the potter hath power over the clay, of the same lump to make one vessel unto honour, and another unto dishonour.* Do you wish to dispute with me? Nay rather, do you wonder with me and exclaim with me: *O the depth of the riches!*[4] Let us both be filled with dread, let us both cry: *O the depth of the riches!* Let us agree together in fear, lest we perish in error. *O the depth of the riches of the wisdom and knowledge of God! How unsearchable are His judgements, and His ways past finding out!*[5]

The divine decisions, however, although they appear mysterious and inscrutable now will not always remain so. In the resurrection, God's counsels will be revealed to the blessed:

Then what is now hidden will not be hidden: when one of two infants is taken up by God's mercy and the other abandoned through God's judgement—and when the chosen one knows what would have been his just deserts in judgement—why was the one chosen rather than the other, when the condition of the two was the same? Or again, why were miracles not wrought in the presence of certain people who would have repented in the face of miraculous works, while miracles were wrought

quod etiam sibi supplicium conveniret, nisi gratia subveniret. si autem gratia, utique nullis meritis reddita, sed gratuita bonitate donata'; *De Dono Persever.*, viii, 16: 'Sed "cur", inquit, "gratia Dei non secundum merita hominum datur?" Respondeo, Quoniam Deus misericors est. "Cur ergo", inquit, "non omnibus?" Et hic respondeo, Quoniam Deus iudex est.'
[1] Rom. 9.21.   [2] Ibid.   [3] Rom. 9.20.   [4] Rom. 11.33.   [5] Aug., *Serm.* 26, xii, 13.

in the presence of those who were not about to believe? For our Lord saith most plainly: *Woe to you, Choruzin; woe to you, Bethsaida. For if in Tyre and Sidon had been wrought the miracles done in your midst, they would have repented long ago in sackcloth and ashes.*[1] Now, obviously, God did not act unjustly in not willing their salvation, even though they could have been saved, if He had willed it so.[2]

The grace by which the elect are saved is conveyed by baptism. This fact, indeed, was one of the key issues of the Pelagian controversy. One of the charges brought against Caelestius at Carthage was that he held that infants, even though not baptized, had eternal life, and he attempted to meet it by replying that he had always said that children needed baptism and ought to be baptized—an answer which Augustine found inadequate, because it did not involve an admission that the sin of Adam had passed into them, requiring the laver of regeneration to wash it away.[3] The Pelagians, indeed, were in a difficult situation. The practice of infant baptism had become steadily more common and, at the same time, the implications of the words of the so-called Nicene Creed,[4] 'one baptism for the remission of sins', were having their effect. If there is but one baptism and that for the remission of sins, then from what sins can a newly born infant be cleansed, except from that which comes from Adam? There was a simple logic about the question and answer to which the Pelagians had on adequate rejoinder. They were not prepared to say as they might have done if they had lived in the twentieth century that baptism was not really necessary;[5] indeed, they agreed that it was required. Pelagius himself placed baptism at the centre of his teaching about the Christian life.[6] When faced with the problem of the fate of unbaptized infants, their explanations were reasonable and humane. Pelagius could say: 'I know where they do *not* go; where they go, I do not know',[7] while Julian of Eclanum, with a generosity which not infrequently appears in his works, assigns them to a third state, intermediate between Heaven and Hell, thereby anticipating the view which was to become orthodox among Latin theologians in the Middle Ages.[8] But this did not explain why, lacking

---

[1] Matt. 11.21.
[2] *Enchir.*, xxiv, 95. Tr. Outler, p. 394. Cf. *De Grat. et Lib. Arb.*, xxiii, 45.
[3] *De Peccato Originali*, iv, 3–4. Cf. *Op. Imp. c. Iul.*, i, 53.
[4] Really the Constantinopolitan Creed of 381; but it has always been regarded as expressing the faith declared at Nicaea in 325.
[5] See N. P. Williams, op. cit., p. 344.
[6] See Bohlin, *Die Theologie des Pelagius und ihre Genesis*, 29–45, esp. 32–36.
[7] *De Pecc. Orig.*, xxi, 23.
[8] *Op. Imp. c. Iul.*, i, 50: '[Augustinus dixit:] Ille vero quem sperat iudicem rationalis creatura, quae in sanctis eius est et fidelibus, lege nobis, praeter regnum bonis et supplicium malis, quem tertium locum praeparavit et promiserit non regeneratis innocentibus tuis.' On the Pelagian attitude to unbaptized infants, see Williams, op. cit., pp. 344–5.

baptism, they must be excluded from the kingdom of Heaven, while Augustine's theory of Original Sin most effectively did, and the saint found it impossible to believe that any infant who was predestined to eternal life would be allowed to die unbaptized. Strangely enough, he recognized that there were certain cases in which baptism could be dispensed with. Indeed, he devotes a chapter of the De Civitate Dei to proving that if a man, being unbaptized, suffer death for Christ, his martyrdom cleanses him from sin as effectively as if he had received the sacrament.[1] Once, he had gone further, and declared that not only baptism but faith and conversion of the heart may supply what baptism conveys;[2] but now he had become more rigorous: apart from martyrdom, there can be no salvation for the unbaptized. The only comfort which he can offer is, that for those who have added no sins of their own commission to that which they have inherited from Adam, the mildest pains of Hell will be reserved. He will even admit that this state of damnation may be preferable to non-existence.[3] To Julian's question: what of the ages before baptism was ordained? Augustine replied by admitting the force of the inquiry but giving no answer, except that it is incredible that no sacrament should have been instituted for those centuries, though what it was the Scriptures do not say.[4]

But, while Augustine holds that there is no salvation without baptism, it does not follow that every baptized person will be an inheritor of the kingdom of Heaven and a citizen of the City of God. Two men may both be pious, but to one will be given perseverance to the end and not the other,[5]

[1] dCD, XIII, vii.　　　　　　　　　　　　　　　[2] De Baptismo, IV, xxii, 29.

[3] C. Iul., V, xi, 44: 'Ego autem non dico parvulos sine Christi Baptismate morientes tanta poena esse plectendos, ut eis non nasci potius expediret; cum hoc Dominus non de quibuslibet peccatoribus, sed de scelestissimis et impiissimis dixerit. Si enim de Sodomis ait, et utique non de solis intelligi voluit, alius alio tolerabilius in die iudicii punietur; quis dubitaverit parvulos non baptizatos, qui solum habent originale peccatum, nec ullis propriis aggravantur, in damnatione omnium levissima futuros? Quae qualis et quanta erit, quamvis definire non possim, non tamen audeo dicere quod eis ut nulli essent quam ut ibi essent, potius expediret.'

[4] Ibid., V, xi, 45: 'Aliis deinde propositis meis verbis, quibus commemoravi quam honeste sancti antiqui patres coniugibus usi fuerint; dicis "eos non hoc intuitu operam dedisse propagini, ut tanquam reos gignerent filios Baptismate diluendos, eo quod Baptisma quo nunc adoptamur nondum fuerat institutum". Hoc de Baptismate verum dicis: nec ideo tamen credendum est, et ante datam circumcisionem famulos Dei, quandoquidem eis inerat Mediatoris fides in carne venturi, nullo sacramento eius opitulatos fuisse parvulis suis; quamvis quid illud esset, aliqua necessaria causa Scriptura latere voluerit.' For this conception of the extension of faith in the Incarnate Lord back to the Old Testament saints, cf. De Pecc. Orig., xxiv, 28: 'Itaque sine ista fide, hoc est sine fide unius mediatoris dei et hominum hominis Christi Iesu, sine fide, inquam, resurrectionis eius, quam deus omnibus definivit, quae utique sine incarnatione eius ac morte non potest veraciter credi: sine fide ergo incarnationis et mortis et resurrectionis Christi nec antiquos iustos, ut iusti essent, a peccatis potuisse mundari et dei gratia iustificari veritas christiana non dubitat'; C. duas Ep. Pel., I, xxi, 39; III, iv, 8.

[5] De Dono Persev., ix, 21: 'Ex duobus autem piis, cur huic donetur perseverantia usque in finem, illi non donetur?'

and 'the end' Augustine defines as 'the end of their lives'.[1] If a man falls from grace before his death, he has not persevered;[2] and it is a matter for wonder that God regenerates some of His children in Christ, and bestows upon them Faith, Hope, and Love, but does not give them perseverance.[3] Such, however, is the condition of the world. Among God's enemies are some concealed who will one day be citizens of the heavenly Jerusalem; while in the Church there now are, and shall be to the end of time, others who are at present partakers of her sacraments, but who will not be partakers of the glories of the saints in the eternal kingdom.[4]

Inevitably, Augustine's assertion of the need for Grace for salvation, antecedent to all good actions on the part of the elect, raised the problem of free will, and his opponents were not slow to argue that his teaching overthrew all true freedom and reintroduced the pagan doctrine of Fate, the appalling deity of the ancient world, from whose power the Gospel offered men liberation.[5] This accusation Augustine indignantly denied. He was not, he said, going to quibble about words; if anyone dared to call the grace of God 'fate' he might do so, provided that his meaning were orthodox, but Augustine himself neither used the word nor taught the thing.[6] He did not say that free will had perished by the sin of Adam, but he held that it could avail only for sin in fallen man, and was powerless for good unless liberated by grace from its servitude and aided in the performance of every good thought, word, and deed.[7] He was able indeed to turn the charge back upon its framers. 'You say that because we hold that the grace of God anticipates all good merits in man and is not given as a reward of merit, that we teach fate; but do not yourselves, by your own

---

[1] De Dono Persev., i, 1: 'Asserimus ergo donum Dei esse perseverantiam qua usque in finem perseveratur in Christo. Finem autem dico, quo vita ista finitur, in quo tantummodo periculum est ne cadatur.'
[2] Ibid.: 'Si enim priusquam moriatur cadat, non perseverasse utique dicitur, et verissime dicitur. Quomodo ergo perseverantiam, qui non perseveravit, accepisse vel habuisse dicendus est?'
[3] De Cor. et Grat., viii, 18: 'Mirandum est quidem, multumque mirandum, quod filiis suis quibusdam Deus quos regeneravit in Christo, quibus fidem, spem, dilectionem dedit, non dat perseverantiam.' See also De Dono Persev., xxii, 58.
[4] dCD, I, xxxiv.
[5] C. duas Ep. Pel., II, v, 10: ' "Sub nomine", inquiunt [Pelagiani], "gratiae ita fatum asserunt, ut dicant, quia nisi deus invito et reluctanti homini inspiraverit boni et ipsius inperfecti cupiditatem, nec a malo declinare nec bonum possit arripere." '
[6] Ibid., v, 9: 'Nec sub nomine gratiae fatum asserimus, quia nullis hominum meritis dei gratiam dicimus antecedi. si autem quibusdam omnipotentis dei voluntatem placet fati nomine nuncupare, profanas quidem verborum novitates evitamus, sed de verbis contendere non amamus.'
[7] Ibid.: 'Peccato Adae arbitrium liberum de hominum natura perisse non dicimus; sed ad peccandum valere in hominibus subditis diabolo; ad bene autem pieque vivendum non valere, nisi ipsa voluntas hominis dei gratia fuerit liberata et ad omne bonum actionis, sermonis, cogitationis adiuta.'

admission, regard baptism as necessary for all ages? Why do you not learn
from the fact of infant baptism, which you agree to be necessary, what you
ought to hold about grace?'[1] Once again, the Pelagians were being forced
to fight upon difficult ground of their own choosing, and were handicapped
by the fact that they accepted the need for infant baptism without having
any theory as impressively coherent as the Catholic doctrine of Original
Sin. However, their accusation was not an idle one, since on the face of it
the doctrine of Grace, as expounded in Augustine's anti-Pelagian treatises,
seems to leave little room for human freedom. Not that Augustine admits
this; to the end of his life he strenuously maintained that his writings did
not, in any way, overthrow the freedom of the will. Thus, when in the
Retractations he came to review the *De Libero Arbitrio*, written in the early
years of his Christian life and directed against the necessitarian conception of sin which he regarded as one of the worst features of Manichaeism,
he reflected that, although written long before the Pelagian heresy, it
might well be regarded as an anticipation of the anti-Pelagian writings.[2] In
one sense, the problem of free will does not exist for Augustine; it is self-
evident. In the *De Libero Arbitrio*, for example, he compels his friend
Evodius to admit that we both wish (*velle*) and have a will (*voluntas*), and
Augustine tends to regard 'to will' as an equivalent for 'to use free will'.[3]
The fact that we have a will is as obvious as the fact that we live; we feel
ourselves will and not will.[4] And the testimony of consciousness is reinforced by the moral sense. The conscience condemns sin, but how can sin
be condemned if the sinner is not a free agent?[5]

[1] *C. Duas Ep. Pel.*, II, vi, 11.
[2] *Retract.*, I, 8 [9], 6: 'Ecce tam longe antequam Pelagiana heresis extitisset, sic disputavimus, velut iam contra illos disputaremus.' See however the comment of Burleigh,
Augustine: The Earlier Writings, 107: '. . . the passages quoted in the *Retractations* as
showing that the *De Libero Arbitrio* is virtually anti-pelagian all come from what must
certainly be regarded as the later parts of the work.'
[3] *De Lib. Arb.*, I, xii, 25: 'A. Nam quaero abs te, sitne aliqua nobis voluntas. E. Nescio.
A. Visne hoc scire? E. Et hoc nescio. A. Nihil ergo deinceps me interroges. E. Quare? A.
Quia roganti tibi respondere non debeo nisi volenti scire quod rogas. Deinde nisi velis
ad sapientiam pervenire, sermo tecum de huiuscemodi rebus non est habendus. Postremo amicus meus esse non poteris nisi velis ut bene sit mihi. Iam vero de tu ipse videris,
utrum tibi voluntas nulla sit beatae vitae tuae. E. Fateor, negari non potest habere nos
voluntatem.' See J. Martin, *S. Augustin*, 2e éd., Paris, 1901, 176–9; Lacey, *Nature*,
Miracle and Sin, 50–51.
[4] *Conf.*, VII, iii, 5: 'Sublevabat enim me in lucem tuam, quod tam sciebam me habere
voluntatem quam me vivere. Itaque cum aliquid vellem aut nollem, non alium quam me
velle ac nolle certissimus eram et ibi esse causam peccati mei iam iamque animadverte-
bam'; *dCD*, V, ix: 'Nos adversus istos sacrilegos ausus adque inpios et Deum dicimus
omnia scire antequam fiant. et voluntate nos facere, quidquid a nobis non nisi volentibus
fieri sentimus et novimus'; *De Duab. Animab.*, x, 14: 'Nobis autem voluntas nostra
notissima est; neque enim scirem me velle si quid sit voluntas ipsa nescirem.'
[5] *De Vera Rel.*, xiv, 27: '. . . usque adeo peccatum voluntarium est malum, ut nullo
modo sit peccatum, si non sit voluntarium.' But see *Retract.*, i, 12 [13], 6 [5].

The establishment of free will is, however, only the beginning of the discussion, so far as Augustine is concerned. We have free will, but free will for what? Nothing marks him off more sharply from the Pelagians than the recognition of the fact that to have free will is not the same as to be free. The man who chooses evil is a slave to his vices;[1] but his free will was given him by God, and once he has thrown it away by choosing vice, it cannot be recovered except through the action of God.[2] No one has anything of himself except lying and sin,[3] but *if the Son shall make you free, ye shall be free indeed*.[4] There is no true liberty but that of those who are blessed and who keep the eternal law.[5] Such a freedom is very different from that envisaged by the Pelagian definitions: 'Free will is nothing other than the possibility of sinning or not sinning.'[6] 'The freedom of the will, by which man is emancipated from God, consists in the possibility of sinning and of abstaining from sin.'[7] This sort of freedom meant little to Augustine, who had understood from bitter experience the paradoxical declaration of the Lord that the only relief for the weary and the heavy-laden was to take the yoke of Christ, whose yoke is easy and His burden light. The ultimate liberty of the saints is the loss of freedom to sin.[8] Nevertheless, Augustine is clear that, in this life, Grace does not override free will. Under the action of Divine Grace, the will remains its own master. It can accept or refuse the call of God,[9] though it cannot in so

[1] *De Vera Rel.*, xlviii, 93: 'Quem ergo delectat libertas, ab amore mutabilium rerum liber esse appetat'; *dCD*, IV, iii: 'Proinde bonus etiamsi serviat, liber est; malus autem etiamsi regnet, servus est, nec unius hominis, sed, quod est gravius, tot dominorum quot vitiorum. De quibus vitiis cum ageret scriptura divina: *A quo enim quis*, inquit, *devictus est, huic et servus addictus est*.'
[2] *dCD*, XIV, xi: 'Arbitrium igitur voluntatis tunc est vere liberum, cum vitiis peccatis-que non servit. Tale datum est a Deo: quod amissum proprio vitio, nisi a quo dari potuit, reddi non potest. Unde Veritas dicit: *Si vos Filius liberaverit, tunc vere liberi eritis*.'
[3] *In Iohan. Tr.* 5, 1: 'Nemo habet de suo, nisi mendacium et peccatum.'
[4] *Iohan.* 8.36.
[5] *De Lib. Arb.*, I, xv, 32: '. . . libertas; quae quidem nulla vera est nisi beatorum et legi aeternae adherentium.'
[6] *Op. Imp. c. Iul.*, vi, 9: 'Liberum arbitrium . . . non est aliud quam possibilitas peccandi et non peccandi.'
[7] Ibid., i, 78: 'Libertas arbitrii, qua a Deo emancipatus homo est, in admittendi peccati et abstinendi a peccato possibilitate consistit.'
[8] *De Corrept. et Grat.*, xii, 33: 'Prima ergo libertas voluntatis erat, posse non peccare; novissima erit multo maior, non posse peccare; prima immortalitas erat, posse non mori; novissima erit multo maior, non posse mori; prima erat perseverantiae po-testas, bonum posse non deserere; novissima erit felicitas perseverantiae, bonum non posse deserere.'
[9] *De Spir. et Litt.*, xxxiv, 60: 'His ergo modis quando deus agit cum anima rationali, ut ei credat—neque enim credere potest quodlibet libero arbitrio, si nulla sit suasio vel vocatio cui credat—profecto et ipsum velle credere deus operatur in homine et in omnibus misericordia eius praevenit nos, consentire autem vocationi dei vel ab ea dissentire, sicut dixi, propriae voluntatis est.'

N

doing defeat His ends.[1] Man has a part to play in the action of the divine Grace, since he is not an insensate object or an animal lacking the use of reason, but a rational creature with a will of his own.[2] God does not force the will of the elect, which He has foreseen and predestinated. To the consideration of this predestination we must now turn.

The difficulty about any discussion of the Augustinian doctrine of predestination lies in the fact that it is possible to interpret it in a variety of ways so diverse that one might have supposed that different authors had inspired the varying interpretations. Thus the sceptical Richard Simon, the father of modern biblical criticism, regarded Augustine as an innovator, favouring Calvinism, a judgement which caused Bossuet to declare that to attack Augustine on the subject of Grace was to attack the doctrine of the Church.[3] J. B. Mozley is among those who find Augustine's doctrine essentially the same as Calvin's,[4] like Jean Adam, the Catholic contemporary of Cardinal Noris, who declared: 'If I restricted myself within the limits of Augustine [on predestination] I should be a Calvinist.'[5] On the other hand, W. A. Cunningham[6] and Eugène Portalié[7] may be mentioned among those who have denied that there is an essential resemblance between the systems. Calvin himself thought highly of Augustine's teaching as approving his own doctrine[8] but was also aware that there were points of difference.[9] One significant distinction may be noted: Calvin is technically supralapsarian in his teaching, holding that God's decrees of election and reprobation are not due to the Fall but were made before it

---

[1] *Conf.*, I, iv, 4: 'Opera mutas nec mutas concilium.' Augustine holds, of course, that grace and justice remain supreme (*Enchir.*, xxv, 98: 'Quis porro tam impie disipiat, ut dicat deum malas hominum voluntates quas voluerit, quando voluerit, ubi voluerit, in bonum non posse convertere?') but this is a conversion *in bonum*, and the will remains free.

[2] *De Pec. Mer. et Rem.*, II, v, 6: 'Adiutor enim noster deus dicitur nec adiuvari potest, nisi qui aliquid etiam sponte conatur, quia non sicut in lapidibus insensatis aut sicut in eis, in quorum natura rationem voluntatemque non condidit, salutem nostram deus operatur in nobis. cur autem illum adiuvet, illum non adiuvet, illum tantum, illum autem tantum; istum illo, illum isto modo; penes ipsum est et aequitatis tam secretae ratio et excellentia potestatis'; *De Perf. Iust. Hom.*, xx, 43: 'Nec adiuvatur, nisi qui et ipse aliquid agit: adiuvatur autem, si invocat, si credit, si secundum propositum vocatus est.'

[3] See W. J. Sparrow-Simpson, *A Study of Bossuet*, S.P.C.K., London, 1937, 55.

[4] J. B. Mozley, *A Treatise on the Augustinian Doctrine on Predestination*, 2nd ed., 266 n^1, 393–409.

[5] Noris, *Vindiciae Augustinianae*, i. *MPL* xlvii, 577B, cited in W. J. Sparrow-Simpson, *St. Augustine's Episcopate*, xiii.

[6] *St Austin*, 82–88.

[7] *DTC*, Art. 'Augustin', cols. 2398–9 (ET p. 214).

[8] *Institutio*, III, xxii, 8: 'Valeat Augustini testimonium apud eos, qui libenter in patrum auctoritate acquiescunt. ... Si ex Augustino integrum volumen contexere libeat, lectoribus ostendere promptum esset, mihi non nisi eius verbis opus esse: sed eos prolixitate onerare nolo.'

[9] Ibid., II, iv, 3: 'Ne Augustinus quidem illa superstitione interdum solutus est.'

and without regard to it, while Augustine's doctrine is infralapsarian: we are condemned because we fell in Adam, who sinned by the abuse of free will. God certainly foresaw the Fall, but He did not compel it. Furthermore, although all humanity is damned as a result of the Fall, and the choice of the elect, as we see it in this life, incomprehensible, it does not follow that the divine decisions are arbitrary. On the contrary, they rest on reasons which will, eventually, be made known.[1] In view of the sombre nature of much of Augustine's writing on the subject of election and reprobation, this distinction may seem to be technical rather than significant; but in fact it reveals, as surely as the contrast between the Calvinist doctrine of the total corruption of fallen man and Augustine's view that some spark of the divine likeness remains even in fallen nature, the gulf which yawns between the bases of Augustinian and Calvinistic thought.

The difficulty about discussing God's prescience and predestination at all lies in the fact that we have to try to speak of God's knowledge of time with the concepts and language derived from our own finite experience. Inevitably, human minds think in terms of past, present, and future; but we are not justified in supposing that God's experience is in such terms. Certainly, He acts in time—is He not the God who is, and was, and is to come?—but He is not limited by time as we are. His day is eternity,[2] and time itself is His creation.[3] Hence it is that the correct answer to the flippant question: what did God do before He made heaven and earth? is: nothing,[4] for the question implies the limitations of a temporal existence.

In this sense, to talk of prescience and predestination is misleading, since it applies to God human conceptions founded upon our understanding of His workings and of His sayings in Holy Scripture, as when He declared to the prophet Jeremiah: 'Before I formed thee in the belly I knew thee; and before thou camest out of the womb I sanctified thee.'[5] Nevertheless, although Augustine was profoundly aware of the limitations

---

[1] *De Grat. et Lib. Arb.*, xxiii, 45: 'Nolite . . . dare iniustitiam vel insipientiam Deo, apud quem iustitiae fons est et sapientiae: sed sicut vos exhortatus sum ab initio sermonis huius, in quod pervenistis, in eo ambulate, et hoc quoque vobis Deus revelabit, et si non in hac vita, certe in altera: nihil est enim occultum quod non revelabitur'; *Enchir.*, xxiv, 95: 'Tunc non latebit quod nunc latet, cum de duobus parvulis unus esset assumendus per misericordiam, alius per iudicium relinquendus, in quo, is qui assumeretur, agnosceret quid sibi per iudicium deberetur, nisi misericordia subveniret; cur ille potius quam iste fuerit assumptus, cum causa una esset ambobus: cur apud quosdam non factae sint virtutes, quae si factae fuissent, egissent illi homines poenitentiam, et factae sint apud eos qui non fuerant credituri.' For Calvin's view, cf. *Institutio*, III, xxi, 1–7.
[2] *Conf.*, XI, xiii, 16: 'Hodiernus tuus aeternitas.'
[3] Ibid., XI, xiv, 17: 'Nullo ergo tempore non feceras aliquid, quia ipsum tempus tu feceras.'
[4] Ibid., XI, xii, 14: 'Antequam faceret deus caelum et terram, non faciebat aliquid.'
[5] Ierem. 1.5.

of language, he does talk about the prescience and predestination of God. To those who complained that divine prescience took away human freedom, he retorted with the obvious rejoinder that, in that case, it took away free will from God.[1] But what then of predestination?

> This is the predestination of the saints, and nothing else: the prescience and preparation of the benefits of God, whereby whoever are set free are most certainly set free. And where are the rest left by the just judgement of God, save in that mass of perdition, where were left the men of Tyre and the Sidonians, who were also capable of belief, had they but seen those wonderful works of Christ?[2]

This is the classical statement of Augustinian predestination: foreknowledge of the elect and preparation of the means whereby they shall be saved, while the reprobate are left in their state of sin, without any positive impulsion to damnation. Unfortunately, the issue is complicated, because Augustine does, on some occasions, speak as if some men are not merely foreknown but actually predestinated to punishment.[3] If we found evidence in his works that these reprobates, these *damnandi praedestinati*, were rejected before the creation of the world, as he specifically says the elect were chosen,[4] then we should have no alternative but to regard his theology as predestinarian in the same sense that Calvinism is predestinarian. However, this is not the case; and it would seem that Augustine is, on this occasion, speaking loosely when he talks of some being predestinated to wrath because they have not been chosen. Inasmuch as all humanity has perished in Adam it is possible (in a certain sense) to say that the reprobate are predestinated to perdition; but this does not mean an arbitrary decree which deliberately creates certain vessels of wrath, who are to be damned simply to the greater glory of God. In view of Augustine's repeated insistence that the lost are justly condemned, such an interpretation seems preferable to a literal acceptance of his words. It is

---

[1] *De Lib. Arb.*, III, iii, 6. [2] *De Dono Persev.*, xiii, 35.

[3] E.g. *Enchir.*, xxvi, 100: '[Deus] bene utens et malis, tamquam summe bonus, ad eorum damnationem quos iuste praedestinavit ad poenam, et ad eorum salutem quos benigne praedestinavit ad gratiam . . .'; *De Anima*, IV, xi, 16: '. . . qui est et illis quos praedestinavit ad aeternam mortem iustissimus supplicii retributor'; *De Pecc. Mer. et Rem.*, II, xvii, 26: 'Ut autem innotescat quod latebat et suave fiat quod non delectabat, gratiae dei est, qua hominum adiuvat voluntates; qua ut non adiuventur, in ipsis itidem causa est, non in deo, sive damnandi praedestinati sunt propter iniquitatem superbiae sive contra ipsam suam superbiam iudicandi et erudiendi, si filii sunt misericordiae.'

[4] *De Praedest. Sanct.*, xvii, 34: 'Electi sunt itaque ante mundi constitutionem ea praedestinatione, in qua Deus sua futura facta praescivit: electi sunt autem de mundo ea vocatione, qua Deus id quod praedestinavit, implevit. Quos enim praedestinavit, ipsos ea vocavit; illa scilicet vocatione secundum propositum: non ergo alios, sed quos praedestinavit, ipsos et vocavit: nec alios, sed quos ita vocavit, ipsos et iustificavit: nec alios, sed quos praedestinavit, vocavit, iustificavit, ipsos et glorificavit; illo utique fine qui non habet finem.'

not that God deliberately damns anyone; the worst we can say—and no one is likely to underestimate how terrible it is—is, that for St Augustine, God has not an absolute will to save all men. Hence his unhappy, and unconvincing, attempts to explain away the Pauline saying that *God willeth all men to be saved*, by asserting that by 'all' is meant 'many' or 'all those predestinated to salvation' or 'from every race and class' or 'all, because no man shall be saved save him whom God wishes to be saved'.[1] In this negative sense, Augustine does teach a sort of predestination to reprobation; but his doctrine is certainly not Calvinism and is, indeed, only a more rigorous expression of what the Christian must hold, if he is not to fall into Universalism—a theology which has never been acceptable to the mind of the Church.

Augustine as a theologian has aroused the most passionate feelings, both of admiration and repugnance, and nowhere more than in his writings on Grace, sin and predestination. On the one hand there is the celebrated boast of Michael de Bay (Baius), that he had read the entire works of Augustine nine times and the writings on Grace seventy times; on the other, the observation of a hostile critic, writing at the beginning of the twentieth century: 'This great man's influence extended for evil, as his writings show, over practically nearly the whole field of human activity, social and political, no less than religious.'[2] It is obvious that the verdict of the majority of those who study the Doctor of Grace will fall somewhere between these widely divided extremes and will be determined very much by the aspect of Augustine's thought under review. It would be possible, though it would require careful selection, to read widely in Augustine without ever considering his doctrine of Grace. Once however a reader has embarked upon it, his feelings are likely to be those of mingled admiration and repulsion—of admiration for religious insight of the highest genius and of repulsion for a theological system which, despite its greatness, is

[1] *C. Iul.*, IV, viii, 44: '*Omnes* positos esse pro Multis, quos ad istam gratiam vult venire. Quod multo convenientius propter hoc intelligitur dictum, quia nemo venit, nisi quem venire ipse voluerit'; *Enchir.*, xxvii, 103: 'Ac per hoc cum audimus et in sacris Litteris legimus, quod velit omnes homines salvos fieri, quamvis certum sit nobis non omnes homines salvos fieri, non tamen ideo debemus omnipotentissimae Dei voluntati aliquid derogare; sed ita intelligere quod scriptum est: *Qui omnes homines vult salvos fieri*, tanquam diceretur nullum hominem fieri salvum, nisi quem fieri ipse voluerit; non quod nullus sit hominum, nisi quem salvum fieri velit; sed quod nullus fiat, nisi quem velit, et ideo sit rogandus ut velit, quia necesse est fieri si voluerit'; *De Cor. et Grat.*, xv, 47: 'Quia ergo nos qui salvi futuri sint nescientes, omnes quibus praedicamus hanc pacem salvos fieri velle Deus iubet, et ipse in nobis hoc operatur, diffundendo istam charitatem in cordibus nostris per Spiritum sanctum qui datus est nobis potest etiam sic intelligi, quod *omnes homines Deus vult salvos fieri*; quoniam nos facit velle; sicut misit *Spiritum Filii sui clamantem, Abba, Pater*, id est nos clamare facientem.' Cf. *De Spir. et Litt.*, xxxiii, 58—an earlier assertion of the text without his later modifications.
[2] Allin, *The Augustinian Revolution in Theology*, 25.

too legalistic and lacking in charity to reconcile with the continual emphasis laid by Augustine himself on the supernatural virtue of charity, from which the God of his predestinarian writings seems wonderfully immune. Such an attitude is understandable and, in the opinion of the present writer, justified. It would be difficult to overestimate the debt which Christian devotion and dogma owe to Augustine for his long struggle against the Pelagian theology and, still more, the principles upon which that theology rested. Whatever may be the verdict of historians concerning the personal character of Pelagius, the system with which his name is associated menaced the Faith no less than the great heresies which arose in the east concerning the Trinity and the Nature of Christ. Indeed, in one sense the menace of Pelagianism was the greater, in that, unlike the Greek heresies, it could be reconciled with perfect credal orthodoxy. Moreover, it had an obvious appeal for precisely the most dynamic and enthusiastic element in the Church—the monks and the ascetics. It was in the face of this menace that Augustine assumed the moral leadership of the Church and held firmly to the belief in the inner necessity for Grace, not merely to assist men to be good or to effect pardon for past sins, but to enable them to accomplish anything good at all. It was, presumably, this aspect of Augustine's thought which Harnack had in mind when he wrote that Augustine 'preached the sincere humility which blossoms only on ruins—the ruins of self-righteousness; but he recognized in this very humility the charter of the soul'.[1] Christ's saying: *Without Me, ye can do nothing*, dominates every line that the mature Augustine wrote.

Furthermore, we must be grateful for the care with which the saint safeguards the freedom of the will while, at the same time, recognizing that in the long run Christian freedom depends upon a willingness to surrender ourselves utterly to God so that, at the last, we may learn from the Master and say with Him: 'Not my will but Thine be done.' It is easy enough to say these words; it is very difficult to mean them. A study of Augustine brings their implication before our eyes.

Again, the value of Augustine's teaching on the subject of sin deserves the highest recognition. His theory of Original Sin, though ingenious, is too much based upon a faulty physiological theory and an untenable conception of responsibility to be acceptable today; but his attitude to sin and the way in which he emphasises its blighting effect upon all aspects of human life until God's Grace comes is one which the Christian theologian will neglect at his peril. Much of the mystery which seems to envelop the

[1] Harnack, *Lehrbuch der Dogmengeschichte*, 4te Aufl., iii, 65. ET v, 65.

condition of the world—the cruelty, the selfishness, the dishonesty—arises because Christians are, unconsciously, Pelagians when they investigate human affairs. This accounts for the failure of noble actions which are not inspired by the love of God. Augustine's denunciation of the virtues of noble pagans—a denunciation which has shocked and continues to shock many worthy persons—is, within its particular limits, perfectly justified. One cannot fail to detect the nature of sin in actions which are not inspired by the love of God. Where the modern christian is likely to introduce a note of caution is in his unwillingness to limit the operations of the divine Mercy and the divine Grace to those who have heard the Word and been baptized into the Church of Christ. The saying in St Matthew: *Inasmuch as ye have done it unto one of the least of these my brethren, ye have done it unto Me*[1]—a saying addressed, not to Christians, but to the nations (πάντα τὰ ἔθνη)—permits us to believe on our Lord's own authority that those who have been deprived of the priceless benefit of the Faith and the Sacraments will not, merely on that account, be excluded from the kingdom of Heaven. And, in our own age, it is possible to see among us persons who lack the grace of faith but who seem, in a certain manner, to be 'waiting on God', to employ the phrase of one of their most distinguished representatives.[2] It would be rash, in the case of such persons, to attempt to limit the degree to which God may give them some measure of Grace in their daily lives, even though they remain outside the Church.

We come to the last point: the authority of Augustine's doctrine of predestination. Of the importance of this doctrine in the history of Latin theology there can be no question and it is tempting to apply to the bishop of Hippo the comment on Julius Caesar put by Shakespeare into the mouth of Cassius:

> Why, man, he doth bestride the narrow world
> Like a colossus.

His influence has extended far beyond the boundaries of any one communion, and Roman and Protestant divines alike have drawn at his fountain and claimed him as their own. In the last century or so, however, there has been a change in theological emphasis, and it is doubtful if more than a handful of Christian thinkers would today give unqualified acceptance to Augustine's doctrine of predestination as he stated it. Nor is there any reason why they should for, despite the large claims which disciples of

[1] Matt. 25.40.
[2] It must, however, be added that in the case of Simone Weil, it is hard to understand and still harder to approve her continued refusal of baptism, a refusal which points to an element of pride in her nature.

the bishop of Hippo have made on his behalf—claims which, indeed, we may feel that he would himself have rejected—Augustinian predestination is not the doctrine of the Church but only the opinion of a distinguished Catholic theologian. Its weaknesses are plain to see: a rigorous logic which, working from arbitrary premisses, emphasizes the power of God and neglects the quality of Love which was revealed by Christ in His Incarnation and Death. Why Augustine, who so often and so eloquently dwells upon the quality of Love, should have so narrowly applied it when he wrote upon God's dealings with His creation is a mystery which may well provoke the reader to echo Augustine's own cry of *O Altitudo!* Nothing is gained by attempting to defend the doctrine, which remains a terrible one and more likely to arouse our awe than to enlist our sympathy. It is not merely the fashion in which Augustine consigns unbaptized infants to eternal pain which repels us, though this has an obvious emotional effect. As terrifying is the detachment with which he contemplates the damnation of the greater part of the human race, among whom there are many who are lost because time or space or their condition of life prevented them from having the Gospel preached to them. We have said that it is not incumbent upon the believer to entertain the sombre beliefs as to their fate which Augustine held and it may be added that, from Augustine's own writings, it is possible to discern suggestions which could be developed into a more optimistic, and a more charitable, attitude. In the treatise *On Original Sin*, Augustine extended the benefits of Christ's mediation back to the saints of the Old Testament[1] since, as he quotes, 'there is none other name under heaven given among men, whereby we must be saved.[2]' It is no very great exaggeration of this conception to extend it to those multitudes of human creatures who, from the beginning of the world, have lived and died in ignorance of the love of God revealed in Jesus Christ. This hope is not, indeed, a matter for the dogmatic theologian; rather, it springs from faith in God, and the conviction that

> Christ's love o'er-flows the bounds His Prophets trace
> In His revealed design.[3]

Nevertheless, when all else is said, the fact that we dissent from Augustine in the matter of predestination does not detract from his personal

---

[1] *De Pecc. Orig.*, xxiv, 28. Quoted above, p. 382 n^4.   [2] Acts 4.12.
[3] Newman, 'Schism' in *Lyra Apostolica* (1836). For an attempt to work out the implications of Augustine's teaching with regard to the virtues of the pagans, see J. Wang, S.J., *Saint Augustin et les vertus des paiens*, Paris, 1933. This work has a particular poignancy, in that it is the work of a Chinese theologian, to whom the knowledge that many of his ancestors died outside the Christian faith must have given his studies a peculiar urgency.

greatness nor from the inspiration which he gives his reader. An excellent summary of the whole matter may be found in the words of the distinguished and original thinker Alexander Knox, who, in his writings, anticipated in some measure the Tractarian movement:

> I have called [Augustine] the great Doctor of Grace, next to the Apostles; and I must now add that I have given him this title, not only because no other individual in the Church so fully deserves it, but because, I conceive, that what Augustine has done in this department, he has done exquisitely. His excesses are easily separable from his excellencies; and when the latter are viewed in themselves, they furnish, to my mind, the best key to St Paul's leading doctrine, in his two Epistles to the Romans and Galatians, that the world has ever seen.[1]

[1] Alexander Knox, *Remains*, 1834, iii, 191, quoted in Sparrow-Simpson, *St Augustine's Episcopate*, 83.

APPENDIX A

Augustine's Knowledge of Greek

AUGUSTINE'S KNOWLEDGE of Greek has been much discussed in the years which have elapsed since the publication by the Danish scholar Clausen of his study, *Augustinus Hipponensis sacrae Scripturae interpres* (Copenhagen, 1827). A general examination of the various investigations made and conclusions reached up to the time of his writing was provided by Berthold Altaner, 'Augustinus und die griechische Sprache', in *Pisciculi: Studien zur Religion und Kultur des Altertums Franz Joseph Dölger . . . dargeboten*, Münster in Westf., 1939, 19–40. To the list of studies there given may now be added Irénée Chevalier, *St Augustin et la pensée grecque. Les relations trinitaires*, Fribourg en Suisse, 1940, 98ff.; Altaner, 'Augustinus und Eusebios von Kaisareia', in *Byzantinische Zeitschrift*, xliv (1951), 1–6; and Luguori G. Müller, *The De Haeresibus of St Augustine* (Catholic University of America Patristic Studies, Vol. 90), Washington, D.C., 1956, 30–37. Particularly important on the subject (besides those already given) are H. Reuter, *Augustinische Studien*, Gotha, 1887, 170–82; S. Angus, *The Sources of the first ten books of St Augustine's De Civitate Dei*, Princeton, 1906, 236–73, 276; Pierre Courcelle, *Les lettres grecques en Occident: De Macrobe à Cassiodore*, 2e éd., Paris, 1948, 137–94; and H. I. Marrou, *St. Augustin et la fin de la culture antique*, 4e éd., Paris, 1958, 27–46, 631–7.

The extent of Augustine's knowledge of Greek might seem to be a purely academic question with little relevance to the understanding of his thought. In fact, this is not the case, because it is important to try to establish to what degree he was affected by Greek patristic theology and how much he had to rely on his own intellect. It cannot be said that a definitive judgement is possible at the present time (cf. Altaner in *BZ* xliv [1951], 1) but some general observations can be made.

The extent of Augustine's capability as a Greek scholar can be established in two ways: (1) by a careful examination of the Greek words, phrases and sentences which occur in his writings and (2) by comparing resemblances between his works and possible influences among the Greek

Fathers. The second method, much relied upon by Chevalier in *St Augustin et la pensée grecque*, tends to be subjective and is of little value if its conclusions are not borne out by the first (see Altaner's review of Chevalier in *Historisches Jahrbuch*, lxii–lxix [1949], 854–5). The first method, however, is both laborious and limited in scope, since much of the evidence turns upon the exegesis of individual Greek words and phrases which might easily have come from a dictionary or a preacher's handbook.

The general results of research at the present time seem to be as follows. Augustine, starting with the barest rudiments of Greek—a language he had hated as a child and never tried to master (*Conf.*, I, xiii, 20; xiv, 23)—in his later years gradually extended his knowledge until by about 415–16 he had a reasonable working knowledge of biblical Greek (see Courcelle, op. cit., pp. 150ff.; Marrou, op. cit., pp. 632ff.). In the Pelagian controversy, he was able to quote from a Greek Father in the original Greek and offer his own translation (*C. Iul.*, I, vi, 21–26). Finally, at the end of his life in 428 he was prepared to undertake the translation of a complete Greek treatise, when he based his work *De Haeresibus ad Quodvultdeum* on the abridgement of St Epiphanius' *Panarion* called the *Anacephalaiosis*. It must however be admitted that Augustine's translation is a very laboured and literal one, the work of the man who relies much on the dictionary, rather than one to whom the original language is a living reality.

Accordingly we may say that, although at the end of his life Augustine had acquired a reasonable familiarity with biblical Greek and was capable of checking and controlling a passage from the Fathers in the original Greek and even, on occasion, venturing upon a translation, there is no evidence of any study of a Greek patristic treatise (other than the *Anacephalaiosis*) which he had not already read in Latin translation, and no proof of direct study of the originals of any non-Christian Greek author. Essentially, the influence of Hellenic culture on Augustine is effected through the medium of Latin translations. Angus's verdict still holds good: 'On the testimony of Augustine's works he had a limited working knowledge of biblical Greek, a very slight working knowledge of patristic Greek and apparently no working knowledge of classical Greek' (op. cit., p. 276).

APPENDIX B

Augustine as a Monastic Legislator

THREE DOCUMENTS have been commonly associated with the name of Augustine as a monastic legislator.

(1) Letter 211 (ed. Goldbacher, *CSEL* lvii, 356–71; *MPL* xxxiii, 958–965) addressed to a community of women over which his sister had previously presided. After her death, disturbances had broken out and the nuns declared themselves dissatisfied with their new superior. Augustine addressed a letter of reproof and exhortation in the course of which (*Ep.* 211, 5–16) he laid down a conventual rule.

(2) The *Regula secunda* (*MPL* xxxii, 1449–52; ed. De Bruyne in *Revue Bénédictine*, xliii [1930], 318–19) otherwise known as the *De Ordine Monasterii* or the *Disciplina monastica*. This is a short document, written in a style unlike that of Augustine.

(3) The *Regula Sancti Augustini* (*MPL* xxxii, 1377–84; ed. De Bruyne, *Rev. Bén.*, xliii [1930], 320–6) also called the *Regula ad servos Dei* and the *Regula tertia*. This is a longer document than the *Regula secunda*, incorporating the rule laid down in *Ep.* 211, but addressed to a masculine community.

Traditionally, it has been held that the original and only genuinely Augustinian document among these three is the letter to the women religious, *Ep.* 211. The *Regula Sancti Augustini* was regarded as an adaptation of the rule laid down in the letter for the use of monks. The *Regula secunda* was regarded as apocryphal. There was, however, a curious feature of the manuscript tradition of the letter and the *Regula Sancti Augustini*. The latter is to be found in a manuscript at Paris (B.N. 12634), which is to be dated to 550–650 and is to be assigned to Vivarium or southern Italy. The letter first appears in a Spanish MS. of the early ninth century (Escorial a I 13)—a feminine version of the *Rule* in a much abridged form of the letter. The earliest complete MS. of the letter (Rheinau 89) dates from the late eleventh to the early twelfth century.

In recent times, a new theory has been put forward, which stems originally from the solutions propounded by P. Mandonnet, *Saint*

Dominique : L'idée, l'homme et l'œuvre, Paris [1937], ii, 107–62 (adopted by Bardy, *Saint Augustin*, 7e éd., 161–4, but see his reservations, p. 161 n^2). This school, of which the prominent spokesman is W. Hümpfner (see his 'Die Monchsregel des heiligen Augustins', in *Augustinus Magister*, i, 241–254), regards the *Regula Sancti Augustini* as a genuine composition of the saint and the *Ep.* 211 as a medieval forgery. It is suggested that the *Regula secunda* was composed by Augustine for his community at Thagaste in 389 and the *Regula tertia* for the monastery at Hippo before 395.

The case for assigning the *Regula secunda* to Augustine is very much weaker on stylistic grounds than that for the *Regula Sancti Augustini*. D. de Bruyne, 'La première règle de saint Benoit', in *Rev. Bén.*, xlii (1930), 316–342 argues that the *Regula secunda* must be assigned to St Benedict, while M. Verheijen, 'Remarques sur le style de la "Regula secunda" de saint Augustin', in *Aug. Mag.*, i, 255–63 tries to prove that it was the work of Alypius, on the ground that its phraseology shows the hand of a lawyer and that Alypius was the only person with legal training in the community at Thagaste. In any case, there seems good reason to reject any claim for an Augustinian authorship for the *Regula secunda*. The case for the genuineness of the *Regula Sancti Augustini* as against *Ep.* 211 is very much stronger. The style makes it clear that one or the other must be the work of the saint, and the problem is to decide which one it is to be. A very strong case for regarding the tradition that *Ep.* 211 is genuine and the original form of the Rule has been made by Dom D. C. Lambot, 'La règle de s. Augustin et s. Césaire', in *Rev. Bén.*, xli (1929), 335–8; 'S. Augustin a-t-il rédigé la Règle pour moines qui porte son nom?', in *Rev. Bén.*, liii (1941), 41–58; and 'Le monachisme de s. Augustin', in *Aug. Mag.*, iii, 65–68.

A convenient summary of the controversy will be found in Maria C. McCarthy, *The Rule for Nuns of St Caesarius of Arles* (Catholic University of America Studies in Medieval History, Vol. 16), Washington, D.C., 1960, 107–26, 164–5, who accepts Dom Lambot's arguments and adds further material to his view. For bibliographies of the literature of the debate see A. Zumkeller, *Das Mönchtum des heiligen Augustinus*, Würzburg, 1950, 215–18; Altaner, *Patrologie*, 5te Aufl., 396–7.

APPENDIX C

Concupiscentia and Libido

BOTH THESE words are so frequently used by St Augustine that it may be helpful to give some outline of their significance and background.

The meaning behind both of them as used in Augustinian theology is expressed by the English word *lust*, used in the sense of illegitimate sexual desire. Augustine is aware of this: 'Cum igitur sint multarum libidines rerum, tamen cum libido dicitur neque cuius rei libido sit additur, non fere adsolet animus occurrere nisi illa, qua obscenae partes corporis excitantur' (*dCD*, XIV, xvi). Here, it will be noticed, Augustine employs *libido* and not *concupiscentia*; and it will be recalled that another form of *libido*, the *libido dominandi*, the lust for rule over others, is the theme of the *dCD*. As a very general principle it may be said that when Augustine wishes to speak of lust in the sense of sexual desire, *libido* and *concupiscentia* are virtually interchangeable; but when any other lust is mentioned (with an exception which we shall see later) *libido* is the word used, very occasionally alternated with *cupido* or a similar form, e.g. *dCD*, V, xii: 'Ista ergo laudis aviditas et cupido gloriae multa illa miranda fecit, laudabilia scilicet atque gloriosa secundum hominum existimationem.'

There is abundant evidence for the interchangeability of *libido* and *concupiscentia* in their sexual significance, e.g. in *De Nuptiis et Concupiscentia* Augustine speaks of *libido* (I, vii, 8: 'libidinis malum'; I, viii, 9; xv, 17; xxi, 23; xxiv, 27); *concupiscentia* (I, vii, 8); *libido carnalis* (I, v, 6); *carnalis concupiscentia* (I, xi, 12); *carnis concupiscentia* (I, xvii, 19); and *carnis pudenda concupiscentia* (I, xii, 13; xvi, 18) always to describe the state of lust called concupiscence. If it is asked why Augustine used alternative words to express the same emotion, the answer lies partly in literary convenience to prevent the too-frequent repetition of the same word, and partly in the history of the Latin language, since of the two words, only *libido* is classical, with a wide range of meaning, while *concupiscentia* is a Christian technical term used predominantly (though not exclusively) of concupiscence. It is desirable to examine them both a little more closely.

Libido is a classical word, common in Latin literature. Basically, it has a neutral sense of desire; so Lucretius, *De Rerum Natura*, iv, 779–80:

Quaeritur in primis quare, quod cuique *libido*
venerit, extemplo mens cogitet eius id ipsum.

Here, *libido* amounts to little more than whim or fancy—why is it, the poet asks, that when anyone has the whim to think about a certain thing, the mind immediately furnishes a mental image of it? In a slightly more positive but still neutral sense, Sallust, *Bellum Jugurthinum*, 84, 3: 'Sed ea res frustra sperata; tanta *lubido* cum Mario eundi plerosque invaserat'— the senate had hoped that the plebeians would not want to go campaigning with Marius, but this hope was disappointed because of the great desire which had taken hold of the commons, filled with hopes of loot and glory. This is the first and essential meaning of *libido*: desire, without a very strong suggestion that the object of the desire is good or evil.

Secondly, there is an implication for desire of a vicious kind. Livy, i, 57: 'Ibi Sex. Tarquinum *mala libido* Lucretiae per vim stuprandae capit.' The point here is that it was a *mala libido*, which implies that *libido* is not in itself evil. More positive is Sallust, *Coniuratio Catalinae*, 28, 4: 'quibus *lubido* atque luxuria ex magnis rapinis nihil reliqui fecerant.' Here the word clearly has an unfavourable meaning; 'ruined by dissolute and extravagant living' seems a reasonable rendering. Cicero, *Tusculanae Disputationes*, III, ii, 4: 'qui pecuniae cupiditate, qui voluptatum *libidine* feruntur, quorum ita perturbantur animae, ut non multum absint ab insania' is more general; *libido voluptatum* covers a wide range of dissolute desire. With this we may compare Tacitus on Nero, *Annales*, xvi, 18: 'ergo crudelitatem principis, cui ceterae *libidines* cedebant, adgreditur.' Tacitus is speaking of the efforts of Tigellinus to poison Nero's mind against Petronius: 'And so he worked on the prince's cruelty, which dominated every other passion' is the rendering of Church and Brodribb. Equally specific is Cicero, *Tusc. Disput.*, III, v, 11: 'Itaque nihil melius, quam quod est in consuetudine sermonis Latini, cum exisse ex potestate dicimus eos, qui ecfrenati feruntur aut libidine aut iracundia; quamquam ipsa iracundia libidinis est pars; sic enim definitur iracundia: *ulciscendi libido*.' This passage unquestionably affected Augustine's thought on the subject of *libido*. We find references to it in *dCD*, XIV, xv: 'Nam et ipsam iram nihil aliud esse quam *ulciscendi libidinem* veteres definierunt'; in *Ep*. 138, ii, 9: 'Quo modo Caesari utique administratori rei publicae mores eius extollens Cicero dicebat, quod nihil oblivisci soleret nisi iniurias? Dicebat enim hoc tam magnus laudator aut tam magnus adulator; sed si laudator, talem Caesarem noverat, si autem adulator, talem esse debere ostendebat principem civitatis, qualem illum fallaciter praedicebat. Quid est autem non reddere malum pro malo nisi abhorrere ab *ulciscendi libidine*, quod est accepta iniuria ignoscere malle quam persequi, et nihil nisi iniurias oblivisci?'; *Conf.*, II, ix, 17: 'O nimis inimica amicitia, seductio mentis investigabilis, ex ludo et ioco nocendi aviditas et alieni damni appetitus nulla lucri mei, nulla *ulciscendi libido*, sed cum dicitur: "Eamus, faciamus" et pudet non esse impudentem.' Finally, there is the famous passage in Sallust, *Coniuratio Catilinae*, 2, 2: 'Post ea vero quam in Asia Cyrus, in Graecia Lacedaemonii et Athenienses coepere urbus atque nationes subigere, *lubidinem dominandi* causam belli habere, maxumam gloriam in maxumo imperio putare.' This is the *libido dominandi*, the lust for rule over others which, with *libido carnalis*, is one of the distinguishing marks of fallen humanity. The passage from Sallust is cited by Augustine in *dCD*, III, xiv, and he returns to the theme again and again (*dCD*, XIV, xxviii; XIX, xiv; XIX, xv).

Thirdly, there is a distinctly sexual connotation. One can find it in Petronius (ed. Baehrens, *Poetae Latinae Minores*, iv, 99, No. 101):

> Foeda est in coitu, et brevis voluptas,
> et taedet Veneris statim peractae.
> Non ergo ut pecudes *libidinosae*
> caeci protinus irruamus illuc,
> nam languescit amor, peritque flamma;

in Tacitus, *De Situ, Moribus et Populis Germaniae*, 17: 'Prope soli barbarorum singulis uxoribus contenti sunt, exceptis admodum paucis, qui non *libidine* sed ob nobilitatem plurimus nuptiis ambiuntur'; and in Seneca (*Hippol.*, 194–5). This last is particularly interesting, because it is actually quoted by Augustine in *Contra Faustum*, XX, ix:

> ... nec solas virtutes ipsius creaturae, sicut Minervam, cuius fabulam, quod de Iovis capite nata sit, ad prudentiam consiliorum interpretantur, quae rationis est propia, cui sedem capitis etiam Plato dedit, sed etiam vitia, sicut de Cupidine diximus. unde quidam eorum tragicus ait:
> > deum esse amorem turpis et vitio favens
> > finxit *libido*.
>
> > > (*CSEL* xxv, 545)

From these passages, it is clear that *libido*, in the sense of evil desire, was common enough in Latin literature, and that although it lacked the strongly sexual overtones of Augustine's *libido carnalis*, examples can be found of it being used in this sense. Furthermore, we must not forget the other source of inspiration open to Augustine—the Latin Bible, where the word *libido*, although much less frequent than *concupiscentia*, occurs, and invariably in the sense of *libido carnalis* (Iudic. 19.24; 20.5; Tobias 3.18; 6.17, 22; Judith 10.4; Ezech. 23.9, 11.20; Col. 3.5).

From the foregoing it will be apparent that Augustine, when discussing lusts other than sexual, is almost certain to employ the standard word *libido*, but that he was also able to employ it as an equivalent to *concupiscentia carnis* because of its literary history and specifically biblical employment.

The case of *concupiscentia* is different. Here we have a Christian technical word (see Alexander Souter, *A Glossary of Later Latin to A.D. 600*, Oxford, 1949, 69 *s.v.*: '[= ἐπιθυμία, ὄρεξις], desire, *generally* evil desire [not found outside Scripture and Christian writings]') with a very wide use in the Bible and generally, but not always, in a bad and sexual connotation. An instance of a good sense, to which Augustine refers, is Sap. 6.21: 'Concupiscentia itaque sapientiae deducit ad regnum perpetuum.' So Augustine writes in *De Nuptiis et Concupiscentia*, II, xxx, 52: 'Non dixi "nulla esset *concupiscentia*" quia est et glorianda concupiscentia spiritalis, qua concupiscitur sapientia; sed dixi "nulla esset pudenda *concupiscentia*".'

An example of *concupiscentia* used of a lust other than sexual is in *In Iohannem Tr.* 73, 1: 'An non videmus Israelitas malo suo impetrasse, quod culpabili *concupiscentia* petierunt [Num. 11.32]. Concupierant enim carnibus vesci, quibus pluebatur manna de coelo. . . . Cuius [sc. Dei] in Israelitis non parva erat offensio, repudiare quod dabat sapientia, et petere quod inhiabat concupiscentia.'

BIBLIOGRAPHY

THE BEST general edition of the works of St Augustine, complete except with regard to the sermons, is still that of the Benedictine editors of St Maur, which appeared between 1679 and 1700. This text was reproduced, not wholly reliably, in the *Patrologia Latina* of the Abbé J. P. Migne which, with all its faults, is the edition most generally available today. The Migne text is gradually being superseded by modern critical editions, notably those of the Viennese *Corpus Scriptorum Ecclesiasticorum Latinorum* and the *Corpus Christianorum* of Brepols, Tournhout. It is in this latter series that the collected sermons of Augustine, both those known to the Maurists and those which have come to light since their edition, have begun to appear.

Throughout the present work, quotations from Augustine have been given from the *Corpus Scriptorum Ecclesiasticorum Latinorum* when available and, failing that, from the *Patrologia Latina*. Exceptions to this rule are the *Confessions*, where the text used is that of Pierre de Labriolle (2 vols., Paris, 1933, 1937); the *De Trinitate*, whose text is that of Luis Arias (*Biblioteca de autores cristianos: Obras de san Agustin en edicion bilingüe*, tomo V, Madrid, 1948); the *Psalmus contra Partem Donati* (ed. Rosario Anastasi, Padua, 1957); and the first fifty sermons, where the text is that of Dom Cyrile Lambot in *Corpus Christianorum* (*Series Latina*, xli, Tournai, 1961).

There is no complete translation of Augustine's works in English. The largest single collection is in the *Select Library of the Nicene and Post-Nicene Fathers of the Christian Church* (Buffalo, 1886). In recent years, a number of series of translations have appeared in England and America. These include the *Library of Christian Classics* (London), which has been employed whenever possible throughout this study, and which is cited as LCC in the bibliography; *The Catholic University of America Patristic Studies* (Washington, D.C.); *Ancient Christian Writers: The Works of the Fathers in Translation* (Westminster, Maryland and London); and *The Fathers of the Church* (New York).

I · ORIGINAL SOURCES

(a) WORKS BY AUGUSTINE

Ad Caesariensis Ecclesiae plebem Sermo   CSEL liii
Ad Donatistas post Collationem   CSEL liii

Ad Simplicianum de diversis Quaestionibus
(LCC)   *MPL* xl
Breviculus Collationis   *CSEL* liii
Collatio cum Maximiano Arianorum Episcopo   *MPL* xlii
Confessionum Libri XIII (LCC)   ed. Labriolle
Contra Academicos (LCC)   *CSEL* lxiii
Contra Adimantium   *CSEL* xxv
Contra Adversarium Legis et Prophetarum   *MPL* xlii
Contra Cresconium   *CSEL* lii
Contra duas Epistulas Pelagianorum   *CSEL* lx
Contra Epistulam Parmeniani   *CSEL* li
Contra Epistulam quam vocant Fundamenti   *CSEL* xxv
Contra Faustum Manichaeum   *CSEL* xxv
Contra Fortunatum Disputatio   *CSEL* xxv
Contra Gaudentium   *CSEL* liii
Contra Julianum Libri VI   *MPL* xliv
Contra Litteras Petiliani   *CSEL* lii
Contra Maximinum   *MPL* xlii
Contra Priscillianistas et Origenistas   *MPL* xlii
Contra Sermonem Arianorum   *MPL* xlii
De Actis cum Felice Manichaeo   *CSEL* xxv
De Baptismo contra Donatistas   *CSEL* li
De Beata Vita   *CSEL* lxiii
De Bono Coniugali   *CSEL* xli
De Catechizandis Rudibus   *MPL* xl
De Civitate Dei   *CSEL* xl
De Continentia   *CSEL* xli
De Correptione et Gratia   *MPL* xliv
De Cura pro Mortis Gerenda   *CSEL* xli
De Diversis Quaestionibus LXXXIII   *MPL* xl
De Doctrina Christiana   *MPL* xxxiv
De Dono Perseverantiae   *MPL* xlv
De Duabus Animabus   *CSEL* xxv
De Fide et Symbolo (LCC)   *CSEL* xli
De Genesi ad Litteram Libri XII   *CSEL* xxviii
De Gestis cum Emerito   *CSEL* liii
De Gestis Pelagii   *CSEL* xlii
De Gratia Christi   *CSEL* xlii
De Gratia et Libero Arbitrio   *MPL* xliv
De Haeresibus ad Quodvultdeum   *MPL* xlii
De Libero Arbitrio (LCC)   *CSEL* lxxiv
De Magistro (LCC)   *MPL* xxxii
De Mendacio   *CSEL* xli

De Moribus Ecclesiae Catholicae et de
  Moribus Manichaeorum — *MPL* xxxii
De Natura Boni (LCC) — *CSEL* xxv
De Natura et Gratia — *CSEL* lx
De Nuptiis et Concupiscentia — *CSEL* xlii
De Ordine — *CSEL* lxiii
De Peccato Originali — *CSEL* xlii
De Peccatorum Meritis et Remissione — *CSEL* lx
De Perfectionis Justitiae Hominis — *CSEL* xlii
De Praedestinatione Sanctorum — *MPL* xliv
De Quantitate Animae — *MPL* xxxii
De Sermone Domini in Monte — *MPL* xxxiv
De Spiritu et Littera (LCC) — *CSEL* lx
De Trinitate (LCC) — ed. Arias
De Unico Baptismo — *CSEL* liii
De Utilitate Credendi (LCC) — *CSEL* xxv
De Vera Religione (LCC) — *MPL* xxxiv
Enarrationes in Psalmos — *MPL* xxxvi, xxxvii
Enchiridion ad Laurentium (LCC) — *MPL* xl
Epistulae — *CSEL* xxxiv, xliv, lvii, lviii
Epistula ad Romanos inchoata Expositio — *MPL* xxxv
Expositio quarundam Propositionum ex Ep.
  ad Romanos — *MPL* xxxv
Opus Imperfectum contra Julianum — *MPL* xlv
Psalmus contra Partem Donati — ed. Anastasi
Retractationes — *CSEL* xxxvi
Sermones — *MPL* xxxviii, xxxix. Morin, *Sermones post Maurinos Reperti* in *Misc. Agost.* i (1931). Lambot, *Sermones Augustini I–L de Vetere Testamento* (*Corpus Christianorum Ser. Lat.* xli)
Soliloquia (LCC) — *MPL* xxxii
Tractatus CXXIV in Iohannis Evangelium — *MPL* xxxv
Tractatus X in Epistula Iohannis ad Parthos (LCC) — *MPL* xxxv

(b) OTHER ANCIENT AUTHORS

Ambrose, *De Excessu fratris sui Satyri* — *MPL* xvi
  De Fide Libri V — *MPL* xvi
  De Paenitentia Libri II — *MPL* xvi
  De Sacramentis — *CSEL* lxxiii

In Evangelium secundum Lucam Expositio	*MPL* xv
AMBROSIASTER, *Commentarius in Ep. ad Romanos*	*MPL* xvii
PSEUDO-AUGUSTINE, *Ad Catholicos Epistula*	*CSEL* lii
Contra Fulgentium	*MPL* xliii
CASSIODORUS, *Expositiones in Psalmos*	*MPL* lxx
COELESTINUS, POPE, *Epistulae*	*MPL* l
CYPRIAN, *De Unitate*	*CSEL* iii (1)
Epistulae	*CSEL* iii (2)
EUSEBIUS, *Historia Ecclesiastica*	ed. Bright, Oxford, 1881
FULGENTIUS, *De Incarnatione*	*MPL* lxv
Ad Trasimundum Libri III	*MPL* lxv
De Veritate Praedestinationis	*MPL* lxv
GENNADIUS, *De Scriptoribus Ecclesiasticis*	*MPL* lviii
Gesta Collationis Carthaginensis	*MPL* xi
GREGORY I, POPE, *Epistulae*	*MPL* lxxvii
GREGORY NAZIANZEN, *Orationes*	*MPG* xxxvi, xxxvii
HILARY OF POITIERS, *Commentarius in Matthaeum*	*MPL* ix
Hypomnesticon contra Pelagianos et Caelestianos	*MPL* xlv
JEROME, *Apologia ad Librum Rufini*	*MPL* xxiii
De Viris Illustribus	*MPL* xxiii
Dialogus adversus Pelagianos	*MPL* xxiii
Epistulae	*CSEL* liv–lvi
In Ezechiel Commentarius	*MPL* xxv
LEO, POPE, *Sermones*	*MPL* liv
MARCELLINUS (AMMIANUS) *Rerum Gestarum Libri quae supersunt*	ed. Gardthausen, Teubner, Leipzig, 1874–5
MERCATOR (MARIUS), *Commonitorium*	*MPL* xlviii
OPTATUS OF MILEVIS, *De Schismate Donatistarum*	*CSEL* xxvi
OROSIUS, *Liber Apologeticus*	*CSEL* v
Historia adversus Paganos	*CSEL* v
PACATUS, *Panegyricus*	ed. in *XII Panegyrici Latini*, Teubner, Leipzig, 1911
Passio Perpetuae	ed. J. A. Robinson (Cambridge Texts and Studies, i, 2), 1891
PELAGIUS, *Epistula ad Demetriaden*	*MPL* xxxiii
PHOTIUS, *Bibliotheca*	*MPG* ciii
PLOTINUS, *Enneades*	ed. Bréhier with Fr. tr.
POSSIDIUS, *Operum S. Augustine Elenchus*	ed. Wilmart in *Misc. Agost.* ii

Vita Augustini	ed. Pellegrino, Edizioni Paoline, 1955
PROCOPIUS, *De Bello Persico*	*CSHB* ii
De Bello Vandalico	*CSHB* ii
PROSPER, *Chronicon*	ed. Mommsen, *MGH* Auctores Antiquissimi ix, *Chronica Minora* i (1892)
PRUDENTIUS, *Contra Symmachum*	*CSEL* lxi
Sententiae Episcoporum num. LXXXVI de Haereticis baptizandis	*CSEL* iii (1)
SOCRATES SCHOLASTICUS, *Historica Ecclesiastica*	ed. Bright, Oxford, 1878
TERTULLIAN, *Ad Scapulam*	*MPL* i
Apologeticus	*CSEL* lxix
De Baptismo	*MPL* i
De Carnis Resurrectione	*CSEL* xlvii
De Praescriptione Haereticorum	*CSEL* lxx
CODEX THEODOSIANUS	ed. Mommsen and Meyer, Berlin, 1905
TYCONIUS, *Commentarius in Apocalypsin*	in Beatus, *In Apocalypsin Libri XII*, ed. H. Florez, Madrid, 1770
ZOSIMUS, POPE, *Epistulae de causa Pelagii*	*MPL* xlv

II · MODERN STUDIES

ABERCROMBIE, Nigel, *The Origins of Jansenism*, Oxford, 1936.

ADAM, Alfred, *Texte zum Manichäismus* (Kleine Texte für Vorlesungen und Übungen Nr. 175), Berlin, 1954.

ALAND, Kurt, 'Eine Wende in der Konstantin-Forschung?' in *Forschungen und Fortschritte*, Bd. xxviii, Heft. 7 (July 1954).

ALÈS, A. de, *Priscillien et l'Espagne chrétienne du IVe siècle*, Paris, 1936. *La théologie de saint Cyprien*, Paris, 1922.

ALFARIC, P., *Les Écritures manichéennes*, 2 vols., Paris, 1918. *L'évolution intellectuelle de saint Augustin*, Tom. I, Paris, 1918. [No more appeared.]

ALLBERRY, C. R. C., *A Manichaean Psalm Book*, Part II (Manichaean Manuscripts in the Chester Beatty Collection, Vol. II), Stuttgart, 1938.

ALLIN, Thomas, *The Augustinian Revolution in Theology*, London, 1911.

ALTANER, Berthold, 'Augustinus und die griechische Sprache' in *Pisciculi: Studien zur Religion und Kultur des Altertums Franz Joseph Dölger . . . dargeboten*, Münster i. Westf., 1939.

'Augustinus und Eusebius von Kaisareia' in *Byzantinische Zeitschrift*, xliv (1951), 1–6.

Patrologie, 5te Aufl., Freiburg i. Br., 1958.

ALTHEIM, Franz, *A History of Roman Religion*, ET by Harold Mattingley, London, 1938.

AMATUCCI, A. G., *Storia della letturatura latina cristiana*, 2a ed., Turin, 1955.

ANGUS, S., *The Sources of the first ten books of St Augustine's De Civitate Dei*, Princeton, 1906.

Augustinus Magister: Congrès international augustinien, Paris, 21–24 September 1954. 3 vols.

BABUT, E. C., *Priscillien et le priscillianisme* (Bibliothèque de l'École des Hautes Études, Fasc. clxix), Paris, 1909.

BARDY, Gustave, *L'Église et les dernières Romains*, Paris, 1948.

'Les origines des écoles monastiques en Occident' in *Sacris erudiri*, v (1953), 86–104.

La question des langues dans l'Église ancienne, i, Paris, 1948. [No more published.]

Saint Augustin. L'homme et l'œuvre, 7e éd., Paris, 1948.

BATTIFOL, Pierre, *Le catholicisme de saint Augustin*, 5e éd., 2 vols., Paris, 1930.

BAUR, F. C., *Das Manichäische Religionssystem*, Tübingen, 1831. [Photographically reprinted in 1928.]

BAXTER, J. H., 'The Martyrs of Madaura' in *JTS* xvi (1924), 21–37.

St Augustine: Select Letters, tr. by J. H. Baxter, Loeb ed., London and New York, 1930.

BAYNES, N. H., *Byzantine Studies and other Essays*, London, 1955.

Constantine the Great and the Conversion of Europe (Proceedings of the British Academy, xv), London, 1929.

and H. St L. B. Moss, *Byzantium: An introduction to East Roman Civilization*, Oxford, 1949.

BEARE, William, *Latin Verse and European Song*, London, 1957.

BENSON, E. W., *Cyprian: His Life, his Times and his Work*, London, 1897.

BERTHIER, André, *Tiddis: Antique Castellum Tidditanorum*, Algiers, 1951.

BESNIER, M., *L'Empire romain de l'avènement des Sévères*, Paris, 1937.

BETHUNE-BAKER, J. F., *An Introduction to the Early History of Christian Doctrine*, revised ed., London, 1954.

BEVAN, Edwyn, *Later Greek Religion*, London, 1927.

BÉVENOT, Maurice, *St Cyprian's De Unitate chap. 4 in the light of the manuscripts*, Rome, 1937.

BOHLIN, Torgny, *Die Theologie des Pelagius und ihre Genesis*, Uppsala/Wiesbaden, 1957.

BONNER, Gerald, 'The Scillitan Saints and the Pauline Epistles' in *JEH* vii (1956), 141–6.

BOUGAUD, L. V. E., *Histoire de sainte Monique*, Paris, 1861.

BOYD, W. K., *The Ecclesiastical Edicts of the Theodosian Code*, New York, 1905.

BOYER, Charles, *Christianisme et Néoplatonisme dans la formation de saint Augustin*, 2e éd., Rome, 1953.

BRIGHT, William, *The Roman See in the Early Church*, London, 1896.
Select Anti-Pelagian Treatises of St Augustine, Oxford, 1880.

BRISSON, J. P., *Autonomisme et Christianisme dans l'Afrique romaine*, Paris, 1958.

BROWN, P. R. L., 'Aspects of the christianization of the Roman Aristocracy' in *JRS* li (1961), 1–11.

BRUCKNER, Albert, *Julian von Eclanum: Sein Leben und seine Lehre. Ein Beitrag zur Geschichte des Pelagianismus* (Texte und Untersuchungen zur Geschichte der altchristlichen Litteratur, Bd. 15, Teil 3), Leipzig, 1897.
Quellen zur Geschichte der pelagianischen Streites (Sammlung ausgewählter kirchen- und dogmengeschichtlichen Quellenschriften, 2te Reihe, 7es Heft), Tübingen, 1906.

BRUYNE, D. de, 'La première règle de saint Benoit' in *Rev. Bénéd.*, xlii (1930), 316–42.

BUONAIUTI, Ernesto, *Il cristianesimo nell' Africa romana*, Bari, 1928.
'La prima coppia umana nel systema manichaeo' in *Saggi sul cristianesimo primitivo*, Città di Castello, 1923, 150–70.

BURKITT, F. C., *The Book of Rules of Tyconius* (Cambridge Texts and Studies, iii, 1), 1894.
'Manichaica' in *JTS* xxxv (1934), 185–6.
The Religion of the Manichees, Cambridge, 1925.
'Xrōštay and Padvāχtay, Call and Answer' in *JTS* xxxvi (1935), 180–1.

BURLEIGH, J. H. S., *Augustine: Earlier Writings* (The Library of Christian Classics, Vol. VI), London, 1953.

BURNABY, John, *Amor Dei. A Study of Saint Augustine's teaching on the Love of God as the motive of Christian Life*, London, 1938.
Augustine: Later Works (The Library of Christian Classics, Vol. VIII), London, 1955.
'The "Retractations" of St Augustine: Self-criticism or Apologia?' in *Aug. Mag.*, i, 85–92.

BURY, J. B., *History of the Later Roman Empire*, 2 vols., London, 1923.

BUSCH, B., 'De initiatione christiana secundum sanctum Augustinum' in *Ephemerides Liturgicae*, Anno 52, no. 2, 159–78.
'De modo quo sanctus Augustinus descripserit initiationem christianam', ibid., Anno 52, no. 4, 385–483.

De initiatione christiana secundum doctrinam sancti Augustini, Rome, 1939.

BUTLER, Cuthbert, *Western Mysticism,* 2nd ed., London, 1927.

BÜTTNER, T. and WERNER, E., *Circumcellionen und Adamiten: Zwei Formen mittelalterlicher Haeresie,* Berlin, 1959.

CARRÉ, M. H., *Realists and Nominalists,* London, 1946.

CAYRÉ, Fulbert, *La contemplation augustienne,* 2e éd., Bruges/Paris, 1954.

CHADWICK, Owen, 'Euladius of Arles' in *JTS* xlvi (1945), 200–5.

John Cassian, Cambridge, 1950.

CHAPMAN, John, *Studies in the Early Papacy,* London, 1925.

CHEVALIER, Irenée, *St Augustin et la pensée grecque,* Friburg en Suisse, 1940.

CHITTY, Derwas, 'St Anthony the Great' in *Sobornost,* Series 3, No. 19 (Summer 1956), 339–43.

CLARKE, M. L., *The Roman Mind,* London, 1956.

COMEAU, Marie, *La rhétorique de saint Augustin,* Paris, 1930.

COURCELLE, Pierre, *Les lettres grecques en occident,* 2e éd., Paris, 1948.

'Plotin et saint Ambrose' in *Revue de Philologie,* lxxvi (1950), 31–45.

Recherches sur les Confessions de saint Augustin, Paris, 1950.

COURTOIS, Christian, 'St Augustin et le problème de la survivance de punique' in *Revue Africaine,* xxiv (1950), 259–82.

CRISTIANI, Léon, *Jean Cassien,* 2 vols., Editions de Fontinelle, Abbaye S. Wandrille, 1946.

CUMONT, Franz, *Recherches sur le Manichéisme,* Brussels, 1908.

CUNNINGHAM, W., *St Austin and his place in the history of Christian thought,* London, 1886.

DAVIDS, J. A., *De Orosio et sancto Augustino Priscillianistarum adversariis commentatio historica et philosophica,* The Hague, 1930.

Dictionnaire d'archéologie chrétienne et de liturgie, Paris, 1907– (*in progress*).

DILL, Samuel, *Roman Society in the last century of the Western Empire,* 2nd ed., London, 1899.

DUDDEN, F. Holmes, *Gregory the Great,* London, 1905.

The Life and Times of St Ambrose, 2 vols., Oxford, 1935.

DUFOURCQ, Albert, *De Manichaeisimo apud Latinos quinto sextoque saeculo,* Paris, 1900.

DVORNIK, F., 'Pope Gelasius and Emperor Anastasius I' in *Byzantinische Zeitschrift,* xliv (1951), 111–16.

Encyclopedia italiana, Rome, 1929–39, art. 'Agostino', vol. 1, pp. 913–28.

ESCHER DI STEFANO, Anna, *Il Manicheismo in S. Agostino,* Padua, 1960.

FARRAR, F. W., *The Lives of the Fathers,* vol. 2, London, 1907.

FEIBLEMAN, J. K., *Religious Platonism,* London, 1959.

FERGUSON, John, *Pelagius. A Historical and Theological Study,* Cambridge, 1936.

FLICHE and MARTIN, Edd., *Histoire de l'Église*, tom. 4, Paris, 1937.

FREND, W. H. C., *The Donatist Church*, Oxford, 1952.

'The Gnostic-Manichaean Tradition in Roman North Africa' in *JEH* iv (1953), 13–26.

'North Africa and Europe in the early Middle Ages' in *Transactions of the Royal Historical Society*, 5th Series, v (1955), 61–80.

'A Note on the Berber Background in the Life of Augustine' in *JTS* xviii (1942), 188–91.

GIBBON, Edward, *The History of the Decline and Fall of the Roman Empire*. Ed. J. B. Bury, 7 vols., London, 1896–1902.

GIESELER, J. C. L., *Lehrbuch der Kirchengeschichte*, 3te Aufl., 2te Bd., 1te Abb., Bonn, 1831.

GILSON, Étienne, 'The Future of Augustinian Metaphysics' in *A Monument to St Augustine*, 289–315.

Introduction à l'étude de Saint Augustin, 3e éd., Paris, 1949.

La philosophie au Moyen Age, 2e éd., Paris, 1947.

GRÉGOIRE, Hippolyte, *Les persécutions dans l'empire romaine* (Academie royale de Belgique: Classe des lettres et des sciences morales, tom. xlvi, fasc. 1), Brussels, 1951.

GRIFFE, Elie, *La Gaule chrétienne à l'epoche romaine*, tom. 2, Paris/Toulouse, 1957.

GSELL, Stéphane, *Cherchel: Antique Iol-Caesarea*, revised by M. Leglay and E. S. Colosier, Algiers, 1952.

GWYNN, Aubrey, *Roman Education from Cicero to Quintilian*, Oxford, 1926.

HAARHOFF, T. J., *Schools of Gaul*, 2nd ed., Johannesburg, 1958.

HAHN, T., *Tyconius Studien. Ein Beitrag zur Kirchen- und Dogmengeschichte des vierten Jahrhunderts*, Leipzig, 1900.

HARNACK, Adolf von, *Lehrbuch der Dogmengeschichte*, 4te Aufl., Tübingen, 1910. ET by James Millar, *History of Dogma*, London, 1898 (from 3rd German ed.).

HENDRIKS, Ephraem, *Augustins Verhältnis zur Mystik. Eine patristische Untersuchung*, Würzburg, 1936.

HENRY, Paul, *La vision d'Ostie*, Paris, 1938.

HEUSSI, Karl, *Der Ursprung des Mönchtums*, Tübingen, 1936.

HIRSCHFELD, O., 'Die *Agentes in rebus*' in *Sitzungsberichte der berlinische Akademie*, 1893, 421–4.

HOARE, Frederick R., *The Western Fathers*, London, 1954.

HOLL, Adolf, *Augustins Bergpredigtexegese*, Vienna, 1960.

HOLME, L. R., *The Extinction of the Christian Church in North Africa*, London, 1898.

HOPKINS, J. F. P., *Medieval Muslim Government in Barbary*, London, 1958.

BIBLIOGRAPHY 411

HÜMPFNER, Winfried, 'Die Mönchsregel des heiligen Augustins' in *Aug. Mag.*, i, 241–54.

INGE, W. R., *The Philosophy of Plotinus*, 3rd ed., 2 vols., London, 1929. *Mysticism in Religion*, 2nd ed., London, 1959.

JACKSON, A. V. Williams, 'The Doctrine of Metempsychosis in Manichaeism' in *Journal of the American Oriental Society*, xlv (1925), 246–268.
Researches in Manichaeism, New York, 1932.

JALLAND, T. G., *The Church and the Papacy*, London, 1944.

JOLIVET, Régis, *Le problème du mal d'après saint Augustin*, 2e éd., Paris, 1936.

JONES, A. H. M., *Constantine and the conversion of Europe*, London, 1948.
'Notes on the genuineness of the Constantinian Documents in Eusebius's *Life of Constantine*' in *JEH* v (1954), 196–200.

JULIEN, Ch. A., *Histoire de l'Afrique du Nord*, 2 vols., Paris, 1956.

KEENAN, Mary E., *The Life and Times of St. Augustine as revealed in his Letters* (Catholic University of America Patristic Studies, vol. 45), Washington, D.C., 1935.

KNOWLES, M. David, *The English Mystical Tradition*, London, 1961.

KOCH, Hugo, 'I rapporti di Cipriano con Ireno ed altri scrittori greci' in *Ricerci religiosi*, v (1929), 137–63.
Vincent von Lérins und Gennadius (Texte und Untersuchungen zur altchristlichen Litteratur, Bd. 31), Leipzig, 1907.

LABRIOLLE, Pierre de, *Histoire de la littérature latine chrétienne*, 3e éd. by G. Bardy, 2 vols., Paris, 1947.
La réaction païenne. Étude sur la polemique antichrétienne du Ier au VIe siècle, Paris, 1948.

LACEY, T. A., *Nature, Miracle and Sin: A Study of St Augustine's Conception of the Natural Order*, London, 1916.

LAGRANGE, P. M. J., 'Les Retractations éxégetiques de saint Augustin' in *Miscellanea Agostiniana*, ii, 373–95.

LAMBOT, Cyrile, 'Le monachisme de saint Augustin' in *Aug. Mag.*, iii, 65–68.
'La règle de saint Augustin et saint Césaire' in *Rev. Bénéd.*, xli (1929), 335–8.
'S. Augustin a-t-il rédige la Règle pour moines qui porte son nom?' in *Rev. Bénéd.*, liii (1941), 41–58.
Sancti Aurelii Augustini Sermones Selecti duodeviginti, ed. C.L. (Stromata Patristica et Mediaevalia Fasc. I), Utrecht/Brussels, 1950.
Sancti Aurelii Augustini Sermones de Vetere Testamento I–L, ed. C.L. (Corpus Christianorum Series Latina xli), Tournai, 1961.

LE BLOND, J. M., *Les conversions de saint Augustin*, Paris, 1950.

LECERF, Jean, 'Notule sur Saint Augustin et les survivances puniques' in *Aug. Mag.*, i, 31–33.

LEGEWIE, B., 'Die körperliche Konstitution und die Krankheiten Augustins' in *Miscellanea Agostiniana*, ii, 5–21.

LEROQUAIS, V., *Les Livres d'Heures manuscrits de la Bibliothèque Nationale*, Tom. I, Paris, 1927.

LESOUSKY, M. A., *The De Dono Perseverantia of St Augustine* (Catholic University of America Patristic Studies, vol. 91), Washington, D.C., 1956.

LOT, Ferdinand, *La fin du monde antique et le début du Moyen Age*, Paris, 1927.

MACALI, Luigi, *Il problema del dolore secondo s. Agostino*, Rome, 1943.

MCCARTHY, Maria C., *The Rule for Nuns of St Caesarius of Arles* (Catholic University of America Studies in Medieval History, vol. 16), Washington, D.C., 1960.

MACKENNA, Stephen, *Plotinus : The Ethical Treatises*, tr. by S.M., London, 1917.

MANDONNET, P., *St Dominique, L'idée, l'homme et l'œuvre*, 2 vols., Paris, 1937.

MANDOUZE, André, 'L'extase d'Ostie' in *Aug. Mag.*, i, 67–84.
'Où en est la question de la mystique augustinienne?' in *Aug. Mag.*, iii, 103–63.

MAREC, Erwan, 'Les dernières fouilles d'Hippo Regius ville épiscopale de Saint Augustin' in *Aug. Mag.*, i, 1–18.
Hippone : Antique Hippo Regius, 2e éd., Algiers, 1954.

MARROU, H. I., *Histoire de l'éducation dans l'antiquité*, 3e éd., Paris, 1955. ET, London, 1956.
Saint Augustin et l'augustinisme, Paris [1956]. ET, *Saint Augustine and his influence through the Ages*, London, n.d.
Saint Augustin et la fin de la culture antique, 4e éd., Paris, 1958.

MARTINDALE, C. C., 'St Augustine's Life and Character' in *A Monument to St Augustine*, London, 1930, 81–101.

MARTROYE, F., 'L'asile et la legislation impériale du IVe au VIe siècle' in *Memoires de la Société des Antiquaires de France*, lxxv (1918), 159–246.
'L'influence de saint Augustin sur la legislation de son temps' in *Bulletin de la Société Nationale des Antiquaires de France*, 1915, 166–8.
'Les plaidoiries devant la jurisdiction épiscopale au IVe siècle' in *Bulletin de la Société Nationale des Antiquaires de France*, 1918, 136–7.
'Une tentative de revolution sociale en Afrique' in *Revue des questions historiques*, lxxvi (1904), 353–416; lxxvii (1905), 1–53.

MEDEA, Filippo, 'La controversia sul "rus Cassiciacum" ' in *Miscellanea Agostiniana*, ii, 49–59.

MEER, F. Van der, *v.* VAN DER MEER.

MENASCE, P. J., 'Augustin Manichéen' in *Freundesgabe für Ernst Robert Curtius*, Bern, 1958, 79–93.

MERLIN, Nicolas, *Saint Augustin et les dogmes du péché originel et de la grâce*, Paris, 1931.

Miscellanea Agostiniana, 2 vols., Rome, 1931.

MOHRMANN, Christine, 'Les éléments vulgaires du latin des chrétiennes' in *Vigiliae Christianae*, ii (1948), 89–101, 163–84.

'Les origines de la latinité chrétienne à Rome' in *Vigiliae Christianae*, iii (1949), 67–106, 163–83.

Review of Courcelle, *Recherches* in *Vigiliae Christianae*, v (1951), 249–54.

MONCEAUX, Paul, *Histoire littéraire de l'Afrique chrétienne*, 7 vols., Paris, 1901–23.

'Saint Augustin et saint Antoine: contribution à l'histoire du monachisme' in *Miscellanea Agostiniana*, ii, 61–89.

Saint Cyprien, Paris, 1914.

MONTGOMERY, W., *St Augustine : Aspects of his Life and Thought*, London, 1914.

A Monument to St Augustine : Essays on some aspects of his thought written in commemoration of his 15th centenary, ed. by M. C. D'Arcy, London, 1930.

MOON, A. Anthony, *The De Natura of Saint Augustine* (Catholic University of America Patristic Studies, vol. 88), Washington, D.C., 1955.

MORIN, Germain, 'Date de l'ordination épiscopale de saint Augustin' in *Rev. Bénéd.*, xl (1928), 366–7.

Sancti Augustini Sermones post Maurinos reperti, ed. G.M., *Miscellanea Agostiniana*, vol. I.

MOSS, H. St L. B., *The Birth of the Middle Ages*, London, 1947.

MOZLEY, J. B., *A Treatise on the Augustinian Doctrine of Predestination*, 2nd ed., London, 1878.

MULLER, H. F. and TAYLOR, P., *A Chrestomathy of Vulgar Latin*, New York, 1932.

MÜLLER, Luguori, G., *The De Haeresibus of St Augustine* (Catholic University of America Patristic Studies, vol. 90), Washington, D.C., 1956.

MÜLLER, Michael, *Die Lehre des hl. Augustins von der Paradiesesehe und ihre Auswirkung in der Sexualethik des 12. und 13. Jahrhunderts bis Thomas von Aquin* (Studien zur Geschichte der kath. Moraltheologie Bd. I), Regensburg, 1954.

MURDOCH, H. Burn, *The Development of the Papacy*, London, 1954.

NEUSS, Wilhelm, *Die Apocalypse des hl. Johannes in der althispanischen und altchristlichen Bibel-Illustration. Der Problem der Beatus Handschriften*, Munster, 1931.

NOCK, A. D., *Conversion*, Oxford, 1933.

NÖRREGAARD, Jens, *Augustins Bekehrung*, tr. by A. Spelmeyer, Tübingen, 1923.

O'MEARA, John J., 'Arripui, aperui, et legi' in *Aug. Mag.*, i, 59–65.
'Augustine and Neo-Platonism' in *Recherches augustinennes*, vol. i, Paris, 1958, 91–111.
St Augustine: Against the Academics, tr. by J. J. O'M. (Ancient Christian Writers, No. 12), Maryland/London, 1951.
The Young Augustine, London, 1954.
OTTLEY, R. L., *Studies in the* Confessions *of St Augustine*, London, 1919.
OUTLER, A. C., *Augustine: The Confessions and Enchiridion* (The Library of Christian Classics, vol. VII), London, 1955.
PARKER, H. M. D., *A History of the Roman World AD 138–337*, 2nd ed., London, 1958.
PELLEGRINO, Michele, *Le 'Confessioni' de sant' Agostino*, Rome, 1956.
Possidio: Vita di s. Aostino, tr. by M.P., Edizione Paololine, 1955.
PEREIRA, Alves, *La doctrine du marriage selon saint Augustin*, 2e éd., Paris, 1930.
PIGANIOL, André, *L'Empire chrétien 325–395*, Paris, 1947.
PLANUDES, Maximus, v. WENDEL.
PLINVAL, Georges de, *Pélage: ses écrits, sa vie, et sa réforme*, Lausanne, 1943.
PONTET, Maurice, *L'exégèse de s. Augustin prédicateur*, Paris, n.d.
POPE, Hugh, *St Augustine of Hippo*, London, 1937.
PORTALIÉ, Eugène, 'Augustin': Art. in *Dictionnaire de Théologie Catholique*.
ET, *A Guide to the Thought of Saint Augustine*, London, 1960.
PUECH, Aimé, *St Jean Chrysostom et les mœurs de son temps*, Paris, 1891.
PUECH, H. C., *Le Manichéisme: son fondateur, sa doctrine*, Paris, 1949.
Recherches augustiniennes, vol. I, Paris, 1958.
REUTER, H., *Augustinische Studien*, Gotha, 1887.
RICKABY, Joseph, *The Manichees as St Augustine saw them*, London, 1925.
RIVINGTON, Luke, *The Primitive Church and the See of St Peter*, London, 1894.
ROBERTS, C. H., *Catalogue of the Greek and Latin Papyri of the John Rylands Library*, vol. III, Manchester, 1938.
ROSE, H. J., 'St Augustine as a forerunner of medieval hymnology' in *JTS* xxviii (1927), 383–92.
ROTTMANNER, Odilo, *Der Augustinismus. Eine dogmengeschichtliche Studie*, Munich, 1892.
RUNCIMAN, Steven, *The Medieval Manichee*, Cambridge, 1955.
SAGE, A., *La Règle de saint Augustin commentée par ses écrits*, Paris, 1961.
SCIACCA, M. F., *Saint Augustin et le Néoplatonisme*, Louvain/Paris, 1956.
SEECK, Otto, Art. 'Bonifatius' in Pauly-Wissowa, *Real-Encyclopädie*, Neue Bearbeitung, 5ter Halbbd., Stuttgart, 1897, 698–9.
    Art. 'Gildo' in Pauly-Wissowa, *Real-Encyclopädie*, 13ter Halbbd., Stuttgart, 1910, 1360–3.

Geschichte des Untergangs der antiken Welt, Bd. III and VI, Stuttgart, 1909–20.

Regesten der Kaiser und Päpste für Jahre 311 bis 476 N. Chr., Stuttgart, 1919.

SESTON, William, *Dioclétian et la Tétrachie*, Paris, 1946.

'Sur l'authenticité et la date de l'édit de Dioclétien contre le Manichéisme' in *Mélanges de philosophie, de littérature et d'histoire ancienne offerts à Alfred Ernout*, Paris, 1940.

'Sur les derniers temps du Christianisme en Afrique' in *Mélanges d'archéologie et d'histoire* (École française de Rome), liii (1936), 101–24.

SODEN, Hans von, *Urkunden zur Entstehungsgeschichte des Donatismus* (Kleine Texte für Vorlesungen und Übungen), 2te Aufl. von H. von Campenhausen, Berlin, 1950.

SPARROW-SIMPSON, W. J., *The Letters of St Augustine*, London, 1919.

St Augustine's Episcopate, London, 1944.

STEIN, Ernst, *Geschichte des spätromischen Reiches*, Bd. I, Vienna, 1928.

Art. 'Maximus (Usurpator)' in Pauly-Wissowa, *Real-Encyclopädie*, 14ter Bd., Stuttgart, 1930, 2546–55.

STOOP, E. de, *Essai sur la diffusion du Manichéisme dans l'Empire romain* (Université de Gand: Recueil de travaux publiés par la faculté de philosophie et lettres, fasc. 38), Ghent, 1909.

STRAUSS, Gerhard, *Schriftgebrauch, Schriftauslegung und Schriftbeweis bei Augustin* (Beiträge zur Geschichte der biblischen Hermeneutik), Tübingen, 1959.

TAYLOR, A. E., *Platonism and its influence*, London [1925].

TEMPLE, William, 'The Divinity of Christ' in *Foundations*, ed. B. H. Streeter, London, 1913, 213–63.

TESTARD, Maurice, *Saint Augustin et Cicéron*, 2 vols., Paris, 1958.

THEILER, W., *Porphyrius und Augustin*, Halle, 1933.

Review of Courcelle, *Recherches* in *Gnomon*, xxv (1953), 113–22.

THOMAS, J. F., *Saint Augustin s'est-il trompé? Essai sur la prédestination*, Paris, 1959.

UGHELLI, Ferdinando, *Italia Sacra sive de Episcopis Italiae*, 2nd ed. by N. Coleti, Venice, vol. VII, 1721.

VAN DER MEER, Frederick, *Augustinus de zielzorger*, Utrecht, 1947. FT *Saint Augustin: pasteur d'âmes*, 2 vols., Colmar/Paris, 1959. ET *St Augustine the Bishop*, London, 1961.

VASILIEV, A. A., *History of the Byzantine Empire*, 2nd ed., 2 vols., Madison, Wisconsin, 1958.

VERHEIJEN, M., 'Remarques sur le style de la "Regula secunda" de saint Augustin' in *Aug. Mag.*, i, 255–63.

VROOM, H., *Le psaume abécédaire de saint Augustin et la poésie latine rhymique*, Nijmegen, 1933.

416   ST AUGUSTINE OF HIPPO

WALDSCHMIDT, E., and LENTZ, W., *Die Stellung Jesu in Manichäismus* (Abhandlungen der preussischen Akademie der Wissenschaften 1926, Nr. 4), Berlin, 1926.

WANG, J., *Saint Augustin et les vertus des paiens*, Paris, 1933.

WARFIELD, B. B., *Studies in Tertullian and Augustine*, New York, 1930.

WARMINGTON, B. H., *The North African Provinces from Diocletian to the Vandal Conquest*, Cambridge, 1953.

WENDEL, Carl, Art. 'Planudes' in Pauly-Wissowa, *Real-Encyclopädie*, Neue Bearb., 40er Halbbd., 1950, 2202–53.

WEST, Rebecca, *St Augustine*, London, 1933.

WILLIAMS, N. P., *The Idea of the Fall and Original Sin*, London, 1927.

WILLIS, G. G., *Saint Augustine and the Donatist Controversy*, London, 1950.

ZEPF, M., 'Zur Chronologie der antidonatistischen Schriften Augustins' in *ZNW* viii (1929), 46–61.

ZERNOV, Nicholas, 'Saint Stephen and the Roman Church at the time of the Baptismal Controversy' in *Church Quarterly Review*, cxvii (1934), 304–36.

ZUMKELLER, A., *Das Mönchtum des heiligen Augustinus*, Würzburg, 1950.

INDEX

o